ArthurSinger

# Life Histories of North American Cardinals, Grosbeaks, Buntings, Towhees, Finches, Sparrows, and Allies

*Order Passeriformes: Family Fringillidae*

**PART TWO**
Genera Pipilo (part) through Spizella

ARTHUR CLEVELAND BENT and COLLABORATORS

*Compiled and Edited by*
OLIVER L. AUSTIN, JR.
*Florida State Museum, University of Florida*
*Research Associate, Smithsonian Institution*

DOVER PUBLICATIONS, INC., NEW YORK

Published in Canada by General Publishing Company, Ltd.,
30 Lesmill Road, Don Mills, Toronto, Ontario.
Published in the United Kingdom by Constable and Company,
Ltd., 10 Orange Street, London WC 2.


This Dover edition, first published in 1968, is an unabridged
and unaltered republication of the work originally published in
1968 by the Smithsonian Institution Press as United States
National Museum *Bulletin 237*.

*International Standard Book Number: 0-486-21978-X*
*Library of Congress Catalog Card Number: 68-55072*

Manufactured in the United States of America

DOVER PUBLICATIONS, INC.
180 Varick Street
New York, N. Y. 10014

## Publication of the United States National Museum

The scientific publications of the United States National Museum include two series, *Proceedings of the United States National Museum* and *United States National Museum Bulletin.*

In these series are published original articles and monographs dealing with the collections and work of the Museum and setting forth newly acquired facts in the fields of Anthropology, Biology, Geology, History, and Technology. Copies of each publication are distributed to libraries and scientific organizations and to specialists and others interested in the different subjects.

The *Proceedings*, begun in 1878, are intended for the publication, in separate form, of shorter papers. These are gathered in volumes, octavo in size, with the publication of each paper recorded in the table of contents of the volume.

In the *Bulletin* series, the first of which was issued in 1875, appear longer, separate publications consisting of monographs (occasionally in several parts) and volumes in which are collected works on related subjects. *Bulletins* are either octavo or quarto in size, depending on the needs of the presentation. Since 1902 papers relating to the botanical collections of the Museum have been published in the *Bulletin* series under the heading *Contributions from the United States National Herbarium.* Since 1959, in *Bulletins* titled "Contributions from the Museum of History and Technology," have been gathered shorter papers relating to the collections and research of that museum.

This work forms number 237, parts 1–3, of the *Bulletin* series.

FRANK A. TAYLOR,
*Director, United States National Museum.*

# Contents

## PART TWO

# List of Plates

Life Histories of
North American Cardinals,
Grosbeaks, Buntings, Towhees,
Finches, Sparrows, and Allies

PIPILO FUSCUS BULLATUS Grinnell and Swarth

## Oregon Brown Towhee

PLATE 33

Contributed by HENRY E. CHILDS, JR.

### HABITS

This, the northernmost subspecies of the brown towhee, is limited to the chaparral areas of southwestern Oregon and northern Siskiyou County, Calif.   In California, John Davis (1951) states it is resident "north of the yellow pine–Douglas fir belt rimming the northern end of the Sacramento Valley, and between the Cascade Range to the east and the Trinity Mountains and their northern continuation to the west." In Oregon, Ira N. Gabrielson and Stanley G. Jewett (1940) consider it "a characteristic bird of the bushy hillsides in the interior valleys of Douglas, Jackson, and Josephine Counties.   There in the lowlands between the Coast and Cascade Ranges in the Umpqua and Rogue watersheds its characteristic metallic alarm note can be heard throughout the year."   In the early 1900's it was found considerably north of its present range near Corvallis, Oreg., where it no longer occurs.

The same authors state: "Patterson (MS.) has found numerous nests about Ashland and Pinehurst with extreme dates of May 2 and 20."   They describe the nest as "In bushes and trees, usually within a few feet of the ground, made of inner bark, twigs, and weed stems and lined with plant stems, wool, and hair.   *Eggs:* 4 or 5, pale blue, spotted with purplish brown."

### DISTRIBUTION

*Range.*—The Oregon brown towhee is resident in the Umpqua River and Rogue River valleys of southwestern Oregon (Roseburg, Takilme, Ashland) and the Klamath River and Shasta valleys of north-central California (Berwick, Hornbrook, Edgewood).

PIPILO FUSCUS CAROLAE McGregor

## Sacramento Brown Towhee

Contributed by HENRY E. CHILDS, JR.

### HABITS

In the dry foothills of the western slopes of the Sierra Nevada, the valley quail is the only bird more conspicuous in the brushland avifauna than the brown towhee.   The principal use of this land area is for grazing, and the white-face Herefords contrast markedly with the somber brown bird which in great measure depends on the cattle troughs for its water supply. The brown towhee is essentially a resident of the upper Sonoran zone, but it may be found occasionally in suitable habitat both above and below it.

As this race, like *petulans*, is largely dependent on "edge" habitat, its abundance depends to some degree on grazing. Tall grass and thick brush do not suit it; consequently the thinning of such vegetation by the grazing and browsing of cattle benefits the towhees. This race also has responded to the artificial habitats produced in residential areas. J. G. Tyler (1913) notes that it occurs among the shrubs and trees along the irrigation canal and creeks from the foothills, and was most common in Kearney Park in the city of Fresno. He found nests 3 to 8 feet above the ground and lined with horsehair. He states:

"The usual complement of eggs is four, but I have found several sets of but three, and in at least three different instances the birds began the duties of incubation with just two eggs to their credit. The sets of two were in each case the first ones laid, so far as I could determine. May and June are the nesting months, my earliest record being May 1 (1906) for considerably incubated eggs. A set well along in incubation was found June 30 of the same year, while all other dates have fallen between these two extremes."

### DISTRIBUTION

*Range.*—The Sacramento brown towhee is resident in California east of the humid coastal region, from Humboldt County (Hoopa Valley) to Napa County, east to the foothills of the Cascade Mountains and the Sierra Nevadas, and south along the eastern side of San Joaquin Valley to Kern County (Piute Mountains, Fort Tejon).

*Egg date.*—California: 1 record, May 9.

### PIPILO FUSCUS EREMOPHILUS van Rossem

## Argus Brown Towhee

### Contributed by HENRY E. CHILDS, JR.

### HABITS

This very restricted race of the brown towhee is considered a relict population of a group formerly more widely distributed but now confined by the deserts surrounding the Argus Mountains. It was described in 1935 from specimens taken in Mountain Spring Canyon at 5,500 feet in the Argus Mountains of Inyo County, Calif. As John Davis (1951) points out: "Nearly all [known] specimens have been collected at this locality and only at this station has breeding

PLATE 33

Azusa, Calif., Sept. 20, 1931　　　　　　　　　　　　　　R. S. Woods

SAN DIEGO TOWHEE

Ashland, Oreg., May 22, 1924　　　　　　　　　　　　　J. E. Patterson

NEST OF OREGON BROWN TOWHEE

PLATE 34

San Mateo, Calif., May 7, 1932            J. S. Rowley

NEST OF SAN FRANCISCO BROWN TOWHEE

Azusa, Calif., Nov. 3, 1930            R. S. Woods

CALIFORNIA BROWN TOWHEE

been established. It seems likely that breeding colonies of this form will be found in other canyons in the Argus Mountains in which willow thickets are present, such as Wilson Canyon."

Nothing is known about possible variations in its patterns of life history and behavior from those of other races. Davis (1951) surmises that a local migration takes place in winter, as he found no brown towhees at Mountain Spring Canyon in December when the ground above 4,300 feet was covered with snow. An apparent vagrant taken at Lone Pine, Inyo County, is the only record for the race away from the Argus Mountains.

## DISTRIBUTION

*Range.*—The Argus towhee is resident in the Argus Mountains of Inyo and San Bernardino counties in California.

### PIPILO FUSCUS PETULANS Grinnell and Swarth
## San Francisco Brown Towhee
### PLATE 34
### Contributed by HENRY E. CHILDS, JR.

## HABITS

The brown towhee is a widespread species over much of the brush-covered areas of California and the southwest. It is, perhaps, as typically Californian as the chaparral it so commonly inhabits. Because of its drab appearance and uninteresting song, it has until recently received little more than casual study by bird enthusiasts. Yet the brown towhee is one of the most common dooryard species in suburban areas near the large cities of California, and an important element of the avifauna of much of the west.

The many subspecies of the brown towhee range from southern Oregon to southern Mexico and east into Texas. In California it occurs from the lower Sonoran to the Transition Zone (A. H. Miller, 1951c). Apparently the species originated in Mexico and spread northward during the Pliocene through a generalized sclerophyll woodland whose elements are called the Madro-Tertiary flora by D. I. Axelrod (1939). This floral association occurred north into California and contained many of the trees and shrubs found in that area today.

John Davis (1951) has shown that the brown towhees of the United States are divisible into two main groups of subspecies, each geographically isolated from the other. The *crissalis* group is characterized by a low degree of contrast between pileum and dorsum, a dark dorsal coloration, and a relatively long tail. These are the birds of California. The *perpallidus* group is distinguished by a high degree of contrast between pileum and dorsum, pale dorsal coloration, and a black pectoral spot. These are the birds of Arizona, New Mexico, Texas, and parts of Mexico.

Throughout its range the species is strictly resident and highly territorial. Movements within each population can only be interpreted as dispersal of young individuals.

The climate varies considerably within the range of this species, with maximum rainfall and lowest temperatures in southern Oregon and minimum rainfall and highest temperatures in the deserts of the southwest. In the coast ranges and in the foothills of the Sierra Nevada, which may be considered typical of the habitat of this species in California, the temperatures are moderate and rainfall is from 10 to 20 inches a year. These factors appear to limit the distribution of this species only when they result in little or no brush vegetation.

Within its range the brown towhee meets with the closely related Abert's towhee (*Pipilo aberti*) to which it is very similar in appearance. Abert's towhee is a bird of desert riparian and lacustrine vegetation, a much more restricted habitat than that of the brown towhee. In southern Mexico another close relative, *Pipilo rutilus*, is found. The brown towhee also comes in contact with the rufous-sided towhee (*Pipilo erythrophthalmus*), a ground-nesting species inhabiting more dense vegetation than that of its congener. The rufous-sided and brown towhees differ considerably in habits, song, and coloration, indicating a much more distant relationship than that between the brown and Abert's towhees. Davis suggests that *fuscus* may be related only distantly to *erythrophthalmus* and may be more closely related to the genus *Melozone*.

The brown towhee is primarily associated with the chaparral and secondarily with riparian vegetation. Davis (1951) describes its vegetation requirements as follows:

The growth form most desirable for protection and for location of the nest may be provided by many plants or combination of plants. However, the association utilized to the greatest extent is Californian chaparral. Of primary importance in this association are *Adenostoma fasciculatum* and *Ceanothus cuneatus*. Both species are widely distributed in the Coast ranges, the Cascade and Sierra Nevada foothills, and the mountains of Southern California. Both extend into northwestern Baja California, and *Ceanothus cuneatus* extends northward into Oregon. Other important chaparral shrubs are *Prunus ilicifolia*, *Pickeringia montana*, *Dendromecon rigida*, *Photinia arbutifolia*, and various species of *Arctostaphylos*, *Rhus*, *Quercus*, *Rhamnus*, *Garrya*, and *Eriodictyon*. The most important trees associated with the chaparral are *Arbutus menziesii*, various species of *Quercus*, *Pinus sabiniana*, and *P. coulteri* (McMinn, 1939:6).

The Californian races are found secondarily in associations other than chaparral. They have been recorded frequently in riparian vegetation, especially in

*Alnus* and *Salix* and in tangles of *Rubus vitifolius, R. parviflora,* and *Ribes.* Plants such as *Baccharis, Diplacus, Vitis,* and *Sambucus* may also be utilized. A few specimens have been taken in *Artemisia.* Disturbed areas may be used when the proper growth form has succeeded the original vegetation or when the original vegetation has been modified to provide suitable habitat for the brown towhees. Grazing, farming, logging operations, road building, and landscaping have opened areas to invasion by towhees. Local spread or increase in numbers has resulted.

Two Californian races occur mainly or entirely in associations other than chaparral. *P. f. petulans* of the humid north-central coast occupies an area in which chaparral is much restricted. This race is found in chaparral where this plant formation occurs within its range, but the birds have been restricted for the most part to the secondary association just listed. *P. f. eremophilis* of the Argus Mountains of Inyo and San Bernardino counties is found in rocky canyons that support extensive thickets of *Salix.*

Within these plant associations the brown towhee is an inhabitant of the brush edges. It is found along roads, trails, clearings, on lawns, wherever it can forage in the open with a clear view of predators and close to safe cover. Edge also appears to be of importance in determining territorial size.

During the winter towhees are found in association with other species of ground-feeding birds, particularly the white and golden-crowned sparrows, song sparrow, and house finch. It is the despot wherever it is found, putting all smaller birds to flight by strongly attacking those in its path. At Berkeley only the larger Steller and scrub jays dominate any chance encounter.

That the brown towhee is a conspicuous bird in its habitat is indicated by T. L. Rodgers and C. G. Sibley (1940), who recorded it in 99.6 percent of trips taken on the Berkeley campus throughout the year.

*Territory.*—Although lacking in brilliance of plumage and beauty of song, the brown towhee is well able to establish and maintain a typical passerine territory providing all the necessities for its comparatively sedentary life. In it are found mating and nest sites, food gathering areas, and escape areas for flight and roosting. A strictly resident bird, the male towhee defends his territory vigorously from all encroachment by others of his species.

Territorial defense is first noted in late fall after a period following the major dispersal of juveniles. Chasing and fighting between individuals becomes more frequent and pronounced in spring with the onset of breeding. Normally a relatively quiet bird, the towhee then becomes a loud, dominating tyrant to the hapless neighbor or vagrant towhee caught trespassing on his territory.

Song plays only a small part in the announcement of territory. Birds of neighboring pairs can see one another over most of their territories and trespass is usually observed and reacted to almost immediately. During the morning twilight hours in early spring, the male moves around the limits of his territory giving a rapid loud *tsip* note. This behavior, constant enough to be useful in census taking, ceases with the onset of nesting activities.

Population density reaches its maximum in disturbed areas such as the campus of the University of California at Berkeley. Here the vegetation is composed of ornamental shrubs, usually in a linear arrangement along buildings, streams, or paths, with much of the area in lawns. This pattern of vegetation provides nesting cover in dense shrubs from 2 to 5 feet tall, foraging areas on the lawns for these primarily ground feeding, seed-eating birds, and escape cover close to the foraging and nesting areas, mandatory because the towhee's short, rounded wings do not allow long or fast flight. The habitat thus provided appears optimum for the brown towhee as indicated by its abundance, 48 pairs per 100 acres. The territories, 1–2 acres in size, are remarkably uniform. In a study of avian responses to artificial habitat near Dillon Beach, Calif., F. A. Pitelka (1942) observed one once in this coastal locality, but found no towhees breeding.

In natural areas such as the Berkeley hills, where the shrub vegetation of the west-facing slopes grows along drainages, territories are larger and longer, following the intersection of shrubs and grass. Here individual territories may be over 5 acres in size.

*Courtship.*—Courtship behavior has not been described in great detail. On several occasions during the breeding season the male has been observed approaching the female with wings slightly drooped and quivering. Both wings may quiver in unison or alternatingly. Copulation may occur on the ground, but on one occasion it was observed on the top of a three-story building. The female assumes a position with the head tipped slightly forward and down and raises her tail. The male then mounts. In all cases observed both sexes were silent during coition.

*Nesting.*—Most brown towhees at Berkeley start nest building by mid-April, and some pairs complete three nestings successfully by the end of summer. Incubation by the female alone takes 11 days and the first clutch of three or four usually hatches in late April. After 8 days in the nest, the young fledge enough to leave it. The period of dependence on the adults varies. If there is no renesting, the young may remain with the adults from 4 to 6 weeks, but when the adults renest they drive the first young from the territory when the next clutch hatches.

The nests are rather bulky affairs of grasses and twigs of many kinds, and not too well constructed. Built from ground level to more than 35 feet up in a variety of trees and shrubs, the optimum height appears to be between 4 and 12 feet. The nest is placed in the densest part of the foliage and is usually supported by several branches. J. Grinnell and M. W. Wythe (1927) report nests being found from mid-April to the first week in September, situated well above ground in thick bushes or low trees.

A series of unusual nest sites have been reported. J. Mailliard (1936) reports a nest built a few inches underneath an apple. When the apple finally fell, it did not break any of the four-egg clutch, but the nest was deserted. J. McB. Robertson (1931) reports that towhees will nest in eucalyptus in accumulations of bark not too far from the ground. It is one of the few species to respond to this exotic tree, so plentiful in California. Brown towhees C. D. Scott (1920) kept in captivity nested on the ground two successive years. W. M. Pierce (1915) found a pair of brown towhees nesting in a berry basket 10 feet inside a barn door, but they deserted it midway in incubation.

*Eggs.*—The measurements of 40 eggs average 24.9 by 18.3 millimeters; the eggs showing the four extremes measure *26.4* by 18.3, 25.9 by *19.7*, *20.9* by 18.0, and 25.7 by *17.5* millimeters.

*Plumages.*—John Davis (1951) has the following to say about the molts and plumages of the brown towhee:

The only molt of real significance in the brown towhee is the fall molt. At this time adults undergo complete feather replacement. Birds undergoing the post-juvenal (first fall) molt retain the primaries and secondaries, and usually the rectrices. This molt pattern offers plumage characters that may be used to separate first-year birds from second-year or older birds. In fresh fall plumage the primaries of first-year (= immature) birds are dull brown and the margins of these feathers are finely erose because of wear. The primaries of second-year and older birds (= adults) at this time are glossy and nearly black and the margins of these feathers are entire. The rectrices of immature birds have pointed tips * * * and show signs of wear. The rectrices of adults are obtuse at the tip * * * and are glossy and unworn. Since rectrices are often replaced in the post-juvenal molt, the amount of wear on the primaries offers the most reliable criterion for judging age.

The period of time over which these criteria may be used depends entirely on the amount of wear to which the plumage of the individual is subjected. As the adult primaries become worn they take on the dull brown color and erose margins of the immature primaries. As the tips of the adult rectrices become worn they become so ragged that it is impossible to distinguish them from the rectrices of immatures. A few individuals may lose the characters of their age group as early as December; others may retain them as late as June. Age determination of most individuals becomes impossible by the middle of February. Occasional immatures are encountered which retain a few of the juvenal upper tail coverts. This has enabled the determination of age of some specimens that were otherwise so worn that the usual criteria were of no use.

The plumage of brown towhees is especially subject to wear. The abrasion of feathers causes a noticeable paling over the entire plumage. This paling is most pronounced on the coloration of the throat, since the color of this region is restricted to the terminal two-thirds of the throat feathers. As the colored portions of these feathers are worn away, the white feather bases are exposed. In examples of extreme wear the throat may appear white, because only the feather bases remain. The coloration of the crissum is also strikingly affected by wear, for the intensity of the coloration of this area is determined largely by the thickness of mass of the under tail coverts. As these become worn the color of the crissum becomes paler, owing to the thinning of the feather mass.

*Food.*—Brown towhees forage on the ground for seeds and insects. Occasionally they pursue large flying insects, but in the main they depend on the small ground surface forms. F. E. L. Beal (1910) made a study of stomach contents of these birds and found weed seeds—51 percent—to be their most important food, followed by grain—28 percent. Insects were the principal animal food—14 percent—and fruit—4.4 percent—probably windfalls, taken occasionally.

To obtain its food the brown towhee does not scratch as frequently or as violently as does the rufous-sided towhee. Birds are seen occasionally feeding on new grass shoots and drinking the dew collected on them in the morning. They respond well to feeding stations baited with various commercial bird seeds and bread crumbs, oat groats being particularly favored. The young, as in most other fringillids, are fed entirely on insect material, largely moth and butterfly larvae.

*Behavior.*—A behavior pattern often mentioned in the literature is the brown towhee's so-called "shadow-boxing," a fighting response aroused when its reflection in a shiny surface suggests the presence of another towhee in its territory. D. P. Dickey (1916) first described this action for *senicula* as follows: "Perching on the sill, the bird would eye his reflection, and then set systematically to work to kill the supposed rival, with all the ire and intolerance of a rutting moose." Reflections from window panes near feeding stations frequently stimulate these attacks, and hub caps often receive the same attention in the Berkeley area from both towhees and robins. W. E. Ritter and S. Benson (1934) describe and discuss the meaning of this phenomenon in terms of breeding activity and territorial behavior:

The Towhee, standing on the ledge, would face the window and assume a threatening attitude by lowering its head, fluffing out its feathers, and drooping its wings. It would then leap up at the window, striking it with its feet, or with the feet and the beak at the height of about ten inches. It would then fall back and immediately leap up to strike again. Sometimes it varied the procedure by continuing up the pane, clawing at its image as it rose.
\* \* \*
After May 1 the bird fought the window every day until July 4. Its last visit for the summer was July 14, but it appeared again on September 23 and fought occasionally for some weeks. The amount of fighting was never constant during this period. Beginning April 28 the bird increased its fighting activity until May 15. During this period it confined its efforts to the windows of our rooms. By May 20 the attacks had fallen off a great deal and the bird had expanded the zone of its operations to include the west-facing windows of the

main room of the Museum. By May 25 the attacks had nearly ceased, but after this date they increased again at our windows until on June 24 they were about as vigorous as ever. Subsequently they dwindled again to cease finally after July 14. On September 23, and for a few days subsequent to it more attacks occurred.

An explanation of the variation in the amount of activity was easy to discover. During the first period of increasing activity the fighting bird always accompanied its mate to the window. Their appearance at the window ledge was always heralded by a medley of mewing and squeaking notes from the oak tree outside the window. While the female fed busily the male would fight the window. The birds would usually fly into the oak tree where the female would sometimes preen awhile, but in a short time the female would fly to the west and disappear among the trees bordering Strawberry Creek. The male always closely accompanied the female. In a short time the male would return to the window to fight. The actions of the pair, and the presence of brood patches on the female, led to the belief that the female was incubating, but it appeared that the male was taking little if any part in the incubation other than guarding the female. * * *

It is clearly apparent from the above description that shadow boxing is intimately connected with breeding and defense of territory. The authors further point out that the attacks dropped off during the feeding of the young and increased again with the second brood.

E. I. Dyer (1931) observed four or five brown towhees respond to the distress calls of rufous-sided towhees when he approached too closely to their nest.

*Voice.*—Just as uninspiring as its plumage is the voice of the brown towhee. With care, however, it is possible to distinguish many variations of the basic chip note and to interpret the meanings of these variations. Indeed, to understand the mechanics of the species' population biology, one must become acquainted with its metallic clatter song. C. W. Quaintance (1938, 1941) has reported at length on the voice of the brown towhee and in the main this discussion comes from his work.

The basic note of the brown towhee's vocabulary is a metallic *chip* or *tsip*, often repeated with monotonous regularity, sometimes as fast as 30 per minute for 25 minutes at a time. Quaintance (1941) thus describes the use of this note:

The *tsip* note is not necessarily correlated with activity, although it does announce the beginning of activity in the early mornings and again, the cessation of activity in the evenings before the towhees go to roost. On the other hand a towhee may *tsip* for fifteen minutes without any activity. In flight it may give several *tsips* or none at all. An emphatic *tsip* may announce the take-off, and a *tsip* or two may be given upon alighting from a flight. A towhee may *tsip* on the ground while it is foraging, or it may forage for minutes without giving a sound. Frequently, in the nesting season, the *tsiping* is done from a high station such as the top of a laurel tree, or thirty or forty feet up in a eucalyptus, or from the peak of the highest available house or telephone pole.

The general *tsip* note seems to have different functions. It may serve as a contact note between birds, especially birds of a pair, as a protest note, or as an alarm or warning note. Further study of this note may yet resolve it into at least three different notes corresponding to the behavior induced. In other words, although the *tsip* may sound the same to us, the variations in manner of delivery or loudness may have meaning.

The *tsips* of a female disturbed at the nest are immediately answered by her mate and if her notes become hurried and excitable, he may come racing in to her side, no matter what part of the territory he may be in. Both birds may then utter loud *tsips* of protest at an intruder. The protest note invariably brings neighboring towhees close to the nest in disregard of territorial boundaries. Birds of other species are also attracted to the region of the nest in apparent curiosity.

The rapidly repeated *tsip* early in the morning is apparently the means by which the male towhee announces possession of his territory and its boundaries. He starts this *tsipping* while moving about over his territory shortly after dawn starts to break, calling it from the tops of bushes, boulders, and other song perches within the territory at the rate of about 60 notes per minute. He continues this activity until sunrise and then stops. I have observed this behavior only during the early part of the breeding cycle from mid-March to June at Berkeley, and mid-April to June at O'Neals, Calif.

During the nesting season the *tsip* note may be accentuated to a *tsink* note which appears to function in the control and warning of the young. It also serves to warn the female of danger while she is on the nest. A faint sparrowlike *tssp* is used to keep in contact with a mate when separated by shrubbery. Conditions of great stress, such as attack by predators or handling by humans, produce a loud squawking. When uttered by a young bird, this squawking acts as a distress signal that brings the parents rushing to the scene.

One of the most interesting combination of notes is the brown towhee's mate-call, which C. W. Quaintance (1941) describes as follows:

"To me, the basic *tsip* note is distinguishable in this particular series of notes. The utterance sounds something like this: *Tss' tss' tss' tsurr tsurr tsurr*, starting with fast staccato notes and getting faster toward the end. Because these unique notes are given almost exclusively between birds of a mated pair, they are referred to in this study as mate-notes or as the mate-call."

A casual observer seeing two birds fly into shrubbery uttering this call might associate the notes with fighting. The observation of banded birds allows only the interpretation of the mate-call as having a "pair reinforcement" function. Quaintance (1941) continues:

In most of these instances the meaning of the mate-call might have been misconstrued if the whole action was not carefully followed. In over a hundred recorded observations these mate-notes were given between members of a known pair when they met and in no instance did the two fight.   Moreover, in approximately one hundred clashes or boundary disputes between birds of different pairs, no mate-call was given * * *.

Outside of the nesting season the mate-calls are given less often.   Before meeting in the morning, the members of a pair may forage separately for awhile; when they meet, the mate-call is given * * *.   Generally speaking, the mated birds forage together in the winter months and since the meetings are relatively fewer, the mate-call is given less.

It is difficult to tell which sex gives the mate-call.   Sometimes it appears that only one of the birds gives the call, but more often it seems to be a duet.

Of particular interest is the brown towhee's only really musical attempt at song, which appears to function chiefly in attracting females to unattached males.   As all birds singing it that have been collected have been males, it is apparently a male trait.   Its prevalence from late January into June suggests that the sex ratio is often unbalanced in favor of the male.

This song is an elaboration of the basic *chip* or *tsip* note repeated three or four times in succession and followed by a rapid, sometimes descending series of notes almost trill-like in quality.   R. Hunt (1922) confines the rhythm of this song to that of a golf ball dropped on a hard surface and allowed to bounce until it stops.   The trill-like ending may vary considerably from a linnetlike trill to the bubbling of a winter wren, and at times may be omitted entirely.   This finch-like warble appears to be a retention of an ancestral song which is gradually being lost.   As the brown towhee lives where members of a pair can almost always see each other and their neighbors, such elaborate advertising as in the song sparrow or mockingbird is not necessary.

The note of the young in the nest calling for food is a *puhlee*, reminescent of the call of the rufous-sided towhee.   The fledgling's hunger note is similar to that of most sparrows, a loud *tst, tst, tst*. As the young bird becomes more active it gives a faint *tssp*.

In territorial clashes between neighbors or wandering intruders and when driving juveniles from their natal territory, a throaty *tschuck* note is repeated rapidly during flight.   There can be no mistaking the peculiar quality of this note or the intent of the bird making it. It means: "Get out and stay out."

In rare instances the males utter a whispered finchlike warble not unlike the song of the house finch, but so faint it cannot be heard more than a few feet away.   A. H. Miller (MS.) heard it from a male fighting his reflection in a window, and another time from a paired male hidden in the foliage of a tree.   Several times I have heard a male give this song near the nest when the incubating female had left it to feed.   From the variety of situations in which it is used, and the fact that it is inaudible at a distance of over 10 feet, the function of this song is not clear. Presumably it is another ancestral remnant of song no longer highly important to the species. A. H. Miller (MS.) reports a similar pleasant finchlike song in brown towhees in northern Mexico.

Its varied repertoire is indeed remarkable for so unmelodious a bird, which seems to act on the premise "one *tsip* is worth a thousand words."

*Field marks.*—This dull brown bird appears as a very plain, large sparrow, slightly smaller than a robin. The moderately long tail and the cinnamon or rusty under tail coverts are the most noticeable field marks. The throat and upper breast are buff, sometimes with faint dusky streaks. Its hunched over posture and ground feeding habits readily identify it from other sparrows.

*Enemies.*—On the Berkeley campus I found the Norway rat the principal predator of the brown towhee, destroying many nests, eggs, and young along the wooded creeks. The domestic house cat was often seen stalking these birds. Man, through destruction of habitat and disturbance of nests, was the greatest single factor in nest desertion.

In November 1948 at Berkeley I watched a pair of towhees chivvy a cat crouched beside an ash can. First one bird, then the other, dropped to the ground about 10 feet from the cat. Both *tsipped* loudly and continuously, one at the rate of 60 per minute. White-crown sparrows and a scrub jay were attracted by the noise. The cat meowed, apparently in frustration, as the birds moved around it just out of reach. After 5 minutes the birds lost interest and departed.

The same year I reported (1948) the reactions of a pair of brown towhees to a pair of scrubjays intent on robbing their nest. Another pair of towhees joined them, and all four flew at the jays, fluttering widespread wings and tail and uttering the squawk note. Several times they dropped to the ground within a few feet of me, showing no fear. In their excitement the resident pair attacked the other towhees trying to help them, territorial defense against their own kind becoming momentarily paramount. One jay was driven off, but the second, after being driven from the nest bush three times, was no longer molested. The following day the nest was empty, the towhees had left the area, and did not return.

In a series of food habit studies of important predators on range lands at the San Joaquin Experimental Range at O'Neals, Calif., H. S. Fitch (1948a, 1948b, 1949) found the towhee to be a minor prey subject. Ground squirrels, although serious predators of valley quail eggs, were seen being chased by adult towhees away from a nest containing four young. Coyotes were abundant, but among 2,250 identified items in their diet he found only two towhees. Of the snakes in the area the Pacific rattlesnake was the only species known to take towhees, and only two were found in 285 identified prey items.   Fitch et al. (1946a), in their study of the red-tailed hawk report only 3 towhees in 625 articles of food brought to the nest, and 7 towhees in 2,094 pellets.   Fitch et al. (1946b) found only 1 towhee in 41 items at two nests of the Cooper hawk.   Apparently the predation rate on towhees in this area is low and has little effect on the population.

J. M. Linsdale (1931), investigating the destructive effects on wildlife of a rodenticide then in common use, found only one towhee killed by this material.   Compound 1080, now widely used for rodent control, particularly ground squirrels, is mixed with oats and colored a bright canary yellow that apparently make the seeds unattractive to birds.

Towhees evince a mobbing reaction to owls during the mating season, but not a very intense one, according to S. A. Altmann (1956), and Fitch found no towhees among the owl foods he identified.

Young brown towhees in the nest are occasionally parasitized by fly (Protocalliphora) larvae.   O. E. Plath (1919) examined eight nests and found two of them heavily infested with 53 larvae per nest. None were observed in the Berkeley population.   C. M. Herman et al. (1942) found five out of eight towhees infected with Isopora. Hippoboscid or flat flies are found on towhees during the warm months.

Because of their liking for roadside vegetation and their poor powers of flight, brown towhees are frequent victims of automobiles. J. McB. Robertson (1930) listed four such casualties in a study in southern California.

### DISTRIBUTION

*Range.*—The San Francisco brown towhee is resident in California in the humid north central coastal region from Humboldt County (Korbel) to Santa Cruz County (Corralitos), and inland to the western edge of the northern San Joaquin Valley.

*Egg dates.*—California: 8 records, May 9 to June 28.

### PIPILO FUSCUS CRISSALIS (Vigors)

## California Brown Towhee

### PLATES 34 AND 35

### Contributed by HENRY E. CHILDS, JR.

### HABITS

Most of our information about this south central coastal race comes from the Hastings Natural History Reservation in the northern

Santa Lucia Mountains in Monterey County near Robles del Rio, Calif., in publications by Jean M. Linsdale. Since the late 1930's many students have recorded information on the animal life of this 1600-acre study area.

An intense banding program was carried out during the winter on a section of the canyon near the living quarters (Lindsale, 1949). Brown towhees are one of five most plentiful species here, the others being the scrub jay, the rufous-sided towhee, the plain titmouse, and the Oregon junco. Brown towhees were banded in some numbers, 452 from November 1937 to June 1948 or about 41 per year. Later recaptures of 361 of these provide some information on survival and longevity in the species: 184 (51 percent) survived to at least 1 year of age, 83 (23 percent) lived 2 years, 51 (14 percent) 3 years, 29 (8 percent) 4 years, 9 (2 percent) 5 years, 3 (0.8 percent) 6 years, and 2 (.06 percent) 7 years, the oldest recorded in the study. Thus seven years may be assumed as the potential ecological life span for this species. From these data the average individual life span is 1.9 years.

*Eggs.*—The measurements of 50 eggs average 24.9 by 18.4 millimeters; the eggs showing the four extremes measure *26.2* by 19.8, 25.7 by *20.3*, and *22.0* by *17.0* millimeters.

### DISTRIBUTION

*Range.*—The California brown towhee is resident in California from the central coast area (Seaside) to the western edge of the San Joaquin Valley (Orestimba Peak) and south to western Kern (Temblor Range), Santa Barbara, and Ventura Counties.

*Egg dates.*—California: 13 records, April 27 to June 20.

### PIPILO FUSCUS SENICULA Anthony
## Anthony's Brown Towhee
### Contributed by HENRY E. CHILDS, JR.

### HABITS

This is by far the darkest colored of the California races of the brown towhee. John Davis (1951) suggests this is due to its habitat. He states that *senicula* is resident in extreme southwestern California in "The area between the seacoast and the western edge of the deserts in Los Angeles County, San Bernadino County * * *, Riverside, Orange, and San Diego counties, thence southeast in Baja California between the coast and the lower edge of the coniferous forest on the Sierra Juarez and the Sierra San Pedro Martir south to latitude 29°." The chaparral the species inhabits in this region contains less *Ceanothus* than the chaparral farther north and more *Adenostoma*, which gives the vegetation, commonly called "black chaparral," its darker aspect. This dark background, augmented by the frequent reduction of illumination by fog (and smog), tends to select the darker variants in the population.

Though essentially an inhabitant of the wild sage and chaparral country, this subspecies has made itself at home in the settled suburbs of Los Angeles, Pasadena, San Diego, and other cities that have sprung up within its range during the past century. Wherever open lawns are adjacent to dense base-plantings and other ornamental shrubbery, the brown towhee becomes as common a dooryard resident as the mockingbird.

At their home in Pasadena, Harold and Josephine Michener (MS.) banded more than 1,300 brown towhees over a 25-year period. From most of these nothing more was ever heard, but a number of individuals came back to their traps year after year, the oldest one 8 years after they had banded it as a juvenal. In common with others who have tried to study this species through banding, the Micheners found that most individuals soon became "trap-wise." Though birds holding territory in the vicinity may visit the feeding trays regularly and glean bait spilled outside the traps, after once being caught they are reluctant to enter the trap again immediately. By marking some of the resident individuals with colored bands, the Micheners were able to keep some track of their movements by observation alone.

One of their most interesting case histories involves a male they banded as a juvenal in August 1933, who established his territory on their property and maintained it there until he was last recorded in March 1938, when he was almost 5 years old. "He lived in the yard as we did, and was so easily found that to record each time he was seen would have seemed absurd. We soon learned that his territory, defined as the space within which a great many sight records were made and beyond which few or none are noted, extended approximately 150 by 175 feet. This area contained a great many shrubs and trees for its size, several water drips, and food was always available at a shelf on the corner of the house, on a window ledge, and on the drive."

During the four breeding seasons this bird lived with the Micheners, though they were unable to keep track of all his nesting activities, they were able to determine he had at least three different mates. Each nest these built within his territory was in a different place. The first nest found, with four eggs in early April 1935, was on top of an old mockingbird nest in a melaleuca bush. This nest was unsuccessful, probably owing to the effects of an unprecedented heavy rain, and its female was last recorded near it on May 3. By June 1 a new female that had been banded as a juvenal 6 years earlier in June 1929, appeared on the territory and, though no evidence of nesting was noted, remained in occupancy with the male throughout the winter. Her first nest was found Apr. 14, 1936, 7 feet up in a buddleia on the opposite side of the yard. This nest fledged its young and on May 2 the female was found sitting on a new nest 4 feet up in a small crataegus, from which she also fledged her brood. Late that autumn her dried remains were found among the broken egg-shells in a thrid nest she had built 20 feet up in a eucalyptus. She was thus 7 years old when she died. No records of the male's nesting activities or mate were obtained in 1937, though he remained on the territory throughout the year. The last time he was taken, in mid-March 1938, he had a new mate, a female banded as a juvenal in June 1935. She built her nest in a small acacia, from which she fledged a single young on Apr. 11, 1938.

The reactions of this male and his various mates to other brown towhees intruding on their territory varied at different times of the year. In the fall and winter they showed no resentment when pairs from adjoining territories joined them at the feeders, but ate with them peacefully. On Mar. 2, 1935, "he and his mate were eating on the ground at the corner of the house in company with the pair holding the adjacent territory to the west. The four birds were in perfect harmony. The following November, December, and January, the color-banded pair holding the territory to the east were frequent visitors as well. There was no fighting. From these and later observations we concluded that this peaceful behavior was due to the fact that the pairs were settled for the season, that they knew each other and, certainly at this time of year, our resident pair did not regard neighboring mated territory holders as a threat."

Most territorial clashes were noted during the nesting season, and they usually involved comparatively strange birds. Whenever one of these managed to enter a trap on his territory, the male always attacked it viciously. "On May 1, 1936, a towhee entered the trap near his nest. At once there was the sound of fighting and commotion. The trap was of 1-inch poultry wire, and the trapped bird kept putting his head through the mesh, where our male could and did inflict severe injuries. By the time I reached the trap the intruder was bleeding badly and in such a serious state that after reading his band number I released him at once. He did not fly, but ran across the yard, our male after him, looking curiously like two rats rather than birds. When he disappeared under an old barn our male returned and seemed to regard the incident as closed. We had banded the intruder as a juvenile July 24, 1935, and this was his only repeat record. The continued and violent attacks on trapped birds within a territory suggest that, as with mockingbirds, an intruder is always at a disadvantage and usually leaves at any sign of hostility. But a trapped bird cannot leave, and this fact is ignored by the territory owner."

In an anlysis of nest-site data in California, John Davis (1951) notes: "In the vicinity of towns and farms the birds seem to nest frequently in trees, especially fruit trees, and to a lesser extent, in ornamentals such as pines, palms, and poplars. Tree nests may be located up to twenty-five feet from the ground." Of 26 nests taken under natural conditions in Reche Canyon, near Colton, Riverside County, "eleven were found in *Eriogonum fasciculatum*. They were placed from two and one-half to three and one-half feet above the ground. Two nests were found in *Ceanothus cuneatus*, two and one-half and three feet above the ground. The rest were found in various situations, including twenty feet up in a sycamore, and one each in *Convolvulus*, *Rhus diversiloba*, sunflower, 'wild holly,' nettles, *Salvia apiana*, scrub oak, and *Lupinus*. One was in a cleft five feet above the ground on the face of a rock wall. Only one was in tuna cactus and only one on the ground."

*Eggs.*—The measurements of 13 eggs average 24.8 by 17.8 millimeters; the eggs showing the four extremes measure 27.7 by 18.2, 26.4 by *18.6*, *21.1* by 17.5, and 23.8 by *17.5* millimeters.

Records of egg weights are not plentiful. Hanna (1924a) recorded the weights of a clutch of six eggs found at Colton, Calif., in a nest in black sage, 2½ feet above the ground. These eggs weighed 4.18, 4.14, 4.05, 4.05, 3.98, and 3.90 grams. As six is an unusual number for a brown towhee clutch, it would be interesting to compare these with the weights of eggs in the normal three- or four-egg clutches.

## DISTRIBUTION

*Range.*—Anthony's brown towhee is resident in southern California, west of the Mohave and Colorado deserts, from Los Angeles County southward through northwestern Baja California, west of the montane coniferous forests, to lat. 29°20′ N. (Yubay). Recorded once from Todos Santos Island, lat. 31°48′ N.

*Egg dates.*—California: 3 records, March 25 to June 6.

### PIPILO FUSCUS ARIPOLIUS Oberholser

## San Pablo Brown Towhee
### Contributed by JOHN DAVIS

### HABITS

Described by H. C. Oberholser (1919), this race differs from *senicula* to the north in the paler and grayer coloration of its pileum and dorsum; whiter, less buffy mid-ventral area; pallor of the posterior part of the throat patch; and longer bill.   In most characters, it is intermediate between *senicula* and *albigula*, which occurs to the south in the cape region of Baja California.   The intermediacy of *aripolius* between *senicula*, a typical representative of the subspecies of the brown towhee found on the Pacific Coast, and *albigula*, which resembles the geographically isolated subspecies of the southwestern United States and northern Mexico, led Oberholser to the conclusion that all the brown towhees were conspecific and should be regarded as belonging to the single species *fuscus*, rather than divided into the species *crissalis*, for the birds of the Pacific Coast, and the species *fuscus* for the towhees to the east and south.   The validity of his conclusion has been upheld by other workers.

The northern limits of the San Pablo brown towhee's distribution occur near the sharp vegetational break between the mixed foothill and desert flora of northwestern Baja California and the extremely rich and varied desert flora that has its northern limits between latitudes 29° and 30° N.   The life history of this form is virtually unknown, although it is a common bird over much of its range.

## DISTRIBUTION

*Range.*—The San Pablo brown towhee is resident in the middle section of the peninsula of Baja California, from Playa María Bay, lat. 28°55′ N. (Grinnell, 1928b) south to Guajademí, lat. 26°35′ N.

*Egg date.*—Baja California: 1 record, April 26.

### PIPILO FUSCUS ALBIGULA Baird
## San Lucas Brown Towhee
### Contributed by JOHN DAVIS

#### HABITS

Described originally by Spencer F. Baird (1859) as *Pipilo albigula*, this well-marked subspecies differs from the race *aripolius* to the north in its paler, more rufescent pileum; paler dorsum, sides, flanks, throat, and under tail coverts; and in its greater area of ventral white. Superficially it resembles the canyon brown towhee (*Pipilo fuscus mesoleucus*), from which it is separated by a broad geographic hiatus, but it is easily differentiated from that form by its generally smaller size and lack of a black breast spot.   Further, its voice is similar to that of the Pacific coast races rather than to that of *mesoleucus* (Marshall, 1964).

The San Lucas brown towhee is restricted to the cape region, or terminal third of the peninsula of Baja California, from latitude 26° 35′

N. south to Cape San Lucas. It is found in the rich desert vegetation of the lowlands, and it also occurs in the mountains of the cape region, in a vegetation containing such highland elements as *Pinus cembroides, Glaucothea brandegeei, Populus monticola, Nolina beldingi, Arbutus peninsularis,* and *Quercus devia.* Most museum specimens of this form have been collected in the lowlands, and this suggests that brown towhees are more common in the deserts of the cape region than in the mountains. Judging by the large number of specimens in collections, it is a common bird over most of its range.

*Nests.*—W. Brewster (1902) stated that three nests collected by M. Abbot Frazar in late July were composed of dry grass, weed stalks, and twigs. Two were lined with horsehair, and one with horsehair and fine grass. Two nests were located in bushes, and one in a tree. All were 6 to 8 feet above ground. Each nest contained three eggs. Baird, Brewer, and Ridgway (1874b) describe two nests found by John Xantus; one, containing four eggs, was located in a wild *Humulus* thicket; the other was found in a thicket of wild roses in a garden fence.

*Eggs.*—Brewster (1902) described the three sets of eggs collected by Frazar as having a ground color "greenish white with a tinge of blue," each egg marked "chiefly about the larger ends, with irregular spots, dashes, and pen-lines of lavender and purplish black." Of the eggs collected by Xantus, Baird, Brewer and Ridgway (1874b) state: "They bear a strong resemblance to those of the *P. fuscus,* but the markings are darker and more distinctly defined, standing out with a clear and striking effect, in marked contrast with the light background. The ground-color of the eggs is a light tint of robin-blue. The markings of dots, dashes, and lines are all about the larger end, and are of a deep dark shade of purplish-brown, so dark as, except in a strong light, to be undistinguishable from black."

H. M. Hill and I. L. Wiggins (1948) found evidence of fall breeding in a male collected five miles northwest of Canipolé, Nov. 18, 1946. The left and right testes of this individual measured 6.0 × 3.5 mm. and 5.0 × 4.0 mm.

The measurements of 32 eggs average 23.5 by 17.2 millimeters; the eggs showing the four extremes measure *25.2* by *18.1, 20.3* by 16.3, and 23.9 by *15.8* millimeters.

## DISTRIBUTION

*Range.*—The San Lucas brown towhee is resident in southern Baja California from lat. 26°35′ N. south to Cape San Lucas.

PIPILO FUSCUS MESOLEUCUS Baird

# Canyon Brown Towhee

PLATES 35 AND 36

Contributed by JOE T. MARSHALL, JR., and R. ROY JOHNSON

## HABITS

It is curious that the arguments over the relationships of similar kinds of birds (like the two kinds of flickers, meadowlarks, and wood pewees) have never touched the canyon towhee as a subspecies of the brown towhee of California. The two have always been considered conspecific, yet they are isolated from each other by the Gulf of California and the Colorado Desert, and they differ from each other in voice, habits, and coloration. The shy canyon towhee calls *sheddap* and has a pleasant jingling song, whereas the bold brown towhee of California calls a sharp *chip* which also serves, in series, as the rare song. Whereas the brown towhee of California is long-tailed and a fairly uniform brown, the canyon towhee of Arizona has a shorter tail, a white belly, a black spot in the middle of the chest, and a reddish-brown crown patch. This line of reasoning unites the two: there is a gradual transition southward from the California brown towhee to a population at the cape of Baja California which resembles the canyon towhee in every detail except the chest spot, which is lacking.

Within their large geographic range canyon towhees live in a variety of habitats. All provide open spaces for feeding on bare ground and dense bushes or trees with low growing limbs for hiding. Examples are desert gullies and foothill canyons in Arizona, where the vegetation is giant cactus and paloverde; around sheds, wood-piles, outbuildings, and chicken-coops of the farm; and in the log fences around corn fields and in scrap lumber piles at sawmills in the forested mountains of Mexico.

*Territory.*—Each pair of canyon towhees lives by itself in an area whose size is such that the pairs are generally spaced about 300 yards apart. Unmated males, singing in spring, cover distances three times that in terrain not held by neighbors. But the lone immature bird in winter also remains in a small area. Nests of adjacent pairs have been found no closer together than 175 yards, and successive nests of the same pair have been as far apart as 120 yards. This spacing of canyon towhees implies that each pair or each solitary bird possesses and holds a territory—its place for successful living and nesting.

Most territorial birds advertise their areas by song and fight for them against encroachment by neighbors. Yet canyon towhees

PLATE 35

Azusa, Calif., June 4, 1946        R. S. Woods

NEST OF CALIFORNIA BROWN TOWHEE

Klondyke, Ariz., May 31, 1936        J. S. Rowley

NEST OF CANYON BROWN TOWHEE

PLATE 36

Big Bend National Park, Texas                    A. D. Cruickshank
CANYON BROWN TOWHEE

Coachella, Calif., Apr. 12, 1936                    J. S. Rowley
NEST OF ABERT'S TOWHEE

have never been seen fighting among themselves. One explanation for this is that the birds are so unobtrusive and shy that they are seldom seen by their neighbors, much less molested. The pair sometimes explores or wanders into the domain of its next-door neighbor, both in winter and when tending its moving offspring, yet the trespass is never challenged. Thus the territory does not seem to be a "defended area," nor is it made conspicuous by advertising song, with the following two exceptions:

The unpaired male in late winter and spring makes himself and his area conspicuous by constant song, but this seems to be to advertise for a mate rather than to proclaim his boundaries to his neighbors. However, should he sing too close to the neighbor, say within 100 yards, the neighboring male will jump on a tree and sing a few songs in reply. These usually suffice to impel the unmated bird farther away at his next change of song-perch. The second exception is a brief few minutes of actual advertisement at dawn in spring and summer, when all the males, mated and unmated alike, sing just after waking.

Canyon towhee pairs simply have strong inclinations to stay at home and to shun company. Although we might criticize them for being antisocial, still their peaceful means of maintaining the necessary space for security, food, and nesting seems worthy of emulation.

*Courtship.*—As canyon towhees probably mate for life (perhaps only 2 or 3 years at best), there is seldom the opportunity to observe the first meeting of two new mates, though it is conceivable that this might take place in fall when groups of young, having become independent of their parents, scatter and cross paths. Judging from the actions of "old married couples," it is likely that the new pair-bond is ceremoniously ushered in with the usual duet of squeals, uttered while the male is perched in a bush a few inches higher than the female. It can also be imagined from the incessant singing of the unpaired male in spring, that should a female appear in response to his song, the same ritual would follow, and that the singing would come to an abrupt halt.

The male canyon towhee works hard and all year round at making his marriage a success, as if the pair were on a permanent honeymoon. While the female feeds along the ground, he watches from a perch in a bush or low tree over her. He solicitously flies to a new lookout post above her when she moves farther away, and when she flies, he too flies to meet her and to join in the ritual duet of squeals mentioned above. When both birds feed on the ground the male stays within a few inches of his mate, and he raises his head more frequently to look about. At the approach of a person he flies up to a perch and watches, while the female continues to feed in perfect security without even glancing up.

*Nesting.*—The following extreme dates of nesting about Tucson, Ariz., encompass a remarkably long nesting season. Marshall saw a pair feeding young out of the nest on Mar. 31, 1958. A. R. Phillips writes, "My latest nest was in a wash at Wilmot Road, Tucson, 5 feet up in a cholla cactus. It had three eggs on Aug. 28, 1939, small young on September 1, young still there September 6, empty and clean on September 12." The normal number of successful nestings by any one pair at Tucson is not known, but one pair had successfully fledged two broods by May 21 in 1958. Both parents had been color-banded the previous winter. The schedule of their two nestings was as follows: stationary juveniles out of nest on March 31, clutch of four eggs in second nest at least from April 15 to 23, young in this nest on April 30, older juveniles following parents from May 21 at least until June 20. As both parents were tending the fully grown young in May and June, we must conclude they had not yet started a third nest, though another 10 weeks still remained of the potential nesting season. July and August nests could be new attempts after repeated failures, or even first attempts by young of the previous year that matured or paired late.

The solidly constructed nest is generally placed against the main trunk of a small tree or tall bush where it is supported by strong branches and well shaded and hidden by foliage or twigs of the tree. Nests have been found around Tucson on the north, shaded side of cholla cacti, mesquites, elderberries, and hackberries at heights from 3 to 12 feet. In the spring of 1958, young were successfully reared before the trees holding their nests had leafed-out. The female canyon towhee is a close sitter. She flushes only when approached to within 2 or 3 feet, and then silently and inconspicuously.

The bulk of a nest collected and analyzed at Tucson was constructed of small twigs, dry composite stems and heads, crucifer stems and inflorescences, leaves of grasses, leafy ends of stems, and large hollow herbaceous stems. It was lined with elm leaves, small shredded hollow herbaceous stems, fine strips of bark, leafy ends of herbaceous stems, and finally with exceedingly fine stems and spikelets of grasses and with animal hair. C. E. Bendire (1890) gives 5½ inches across and 3½ inches in height for outside measurements with 3 inches across and 2 inches in depth for inner dimensions. Brewster (1882a) differs slightly with 5 inches across outside, 2 inches in height, 2 inches across inside, and 1½ inches in depth.

F. C. Willard (1923) lists some unusual nesting sites. One pair built inside a porch in a robin-like situation. Also listed are the tops of cottonwood trees and honeysuckle vines. H. Brandt (1951) tells of a nest made of plant stems bearing yellow flowers, he thought of the mustard family, "forming a gay golden garland." He also mentions yucca tresses as nesting sites. A. W. Anthony (1892) lists cholla cactus and yucca as favorite nesting sites.

*Eggs.*—C. E. Bendire (1890) gives the following description of the eggs:

The eggs are usually three in number; about one nest in ten contains four; occasionally I have found the bird sitting hard on but two, probably a second or third brood. * * *

The ground color of the eggs of the Cañon Towhee is a very pale bluish white, or very light pearl gray, scarcely an egg in a series of one hundred and three specimens can be called pure white. As far as markings are concerned, these eggs can be divided into two types. In one the spots are sharp, well defined, occasionally connected with each other by lines and scrawls, and principally concentrated about the larger end. Their color is a very deep brown, almost a black. This pattern includes the less heavily marked specimens. In the second type, the markings are less clearly defined, more irregular in shape, mere blotches, and much more profuse. The color is less deep, more of a claret brown or vinaceous rufous. In addition fine shell markings of lavender and heliotrope purple are scattered more or less profusely over the entire egg in both types. The eggs bear a certain resemblance to those of *Sturnella*, especially to heavily marked specimens of the western race, *Sturnella magna neglecta*. Nearly all the eggs of *Pipilo fuscus mesoleucus* are much more heavily marked than those of the other two races, aside from the racial difference of the ground color, which is also more lustrous. In a series of one hundred and three specimens before me, all but eleven collected by myself, there is considerable difference both in size and shape. The eggs are mostly ovate, some elliptical ovate. The average size of the series before me is .92 x .69 inch. The largest egg measures 1.04 x .71, the smallest .81 x .66 inch, and a runt egg of this species in the collection measures but .70 x .56 inch.

W. G. F. Harris adds: "This subspecies usually lays three or four ovate or short ovate eggs, sometimes only two or as many as five and less frequently six. They are slightly glossy. The ground is very pale greenish or creamy white, with markings of very dark brown and black with under spots of 'light Quaker drab,' or 'light mouse gray.' These markings are in the form of speckles, spots, scrawls, or scribblings rather sparingly scattered over the entire egg, but more numerous toward the large end where frequently a loose wreath may be formed. The eggs with the creamy white ground usually are spotted with dark browns such as 'liver brown,' 'Carob brown,' or 'Hessian brown,' and black with a few spots of gray; those with the greenish white grounds tend to be marked almost entirely with black and gray undermarkings with only an occasional spot of very dark brown such as 'chestnut brown.' Many eggs are marked only with spots or small blotches of the grays with a few spots or scrawls of black. The measurements of 50 eggs average 23.4 by 17.5 millimeters; the eggs showing the four extremes measure *26.9* by 16.8, 25.4 by *18.8*, *20.6* by 16.8, and 20.8 by *15.2* millimeters."

*Incubation.*—Only the female incubates. Every few hours she leaves the nest to feed under the watchful eye of the male, solicitous as usual. A sure sign of incubation is the singing of the male past the normal short period at dawn. He sings loudly and constantly from a conspicuous perch in a tree almost all the time she is incubating; he stops singing and joins her the moment she leaves the nest to feed. No accurate data are available on the length of the incubation period in this race.

*Young.*—Upon leaving the nest, the young climb up into the bushes or low trees and remain stationary for long periods while uttering a high, thin *sip* food call. The parents use the same note, but much louder and more piercing, as an alarm note; when uttered it silences the food-calls of the young. Only when much older do the young begin to move after the parents to be fed. Then their note has filled out to the ordinary locative *see*.

Groups of canyon towhees seen in some autumns may be families of young still staying near their parents. Thus in mid-November Marshall saw two birds with a color-banded adult female in an area where canyon towhees are rather uncommon. They may have been her young, as they were all feeding together at a feeding station about 10 yards from a bush in which she had nested the previous spring. A. R. Phillips writes that his latest record of a "flock" (family?) of three or four birds was on Feb. 19, 1939.

*Plumages.*—The natal down is brown. At the time of leaving the nest the fully-feathered juvenile has a bobbed tail and is in a lacy brown coat with spotting on the chest, somewhat like that of a thrush. During October the post-juvenal molt is completed. This replaces the thin lacy body and head feathers with firmer, more solidly colored feathers like those of the adult. However, the nestling wing and all or most of the tail feathers are retained. A year later, in fall, a complete molt renews the adult body plumage and at last endows the now mature bird with adult wing and tail feathers. These have perfect margins and are broader, blacker, and more square-ended than are the corresponding juvenal feathers of fall immature birds. Therefore, the bird bander can easily tell the sex and age of his captured birds by these plumage criteria (for age) and measurements of the wing and tail (for sex) as set forth and explained in detail in John Davis's (1951) monograph of the brown towhees.

*Food.*—All the feeding is done on the ground, where seeds in winter and insects in summer are picked up in the bill by repeated dabs while the body is held horizontal. Birds often scratch the ground by jumping and moving both feet simultaneously to scuff dirt and leaves out toward the rear. But scratching is not as incessant in the canyon towhee as in the rufous-sided and green-tailed towhees, nor does it seem as frequent as in the Abert's towhee. In winter-taken stomachs, in addition to a great variety of seeds, there are little colorful crystals the birds pick up daily to help grind the seeds in the stomach.

During the nesting season parents gather insects by the beakful for their young. Both parents have been seen to feed young out of the nest, each parent apparently providing for a certain offspring. In one family, the male seemed not to be gathering food. Instead, he sang while the female was out of sight, then carefully supervised her approach to feed the stationary young out of the nest by duplicating her path higher up.

*Behavior.*—The canyon towhee is normally one of the shyest birds of southern Arizona. A few fortunate persons who live in foothill homes where natural vegetation of saguaro and palo verde is preserved have birds about their yards, visiting their drinking or feeding stations, which become fairly tame. So are those that live about Indian homes and dooryards in rural Mexico. But in wild country the birds, though known to be present, can avoid being seen from dawn until dusk. In fall and early winter, when they call least often they may utter the call-note only five or six times at dawn, and perhaps a few more times in succession at dusk. During the rest of the day they may have only three or four other periods of brief calling, or of squealing in the case of a pair. In winter the towhee calls as much while going to roost as it does during the rest of the day. In the gloom of dusk it will ascend to a post to call for a few minutes before flying to a dense bush to roost 4 to 8 feet off the ground.

The canyon towhee especially likes to feed under things—under bushes, log fences, old buildings, and chicken-houses. Lew Blatchley reports that at Silver City, N. Mex., a favorite resort for the canyon towhees is under his parked car. At Tucson they have been seen feeding under trailers, under wagons on the farm, under dense patches of tumbleweeds, under mesquites, and within tall grasses.

When it feeds in the open, the canyon towhee always stays within a few feet of dense bushes, to which it retreats even when other kinds of birds of lesser size fly by or alight, as at a feeder. Also the towhee keeps on the move, no matter how abundant the food at a particular spot. It may scratch in one place for five minutes or more, but usually it samples the feeder's offering, runs back into the bushes, and moves on.

C. F. Batchelder (1885) encountered the canyon towhee at Las Vegas Hot Springs, N. Mex., in December 1882. He had this to say of the behavior of this race:

In the willows along the river bank the Cañon Towhees (*Pipilo fuscus mesoleucus*) were sometimes to be seen, though they frequented other places as well.

Among their resorts were the small cliffs scattered along the river, where they poked about among the masses of fallen rocks at their bases, and in the clefts and gullies by which they were intersected. They were apt to be found, too, about the Mexican villages, where they might be seen perched on the high adobe walls surrounding a courtyard, or exploring the ruins of some deserted house that offered a safe retreat in case of alarm. Perhaps, however, the places where they were most numerous were some small irrigated fields on the outskirts of one of these little villages. Where these fields bordered the river or an irrigating ditch, they were fringed with bushes, chiefly willows, that were a favorite haunt of the Towhees. Here one would sometimes be seen running along and then stopping, somewhat like a Robin on an earthworm hunt. Their run really consists, however, of a series of rapid hops. There is much that is Thrush-like about their air and motions, and if seen from behind one might almost be mistaken for a Robin, its form and attitudes are so similar, though it does not stand as upright as a Robin very often does. As a rule they kept on the ground but now and then they would get up in a bush or even in a low tree, but as soon as a Towhee saw he was attracting attention he immediately shifted his position or retired silently with a swift low flight to some safer place.

Though they commonly go in small flocks I am inclined to think that some at least remain paired throughout the year. They are not infrequently found in couples; in one such case dissection proved them to be male and female; in another when I had shot one bird the survivor showed evident signs of distress.

F. M. Bailey (1923) says of the canyon towhee: "It was one of the commonest birds of the mesquite and catsclaw as well as of the canyons in the region of McCleary's (Nicholson's) during the winter and spring of 1920–1921. Several were caught in traps set for live mammals, evidently attracted by the popular rolled oats." She also mentions finding it in January 1923 in groups of two, three, or four on the ground along roads.

*Voice.*—The usual song of the canyon towhee is a series of six or seven double syllables, all alike and evenly spaced, as *chili-chili-chili-chili-chili-chili*. The song may begin or end with a different note, or it may begin with a faint rendition of the usual call note. Some series are of single notes, others are in fine trills like those of juncos. At its worst the song is a dull series of *chilps*, but at its best it is a gay, sustained jingle to be compared with that of a titmouse. A male whose dawn singing has been dull and perfunctory during late winter and early spring will become transformed into a polished singer when his mate disappears to incubate. At that time it is evident, as it has been in unpaired males, that the charm is lent by the variety of the songs resorted to, each variation prevailing for a series of several songs. The more brilliant the songs, the more frequently are their patterns changed.

The ordinary call note, used also as an alarm note, is a two-syllable *tscheddap*, of which the second syllable may be suppressed to *tschedd'p*. This call is explosively uttered and is "rusty," that is, rather hoarse.

The duet squeal is exactly the same as that of the California brown towhee and is uttered under the same circumstances, in ceremonial reaffirming of the pair relationship. It can be represented as *squeal-churrrr* or *squeal—squeal-squeal-squeal,* which can readily be told in the field from the laughing *squeal-cha-cha-cha* or *squeal—hah-hah-hah* of the Abert's towhee.

Birds keep in touch by an occasional unquavering locative note, *see.* It is similar to the food call of the young and to the louder warning call of the parent mentioned earlier. Finally there is a light *tic* of alarm, uttered when an intruder comes near the nest.

Bailey (1923) reports that the commonest call resembles that of the California towhee, *scree-kee-gee, kee-gee-kee.* She likens the one quick call note to that of the Gila woodpecker.

*Field marks.*—The traveler of country roads through river-bottom farmlands in southern Arizona will flush before his car numerous nondescript brown birds of medium size from the mesquites and hackberries of the fence rows. These are Bendire thrashers, curve-billed thrashers, crissal thrashers, female cardinals and pyrrhuloxias, Abert's towhees, and canyon towhees. Of all these, the canyon towhee has the broadest and shortest tail for its size. It does not constantly jerk or bob the tail, as do the pyrrhuloxias. The canyon towhee is the only member of this group with a lone central dark breast spot. This attribute eliminates everything but the strikingly handsome, white-flashing lark sparrow. Of course when the bird is on the ground its spot cannot be relied upon, especially if it is under shady bushes. Then it can easily be mistaken for an Abert's towhee. However the light face and fairly dark bill of the canyon towhee is in great contrast to the whitish bill and black area around its base, by which the Abert's towhee presents a different appearance almost as far as it can be seen.

*Enemies.*—Apparently little is known of the enemies of the canyon towhee. Herbert Friedmann (1934) states that Griffing Bancroft has two sets of eggs from Santa Fe County, N. Mex., which had been parasitized by brown-headed cowbirds (*Molothrus ater*).

External parasites of the families Ricinidae and Hippoboscidae have been found on specimens banded near Tucson.

### DISTRIBUTION

*Range.*—The canyon towhee is resident from western Arizona (Black Mountains, Kofa Mountains, Papago Well) east through New Mexico (except Union County in northeast), south to northern Sonora (lat. 30° N.), northern Chihuahua (lat. 31° N.), and extreme western Texas (El Paso, Guadalupe Mountains).

*Casual record.*—Casual north to Grand Canyon, Arizona.

*Egg dates.*—Arizona: 73 records, March 3 to September 8; 38 records, May 2 to June 12.

New Mexico: 20 records, March 22 to July 8; 10 records, May 21 to June 13.

## PIPILO FUSCUS RELICTUS van Rossem

## Harquahala Brown Towhee

### Contributed by JOHN DAVIS

#### HABITS

This race, described by A. J. van Rossem (1946b), has a very limited distribution in Yuma and Maricopa counties, Ariz., where it is restricted to the Harquahala Mountains and Eagle Eye Peak. *P. f. relictus* allegedly differs from *P. f. mesoleucus* in the relatively darker coloration of its dorsum, sides, flanks, and throat. However, the brown towhees of the Harquahala Mountains vary considerably in color, and many individuals are indistinguishable from *mesoleucus*.

The Harquahala brown towhee is resident in a vegetation composed in part of scrub oak, manzanita, mountain mahogany, *Ceanothus*, and laurel, which differs markedly from the surrounding desert vegetation at lower elevations. Nothing is known of its life history.

#### DISTRIBUTION

*Range.*—The Harquahala brown towhee is resident in the Harquahala Mountains in southwestern Arizona, above 2,500 feet.

## PIPILO FUSCUS MESATUS Oberholser

## Colorado Brown Towhee

### Contributed by JOHN DAVIS

#### HABITS

This subspecies, described by H. C. Oberholser (1937), is differentiated from *P. f. mesoleucus* by its paler pileum, browner coloration of the dorsum, sides, and flanks, longer wing, and higher wing-tail ratio. A locally common resident of the piñon–juniper association of southeastern Colorado, northeastern New Mexico, and northwestern Oklahoma, the Colorado brown towhees are limited in their occurrence to the west by the eastern ranges of the Rocky Mountains, and to the north by the constriction of the piñon–juniper association north of the Arkansas River.

Cooke (1897) states that *mesatus* breeds in the latter part of April, nesting in juniper and sometimes in cacti. Nice (1922) found three nests near Kenton, Okla., on June 1 and 2. Two nests contained three eggs each, and the third held three young. One nest was in a piñon, one in a juniper, and the third in a tree cactus. Late nesting of some individuals is indicated by the collecting of a female almost entirely in juvenal plumage on Oct. 4, 1932 (Sutton, 1934).

## DISTRIBUTION

*Range.*—The Colorado brown towhee is resident in southeastern Colorado (mainly south of the Arkansas River, sparingly north to Boulder), northeastern New Mexico (Union County), and extreme northwestern Oklahoma (Kenton).

### PIPILO FUSCUS TEXANUS van Rossem

## Texas Brown Towhee

### Contributed by JOHN DAVIS

#### HABITS

Described by A. J. van Rossem (1934c), the race *texanus* resembles *mesoleucus* in color, but can be distinguished from that race by its darker pileum, shorter tail, and higher wing-tail ratio.

The Texas brown towhee occupies two main centers of distribution—the broken, mountainous country west of the Pecos River and the Edwards Plateau. Recently, its range has been extended south to the Sierra del Carmen, in northern Coahuila, Mexico (Miller, 1955a). West of the Pecos River, *texanus* occurs in the piñon–juniper association. On the Edwards Plateau, brown towhees have been found in oak–savanna pastures, juniper brakes, and dense thickets of "shinnery" oak. Lloyd (1887) found a nest of this towhee containing three incubated eggs in the fork of a small live oak tree in Tom Green County. He states that nests found farther west contained five eggs each, and he considered three eggs an exceptionally small clutch. Van Tyne and Sutton (1937) found three nests in Brewster County on May 20, 30, and 31. One nest contained two eggs and two contained three eggs each; all eggs were fresh. Parents were seen feeding short-tailed but fully fledged young on May 2 and 4.

## DISTRIBUTION

*Range.*—The Texas brown towhee is resident in northern Coahuila (Sierra del Carmen) and in the plateau area of western and central Texas from Reeves, Tom Green, and Kerr counties to Val Verde County.

PIPILO ABERTI Baird

# Abert's Towhee*

PLATE 36

Contributed by WILLIAM R. DAWSON

## HABITS

The Abert's towhee comprises two subspecies, the ecology and the behavior of which appear similar, and both forms are treated in this account. They are abundant residents in the vicinity of water courses, either permanent or intermittent, in parts of the deserts of southwestern United States, and they actively penetrate the thickest parts of the riparian vegetation with which they are characteristically associated (E. Coues, 1866; C. B. R. Kennerly, 1859; W. Brewster, 1882a; W. W. Price, 1899; and John Davis, 1951). However, they will exploit edge vegetation, and I was successful in trapping birds of the subspecies *P. a. dumeticolus* at the junction between riparian growth and what A. H. Miller (1951c) has termed "desert scrub" vegetation.

The plant associates of the two forms of the Abert's towhee are generally similar. In New Mexico and Arizona, *P. a. aberti* has been recorded most frequently in mesquite (*Prosopis* sp.) (H. W. Henshaw, 1875; F. Stevens, 1878; W. Brewster, 1882a; H. K. Coale, 1894; G. F. Breninger, 1901; and H. S. Swarth, 1905a) and to a lesser extent in cottonwoods (*Populus fremontii*) and willow (*Salix* sp.). According to Davis (1951), the late A. J. van Rossem and L. H. Miller collected them in arrowweed (*Pluchea sericea*) along the Bill Williams River in western Arizona. They have also been observed in Arizona about farms, citrus groves, and urban areas (F. M. Dille, 1935). The increased irrigation of desert lands in this state undoubtedly is increasing the amount of habitat suitable for Abert's towhees.

Birds of the subspecies *P. a. dumeticolus* have been most frequently recorded in willow, mesquite, and arrowweed growth (W. W. Price, 1899; N. Hollister, 1908; van Rossem, 1911; G. Bancroft, 1922; and W. R. Dawson, 1954), but J. Grinnell (1914b) concludes that they are most commonly associated along the Colorado River with quail brush (*Atriplex lentiformis*) and mesquite. In the Imperial Valley of California I have observed them occurring frequently in a reed (*Phragmites communis*), and somewhat less commonly in a species of

---

*The following subspecies are discussed in this section: *Pipilo aberti aberti* Baird and *P. a. dumeticolus* van Rossem.

*Baccharis* and in an introduced tree, *Tamarix gallica*. I believe that a marked enlargement of habitat suitable for Abert's towhees has occurred in southeastern California, as in Arizona, as a result of the enlargement of irrigation facilities there in the past few decades.

*Nesting.*—Abert's towhees of both subspecies nest most commonly in willows, and three quarters of the 80 nests of *P. a. aberti* C. E. Bendire (1890) found along Rillito Creek near Tucson, Pima County, Ariz., were in plants of this type, particularly stumps. Mesquite also appears to be regularly used as a nest site (Gilman, 1915; Bendire, 1890). *P. a. aberti* has also been recorded nesting in a Mexican elderberry shrub (*Sambucus mexicana?*) (Brandt, 1951); a species of ash (*Fraxinus* sp.) (Bendire, 1890); *Suaeda torreyana*, umbrella tree (*Melia azedarach*), and *Zizyphus* (M. F. Gilman, 1915); cottonwood (F. C. Willard, 1923), and a mistletoe clump (*Phoradendron* sp.) in a cottonwood (F. Stevens, 1878). *P. a. dumeticolus* is known to nest in willows and mesquite and has also been recorded nesting in arrow-weed and mistletoe clumps (*Phoradendron* sp.) probably located in mesquite (van Rossem, 1911), and in such introduced plants as pepper trees (*Schinus molle*) and orange trees near Palm Springs, Riverside County, Calif. (M. F. Gilman, 1903).

The nest of the Abert's towhee is rather bulky and loosely constructed (H. Brandt, 1951; H. Brown, 1903; and F. M. Bailey, 1928). W. L. Dawson (1923) describes a typical one as follows:

"A typical nest of this towhee is a bulky assemblage of weed-stems, dead vines, bark-strips, green leaves; and, interiorly, coiled bark, dried grasses, and horsehair. Bark is a favorite material, and I have seen nests which contained nothing else. Occasionally, the taste inclines to green grass, and the superstructure may be composed of green, or recently dried, grass or leaves of a single sort. * * *"

Bendire (1890) reported the dimensions of one nest to be: outer diameter, 5.5 inches; overall depth, 4 inches; inner diameter, 3 inches; inside depth, 2.5 inches. Brown's (1903) and Brewster's (1882a) measurements of other nests of this species are comparable.

The nests are placed off the ground usually in low bushes. There are several records of them placed in trees. Bendire (1890) found one such along Rillito Creek in an ash fully 25 feet above the ground, and Stevens (1878) found another apparently along the Gila River in a clump of mistletoe about 30 feet above the ground. Perhaps the most unusual nest site on record was a cavity near the top of a rotten cottonwood stump 12 feet above the ground (F. C. Willard, 1923).

*Eggs.*—The clutch size for birds of both subspecies ranges from two to four (C. K. Averill, 1933; F. M. Bailey, 1928; Bendire, 1890; van Rossem, 1911; and M. F. Gilman, 1903), with the usual number three. There is a single record of a clutch of five eggs, apparently for *P. a. dumeticolus* (H. Brown, 1903).

The eggs are generally ovate, though elliptical or elongate-ovate examples are found occasionally. Characteristically their ground color is a plae clay blue, and Bendire (1890) thought it to be paler than that of the eggs of either *Pipilo fuscus crissalis* (*senicula?*) or *P. f. albigula*. The markings of the eggs of Abert's towhees are sparse but well defined. They are usually heaviest about the larger end, and are dark brown in color. Eggs with almost black markings occur occasionally. Some have been described with brown markings bordered by vinaceous and rufous. Infrequently the markings, whatever their color, are connected by fine pigmented lines. Paler shell markings of lavender or purple have been described in some eggs.

Measurements of 83 eggs of *P. a. aberti* yielded the following data—mean dimensions, 0.94 by 0.70 inches (23.8 by 17.8 millimeters); largest egg in the series, 1.08 by 0.70 inches (27.4 by 17.8 millimeters); and smallest egg in the series, 0.82 by 0.69 inches (20.8 by 17.5 millimeters). Brewster's (1882a) measurements of three eggs fall within these ranges.

W. G. F. Harris writes: "The Abert's towhee usually lays three or four slightly glossy eggs, sometimes only two and less frequently five. They are ovate or short-ovate and practically indistinguishable from those of the canon towhee. The ground may be very pale greenish or creamy white with scattered spots and scrawls of black and very dark browns such as 'chestnut brown,' 'Carob brown,' or 'mummy brown,' with undermarkings of 'light neutral gray,' or 'dark purplish gray.' The eggs generally are rather sparingly marked, and mostly toward the large end. Often a loose wreath is formed of small black scribblings interspersed with a few gray spots. The measurements of 50 eggs average 24.1 by 17.8 millimeters; the eggs showing the four extremes measure *27.7* by 17.3, 23.4 by *19.3*, *20.8* by 17.5, and 25.4 by 16.3 millimeters. The measurements of 17 western Abert's towhee eggs average 24.8 by 18.2 millimeters; the eggs showing the four extremes measure *27.3* by *19.9*, *23.3* by 18.2, and 25.1 by *17.3* millimeters."

*Plumages.*—The following information on the molts and plumages of all the brown towhees (*Pipilo fuscus*, *Pipilo albicollis*, and *Pipilo aberti*) is taken directly from John Davis (1951):

The molt pattern of the brown towhees has been determined through the study of fall-taken specimens, the ages of which were ascertained by the degree of skull ossification. The only molt of real significance in the brown towhees is the fall molt. At this time adults undergo complete feather replacement. Birds undergoing the postjuvenal (first fall) molt retain the primaries and secondaries, and usually the rectrices. This molt pattern offers plumage characters that may be used to separate first-year birds from second-year or older birds. In fresh fall plumage the primaries of the first-year (=immature) birds are dull brown and the margins of these feathers are finely erose because of wear. The primaries of second-year and older (=adults) at this time are glossy and nearly black and the margins of these feathers are entire. The rectrices of immature birds have pointed tips * * * and show signs of wear. The rectrices of adults are obtuse at the tip * * * and are glossy and unworn. Since rectrices are often replaced in the postjuvenal molt, the amount of wear on the primaries offers the most reliable criterion for judging age. * * *

Juveniles are at once distinguished from immatures and adults by the extensive streaking and spotting of the underparts and by the very soft and lacy texture of the head and body plumage.

Coues (1866) considered the molt of the Abert's towhee to occur from July well into October. Henshaw (1875) found all of the six specimens he obtained along the Gila River in mid-September to be molting. I did not observe towhees in this condition in the Imperial Valley of California until late August.

The Abert's towhee has a grayish brown pileum and a slightly paler and grayer dorsum. Its breast, sides, and flanks are pinkish gray. The chin is black and the throat is grayish pink streaked with black. The under tail coverts are dull cinnamon, and the primaries are dark grayish brown with the rectrices blackish brown. *P. a. aberti*, originally described by S. F. Baird (1852), differs from *P. a. dumeticolus*, originally described by van Rossem (1946a), in having a darker, grayer pileum and dorsum, and grayer underparts with a pinkish rather than a cinnamon tinge. The bill in both forms is horn colored and contrasts strongly with the black face patch. Immatures and adults show no consistent differences in coloration (Davis, 1951).

*Food.*—No comprehensive study of the food habits of Abert's towhees has been published, but presumably the general nature of their diet approximates those of the brown and the spotted towhees (*P. fuscus* and *P. erythrophtalmus*) analyzed in California by F. E. L. Beal (1910)—animal material constituted 14 percent of the total food taken by the former and 24 percent of that by the latter. I have observed Abert's towhees foraging extensively around quail brush, apparently obtaining the fallen seeds of this plant, and I have trapped these birds successfully using millet seed as bait. Like most other passerines, they will readily eat meal worms (*Tenebrio larvae*) in captivity. Their utilization of insects in nature is suggested by Stevens's (1878) and Stephens's (in Brewster, 1882a) observations of their hunting in the bark of large trees like wrens or nuthatches.

*Behavior.*—The wariness of Abert's towhees has impressed many ornithologists, and Bendire (1890) rated them among the shyest birds of his acquaintance. They are generally difficult to approach and to observe, because of the denseness of the riparian growth which they frequent much of the time. However, it is usually easy to detect their presence in an area owing to their habit of calling frequently under most conditions. As indicated above, they are not strictly confined to riparian vegetation, but will venture forth a few yards into adjacent, more open situations to forage and dust bathe. When disturbed, they usually retreat directly back into riparian growth, even though closer shelter may be available.

Abert's towhees live in areas marked by very hot summers; environmental temperatures above 40° C. and intense solar radiation are common. During hot weather these birds generally confine their activity to the cooler parts of the day—the early morning and late afternoon. In the hottest part of the day, between approximately 11:00 a.m. and 3:30 p.m., they apparently take shelter in the densest part of their riparian habitat and remain inactive. Along the Alamo River, Imperial County, Calif., I (1954) never found them in open areas during mid-day in hot weather. This pattern of behavior, which minimizes their metabolic heat production in the coolest surroundings available, appears to be of critical importance in their coping with heat stress. Activity of Abert's towhees declined to a much smaller degree during the middle of the day in cooler weather, when birds were observed frequently in the more open parts of their habitat.

Various opinions have been expressed concerning the social tendencies of these birds. Bendire (1890), on the basis of experience with *P. a. aberti*, considered them to be less social than brown towhees (*P. f. mesoleucus*), whereas Coues (1866), on the basis of experience with the same form, thought them to be more gregarious than other members of the genus *Pipilo*. Coues, according to Baird, Brewer, and Ridgway (1874b), observed small flocks of this form in September. Henshaw (1875) also observed them to be gregarious in this month. Coues (1866) noted Abert's towhees to associate occasionally with brown towhees along Rillito Creek in Arizona. I have always considered Abert's towhees to be rather gregarious during the nonbreeding season, and this is consistent with the observations of Brown (1903), who repeatedly saw them in rather large flocks in the early winter months along the Colorado and lower Gila rivers "scratching in the earth and sunning themselves like a lot of quail."

In the vicinity of Tucson, Arizona, *P. a. aberti* and *P. fuscus mesoleucus* occur together in the same mesquite river-bottom woodlands. J. T. Marshall (1960) considers that they are in direct competition with each other there, though he found little indication of antagonism between the two species.

*Voice.*—The call of the Abert's towhee is reminiscent of that of the brown towhee, but it seems to me to be less metallic and to have a more whistlelike quality. It has been variously described as "sharp, high pitched" (F. M. Bailey, 1928); a "loud, clear, sharp chirp"

(Coues, 1866); a "loud chuck" (Coale, 1894); a "huit, huit" (Bendire, 1890); and a "sharp chirp" (Brewster, 1882a). The Abert's towhee will occasionally produce a succession of notes which progressively increase in frequency, characterized by Baird, Brewer, and Ridgway (1874b) as *"chip, chip, chee-chee-chee."*

Marshall (1960) provides the most comprehensive account of the voice of this species. He characterizes the call note as a "sharp peep," the male song as an "accelerating series of its ordinary call note, *peep*, often terminating in coarse phrases like the song of a Tolmie Warbler," the locative note as a quavering *"seee,"* the alarm note near a nest with young as a *"tic,"* and the pair reinforcement call as a *"squeal-cha-cha-cha."*

*Field marks.*—Abert's towhees are light brown birds about 9 inches in total length and weighing approximately 45 grams. The most conspicuous field mark is the black face patch which contrasts sharply with the light-colored conical bill.

*Enemies.*—Abert's towhees of both subspecies are occasionally parasitized by cowbirds (*Molothrus ater obscurus*). Brown (1903) found nests with cowbird eggs in them along the Colorado and lower Gila rivers, A. B. Howell found a nest containing a cowbird egg near Gadsden, Yuma County, Ariz. (Friedmann, 1929), and H. Friedmann (1931) records several others near Mesa, Maricopa County, Ariz.

A number of predators appear to prey on Abert's towhees at all stages in their life history, and Bendire (1890) suggests that snakes, jays, squirrels, hawks, and owls all take a toll of eggs, young, and, in some cases, adults. Gilman (1915) recorded discovering an empty nest with a blacksnake coiled around it near Sacaton, Pinal County, Ariz.; a pair of adult towhees obviously agitated by its presence remained nearby. Roadrunners (*Geococcyx californicus*) may prey on young birds, because one H. C. Bryant (1916) collected at Palo Verde, Imperial County, Calif., contained a nestling Abert's towhee. However, the possibility that the roadrunner had obtained it dead could not be discounted.

Two helminth parasites have been found in Abert's towhees of the subspecies *dumeticolus*, collected in the Imperial Valley of California. One of these was a tape worm, *Anonchotaenia longiovata* (M. Voge and B. S. Davis, 1953); the other, a nemotode crop worm for which the identification is not at this time available (W. R. Dawson, notes).

## DISTRIBUTION

*Range.*—The eastern Abert's towhee (*P. a. aberti*) is resident along the Gila River and its tributaries in southern Arizona and southwestern New Mexico (Cliff, Redrock). The western Abert's towhee (*P. a. dumeticolus*) is resident in the valleys of the Virgin and lower Colorado rivers from southwestern Utah (St. George) to northeastern Baja California and northwestern Sonora, and in the Salton Sea Basin of southeastern California (west to Whitewater).

*Egg dates.*—Arizona: 92 records, February 28 to September 4; 46 records, April 1 to May 31.

## CALAMOSPIZA MELANOCORYS Stejneger

### Lark Bunting

#### PLATES 37 AND 38

#### Contributed by HENRY E. BAUMGARTEN

#### HABITS

The lark bunting was first reported by Townsend who, in the company of Nuttall, discovered it on May 24, 1837, shortly after crossing the north branch of the Platte River in central Nebraska. Nuttall regarded the lark bunting as a close relative of the bobolink and assigned it to the same genus. Indeed, there is considerable resemblance between the two birds in general appearance and behavior, and many less experienced observers in some parts of the lark bunting's breeding range call it "bobolink." Other names that have been used to describe this species are: white winged blackbird, white-winged bunting, and buffalo-bird.

Roberts (1936) has expanded Coues's (1874) earlier observations of the specialized character of the lark bunting, "pointing out that in some ways it is like a Lark, has the bill of a Grosbeak, the seasonal plumage changes of the Bobolink, notes and manner of singing like the Yellow-breasted Chat, gregarious habits of the Blackbirds," and a nest and eggs "almost indistinguishable from those of the Dickcissel, with which bird it is somewhat akin in its nomadic habits." These characteristics do render the lark bunting unique and endear it to those with whom it spends the late spring and summer.

The lark bunting breeds in Transition and Upper Sonoran Zones from southern Alberta, southern Saskatchewan, and southwestern Manitoba, south to northwestern Texas and New Mexico, east to Nebraska and western Minnesota. Unfortunately during the past 50 years the lark bunting has all but abandoned the eastern and northeastern portions of its breeding range. Thus, Roberts (1936) wrote that "it was a keen disappointment to the bird-students of the state that the breaking up of the native prairie caused it to leave after it had become well established for so many years over a wide area and was apparently on the way toward occupying all the prairie region of Minnesota." Similarly, William Youngworth (MS.) has concluded "after nearly 40 years of field work in the area under discussion, that the Lark Bunting has deserted Iowa and Minnesota in the main as a nesting bird. A stray pair now and then nests in northwestern Iowa, but the main nesting area has now been pushed back roughly from a line west of Lincoln, Nebr., through Norfolk, Nebr., to Yankton, S. Dak., to about Sisseton, S. Dak. There still would be a few nesting on this line and it would not be improbable east of the line."

Although the lark bunting has disappeared from parts of its breeding range, its propensity to wander carries it far from its usual haunts in migration. It is not at all unusual for the lark bunting to appear, sometimes in goodly numbers, in southern California in late winter or spring, or to visit nearby Nevada and Utah, but its occasional appearance in Oregon, Ohio, Virginia, Massachusetts, Quebec, and New Brunswick represent a rare ornithogical reward for the alert observers who have recorded it so far from home.

In addition to somewhat irregular movements during migration, the lark bunting shows some tendency to fluctuate greatly in abundance in given localities from year to year. The species apparently shows no great attachment for any particular nesting grounds, and may be abundant one year in a given area and uncommon the next. Tout (1902) has suggested that the lark bunting is more abundant in dry than in wet years. Its variation in numbers from year to year has led many local people to associate good crop years and even the best planting times with the abundance of lark buntings. Thus, Gerbracht (1944) writes of the species in North Dakota:

Their arrival means settled warm weather, and everything subject to frost may be planted safely. * * * We get our corn ground ready, and then wait for the buntings to appear * * *. And it always proves to be the pick of the season, better than either earlier or later.

* * * The buntings seem to know whether the season will be propitious or otherwise. If they arrive in great numbers and every fence and weed stalk is hanging full of them, and the air from the first streak of daylight until after dark is full of their song, and they immediately start housekeeping, we know that they know a good season is ahead, and there will be plenty of everything for both us and them. But if their numbers are scanty and they are mute and uneasy, apparently unsatisfied with the prospects and disappear in a few days, we know the season will be poor and the harvest meager.

In "good" years the lark buntings are indeed abundant. Pettingill and Dana (1943) estimated that, in driving the 275 miles from Brooking, S. Dak., to the edge of the Badlands on June 2 and 3, they saw roughly 4,125 lark buntings on or within the fence paralleling the road.

*Spring.*—From its winter home in northern Mexico, and less commonly in southern Texas, southern New Mexico, and southern Arizona, the lark bunting begins its northward migration in early March. However, it wends its way northward so slowly that it does not reach the northern limit of its breeding range, southern Canada from southern Alberta east to southwestern Manitoba, until the first of June. W. W. Cooke (*in* Bailey, 1928) has described its passage through New Mexico as follows:

"In the spring of 1904 it arrived at Rinconada on April 23 * * * and this is probably not far from an average date for northern New Mexico. * * * The larger part have passed across the State by the middle of May, but a flock of about thirty birds was seen at Shiprock as late as June 2, 1907 * * *. The fact that they were still in a flock would seem to indicate that they were late migrants, rather than local breeders."

By late March the vanguard reaches southwestern Kansas, although the main body of migrants does not appear there until mid-April (R. and L. Graber, 1951). About 2 weeks later lark buntings penetrate to the eastern plains of Colorado. The following charming account of the species' appearance on the Colorado prairies was written by Langdon (1933):

May adorns the prairies and hills with flowers and summons her choralists to sing the joy of living. Heeding her call, as they have heeded it from time immemorial, the Lark Buntings begin to arrive in Colorado during the first week of the Month of Flowers. The male is robed in black and white, but, infrequently, his black coat is overcast with slaty gray, as if he had put on a silken duster. * * * And what of the subject of this Dandy's chivalrous attentions. If we call the coat of the Western Lark Sparrow beautiful, we shall be obliged to say, as alas we too often cannot truthfully say of the feminine-in-feathers, Lady Lark Bunting wears a beautiful gown. Indeed, were it not for the light buff where her spouse wears white, and for her "grosbeak", it would take close scrutiny to distinguish her from the Western Lark Sparrow, often seen in the Lark Bunting company during migration. Lady Bunting's large wing-patch, so evident in flight, is, however, a certain badge of identity.
* * *
Some authorities say the males precede the females in the spring by about a week, but I do not remember seeing a segregated flock. I have seen a lone scout travel in advance of the flocks a few days. In my experience, the Lark Buntings return, singing joyously, in choruses of various numbers, from a few to two or three hundred individuals, the average flock numbering perhaps twenty to forty.

On the average the lark bunting appears in central and western Nebraska during the first week of May and in South Dakota and eastern Montana a week later. Cameron (1908), in describing the status of the species in Custer and Dawson counties in Montana, stated that the lark bunting arrives "about the second week in May. It is invariably called Bobolink and confused with that bird. The males precede the females by about five days and, when all have arrived, flying hosts are seen strung out for about a quarter of a mile. * * * Although essentially prairie birds, the flocks rest in the trees when migrating through pine hills." Continuing their push northward, the most venturesome of the migrants reach their northernmost breeding grounds in southern Manitoba, Saskatchewan, and Alberta by the last week in May.

*Courtship.*—We note the courtship of the lark bunting chiefly in the approximately 2-week period between their arrival in flocks and their gradual dispersal to the nesting areas. Langdon (1933) describes courtship among lark buntings in Colorado as follows: "Courtship, delightful to behold, takes place in the flocks. Females seem receptive as the males, with fluffed feathers and uplifted crowns, sing to them individually during the brief pauses in the busy journeyings. Soon after this home-coming jollity has spent itself, the flocks break up into pairs and homestead the plains and plateaus to an elevation of almost 9000 ft. above sea level."

It seems probable that the spectacular flight song of the lark bunting is an important part of the courtship performance, although, in general, this type of singing is continued well past the courtship period, perhaps to about the middle of July. During courtship the male sings almost continuously, sometimes perched on fence posts or tall weeds, but more commonly on the wing. For a description of this striking flight, see *Behavior*.

Published evidence indicates that the lark bunting does not attempt strongly to establish or maintain territories. Thus, Whittle (1922) reports that after dispersal of the larger flocks, the lark buntings nested in colonies in which five or six nests were "so close together that the males often sang from a series of fence posts at the same time." A. A. Saunders (MS.) has pointed out that "if there were territories, the birds crossed over each other's frequently while singing, but it may have been that when they alighted they did so only in their own territories." This tolerance of other buntings seems to be extended to other prairie species as well. Thus, Langdon (1933) writes: "Our Troubadour of the Plains is gentle of manner and pleasingly sociable among his fellows. He lives a beautiful family and community life. Amiability is a characteristic trait. I have yet to see him quarrel with the Desert Horned Lark or the McCown Longspur much less with one of his own kind, even when the plains are populated with many pairs of all three birds."

Bailey and Niedrach (1938) report that the lark bunting commonly nests with chestnut-collared longspurs, McCown's longspurs, desert horned larks, and mountain plovers as near neighbors.

*Nesting.*—The nest of the lark bunting typically is a rather simple affair, usually laid in a depression in the ground and made of grasses, slender weed stems, and fine roots, often lined with finer material of the same sort, plant down, or hair. It is very similar to the nest of the dickcissel. A. D. Du Bois (MS.) described a nest found in Teton

County, Mont., which was situated "on the ground, in the grass, on the slope of a coulee bank." It was "sunk almost flush with the surface of the ground" and was "composed of weed and grass stems and grass leaves." The nest was "lined with grass in a more or less shredded condition. A flat outer rim, just above ground, was composed of coarse weed stems." Internal measurements of the nest were: diameter, 2.75 inches; depth, 1.75 inches. He describes a second nest he found "in the flat bottom area of the coulee, well concealed by thick grass which surrounded it. One long, thick tuft of green grass leaned over it. The nest rim was perhaps an inch above ground, in matted dry grass." The nest was "constructed of dried grass stems and blades, lined with dried grass, some fine rootlets, and a few hairs."

Langdon (1933) published several photographs of male and female lark buntings as well as their young at the nest and describes the typical nest in the following terms:

"The nest is usually sunken flush with the ground, although sometimes it is slightly elevated. It is made of grasses and fine roots and lined with fine grasses, plant down, or hair. Sometimes it is sheltered by prairie plants and almost always difficult to find. To avoid revealing its location, the birds will remain away from the nest for long periods of time."

The nest is often located near or is hidden by some species of plant or plant debris. Thus, Whittle (1922) reports that lark buntings in the Missouri valley of Montana often selected "nesting sites in weedy tracts, under thick cover of tumble weed (*Cycloloma atriplicicolium*) accumulated by the wind against some obstruction, usually a wire fence, or even under a single plant of this species over-turned on the prairie." One such nest was "built entirely of grass and, as is customary, was placed on the ground with its rim flush with the surface, the inside diameter being two and one-quarter inches, and the depth the same." Benckeser (1957) reported finding a nest in pasture lands north of Brule, Nebr., that was constructed among prickly pear cactus foliage. Quillin (1935) found that lark buntings nesting near El Dorado, Tex., had built two nests in shallow hollows "in the center of an open clump of acacia a few inches high growing in a level meadow that was dotted with similar bushes." Sclater (1912) reports a nest found near Greeley, Colo., "in a slight hollow in the ground, in a freshly cut alfalfa field, and was made up of alfalfa stems and leaves." Reed (1904) noted that eggs had been collected from a nest in a cornfield at the base of a stalk. Cary (1902) observed that out of a dozen nests examined "all but one were hidden under a sage brush. The exception was a nest which the birds had built right in the middle of a thick bunch of cactus."

Cameron (1908) found that in Dawson and Custer counties in Montana nests were more plentiful in fenced pastures than elsewhere and suggests that this observation is explained by the bird's fondness for perching on the wires.

Various observers have encountered greater or lesser difficulties in attempting to locate the nest of the lark bunting, although perhaps the majority report no special trouble. A typical report of the difficulties occasionally encountered is that of Keyser (1902):

At first only male buntings were seen. Surely, I thought, there must be females in the neighborhood, for when male birds are singing so lustily about a place, their spouses are usually sitting quietly on nests somewhere in bush or tree or grass. I hunted long for a nest, trudging about over the meadow, examining many a grass-tuft and weed-clump, hoping to flush a female and discover her secret; but my quest was vain. It is strange how difficult it is to find nests in Colorado, either on the plains or in the mountains. The birds seem to be adept in the fine arts of concealment and secret-keeping. Presently several females were seen flying off over the fields and returning, obviously to feed their young. There was now some colorable prospect of finding a nest. A mother bird appeared with a worm in her bill, and you may rely upon it I did not permit her to slip from my sight until I saw her drop to the ground, hop about stealthily for a few moments, then disappear, and presently fly up minus the worm. Scarcely daring to breathe, I followed a direct course to the weed-clump from which she had risen. And there was a nest, sure enough—my first lark bunting's—set in a shallow pit of the ground, prettily concealed and partly roofed over by the flat and spreading weed-stalk. Four half-fledged youngsters lay panting in the little cradle * * *. I stepped back a short distance and watched the mother bird returning with another mouthful of "goodies", and feeding her bantlings four. She was not very shy, and simply uttered a fine chirp when I went too close to her nestlings, while her gallant consort did not even chirp, but tried to divert my attention by repeatedly curveting in the air and singing his choicest measures.

On the other hand, Cameron (1908) wrote that he observed five nests in a small pasture while merely riding through it on horseback. Similarly, Saunders (1921) reports that the lark bunting was so abundant in the Gallatin Valley of Montana that many people not acquainted with birds described the species to him, "telling how common it was, and how easily nests could be found."

*Eggs.*—The lark bunting lays from three to six eggs to a set, usually four or five, rarely seven. Sometimes two broods are raised in a season. The eggs are ovate, approaching short-ovate, in shape. Their color is a light greenish-blue, rarely lightly sprinkled with reddish-brown spots. The measurements of 50 eggs average 21.9 by 16.8 millimeters; the eggs showing the four extremes measure *24.1* by 17.0, 21.8 by *18.0*, *19.1* by 16.3, and 21.8 by *13.7* millimeters.

*Young.*—The period of incubation for the lark bunting is given by Cameron (1908) as about 12 days. Cameron also states that the male shares the incubation duties with his mate. A few other reports in the literature tend to support this. Benckeser (1955) is said to have flushed a male lark bunting from a nest containing six eggs near Brule, Nebr., and Cary (1902) reports that from seven nests he examined in Nebraska the male bird was flushed from five. Most other observers agree with Roberts (1936) who reports that: "The male was never discovered assisting in incubation but did take part in the care of the young and was always close by to join the female in protesting any intrusion upon the nest." As Langdon (1933) describes it: "The less-conspicuous female does all the incubating. The male makes his family glad they are alive, not only by singing to them constantly but also by helping feed the dark bluish nestlings."

Cameron (1908) gives the following description of the development of young lark buntings in Montana: "The usual number of five eggs is laid by June 1 * * *. The young are fledged by July 1, and, as soon as they can fly weakly (about the middle of the month), sit on the wires with their parents which feed them on grasshoppers."

*Plumages*.—Roberts (1936) has provided the best published description of the striking changes in plumage of the male lark bunting:

*Juvenal plumage*.—Resembles the female but paler above, because of lighter feather edgings causing a scaled effect as in the young horned lark; the markings below are more diffuse; the characteristic wing-patches are present and will serve to identify the bird; the lower mandible is yellowish, upper as in adult. The first prenuptial molt [April] produces the black and white breeding male, except the brown inner primaries, secondaries, and coverts, as described [below], and in some birds various patches of gray and buffy feathers are retained from the winter plumage.

*Second-year breeding*.—Secondaries, and all but four outer (black) primaries and their coverts, brown, retained from the juvenal (winter?) plumage; central pair of tail-feathers brown, others black not so pure above.

*Fall and winter adult*.—At a complete postnuptial molt, in late July and August, the male becomes somewhat like the female, but the wing-patches are brighter buff, the head and back more rusty, and the feathers of the abdomen are black beneath the light edgings.

*Adult breeding male*.—General color black, above grayish or faintly brownish in some specimens; middle and lesser wing-coverts white, forming *a large white patch in wing*; primaries black, brownish at tips; secondaries tipped with white, and tertiaries margined with white; tail brownish-black, all but middle pair of feathers with terminal white spots on inner web; under tail-coverts tipped with white. Bill bluish-horn color, paler below; leg brownish, darker on feet; iris hazel.

*Adult breeding female*.—Very different from breeding male. Above and on sides of head and neck pale grayish-brown streaked with dusky, more sparsely on rump and upper tail-coverts; a light line back of eye and a narrow light eye-ring; below white, streaked with dusky except on throat and belly; some of the feathers on upper abdomen may have concealed blackish centers; markings on breast may coalesce too from a central dark spot, as in Song Sparrow; a dark stripe on either side of throat, bordered above by dull white; wings brown, the middle and greater coverts dark centrally, margined widely with dull white or light buff, to form an interrupted wing-patch, less conspicuous than in the male; tertiaries dark, tipped and margined with dull white and buffy; tail as in male,

PLATE 37

P. B. Witherspoon

P. B. Witherspoon

MALE AND FEMALE LARK BUNTING AT NEST

PLATE 38

Phillips County, Mont., June 1936            L. H. Walkinshaw

NEST OF LARK BUNTING

Plattsburg, N.Y., July 4, 1940            B. Meanley

JUVENILE EASTERN SAVANNAH SPARROW

with addition of light edgings, especially on middle pair of feathers. Bill, legs, and feet lighter than in male.

Chapman (1914) describes the sequences of plumages as follows:

The nestling male is buffy white, faintly streaked below; above the feathers are blackish margined with buffy, producing a somewhat scaled appearance. At the postjuvenal molt the tail and wing-quills are retained, the rest of the plumage molted. The new plumage (first winter) resembles that of the female but the wings and tail are blacker and there is more black on the underparts, particularly on the throat.

The breeding or nuptial plumage is gained by a spring or prenuptial molt, in which, as in the postjuvenal or first fall molt, the tail and wing-quills are retained. The body plumage, wing coverts and tertials are shed and replaced by the black-and-white breeding-dress. Birds in their first nuptial plumage may now be distinguished from fully mature birds by their browner wings and tail and, often, less intensely black body feathers.

At the post nuptial or fall molt, which, as usual, is complete, the bird assumes a costume somewhat like that of the first winter, but the tail and wing-quills are now fully black and there is more black on the underparts.

Albino lark buntings apparently are not common, but a few have been observed, and at least one specimen has been collected.

*Food.*—Although the feeding habits of the lark bunting have not been studied as systematically as one might expect for so prominent and abundant a species, it is clear that the food in summer consists predominantly of insects together with a considerably lesser quantity of seeds of useless plants. The young are fed almost exclusively on insects. Langdon (1933) summarizes data in the files of the Bureau of Biological Survey as follows: "An examination of thirty-six stomachs, mostly collected in July and August, revealed 79.08 per cent animal matter and 20.92 per cent vegetable matter in the bird's total diet. The percentages of insects were: Grasshopper, 62.44; beetle, with weevils predominating, 11.33; true bugs (Hemiptera), 2.67; Hymenoptera (mainly wild bees and ants), 2.08; and miscellaneous (flies, moth larvae, etc.), 0.56. Seeds eaten were: Grasses, 7.47 per cent (2.36 per cent of these were cultivated grain seeds, probably mainly waste material). The remaining 13–45 per cent of the total diet was made up of seeds of pigweed, knotweed, gromwell, prickly poppy, verbena, goosefoot, etc."

Numerous less detailed observations from the field tend to substantiate these data. Thus, Knowlton (1947) described the stomach contents of a lark bunting collected among the sagebrush and rabbit-brush fence rows in central Utah in 1941 as containing "1 fly, 1 beetle, and 1 harvester ant, besides insect fragments. Also present was a spider, 65 seeds, mostly of weeds, and two Russian thistle plant fragments." The stomach contents of a second specimen collected at about the same time consisted of: "2 beetles (1 a weevil), 3

Hymenoptera, 2 of which were ants.  * * * 5 kernels of wheat, 1 sunflower seed, 7 other weed seeds and a few plant fragments."

May (in Forbush, 1929) describes an accidental visitor to Marchville, Mass., June 9, 1907, as feeding "by the roadside with a small flock of House Sparrows.  * * * The bird was feeding avidly upon the seeds of wayside dandelions, which it procured by jumping up from the ground and nipping, with its powerful beak, through the base of the ripening flower heads, each time alighting with a beakful of white pappus." Other weed seeds eaten by this species are those of the smartweed and amaranth.

Considerable evidence shows that when grasshoppers are available, this insect becomes the bird's favorite food. Thus, Kalmbach (1914) reported that near Koehler Junction, N. Mex., about 78 percent of its animal food was formed of grasshoppers, and Aughey (1878) stated that, out of nine specimens collected in southern Nebraska, seven had grasshoppers in their stomachs, the lowest number being 11 and the highest 19. R. L. Shotwell (1930) says of the bird foes of the grasshopper: "The most important predatory enemies of this insect in Montana are the Lark Bunting (Calamospiza melanocorys), Western Meadowlark (Sturnella neglecta), Sparrow Hawk (Falco sparverius), Sage Hen (Centrocercus urophasianus), Sharp-tailed Grouse (Pedioecetes phasianellus), and domestic turkeys and chickens. Of these the most important is the Lark Bunting, which is very abundant on the prairie lands. Swarms of grasshoppers can often be located by the presence of large numbers of these buntings." This is supported by the observations of Welch (1936), who reported that on "a trip through the wheat country near Broadview [Mont.] on August 4, there were encountered hordes of grasshoppers. The country roads were literally covered with these insects. Thousands of Lark Buntings and Desert Horned Larks were found in this territory, evidently attracted by the grasshoppers."

Behavior.—Probably the most outstanding behavioral characteristic of the lark buntings is their gregariousness. Except when on their nesting grounds, lark buntings live largely in flocks of considerable size. W. F. Rapp, Jr., tells me that for a short period of time after their arrival in western Nebraska the males and females remain in segregated flocks before their gradual dispersal to the nesting areas.

Apparently even when a lone lark bunting is separated from others of his kind, he seeks the company of other birds. Thus, F. M. and A. M. Baumgartner (1950) report that a lone female lark bunting appeared at their banding station at various times from Feb. 5 to Apr. 9, 1949, in the company of a flock of Harris's sparrows. The flock disappeared at about the same time as the bunting's final

appearance.  They report, further, that although "very similar to
the Harris's Sparrows in coloring, the bunting could always be distinguished from a distance by its characteristic behavior.  At our
approach to the trap the Harris's Sparrows usually flew *up*, flitting
from side to side.  The bunting always dove *down* into the farthest
corner, and continued to push and flutter in one spot until released."

The gregarious character is especially prominent on the lark bunting's wintering grounds in northern Mexico.  Thus Baird, Brewer,
and Ridgway (1874b) report that "Dr. Kennerly, who met with these
birds both in Sonora and Espia, on the Mexican Boundary Survey,
states that he observed them in the valley of the river early in the
morning, in very large flocks.  During the greater part of the day
they feed on the hills among the bushes.  When on the wing they
keep very close together, so that a single discharge of shot would
sometimes bring down twenty or thirty.  Mr. J. H. Clark, on the
same survey, also states that he sometimes found them occurring in
flocks of hundreds.  The greatest numbers were seen near Presidio
del Norte.  Great varieties of plumage were observed in the same
flock.  The food seemed to be seeds almost exclusively.  They were
very simultaneous in all their movements.  Stragglers were never
observed remaining behind after the flock had started.  They are,
he states, the most absolutely gregarious birds he has ever met with."

As characteristic of the lark bunting as its gregariousness is the
spectacular song or nuptial flight of the males over their nesting
grounds or when courting their mates.  Whittle (1922) describes
these flights as follows:

* * * in every direction, first here and then there, often in a dozen places at once,
Lark Buntings shot into the air, usually from the ground, as though propelled
from guns, pouring out the most infectious and passionate song, perhaps, sung
by any bird in the United States.  * * * there were at least a hundred singing
males, and with them there were, no doubt, a similar number of silent and inconspicuous females feeding on the ground.  If the females were impressed by
the singing, or were even aware of it, their behavior did not indicate it.

In one weedy field I counted twenty singing males.  They sing while resting
on the ground, on weeds, or on fence posts, but commonly the song begins as the
bird leaves the ground, moving directly upward at an angle of about 50° to a
height of ten to thirty feet and occasionally higher.  The descent is slower,
usually indirect and more gradual, the song culminating as the bird comes to
rest on the ground or on a fence post.  * * * Very frequently these flights,
which are doubtless courtship performances, are accompanied by unusual wing
motions.  Sometimes the wings are set at the apex of the flight and are often
upturned over the back in an acute V, after the habit of McCown Longspurs,
with which the Lark Buntings are often associated during such exhibitions, the
wings being slowly lowered as they glide or float to the ground.  At other times,
in place of setting the wings, the birds fly downward, the wing strokes not being
perfectly synchronized, giving the birds a rocking motion.  This alternation of
wing strokes, which is only practised during flight singing, is often at a maximum,

namely, when one wing is at the top of its describing arc and the other is at the bottom of its arc. * * *

F. H. Allen has advanced the theory that the ecstatic mating song is an elaborated older song, one which has been evolved from the perch song. Nevertheless, flight songs often contain even more primitive sounds, such as call notes, and it is interesting to note that alternate wing motions in birds, which is a survival of the alternate leg motion of their reptilian ancestors, is still occasionally practised by Lark Buntings during their flight singing.

Zimmer (1913) described the unusual song-flight of the lark bunting in the following terms: "When the birds sings thus in flight it rises regularly and directly into the air with rapid wing beats until, at the summit of its ascent, it pauses and begins to descend by a series of awkward, jerky motions of its set, extended wings, the motion being more like that of a butterfly than of a bird."

Although the song-flight of the lark bunting has been likened to that of the bobolink, Keyser (1902) has pointed out that—

a striking difference between his intermittent song-flights and those of the bobolink is to be noted. The latter usually rises in the air, soars around in a curve, and returns to the perch from which it started, or to one near by, describing something of an ellipse. The lark bunting generally rises obliquely to a certain point, then descends at about the same angle to another perch opposite the starting-point, describing what might be called the upper sides of an isosceles triangle, the base being a line near the ground, connecting the perch from which he rose and the one on which he alighted. I do not mean to say that our bunting never circles, but simply that such is not his ordinary habit, while sweeping in a circle or ellipse is the favorite pastime of the eastern bobolink. The ascent of neither bird is very high. They are far from deserving the name of skylarks.

Several authors have observed that the lark bunting appears to enjoy flying and singing in the face of winds of sufficient force to cause other birds to take cover. Thus, J. A. Allen (quoted in Coues, 1874) wrote that the lark bunting "is a very strong flier, and seems to delight in the strongest gales, singing more at such times than in comparatively quiet weather." Langdon (1933) says: "Several times I have heard him in the sunlit, sparkling rain. He is vocal when other birds seek shelter. Being strong of wing, he flies up to greet with song the cooling breeze or the gale that brings the storm. Sometimes he flies almost vertically up the wind, turns, and sails rapidly down the wind, bubbling with glee."

Baird, Brewer, and Ridgway (1874b) quote Coues as writing that the "ordinary flight of this species is altogether of a different character, being a low gliding motion, overtopping the weeds and bushes."

An interesting pattern of behavior was noted by Youngworth (1930), who observed hundreds of lark buntings seeking shade from the heat of the afternoon sun. Thus, during the "intense heat of the afternoon numerous lark buntings were found perching on barbed wire fences. The birds were, however, sitting close to the posts and on the side opposite to the sun."

Although some observers have reported that the lark bunting is shy and difficult to approach, this appears to be more characteristic of the bird on its wintering grounds than on its breeding grounds. Thus, Coues (quoted in Baird, Brewer, and Ridgway, 1874b) wrote that the lark buntings "were very heedless of approach, and any number could have been destroyed." Similarly, Langdon (1933) says that in his experience the lark bunting is friendly but not intimate with man, and that he has had the bird sit on his car while he was in it. On the other hand, Allen (1872) found the lark bunting to be exceeding shy and difficult to collect during the breeding season.

In general during the spring migration and breeding season, when approached by a human being, the lark bunting rises up from the prairie and bursts into song. The same response is elicted by 'the approach of automobiles on the highway or railway trains. However, on its wintering grounds the lark bunting is a less amiable and sociable bird. Thus Dille (1935) writes: "No bird has yet fooled me so completely as did the winter flocks of this old friend of my Colorado and Nebraska experience. If there is one bird on its northern nesting ground that I have known longer than any other it is the Lark Bunting. But what were these birds in this nervous, closely packed, quickly startling moving flock, acting just like a flock of wild scaled quail? There were no males of full colors in the bunch, which did not help my recognition. * * * How they must tame down during their tedious journey northward, for when they arrive with us in Colorado and take location, they are very sociable, and full of song."

These observations are in accord with those Coale (1894), who reported from the Tucson, Ariz., area that in the winter "these birds were on the ground in immense flocks, thousands I should judge, and were quite hard to approach. They kept running and flying over each other, always keeping well ahead of me."

*Voice.*—A. A. Saunders (MS.) has contributed the following study of this subject: "The lark bunting is commonly a flight singer. The bird flies up into the air, then wheels about and floats back to the ground, singing and circling around as it does so. In a way it resembles the song flights of longspurs, but the wings are not held at the same angle, and the longspur flight is straight and not circling.

"The song is a long mixture of series of short notes, two-note phrases or slurs. It is quite musical and pleasing, but of a peculiar quality that seemed to me indescribable. Consonant sounds are prominent. I wrote the phonetics of one song as follows: *kazee kazee kazee kazee zizizizizi tō kayeekayeekayeekayee trrrrrrrrrr tee tō wewewewewe tur tur tur tur quit quit quit quit quit quit quit.* This song lasted eight seconds, and varied in pitch from E″ to B″. Other songs range as high as F″.

"These studies were all made in a single morning, June 12, 1951, in the vicinity of Crosby, N. Dak. Seven or eight male birds were singing in a shrubby pasture, and two or three birds would be in the air singing at almost any minute of the time.

"I recorded one quite musical call-note of two syllables, that I wrote: 'Wheetwer.' "

J. E. and N. J. Stillwell (1955) recorded the songs of two lark buntings, one near Hugo, Lincoln County, Colo. (June 13, 1954) and the second near Cimarron, Gray County, Kans. (June 14, 1954). They report that the birds sang fully as well from fence posts as when on the wing and they described the songs in the following terms:

Boadly, the songs of the two Lark Buntings we recorded on tape, and of others heard but not recorded, consisted of the random use of several distinct phrases, with considerable variation in both the musical quality and pitches of the several phrases. A phrase might consist of a trill, or a buzz, or one or two notes repeated three to ten times.

In all, we recorded 16 songs from the Lark Bunting near Hugo, and 10 from the Cimarron bird. The Hugo bird averaged three to four phrases per song, and the Cimarron bird averaged six to seven phrases per song. For both birds we were able to recognize 11 different phrase types or patterns, although the repetitions of a given phrase-type were not always exactly identical.

The 11 phrase-types of these two Lark Buntings may be placed in four groups. Group A contains three types, Cardinal-like and gliding in pitch: (1) a single-note *sweet*, rising rapidly in pitch for about an octave, this note repeated four to eight times; (2) a slurred double-note *cher-wheat*, rising in pitch, usually repeated about three times; and (3) *weeta*, falling in pitch. Group B contains two types, chat-like and unmusical: (4) *chug* repeated three or four times; and (5) *chut*, repeated more rapidly, usually nine or ten times. Group C contains three types, trills or buzzes; (6) a low-pitched *buzz;* (7) a junco-like trill; and (8) a high-pitched, insect-like trill. Group D contains three types: (9) *toot* repeated four to twelve times, quality clear and piping; (10) *churt* less clear and musical than type 9; and (11) *chew*, rather Cardinal-like, but not conspicuously gliding in pitch as in Group A. [For a description in tabular form of the use of these song types by the two males the reader is referred to the original article by the Stillwells.]

With three exceptions, both birds began each song with Type 1 phrase. Seven of the 11 types (no. 1, 2, 4, 7, 8, 9, and 10) were used by both birds. Type 5 was used only by the Hugo bird; and Types 3, 6, and 11 were used only by the Cimarron bird. Type 4 was used eight times by the Cimarron bird as the second phrase in his songs; and Type 9 was used eight times by the Hugo bird as the second phrase in his songs.

A typical song of the Hugo Lark Bunting might be written: *sweet, sweet, sweet, sweet, sweet, sweet: toot, toot, toot, toot, toot, toot: chug, chug, chug: tr-r-r-r-r-r.*

A typical song of the Cimarron bird would be: *sweet, sweet, sweet, sweet, sweet: chug, chug, chug, chug: tr-r-r-r-r-r-r: toot, toot, toot, toot, toot: buz-z-z-z-z: churt, churt, churt.*

Zimmer (1913) describes the call note and song of the lark bunting as follows:

The call note of the Lark Buntings, a gentle "who-ee-ee", with gradually rising inflection, was heard frequently, and when given by a flock in chorus as the birds rose from the ground before you or settled again a short distance away was most pleasing.    The true song, which is given by the males, as I have heard it here [Thomas County, Nebr.] and on the high plains where the buntings breed abundantly, is, to me, suggestive of the notes of the Long-tailed Chat.    In addition to the similarity of the notes the singing bird frequently performs in a manner that also calls to mind the same other feathered clown, and if the proceeding be seen at a distance and in such a light that the colors and markings of the bird are obscured, the illusion is all the more complete except that wonder may arise as to what a Chat is doing in the open hills.    The song is composed of syllables or repetitions of syllables pieced together in a more or less regular fashion.    Some of the notes may be expressed as "cheerp'–cheerp'–cheerp'–cheerp'–chee-ee-ee-ee-ee-hir'–ta-hir' ta-hir' ta-who-oo-oo-oo-oo-yor' da-yor' da-hurt'–hurt'–hurt'–ee-ee-ee-ee-ee-ee—."    This is delivered most frequently by a bird on the wing, but it may be given from a perch on a fence post or weed stalk.

## Keyser (1902) describes the song of the male lark bunting as follows:

* * * his voice has not the loud, metallic ring, nor his chanson the medley-like happy-go-lucky execution, that marks the musical performance of the bobolink; but his song is more mellow, rhythmic, themelike; for he has a distinct tune to sing, and sing it he will.    In fine, his song is of a different order from that of the bobolink, and, therefore, the comparison need be carried no further.

As one of these minstrels sat on a flowering weed and gave himself up to a lyrical transport, I made careful notes, and now give the substance of my elaborate entries.    The song, which is intermittent, opens with three prolonged notes running high in the scale, and is succeeded by a quaint, rattling trill of an indescribable character, not without musical effect, which is followed by three double-toned long notes quite different from the opening phrases; then the whole performance is closed by an exceedingly high and fine run like an insect's hum—so fine, indeed, that the auditor must be at hand to notice it at all.    Sometimes the latter half of the score, including the second triad of long notes, is repeated before the soloist stops to take a breath.    It will be seen that the regular song consists of four distinct phrases, two triads, and two trills.    About one-third of the songs are opened in a little lower key than the rest, the remainder being correspondingly mellowed. The opening syllables, and, indeed, some other parts of the melody as well, are very like certain strains of the song-sparrow, both in execution and in quality of tone; and thus even the experienced ornithologist may sometimes be led astray. When the bunting sails into the air, he rehearses the song just described, only he is very likely to prolong it by repeating the various parts, though I think he seldom, if ever, throws them together in a hodge-podge.    He seems to follow a system in his recitals, varied as many of them are.    As to his voice, it is of superb timbre.

Another characteristic noted was that the buntings do not throw back their heads while singing, after the manners of the sparrows, but stretch their necks forward, and at no time do they open their mouths widely.    As a rule, or at least very often, when flying, they do not begin their songs until they have almost reached the apex of their triangle; then the song begins, and it continues over the angle and down the incline until another perch is settled upon.

Langdon (1933) has to say of the song: "This mellow, rhythmic tune has several, perhaps a half-dozen, distinct themes of about equal length which are sung one after the other, Canary-like until the bird alights or

ceases to sing from some lowly perch.   I have often seen three or four
birds fly toward each other, mount together, pour out their hearts in
friendly rivalry, then separate, each sailing and singing to his own
territory.   The Bunting's song is highly inspiring whether sung solo
or ensemble.   Surely this prairie bird must be ranked as one of our
very best feathered songsters."

Attempts have been made to render the song in human words; however, such attempts usually give only an impression of the rhythm,
not of the musical quality of the song.   Gerbracht (1944) describes
the singing of the lark bunting in this way: "Most birds slip in quietly,
but everyone knows when the buntings arrive.   Everybody is glad
to see them, for they are the answer to the things everybody wants
to know, as they are both measuring stick and seasonal synchronizers.
Just as the meadowlark says, 'Time to sow wheat; time to sow wheat,'
the bunting says, 'Click, click, click, get busy, busy, busy, plant corn,
corn, corn, wiggle, wiggle, wiggle, click, click.' "

*Field marks.*—The adult male lark bunting in spring plumage is a
wholly black or dark slate color except for conspicuous white patches
on the wing.   Although one would expect that so strikingly marked
a bird would rarely be misidentified, where the ranges of the two birds
tend to overlap, the lark bunting and bobolink are not infrequently
mistaken for each other (cf. Cameron, 1908; Tout, 1936).   The adult
female in spring plumage is much less striking, being a grayish-brown
above and nearly white below and streaked with dusky both above
and below.   The wing patch in the female is smaller and is tinged with
buffy.   In the fall, all ages and sexes look much alike, resembling the
adult female.

*Enemies.*—There is little doubt that the breaking up of the prairies
and their intensive cultivation in Minnesota, western Iowa, and extreme eastern Nebraska and South Dakota have largely driven the
lark bunting out of these areas as a breeding bird.   In addition man
in his speeding automobile undoubtedly takes an additional toll of
lark buntings along the highways during migration.   Baumgartner
(1934) reports finding dead lark buntings on the highways in both
Kansas and Colorado.   Both in spring and fall migrations, lark buntings are common along the roadsides and, although the flushed birds
tend to fly away from the highway, inevitably a few fly into the path
of the automobile.

Inasmuch as the lark buntings are late migrants, they are not generally susceptible to the vagaries of springtime weather in the central
plains.   However, occasional late spring snowstorms trap large
numbers.   One such storm was that on May 28–29, 1947, in northwestern Nebraska, which dumped more than a foot of heavy, wet
snow on the ground and brought temperatures down to 18° F. or lower.

As reported by H. J. Cook (1947), lark buntings had arrived a week earlier, but after the storm the migrants were not to be found. In his words:

We have immense numbers of Lark Buntings here each summer; when they migrate in the spring and fall very large flocks are in abundance. I had seen such flocks here for a week before this storm hit. On June 1 Mrs. Cook and I drove to Lusk, Wyoming, and back. I have never seen such a lack of bird life in this region, even in the lead of winter. Coming back in the afternoon we counted the birds we saw along the highway in that 55-mile drive over the high country of Nebraska–Wyoming borderland, near the headwaters of the Niobrara River. Instead of the thousands of Horned Larks and Longspurs normally along this road, we did not see a living bird of those two species. Instead of the numerous flocks of migrating and scattering Lark Buntings, we saw just 23 individuals; all but 3 of these were males and were widely dispersed, one to three in a place.
* * * Dead birds are everywhere.

The extent to which the lark bunting is imposed upon by the cowbird has not been accurately determined. J. A. Allen (1874) described the lark bunting as one of the favorite foster parents of the cowbird. In a series of 18 nests that he examined, five contained cowbird eggs; two of them contained two cowbird eggs and one contained three At the same time in 29 nests of other ground-nesting prairie birds not one cowbird egg was found. Strangely, Friedmann (1963) notes only a single subsequent record, a parasitized set of eggs taken in North Dakota, June 9, 1963, and now in the Carnegie Museum.

Cameron (1913) has noted that lark buntings were often numerous around the nesting sites of Swainson's hawk in Montana. Occasionally when this hawk could not obtain its favorite food (frogs, grasshoppers, and mice), it attacked the lark bunting. Since no other species of bird was taken, Cameron concluded that the color of the male lark bunting and his soaring habits render him particularly conspicuous and vulnerable to attack. He reports collecting one female Swainson's hawk whose stomach contained an entire lark bunting and describes one unsuccessful assault as follows:

I have only once myself seen a Swainson's Hawk in pursuit of a flying bird, although such a chase must not infrequently occur when the hawk is famished or ground game is scarce or absent. In this flight, at any rate, the hawk acquitted herself with considerable dash, and, so far as I know, has added a new record to the hitherto published history of the species. During August, 1909, I saw the female of the pair of Swainson's Hawks which had been under observation, and whose young had then flown, make a determined swoop at a Lark Bunting on the ground. The quarry crouched under the lowest wire of a protecting fence, and there was no wind to aid the hawk which was obviously so hungry that her valor overcame her discretion. The consequence was that she just missed the bird but collided with the fence, and, losing her balance, fell over. The terrified bunting was the first to recover its wits, and justified its name by soaring straight upwards like a true lark before it flew swiftly away. To my great astonishment the flustered hawk rose in the calm air and flapped after the now distant bunting. With steady beats of her long wings she appeared to be making but slow progress, whereas, in reality, her speed was more than double that of the fugitive, and she soon overtook it. When, as it appeared to me, about a yard above her quarry, the hawk made a sudden dash to seize the bunting in her claws, which the latter cleverly evaded and then flew off in a different direction. Being assailed only by a clumsy buzzard, which could not "throw up" like a falcon, the little bird escaped rejoicing, although by a narrow margin.

According to Webster (1944) the lark bunting is also preyed upon by the prairie falcon.

*Economic status.*—While it is with us on its breeding grounds there is no doubt that the lark bunting is a beneficial species. The insects it eats (particularly grasshoppers) are of harmful species, or of species of little or no value. Most of its vegetable food consists of weed seeds, or seeds of useless plants. There is less information available as to the food taken during its migration to the south, but Mrs. Bailey (1928) has said that on "isolated ranches, the Lark Buntings sometimes do serious injury to the grain crops in passing, especially in seasons when desert grass seed is scarce, but it is believed that when the country settles up the loss to individuals will be negligible, and the destruction of weed seed and injurious insects is important." Similarly, Langdon (1933) quotes the conclusions of the Bureau of Biological Survey: "In summer, therefore, under normal conditions in most localities of its range, the Lark Bunting should be regarded as a highly beneficial bird."

*Fall.*—As the mating and nesting season draws to an end the male lark bunting loses his dark splendor and stills his glorious song, becoming a quiet, sparrowlike imitation of the female. Like the bobolink the buntings gather in flocks of ever-increasing size, which rise and wheel in unison across the prairies, stopping now and then to feed in grassy places, weed patches, or grain fields. According to Wood (1923) on the prairies of North Dakota during this time occasional large flocks of adults and young may be seen feeding about ranch buildings like house sparrows.

The lark bunting is a fairly early migrant. According to W. W. Cooke (1914), the first migrants reached Brownsville, Tex., on July 27, 1881. More commonly the southward migration begins in late July or early August but, as in the spring migration, proceeds so slowly that the stragglers are still in New Mexico during the last week of October. The fall migration is started and is occasionally finished before the annual molt is accomplished; some young birds arrive at the northern edge of their winter range while still in juvenal plumage, and many adults are still molting when the first migrants arrive. Thus, Mrs. Bailey (1928) writes of the migrants arriving in New Mexico:

The Lark Buntings or White-wings, black in the breeding plumage and brown in winter, were first seen in northwestern New Mexico by Mr. Hollister on July 22, 1905. * * * He writes regarding them: "The males were in excellent black plumage, but I think they were fresh arrivals from the north, although it may seem early for migration." Three years previous, in the southeastern part of the State, he had found them five weeks later (September 2–3, 1902). * * * At that time they were all "in brown plumage."

Previous to August 8, 1908, Major Goldman writes, "When we entered the Animas Mountains from Animas Valley none of the birds had been seen. When we returned to the valley on August 9, we found them numerous in large [black] flocks and they were seen every day until I left the valley, August 19. They were common in flocks, apparently consisting almost entirely of black males, at Socorro, August 11–24, 1909." The thousands found by Doctor Dearborn at Carlsbad, August 1–14, 1910, were also mainly in the breeding plumage, although beginning to molt.

Near Las Vegas, from August 29 to September 1, 1903, small flocks were frequently seen passing over our camp, while numbers were flushed from the fences. At this time they were all in the brown plumage. Near Espanola early in September, 1906, they were also numerous in the fields and along the roads. In one place perhaps three hundred were seen on a wire fence, mostly in the brown plumage.

*Winter.*—The lark buntings, having withdrawn from their breeding range, spend the winter south from southern California, southern Nevada, central Arizona, southern New Mexico, and north-central Texas to southern Baja California, Jalisco, Guana, Vato, and Hildalgo. On their winter range the birds forage in sizeable flocks in the open fields or out on the desert plains and plateaus.

Dawson (1923) says of the winter habits of the lark bunting: "Winter flocks may be composed of both sexes in equal or very unequal proportions. They feed quietly upon the ground in the open, whether along a river bottom or over the baldest desert. The Lark Buntings are not averse to civilization, and they sometimes frequent Mexican dooryards or barnyards with much the freedom and something of the manner of blackbirds."

### DISTRIBUTION

*Range.*—High plains of the southern prairie provinces south to central Mexico.

*Breeding range.*—The lark bunting breeds from west central Montana (Missoula), southern Alberta (Waterton Lakes Park, Castor), southern Saskatchewan (Skull Creek, Indian Head), southwestern Manitoba (Brandon), southeastern North Dakota (Valley City), and southwestern Minnesota (Otter Tail and Jackson counties, irregularly) south to central southern Montana (Bozeman, Billings) and, east of the Rocky Mountains, to southeastern New Mexico (Vaughn Lovington), northern Texas, north central Oklahoma (Grant County), and south central and central eastern Kansas (St. John, Rantoul);

also locally or sporadically in Utah (Murray) and southwestern Colorado (Navajo Springs).

*Winter range.*—Winters from southern California (San Fernando Valley), southern Nevada (Corn Creek), central Arizona (Camp Verde, San Carlos), southern New Mexico (Deming, Carlsbad), and north central Texas (Colorado, Indianola) south to southern Baja California (Cape San Lucas), Jalisco, Guanajuato (Guanajuato), Hidalgo, northern Tamaulipas (Matamoros), and southern Louisiana (near Grand Isle).

*Casual records.*—Casual, chiefly in migration, west to British Columbia (Wistaria, Okanagan Landing), western Alberta (Banff), Idaho (Minidoka, Grays), and central California (Dudley, Colusa); and east to Ontario (Lowbush), New Brunswick (Grand Manan, West Quaco), Nova Scotia (4 sight records), Massachusetts (10 localities), New York (5 Long Island localities), New Jersey (Island Beach), Pennsylvania (Graterford, Chambersburg), Maryland (Smithville), Virginia (Lexington, Sandbridge), South Carolina (Christ Church Paris), Georgia (Tybee Island) and Florida (near St. Marks light).

*Fossil record.*—Fossil, late Pleistocene of California.

*Migration.*—Early dates of spring arrival are: Iowa—Mason City, May 2. Wisconsin—Milton, April 30. Minnesota—Sherburn, April 12 (average of 7 years for southern Minnesota, May 23). Oklahoma—Red River, March 15; Jackson County, March 27. Nebraska—Red Cloud, April 10 (average of 10 years, May 3). South Dakota—Rapid City, April 8; North Dakota—Jamestown, May 10. Manitoba—Treesbank, May 18 (average of 6 years, May 26). Saskatchewan—Wiseton, April 12. New Mexico—60 miles west of El Paso, April 3. Colorado—Colorado Springs, April 14. Wyoming—Laramie, May 3 (average of 13 years), May 10. Montana—Huntley, April 28. Alberta—Warner, April 28. Oregon—Saddle Butte, May 14. British Columbia—Wistaria, May 28.

Late dates of spring departure are: Texas—Somerset, April 10. Arizona—Tucson, April 25.

Early dates of fall arrival are: Oklahoma—Ivanhoe Lake, August 12. Texas—Midland, July 14. Ohio—Henry County, August 6. Louisiana—Grand Isle, September 4. New Brunswick—West Quaco, July 26. Maine—Hog Island, August 25. Massachusetts—Princeton, July 28; Martha's Vineyard, August 5. New York—Easthampton, August 31. New Jersey—Island Beach, September 7. Maryland—Smithville, July 10.

Late dates of fall departure are: Oregon—White City, November 13. Montana—Huntley, September 29. Wyoming—Laramie, September 9 (average of 10 years, August 26). Colorado—Walden, October 2. Saskatchewan—Indian Head, September 10. North

Dakota—Jamestown, September 5. South Dakota—Rapid City, October 15. Minnesota—Wilder, October 21. Nova Scotia—Cape Island, Shelburne County, October 12. Massachusetts—Wayland, November 11. New York—Wainscott, November 27. Virginia—Sandridge, September 5.

*Egg dates*—Alberta; 8 records, May 15 to June 2.

Colorado; 23 records, May 22 to July 25; 14 records, June 1 to June 10.

Kansas; 25 records, May 26 to June 24; 12 records, June 6 to June 14.

Montana; 17 records, May 25 to July 21; 9 records, June 13 to June 20.

North Dakota; 1 record, July 20.

Wyoming; 12 records, May 21 to July 8.

## PASSERCULUS PRINCEPS (Maynard)

## Ipswich Sparrow

### Contributed by JOHN JACKSON ELLIOTT

#### HABITS

Ornithologists have long suspected that the Ipswich sparrow may prove eventually to be a geographical race of the Savannah sparrow (*Passerculus sandwichensis*). Richard H. Pough (1946) points out that actually no one knows whether or not this strongly marked form of Sable Island can interbreed with mainland Savannah sparrows and remarks that: "It is merely assumed on the basis of the differences which we observe between them that they would not." He then adds: "Should Sable Island eventually wash completely away, as seems likely, forcing the Ipswich sparrow to breed on the mainland or perish, it will survive as a distinct form only if it has actually achieved reproductive isolation from the Savannah. Should this be lacking (in which case it is not a species), interbreeding with mainland Savannahs would soon obliterate the distinctive Ipswich characteristics." The 1957 A.O.U. Check-List, however, still retains it as *Passerculus princeps*.

The Ipswich sparrow was discovered in 1868, when C. J. Maynard shot one on December 4 among the sand dunes of Ipswich, Mass. It was at first mistaken for Baird's sparrow (*Ammodramus bairdii*) of the far west. Previous to this it was known as "gray bird" by the residents of Sable Island, Nova Scotia, a name that it retained there for many years. As early as 1858, Dr. Gilpin mentioned a sparrow resident there and on the mainland; some years before this,

Alexander Wilson presumably mistook one for the male of the Savannah sparrow along the New Jersey coast.

The complete winter range of the Ipswich sparrow was unknown for many years, but by early 1890 specimens had been collected intermittently southward to Glynn County, Ga. Its breeding ground was not suspected until 1884, when eggs in the National Museum in Washington, D.C., uniformly larger than those of the Savannah sparrow and labeled Sable Island, July 1862, were believed by Robert Ridgway to be those of the Ipswich sparrow. Shortly afterward, C. Hart Merriam sent for and received a summer specimen of the Sable Island "gray bird" from Rev. W. A. DesBrisay, resident missionary there, which proved to be an Ipswich sparrow.

Jonathan Dwight, Jr. (1895) arrived on Sable Island May 24, 1894, and studied the species' nesting behavior until June 14. Later W. E. Saunders (1902a,b) visited there in May and made similar observations. Apparently no further studies were made of the summer behavior until I went to Sable Island in late July 1948.

The Ipswich sparrow is unique in that its summer breeding ground on Sable Island is less than 20 miles long, and its wintering range on the mainland is more than 1,000 miles, although this coastal strip is not over a few hundred feet wide in spots. A small segment of the population, perhaps 20 percent, winters on Sable Island.

This sparrow makes its winter home where the strong winds blow flying beach sand over the hillocks within the sound of the pounding sea, and the grass-clumped sand dunes, humped in jumbled confusion, parallel the shore line to the horizon. The search to find one may take some time or be relatively short, because the birds vary in numbers from year to year. Suddenly, with a seemingly effortless lifting of wings, a pale gray sparrow tosses itself aloft. The wind catches it, 'and with rapid, erratic flight it passes over the waving clumps of beach grass, or perhaps along a sandy gulch, to alight near the top of a dune 100 or so yards away. The chase is on and, if fortunate, one may arrive in time to see the quick-running bird traveling a nearby slope, unless another low flight has taken it unseen out of the neighborhood. A slight delay on the observer's part in taking up immediate pursuit in windy weather usually requires a renewed search, often unsuccessful.

In calmer weather in winter, the Ipswich sparrow has the habit, when not pursued too closely, of running along the sand. During mild periods in fall it may perch on a weed stalk or on beach wreckage and eye the observer momentarily before flying off. In late October and early November the birds are often quite tame.

*Spring.*—Roy Latham, at Orient, N.Y., says he has fewer records during February in that area along the eastern end of Long Island

Sound than for other winter months, and that the northern movement comes in March when an increase of song sparrows also occurs. At that time, he says, the birds are not confined to the dunes as in winter but may be found in grassy fields near the beaches. At Jones Beach I once found an individual in dune-bordering marsh grass (*Spartina patens*). This is also true of Long Island farther west, where spring birds are sometimes found along the grassy borders of the north side of Jamaica Bay, well away from the sea and the flattened, built-upon sands of Long Beach and the Rockaways.

George B. Rabb (*in* litt.) of the Charleston Museum remarks that the Ipswich sparrow does not become common enough in South Carolina in spring to indicate a "marked migration of more southerly individuals." Alexander Sprunt, Jr., also in correspondence, gives April 8 as his latest date of spring departure for South Carolina and adds that Arthur T. Wayne once collected a spring specimen 7 miles from the ocean on a bush at the edge of an oat field. Many sand dunes in spring are quite wind-blown and sterile, which probably accounts for the dispersal into other habitat at this season.

Spring migration becomes more marked northward, and in New Jersey Charles K. Nichols (*in* litt.) notes that the largest daily numbers are recorded in March, and that the end of migration generally occurs by the second week in April. Julian Potter, in sending records from Brigantine, N.J., from 1932 to 1942, gives his latest date as March 25. Potter reports a fair representation of New Jersey records for February, most of them from the ocean beaches at Stone Harbor, Brigantine, Beach Haven, and Barnegat.

Forbush (1929) says the Ipswich sparrow is uncommon in spring in Massachusetts and a rare local migrant in New Hampshire and Maine. W. A. Squires of the New Brunswick Museum writes me that it is a rare transient in spring migration in that Canadian province; in fall it apparently crosses the Gulf of Maine without reaching New Brunswick. Records from Grand Manan, Point Lepreaux, St. John, St. Stephen, St. Andrews, and Kent Island run from March 26 to May 7, the latter being the latest spring date I know away from Sable Island. The St. John record is an old one reported by Chamberlain (1883), in which Alfred Morrissey took several out of what he claimed to be a flock of 20 Ipswich sparrows on Apr. 11, 1882. Regarding this, W. Earl Godfrey of the National Museum of Canada, writes me: "Whether or not Morrissey could separate the Ipswich sparrow from the other races of the Savannah sparrow casts a shadow on the validity of this record." Other than this, three was the largest number reported at any one time in New Brunswick, according to Squires's records.

On Apr. 11, 1876, on Point Lepreaux, New Brunswick, William Brewster collected a female that was sitting on a rock out on the end of the point. An Ipswich sparrow I watched at Atlantic Beach, Long Island, two decades ago often left the dunes to forage among the large rocks on the land side of the breakwater.

Grassy strips bordering the ocean parkway at Gilgo on Jones Beach, Long Island, were formerly productive of many records during spring migration. During a good infiltration of song and tree sparrows, an Ipswich sparrow or two often fed along with them and offered good opportunities for study in the short grass. On Apr. 1, 1950, I counted six Ipswich sparrows on these grassy tracts and on Mar. 29, 1940, I estimated 10 or 11 to be present. A dual parkway has since obliterated these grassy strips.

*Courtship.*—Jonathan Dwight, Jr. (1895) writes of his Sable Island experience: "It was impossible to pry much into their domestic affairs, they were so retiring. All seemed to be mated at the time of my arrival (May 24), and they appeared to take life very quietly. The demeanor of the males, when paying court to their admiring mates, was largely a parade of bowing flutterings, accompanied by a low, murmuring chirruping." Regarding male competition he states: "Only once did I actually catch the males quarreling among themselves; but toward the end of my stay I secured several with heads so denuded of feathers that it was evidently not a question of whether they had been fighting, but of how much."

*Nesting.*—The general nesting range of the Ipswich sparrow extends down the interior of Sable Island from a little west of where the old main station stood in 1948 to the east lighthouse, a distance of about 17 miles. To understand the Ipswich sparrow's nesting activities and the extent of its breeding ground, the unique physical features of Sable Island should be described. To quote from my own (1956) report:

On the eastern half of Sable Island Bank lies unique Sable Island, "Graveyard of the Atlantic." * * * It is gradually shrinking in size and its predicted fate is that in time it will disappear, the last of many tracts believed to have occurred in this region. Submergence of the others has isolated the Ipswich sparrow to this, its present insular and only nesting grounds.

To this island, sometimes fog-bound for weeks at a time, Ipswich sparrows must travel from the mainland each spring, although an estimated one-fifth winter on the island. Residents there say returning numbers increase over the wintering population in late April and May.

Sable Island (sable means sand in French) is about 24.5 miles long with a maximum width of about one mile. It is gradually washing away on the west end and building up more slowly on the east. Its east end is about 100 miles out in the Atlantic off Nova Scotia, east-southeast from Halifax. From shipboard it appears as a long, sandy cliff facing the ocean and tapering down on the ends. Its western tip is low, flat sand, and eastward for about two miles supports a few windrows or sand dunes with shaggy crests of beach grass (*Ammophila*). This broadens a mile further east into an attractive, peaty interior, protected from the ocean and containing five or six semi-fresh-water ponds, well-vegetated around the borders. Near this area, about four miles from the west end, on higher, grassy slopes are the west lighthouse, main station and radio station. A mile further east is the weather station. For some nine miles this portion of the island is narrowed by Wallace Lake. About 100 years ago it had an inlet from the ocean, but shortly afterward became completely rimmed with an outer beach as it is today. About 1913 Wallace Lake was divided by a broad, sandy flat. East of Wallace Lake the substantial "backbone" of the island extends about six miles to the east lighthouse. It is in this stretch that Sable Island reaches its maximum width, and the well vegetated tracts are known as the "old land." It is here also that the island attains its maximum height of about 80 feet. From the east lighthouse the island tapers gradually into a curved projection of bare sand jutting out into the ocean for four or five miles like a long serpentine tail.

Exposed on all sides, the treeless island is subjected to excessive wave action and the object of severe sand storms. It is composed almost entirely of white quartz sand, and old dunes are continually blown down and new dunes formed by the high winds. On windy days flying sand discourages travel abroad except during emergencies. Well-vegetated tracts are buried during these periods, and revegetating of the newly formed dunes begins as the beach grass shoots out its runners. Fog is prevalent sometimes for weeks at a time in late spring and early summer, and the dampness appears to help the grasses gain a foothold and grow rapidly.

The island's tallest vegetation of stunted bayberry, blueberry, wild rose bushes, here and there intermingled with vines, ranges to waist-high in the shelter of the high dunes in the "old land" of the island's main backbone. Elsewhere it is usually less than knee-deep, such as around the turfy tracts on the western half. What it lacks there in height, however, it makes up in density in the thick growth of crowberry, bayberry, and blueberry, making good nesting areas which are largely free of infiltrating sand.

Saunders (1902b), who apparently visited only the west end of the island, makes no mention of the prostrate juniper (*Juniperus hori-zontalis*) which is prevalent on the eastern half, and in describing the finding of numerous nests, many unfinished, he writes only of the western ponds and the superintendent's grounds. He was able to find nests readily by locating the nest cavity as it was just started, when the excavation showed some black soil. In this way he discovered nearly 30 sites. Few nests were completed during his stay. All but five were placed in long grass where the former year's bleached stems had fallen over. One was in a clump of crowberry and one among dark green rushes; three were in a small field of clover near the superintendent's house at the main station. He describes the nests as large, thick, and deep. A few were in holes in hillsides or terraces, perhaps with a projecting piece of sod protecting the nest from above. They were made principally of fine, dry grass with stronger weeds supplying the base. Coarser grasses formed the upper edge of the rim. Eel grass often was added and sometimes moss. He states that the smallest nest, found in crowberry, was much heavier than a Savannah sparrow's usual nest. Nests were built mostly in dry locations with two exceptions: one was on low, damp ground under rushes; another, was on drier ground near water among long grass.

Dwight (1895) examined 9 or 10 nests. He visited the vegetated juniper tracts on the eastward end of the island as well as the dark turfy areas on the western half. He remarks that all of the nests were carefully concealed and not easy to find, especially those deep in the juniper. Residents told him that the most favored nesting sites were the steep, grassy slopes, often terraced by zigzagging cattle paths, where the bleached and storm-matted grasses afforded ample protection. Of the western end, he remarks that everywhere the trailing stems of crowberry and juniper lend a canopy for nests that sometimes reposed in beds of mosses and lichens. Each nest was placed in a cup-shaped hollow the birds scratch in the sand, about 4 inches in diameter and fully 2 inches deep.

According to Dwight (1895) the nest is compactly woven and much more pretentious than that of the Savannah sparrow. It has the effect of a nest built of hay and stubble lined with paler, finer straw. He writes: "It has two distinct parts, an outer shell of coarse material disposed, as a rim and an inner cup finely woven. The excavation is filled in at the sides and around the margin with dead weed stalks, various coarse grasses and sedges, bits of moss or similar materials. These form a shell rising about an inch above the surface of the sand and straggling out over it for an inch or two. The shell is lined almost wholly with the finer bleached blades of an unidentified species of Carex, a few wiry horse hairs, or tufts from the shaggy ponies or cattle, being sometimes added." He says the lining is circularly disposed leaving an inch, more or less, of closely woven grasses between the eggs and the sand beneath. Higher up the walls are considerably thicker on account of the added shell.

He found two unusual nesting sites on June 2, one in a small tuft of beach grass, and one in a little hollow under a short bit of board on a flat stretch of bare sod. Later the same day he discovered two more nests, one in crowberry and one in a clump of rose bushes.

W. E. Saunders (1902b) states nest measurements averaged an inside diameter of 2½ inches, outside 5 inches, depth 2 inches, outside 3 inches. The thickness of the walls varied from a half an inch to 2 inches. Dwight gives six nests the average inside diameter in millimeters as 58.33, outside diameter 114.5, the inside depth as 45.5, outside depth 72.

With permission of the Canadian Board of Transport "to study the nesting ground of the Ipswich sparrow," I sailed to Sable Island on the supply ship *Lady Laurier* out of Halifax, Nova Scotia, on July 29, 1948, and returned August 2. I found that conditions had changed somewhat since Dwight's and Saunders's time. There had been no cows or sheep on the island for many years, but an estimated 200 to 300 wild horses were then roaming over it. On this visit I found the Ipswich sparrow still in a state of breeding agitation in one or two locations, although apparently practically at the end of its nesting season elsewhere. The terraced, horse-trodden paths and the well-vegetated hillsides sloping down to the some half-dozen small ponds 3 or 4 miles from the western end were attractively dotted with pink wild roses facing upward, barely 2 or 3 inches out of the sand. Flowering meadow rue, some 2 feet tall, stood above the vegetation, and the attractive little yellow-flowering silver weed (*Potentilla anserina*) blossomed in damp places. The low vegetation hugs the contour of the treeless island. Stunted blueberry and bayberry bordering the higher terraces and the crowberry growing profusely in strung-out tracts emphasize these more strongly. I found one nesting site in stunted blueberry beside a foot path.

The entire area, which the inhabitants regarded as a very favorable one for nesting, was still frequented by agitated birds on August 1. Ipswich sparrows were still bobbing and twisting in the stunted growth around the ponds the same way Dwight (1895) and Saunders (1902) described them during their visits in May and June. I saw one adult bird carrying food and found some young in the last stages of parental care. The incessant *tsick* of the agitated adults was delivered at a very fast tempo, one adult being timed at 132 times a minute. On all sides about the ponds were Ipswich sparrows, a dozen or more being in evidence at a time. Some of these were young birds, and many adults, apparently finished nesting, occasionally drifted out on the dunes and perched in little groups on the nearby telephone wire or on the poles. The incessant chipping of the agitated birds began before a near approach was made to the turfy tracts and lasted as long as one lingered in the neighborhood.

The Ipswich sparrows were more plentiful and more closely associated here than I have ever found Savannah sparrows on the mainland or Long Island. Their agitation also seemed greater and the tempo of their call notes faster. Except around these ponds and in a favorable tract around the superintendent's house and small garden, observations elsewhere on the island, especially eastward, revealed practically no nesting activity.

*Eggs.*—Saunders (1902a) took seven sets of eggs during his May visit; four nests contained five eggs and the remaining three contained four.  He describes them as having a great variety of markings and color, some resembling those of the Savannah sparrow; others were light brown with larger blotches like eggs of the vesper sparrow. One set was slaty with very small spots resembling the eggs of the horned lark; another set were like the eggs of the bobolink.  Dwight (1895) found his first nest containing three eggs on June 2.  Apparently an egg a day was laid, because by June 4 the nest contained five.  Another nest which had just been completed June 2 was abandoned.  On June 2 he found three more nests on the eastern part of Sable Island, each containing four eggs.  Of 22 eggs taken, Dwight remarks that they average a little larger than the eggs of the Savannah sparrow, from which they are otherwise indistinguishable, and adds: "They resemble the eggs of several other sparrows.  The ground color is bluish or grayish-white, often so washed with brown as to appear olive-brown and usually so splashed and sprinkled with different shades of umber and vandyke brown as almost to conceal the color of the shell.  There are also purplish and grayish-brown markings that are less apparent on most of the eggs than are the bolder blotches of the deeper browns that in the majority of cases aggregate about the larger end and form there a ring."

Dwight also noted considerable variation in the eggs of a single clutch.  Their shape was usually ovate, but in one set they were long and slender.  The average size was 21.6 millimeters (.85 inch) by 15.5 millimeters (.61 inch).  The lengths of extremes were 23.1 millimeters (.91 inch) to 20.3 millimeters (.80 inch); extremes of diameter were 15.7 millimeters (.62 inch) to 15.2 millimeters (.60 inch).

W. G. F. Harris adds: "The usual number of eggs laid by the Ipswich sparrow are from three to five.  They are ovate to elongate-ovate and have very little gloss.  The ground color may be very pale greenish-white or dirty white; heavily speckled, spotted, or blotched with browns and reddish browns, and undermarkings of 'pale neutral gray.'  The two sets at the Harvard Museum of Comparative Zoology differ both in shape and coloring.  The eggs of one set are elongate-ovate.  The ground is dirty white profusely spotted and blotched with reddish browns such as 'pecan brown,' 'russet,' 'auburn,' and 'snuff brown' with a few short streaks of black and undermarkings of 'pale neutral gray.'  The spottings are concentrated toward the large end, and on some they form a solid cap.  The eggs of the second set are ovate.  The ground is creamy white and the markings tend more toward the yellow browns such as 'Verona brown,' 'Brussels brown,' 'snuff brown,' and 'Argus brown' with underlying spots of the same 'pale neutral gray.'  The fine speckles, spots, and large blotches are well scattered over the entire eggs becoming confluent at the large end. The measurements of 50 eggs average 21.0 by 15.2 millimeters; the eggs showing the four extremes measure *22.5* by 15.3, 21.3 by *16.3, 18.8* by 15.8, and 20.0 by *14.4* millimeters."

*Young.*—Both Dwight and Saunders visited Sable Island in spring, from May to early June, and I went there in midsummer, from late July to early August. As apparently no one else has studied the nesting of the Ipswich sparrow, no data on its incubation and fledging periods are available. Ralph S. Palmer (1949) gives the incubation period of the closely related Savannah sparrow, across on the mainland in Maine, as 12 days and fledging as 14 days. Assuming that the Ipswich sparrow has similar incubating and fledging periods, my discovery of a fledgling on July 31 near the weather station on Sable Island during my 1948 visit suggests the possibility of two broods annually. This buffy juvenile was barely able to flutter along a path and could not have been out of the nest more than a day or two. Its hatching date was probably about July 15, and the egg must have been laid early in the month. Other evidence suggestive of second nestings was the adult I saw carrying food in early August and the preoccupied and very agitated adults I found about the ponds. I saw other juveniles abroad on the island still being cared for by their parents and calling to be fed.

The young of the year were not only trimmer than the molting and raggedy adults, but were noticeably buffy. On July 31 four young accompanied by one or two adults flew up out of the grass to the ridge of an old unroofed barn east of Wallace Lake. Another young bird, apparently calling for food, displaced a juvenile English sparrow from the top of a pole. Both young and adults proved to be rather tame, and a cautious approach brought me within 15 feet of individuals sitting on wire or pole. My approach did not send them flying out of the area as Dwight described spring birds; they proceeded by flitting short distances along the island's single telephone wire, or by alighting in turn on the insulators or poles. The adults that were through nesting and the unattached young appeared to be enjoying an auspicious season in this midsummer period of good weather and plentiful food.

*Plumage.*—Dwight (1900) saw no specimen in natal down. He describes the juvenal plumage as buff above streaked with brown; below pale yellow buff, palest on the chin, abdomen and crissum; sides of throat narrowly streaked across jugulum and on sides; wings and tail clove brown, the quills and coverts with whitish or pale cinnamon edgings becoming russet on the tertiaries.

He describes the first winter plumage as "acquired by a partial postjuvenal moult in August which involves the body plumage, and apparently the wing coverts, but not the rest of the wings nor tail, young and old becoming practically indistinguishable. *** Above, chiefly drab-gray which edges feathers clove-brown centrally bordered by a zone of Vandyke-brown so that the streaking above is suffused. The nape and median crown stripe are yellowish. The edgings of the wing coverts, secondaries, and tertiaries are of a vinaceous cinnamon which rapidly fades. Below, white, buff tinged on sides of head, across throat and on sides, streaked on sides of chin, across jugulum and on sides and flanks with russet bordered by clove-brown which is veiled by overlapping whitish feather edgings. Superciliary line ash gray. No yellow above the eye."

The first nuptial plumage is acquired by a partial prenuptial molt involving the head, throat, part of the breast, and a few stray feathers of other tracts, but not wings or tail. The chin and throat become whiter and their streakings darker; the yellow of the superciliary line is acquired. Elsewhere the buffy tints fade out and the streakings become more prominent beneath the veiling owing to abrasion. The prenuptial molt begins in February and lasts through March in the vicinity of New York City.

The adult winter plumage, acquired by complete postnuptial molt in July and August, is indistinguishable with certainty from the first winter dress, but is usually grayer or more hoary, the russet above deeper on the wings, everywhere less suffused with buff. Some specimens are tinged with yellow before the eye. The adult nuptial plumage is acquired by a partial prenuptial molt as in the young bird.

The sexes are practically indistinguishable according to Dwight, although females average rather browner and duller, and their molts are identical except that the prenuptial molt of the female is more limited than that of the male.

Dwight (1900) states, from examination of birds sent him, that the first winter plumage is acquired by a partial post-juvenal molt in August. During my 1948 visit to Sable Island the many ragged and tailless adult birds I saw showed postnuptial molt progressing in late July. Some showed considerable loss of feathers about the face; in others the superciliary line was mostly gray with a few very small yellow patches still showing. One or two almost bald individuals recalled the fighting by males during courtship that Dwight described. The trim juveniles were readily distinguishable from the gray adults by their buffier and browner tones.

*Food.*—A Department of Agriculture report by Beal on 56 stomachs Dwight sent him lists the contents of 19 Sable Island summer specimens and 37 winter birds from Long Island and New Jersey. The food of the summer birds consisted of 75.5 percent animal matter, 15.2 percent vegetable matter, and 9.3 percent gravel or sand. The 35 winter specimens contained 7.3 percent animal matter, 57.8 percent vegetable matter, and 34.9 percent gravel and sand; 24 of these showed no animal food or only a trace. The increase of gravel to grind the higher proportion of seeds is notable.

The animal matter eaten by the Sable Island birds consisted of beetles and larvae representing scarabaeids (*Aphodius fimentarium* identified), carabids, elaterids, cicindelids, and weevils; caterpillars, as well as pupae and pupae cases; grasshoppers; ants (including one pupa) and other hymenoptera; hemiptera; diptera; spiders (also eggs and cocoons); snails; also seeds, herbage, and unrecognizable material except seeds or granules of *Myrica cerifera*, *Cornus canadensis*, *Rumex acetosella*, and *Vaccinium*. The winter diet consisted largely of the seeds of grasses, including *Chenopodium* sp.?, *Eragrostis* sp.?, *Polygonum articulatum*, and rye, and other unidentifiable plants. The animal food in winter included beetles, among them scarabaeids and weevils; caterpillars and their cocoons; hymenoptera, including some ants; diptera; spiders' cocoons; and snails.

W. Earl Godfrey sends in food data on three museum specimens from Sable Island collected by W. E. Saunders. The stomach of one female taken May 22, 1901, contained small beetles, that of a male on the same date contained 85 percent seeds and 15 percent beetles, while the stomach of the third, a female taken on May 15, contained a few insects but mostly seeds.

William Dutcher (1886) remarks of birds received Apr. 1, 1885, with stomachs filled with small black insects and claims this to be the first instance of anything but vegetable food found among birds examined.

Charles W. Townsend watched Ipswich sparrows foraging along the seaweed drifts thrown up on a Massachusetts beach Apr. 3, 1910, and actually saw birds jump into the air for insects; beetles and small flies were the chief forms present. George M. Sutton, with Roger T. Peterson on an Audubon field trip, saw an Ipswich sparrow at Moriches, Long Island, on Oct. 17, 1948, feeding on sand grass (*Triplasis purpurea*).

No doubt the Ipswich sparrows would fare badly without beach grass (*Ammophila arenaria*) with its elevated panicles that stand well up out of the snow during severe weather. Some winters ago a sleet storm encased every branch, weed stalk, and blade of beach grass on Long Island in a casing of crystal-clear ice. The top-heavy seed panicles hung over within 5 or 6 inches of the ice-coated sand and only an occasional underside escaped the glazing. Alternately jumping and sliding on the ice, the sparrows had difficulty finding husks to pluck which were not encased in ice.

During open winters Ipswich sparrows used to fly out of the dunes and feed on the grassy strips that formerly bordered the ocean parkway at Gilgo on Jones Beach. Here crab grass (*Digitaria*) was plentiful. The birds fed by manipulating the seed heads, picking off and swallowing the seeds as the stems passed through the mandibles. Beach goldenrod, *Agrostis*, and *Andropogen* are among the plants this species was observed to feed upon. Once I watched an Ipswich sparrow feeding in a patch of salt grass (*Spartina patens*).

In New Jersey during the winter of 1940, Julian Potter counted 14 Ipswich sparrows near Stone Harbor along the shoulders of the "Sea Gull" highway. Driven off the low dunes by an extremely high tide, they were scattered for about three-quarters of a mile on both sides of the road, and were feeding along the grassy and weedy edges with many Savannah and several sharp-tailed sparrows. When approached they flew short distances and again alighted on the borders of the road.

Roy Latham states that in times of deep snow at Orient, Long Island, Ipswich sparrows enter the tracts of high tide bush (*Iva*) and feed on its seeds. W. Earl Godfrey took a winter specimen in Nova Scotia on Feb. 2, 1929, in an area where a system of dikes keeps the salt water out of the hay meadows. He writes me: "As you know snow usually blows off the top of these dikes, which average about 6–8 feet in height. This Ipswich sparrow was feeding on weed seeds (unfortunately I do not now know what kind). There are no dunes in that area. An autumn bird I collected was on the flat, hay meadows behind the dikes and separated from salt water by them."

One shot at Lawrencetown, near Halifax, Nova Scotia, around the end of March 1878, was feeding on bent grass (*Agrostis*). Regarding its feeding in South Carolina, Alexander Sprunt, Jr., writes me that "as to the food on this coast, I am convinced (and so was Wayne) that its mainstay is seeds of the sea-oats (*Uniola paniculata*)."

During the summer of 1948 Ipswich sparrows on Sable Island were observed to feed largely on the ground, often in damp, boggy tracts where they picked up both seeds and insects. I saw one bird pluck the center out of a seeding flower of the silver-weed (*Potentilla anserina*). Fecal matter examined consisted largely of animal matter, principally remains of beetles.

The few Ipswich sparrows that winter on Sable Island come regularly to bread crumbs and other food the inhabitants put out for them. R. S. Boutillier, superintendent of Sable Island station for many years, made a practice of feeding the Ipswich sparrows in winter. Captain Patrick Solawan, superintendent during my 1948 visit, wrote me that he and his family fed them regularly during the winters of 1948–49 and 1949–50. In Dwight's and Sanders's time, the Ipswich sparrow was the only resident land bird on the island. Unfortunately, the English sparrow, arriving about 1930, is now resident there, and although not overly abundant in 1948, it no doubt got more than its share of the food the inhabitants put out for the birds.

*Behavior.*—In its actions the Ipswich sparrow resembes the Savannah sparrow in many ways. One April morning I watched one of each standing a foot apart on the grassy strip at Gilgo, Long Island. They stretched their necks to the utmost to watch my approach, then relaxed and assumed identical crouching postures as they crept along feeding in the short grass. Again they reared, on the alert, standing high, necks upstretched, bills pointed upward. The Ipswich sparrow stood well above the Savannah sparrow and appeared much more robust. While stretching its head it still maintained its well-rounded proportions, while the Savannah's head and neck, normally thinner in profile, looked quite pointed in comparison.

Both species run rather loose-legged through the short grass, and, although the Savannah sparrow is likely to hop more than the Ipswich in winter, on the grass strip both species show essentially the same slow crouching or creeping advance and occasional scratch before picking up seeds in the short grass. The hopping tree sparrows that appear along the grassy strips with them in spring stand fairly high on their legs and are generally separable by shape alone from Savannah and Ipswich sparrows.

Edward H. Forbush (1929) cites Charles W. Townsend's description of the flight of the Ipswich sparrow as flickering and undulating like that of the Savannah sparrow. He notes that both drop abruptly into the grass with the tail down and that, like the Savannah, Ipswich sparrows frequently chase one another and associate with various other species, but are often by themselves. Townsend (1912b) writes: "Pipits, Horned Larks and Ipswich Sparrows have so completely departed from arboreal habits, that they run easily and walk with grace. Walking appears to be acquired later than running. It is a very interesting fact that the Savannah Sparrow, frequenter of meadows and marshy pastures, generally hops even when on smooth ground, although it is also a good runner, while its near relation the Ipswich Sparrow, frequenter of sandy wastes, almost never hops and is a good walker." Townsend also remarks that the Ipswich sparrow walks with a dovelike back-and-forth nodding of its head.

While I am in full agreement with Townsend's remarks for winter and early spring, the Ipswich sparrows on Sable Island in mid-summer hop perhaps as much as any of our sparrows. To quote from my field notes for 1948: "One bird flew out on the clean white sand, hopped several feet, picked at scattered seeds and to my surprise continued to hop through a patch of short sedges where it fed and then flew off into the crowberry. A moment later it returned and hopped around for 20 feet, once breaking into a run of several feet and then resorting to hopping for another minute before flying off.  On eastern Sable Island a tailless bird hopped for several minutes and continuously flipped its wings together rapidly as it circled on the bare sand in a small depression out of the wind.  The small hopping steps ranged from 4 to 6 inches between the center of footprints.  The hopping and wing-flipping continued for 5 minutes, and in that time the bird took a few running steps only once.  Occasionally Ipswich sparrows are seen to hop on our beaches during early fall migration.  Measurement of prints of fast hopping birds on Long Island sand beaches showed they average about 9 inches from center to center."

Julian Potter writes me of its behavior in New Jersey: "As the bird comes out into the open spaces between grass clumps on the dune it runs from one grassy spot to another.  Once in a while a bird will pause, stretch its head up high for an instant to notice my approach and then proceed on its skulking retreat.  When approached too closely, the bird flies a short way, then drops into the grass."  Alexander Sprunt, Jr., writes me from South Carolina: "The behavior of this bird is very similar to that of the Savannah sparrow, with which it is often found in company.  It is certainly adept at hiding amid clumps of grass, and usually prefers running to flying."

*Voice.*—W. E. Saunders (1902a) writes that he heard singing almost every moment of the day during his May 1901 visit.  J. H. Dwight (1895) tells of a rolling chatter uttered by quarreling males. He remarks than the song is a more polished and tuneful effort than that of the Savannah sparrow and lower in tone.  He describes it as two or three high-pitched and slightly sibilant introductory notes followed by a prolonged, still more sibilant, grasshopperlike lisp, and concluded without pause by a trill which carries farthest and is swung "out with a vim" unlike the weaker ending of the Savannah's song.

When heard by Dwight during May and June, the birds sang several times a minute, but rarely for more than a few minutes at a time, followed by perfect silence for up to 20 minutes when the chorus would start once more.  They were partial to early morning and dusk singing, when five or six might be heard at one time.  He states that the birds might start regardless of the fog and didn't greet the sun with an outburst of song.  According to him, they sang from the top of a dune, fence post, or telephone pole, sometimes starting from one individual's song.

Regarding midsummer song on Sable Island, I (1956) wrote "On July 31, singing was heard in mid-afternoon and continued irregularly until after dark.  Although that day broke clear and sunshine continued all morning, fog swept in, covering landmarks, at 2:30 p.m. and remained into the night.  As dusk came on singing increased until four or five could be heard from various directions. The muffled hoof beats of wild horses as under darkness they approached the dwellings, the continual distant roar of heavy surf along the south shore, and the rhythmatic musical and hylalike piping of arctic terns in a nearby colony, all served as a subdued chorus which made singing Ipswich sparrows the principal performers and this the only place on earth where such a combination could be heard."

The next morning, August 1, singing began in mid-morning bright sunshine and followed Dwight's May–June pattern of starting and stopping, even though it was late in the season. Singing perches ranged from invisible ones low in the contour-hugging growth to the tops of poles and to some 20 feet up on the wireless stays. To my ears the song sounded slightly louder and more musical than that of the Savannah. One repeated and completely different song by a bird perched on a radio strut consisted of two trills, as if it had left off the first three opening notes, *tswiteee, tswaaah.* The last trill was buzzy like the first, and quite dissimilar to the usual musical Ipswich ending. Richard H. Pough (1946) writes that the Ipswich sparrow's song ends "with a sound like a common tern's *tee-arr.*" This is the ending which Dwight says usually "swings out with a vim," and I noted it in some but not all of the birds singing in July and August 1948. Occasionally a song ends softly, and less emphatically, resembling the Savannah's.

Besides the musical *tsip* heard in winter, adults use a thicker *tsick* or *tsuck* repeatedly on the nesting grounds. Young call for food after leaving the nest with a similar chirp. I have heard this coarser note twice on Long Island in November, but the more musical *tsip* is the usual note on the mainland. I know of only three records of off-island singing—all heard in April—two on Long Island and one in Massachusetts.

*Field marks.*—The similarly sized, grayish vesper sparrow is sometimes found with Ipswich sparrows in early spring migration in grassy strips along ocean boulevards, such as at Jones Beach. The vesper sparrow lacks the Ipswich's facial streaking and its yellow over the eye, and has a plainer back and darkish ear patch. In flight the vesper's distinctive white outer tail feathers prevent confusion between the two.

Savannah sparrows are smaller, darker, and browner compared to the large, pale male Ipswich sparrows, which appear almost ghostly when out of the dunes. Female Ipswich sparrows often resemble the males but, according to Dwight, are sometimes slightly browner and smaller, approaching male Savannah sparrows in size. Generally the Savannah sparrow has a darker crown bordering the median line and shows considerably more black streakign on the back. Some spring Savannah sparrows are broadly streaked with white on the upper back and scapulars. These, however, are contrasty brown and white and lack the washed-out appearance of the Ipswich. Nevertheless, great care must be taken to distinguish the two, particularly in late spring.

*Enemies.*—On Sable Island, cats, foxes, and rats—the latter from shipwrecks—have threatened the Ipswich sparrow population for many years. Dwight found fewer in 1894 than Saunders did in 1901, and Saunders (1902a) reported the extermination of the foxes. In 1948 I found few apparent enemies of the Ipswich sparrow on Sable Island and the birds fairly abundant. Inquiry revealed two or three cats—household pets—on the island, and comparatively few rats. Some unidentified predator, however, had killed six adults and about a dozen half-grown young of the arctic tern in a colony near the western end of the island.

Undoubtedly, some birds are lost in migration to and from this fog-bound and storm-battered island some 100 miles off Nova Scotia's coast. Of those that do not migrate some must perish from the rigors of its severe winters. Saunders (1902a) tells how the inhabitants sometimes picked up exhausted and chilled Ipswich sparrows during winter and sheltered and fed them until better weather arrived. After the severe winter of 1947–48, Arthur MacDonald, a crewman at the main station on Sable Island, told me that he had found fully a dozen dead Ipswich sparrows here and there on the upper edges of abrupt dunes. Several groups lying in and about matted grass roots torn away by the wind he thought had apparently died of exposure.

On the mainland the shrinking of suitable habitat as the shore line is developed for real estate up and down the coast is a factor of moment. Cats, rats, hawks, and specimen collectors no doubt also take their share of Ipswich sparrows. Collectors have always exacted their toll, from the time of professional collectors on Long Island in the 1880's and 1890's to present-day "scientific" collecting in the southern part of their wintering range—Maryland, Virginia, the Carolinas, and Georgia. I feel it is time the collecting of this relict species be sharply restricted. Its nesting range is only some 17 miles of narrow, shrinking Sable Island, and its winter range, already despoiled in the northeast, is shrinking too, progressively forcing this unfortunate bird of many perils nearer to oblivion. Although occasional Savannah sparrows are found dead from time to time along the ocean boulevard at Jones Beach, I know of only one Ipswich sparrow ever having been struck by a motor car, and this one was able to fly away.

*Fall.*—W. A. Jeffries (1879) writes of his collecting experiences in Massachusetts. When they first arrived in the fall, the Ipswich sparrows were very tame, but they flew so fast and low and then ran along the sand so far before stopping that they were hard to find without a good dog. "Later comers," he remarks, "were very shy, never allowing a very near approach, but running before the dog for a few yards, would then rise wildly."

Allan D. Cruickshank (1942) calls the species a common transient visitor in the New York area, commonest in November during which he had seen "as many as twenty-seven individuals along the Jones Beach stretch in a single day." On Nov. 11, 1950, John Mayer of Idlewild and I counted 10 in a half-mile stretch at Gilgo, also on the Jones Beach stretch. Hurricanes, developments, and road building now cause migrants to pass more rapidly through the rather sterile Jones Beach dune tracts, and during the past few years, smaller numbers have been observed there.

One fall day at Jones Beach I watched two Ipswich sparrows allow a large black dog to come within six feet of them in its heedless wandering. The birds' reaction to the dog's approach was to crouch motionless. As the dog moved off, the birds resumed their feeding. When it returned, they again froze. Despite my greatest care, I was unable to approach them nearer than about 25 feet before they flushed.

On windless fall days, but generally less so in cold weather, Ipswich sparrows may often be approached closely. A group of members of the Delaware Valley Ornithological Club told me that while photographing one on the New Jersey dunes in late fall, they encircled and slowly approached it until they were about six feet away before the bird flew off. G. M. Sutton writes me of a bird a group encountered at Moriches, Long Island, in October, that was similarly tame: "At times the half-circle of observers almost closed in on it, yet it did not fly off in haste. As a rule when it moved on it walked or ran. We all watched the bird for about 20 minutes or more."

*Winter.*—With cold winds and wintry weather, the Ipswich sparrow becomes mainly terrestrial, walking, running, and crouching close to the ground as it traverses the blustery sand dunes. At times as it stands back to the wind, the long feathers covering its lesser wing coverts blow out loosely like a partly open cape, and the long upper tail coverts blow in a curve away from its body. As, unheeding, it picks up seeds in some exposed spot, its creeping crouch, short bill, and rounded head are reminiscent of a snow bunting or a longspur.

In Nova Scotia records of Robie W. Tufts from Queens, Shelbourne, and Halifax counties show this species a rather uncommon fall and winter visitor. Apparently the bird is also a local winter resident in Maine. Wendell Taber (1952) remarks that he and two

companions watched at length one of these birds at Popham Beach
on Feb. 23, 1952:

The bird was out of habitat, feeding voraciously in the wet seaweed left but
a few minutes earlier at high water mark on a sandy beach bordered by cottages.
Hunger, apparently, made this bird unusually tame. Once having accepted
our presence the bird seemed to ignore almost completely our movements as we
walked about to obtain better light and to approach to within perhaps 25 feet
or less. More often, one can spend an interminable amount of time attempting
to obtain a clear and lengthy look at the species. The bird scurries in rapid order
through one clump after another of beach grass in some sandy area close to the
sea—and success in one's attempts to obtain more than a fleeting glimpse is far
from being a certainty. Such habitat existed a few hundred yards distant—or
had existed. The snow storms which placed Portland in a state of "Emergency"
had shown no partiality towards Popham and in all probability the habitat had
vanished overnight.* * *

Palmer in "Maine Birds", 1949, supplies at the outside but three winter records.
Of these, one is December 6, 1946, by William H. Drury, Jr., who was a member of
my party at Popham Beach. I had the misfortune to be elsewhere at the particular moment and failed, myself, to see the bird. The location was about a half-mile
distant from that of the subject bird and was in appropriate territory. (According to Mrs. Genevieve D. Webb the Ipswich sparrow is a fairly common fall and
winter bird at Ocean Park, Maine. Maine Aud. Bull., 8 (3): 51.)

Sable Island boatman Arthur MacDonald told me of the Ipswich
sparrow feeding in the tidal drift in late winter, usually when the strong
winds blowing flying sand abated in late afternoon.

In Rhode Island, Douglas L. Kraus writes: "As you know the
Ipswich sparrow is a bird which must be sought hard and my own
records are scanty more because of my negligence than a real scarcity.
I do know that the hurricanes of 1938 and 1944, as well as the more
severe winter storms, have greatly affected the habitat of the Ipswich
and certainly reduced the wintering population. The influence of
filling, dredging, leveling and building along the R.I. shore is also
having a significant adverse effect." He sent me 29 records for that
state, many of them February birds, and 5 records for offshore Block
Island.

### DISTRIBUTION

*Range.*—Coastal dunes, Nova Scotia to Georgia.

*Breeding range.*—The Ipswich sparrow breeds only on Sable Island
off Nova Scotia. Reported in recent years in reduced numbers, due
probably to decrease in the size of Sable Island through erosion.

*Winter range.*—Winters along the Atlantic coast from Nova Scotia
south to southern Georgia (Cumberland Island); casually north to
southern Maine (Old Orchard) and central Nova Scotia (Wolfville).

*Casual records.*—Casual inland in Massachusetts (Cambridge) and
Connecticut (New Haven, West Haven) and along Chesapeake Bay.

*Migration.*—Early dates of spring arrival are: Maine—Cape

Elizabeth, March 15.  New Brunswick—Grand Manan, March 26.
Nova Scotia—Summerville, April 1.

Late dates of spring departure are: Georgia—Cumberland Island,
April 14.  South Carolina—Charleston, April 8.  Virginia—Cobb
Island, March 13.  Maryland—Gibson Island, April 15.  New
Jersey—Cape May, April 12.  New York—Long Beach, April 25.
Massachusetts—North Truro, April 22.  New Brunswick—Kent
Island, May 7.

Early dates of fall arrival are: Nova Scotia—Martinique Beach,
September 24.  Maine—Scarborough, October 1.  Connecticut—
West Haven, October 19.  New York—Long Island, October 23.
New Jersey—Cape May, October 23.  Maryland—Worcester County,
November 9.  Virginia—Cobb Island, November 22.  North Caro-
lina—Cape Hatteras, November 4.  South Carolina—Charleston,
November 3 (median of 10 years, November 20).

Late dates of fall departure are: Nova Scotia—Grand Pré, November 28.  Maine—Scarborough, November 27.

*Egg dates.*—Sable Island, Nova Scotia: 5 records, June 4 to June 11.

## PASSERCULUS SANDWICHENSIS LABRADORIUS Howe

## Labrador Savannah Sparrow

### Contributed by JAMES BAIRD

### HABITS

This dark northeastern race of the Savannah sparrow breeds from
northeastern Quebec and Labrador south to southeastern Quebec
(Anticosti Island), Newfoundland, and the St. Pierre and Miquelon
Islands.  It would appear, however, that *labradorius* is not equally
plentiful over the whole of this territory.

It has been referred to as abundant along the Labrador coast
(Austin, 1932; Todd, MS.), in Newfoundland (Peters and Burleigh,
1951a), and on the St. Pierre and Miquelon Islands (Peters and
Burleigh, 1951b).  That it is less abundant in the interior can be
seen in the reports of Godfrey (1949), who considered the Savannah
sparrow only a migrant in the Lake Mistassini and Lake Albanel
region of Quebec; of Harper (1958) who investigated the area around
Knob Lake in 1953 and found only one bird; and of Clement and
Baird who in 1958 worked the same area and found only 13 birds,
with no more than two pairs per bog, regardless of the size of the
bog.

Todd (1963) summarizes the situation well: "The Savannah sparrow
appears to have a wide but peculiar distribution in the Labrador
Peninsula.  The race *labradorius* is * * * primarily a coastal bird in

the Canadian Life–Zone, except where local ecological conditions permit its presence elsewhere, but in the Hudsonian and Arctic life–zones it has invaded the interior country, and has spread northward even to Hudson Strait."

*Nesting.*—Peters and Burleigh (1951a) found Savannahs "abundant in the meadows of southwestern Newfoundland, in the barrens of the Topsail country and in the ptarmigan barrens on the Avalon Peninsula. They also occur on the tops of hills and mountains * * *. We have seen many nests all containing either five eggs or five young birds. There are evidently two broods raised commonly * * *, for on several occasions we have foung flying young in the same areas with nests containing eggs."

Braund and McCullagh (1940), reporting on the birds of Anticosti Island, have this to say about the Savannah sparrow:

* * * We found the Savannah Sparrow common inland, on the dryer areas surrounding the muskeg, as well as along the coast. In the vicinity of the Eel Falls camp on June 29 fifteen were observed, and in the numerous bogs bordering Fox River, several pairs were seen. On a low ridge between the sea and one of these bogs a nest with 3 fresh eggs was found, concealed in a tuft of grass. The nest was composed of coarse native grasses, becoming progressively finer inward, to the lining, which was composed of fine dry grasses. The outside dimensions of the nest were 6 inches across by 3 inches deep; the bowl had a diameter of 2¼ inches, and a depth of 1¼ inches.

In coastal Labrador, Austin (1932) found a nest at Battle Harbor which was "composed of fine grasses and lined with rootlets, [it] was level with the ground in a little cup under an overhanging tuft of *Empetrum nigrum.*"

In the Knob Lake area of central Labrador, I examined several nests, each in one of the numerous sedge bogs that are interspersed between the spruce-lichen forests of the Labrador trough. Each nest was deeply sunk into a sedge clump, its top even with the matted basal stems, and the sparse sedge blades forming the thinnest of canopies over the nest. Although it seemed inevitable that the bottom of such a nest should be wet, the cup was quite dry in every nest inspected.

One of these nests in a bog east of Lake Matemace on June 26, 1958, contained four eggs which hatched on July 3. The newly hatched young had down on the capital, dorsal, alar, and femoral tracts, and their red gape was outlined with bright yellow.

Peters and Burleigh (1951a) say that in Newfoundland, the Savannah sparrow "Nests in a slight hollow in the ground, usually hidden by overhanging grasses. The nest is constructed of fine grasses. Usually 5 eggs are laid, of greenish-white or bluish-white, spotted with reddish-brown or purplish-brown, but variable."

*Plumages.*—Peters and Griscom (1938) state that *labradorius* is a dark Savannah sparrow with a relatively stout bill; similar to *P.s. savanna* and about the same size but darker throughout, the black areas more extensive. They continue:

"In spring general coloration above black, grey and brown, the black areas conspicuously developed, browns reduced, the white interscapular edges less developed than in *savanna;* lateral crown stripes largely black with little or no brown in extreme specimens; lores and superciliary stripe bright yellow, entire auricular region averaging darker than in *s. savanna;* streaking beneath dark brown or black, and heavier."

Norris and Hight (1957) characterize the race as follows:

"Dorsal surface: very dark, black and brown; feathers with extensive black markings and rich brown edgings. Sides of head: relatively dark, especially in auricular region, with brown and buff elements noticeable; loral region usually bright yellow. Ventral streaks: heavy, usually deep brown or black. Greater secondary coverts: dark, warm brown."

Harper (1958) describes the soft parts of an adult male: iris—olive brown; maxilla—dusky; tomium and mandible—horn color; tarsus and toes—light brownish, straw colored.

*Winter.*—*P. s. labradorius* winters from northwestern Mississippi and southeastern Maryland south to southeastern Texas, southern Louisiana, southern Mississippi, southern Florida, and western Cuba.

Throughout most, if not all of this wintering area, *labradorius* is found intermingling with other races of the Savannah sparrow in old fields and other similar herbaceous communities (Norris and Hight, 1957; Lowery, 1947; Quay, 1957). There is no evidence of any ecological segregation between the races (Norris, 1960). In South Carolina, *labradorius* made up 20.7 percent of a sample population of 1,758 Savannah sparrows, while in Louisiana, another sampling technique showed *labradorius* to comprise 9 percent of a sample of 107 collected birds (Lowrey, 1947).

## DISTRIBUTION

*Range.*—Eastern Quebec, Labrador, and Newfoundland south to the Gulf Coast and Cuba.

*Breeding range.*—The Labrador savannah sparrow breeds from northeastern Quebec (Wakeham Bay, George River) and Labrador (Ramah, Battle Harbour) south to southeastern Quebec (Mingan Island, Anticosti Island), Newfoundland, and St. Pierre Island.

*Winter range.*—Winters from northwestern Mississippi (Rosedale) and southeastern Maryland (Ocean City) south to southeastern Texas (Matagorda), southern Louisiana (New Orleans), southern

Mississippi (Gulfport), southern Florida (Tortugas), and western Cuba (Havana); casually north to Massachusetts (Newburyport) and Rhode Island (Warren).

*Egg dates.*—Labrador: 5 records, June 5 to July 17.

## PASSERCULUS SANDWICHENSIS SAVANNA (Wilson)

### Eastern Savannah Sparrow*

#### PLATES 38 AND 39
#### Contributed by JAMES BAIRD

#### HABITS

Ask ornithologists to think about Savannah sparrows and there is no telling what mental imagery will be conjured up. One will think immediately of a lush, spring-green meadow visited on a misty May morning; there, the thin song of the Savannah could barely be heard over the more robust songs of the redwing, meadowlark, and bobolink. Then he will remember, with a certain lingering discomfort that same field during the heat of a hot July day. Another will think of sand in his shoes, the roar of the nearby surf, and see once again a Savannah's nest hidden under some flotsam at the base of a Cape Cod sand dune. Still another bird man will remember cussing out a persistent yellowlegs that yodelled his alarm from atop a black spruce while he was trying to observe, unseen, a pair of Savannahs on a Labrador sphagnum bog. To the next, to think of Savannah sparrows will recall a bleak Alaskan tundra, longspurs, jaegers, godwits, lemmings and ice in the coffee pot on a midsummer morning.

That the Savannah sparrow should be able to evoke such a variety of climatic, geographic, and ecological memories is primarily due to its extensive breeding range, which covers nearly the whole of the North American continent from the arctic circle to the tropics. Throughout this vast range the racial populations form the links in the Savannah sparrow chain. And, just as the links of a chain pass one through the other, most of the racial populations merge into one another at their boundaries, thus creating the intermediates, that are, in part, the reason for considering each to be a part of the whole, rather than specific entities.

---

* When dealing with a species that has as many races as the Savannah sparrow, it is sometimes difficult to remember that it is the species that is important. Therefore, the following account deals not only with *savanna* as a race but more importantly with *savanna* as exemplary of the species. This seems appropriate because (1) the Savannah sparrow has a long history of taxonomic confusion, which makes it difficult to separate the races in the literature and (2) it seems probable that *P. s. mediogriseus* Aldrich will eventually be recognized as valid, thus restricting *P. s. savanna* to the maritime provinces of Canada.

In view of its extensive distribution, it is interesting to note that while the common name, Savannah sparrow, truly indicates its preferred habitat, it was actually named by Wilson for the town of Savannah, Ga., where the type specimen was collected. It is also something of a paradox that the species should acquire its familiar name from a town in the only section (southeastern United States) of the continent in which it does not breed.

*Nesting.*—Although the Savannah sparrow is confined in its choice of breeding sites to grassy or grasslike vegetation, these conditions are met in a wide variety of ecological situations across the continent. Therefore Savannah sparrows are found nesting from the sedge bogs of Labrador to the grass-capped islands of the Aleutians, from the New England hayfields to the short-grass prairies of mid-western Canada, from the salt marshes of the northeastern coast to the coastal marshes of California.

Throughout this extensive range there is remarkable uniformity in nest location and construction. With the possible exception of some of the "large-billed" Savannah sparrows of Baja California, the nest is built on the ground, almost always in a natural hollow or depression (the hollow may be scratched or dug out by the bird as indicated by Townsend, 1905; Forbush, 1929; Palmer, 1949), with its edges even with the ground or the tussock. By the very nature of the low rank vegetation of the nest site, the nest is well concealed, but further concealment is sometimes effected by a loose canopy of grasses and forbs overhanging the nest.

The nest is usually made of coarse grass stems, the cup lined with finer grasses. Sometimes mosses and other coarse plant materials are used in the bulky exterior, while hairs and rootlets may be used alone or in combination with the fine grass lining.

The following descriptions drawn from widely separated areas illustrate the similarities of nest construction despite the diversity of habitat.

From Cuyahoga County, Ohio, Donald L. Newman (in litt.) describes two nests located in an upland meadow: "The nest, which measured 3 inches at the widest point and was about 1⅝ inches deep, was made entirely of grasses—coarse and heavy on the outside, finer on the inside. It was placed in a perfect cuplike cavity on a small hummock of earth, perhaps 12 to 14 inches wide and about 6 inches above the general level of the field. Short over-arching grass and a narrow border of strawberry vines served to shade and conceal the nest. * * * A second nest * * * was constructed of coarse dead grass with a somewhat finer grass lining, was located in a slight depression or pocket of ground and was well concealed by the surrounding vegetation, consisting chiefly of cinquefoil, daisies, and coarse grasses."

Townsend (1905) refers to the Savannah sparrow in coastal New England as an abundant summer resident among the sand dunes, on the borders of the salt marshes, and among the adjoining grassy fields. He describes a nest found at Ipswich, Mass., which was built in the dunes just above the level of the highest tides. "The nest was concealed by a tuft of grass, and its bottom, which must have been excavated for the purpose was below the level of the sand which was rounded up about it. It was made of coarse grass, and neatly lined with fine grass."

From the mid-coastal areas of Delaware, Maryland, and Virginia, John H. Buckalew writes me:

"June 6, 1936. Two nests found near Indian River Inlet, Delaware, were each located near the base of a small sand dune, in the base of a clump of sedge. The nests were in slight hollows, the rim almost even with the sand, and were constructed of fine, dead marsh grass, lined with what appeared to be very fine marsh hay (*Spartina patens*).

"June 1, 1941. One nest found approximately one mile south of the Delaware–Maryland line, in Maryland, was at the edge of the salt marsh under a clump of *S. patens*, and apparently constructed entirely of the same grass."

Although colonial nesting by the Savannah sparrow has been alluded to several times in the literature (Baird, Brewer, and Ridgway, 1874a; Butler, 1897; Griscom, 1938), it is not frequent. These few observations might well only reflect a semicolonial tendency enforced by a scarcity of suitable nesting territory for the available population.

Since the success or failure of any bird population is to a large extent dependent upon the adaptability of the species to new situations, especially during the breeding season, an unusual nesting site for the Savannah sparrow Allen H. Morgan and I found in Carelton, Quebec, Canada, June 29, 1957, is of interest. Near the center of this little Gaspesian town was a small parklike area (150 × 500 ft.) between Chaleur Bay and Route 6. One-sixth of the area was a hard-topped parking lot that exited onto the main road; the remainder was mowed grass, interspersed with such ubiquitous plants as dandelion, burdock, plantain, white clover, and yarrow. The nest was sunk in the ground about 20 feet from the main road and 6 feet from the parking lot. We were not the first to discover the nest, for its location had been marked with a stick and the nest had been carefully circumnavigated by the mower. The female became disturbed when people came too close to the nest, but seemingly paid no attention to persons walking down the sidewalk, or such noises of civilization as cars, trucks, doors slamming, the rattle of milk bottles, or the yelling of children. While we were there the male sang from various pieces of playground equipment and picnic furniture scattered about the nearby beach. During one of these song periods, he seemed oblivious to a woman who walked within 10 feet of him.

Perhaps it is from such small beginnings that the Savannah sparrow will continue to find a niche that will secure its place in this constantly changing world.

*Eggs.*—W. G. F. Harris writes: "The Savannah sparrow lays from three to six eggs, with four or five comprising the usual set. They are only slightly glossy and generally ovate, though some tend to either short-ovate or elongate-ovate. The ground color may be pale greenish bluish, or dirty white, with markings of 'snuff brown,' 'russet,' 'Mars brown,' 'Prout's brown,' 'chestnut brown,' or 'auburn,' and occasional undermarkings of 'pale neutral gray.' The eggs of this species are particularly interesting because of the wide variation even of eggs in the same clutch. They may be finely speckled, either scattered over the entire egg or concentrated toward the larger end, or be so heavily blotched, spotted, or clouded that the ground is obscured, giving the egg the appearance of having a pale russet ground with superimposed blotches of darker tones of the same color. There is often a tendency for the markings to be somewhat blurred, and frequently eggs have a few distinct scrawls of black. The measurements of 50 eggs of *P. s. savanna* average 19.5 by 14.7 millimeters; the eggs showing the four extremes measure *21.3* by 15.2, 20.0 by *15.3* *17.3* by 13.9, and 18.0 by *13.5* millimeters."

The widely observed variation in clutch size probably results in part from whether the egg count represents a first or second nesting. First clutches are frequently larger than the second (Lack, 1954; Van Tyne and Berger, 1959).

Both male and female share the incubation (Baird, Brewer, and Ridgway, 1874a), and I have personally observed one instance where the male took over the feeding of the nestlings after the death of the female. According to Palmer (1949) "Incubation requires 12 days and fledging about 14."

*Plumages.*—The sexes are alike in all plumages. The natal down according to Sutton (1935) is dull brownish gray. Wetherbee (1957), attempting, with the 1912 Ridgway color plates, a more refined color determination, refers to the down as being bister anteriorly and wood-brown or olive-brown posteriorly.

The postnatal molt is effected by the down being "pushed out by the incoming nestling plumage" (Sutton, 1935). This down may cling to the feather tips of the heavily streaked juvenal plumage for some time after the bird has left the nest. Graber (1955) describes the juvenal plumage of *P. s. savanna* as follows: "Forehead and crown profusely streaked golden brown, buff and black. Median stripe of buffy yellow, sometimes obscure, and light superciliaries. Nape similar to crown but black streaking much reduced. Back streaked black (heavily), and shades of golden brown and buffy yellow. Rump buffy or buffy brown streaked with black. Upper tail coverts dark brown, broadly edged with buffy brown. Remiges black, outer primary edged white. Other remiges edged with rusty brown. Tertials broadly so, except uppermost which is edged with buffy white. Coverts black, lessers and medians edged with buffy white. Greaters edged with rust and tipped with buffy white (definite wing bars). Lores buffy, anterior end of superciliary yellow. Superciliary whitish streaked with black. Eye-ring white or buffy white. Auriculars buff or sandy, partially margined in black. Post-auriculars white streaked with black. Sub-auriculars buffy yellow (cheek patch about auriculars). Underparts buffy yellow, marked with black 'mustaches.' Jugulum, chest, sides, and flanks streaked with black or dark brown. Buffy yellow darkest on chest, lightest on belly (white in worn specimens). Crissum whitish or buffy yellow."

While working with several species of juvenal sparrows in Michigan, Sutton (1935) discovered what appears to be two color phases in the juvenal plumage of the Savannah sparrow. This first came to his attention when he collected two strikingly different juvenile Savannahs. He later brought together a small series of juvenal-plumaged specimens which bore out his original observation. And he stated: "It is my present opinion that the Savannah Sparrow's juvenal plumage has two color phases, one with dull, gray-brown tones predominating, the other with much brighter, yellowish buffy and red-brown tones. Whether the differences * * * are entirely a matter of color-phase I cannot say, but I cannot help feeling that they demand explanation beyond that of mere individual variation; and I feel furthermore, that some mention should be made of these two plumage-phases in any really adequate treatment of the species."

The first winter plumage is acquired by a partial post-juvenal molt which is initiated shortly after the juvenal plumage is acquired; possibly even before the "full" juvenal plumage is acquired (Sutton, 1935). Therefore, this incomplete molt involving only the body plumage and some of the wing coverts may begin as early as July and be completed in early September. Sutton (1935) regards the molting process as particularly rapid.

Peters and Griscom (1938) describe *savanna* as being a medium-sized, brown Savannah sparrow with a relatively stout bill. Similar to *oblitus* but browner throughout, the brown and buff elements strongly developed. Norris and Hight (1957) characterize *savanna*

PLATE 39

Pennington County, Minn., June 1933                    S. A. Grimes
NEST OF EASTERN SAVANNAH SPARROW

Tillamook, Oreg., May 28, 1916                         A. Walker
NEST OF WESTERN SAVANNAH SPARROW

PLATE 40

National Bison Range, Mont.             A. D. Cruickshank

NEVADA SAVANNAH SPARROW AT NEST

Newport Bay, Calif., Apr. 17, 1952            R. Quigley, Jr.

NEST OF BELDING'S SAVANNAH SPARROW

as follows: "Dorsal surface: generally medium brown; feathers with dark centers and light brown edgings. Sides of head: relatively light-colored, often with buffy suffusion; loral region usually yellow or yellowish. Ventral streaks: somewhat reduced (as compared with dark races), medium to dark brown. Greater secondary coverts: medium brown."

At the end of the nesting season, generally August, the adults acquire their winter plumage by a complete postnuptial molt. With the completion of the post-juvenal and the postnuptial molts, young and adult become virtually indistinguishable in the field. But in the hand, it can be seen that, in the eastern races at least, the buffy suffusion about the head of the immature clearly contrasts with the grayer head of the adult.

Both the first and later nuptial plumages are acquired by a partial prenuptial molt in March and April. This "involves the head, throat, breast, often the anterior part of the back, the tertiaries and stray feathers elsewhere even on the thighs, the abdomen, the lumbar tracts and the tail coverts, but not the remiges nor rectrices." (Dwight, 1900.)

Taverner (1932) and others have commented upon what they regard as extraordinary variation in plumage wear in the Savannah sparrow. While there can be no doubt that some breeding adults can acquire a "very frowsy, worn plumage," it is doubtful that such wear is excessive and peculiar to the species. It is probable that the worn plumage is simply more noticeable in the Savannah sparrow than in some other species because of the feather patterns.

*Food.*—Judd (1901) examined the stomach contents of 119 Savannah sparrows collected "in 12 states ranging from Massachusetts to California and in the District of Columbia, Nova Scotia, and Newfoundland." They represented all the months of the year except December and February. Overall, their food contents consisted of 46 percent animal matter, and 54 percent vegetable matter, mostly seeds. The Savannah is more highly insectivorous than other sparrows and the food items eaten were as follows: *Coleoptera,* 15 percent; *Lepidoptera,* 9 percent; *Orthoptera,* 8 percent; *Hymenoptera,* 5 percent; *Hemiptera,* 2 percent; other insects, 4 percent; spiders and snails, 3 percent.

Judd elaborates further to add that the Savannah sparrow—

appears to be the greatest eater of beetles of all the sparrow family. Beetles constitute the most important element of its animal food, and are eaten during every month in which stomachs were obtained, though of course in very small quantities during the winter months. In May and June * * * they form one-third of the entire food of those months. * * * it takes grasshoppers in quantity from June to August, and in July eats them to such an extent that they constitute 34 percent of its food * * *

The character of the vegetable food shows the savanna sparrow to be a great consumer of grass seeds. * * * Other seeds, mainly * * * weed seeds * * * make practically all of the remaining 22 percent of the vegetable matter, the only exception being a few blueberries found in one of the stomachs."

Martin, Zim, and Nelson (1951) show that for Savannah sparrows in the United States, the diet consists largely of plant food, mostly seeds. When considered seasonally, plant food composes 92 percent of the diet in winter, 63 percent in spring, 26 percent in summer, and 84 percent in fall. Animal food, mostly insects, is most heavily utilized in the late spring and summer. The most frequently utilized food plants (5 to 25 percent of the diet) in the northeast are bristle-grass, crabgrass, ragweed, and panicgrass; in the southern prairies, panicgrass, goosegrass, and pigweed; in California, knotweed, turkey-mullein, pigweed, and oats; in southern California and Mexico, wild oats, nightshade, and barley.

The early food habits studies carried on by Judd et al. were, of necessity, qualitative and "economic" in character; they fulfilled a definite need and are singularly useful even today. But these are yesterday's studies; today, food habits studies must meet the challenge of such concepts as "biomass" and "energy cycle." The Savannah sparrow, because of a decided predilection for fields in early stages of succession on its wintering ground, has been the subject of several recent papers dealing with old-field ecosystems (Odum and Hight, 1957; Quay, 1947, 1957, 1958; Norris, 1960).

To Odum and Hight (1957) the Savannah sparrow is an "herb sparrow," which they define as a sparrow that does not require woody vegetation but finds all food and habitat requirements in herbaceous vegetation. Quay (1957) defines the Savannah sparrow's winter habitat requirements: "Thus, the habitat niche of the Savannah sparrow in winter around Raleigh [North Carolina] was found in the ground level stratum of a particular facies (*Digitaria*) of one life-form of vegetation (grass). This niche was composed in large measure of: (1) bare ground on which to move and forage, (2) an abundance of small seeds easily visible from the ground surface and available without scratching, (3) an overhead cover of low to mediumly tall grass."

However, the Savannah sparrow is moderately abundant in many grassland associations and is concentrated only around favored seed sources. In South Carolina, an abundance of *Paspalum* attracted and maintained a large concentration of Savannahs (Odum and Hight, 1957), while in North Carolina, there was an almost linear relationship between the abundance of *Digitaria* (crabgrass) and the number of Savannahs (Quay, 1957).

Quay (1958) summarizes his work on the Savannah's foods and feeding habits as follows:

Total foods averaged 97 percent seeds and 3 percent insects and spiders. *Digitaria* seeds formed 70 percent of all foods eaten * * *. Seeds of secondary importance were *Ambrosia, Sorghum,* and *Eleusine.* * * * The seeds of greater use shattered from the plants later and more gradually than the ones of lesser use, thus being more steadily available both on the plant and on the ground (although seeds are seldom taken directly from the plant). * * * Feeding was characteristically local at any one period, on some one to four kinds of seeds. * * * Feeding was a continuous process, unhurried during most of the day but accelerated early in the morning and late in the afternoon. The crop was filled only once a day, at sunset.

*Behavior.*—The most frequently occurring description of Savannah sparrow behavior is that "it runs like a mouse through the grass." This is certainly an apt phrase since it has connotations of color, behavior, and habitat and, in addition, neatly summarizes the Savannah's mien.

Quay (1957), in his paper on wintering Savannahs, summarizes his observations as follows:

The Savannah sparrow was not an easy bird to watch. When disturbed, it ran on the ground more often than it flushed. Crouched low to the ground, head down and stretched forward, it ran quickly and quietly, taking advantage of all cover and resembling a mouse more than a bird.

When disturbed by a man walking, Savannahs either moved onward on the ground or took flight. Flights were usually short, 20–70 feet, and practically never carried the bird out of the plot. Flight was quick, erratic and only a few inches above the vegetation.

Although the Savannah sparrow runs when disturbed, it hops when it feeds, and sometimes scratches like a towhee. Quay (1958) reports that the Savannahs "typically fed on the ground, picking up seeds from the ground like a chicken. The only times they were seen to take seeds directly from plants were when snow and sleet covered the bare ground." However, as the seeds continue to shatter from the plants, the Savannahs soon resume feeding on the surface of the snow.

Quay (1957) notes: "The Savannah Sparrow proved to be at most only a weakly flocking species. Closely-knit flocks, of the type exhibited by field sparrows or starlings, were never observed. * * * As come upon in the undisturbed state, Savannah Sparrows commonly were found from singly up to loose groups of 20 to 60. Most commonly, the aggregation numbered fewer than ten birds." Norris (1960) who also worked with the Savannah on its wintering ground drew similar conclusions: "Thus, Savannah Sparrows exhibited a tendency toward being scattered over the fields, and although they were concentrated in some places they were nowhere bound, as it were, into closely knit, easily defined flocks." F. H. Allen reports in a letter to Mr. Bent that a flock of Savannahs seen in Massachusetts in April 1922 "exhibited traits of an imperfectly gregarious species, not rising in a flock and flying together, but rising singly and in small numbers and scattering in different directions. They often, if not always, ran a little way before they flew."

Norris (1960) describes a hostile display "of a warning nature" as follows: "The most prominent features of this display consist of the bird's facing its opponent, lowering and apparently "pulling in" its head, opening its bill, and raising its wings. The intensity is variable. Sometimes the bill is opened but little, and the wings raised slightly. At other times the mouth gapes rather widely and the wings are raised over the back. A warning display would normally last but two or three seconds, but it might be repeated."

Hailman (1958) describes a similar hostile display: "The aggressive posture is the same for both species. The head is thrust forward toward the opponent, and the bill is opened, displaying the gape. In addition, the wings are raised in a quick upward jerk, and the tail may be raised slightly, although the feathers are not spread. The threat posture is frequently accompanied by a running chase by the dominant individual, but rarely ends in flight of either. A note 'buzt' or 'buzt-buzt-buzt' is sometimes uttered by the dominant individual and so is assumed to be an aggressive note." He also states that supplanting flights were infrequent and that the associated fear response "seems to be relatively simple and unritualized, and consists of sleeking the body feathers as in flight intention * * *."

R. A. Norris (1960) notes that in his seminatural experimental group of Savannahs "The presence of a rather loose social hierarchy soon became apparent; among the dominant individuals, certain males belonging to dark races were especially well represented." However, it should be added that "many of the sparrows tended to feed and associate peacefully, and it was not uncommon for two or more to feed only inches apart, or for two to bathe at the same time."

Little or nothing has been published on maintenance behavior, therefore the following brief note I made at Knob Lake, Labrador, in 1958, will have to suffice: "A male Savannah sparrow has been singing and moving constantly along the edge of a large sphagnum bog. At one stage of his 'patrol' he stopped in the top of a small tamarack and proceeded to preen himself between songs. He first worked on his breast, then his back and wings. He then dipped his bill into the feathers of the rump (uropygial gland?) and worked on his legs and feet. He would thrust his bill into his rump and then nibble down his legs or toes, an action he repeated a number of times. He seemed to pay particular attention to his toes. Although the sequential occurrence was not noted, he was seen to scratch his head a number of times over the wing (indirectly)."

So little has apparently been published on the courtship behavior of the Savannah sparrow that the only account I can find is by

Townsend (1920) who states that "In courtship the male stands on the ground and vibrates his wings rapidly above his back. He also flies slowly a short distance above the ground with head and tail up and rapidly vibrating wings." And presumably as part of the courtship display, Townsend writes: "I have heard the song given on the wing."

Also of some possible significance in this regard is an observation I made at Middletown, R.I., in May 1958: "A male Savannah has been vigorously patrolling his territory along a stone wall. He fell silent for some 15 minutes and then flew back to the stone wall. He crept about the top of the wall, singing as he went, then eventually flew to the top of the tallest fence post along the wall and sang steadily. What I presumed to be the female came to the wall a few minutes later and also crept (and hopped) along the stones towards the male. She then dropped into the grass and the male followed. The significance of the creeping action is obscure, but it may be related to either courtship or pair formation."

Injury feigning by the female (and male?) is a well-known behavioral trait, and accounts can be found as far back as 1832, when Wilson and Bonaparte described a female who "counterfeited lameness, spreading her wings and tail, and used many affectionate stratagems to allure me from the place." However I have flushed a number of Savannahs from nests containing eggs or young that gave no distraction display. It would be interesting to know what actually triggers this maneuver.

Evans and Emlen (1947) in discussing barn owl prey state that Savannah sparrows commonly roosted at night in the grassy fields at Davis, Calif. McIlhenny (1942) adds: "I learned an interesting thing about Savannah sparrows that night, which is—they sleep in small compact groups on the ground in short grass."

One last observation that is perhaps more physiological than behavioral relates to the fact that the Savannah sparrow is found in a number of habitats that are either actually dry (weedy upland fields) or devoid of fresh water (salt marshes or sand dunes). To utilize these habitats the birds must be able either to subsist on a limited supply of water (dew) or to satisfy their moisture requirements from metabolic water. However, they do use fresh water for bathing and drinking when it is available (Norris, 1960), and in the winter when all water is frozen I have seen them eat snow.

*Voice.*—The song of the Savannah sparrow can only be described as utilitarian. That it obviously does not delight the ear of man can be seen by the comments of those who have described it in print: "insignificant" (Dwight, *in* Chapman, 1897), "buzzy and insect-like" (Saunders, 1935), "high-pitched and thin in quality" (Roberts, 1936), shrilly musical (Hausman, 1946). But to the male patrolling his breeding territory, his song, insectlike though it may be, is a vital part of the nesting cycle.

Aretas A. Saunders (MS.) sent the following analysis to Mr. Bent:

"The Savannah sparrow is one of the 'buzzy-voiced' sparrows, but its song is rather more pleasing and musical than the others of that group. In form it suggests the song sparrow, as it begins with several (usually three) short staccato notes. These are usually followed by two buzzes on different pitches. The introductory notes are commonly three, but vary from one to seven. There are usually two trills, but a few songs have only one and still fewer have three. I have 46 records; 35 have two trills, 8 have one only, and 3 have three.

"Songs vary from 1.8 to 3.4 seconds in length, averaging about 2.3 seconds. The longest one begins with five introductory notes, the first two with pauses between them. Except for this one, no song I have is longer than 2.5 seconds.

"The pitch of songs varies from D#′′′ to G′′′′. The pitch interval varies from 1 to 4 tones, averaging about 2¼ tones. The three parts of the most typical songs, the introductory notes and the two trills, are ordinarily each on a different pitch, one high, one medium, and one low. There are six possible arrangements of three different pitches, and by using numbers, 1 for the highest note, 2 for medium, and 3 for low, these six arrangements are 123, 132, 213, 231, 312, and 321. All of these arrangements occur in Savannah sparrow songs, and I have from four to six records of each arrangement, showing that they probably occur in nearly equal frequency. The ones most numerous in my records are 132 and 123.

"The first songs of this bird are generally to be heard in April, and the song continues on the breeding grounds until late July, or occasionally to early August."

In his guide Saunders (1935) lists four phonetic renditions of the Savannah sparrow's song:

1. C′′′′ *tiptiptip seeeee saaaay*
2. C′′′′ *tiptiptip saaaaaay seeeeeee*
3. E′′′′ *taptaptap saaaaaaaah seeeeee*
4. E′′′′ *tap tap tuptuptup saaa weeeee*

He further states that "The call note, '*tthlip*', is short and rather curious in its combination of explosive, fricative, and liquid sounds at its beginning."

Ralph Hoffmann (1904) states that the Savannah sparrow "rarely sings on migration" and that on the breeding ground "the song continues through July. * * * It is uttered from a rock or a low post, and consists of two or three preliminary chips, followed by two long, insect-like trills, the second in a little lower key than the first, tsip,

tsip, tsip, tseeeeeeeee tsee-ee-ee-ee. * * * When the birds have young about * * * [they are] continually uttering a sharp tsup. When two birds quarrel, they utter a harsh bsss."

Jonathan Dwight, Jr. (*in* Chapman, 1898) has this to say:

The song is insignificant—a weak, musical little trill following a grasshopperlike introduction, and is of such small volume that it can be heard but a few rods. It usually resembles tsip-tsip-tsip' sē'-ē-ē-s'r-r-r. More singing is heard towards sunset, when of a quiet evening the trills are audible at greater distances. Each male seems to have a number of favorite perches, weeds or fence posts, which are visited as inclination dictates, but he has too restless a disposition to remain long on any of them. The most familiar note is a sharp *tsip* of alarm or expostulation heard during migration, but so constantly employed by both sexes in the breeding season, even on slight provocation, that one gets to think of them as veritable scolds.

Norris (1960) in describing hostile intraspecific displays says that "the sparrows occasionally had short-lived fights, usually accompanied with rather buzzy or harsh call notes (schwurt-t) * * *."

Quay (1957) has this to say about the call note and its relation to social behavior:

There was one definite aggregating mechanism which served, though at times rather ineffectively, to maintain the weak type of flocking—the call note. The single call note was a faint and sibilant "tseep" (variations: tseeep, tseeh, tseeeh, tseh, tsip). The note was not given while the bird was on the ground and undisturbed. Typically, the first note was given just before or as the bird took flight and then an additional one each two or three seconds while in flight. This note had a disturbing or alerting influence on other Savannah sparrows nearby. The note was usually effective as a signal to the others to follow the caller, not quickly and all at once but slowly and as singles and groups of two and three, which birds themselves also "tseeped" as they flew.

*Field marks.*—The Savannah sparrow is a medium-sized open-country sparrow. Streaked above and below, it is whiter below than most other sparrows, with the crisp, black or brown streaks sometimes clustering into a breast spot as in the song sparrow. It has a light stripe through the crown and another over the eye, the forepart of which becomes yellow in the breeding season. The tail is relatively short and forked (an important field character, since the other sparrows which resemble the Savannah have rounded tails). The legs are pinkish or flesh-colored.

*Enemies.*—The enemies of the Savannah sparrow are many. Depending upon how broad a definition one applies to the word "enemy," they could include the nest-robbing crow, the hazards of migration, the nest-usurping cowbird, and the competing song sparrow, as well as, in the more classical sense, the hungry predator, whether it be hawk, fox, cat, or owl. Basically of course, the main enemy is the predator. And since the Savannah is widespread, plentiful, small, and a ground nester, it is a perfect prey species. Data on its use by predators are relatively few; the observations that follow afford us only token insight into this important control on the species' numbers.

Owls. Richard M. Bond (1939) found them frequently used as food by either horned owls or barn owls. Evans and Emlen (1947) state more definitely that the Savannah sparrow was the only common wintering bird in Davis, Calif., that was represented in appreciable numbers in barn owl pellets. Errington (1932) records Savannah sparrows as prey of the long-eared owl in southern Wisconsin. J. A. Munro (1929) reported two Savannahs killed by short-eared owls at Beaver Lake, Alberta, Canada.

Hawks. J. Grinnell (1923b) watched a sharp-shinned hawk pursue and successfully capture a Savannah sparrow, which later proved to be *anthinus*. W. J. Breckenridge (1935) includes Savannahs as part of the diet of the marsh hawk in Minnesota, and E. W. Martin (1939) lists them among prey of the pigeon hawk. I have several times seen a sparrow hawk slip off a telephone pole, fly fast and low over the grass tops, and make an unsuccessful grab at a feeding Savannah sparrow.

While parasites are not enemies in the strictest sense, they do have their effect upon their host. However, in most cases this effect is not measurable. For instance, although the brown-headed cowbird victimizes the Savannah sparrow rather infrequently (Friedmann, 1963) each parasitized nest means a loss of potential parent replacement, and how this affects the aggregate population has never been assessed accurately. Similarly the effect of body parasites upon the Savannah sparrow has not been determined.

R. O. Malcomson (1960) reports the presence of the bird louse *Ricinus diffusus* (*Mallophaga*) on Savannah sparrows.

Carlton M. Herman (1937) reports Savannah sparrows as hosts to the Hippoboscid louse flies *Ornithomyia fringillina*, which Bequaert also identified in a sample collected from Savannahs in Rhode Island.

Herman (1944) lists the following blood protozoans from the Savannah sparrow: *Trypanosomidae* (*Trypanosoma* sp?), *Plasmodiidae* (*Plasmodium* sp?), *Haemogregarinidae* (*Toxoplasma* sp?).

*Fall.*—For the period between the close of the nesting season and the onset of migration, Forbush (1929) reports that in Massachusetts "The birds gather in family groups and roam the fields and meadows." Palmer (1949), speaking of Maine birds, says that "In August, after nesting is ended, hundreds of the birds often are found in a small area of salt marsh. These are mostly young of the year, that linger in these areas of adequate food and shelter before flying south."

While we may not know exactly where the birds spend the postbreeding period, it seems reasonably certain that little, if any, long range dispersal from the breeding grounds occurs immediately. The first really large migratory movement begins in mid-September, with the peak occurring from the last week of September to mid-October. In the eastern populations the migration from north to south shows a definite progression: Maine—September 15 to October 25; peak period, end of September to October 13; Massachusetts and Rhode Island—peak period from third week of September to second week of October; Maryland—September 15–25 to November 1–10, peak period October 5 to October 30. The birds arrive on the wintering grounds in North Carolina in late September, gradually increase during October and become "commoner and more widely distributed" by early November (Norris and Hight, 1957).

The Savannah sparrow is a nocturnal migrant, but in some instances the migration may continue into the morning either as a manifestation of continuing migratory restlessness, or as a redirected movement away from the coast (Baird and Nisbet, 1960). The stimulus to migrate in the fall is provided by the passage of the leading edge (cold front) of a high pressure cell that, by late September and October, is characterized by a sharp drop in temperature, fair strong north or northwest winds, and clear skies.

As with most small birds, the migratory period presents certain hazards. Some are natural, but many are created by man. W. E. Saunders (1907) reports on what may be considered a typical but infrequent natural migration disaster. An early snowstorm over Lake Huron in western Ontario on the night of Oct. 10, 1906, killed thousands of birds, of which Savannahs formed a small percentage. Another natural disaster, which may take an annual toll far greater than any recorded mortality, is the danger of being blown out to sea (Scholander, 1955, and others). Savannahs have been recorded at sea in both the Atlantic and the Pacific and, while some Savannah populations fly over the ocean as part of their regular migration path, as the Newfoundland birds must, the evidence suggests that most sightings of Savannahs at sea are of birds blown off course (Baird and Nisbet, 1960).

Man has long rivaled nature in his ability to cause mass mortalities of migrating birds. Lighthouses were perhaps the first of the man-made structures to cause significant bird destruction, and have presumably been doing so since they were first constructed. Savannah sparrows have frequently appeared in the lists of birds killed (Dutcher, 1884; Merriam, 1885).

With the advent of ample electricity, the electric light, and the increasing height of buildings, the lighted building became a beacon of destruction under certain weather conditions, and continues to attract and kill varying numbers of nocturnal migrants, Savannahs included.

But the greatest menace to migrants has resulted from two fairly recent innovations: the television tower and the airport ceilometer. Both these instruments have taken a fantastic toll of migrants; for example, 50,000 birds were killed during one October night at a ceilometer in Georgia (Johnston, 1955). Stoddard (1962) reports 15,000 birds killed at a Florida TV tower in 6 years; the Savannah sparrow is nearly always represented in these mass kills.

*Winter.*—The southeastern United States forms the major wintering ground for not only the eastern races (*oblitus, labradorius, savanna*), but for at least part of the population of the more western *nevadensis*. Here the races intermingle without apparent habitat or social segregation (Johnston, 1956; Norris and Hight, 1957; Quay, 1957; Norris, 1960).

As noted earlier, the Savannah sparrow becomes common in South Carolina (Savannah River Plant) by November, and remains abundant throughout the winter. The population gradually builds up to a December peak, which then drops until it becomes stabilized during February and March (Norris and Hight, 1957). During this period the total population fluctuates to some extent, but Norris (1960) estimates that on the average there are about four or five birds per acre, and more—up to 30 per acre—in particularly favorable fields. Odum and Hight's (1957) estimate of the same population in the same area with a different census technique showed about 10 birds per acre. This represents no real discrepancy for even the short-term home range of a Savannah sparrow is about 8 acres, and Norris (1960) found evidence that some birds exhibited even greater vagility over an extended period.

If the post-December drop in the numbers of Savannah sparrows at the Savannah River Plant occurs annually, it suggests the presence in the December population of birds who have not yet reached their usual winter quarters farther south. If this drop occurs only sporadically, it may be a "hard weather" movement, such as Quay (1957) noted in North Carolina:

The month from January 14 to February 14, 1948, was a time of continuously below-normal temperatures and repeated sleetfalls, snowfalls, and ice glazes. * * * During January 14–23 there were daily freezing temperatures, frequently down to 10–15 degrees Fahrenheit. This sharp drop in temperature alone caused no visible change in the savannah sparrow population. On the 24th of January two inches of snow and fine sleet fell, accompanied by a glaze of ice on the vegetation. The sleet and snow covered the bare ground completely through the 26th, and thirty per cent of the ground still by the 30th. The ice glaze melted by the afternoon of the 25th.

The savannah sparrows were entirely gone on the 25th from all the Tall Weeds and *Andropogon* Plots, from all the *Digitaria-Medicago* Plots except for 24 birds in a sheltered spot of *Digitaria* in the lee of a Tall Weeds' edge of Plot 11, and from the mowed *Digitaria-Sorghum* Plot. Thereafter until the middle of February, except for 2 birds in Plot 11 on February 6, none of these plots contained any savannah sparrows. During the clear and warmer weather of the second half of February there was only about 25 per cent recovery.

He further states that "The savannah sparrows which disappeared could have either died or moved farther south. Careful search was made for dead birds, both in the regular and other habitats, but none were found. The writer believes that the savannahs made a wholesale, mid-winter, southward 'weather movement'."

It has been amply demonstrated that birds return year after year to the same breeding area, but it is not so well known that many birds return to the same wintering area. This winter "homing" tendency has been particularly well demonstrated for sparrows, and the Savannah sparrow has been no exception. Wharton (1941) reports that of 453 Savannahs banded in South Carolina, 33 or 7.28 percent returned in successive winters.

Based on a comparison of the actual returns compared with a figure that they believe represented the total population, Odum and Hight (1957) estimated a return ratio of 38 percent in 1956 and 41 percent in 1957. From this they estimate that 40 out of 100 birds wintering in the area return the next year.

## DISTRIBUTION

*Range.*—Southern Ontario, southern Quebec, and Nova Scotia south to Veracruz, the Yucatán Peninsula, Cuba, and the Bahamas.

*Breeding range.*—The eastern savannah sparrow breeds from southern Ontario (Bigwood), southern Quebec (Montreal, Kamouraska, Magdalen Islands) and Nova Scotia (Cape Breton Island) south to northwestern and central Ohio (Toledo, rarely Columbus), West Virginia (Maxwelton), western Maryland (Accident, Buckeystown), southeastern Pennsylvania (Carlisle, Reading), northern New Jersey (Morristown, Newark), and southeastern New York (Hicks Island, Plum Island); once in southern New Jersey (Seven Mile Beach).

*Winter range.*—Winters from Massachusetts (casually) south on the Atlantic coast to Florida and the northern Bahamas, and from Kansas (rarely), Arkansas, Tennessee, North Carolina, and eastern Virginia south to Veracruz (Tlacotalpam, Tehuatlán), Yucatán (Río Lagartos), Quintana Roo (Holbox and Cozumel islands), Grand Cayman, Isle of Pines, and Cuba; rarely north to Nova Scotia (Wolfville).

*Migration.*—The data apply to the species as a whole. Early dates of spring arrival are: Florida—Leon County, February 1. District of Columbia—average of 37 years, March 26. Maryland—

Harford County, March 6; Laurel, March 11 (median of 8 years, March 21). Pennsylvania—State College, March 17. New York—Cayuga and Oneida Lake basins, March 14 (median of 21 years, March 31). Connecticut—New Haven, March 24. Rhode Island—Providence, March 31. Massachusetts—Martha's Vineyard, March 7. Vermont—Rutland, March 27. New Hampshire—Concord, March 26. Maine—Portland, April 6. Quebec—Hatley, March 20. New Brunswick—Grand Manan and Scotch Lake, April 3. Nova Scotia—Wolfville, April 1. Prince Edward Island—North Bedeque, April 9. Newfoundland—St. John's, April 28. Arkansas—Hot Springs, April 2. Tennessee—Nashville, March 8 (median of 10 years, March 20). Kentucky—Bardstown, March 3. Missouri—St. Louis, February 26 (median of 13 years, March 10). Illinois—Urbana, March 5 (median of 13 years, March 24); Rantoul, March 13; Chicago, March 23 (average of 16 years, April 8). Indiana—Sedan, March 9. Ohio—central Ohio, March 10 (median of 40 years, March 23); Oberlin, March 30 (median of 13 years, April 18). Michigan—Detroit area, March 27; Battle Creek, April 4 (median of 29 years, April 15). Ontario—Toronto, March 20; Ottawa, March 31 (average of 14 years, April 14). Iowa—Sioux City, March 27. Wisconsin—Dane County, March 19. Minnesota—Pipestone, March 21 (average of 11 years for southern Minnesota, April 15). Texas—Sinton, March 22. Oklahoma—Cleveland County, March 2. Kansas—northeastern Kansas, February 21. Nebraska—Holstein, March 18; Red Cloud, April 14 (average of 10 years, April 29). South Dakota—Lake Poinsett, April 12; Sioux Falls, April 24 (average of 5 years, May 2). North Dakota—northeastern North Dakota, April 3 (average of 8 years, April 17); Jamestown, April 15. Manitoba—Treesbank, April 20 (average of 22 years, April 28). Saskatchewan—Lake Johnston, April 27. Mackenzie—Mackenzie River, May 19. Arizona—Ganado, February 10; Tucson, February 15. Utah—Brigham, March 15. Colorado—El Paso County, March 19. Wyoming—Laramie, April 13. Idaho—Meridian, March 12. Montana—Bozeman, April 18; Libby, April 21 (median of 5 years, April 23). Alberta—Glenevis, April 20.

Late dates of spring departure are: Florida—Tallahassee, May 20. Alabama—Birmingham, May 26. Georgia—Savannah, May 28. South Carolina—Charleston, May 13. North Carolina—Buncombe County, May 17; Raleigh, May 13 (average of 8 years, May 6). Virginia—Smith Island, May 19. District of Columbia—May 18 (average of 24 years, May 3). Maryland—Laurel, May 23 (median of 7 years, May 7). Connecticut—Portland, May 27. Louisiana—Covington, June 15; Baton Rouge, May 14. Mississippi—Rosedale, May 14. Tennessee—Knox County, May 20. Kentucky—Bowling

Green, May 11. Missouri—St. Louis, May 30 (median of 13 years, May 12). Illinois—Chicago, June 2 (average of 16 years, May 25); Urbana, May 21 (median of 13 years, May 10). Indiana—Wayne County, May 2. Ohio—Oberlin, May 25 (median of 13 years, May 12); Buckeye Lake, May 16 (median, May 7). Texas—Sinton, May 26 (median of 7 years, May 11). Kansas—northeastern Kansas, June 3 (median of 5 years, May 13). Nebraska—Holstein, May 25. South Dakota—Yankton, May 13. New Mexico—Mosquito Springs, May 16; Rio Grande, May 12. Arizona—Topock, May 22.

Early dates of fall arrival are: Arizona—Camp Verde, August 13; Bill Williams delta, August 24. Nebraska—Holstein, August 25. Texas—Sinton, September 9 (median of 5 years, October 1). Ohio— Buckeye Lake, September 10 (median, September 15). Illinois— Chicago, August 27 (average of 16 years, September 7). Missouri—St. Louis, September 1. Tennessee—Nashville, September 4. Mississippi—Rosedale, October 2. Louisiana—Baton Rouge, September 28. New York—Long Island, September 3. New Jersey—Cape May, August 21. Maryland—Baltimore County, September 4; Laurel, September 13 (median of 5 years, September 26). District of Columbia—September 21 (average of 10 years, October 9). Virginia—Cobb Island, August 22. North Carolina—Raleigh, August 20. South Carolina—Charleston, September 26 (median of 7 years, October 22). Georgia—Athens, September 19. Alabama—Birmingham, September 15. Florida—northwestern Florida, September 15.

Late dates of fall departure are: Alberta—Glenevis, October 1. Idaho—Lewiston, November 1. Wyoming—Laramie, October 16 (average of 6 years, September 23); Albany County, October 15. Colorado—Pueblo, November 4. Arizona—Tucson, November 26. New Mexico—Silver City, November 5. Mackenzie—Fort Simpson, September 15. Saskatchewan—Wiseton, September 25. Manitoba—Treesbank, October 19 (average of 10 years, October 8). North Dakota—Cass County, October 27 (average, October 20). South Dakota—Yankton, November 2. Nebraska—Holstein, November 10. Kansas—northeastern Kansas, December 1 (median of 16 years, October 20). Oklahoma—Tulsa, November 6. Texas— Sinton, November 10. Minnesota—Minneapolis-St. Paul, October 31 (average of 6 years, October 19). Wisconsin—Madison, October 25. Iowa—Sioux City, October 20. Ontario—Toronto, October 31; Ottawa, October 21 (average of 14 years, October 3). Michigan— Battle Creek, October 25 (median of 13 years, October 5). Ohio— central Ohio, November 13 (average, October 27). Indiana—Bloomington, November 6. Illinois—Chicago, November 8 (average of 16 years, October 24). Missouri—St. Louis, December 10 (median of 12 years, October 2). Kentucky—Roundhill, November 12.

Mississippi—Rosedale, October 22. Newfoundland—Tompkins, October 4. Prince Edward Island—North River, September 20. New Brunswick—Scotch Lake, November 10. Quebec—Montreal, October 23. Maine—Pittsfield, October 10. New Hampshire—Exeter, November 13. Vermont—Rutland, November 1. Massachusetts—Belmont, November 8. Rhode Island—Charlestown, November 4. Connecticut—Hartford, November 29. New York—New York City, November 30; Cayuga and Oneida Lake basins, November 27 (median of 19 years, October 30). Pennsylvania—State College, November 4. Maryland—Baltimore County, November 16; Laurel, November 1 (median of 5 years, October 30). District of Columbia—November 22 (average of 7 years, October 30).

*Egg dates.*—Illinois: 19 records, May 6 to June 20; 11 records, June 1 to June 10.

Massachusetts: 30 records, May 9 to July 21; 20 records, May 26 to June 8.

New Brunswick: 29 records, May 29 to July 30.

New York: May 5 to June 28 (number of records not stated).

Nova Scotia: 32 records, May 16 to July 10; 18 records, June 6 to June 16.

Rhode Island: 7 records, May 22 to June 18.


### PASSERCULUS SANDWICHENSIS OBLITUS Peters and Griscom
## Churchill Savannah Sparrow
### Contributed by JAMES BAIRD


#### HABITS

*P. s. oblitus* is a dark-colored interior race that bridges the clinal gap between *labradorius* and *nevadensis*. It breeds from northeastern Manitoba, northern Ontario, and northwestern Quebec south to southern Minnesota, southern Michigan, central eastern Ontario and central southern Quebec.

*Nesting.*—Godfrey and Wilk (1948) say that *oblitus* is a common breeder in the meadows and hay fields in the Lake St. John region of Quebec. "In the St. Felicien region, where it was especially common, Wilk estimated a breeding population of thirty-two pairs for the 80 acres of hay field near camp. Here a nest on June 16 contained five eggs, and on June 27 three young and two eggs. Flying juvenals were noted first on July 1. The species became increasingly common in late August and early September."

Although apparently local in distribution in the southern counties of Michigan, it is an abundant breeding bird in the Upper Peninsula

(Wood, 1951). In Luce County, in the Upper Peninsula, nests with eggs were found from May 18 to August 1.

In Minnesota, Roberts (1936) states of the Savannah sparrow, which he lists as *savanna:* "In the heavily timbered northern portion of the state it is confined to meadows adjoining lakes and marshy land and to old grass grown clearings. It is especially abundant on the western prairies, where it inhabits not only the lowlands but also upland thickets * * *."

Most of the nest and egg records Roberts cites are in June, with clutch size usually either four or five. He describes the nest as being "on the ground, well concealed in thick grass in a meadow, field, or on low prairie; built of grasses, lined with finer grasses, and a few hairs if available." The three to five eggs are grayish–white and speckled with reddish-brown, and the incubation period is 12 days.

*Plumages.*—Peters and Griscom (1938) in their original description of *oblitus* say:

A medium sized gray Savannah Sparrow with relatively stout bill, its depth more than half the length of the culmen. Similar to *P. s. savanna* and of about the same size, but grayer throughout; the brown and buff elements reduced or lacking: similar also to *P. s. labradorius* in the depth and extent of the streaking of the under-parts and development of black areas above, but browns much paler and reduced in area, often lacking; reddish wing edges much paler. In spring plumage recalling *P. s. nevadensis* in gray, black, and white coloration above, but with black areas more extensive, streaking below much heavier, and yellow superciliary brighter and more extensive.

In autumn most nearly resembling *P. s. labradorius*, but blacker, less brownish; distinguishable at a glance from *P. s. savanna* by almost complete absence of reddish brown; the color which predominates in the Atlantic slope bird at that season. *P. s. nevadensis* in fall is *paler* and *grayer* than *oblitus*, and is always readily separable by its slenderer bill. * * *

As would naturally be expected, *oblitus* intergrades with *nevadensis* where the two forms meet. On the area of intergradation we find two types of intergrades; thick-billed birds with the paler coloration of *nevadensis* and slender billed birds like *oblitus* in color.* * *

Norris and Hight (1957) provide us with a more succinct description: "Dorsal surface: dark to very dark, black and gray; feathers with extensive black markings and light gray edgings. Sides of head: relatively dark, especially in auricular region, with brown and buff elements lacking; loral region usually bright yellow. Ventral streaks: heavy, usually deep brownish black or black. Greater secondary coverts: medium or relatively light brown or grayish brown."

*Winter.*—The 1957 A.O.U. Check-List states that *oblitus* winters from northern Oklahoma, northern Mississippi, and northern Georgia south to Coahuila, Nuevo León, southern Texas, southern Louisiana, southern Mississippi, and southern Georgia; casual in Virginia and North Carolina.

However, recent field work in the Carolinas, especially South Carolina, has shown that *oblitus* occurs as a regular winterer in old fields on the piedmont and coastal plain (Johnston, 1956; Quay, 1957; Norris and Hight, 1957). Norris (1960), in analyzing the racial types of a sample of over 1700 wintering Savannah sparrows in the Savannah River Plant in South Carolina, found that more than 15 percent were referable to *oblitus*.

### DISTRIBUTION

*Range.*—Hudson Bay to northeastern Mexico.

*Breeding range.*—The Churchill savannah sparrow breeds from northeastern Manitoba (Churchill, Cape Tatnam), northern Ontario (Fort Severn, Cape Henrietta Maria), and northwestern Quebec (Kogaluk River, Mistassini Post) south to southern Minnesota (Minneapolis), southern Wisconsin (Friendship, Beaverdam), southern Michigan (East Lansing, Ann Arbor), central eastern Ontario (Biscotasing, North Bay), and central southern Quebec (Lake St. John); southern records of breeding, probably relating to this sub-species, are known from Missouri (Pierce City, Bolivar), Illinois (Pekin, Leroy, Mount Carmel), and Indiana (Bloomington, Waterloo).

*Winter range.*—Winters from northern Oklahoma (Oklahoma City, Tulsa), northern Mississippi (Rosedale), and northern Georgia (Athens) south to Coahuila (Sabinas), Nuevo León (Linares), southern Texas (Brownsville, Matagorda), southern Louisiana (Chenier au Tigre, New Orleans), southern Mississippi (Biloxi), and southern Florida (Ochopee).

*Casual records.*—Casual north to Cornwallis Island (Resolute Bay), Maryland (Ocean City), western Virginia (Blacksburg), and western North Carolina (Buncombe County).

*Egg dates.*—Michigan: 14 records, May 5 to June 21; 9 records, May 19 to June 21.

Quebec: 121 records, May 22 to June 28; 70 records, June 3 to June 14.

### PASSERCULUS SANDWICHENSIS BROOKSI Bishop

## Dwarf Savannah Sparrow

### Contributed by WENDELL TABER

#### HABITS

This race is the smallest of the Savannah sparrows and has a narrow breeding range. Miller (1951c) says that the California population of *brooksi* is narrowly restricted to the coast and is not numerous. Peters and Griscom (1938) state that *brooksi* "occupy a very definite though limited geographic area, * * * they differ from * * * other Savannah sparrows in being largely resident."

*Nesting.*—Joseph Mailliard (1921) describes a breeding site of *brooksi* at the mouth of the Klamath River opposite Requa, Del Norte County, Calif., on an alluvial flat about a mile long and a half-mile wide, shut off from the ocean by a bar of low sand dunes. The birds were observed only at the ocean end of the flat, on meadow land bisected by a small stream backed up by the tides. The birds were seen most often on the scattered bushes of lupine that covered most of the drier parts of the flats.

W. L. Dawson (1923) found a nest of *brooksi* with five eggs in northern California resting on the surface of damp earth, perfectly concealed by the edge of some cow dung held aloft by stiff grass. Another similarly situated nest contained two eggs and two freshly hatched young.

*P. s. brooksi* is considered the breeding form in the Willamette Valley of Oregon and the coastal counties where it is common in the open grasslands (Gabrielson and Jewett, 1940). A set of five eggs was taken at Tillamook on May 26, 1928.

Both J. H. Bowles (1920) and Allan Brooks (1917) refer to the early nesting of *brooksi* in coastal Washington. Bowles says that the very small, light-colored *brooksi* usually arrives in the latter part of March, sometimes a few birds appear much earlier. By the time *anthinus* reaches Tacoma, about April 20, *brooksi* is busy with nests and eggs. Brooks points out that in the Chilliwack Valley, a wide alluvial flat on the south bank of the Fraser River near Vancouver, *brooksi* was sitting on eggs and in some cases feeding young when the larger race passed through in great numbers.

*Plumages.*—Peters and Griscom (1938) state that *P. s. brooksi* is the smallest of the races of the Savannah sparrow. The bill is intermediate between the stout-billed and the slender-billed forms, with the depth of the bill averaging about one-half the length of the culmen. In spring, the general coloration is nearest *nevadensis*, averaging very slightly browner, but distinctly grayer than *anthinus*. The supraorbital stripe is the same depth of yellow as in *anthinus*, and much deeper than in *nevadensis*. The lateral crown stripes are more diffuse with the edgings broader and dark centers reduced. They feel that it is difficult to distinguish in winter except by its definitely smaller size. They also state that *brooksi* is roughly intermediate in coloration between *anthinus* and *nevadensis*.

*Voice.*—W. L. Dawson (1923) describes the song of *brooksi* as a series of lisping and buzzing notes, fine only in the sense of being small, and quite unmusical, *tsut, tsut, tsu, wzzzzztsubut.* The sound instantly recalls the grasshopper sparrow, *Ammodramus savannarum perpallidus,* but the preliminary and closing flourishes are a good deal longer and the buzzing strain shorter.

## DISTRIBUTION

*Range.*—Southwestern British Columbia south along the Pacific coast to Baja California.

*Breeding range.*—The dwarf Savannah sparrow breeds from Vancouver Island and the coast of southwestern British Columbia through western Washington and western Oregon to the coastal district of northwestern California (south through Del Norte County).

*Winter range.*—Winters in the breeding range and south through western California to central Baja California (Rosario); also in southern Arizona.

## PASSERCULUS SANDWICHENSIS ANTHINUS Bonaparte
## Western Savannah Sparrow
### PLATE 39
### Contributed by WENDELL TABER

## HABITS

The common name of this race would be more nearly correct were it northwestern instead of western Savannah sparrow, for its breeding range occupies most of the northwestern North American continent. The vastness of this summer range can be imagined only when one realizes that it includes nearly all of the land between the northern continental coastline (Alaska to Keewatin) to a southern boundary that extends from central British Columbia to southern Keewatin.

*Nesting.*—Of all the races of the Savannah sparrow, *anthinus* is the hardiest, and by its ability to adapt to the rigorous climatic and environmental extremes of boreal North America, it has added more than one and one-half million square miles to the breeding range of the species.

In the Arctic tundra along the Upper Kaolak River in northern Alaska, Maher (1959) found the Savannah sparrow nesting abundantly in the dwarf shrub-sedge tundra of the uplands. It was the second most abundant species, being about one-third to one-half as common as the Lapland longspur. He found no nests, but young were first seen on July 12 in 1957, and on July 10 in 1958. From mid-July until the end of the month, Savannahs were abundant, but the numbers declined rapidly in early August, and only a few were present on August 14.

Maher also gives us some idea of the weather conditions in this area: "The climate of this region is severe; the winters are long and cold but the summers are comparatively warm. The mean annual temperature is 10° F. * * * The temperature rises above freezing in May and the snow pack begins to melt. The mean temperature is above freezing only for the months of June, July and August. July is the warmest month, with a monthly mean of 43° F." Maher makes no comment on the wind, which must be severe at times. Bee (1958), who worked in the Kaolak area in 1951, cites one instance when the wind forced most of the tundra birds to seek the shelter of the willow-lined creek beds.

L. H. Walkinshaw and J. J. Stophlet (1949) state that in the John-son River region of Alaska, near Bethel, nests of the Savannah spar-row were built in lowland or highland tundra, under the grasses and sedges, often under dwarf birch and crowberry, and sunk into the moss so that their rims were even with the surface of the moss. Nests were made of grasses and sedges and were lined with fine grasses. This was one of the few small bird species whose nests were *not* lined with ptarmigan feathers. Nests observed between June 4–12, 1946, contained from three to six eggs.

F. L. Williamson (1957) provides a detailed description of the Napaskiak area in the delta of the Kuskokwim River not distant from Bethel, Alaska. He says that the race *anthinus* is common to abundant in nearly all formations of open character where grasses predominate in May and June. Habitats included fresh-water marshes, dwarf birch-alder thickets, wet tundra, and the cleared areas about the village.

J. Grinnell (1900a) found this species fairly numerous in July 1898, in the vicinity of Cape Blossom in the Kotzebue Sound region of Alaska. Grassy meadows bordering lagoons were favored, although a few birds were noted on the interior hillsides. Young were half-fledged by July 10.

A. L. Rand (1946) states that in Yukon territory, Canada, the Savannah sparrow was fairly common in summer above timberline and in grassy areas in the lowlands, from the southern border to Herschel Island. A nest at Burwash Landing, July 2, 1943, contained three young. Below timberline the birds favored sedge-covered grassy margins of lake shores, marshy ponds, and grassy country.

Herbert Brandt (1943) stated the favorite breeding area of *anthinus* in the Hooper Bay region of Alaska was the long grass of an Eskimo graveyard. One nest was only a few feet from a white bleached skull, which often served as a lookout station for the male. Brandt found another nest when a bird darted from his feet in old grass close to a small pond on the valley floor. Lifting the long, matted hay, he saw a runway like that of a lemming, which he traced four feet to a well-made circularly woven grass nest. Nests were invariably placed under a matted screen of long, snow-bent grass stems.  The nests are made of frost-ripened grass straws usually free from paleae, glumes, and panicles, and have a lining closely interwoven of finer grasses with the occasional addition of curled dog hair.  Not once was a foreign feather found in the nest of this species.

Although Brandt first recorded the species on May 18, not until June 4 did he observe a nest.  New-laid clutches were noted as late as June 21.  Of 15 nests examined, 9 contained six eggs each, and 6 contained five eggs each.

R. Rausch (1958) describes the nesting of *anthinus* on Middleton Island, south of Prince William Sound, Alaska, where he found it most numerous on the drier upper terraces of the "Upland Meadow," particularly on the highest terrace where *Calamagrostis nutkaensis* was abundant.  A nest containing five eggs was found June 5.  On June 25 the birds were feeding young, most of which had fledged. Fully feathered young were collected on June 25 and 26.  This sparrow was also quite numerous in the "Lowland Marsh," containing freshwater ponds and appropriate vegetation, and brackish ponds. The sparrows favored especially the shrubby willows along the east side of the marsh.

J. C. Howell (1948) found this Savannah sparrow common in the moist, grassy areas of Kodiak Island (the type locality for the race), both in the valleys and on the slopes of the mountains up to about 1500 feet.  Arriving there in late April 1944, he first recorded the species, three birds all in song, at Middle Bay on May 9.  A nest he found there June 9 containing five fresh eggs was in a tussock of grass in an open swampy area over which stood a few inches of water.  Another nest, on the slope of "The Old Woman" at an altitude of about 1500 feet, held four eggs, about half incubated, on June 17.

K. Racey (1948) stated that *anthinus* was numerous from Avalanche Valley in the Alta Lake region of British Columbia toward the main peak of Mt. Whistler, between 5,800 and 7,000 feet altitude. A breeding female was collected on Mt. Whistler on June 25, 1924, at an altitude of 5,800 feet, and young female was taken at 6,650 feet on Aug. 28, 1932.

*Eggs.*—The measurements of 67 eggs average 18.8 by 14.2 millimeters; the eggs showing the four extremes measure *21.8* by 14.6, 20.3 by *15.2*, *17.5* by 13.7, and 18.9 by *12.7* millimeters.

*Plumage.*—J. L. Peters and L. Griscom (1938) diagnose *P. s. anthinus* (formerly *alaudinus*) as a medium sized Savannah sparrow with slender bill, its depth at base averaging less than half the length of the culmen.  In spring, the general coloration above either with black and brown or gray and brown predominating, but whitish edgings of the scapulars always narrow, and more or less washed with gray. In fall, similar to spring plumage but coloration richer. They state there is a larger degree of size variation in this race than in the other western races, and cite as a case in point the fact that some birds from Nunivak Island are larger than usual. They point out that worn breeding specimens are separable from *nevadensis* only with great difficulty, but the greater amount of pale or whitish streaking above in *nevadensis* is ordinarily apparent. Peters and Griscom also note a certain amount of dichromatism "since grayer and browner specimens of *anthinus* may appear in the same series from the same place, shot in the same week or even on the same day."

As these series also included birds in fresh fall plumage, the color variations were not produced by the feather wear so common in breeding specimens.

J. W. Bee (1958) noted that molt had commenced on two adult males collected at Kaolak, Alaska, on July 22 and 24, 1951.

*Migration.*—J. A. Munro and I. McT. Cowan (1947) state (without reference to race) that the Savannah sparrow is a transient in all of the biotic areas of British Columbia, with a particularly heavy coastal migration.

H. S. Swarth (1924) found Savannah sparrows migrating through Hazelton in the Skeena River region of northern British Columbia during the last week of May 1921, and during the third week of August migrating Savannah sparrows swarmed through the Kispiox Valley, reaching a maximum abundance about the middle of September. Migrants were still present on September 26 when he left the area.

Gabrielson and Jewett (1940) state that *anthinus* is an abundant migrant throughout Oregon, especially in the fall, and is common in the summit meadows of the Cascades as well as in the valleys throughout the state.

Jewett, Taylor, Shaw, and Aldrich (1953) have this to say about the migration of *anthinus* in Washington:

The western Savannah sparrow is a common spring and fall migrant, particularly in western Washington, and in larger numbers in the fall. In the spring of 1915, Bowles says, the species passed through between April 21 and May 11, the sparrows being watched each day. During the fall migration of 1919, the first were seen on September 2. The bulk of the migrants went through between September 12 and 15, with a large number on September 23 also. The birds were seen nearly every day until October 22. Bowles (1920b:109) says the western Savannah sparrow reaches Tacoma about April 20 on its northward migration, remaining until about May 10. Records now available seem to indicate that a principal route of the fall migration of the western Savannah through Washington is along the Cascade Mountains. We found this subspecies common toward the end of August and early in September in the alpine parks of Mt. Rainier, where it was observed in the lush grass or heather of the open Hudsonian country, or occasionally on the ground near clumps of mountain hemlock close to the upper limit of tree growth.

E. Z. Rett (1947) comments that San Nicolas Island, some 70 miles due south of Carpinteria, Santa Barbara County, Calif., and the most distant offshore of the Channel Islands, is a stopping place for *anthinus* in the spring and fall migrations.

Chester C. Lamb's (1929) comments on a 15 day cruise in September from San Francisco to La Paz in lower California are of interest: "The steamer kept at a distance of from 8 to 20 miles offshore most of the way. The weather was windless and the sea calm the whole distance. Among the many species of birds which came aboard were two Savannah sparrows, which he identified as *alaudinus* (now *anthinus*). He went on deck at 6:00 a.m. on September 26 and observed these birds hopping around the deck cargo. The steamer was about 10 miles off San Antonio del Mar. These birds were not seen after 10:00 a.m. On September 28, off Magdelena Bay, at 8:00 a.m. another came aboard but remained only two hours."

## DISTRIBUTION

*Range.*—Northern Alaska and arctic Canada south to southern Mexico and El Salvador.

*Breeding range.*—The western Savannah sparrow breeds from northern Alaska (Cape Prince of Wales, Barrow, Colville Delta), northern Yukon (Herschel Island), northern Mackenzie (Richards Island, Coronation Gulf), and northern Keewatin (Thelon River, Perry River) south to southwestern Alaska (Nunivak Island, Nushagak) and through coastal districts in southern Alaska; inland to central British Columbia (Telegraph Creek, 149 Mile), southeastern Yukon (Pelly River), southern Mackenzie (Fort Providence, Fort Resolution), northwestern Manitoba (Cochrane River, Fort Du Brochet), and southeastern Keewatin (50 miles south of Cape Eskimo).

*Winter range.*—Winters from southwestern British Columbia (Departure Bay, Crescent), southern Nevada (Searchlight), southwestern Utah (Santa Clara), central Arizona (Oak Creek), central New Mexico (Socorro), and western and central Texas (Frijole, San Antonio) south to southern Baja California (San José del Cabo), Guerrero (Chilpancingo), El Salvador (Lake Olomega), and Tamaulipas.

*Casual record.*—Casual on the Pribilof Islands (St. George Island).

*Egg dates.*—Alaska: 41 records, May 10 to July 16; 28 records, June 5 to June 26.

PASSERCULUS SANDWICHENSIS SANDWICHENSIS (Gmelin)

## Aleutian Savannah Sparrow
### Contributed by WENDELL TABER

#### HABITS

The Krenitzen Islands, Alaska, between the islands of Unimak and Unalaska, have for the most part abrupt rocky shores but do not reach any great elevation. Where their surface is not rocky, it is covered with tundra or with long grass. Willows, the only trees, are a stunted type, being for the most part prostrate and buried in the tundra (McGregor, 1906).

Such is the bleak habitat of the Aleutian Savannah sparrow (*P. s. sandwichensis*) over the greater part of its breeding range. In view of the comments of Lucien M. Turner (1885) that the Savannah sparrow is a "summer visitor. Breeds. Not common." in the "Nearer Islands, Alaska" (which includes the well-known Attu), it would appear that the race formerly occupied more of the Aleutian Islands than it does at present.

*Nesting.*—A. R. Cahn (1947) says the Savannah sparrow "Apparently arrives in numbers almost overnight," in the Dutch Harbor region, and by late May or early June is suddenly everywhere among the tundra grasses and in full song at once. It nests in the open tundra.

R. C. McGregor (1906) describes a nest of *P. s. sandwichensis* on the Krenitzin Islands in Alaska as being composed of uniformly sized, dry, yellow grass stems and sunk in dry moss on the ground.

*Plumages.*—J. L. Peters and L. Griscom (1938) state that *P. s. sandwichensis* averages the largest of the races of Savannah sparrow, with long and proportionately slender bill. "In spring, general coloration above the black and gray predominating, brown element reduced; interscapulars with black centers separated from the conspicuous grayish white edges by a very narrow area of grayish or rusty brown; lores and superciliary stripe bright yellow, the latter extending well beyond posterior border of the eye; wing coverts and inner secondaries more or less broadly edged with pale or rusty isabelline. Streaking beneath not conspicuously broad or blackish." They state, further, that *sandwichensis* is "the most satisfactory of the western subspecies; there seems to be no great variation in size, and the variable color characters that make a diagnosis of some of the other races so difficult, are reduced to a minimum. An occasional specimen is found with a greater extent of brown on the dorsal surface and more rufescent wing edgings than is commonly shown by the average bird, but even such specimens are readily determined by the large bill, long wing and longer wing tip."

Robert Ridgway (1901) gives the wing as not less than 68.58 millimeters, averaging about 76.20, and the exposed culmen not less than 11.18, averaging 11.94. He also describes the young as similar to adults, but paler streaks of upper parts more buffy, dusky streaks of under parts less sharply defined, ground color of under parts more buffy, the superciliary stripe usually without yellow anteriorly and finely streaked with dusky.

*Migration and winter.*—It is always fascinating to consider how a land bird that nests on an island manages to migrate twice a year across a featureless ocean. Such a problem exists for that segment of the *P. s. sandwichensis* population that nests along the Aleutian chain. Basically, the problem is whether *sandwichensis* migrates across the Gulf of Alaska or whether it takes the more circuitous route around the southern Alaskan coast.

Peters and Griscom (1938) appear to be in general agreement with Swarth's (1911) suggestion that the migration route of *sandwichensis* after leaving the Alexander Archipelago is directly across the Gulf of Alaska to (and from) its breeding grounds, and cite as support of this statement a specimen of *sandwichensis* taken at sea at lat. 47° N., long. 152° W. However, this position is considerably south of the Gulf of Alaska, and is more suggestive of a bird off course than of a direct trans-gulf migration. Such a view seems to be supported by the observations of Serventy (1939), who stated that on Sept. 29, 1938, when his ship was 278 nautical miles from Victoria, British Columbia (noon position lat. 46° 18′ N., long. 129° 02′ W.) there were a number of land birds resting on the vessel's deck. "The most numerous was the savannah sparrow (*Passerculus sandwichensis*). Several birds were seen flying over the water like storm petrels and a number rested for quite a while on the boat deck aft. Several were tame, evidently because of exhaustion, and I was able to catch one and handle it. The superciliary stripe, lores, and medial crown stripe were quite yellow. The coloration was distinctly brighter than that of the form nesting in the Seattle region (*P. s. brooksi*) and I felt that the birds belonged to the Aleutian breeding race, *P. s. sandwichensis*. The birds were seen up till noon but there was none in the afternoon."

The next day with a noon position of lat. 41° 58′ N., long. 136° 24′ W. (688 miles from Victoria), a slight rain was falling and the weather, which was rough in the morning, subsided in the afternoon. A pair of Savannah sparrows on deck at 8:30 a.m. looked wet and rather bedraggled. Later he saw three more all in bright plumage, which haunted the deck all morning. At 1:00 p.m. an obviously tired bird appeared on deck. Another was seen in the late afternoon. The ship's cat was reported to have taken several birds. Serventy recovered one bird from the cat in the evening. Subsequently, Grinnell and Miller confirmed the identification at the Museum of Vertebrate Zoology in Berkeley as the race *P. s. sandwichensis.*

Similarly Savannah sparrows occur at sea in the spring. G. D. Hanna (1917) reports that on June 10, 1916, in the pack ice south of St. Matthew Island, the largest of the Pribilof Islands, a Savannah sparrow came aboard ship and stayed all day.

Gabrielson and Jewett (1940) state that in the fall *sandwichensis* appears in eastern Oregon by September 27 and stays until November 5; in the spring they first appear about March 24 and are present until May 10.

In the winter *sandwichensis* is found along the Pacific coast from southwestern British Columbia south to central western California and in the Great Valley of California. In California, at least, it mingles with other races of Savannah sparrows, from which it can be readily distinguished by its larger size (R. R. Talmadge, pers. comm. to Mr. Bent).

The 1957 A.O.U. Check-List lists this race as casual in the Pribilof Islands and east of the Cascade Mountains in Oregon. To this must be added a record made by A. M. Bailey (1926), who collected an adult female *sandwichensis* at Wainwright, Alaska, on Oct. 5, 1921. This record certainly qualifies as a "casual," because Wainwright, on the northern Alaskan coast far inside the Arctic Circle is nearly 1000 miles outside of its normal range, and at that date snow covered the tundra and the ice was already 8 inches thick on the tundra ponds.

### DISTRIBUTION

*Range.*—Eastern Aleutians east and south to central California.

*Breeding range.*—The Aleutian Savannah sparrow breeds on the eastern Aleutian Islands (west to Amukta Island) and the western Alaskan Peninusla (Kings Cove, Shumagin Islands).

*Winter range.*—Winters along the Pacific coast from southwestern British Columbia (Vancouver Island) south to central western California (Berkeley), and in the Great Valley of California (south to Merced County).

*Casual records.*—Casual in the Pribilof Islands (St. Paul Island) and east of the Cascades in Oregon (Crooked River, Fort Klamath).

*Egg date.*—Alaska: 1 record, June 18.

PASSERCULUS SANDWICHENSIS NEVADENSIS Grinnell

# Nevada Savannah Sparrow

PLATE 40

Contributed by WENDELL TABER

## HABITS

This medium-sized, pale-gray race of the Savannah sparrow occupies a vast area in the western half of the continent. Roughly rectangular, with its corners in British Columbia, central Manitoba, western Nebraska, and northern California, its breeding range covers over a million square miles.

*Nesting.*—Despite the vastness of this breeding area, the ubiquitous *nevadensis* breeds plentifully throughout it, whether the locality be a mountain meadow, a prairie slough, or a lakeside marsh.

C. S. Jung (1930) found the Savannah the most abundant sparrow in the joint delta region of the Athabasca and Peace Rivers in northeastern Alberta in June 1928. He found five nests in an area 100 yards square in the swamp meadows on the southeast shore of Lake Claire. For more than 5 square miles in the immediate vicinity the birds seemed to average better than one nest to every 100-yard square block. On June 15 he found nests in every stage of development from those with a single egg to some with fledgings almost ready to fly.

J. S. Rowley (1939) reported a nest of *nevadensis* found on the ground in a natural depression well concealed by grasses in a marshy place at about 6,000 feet elevation near Convict Creek, Mono County, Calif.

D. S. Farner and I. O. Buss (1957) observed Savannah sparrows, presumed to be breeding, at an altitude of about 6,500 feet near Hart's Pass on the summit of the Cascade Mountains in Okanogan County, Wash., in July 1956. Most of the ground was covered with alpine vegetation. The habitat contained small clumps of alpine firs (*Abies lasiocarpa*) which were widely scattered over sloping meadows. Dwarf willow (*Salix* sp.) grew densely in moist sites. At Hart's Pass (altitude 6,200 feet), July 1–4, 1959, R. C. Banks (1960) found much of the snow had melted from the large, open, south-facing meadows, making them very wet. Shaded and drifted areas retained up to 2 feet of snow, and most of the forest floor was similarly covered. Temperatures at night dropped to freezing. The Savannah sparrow was one of the most common species, and proved to be the race *nevadensis*. A nest containing five eggs was found on July 2.

In extreme northeastern North Dakota, F. B. Philipp (1936) found a nest of *nevadensis* containing five slightly incubated eggs in a furrow in a large, shallow, dry slough in rolling prairie country. It was flush with the ground and extremely well hidden in a tuft of dead grass. Compactly constructed of dried grass and fine weed stems, it was lined with finer grasses and a few strands of black horsehair.

J. F. Ferry (1910) found the Savannah sparrow abundant in southeastern Saskatchewan. Nests were usually sunk deep in the ground at the base of a bunch of grass on the prairie. The eggs were usually four, occasionally five, and were fresh from June 10 to 20. A number of fledglings just able to fly were seen on July 3.

W. W. Cooke (1897) considers the Savannah sparrow a not uncommon breeding species in Colorado from the base of the foothills through the mountains up to nearly 12,000 feet, arriving early in April and remaining until mid-October. In the Mesa County region of Colorado, R. B. Rockwell (1908) states the Savannah sparrow arrives in mid-April and breeds during May, June, and July, ranging up to at least 8,000 feet and raising two broods. Favorite nesting sites are the alfalfa fields, with the nests concealed in the dense alfalfa plants close to or upon the ground. In late summer he found the species abundant in hay fields where it associated with vesper sparrows, lark sparrows, and chipping sparrows.

W. P. Taylor (1912) found a nest of *nevadensis* in northern Nevada in a slight depression on a low hummock covered with sparse grass and completely surrounded by mud and water in a marsh. The nest was built between a large clod of earth and a piece of cow dung, and was composed of coarse pieces of wild hay and marsh grass and lined with fine grasses and threads of horsehair. Dimensions of the cavity were: diameter 2⅛ inches, depth 1⅝ inches. Incubation had just commenced on the five eggs.

*Eggs.*—The measurements of 40 eggs average 19.1 by 14.0 millimeters; the eggs showing the four extremes measure *20.5* by 15.2, 19.8 by *15.2*, *16.3* by 13.2, and 18.8 by *12.7* millimeters.

*Plumage.*—Joseph Grinnell (1910) describes *P. s. nevadensis* as resembling *anthinus* (then *alaudinus*) but much paler throughout in all plumages: white replacing buff, black streaks thus more conspicuously contrasted, there being a minimum amount of hazel marginings; size slightly less. From *P. s. savanna*, *nevadensis* differs in coloration in the same ways as above but in greater degree; the bill is proportionally much smaller, though the wing length is nearly the same.

In the juvenal plumage the throat, postpectoral region, and crissum are pure white; the flanks narrowly black-streaked on a white ground; pectoral region sharply black-streaked on a very pale creambuff ground; sides of head and neck flecked with black on a pale cream-buff ground; superciliary and median crown stripes whitish, the former minutely flecked with blackish; lateral crown stripes to hind neck broadly black-streaked on a ground of pale clay color; feathers of dorsum with broad coal-black central areas margined with whitish; tippings of wing coverts and edgings of inner wing quills broadly whitish; edgings of wings, scapulars, and tail, clay color.

He summarizes by stating that *nevadensis* differs from its presumably nearest relatives in its extremely pale coloration. This paleness is not due to less black-streaking, but to a replacement of buff and clay color by white or whitish, and to a restriction and dilution to clay color of the hazel areas on each feather. He considers the appearance of white edges on the rectrices an incipient manifestation of the condition among certain terrestrial birds where the outer rectrix on either side is chiefly white, as in *Pooecetes*.

*Food.*—G. F. Knowlton (1950) analyzed the stomach contents of 14 specimens of *nevadensis* taken in Utah. Recognizable insect food consisted of: 1 Orthoptera (grasshopper); 50 Homoptera (clover and beet leafhoppers, pea and European grain aphids); 39 Hemiptera (lygus and damsel bugs, false chinch bugs); 28 Coleoptera (chrysomelid leaf beetles–adults and larvae, alfalfa and pea weevils); 8 Lepidoptera (all larvae plus 17 eggs); 15 Diptera (chironomids); 4 Hymenoptera (ants). In addition, numerous insect fragments and 136 weed seeds were recognized.

*Migration and winter.*—F. M. Bailey (1928) says that in New Mexico *nevadensis* is an abundant fall migrant, common by the first of September and ranging between 5,000 feet at Apache and Cactus Flat and 10,500 feet near Costilla Pass. Most of the birds leave in October.

In the Navaho country of southeastern Utah and northeastern Arizona, Woodbury and Russell (1945) found *nevadensis* a sparse winter visitor and a migrant, with an increase in the population in late August and September.

While the bulk of the population winters west of the Mississippi, and therefore migrates almost due south from the breeding grounds, there appears to be a small but apparently regular movement to the southeast. Lowrey (1947) in reviewing some recent Savannah sparrow specimens collected in Louisiana, showed that about 6 percent of the 107 specimens were referable to *nevadensis*. Norris and Hight (1957) had similar results in South Carolina, where 6 percent of the 559 wintering Savannah sparrows examined were *nevadensis*. In a later reanalysis of these, plus additional data from the same area, Norris (1960) showed that *nevadensis* comprised 4 percent of the total sample of the 1,758 wintering Savannah sparrows examined.

Little information is available concerning the spring migration. J. Grinnell (1923a) recorded a moderate number of *nevadensis* mingling with a larger number of *anthinus* at about 178 feet below sea level in Death Valley, Calif., near Furnace Creek Ranch, in April 1917. There was no indication of breeding.

## DISTRIBUTION

*Range.*—British Columbia and the prairie provinces south to southern Mexico.

*Breeding range.*—The Nevada Savannah sparrow breeds from central southern and northeastern British Columbia (Lillooet, Charlie Lake), northern Alberta (Athabaska Delta, Sand Point on Lake Athabaska), and central Manitoba (Oxford House) south through eastern Washington and eastern Oregon to eastern California (Battle Creek Meadows, Owens Lake, Bodfish, Big Bear Lake), southern Nevada (Pahranagat Valley), southern Utah (Zion Canyon), northern Arizona (Kayenta), central Colorado (Salida, Fort Morgan), western Nebraska (Mitchell), and northeastern South Dakota (Fort Sisseton). Recorded in summer in southeastern Alaska (Petersburg).

*Winter range.*—Winters from northern California (Nicasio, near Red Bluff), southern Nevada (Indian Springs), southwestern Utah (St. George), central Arizona (Oak Creek), central Texas, central Oklahoma (Okmulgee County), and northwestern Mississippi (Rosedale) south to northern Baja California (Colnett), Guerrero, State of Mexico, Veracruz, southern Texas (Brownsville), and southern Mississippi (Lyman).

*Casual records.*—Casual east to Michigan (Isle Royale), Ohio (Clermont County), Kentucky (Carrollton), Tennessee (Bartlett, Ellendale), South Carolina (Aiken County), and Georgia (Grady County).

*Egg dates.*—North Dakota: 3 records, June 3 to June 5. Utah: 1 record, June 6.

## PASSERCULUS SANDWICHENSIS RUFOFUSCUS Camras

### Chihuahua Savannah Sparrow

#### Contributed by WENDELL TABER

## HABITS

Sidney Camras (1940) described *rufofuscus* as being nearest to the race *P. s. brunnescens*, but with the brownish tones brighter throughout and the black markings heavier and distinguishable from all other members of the genus by its brighter coloration.

Although the 1957 A.O.U. Check-List states that this race breeds from central Arizona and central northern New Mexico south to central Chihuahua, Duvall (1943) points out that "so far as known no Savannah Sparrows have been found breeding between the type locality of *rufofuscus* (Babicora, Chihuahua), the White Mountains of Arizona (Springerville and Big Lake), and the mountains of central northern New Mexico (Taos and Lake Burford). Approximately 400 miles separate the Chihuahua breeding birds from the birds of central eastern Arizona and approximately 375 miles separate the Arizona colony from the birds apparently breeding in New Mexico. Thus it would appear that over that part of its range which lies in the southwestern United States and northern Mexico the Savannah Sparrow breeds only in very local, isolated areas."

### DISTRIBUTION

*Range.*—Arizona, New Mexico, and Chihuahua.

*Winter range.*—Winter range unknown; recorded casually from Jalisco (Ocotlán) and western Texas (east to Fort Clark).

### PASSERCULUS SANDWICHENSIS ALAUDINUS Bonaparte

## Coastal Savannah Sparrow

### Contributed by RICHARD F. JOHNSTON

### HABITS

Compared to other subspecies of Savannah sparrow, this coastal, marsh-inhabiting savannah sparrow is relatively small and dark. It maintains populations in two main types of habitat in coastal California: the *Salicornia* association of tidal marshes and the grassland associations of the coastal fog belt. The grassland habitats are ordinarily not extensive in any one place, being found chiefly on ridges of the coastal hills and mountains; grasslands today are not found in broad conjunction with salt marshes, though perhaps they were before extensive human modifications of the habitats took place.

The populations of this Savannah sparrow inhabiting salt marshes are the best known. Ecologic distribution of the sparrows on salt marshes is nearly limited to the broad expanses of low-lying salicornia (*Salicornia ambigua*) on the older and higher parts of marshes; on San Francisco Bay marshes these reaches stand about five to ten feet above mean sea level and lie back of that salt marsh vegetation (cordgrass, *Spartina foliosa*) best suited to frequent submergence by tidal flooding (R. F. Johnston, 1956). It is in this lower marsh region that the song sparrows *Melospiza melodia samuelis* and *M. m. pusillula* live; these and Savannah sparrows do not overlap significantly either in breeding territories or in foraging beats. There seems to be no competition between the two species for any environmental requisite (J. T. Marshall, Jr., 1948), and their ecologic distributions probably reflect the habitat preferences of the two species.

*Breeding.*—In early spring when the territorial males have apportioned the available suitable area, it is possible to walk out on the vast, damp salicornia flats and see them perched on their song-posts, usually no more than a foot higher than surrounding vegetation, singing their thin abstraction of an emberizine song: *sic-sic-sic-seeee, seer.* As notes of very high frequency are dominant components, in a wind the listener usually misses part of the song. The males flush while the intruder is yet 30 to 40 yards away and move to the farthest corner of the area with which they are familiar. Females seemingly avoid human observation by running along the mud away from the intruder (see *Foraging behavior*).

The breeding season around San Francisco Bay extends from February to June. Males with testes enlarged to sizes typical of breeding males have been taken in mid-February on San Pablo salt marsh, Contra Costa County. Eggs are laid between March 12 and June 15 (sample of 61 records) with the peak of egg-laying (22 clutches) occurring between April 1 and April 10. The species is probably double-brooded, but the data at hand curiously indicate only one, clear-cut peak to egg-laying.

Nests, apparently constructed by females alone, are tightly formed, relatively deep cups composed of dead stems of a variety of grasses, salicornia stalks, and hairs; around Humboldt Bay, eelgrass (*Zostera*) is occasionally used (Robert Talmadge, in litt.). Nests are placed most frequently in salicornia, less so in saltgrass (*Distichlis spicata*) or in upland grasses on the high parts of marshes. Position of nests is low: of 11 nests in one sample, 8 were on the ground surface, 1 was one inch high, 1 three inches, and 1 four inches; this is to be contrasted with the statement of J. Grinnell and S. H. Miller (1944) that nests are "usually slightly above the mud."

Nests are well-concealed by overhanging vegetation. The incubating and brooding birds are exceedingly tight sitters and do not flush until an intruder steps almost upon the nests. At flushing, most individuals give a distraction display (Johnston, 1957) consisting of flight with shallow wingbeats, barely skimming the tops of the salicornia stalks. The displaying individuals usually soon alight, perhaps 30 yards away, and give thin, high-pitched alarm notes.

*Eggs.*—Clutch size is $4.02 \pm 0.08$ eggs (range 3 to 5; 50 records) around San Francisco Bay. Clutches deposited in March average 3.50 eggs and the remainder average 4.09 eggs. The incubation period in one nest was 12½ days, last egg laid to last egg hatched. The young are typically altricial and the natal down is sparse.

The measurements of 40 eggs average 19.0 by 14.7 millimeters; the eggs showing the four extremes measure *21.4* by 14.0, 19.5 by *15.9*, *16.9* by 13.8, and 17.2 by *13.4* millimeters.

*Plumages.*—The juvenal plumage "is similar to savanna * * * but black streaking of crown and back much narrower, buffy yellow coloration paler * * * finely streaked on chest, sides, and flanks" (R. R. Graber, unpublished Ph. D. thesis, Univ. Oklahoma).

First winter and subsequent plumages are "very different from the adjacent breeding or migrant races in being very much darker and browner, with a great development of black streaking above, and more heavily streaked with black (not brownish or blackish brown) below" (J. L. Peters and L. Griscom, 1938).

There is no prenuptial molt or feather growth.

*Foraging behavior.*—This Savannah sparrow forages on the marsh mud and in tangles of salt grass, salicornia, and gumplant (*Grindelia cuneifolia*). The foraging mannerisms seem qualitatively the same as those characteristic of upland Savannah sparrows. On San Pablo Marsh in late autumn to early spring many of the marsh Savannahs work over the soft mud of the tidal sloughs, and some even venture out to the very edge of the marsh fronting on the bay; here they feed on small intertidal invertebrates, including the exceedingly abundant small snails. There is a tendency for the birds to forage together in loose flocks of perhaps 8 to 12 individuals at this time. Thus there is some overlap in foraging beats of the Savannahs and song sparrows of San Francisco Bay marshes. Yet the amount of time the Savannah sparrows spend on the soft mud is small in comparison to that spent there by song sparrows.

### DISTRIBUTION

*Range.*—Resident on salicornia marshes and grasslands in the coastal fog belt from Humboldt Bay, Humboldt County, to Morro Bay, San Luis Obispo County, Calif.

*Egg dates.*—California: 70 records, March 12 to June 15; 35 records, April 1 to April 22.

### PASSERCULUS SANDWICHENSIS BELDINGI Ridgway

## Belding's Savannah Sparrow

PLATE 40

Contributed by WENDELL TABER

### HABITS

In the prefatory remarks to his paper on the Savannah sparrows of northwestern Mexico, Van Rossem (1947) made a particularly lucid and succinct statement on this interesting racial complex. In order that the following accounts may receive a proper foundation and perspective, his statement follows:

Along the Pacific coast of Baja California from the international boundary south to Magdalena Bay, on the San Benito Islands, and on the coast of northwestern Mexico from the mouth of the Colorado River south to Sinaloa, there exists a series of populations of the Savannah Sparrow (*Passerculus sandwichensis*) which are separated ecologically from those of the interior of the continent. The habitat of this group, save for two instances of insular adaptation, is rather rigidly restricted to tidal marshes, a fact long recognized and reflected in past vernacular usage of the name "Marsh Sparrow." Because of environmental limitations, distribution is not continuous and through the same circumstance the transition from one population to another tends at times to be more abrupt in one or more characters than otherwise would be the case. This abruptness is expressed in the nomenclature of only a few years ago, as witness the binomials *Passerculus beldingi*, *Passerculus rostratus*, and *Passerculus guttatus*.

Considerations which have altered the concept of closely related but distinct species are the discovery of geographically intergrading populations in some cases and breakdown of supposed specific characters through individual variation in others. There now is no valid reason to dispute the revaluation of these initially conceived species as geographical variants of the continentwide Savannah Sparrow, *Passerculus sandwichensis*.

This race of the Savannah sparrow is a permanent resident and abundant occupant of the coastal salt marshes from Santa Barbara south through San Diego County. Rarely, the race extends inland to alkaline marshes as much as 8 miles from the coast, but such localities are usually within 100 feet of sea level. The range continues to the Todos Santos Islands, El Rosario, in Baja California.

*Nesting.*—W. L. Dawson (1923) commented on the colonial nesting of *beldingi* and mentions a 5-acre stretch of salt marsh that harbored about 20 pairs in April. Nesting occurs in April and by May 1 most of the broods have hatched. Nests are difficult to find unless the adult sits closer than usual and flushes at close range. When the colony is aroused the females seem to slip away at long range and a person may search for an hour among 40 pairs of birds without finding a nest. A female flushed at close range flutters over the tops of the plants for a great distance as though seeking to decoy, but if the nest is approached she will not return nor evince further interest. *P. s. beldingi* nests indifferently in the shelter of the salicornia itself, or in the protection of nearby larger growth. The nest is settled firmly upon the ground among interlaced stems or grasses and under adequate cover of grass or weed. One nest was composed of dried salicornia stems and lined with duck feathers. Another nest, deeply cupped, was composed of frayed weed stems and finely woven grasses, with a single horsehair.

Howard Robertson (1899) discovered three nests of *beldingi* near Santa Monica, Calif., on Apr. 21, 1899, of which two contained eggs and one young. The nests were placed in salt grass about 6 inches above the ground and were composed principally of large and small straws of the salt grass interwoven with a few straws of Bermuda grass. The first nest, containing four eggs, was well lined with horsehair while the second nest was lined mostly with fine straws, some hairs, and a few gull feathers.

J. Van Denburgh, on the Todos Santos Islands from May 24–30, 1923, found young and old birds very common. A nest on the ground held two half-grown young and one infertile egg. Another nest was about 14 inches up in a small bush. H. B. Kaeding (1905) found fresh eggs on these islands Mar. 10, 1897.

*Eggs.*—Dawson (1923) writes: "3, or rarely, 4; greenish or bluish white, speckled and spotted or washed and clouded with verona brown. Average of 10 eggs in the M.C.O. coll.: 18.5 × 14.2 * * *. Season: April–June, two broods." W. C. Hanna (1924b) gives the average weight of three eggs as 2.25 grams.

W. G. F. Harris writes: "The measurements of 40 eggs average 20.0 by 14.8 millimeters; the eggs showing the four extremes measure *21.0* by 15.1, 20.9 by *15.4*, and *18.9* by *14.1* millimeters."

*Voice.*—Hoffmann (1927) described the song of *beldingi*, which at that time was treated as a distinct race, as a fine-drawn, wheezy song, *tsip, tsip, tsip, tsrree, tsick-a-tsee*, differing from the song of the eastern Savannah sparrows in the emphatic ending. Dawson (1923) describes the song as high-keyed and insectlike, *tsit tsit tsu weezz tsit tsit*.

*Behavior.*—After the nesting season the birds deploy more widely through the more elevated weedy stretches which surround the marsh proper, or take up station in the sand dunes. They invade the beaches also at that time, nimbly pursuing the kelp flies or snatching salty comfits from the wet sand. Momentarily the birds may hide from an approaching person, skulking behind driftwood or stranded kelp roots, but shortly they bolt for weedy regions (Dawson, 1923).

*Field marks.*—Hoffman (1927) describes *beldingi* adults as having the upper parts dark brown streaked with black; an indistinct light stripe through the crown and another over the eye, the latter ending in front in yellowish; under parts whitish, heavily streaked with black. Bill slender, dusky above, flesh-colored on the sides and below; feet light brown. The immatures are similar but lack the yellow between the eye and the bill.

Peters and Griscom (1938) diagnose *beldingi* as being similar to *alaudinus* (formerly *bryanti*), but more heavily and extensively streaked with black below; upperparts more olivaceous, less markedly streaked with brown and black; bill distinctly larger.  Van Rossem (1947) says that:

Within the group characterized above, bill smaller both in length and depth than that of *Passerculus sandwichensis anulus* of Scammon Lagoon, and tail slightly longer than in that form.  Compared with *Passerculus sandwichensis* ["bryanti"] *alaudinus* of the San Francisco Bay area of California, bill longer and more attenuated (less conical), and upper parts with black streaking less prominent. This race is dichromatic in that a gray tendency or manifestation is present in many individuals.  The extreme gray phase is not dissimilar in color to the essentially gray, black, and white *P. s. nevadensis* of the Great Basin but the shorter wing and tail, longer and larger bill, and broad ventral streaking of *beldingi* serve to distinguish such rare extremes without difficulty.  It follows that individual variation in color is very pronounced in *beldingi* but a sharp, contrasting pattern is always present and in this feature *beldingi*, together with *anulus*, is well set off from the other races of northwestern Mexico.

## DISTRIBUTION

*Range.*—Belding's Savannah sparrow is resident in coastal south-western California (Santa Barbara south to San Diego) and north-western Baja California (Todos Santos Islands, El Rosario).

*Egg dates.*—California: 2 records, April 30 and May 27.

### PASSERCULUS SANDWICHENSIS ANULUS Huey

## Scammon Lagoon Savannah Sparrow
### Contributed by WENDELL TABER

### HABITS

A permanent resident at Scammon Lagoon and the adjacent Santo Domingo Landing on the Pacific coast of central Baja California and one of the "*beldingi*" group, this race is the link which in bill size connects that group with the "*guttatus*" group to the south (van Rossem, 1947).  In color it is similar to *P. s. beldingi* from which, though usually lighter, it is not certainly distinguishable.  However, the bill is distinctly larger and longer and the tail shorter.

*Nesting.*—Griffing Bancroft (1927) reports these Savannah sparrows as very common in the marshes of the Scammon Lagoon, both insular and mainland, and closely resembling in behavior both *beldingi* and *rostratus*.  Birds were "forever making short flights to thick tufts of grass or branches of dead bushes, never paying much attention to us, yet not for an instant losing their keen perception of our presence." Close approach was not possible.  Birds were fully as thick in suitable spots as the race *beldingi* in similar habitat in southern California.

Bancroft further comments that the neat nests of *anulus* are so like those of *beldingi* as to be indistinguishable.  The nests of both are nicely rounded and fairly well lined with slender leaves and feathers, but so poorly put together that with the least careless handling they fall to pieces. Ordinarily they are made of shreds of seaweed or leaves and some dead grass stems. The preferred nest site is "a runt growth of *salicornia* just a few inches high. This occurs not infrequently in small patches where the tide moistens but does not overflow. Here the sparrow hides his home cleverly, utilizing to the utmost the cascades of weed growing over rough ground or small mounds."

Bancroft also mentions a small island well back from the mouth of the lagoon that was fairly covered with cactus, a chollalike growth supporting long drapings of gray moss. *P. s. anulus* apparently bred in it, sometimes as much as four feet above the ground, concealing the nests most carefully where the moss was thickest. These sparrows also nested on the dry alkali itself, sometimes a hundred yards from the water, always hiding the nest under a spreading branch. That *anulus* may tend to colonial nesting is indicated by the fact that he once flushed three birds within a yard of his feet: two had young and one a fresh set of three eggs. In each case the bird gave the most convincing demonstration of the broken wing act Bancroft had ever witnessed.

### DISTRIBUTION

*Range.*—The Scammon Lagoon Savannah sparrow is resident around the shores of Viscaíno Bay, western Baja California (Santo Domingo Landing, Scammon Lagoon).

### PASSERCULUS SANDWICHENSIS SANCTORUM Ridgway

## San Benito Savannah Sparrow

### Contributed by WENDELL TABER

#### HABITS

*P. s. sanctorum* is resident on the San Benito Islands off central western Baja California, which J. E. Thayer and Outram Bangs (1907) describe as a group of three small, rocky, barren islands surrounded by outlying rocks and kelp. They lie about 50 miles from the mainland, 15 miles west of the northern end of Cerros Island, and cover an area nearly 4 miles long by 1½ miles wide. West Benito, the largest, has bold rocky shores and consists of an elevated plateau with a mound near the center 600 feet above the sea. Middle Benito is a low flat island, its highest part only 82 feet above the sea, separated from West Benito by a passage 200 feet wide. East Benito is the second largest and is marked by four prominent hills, the highest 421 feet in altitude. The vegetation consists of the tall cactus and a few shrubs. During a stay of two days, no mammals and only a few lizards were seen. Only five species of small land birds were found, and only one of these was at all abundant—the "large-billed" Savannah sparrow. Young were just out of the nest at the time of the visit, about Apr. 24, 1906. One young male, in post-juvenal molt, that was possibly a straggler from San Benito Island, was found on Cerros Island on April 21. William Brewster (1902) points out that this habitat is "essentially different from that of any of the salt marsh *Ammodrami* [now *Passerculus*]."

This subspecies was formerly considered a race of the species *rostratus*, which is now regarded as a well-marked subspecies of the *sandwichensis* complex. In color and size it more nearly resembles the races *rostratus* and *atratus* of the Sonora coast than it does the populations of the *"guttatus"* group resident on the adjacent coast of Baja California. As van Rossem (1947) points out, "The obviously close relationship of *sanctorum, rostratus,* and *atratus* can easily lead to the speculation that the colony on the San Benito Islands is a remnant population. At any rate, it is obvious that the three are more closely interrelated than are any of them to the present-day occupants of the intervening peninsula."

*Nesting.*—William Brewster (1902) quotes R. C. McGregor who found three nests of *sanctorum* on the San Benito Islands. All the nests were placed on the ground under small bushes. A nest found March 30 was sunk level with the ground, which served to support the thin walls. The outside was composed of large grass straws while the lining was of finer grass and a few feathers. The three eggs were slightly incubated.

A. W. Anthony (1906) mentions a nest of *sanctorum* about a foot from the ground in a low bush. Other nests were well hidden in shallow depressions in the soil and overhung with vegetation. The nests were very similar, in fact, to those of *beldingi*.

*Plumages.*—Van Rossem's (1947) exhaustive treatment furnishes the following subspecific characters:

Bill large, stout, and deep at base as in *Passerculus sandwichensis rostratus* and *Passerculus sandwichensis atratus*, but culmen outline normally straight or nearly so rather than convex. Tarsi slightly shorter than in those races, but notably stout and, together with the feet, horn color or plumbeous brown rather than flesh color or light brown, a distinction which persists in most dried specimens. Wing slightly shorter and tail decidedly so, the latter relatively as well as actually. Dorsal pattern moderately variegated or contrasted as in *rostratus* and *atratus*, but differs in the presence of a more or less extensive intermixture of light gray or grayish white edgings in the inter-scapular area. Brown phase with tones tending to chestnut rather than pinkish. Ventral streaking relatively narrow as in *rostratus* but black, or nearly so, instead of brown.

## DISTRIBUTION

*Range.*—The San Benito Savannah sparrow is resident on the San Benito Islands off central western Baja California.

*Egg date.*—San Benito Islands: 1 record, April 1.

## PASSERCULUS SANDWICHENSIS GUTTATUS Lawrence

# Abreojos Savannah Sparrow

## Contributed by WENDELL TABER

### HABITS

The "*guttatus*" group occurs in the southern part of the western Baja California peninsula from Pond and San Ignacio Lagoons south to Magdalena Bay. It is distinct from *beldingi* and *anulus* in the notably diffused and blended character of the dorsal plumage with much less contrast between feather centers and edgings, even in fresh fall plumage. The color tone dorsally is olive and the superciliary streak is normally yellow at all seasons. When compared with *anulus* to the north, the bill of *guttatus* averages decidedly larger, the tail longer, and the dorsal coloration distinctly dull, olivaceous gray with the pattern relatively inconspicuous and diffused instead of contrasted. When compared with the other member of the "*guttatus*" group, *magdalenae*, the size averages smaller in all dimensions except for the slightly longer bill. Also, the coloration is darker and the dorsal pattern is less conspicuously contrasted.

McGregor (1898) described, at Abreojos Point, what he thought at the time was the habitat, nest, and eggs of a new species, *Ammodramus halophilus*, which has since been reduced to the synonomy of *P. s. guttatus*. He states the birds were "found in a salt marsh about five miles long by half a mile wide. The common amphibious plant known as glasswort (*Salicornia ambigua*) covers the moist ground. The entire marsh is cut by tide creeks, which empty into a salt lake or pond lagoon. As the marsh is surrounded by ocean on one side and hot desert on the others, it is probable that *A. halophilus* [*P.s. guttatus*] is confined to that region."

The single nest McGregor found was 16 inches from the ground in a tall bunch of glasswort, the top of which was bent over and in to form a covering. The nest was made of salt grass and lined with fine shreds of grass and a few gull feathers. The three bluish-white eggs were heavily marked all over with large blotches of raw umber and smaller spots of lilac. As he found a nest and eggs in mid-April and collected females ready to lay in mid-June, McGregor (1898) felt that two broods were probably raised in a year.

Van Rossem (1947) states that the winter dispersal of *guttatus* is limited, with only a very few individuals wintering in the Cape region.

## DISTRIBUTION

*Range.*—The Abreojos Savannah sparrow is resident in central western Baja California (Pond Lagoon, San Ignacio Lagoon). It winters casually south to southern Baja California (San Jorge, San José del Cabo).

## PASSERCULUS SANDWICHENSIS MAGDALENAE van Rossem
## Magdalena Savannah Sparrow
### Contributed by WENDELL TABER

### HABITS

The more southerly of the two races forming the *"guttatus"* group, *P. s. magdalenae* is resident in the marshes of Magdalena Bay, southwestern Baja California, and winters south to the Cape district of Baja California. According to its describer, A. J. van Rossem (1947), it is similar in coloration to *P.s. guttatus* but is "lighter and more greenish (less grayish) olive; dorsal markings more prominent (less diffused) due to the lighter edgings. Size averages larger in all dimensions save for the bill which is lightly shorter and thicker at the base; culmen outline more convex."

Van Rossem (1947) continues: "This race is the culmination of the strongly yellow-browed, peninsular Savannah Sparrows with relatively slender bills which average less (usually much less) than a 7.0 millimeter depth at the base. It forms a good connecting link between the smaller-billed, more northern *guttatus* and the larger-billed *rostratus* group of the continental mainland and the San Benito Islands in that it possesses the essential coloration of the former combined with the general larger size of the latter."

### DISTRIBUTION

*Range.*—The Magdalena Savannah sparrow breeds, and is largely resident, in the marshes of Magdalena Bay, southwestern Baja California (San Jorge, North Estero, Santa Margarita Island). It winters in the breeding range and also south to the Cape district of Baja California (Todos Santos, Cape San Lucas).

PASSERCULUS SANDWICHENSIS ROSTRATUS (Cassin)

## Large-billed Savannah Sparrow

### Contributed by WENDELL TABER

#### HABITS

Until recently this well-marked race was considered a distinct species, to which also were assigned the several other large-billed "marsh sparrows" of coastal southern and Baja California and western Sonora. The *"rostratus"* group, as these are still referred to within the *sandwichensis* complex, are characterized by a large gross bill with a culmen outline varying from straight to strongly convex, and in addition by a generally ill-defined and diffuse breast streaking.

*Nesting.*—Bancroft (1927) states that *rostratus* nests in tall grass subject to tidal overflow near the mouth of the Colorado River. He says the nests are constructed of grass stems solely; they are not lined and there is no thinning of grass stems toward the inside.

*Behavior.*—J. Grinnell (1905) records *rostratus* as common in winter in the salt marshes and along the beaches of Los Angeles County, Calif., but less numerous than the race *beldingi*. In San Pedro harbor *rostratus* frequents wharves and breakwaters and even hops fearlessly about the decks of vessels, feeding on crumbs and flies. J. H. Bowles (1911) attributes this behavior to spilled grain.

A. W. Anthony (1906) states that the races *rostratus* and *sanctorum* are equally abundant in September along the beaches of Los Benitos Island, gleaning a livelihood from beds of stranded kelp, over which the birds scurried like mice in search of insects and small marine life. The Benito Islands offer no tidal flats or marsh lands. He also says that the ocean beaches as far as Cape St. Lucas provide winter range for *rostratus*. ·While the birds are by no means rare on both sandy and rocky shores they are nowhere really abundant away from the tide flats of the bays. He had never seen *rostratus* over half a mile from tide water and a bird that wanders over a few hundred yards from the tide flats or beach is at once noticed as out of place. He considered the race strictly littoral and states (1893) that he shot a female *rostratus* at San Ramon in April 1887. He amplified this statement (1906) pointing out that San Ramon was about 25 miles north of San Quintin Bay on the coast of Lower California. The beach was thickly covered by driftwood which reached 'back some 200 feet to the sand dunes and was often piled up several feet high. Through these tangled piles of drift *rostratus* were running, dodging in and out very much after the manner of rock wrens in a pile of rocks.

*Plumages.*—Van Rossem (1947) refers to the plumage coloration as being varied "but usually with a definite pinkish or reddish tone pervading the gray of the entire upper parts and the streaking of the under parts." From the "normal" coloration, there are endless variations which reach a pale gray at one extreme and a pale rufescent or brick red at the other. He further states that "Sexual dichromatism as well as individual variation is more in evidence in *rostratus* than in any other Savannah Sparrow * * *."

*Food.*—C. Cottam and P. Knappen (1939) examined 28 stomachs of *rostratus* (14 in December, 3 in January, and 11 in March), 26 of which were taken at Alamitos Bay, Calif., or San Luis Island, Gulf of California. The other specimens were taken at Pasadena and El Monte, Calif. Food was 39.21 percent animal, 60.79 percent vegetable. A full stomach contained about three-quarters of a cubic centimeter. Of the animal foods, crustaceans represented 22.67 percent of the total intake; of these, various species of crabs formed 10.71 percent. A variety of insects were next in order of importance, supplying 8.36 percent of the food. Beetles (*Coleoptera*) composed 4.68 percent and unidentified insects, ants, and a lepidopterous cocoon (*Tineidae*) made up the remaining 3.68 percent. On the average, spiders composed only 0.39 percent of the total food, but one bird had 11 percent of its last meal composed of spiders.

That small gastropods are readily acceptable is shown from the fact that 10 of the 11 birds collected in March at San Luis Island had ingested a relatively thin-shelled snail (*Marinula rhoadsi*) in amounts varying from a trace to 55 percent of their meals. Snails supplied 18.45 percent of these 11 birds, but averaged only 7.25 percent for the entire 28 birds. Miscellaneous gastropods contributed another 0.54 percent, making the total consumption of these mollusks 7.79 percent.

Of the plant material 30.87 percent could not be identified other than as seed fragments, woody debris, or rubbish. Grain supplied 22.96 percent, with wild oats (*Avena fatua*) present in the greatest quantity (12.25 percent) and oats (*Avena sativa*), storksbill (*Erodium* sp.) and *Solanum* sp. each contributing less than 4 percent of the total.

A considerable difference was noted in the food of birds collected in March at San Luis Island from those taken in December at Alamitos Bay. The former group had subsisted on animal food, mostly crustaceans and gastropods, to the extent of 53.73 percent, while the Californian birds had taken insects, crustaceans, and gastropods only to the extent of 22.29 percent. This would indicate that the species is adaptable, feeding within limits on whatever is most readily available.

*Voice.*—W. L. Dawson (1923) describes a midwinter song of *rostratus* (probably not at its fullest volume) as squeaky, and ending in a pookish trill: *Tsut tsut tsu wzzz tsut tsu wizzy weee.* Having little musical quality, the song is delivered with visible effort as though it had to be squeezed out.

*Range.*—Baja California, California, and northwestern Sonora.

*Breeding range.*—The large-billed Savannah sparrow breeds in northeastern Baja California (delta of the Colorado River, San Felipe) and northwestern Sonora (mouth of Colorado River south to Isla Patos, intergrading with *P. s. atratus*).

*Nonbreeding range.*—Ranges in nonbreeding seasons from central coastal and southern California (Morro Bay, San Miguel Island, San Clemente Island, San Diego, Mecca, rarely from Santa Cruz) south along both shores of Baja California to the Cape district, to islands of the Gulf of California, the Sonoran coast, and northern Sinaloa (to lat. 25° N.).

*Egg date.*—Baja California: 1 record, April 6.

## PASSERCULUS SANDWICHENSIS ATRATUS van Rossem

### Sonora Savannah Sparrow

Contributed by WENDELL TABER

#### HABITS

This most southerly member of the *rostratus* group is found in the tidal marshes of the coast of central and southern Sonora at least to the Sonora-Sinaloa boundary. The winter range is imperfectly known, although some individuals occur at various points in the breeding range at that season. It is found also, perhaps only casually, in the Cape region of Baja California.

Van Rossem (1947) states that it is similar in size and proportion to *rostratus* but averages slightly larger in all dimensions. Coloration grayer and much darker, the central streaking on dorsal feathers fuscous black; ventral streaking wider and black rather than brown, reddish, or gray. He also says that although specimens from the northern part of the range show marked approach to *rostratus*, there seems to be relatively little variation in *atratus*. However, there is the same marked sexual difference seen in *rostratus* in the character of the interscapular streaking, the pattern of which is much more sharply defined and less diffuse in females than in males.

#### DISTRIBUTION

*Range.*—The Sonora Savannah sparrow is resident in coastal marshes from central Sonora (Tepopa and Kino bays) south to central Sinaloa (El Molino). It is casual in winter in southern Baja California (Todos Santos).

## AMMODRAMUS SAVANNARUM (Gmelin)
## Grasshopper Sparrow*
### PLATE 41
### Contributed by ROBERT LEO SMITH

### HABITS

Although the grasshopper sparrow, *Ammodramus savannarum*, ranges from the Atlantic Coast to California and from southern Canada to southern Florida, Arizona, and Mexico, it is one of our more obscure birds. It is seldom noticed, even by those who are familiar with other birds. It usually keeps well hidden in the depths of the grass, and when pursued it flies only when nearly tramped upon. Its courtship, nest building, and rearing of young are carried on in a grass-world of its own, well hidden from human eyes. Its song so closely resembles the stridulations of the grasshopper that many persons do not recognize it as a bird song.

The eastern race, *A. s. pratensis* (Vieillot), is found from the northeastern Atlantic seaboard through the tall grass prairie country to eastern Oklahoma and northeastern Texas, and from extreme southern Ontario and Quebec to central North and South Carolina, central Alabama, and Georgia. Thomas Burleigh (1958) writes that the birds nest locally in northern Georgia where grassland farming makes more habitat available. In recent years they have been found breeding south of the fall line in Macon County.

The western race, *A. s. perpallidus* (Coues), ranges from western Ontario, Minnesota, western Oklahoma, and central Colorado west to the Pacific Coast, and from the extreme southern prairie provinces of Canada south through eastern Washington and Oregon to central Nevada and southwestern California. So much of its habitable range is broken by mountains and deserts, its distribution is very spotty. The bird, however, may be more common than supposed, its absence in many regions reflecting the absence of observers rather

---

*The following subspecies are discussed in this section: *Ammodramus savannarum pratensis* (Vieillot), *A. s. floridanus* (Mearns), *A. s. perpallidus* (Coues), *A. s. ammolegus* Oberholser. Most of this account is based on the author's study of the eastern race of the grasshopper sparrow (Wilson Bulletin, 1959, 1963). Alexander Sprunt contributed a brief account of the Florida grasshopper sparrow, but kindly consented to withhold it so that all subspecies could be incorporated into the one account.

than birds.  D. W. Johnston (1949), who collected the first grass-hopper sparrow in Idaho in 1947 in Latah County, writes (in litt.) that "here, too, it seemed to me that the birds were not unduly rare, although there had been much ornithological field work in the area previously."

The Florida grasshopper sparrow, *A. s. floridanus* (Mearns), in-habits the Kissimmee Prairie region.  It was described in 1902 by Edgar A. Mearns, who based his description on a pair of birds collected on the Kissimmee Prairie near Alligator Bluff, Osceola County.  Not until a quarter-century later were additional specimens collected. According to W. H. Nicholson (1936) its range begins at a point 20 miles southwest of St. Cloud and extends to Okeechobee City.  D. J. Nicholson writes that the center of abundance of the Florida grass-hopper sparrow is "from 7 to 10 miles west of Kenansville, Osceola County, Florida, on the Kissimmee Prairie to within 10 miles of Bassenfer, Okeechobee County, Florida."  The species does not breed over all the area, but forms scattered colonies, sometimes 30 miles apart.

An interesting situation occurs in the wide territorial gap between the ranges of *pratensis* and *floridanus*.  David W. Johnston writes that the species' absence from the coastal plain is difficult to account for, as "much of this physiographic province has been converted to grassland.  My only explanation is historical, namely the possibility that this species simply has not yet had time to invade or perhaps to develop a physiological toleration of the climatic conditions there."

Also isolated on its breeding area is the Arizona grasshopper sparrow, *A. s. ammolegus* Oberholser.  This race, described by H. C. Oberholser (1942) from a series of breeding specimens collected by Alex Walker in 1932, breeds in central southern Arizona, chiefly in the Huachuca Mountain region.

The grasshopper sparrow is a grassland bird, most plentiful in managed grasslands and absent from fields with 35 percent of the area in shrubs.  They inhabit small grain fields to a limited extent, but their densities in such areas are a fraction of those found in grass-land.  Johnston and Odum (1956) observe that the grasshopper sparrow and the meadowlark (*Sturnella magna*) are the only true grassland species of the Athens, Ga., area, and in fact of most of the southeastern United States.  Alden Miller (1951) writes that it is confined exclusively to grassland formation in California.

The eastern race appears to be most abundant on cultivated grass-lands, particularly those containing orchardgrass (*Dactylis glomerata*), alfalfa (*Medicago sativa*), red clover (*Trifolium pratense*), lespedeza (*Lespedeza* spp.), all of which form the clumps the species seemingly requires.  Old fields of poverty grass (*Danthonia spicata*), dewberry

PLATE 41

Convis Township, Mich., July 11, 1935        L. H. Walkinshaw

Butler County, Pa., June 12, 1946        H. H. Harrison

EASTERN GRASSHOPPER SPARROW AND NEST

PLATE 42

Brandon, Manitoba, July 9, 1965        J. Lane

BAIRD'S SPARROW AT NEST

Brandon, Manitoba, Aug, 2, 1965        J. Lane

9-DAY OLD BAIRD'S SPARROW WITH PARENT

(*Rubus* spp.) and broomsedge (*Andropogon* spp.), also are inhabited by the grasshopper sparrow, but the birds leave as the shrubs fill in the fields. On the islands off the New England coast this bird is found in old fields with red cedar (*Juniperus virginiana*) and bayberry (*Morella pensylvanica*).

Prime habitat for the western subspecies *perpallidus* and *ammolegus* is the prairie. Kendeigh (1941) notes that grasshopper sparrows are more plentiful in prairie grasses than in bluegrass.

In the forested regions of the east grasshopper sparrows originally were restricted to extensive natural clearings and sparsely wooded areas. They are found in such situations today in Minnesota (Roberts, 1936) and Michigan (Walkinshaw, 1940). Walkinshaw writes: "In Crawford County in natural clearings, grown sparsely to grass, the species was found on open areas only a few acres in extent where no stock was pastured and no haying was done. Here the birds were found in the natural wild state before man had taken over the land for his use."

Clearing the land for agriculture permitted the species to spread. Todd (1940) writes: "Undoubtedly the species has greatly increased in number during the past century and it is interesting to find that in extending its range it has invaded territory far beyond its usual altitudinal and faunal limits." Forbush (1929) notes that the grasshopper sparrow is a bird "of the coastal plains, river valleys and lower uplands. It is rarely found at elevations much above 1,000 feet." But in Pennsylvania on the western flank of the Alleghenies, the species is found at elevations over 2,000 feet when local conditions are suitable, and Maurice Brooks (1944) found it in West Virginia "on the Allegheny Backbone, in Pocahontas County, at an elevation of 4,300 feet."

The Florida grasshopper sparrow occupies an aberrant type of habitat for the species. Howell (1932) writes that this race "lives among the stunted growth of saw palmetto and dwarf oaks (*Quercus mimina*) a foot or two high, seemingly preferring this habitat to the grassy areas." D. J. Nicholson writes it inhabits the more open parts of the Kissimmee Prairie "where the saw palmettos are small—10 to 15 inches high—and the grass is sparse with patches of bare ground showing here and there. * * * they avoid heavy growth of palmettos or dense grass. * * * Frequently the cattlemen burn the prairie, and the birds seem to prefer these burned-over areas where the cover is very light and rather open."

*Spring.*—The grasshopper sparrow returns to its nesting grounds, often unnoticed, usually from mid-April to early May, although it may appear as early as the last of March. My earliest arrival date for north central Pennsylvania is Mar. 31, 1945, when a resident male returned to his old territory on the study area. A second male arrived two days later, but a short cold spell delayed the arrival of the rest of the population until April 12.

Cruikshank (1942) states that the species arrives in a marked wave about New York City during the first week of May, and stragglers pass through as late as the first week of June. I have never observed any marked wave in central or western Pennsylvania; there a few birds appear first, then the population builds up over a period of 1 to 2 weeks. My observations indicate that the first arrivals are males. They generally do not appear on the nesting areas until the grass is tall enough to conceal them.

*Territory.*—Upon arrival at their nesting grounds, male grasshopper sparrows undertake territorial establishment. The first arrivals have the area to themselves and generally confine their singing to the morning hours. As more birds return, territorial activity increases in intensity, reaching a climax about 2 to 3 weeks after the first birds arrive. Then song is heard throughout the day.

The male proclaims territory by singing the "grasshopper" or territorial song (see *Voice*). When engaged in a song duel, the male alternates song with display. Crouching with head lowered between the shoulders, he raises and flutters one or both wings. Then after hearing the song of his neighbor, he stands erect and sings back. The song completed, he again crouches and flutters his wings while his rival sings. The wing fluttering, conspicuous only during territorial establishment, is never accompanied by a song or a call, and is confined to the intervals between songs.

I regard the wing fluttering of the grasshopper sparrow as a hostile display. During the period of territorial establishment the song of a rival is a sufficient stimulus to release it. Often the birds are hidden by the vegetation or the topography of the field so they can not see one another. They sense the presence of a rival by the sound of his song and manifest this by a hostile display, as if the rival were nearby in the grass.

I have never observed a territorial dispute that elicited an intimidation display of high intensity, although some could have taken place in the grass, out of sight. The only physical encounters I observed during hundreds of hours spent with the species occurred after a bird saw another invade its aerial territory. In each instance the bird chased the intruder, then retired to a singing perch, fluttered his wings, and sang the grasshopper song. I have witnessed a number of such clashes at disputed boundaries. Since the deep grass conceals territorial infringements on the ground, this mode of defense could be most important. Perhaps the grasshopper sparrow recognizes the limits of its territory only from a grasstop point of view.

The territorial "grasshopper" songs usually are delivered from the highest perches in the territory. These may include a clump of grass, an alfalfa stalk, a tall weed, a small bush, fence post, utility wire, tree, or farm equipment left in the field, hay cocks, or grain shocks. The birds appear restricted to low perches only by their habitat, and use low ones simply because no higher ones are available. This was demonstrated experimentally. When a wooden stake tall enough to stand two feet above the grasstops was placed in a bird's territory, the bird claimed it within minutes. When a still higher perch was introduced the next day, the bird abandoned the first for the new, higher perch.

Song perches are clustered about certain singing areas, usually near the periphery of the territory, apart from the nesting areas. Among the birds I have studied, singing perches were from 165 to 412 feet from the nest. Their position may be influenced by row crops in the territory when grasshopper sparrows then confine their singing perches to the vicinity of grass plots.

The size of 22 territories plotted on my study area ranged from 1.2 to 3.3 acres; 11 were between 1 and 2 acres, 9 between 2 and 3 acres, and 2 were over 3 acres. Their average size was 2.03 acres. Kendeigh (1941) reports the average size of 6 territories was 3.4 acres.

Territorial boundaries are maintained rigidly during the periods of territorial establishment, nest building, and incubation. After the young hatch, territorial defense declines and considerable movement of birds into other territories occurs. The movement is often initiated by young birds just able to fly, that flutter into adjoining territories where the parents follow in answer to the feeding call.

Prior to second nesting, territorial defense increases sharply for 2 to 3 days. The males sing the "grasshopper" song and flutter their wings. Territorial boundaries may be shifted in response to disturbances made by harvesting of hay and small grains. In one instance a male grasshopper sparrow shifted his territory for the second nesting to include the eastern half of his neighbor's territory. The hay on this portion had been mowed early, and new growth afforded cover lacking in the original territory. The neighboring male in turn took over the western half of the first male's old territory. In the end both birds had new growth and newly mowed hayfields in their respective territories. Interestingly, these two birds occupied approximately the same territories the following year. Another male, whose territory was bisected by a strip of field corn, took over a corner of his neighbor's territory when the increasing height of the corn walled off the lower half of his own territory and made it useless.

After the second broods leave the nest, grasshopper sparrows no longer defend territorial boundaries, although adults and young remain in the general vicinity until they disappear in the fall.

*Courtship.*—Within 10 to 14 days after their arrival, the males introduce the sustained song (see *Voice*), which for a short time almost replaces the grasshopper song and signifies that courtship is at its height. Most courtship activity is hidden in the grass, but occasionally a male rises above it on quivering wings, delivers this song in a low fluttering flight, and then drops out of sight again. The female may answer this song with a trill of her own (see *Voice*), which she often sings alone. The male responds by singing the sustained song or by flying to her. At times the male pursues the female and sings the sustained song as he gives chase.

W. H. Nicholson writes that the male Florida grasshopper sparrow "has a fluttering mating flight similar to that of the seaside sparrow except that it is low, 3 to 5 feet above the ground for 50 to 100 feet; upon alighting on a twig or saw palmetto it bursts into song."

*Nesting.*—Nests of the grasshopper sparrow are extremely hard to find. During the course of my study I was able to locate only four. All were hidden at the base of clumps of grass, alfalfa, clover, dead vegetation, or other cover, and often had one or two paths leading to the entrance. The nest itself is built of stems and blades of grass and lined with fine grass and rootlets, occasionally with horsehair (Burleigh, 1923; Simmons, 1925; Trautman, 1940). Sunk in a slight depression, the rim is level with or slightly above the surface of the ground. The top is usually arched or domed at the back, giving it an ovenlike appearance. Nest measurements range as follows: outside, 4.50 to 5.50 inches; height, 2 to 2.25 inches; inside, 2.50 or 3 by 3.25 inches; inside depth, 1.25 to 1.30 inches (Simmons, 1925; Dixon, 1916).

W. H. Nicholson (1936) describes the nest of the Florida grasshopper sparrow as follows: "Many of the nests were a single dead palmetto leaf without any other vegetation to conceal them; others were under dead drooping palmetto leaves with small dwarf oaks and wire grass growing on all sides, while several others were in thin tussocks of dead wire grass which looked too small to hide the bird, much less the nest." Nests were "lined with fine wire grass and arched over with grass blades."

Nest-building of the eastern and western grasshopper sparrows reaches its height in late May. This is followed by a second nest-building period in very late June and early July. D. J. Nicholson writes that the nesting of the Florida grasshopper sparrow begins "about the middle of April to the first week in May; second nestings are begun about the first of June; and again in July they breed a third time."

*Eggs.*—The grasshopper sparrow commonly lays 4 or 5 eggs; although frequently sets of 3 are found and occasionally as many as 6. They are generally ovate and have a slight gloss. The ground color is creamy white, speckled and spotted with shades of reddish browns such as "Rood's brown," "russet," "Mars brown," or "chestnut brown," and undermarkings of "pale purplish gray," or "pale neutral gray." The spots are usually sharp and well defined; they may be scattered over the entire egg or concentrated toward the large end where they often form a loose wreath or become confluent over the cap. Many eggs show as many gray undermarkings as spottings of the red browns. The pattern of markings of this species might be considered somewhat delicate, especially as compared with the eggs of the Savannah or song sparrow. The measurements of 92 eggs average 18.7 by 14.4 millimeters; the eggs showing the four extremes measure *20.8* by 14.7, 18.3 by *15.8*, *16.3* by 13.7, and 17.9 by *13.6* millimeters.

*A. s. pratensis.* The measurements of 50 eggs average 18.6 by 14.4 millimeters; the eggs showing the four extremes measure *20.8* by 14.7, 18.3 by *15.8*, *16.3* by 13.7, and 17.8 by *13.7* millimeters.

*A. s. perpallidus.* The measurements of 32 eggs average 18.7 by 14.3 millimeters; the eggs showing the four extremes measure *20.3* by 15.0, 19.6 by *15.2*, *17.8* by 14.2, and 17.9 by *13.6* millimeters.

*Incubation.*—The exact incubation period of the grasshopper sparrow is unknown, as it is only with considerable luck that a nest with a partial or a recently completed clutch can be found. King (1940) reports finding a nest on May 29, 1940, containing five eggs. On June 10, the same nest contained four young and one egg. Assuming that the young were shortly out of the egg and the fifth had yet to hatch, the incubation period would have been 12 days. D. J. Nicholson writes that the incubation period of the Florida grasshopper sparrow is "11 to 12 days—not more." Simmons (1925) writes that the incubation period of *perpallidus* "lasts for about 12 days."

The female alone incubates the eggs and broods the young. She sits very closely on the nest. When leaving, she slips off, runs a distance through the grass and then flies. On her return she never flies directly to the nest, but drops down into the grass some distance away and goes to it on foot, by one of the several paths.

If flushed from the nest the female may dart off, run a short distance, arise in a short fluttering flight, then drop to the ground again where she spreads her tail and trails her wings as if injured. At other times the female may flutter directly off the nest as if crippled or may fly from the nest to a point 25 to 30 feet away and hide in the grass.

W. H. Nicholson writes that some female Florida grasshopper sparrows "will run off the nests before they are found; others will sit tightly until almost stepped upon before they flutter off uttering weak squeaking notes not unlike a mouse." He (1936) writes further: "When they did leave they did not fly, but ran off dragging tail and fluttering the wings as if crippled. If followed they would lead the intruder off about twenty feet from the nest and then fly to some nearby palmetto and begin scolding. Several times the bird would run along the ground within eight feet of me scolding with a weak *tik-tik-tik*."

During the incubation period the male spends his time singing and defending the territory, but shows little concern over human intruders. When they appear he simply stops singing and hides in the grass. The actions of both sexes are such that they attract no attention to the nest location.

The behavior of both male and female changes after the young hatch. One male I observed sang both songs throughout the day his young hatched. The female flushed from the nest but did not feign injury. She flew a short distance, hid in a swath of hay and chipped softly. The male chipped several times, broke into the grasshopper song, fluttered both wings, and then continued to chip vigorously. As I left the area the male sang the sustained song, interrupted it with a grasshopper song, followed by the trill (see *Voice*).

*Young.*—Grasshopper sparrows at hatching are blind and covered with grayish-brown down. Walkinshaw (1940) gives the weight of young at hatching as between 1.7 and 2.3 grams. This is approximately the same weight as the egg. At 4 days wing feathers break through the sheath; breast and side feathers still are in the sheath; back, belly, and rump are bare. At 6 to 7 days body feathers emerge from the sheath and appear dark brown to blackish with yellowish buff edge. A distinct buffy crown patch is present; the commissure is bright yellow. By day 9 to 10 the young are well feathered, though the tail feathers are still short. Walkinshaw gives the weight increases as of the second day, 2.9 grams; sixth day, 8.7 to 9.1 grams; and seventh to eighth day, 9.7 to 10.5 grams. Wetherbee (1934) reports the weight of 14 immature birds as ranging between 14.0 and 18.3 grams, averaging 16.09.

Upon my approach to the nest the young invariably gaped for food, but expressed no sign of fear. On June 7, 1944, my dog discovered the nest of one pair and threw two of the four out of the nest. As I replaced these, the two in the nest gaped for food. Later in the day, immediately after the female fed the young, one bird gaped and three did not respond. This same pattern was followed at other nests. Recently fed young did not respond in any way; if hungry they gaped when I moved near the nest.

Young birds on my Pennsylvania study area remained in the nest 9 days. Michigan birds observed by Walkinshaw (1940) remained in the nest the same length of time. When out of the nest, the young run mouselike through the grass and rarely appear above the grasstops.

Both male and female are very solicitious about the young. During incubation the birds exhibit little concern about human and animal intrusions in their territories except those of cats. After the young hatch, the birds react to human intrusion with vigorous alarm. They may fly in wide circles above the trespasser, raising their crest feathers and flicking their wings and tail. On the ground they bob up and down on their legs like a spotted sandpiper (*Actitis macularia*) and utter a sharp *chi-ip*. When highly alarmed they give this double note so rapidly it almost runs into a trill. Often the male will interrupt his chipping to break into a grasshopper song. If the birds are carrying food to the young at the time, they invariably eat the insect and continue their alarm behavior. When a dog enters the territory, the birds drop into the grass, crouch low, and remain silent until the animal passes.

*Plumages.*—The juvenal plumage and post-juvenal molt of the grasshopper sparrow have been studied in detail by George M. Sutton (1935, 1936). He found a number of discrepancies in the descriptions by Dwight (1900), which were apparently based on a poorly aged specimen.

According to Sutton, the natal down is replaced by the juvenal plumage in a complete postnatal molt. It is worn for a short time as a complete plumage and is probably complete at 10 to 12 days of age. At this time the rectrices are stubby; the feathers of the back and scapulars are plain dark olive-brown or blackish brown, edged with buff, and totally lack any sort of russet spots on the tips. Richard R. Graber (1955) describes the juvenal plumage in detail as follows:

"No sexual dimorphism. Forehead and crown streaked, brown and black, with median and superciliary stripes of light buff or buffy white. Nape mottled, buffy white and black. Back, feathers black, edged with buff or buffy brown. Upper tail coverts black, edged with buff. Rectrices black, narrowly edged with buff, except median pair (broadly edged). Remiges slate gray or black, edged with buff or buffy brown. Tertials black, edged with white. Superciliary buffy white, streaked with black. Auriculars buffy brown. Post-auriculars concolor with nape. Underparts white or buffy white more strongly tinged with buff on chest, sides, flanks, and crissum. Upper chest rather sparsely streaked with blackish or dark brown. Other underparts unmarked. Stub-tailed birds much darker throughout than older birds."

The post-juvenal molt, according to Sutton (1936), takes place in late June or early July with the young of the first brood. Second and third brood young may be wearing part of the juvenal plumage as late or even later than mid-September. The body feathers of the juvenal plumage are lost first, while the flight feathers and tertials may be held for a longer period. At 20 days russet-tipped feathers appear on the back; the superciliary line still is sharply streaked; the rectrices are sheathed at the base. At 4 weeks the juvenal feathers are lost on the crown and the superciliary line, together with all remaining body feathers lacking russet tips. At 36 days the buff-margined juvenal feathers are practically gone, replaced by buffy feathers on the chest, sides, flanks, and lower throat. The back is thickly set with incoming fully-sheathed feathers, and new lesser wing coverts with a strongly yellowish cast appear. At about 6 weeks the juvenal rectrices are lost almost simultaneously. The molt of the juvenal primaries starts from the innermost outward.

A dull yellow superciliary is present in some juvenal males, but apparently is absent in juvenal females. The yellow superciliary spot is acquired by both male and female birds with the post-juvenal molt in the latter part of summer and fall, and not in April with a partial prenuptial molt as described by Dwight (1900).

The first winter pumage contains no streaked feathers on the chest. The back feathers are black with apical chestnut spots edged with pearl gray. The median crown stripe, edging of tertiaries and wing coverts, sides of the head, superciliary line, and underparts are rich buff. New feathers above and in front of the eye are deep yellow. The neck feathers are red-brown medially. Middle of the abdomen is pure white.

There is no evidence of a prenuptial molt except for replacement of feathers lost accidentally. Sutton (1936) states that "the large majority of spring birds are exactly like fall adults except that the plumage is a little more worn. Fall birds are beautifully fresh, breeding birds are noticeably worn, late summer birds are very decidedly worn, and spring birds are in an exactly intermediate position between fall and summer."

The second winter plumage is acquired by a complete postnuptial molt. According to Dwight (1900) it differs little "from the first winter dress, the buff less obvious and the colors deeper."

The adult western grasshopper sparrow, *A. s. perpallidus*, is paler and grayer than the eastern race, with more chestnut and rusty brown and less black above.

Oberholster (1942) describes the Arizona race as similar to *A. s. perpallidus*. The upper parts are decidedly paler, with more chestnut and rufous and also with much less, sometimes almost no, black on the back. The lower parts are lighter and not so dull.

The Florida race, *A. s. floridanus*, is much darker above than *A. s. pratensis*, paler and less buffy below. Feathers of the upper parts are mainly black, edged with grayish, with little or no brown. The underparts are less heavily washed with pinkish buff than *A. s. pratensis*.

*Food.*—Insects form the staple food of the grasshopper sparrow; and the most prominent among these is the grasshopper. Judd (1901) found that grasshoppers (genera *Xiphidium*, *Scudderia*, *Hippiscus*, and *Melanopus*) formed 23 percent of the bird's food during eight months of the year, 60 percent of its food in June and 37 percent of its diet from May to August. Thus the name of the bird is appropriate from the standpoint of its diet as well as its song.

Judd examined 170 stomachs of this sparrow collected between February and October from both the east and west. Food consisted of 63 percent animal matter and 37 percent vegetable matter. Insects comprised 57 percent of its total food, spiders, myriapods, snails, and earthworms, 6 percent; harmful beetles made up 8 percent and caterpillars 14 percent. Beetles were of three families: click beetles (*Elateridae*), weevils (*Sitones* and related genera), and smaller leaf beetles (*Systens* spp). Judd writes: "Caterpillars are eaten more freely in May than at any other time, and constitute 33 percent of the food of that month. More than half of the caterpillars destroyed are cutworms * * *. In one stomach from Bourbon County, Ky., were six cutworms (*Nephelodes violans*), each an inch long. The army worm seems to be also a favorite article of diet." Eleven percent of the total food consists of ants, dung beetles (*Atoeniys* and *Apodius*), and 1 percent bugs, including leaf hoppers (*Jassidae*), leaf bugs (*Capsidae*), assassin bugs (*Reduviidae*), and smaller soldier bugs (*Hymenarcys* and *Trichopepla*).

Vegetable food consists of grain, chiefly waste, 2 percent; wood sorrel (*Oxalis*) 2 percent; ragweed (*Ambrosia*) 5 percent; pigeon grass (*Setaria*), panic grass (*Panicum*), and others 17 percent; smartweed (*Polygonum*), purslane (*Portulata*), ribgrass (*Plantago*), and sedges (*Cyperaceae*) 11 percent.

Howell (1932) writes of the Florida race: "Examination of the stomachs of 10 specimens taken on the Kissimmee Prairie showed the bird's food to consist of animal matter (insects and spiders), 69 percent, and vegetable matter, 31 percent. The insects taken in greatest quantity were grasshoppers and crickets, beetles, weevils, and moths and their larvae, with a few flies and bugs. Seeds of sedges composed most of the vegetable matter, with some grass seed and seeds of star grass (*Hypoxis*)."

*Behavior.*—The grasshopper sparrow is a secretive bird, difficult to observe. It seldom flies, but runs ahead of the searcher through the grass and flushes only when hard pressed. As William Brewster (journal) describes it: "when flushed the sparrows rise swiftly and vigorously, twisting a little * * * the flight then becomes steady and direct and is performed in long, regular undulations, the wings being vibrated rapidly." He adds: "On the ground they both run and hop." Witmer Stone (1937) notes that in flight the bird "turns to one side or the other like a snipe." Simmons (1925) writes that when flushed the western grasshopper sparrow rises "in a zig-zag flight for a few yards" and then "dives back into the weeds. * * * In open fields, flight is extended and rapid."

The bird perches in a peculiar crouched position, as if ready to dart off in an instant.

D. J. Nicholson comments on the colonial nature of *floridanus:* "They breed in small colonies—three or four to a dozen pairs. These colonies are very local and are not found everywhere over this vast prairie, many apparently suitable spots being unoccupied."

These same words might well apply to the eastern and western grasshopper sparrows as well, for they show the same colonial nature and fluctuate considerably in abundance from year to year.

One cause of population changes might be attributed to grassland management practices. On my study area, for example, the fields during the early part of the study were run down and supported a poor growth of timothy, alfalfa, and red clover. From 1944 on, the fertility of the fields increased considerably and the grass mixture was changed to a thick, vigorous growth of alfalfa, ladino clover, and brome grass (*Bromus inermis*). The grasshopper sparrows in the area settled in hay and abandoned fields where the vegetation was not so heavy.

Oscar Root (1957, 1958, letter), who kept a long-time record of local population fluctuations on a level, artificially drained airport of 100 acres at North Andover, Mass., found the grasshopper sparrow populations there built up to highs, followed by severe reductions in numbers the following year. He believed mowing the grass on the area prior to his counts reduced the population. However, when mowing was postponed to allow completion of nesting by the sparrows, the population still remained low. He states that certain areas always productive in the past were without grasshopper sparrows, though in prime shape and undisturbed.

The birds about Concord, Mass., have shown a similarly fluctuating pattern of abundance through the years (Griscom, 1949).

An unusual concentration of grasshopper sparrows is described by Brewster in his Nantucket journal. Here on June 27, 1874, he and Maynard found grasshopper sparrows extremely plentiful. He writes that "they were equally distributed for an extent of three to four miles. Often there were three or four pairs breeding in an area a hundred yards square." This species was fairly common on the Islands in the 1920's, but in recent years it has become local and uncommon and appears to have been replaced by the Savannah sparrow (*Passerculus sandwichensis*) (Griscom and Folger, 1948). Mrs. A. B. Davenport writes that the same situation is true on Conanicut Island, off Rhode Island. The bird was formerly abundant on Martha's Vineyard and north to Essex County, Mass.; today it is rare and local, replaced by the Savannah sparrow (Griscom and Snyder, 1955).

Thus it appears that populations of grasshopper sparrows fluctuate sharply at times in spite of the availability of suitable habitat. No reason can be given, but in some areas it appears to be giving way to the Savannah sparrow, a bird that occupies the same fields and is able to maintain its numbers when shrubs invade the area.

*Voice.*—The male grasshopper sparrow possesses three primary forms of vocalization, the grasshopper song, the sustained song, and the trill; the female has only one, the trill.

Of these the most familiar is the grasshopper song from which the bird derives its name. The song consists of one to three introductory notes followed by a long, very high-pitched trill. The length of this song varies from 1 to 2⅛ seconds, and averages about 1⅔ seconds. The pitch, according to Saunders (MS.), varies from F#[7] to D[8]; and the pitch interval varies from 1 to 3½ tones. The introductory notes "are usually of lower pitch than the trill." The trill is simple and nearly always on the same pitch throughout.

Brand (1938) determined the pitch of this song to range from 9,500 to 7,675 vibrations per second, with a mean of 8,600. By contrast the frequency of a piccilo is 4,608 cycles per second.

The songs of the other races resemble closely those of *pratensis*. Zimmer (1913) describes the song of the western grasshopper sparrow as a *pit-tuck zee- ee- ee*. Simmons (1925) describes it as a "thin, wiry monotonous grasshopper like *pit-tuck zee-ee-e-e-e-e-e-e-e-e* or *kalsick ha tsee-e-e-e-e-e-e-e-e-e-e.*"

W. H. Nicholson (1936) describes the song of the Florida grasshopper sparrow "as sounding like *twittle-e-dee* repeated several times in rapid succession with a *tik-tik-tok-buzzzzzz* at the finish. Many times I have heard them sing the latter part of this song without the former, but never the former part alone. The latter part has a distinct insect-like sound."

The sustained song is more elaborate and more musical than the grasshopper song and is subject to considerable individual variation. It ranges up to 5 seconds in length. The sustained song in its entirety consists of a grasshopper introduction followed by a sustained series of melodious notes. The song may be written as *tip-tup-a-zee-e-e-e-e-e-e-e zeedle zee-e-e-e zeedle zeedle zee-e-e-e-e-e-e*. The grasshopper introduction often is omitted, especially after territories are well established.

Jouy (1881) mistakenly attributed this song to Henslow's sparrow (*Passerherbulus henslowii*). He writes: "Besides their characteristic note of *te-wick*, they have quite a song which may be fairly represented by the syllables *sis-r-r-rit-srit-srit*, with the accent on the first and last parts. The song is often uttered while the bird takes a short flight upward; it then drops down again into the tangled weeds and grasses where it is almost impossible to follow it."

This is an adequate description of the sustained song of the grasshopper sparrow which is often given in flight. During 5 years of concurrent observations of both species in the same fields, I never heard a Henslow's sparrow sing a song that even remotely resembled the sustained song of the grasshopper sparrow.

The primary function of the sustained song is to attract and hold a mate. The grasshopper introduction, however, is hostile in character and serves as a warning early in the season. Later, when the grasshopper introduction is dropped, the males respond to the sustained song with a grasshopper song. Then both birds launch into a duel of grasshopper songs.

The least common vocalization of the male grasshopper sparrow is the trill. Unless one is frequently in the field among these birds, the observer is apt to miss it entirely. Walkinshaw (1940) calls it a nesting song, and Saunders (1951, MS.) describes it graphically. It can be written *ti-tu-ti-tu-ti-i-i-i*. The song consists of a series of moderately loud, short, alternate notes, given rapidly and ending in a downward trill. It is delivered on the ground or from a perch. The trill generally is not given until the pair is formed, and is then uttered only in the vicinity of the nest. It may follow one of the other two songs, or it may be given alone, often in answer to the female. This song apparently serves as a bond to hold the pair together, and as a signal to the female and young that the male is approaching the nest.

The female grasshopper sparrow has a song quite similar to the trill of the male, but softer, lacking the downward trill, and more suggestive of the song of the chipping sparrow (*Spizella passerina*). It may be written *ti-ti-i-i-i-i-i-i-i*. Its primary function is apparently to declare her presence on the territory to the male. She also gives the trill when she is approaching or is near the nest. When so used it serves to announce her location, to maintain the pair bond, and to signal both the male and the young that she is approaching the nest.

Song falls into seasonal and daily patterns. The male sings the grasshopper song from arrival until mid-August. The sustained song is introduced approximately at the time of the females' arrival. After pairing, the volume of song drops for a few days, but singing does not cease entirely. The sustained song is confined mostly to evening twilight; the grasshopper song is the common daytime song. During the periods of egg laying and incubation the male sings both songs frequently, especially in early morning and late evening, continuing until darkness. Song wanes during June when the birds are busy feeding young. Prior to renesting the sustained song is heard frequently for several days before it wanes again. The trills of both male and female are given from the period of pair formation to the completion of nesting.

The grasshopper sparrow does not have an extended morning awakening song. When it wakes the bird may start to feed in silence, or it may utter a few call notes, or snatches of the grasshopper or sustained songs. Once the bird starts singing, it interrupts the song sequence frequently with feeding. By mid-July the morning singing has almost ceased, and daytime song is rarely heard, but in the cool of evening, as feeding activity stops, twilight singing may still be heard until darkness falls. At this period the sustained song with its greater carrying power seems to be the most conspicuous, and for this reason has been erroneously described as a postseason elaboration of the regular song of the species. Night singing, particularly when the moon is full, is a common habit with all races of the species.

The call note of all races of the grasshopper sparrow most commonly heard is a two-syllabled *chi-lip* or *til-lic*. Given by both sexes, the call functions primarily as an alarm note; as such it varies in intensity. When rapidly given in high intensity alarm, the notes suggest the slow clicking of a fishing reel. Less frequently, especially under situations of low intensity alarm, the call note is only a sharp *tik*.

While feeding the grasshopper sparrow utters a single note *tik* or *chip*. It is similar to the alarm note, but is higher pitched and less sharp and vigorous. The food call of the young is a double note *chi-ip* similar to that of the adult but with a more liquid quality.

*Field marks.*—Adult grasshopper sparrows are short-tailed, flat-headed, and the only sparrows of the grasslands that lack streaks or markings on the breast. Young birds of the year have streaked breasts and are often confused with adult Henslow's sparrows, which are more sharply streaked with black on the breast, sides, and flanks. The young Henslow's sparrow with relatively unstreaked breast may be confused with the adult grasshopper sparrow, but the distinctly chestnut wings of Henslow's sparrow separates this species at all ages from the grasshopper sparrow.

The only other bird with which the grasshopper sparrow might be confused is Leconte's sparrow (*Passerherbulus caudacutus*). This sparrow, however, inhabits prairie marshes, an environment too wet for the grasshopper sparrow. Both adult and young Leconte's sparrows are streaked, but the underparts are light yellowish brown instead of cinnamon buff, and they lack the yellow before the eye and on the bend of the wing.

*Enemies.*—It is ironical that the grasshopper sparrow's greatest benefactor is also his greatest enemy. This sparrow depends upon man for maintenance of its habitat through grassland management but these fields are cut for hay. Haying usually begins in mid-June, the height of this bird's nesting season. The nest usually escapes destruction from mower blades, but some nests may be crushed by implement wheels. If the nest escapes destruction by haying opera-tions, it is exposed to weather and predators. Grass used for silage is cut early, around the first of June. This is the height of nest build-ing by the grasshopper sparrow. I have found that in fields regularly cut for grass silage, resulting in early loss of cover, the population of grasshopper sparrows is very low. The loss of cover later in the nesting season does not result in abandonment of the field or the nest, if the nest has not been destroyed. I have never noted grasshopper sparrows leaving a field after haying, despite the loss of cover. This is in sharp contrast to Henslow's sparrow, which leaves a field when the grass is cut.

Among the predators of the grasshopper sparrow are the skunk (*Mephitis mephitis*), weasels, spermophiles (*Citellus* spp.), foxes, and cats. Cats take their toll of grasshopper sparrows, especially after the hay is cut, although they probably catch fewer of these birds than of other sparrows. Dogs at times discover grasshopper sparrow nests accidently.

W. H. Nicholson writes that hogs, snakes, spotted skunks (*Spilogale ambarvalis*), and striped skunks seem to be the major enemies of the Florida grasshopper sparrows. He states; "I have found 25 to 30 nests under construction; upon returning later I found practically all of them destroyed by the above."

As the nests are well concealed and the birds stay close to the grass, hawks probably are insignificant as predators, except after the hay is cut. Marsh hawks (*Circus cyaneus*), though common in grasshopper sparrow habitat, appear to have little influence on the species. The grasshopper sparrow apparently pays no attention to them, for I have observed males singing while marsh hawks were hunting nearby. When, however, a sharp-shinned hawk (*Accipiter striatus*) approaches, the grasshopper sparrows stop singing at once, give a few alarm notes, and drop into the grass. After the hawk has disappeared, they come out of hiding and resume their singing.

The cowbird (*Molothrus ater*) parasitizes a few nests of the grasshopper sparrow, but the incidence is extremely low. Friedmann (1938) lists three known occurrences of parasitism of the eastern grasshopper sparrow and three for the western race. Hicks (1934b) found one grasshopper sparrow nest containing a cowbird egg in Ohio. This low incidence reflects the difficulty cowbirds must have in locating nests of this species.

Walkinshaw (1940) observed small red ants attacking young birds in the nest and entering two pipped eggs. The female ate all the ants in and around the nest.

Terres (1939) reports that an immature grasshopper sparrow was caught in the vertical web of a golden garden spider (*Miranda aurantia*). The bird was released, apparently unharmed.

*Fall and winter.*—By late August the nesting season is over, the young grasshopper sparrows are independent, and the adults are silent and more retiring than ever. The birds stay close to the grass and refuse to fly unless very closely pressed and when flushed quickly seek cover again. Unlike many other sparrows, they do not flock. During migration they may join other migrant fringillids, like the field and song sparrow, and appear in rather unlikely places. I have observed migrating birds along brushy fencerows, and I caught one immature individual in a trapping station in an elderberry thicket. By late September most grasshopper sparrows have left the breeding grounds, although a few may linger on until late October and early November.

Simmons (1925) writes that the eastern grasshopper sparrow during migration in the Austin region of Texas is found in "closely cropped pastures dotted with mesquite, floored with some stubble and buffalo grass, and edged with weed patches, brush thickets, weedy fencerows, and plowed ground."

Skinner (1928) writes that in the sandhills of North Carolina wintering grasshopper sparrows inhabit sandy grassy fields, especially those with broomsedge. Lowery (1955) states that this species is a "rather uncommon or at least seldom observed winter resident" in Louisiana, where it inhabits "broomsedge fields with a few small trees or brush piles." Tyler (1913) writes that in California wintering grasshopper sparrows inhabit "old weedy fields, weed-grown vineyards and berry patches."

There are few winter records north of the above range. Trautman (1940) reports a male bird found on Dec. 29, 1928, in the Buckeye Lake, Ohio, region with a "pathological condition present in the bill

and feet, for both were considerably swollen and a toe was gone."
Griscom and Snyder (1955) cite a winter record for Dec. 6, 1892, at
Arlington, Mass. A grasshopper sparrow banded by Oscar Root at
North Andover, Mass., on Nov. 30, 1940, was collected nearby on Jan.
19, 1941. Another bird was collected at Rose Blanche, Newfound-
land, Nov. 27, 1950 (Peters and Burleigh, 1951a). Easterla (1962)
records two, of which one was collected, wintering near Sedalia, Mo.,
Jan. 14, 1961.

The Arizona race, *ammolegus*, winters from northwestern Mexico
to Guatemala. The Florida grasshopper sparrow is resident and
remains on the breeding grounds all through the year.

## DISTRIBUTION

### Eastern Grasshopper Sparrow (*A. s. pratensis*)

*Range.*—Great Lakes region and New England to Guatemala,
Yucatán Peninsula, Cuba, and the Bahamas.

*Breeding range.*—The eastern grasshopper sparrow breeds from
Wisconsin, northern Michigan (Beaver Island, Douglas Lake), southern Ontario (Palgrave, Ottawa), southwestern Quebec (Chambly
Basin, Charlesbourg), northern Vermont (Swanton, St. Johnsbury),
central New Hampshire (Boscawen), and southern Maine (Berwick)
south to eastern Oklahoma, northeastern Texas, Arkansas, central
Alabama (Greensboro, Barachias), central Georgia (Marshallville),
central South Carolina (Aiken), central North Carolina (Raleigh),
and southeastern Virginia (Buckroe).

*Winter range.*—Winters from Arkansas (Fayetteville), Tennessee
(Memphis), central Georgia (Athens), northern South Carolina (Green-
ville County), eastern North Carolina (Lake Mattamuskeet), coastal
Virginia, and coastal Maryland (Ocean City) south to Guatemala
(Motagua Valley), Quintana Roo (Cozumel Island), Isle of Pines, the
Bahamas (Bimini to Cay Sal) and Bermuda; occasionally north to
Illinois (Champaign), Ohio (Fairfield County), New York (Livingston),
Pennsylvania (Wrightstown), and Rhode Island (Portsmouth).

*Casual records.*—Casual north to central Ontario (Burks Fall,
Lake-of-Two-Rivers), and east to New Brunswick (Grand Manan),
Prince Edward Island (St. Peters), and Newfoundland (Rose Blanche).

*Migration.*—The data apply to the species as a whole. Early dates
of spring arrival are: Florida—Whitefield, March 17. Alabama—
Decatur, April 2. Georgia—Athens, March 16. North Carolina—
Raleigh, March 25 (average of 10 years, April 19). Virginia—Rich-
mond, April 10. West Virginia—Wheeling, April 4. District of
Columbia, March 30 (average of 34 years, April 21). Maryland—
Dorchester County, March 17; Prince Georges County, March 18.
Pennsylvania—State College, April 3. New Jersey—West Orange,

March 20. New York—East Hampton, April 1; Cayuga and Oneida Lake basins, April 18 (median of 21 years, April 29). Connecticut— New Haven, April 22. Rhode Island—Providence, April 12. Massachusetts—Martha's Vineyard, April 6. Vermont—St. Johnsbury, April 18. New Hampshire—Bedford, April 3. Maine—Winthrop, May 3. Quebec—Montreal and Hudson, May 24. Louisiana—New Orleans, March 19. Arkansas—Winslow, March 23. Tennessee— Nashville, March 23 (median of 12 years, April 10); Knox County, April 8. Kentucky—Danville, March 21. Missouri—St. Louis, April 15 (median of 13 years, April 23). Illinois—Chicago, March 22 (median of 16 years, April 13); Rantoul, March 31. Indiana—Wayne County, March 29 (median of 15 years, April 19). Ohio—central Ohio, March 26 (median of 40 years, April 17); Oberlin, April 10 (median of 19 years, April 25). Michigan—Washington County, April 2. Ontario—Toronto and London, April 7. Iowa—Fairfield, April 7. Wisconsin—Madison, April 16. Minnesota—St. Paul, April 17 (average of 9 years, April 29). Oklahoma—Cleveland County, April 6. Kansas—northeastern Kansas, April 12. Nebraska—Lincoln, March 5; Red Cloud, March 8 (average of 20 years, April 6). South Dakota—Hermosa, April 11; Sioux Falls, May 5 (average of 5 years, May 9). North Dakota—Cass County, April 26 (average, May 12). Manitoba—Kildonan, May 2. Saskatchewan—Wiseton, April 5. New Mexico—Rodeo, April 9. Arizona—Huachuca Mountains, March 30. Colorado—Weldona, May 1, Wyoming—Hawk Springs Reservoir, May 18; Republican River, May 22. Idaho—Rupert, April 9. Montana—Columbia Falls May 2. Alberta—Marrin, May 15. California—East Park, April 14. Oregon—Salem, May 4. Washington—Tacoma, May 3. British Columbia—Okanagan Landing, May 12.

Late dates of spring departure are: Florida—Dry Tortugas, May 19. Georgia—Atlanta, April 17. South Carolina—Charleston, May 8. Louisiana—Baton Rouge, June 18. Mississippi—Gulfport, April 22. Illinois—Chicago, May 31 (average of 16 years, May 20). Ohio—Buckeye Lake, median May 22.

Early dates of fall arrival are: Arizona—Elgin, August 7. Texas— Sinton, September 30. Illinois—Chicago, August 9; Rantoul, August 12. Louisiana—Baton Rouge, October 3. New Jersey—Island Beach, September 6. South Carolina—Charleston, September 20. Alabama—Foley, October 19. Florida—Tallahassee, September 27.

Late dates of fall departure are: British Columbia—Okanagan Landing, October 13. Washington—Seattle, September 11. Nevada—Ruby Valley, September 15. Montana—Terry, September 16. Idaho—Moscow, October 9. Wyoming—Lyman, September 17. Colorado—Colorado Springs, October 15. Utah—Salt Lake

City, September 20. Arizona—Colorado River, September 26. New Mexico—Mesa Jumanes, September 26. Manitoba—East Kildonan, October 6. North Dakota—Cass County, September 14 (average, September 10). Nebraska—Lincoln, November 4. Oklahoma—Tulsa, November 25. Minnesota—Lakeville, October 13. Iowa—National, October 21. Michigan—Detroit area, October 11. Ohio—Cleveland, November 8; central Ohio, October 13 (average, September 15). Illinois—Chicago, November 12. Missouri—St. Louis, October 31 (median of 13 years, September 12). Kentucky—Bardstown, November 7. Tennessee—Nashville, November 4. Arkansas—Delight, December 1. Newfoundland—Rose Blanche, November 27. New Brunswick—Grand Manan, October 1. New Hampshire—Concord, September 5. Vermont—Putney, October 8. Massachusetts—Martha's Vineyard, November 1. Rhode Island—Providence, October 20. Connecticut—East Hartford, October 21. New York—Staten Island, October 27; Cayuga and Oneida Lake basins, November 8 (median of 9 years, October 17). New Jersey—Island Beach, November 2 (median of 5 years, October 23). Pennsylvania—Greensburg, October 31. Maryland—Somerset County, November 23; Laurel, October 27. District of Columbia—November 30 (average of 9 years, October 21). West Virginia—Bluefield, October 24. Virginia—Lexington, October 10. North Carolina—Raleigh, November 8. Georgia—Atlanta, November 21. Alabama—Decatur, November 6. Florida—Sombrero Key, December 17.

*Egg dates.*—Alabama: May 11 to July 15 (number of records not stated).

Georgia: 6 records, May 16 to June 28.

Illinois: 24 records, May 18 to July 10; 18 records, May 18 to May 31.

Maryland: 78 records, May 15 to August 19; 39 records, June 6 to July 9.

Michigan: 4 records, May 28 to July 14.

Minnesota: 6 records, May 27 to July 26.

New York: 9 records, May 29 to August 8.

Ontario: 3 records, May 26 to July 8.

Pennsylvania: 3 records, June 2 to July 19.

### Western Grasshopper Sparrow (*A. s. perpallidus*)

*Range.*—Southeastern British Columbia and southern portion of the prairie provinces south through Mexico to El Salvador.

*Breeding range.*—The western grasshopper sparrow breeds from northwestern California (Hayfork), southwestern Oregon (Medford), eastern Washington (Toppenish), southeastern British Columbia (Vernon), southern Alberta (Lost River), southern Saskatchewan

(Wiseton, Regina), southern Manitoba (Brandon, Winnipeg), and western Ontario (Port Arthur) south to southwestern California (San Diego), central Nevada (Eureka), northern Utah (Parley's Park), central Colorado (Colorado Springs), western Oklahoma (Comanche County), and central Texas (San Angelo, Waco).

*Winter Range.*—Winters from central California (Clovis), western and southeastern Arizona (Big Sandy River, Santa Catalina Mountains), and central Oklahoma (Creek County) south to southern Baja California (San José del Cabo), Guerrero (Chilpancingo), El Salvador (Los Esesmiles), Veracruz (Mirador), southern Louisiana (Baton Rouge), southern Mississippi (Saucier), and southwestern and northern Georgia (Newton, Athens).

*Casual record.*—Casual in Virginia (Blacksburg).

*Egg dates.*—British Columbia: 2 records, June 22.

California: 11 records, April 4 to June 12; 4 records, April 14 to June 12.

Texas: 7 records, April 20 to June 7.

### Florida Grasshopper Sparrow (*A. s. floridanus*)

*Range.*—The Florida grasshopper sparrow is resident in central peninsular Florida (Alachua County, Lake Hicpochee).

*Casual record.*—Casual in southern Florida (Cape Sable).

*Egg dates.*—Florida: 15 records, April 2 to June 21; 9 records, April 23 to May 8.

### Arizona Grasshopper Sparrow (*A. s. ammolegus*)

*Range.*—Central southern Arizona south to Sinaloa and Morelos.

*Breeding range.*—The Arizona grasshopper sparrow breeds in central southern and southeastern Arizona (Huachuca Mountains, Fort Grant) and adjacent northern Sonora (Nogales).

*Winter range.*—Winters from southern Arizona south to Sinaloa (Rosario), Morelos (Cuernavaca), and Guatemala.

### AMMODRAMUS BAIRDII (Audubon)
## Baird's Sparrow
### PLATE 42
### Contributed by JOHN LANE
#### HABITS

On June 4, 1840, a 17-year-old youngster named Spencer Fullerton Baird overcame his boyish diffidence and wrote the great naturalist, John James Audubon, to inquire about a strange flycatcher he had collected. When the bird proved to be a new species (the yellow-bellied flycatcher, *Empidonax flaviventris*), Audubon, then 60, was so impressed by the ability of his new acquaintance that a firm April-

November friendship developed. This episode marked the first faint glimmering of what Coues (1903) called the "Bairdian Epoch."

Three years later, on July 21, 1843, John G. Bell, a member of Audubon's western exploring party, shot a male and female of a strange sparrow near the junction of the Missouri and Yellowstone rivers. When Audubon (1844) described it, he named the species "Baird's bunting" (*Emberiza bairdii*), in honor of his young friend.

In her biography of her illustrious grandfather, Maria R. Audubon (1897) includes a footnote by Elliott Coues which states: "Special interest attaches to this case; for the bird was not only the first one ever dedicated to Baird, but the last one named, described, and figured by Audubon; and the plate of it completes the series of exactly 500 plates which the octavo edition of the 'Birds of America' contains."

The strange history of Baird's sparrow for the 30 years following its discovery is admirably traced in a monograph by three Winnipeg, Manitoba, field naturalists, Bertram W. Cartwright, Terence M. Shortt, and Robert D. Harris (1937). Their authoritative study of the species is quoted often in this history, beginning with the account of the rediscovery of Baird's bunting:

> Twenty-nine years elapsed before the species was again encountered by ornithologists and when it was re-discovered by Aiken, 11 miles east of Fontaine, El Paso Co., Col., on October 9, 1872, he thought he had a new species. Ridgway shared his views and named the bird *Centronyx ochrocephalus*, the type specimen being No. 162696 in the United States National Museum. It was later shown that the difference between Audubon's *Emberiza bairdii* and Ridgeway's *Centronyx ochrocephalus* was due to seasonal plumage changes. The following year Coues found them breeding abundantly in North Dakota, collected about 75 specimens, secured young birds and made many field observations. Coues supplied the principal museums with specimens for the first time and in the fall of that year, 1873, Henshaw encountered them in great abundance in Arizona and also secured many specimens. We see, then, that following a hiatus of nearly thirty years, in one year—October, 1872, to October, 1873—the breeding range, migration routes, winter quarters, nest and eggs, plumage changes and juvenal plumage were all more or less established.

The above account gives no actual data on the nest and eggs of the species, and credit for the first nesting record goes to Joel Asaph Allen (1874), who found a nest with four eggs at Big Muddy Creek, N. Dak., July 1, 1873.

During its 29-year hiatus, *A. bairdii* may have been out of sight, but it was certainly not out of mind, for at one time or other during that period, ornithologists gave the bird four different generic or subgeneric names. From *Emberiza* the name was changed to *Coturniculus* in 1850, to *Centronyx* in 1858, and to its present name, *Ammodramus*, in 1872. The British naturalist Sharpe referred to it as *Passerculus* in 1888. In 1903 Coues gave the species two vernacular names: "grass sparrow" and "Baird's savannah sparrow."

Significant changes have occurred in the ecology of Baird's sparrow since Elliott Coues (1878) found it in such numbers on the Dakotan prairies in 1873 that "In some particular spots it outnumbered all the other birds together." This plenitude is now but a memory, and the Encyclopedia Americana gives the prime reason: "Few states in the Union have a larger percentage of tillable land than has North Dakota. * * * there are but small areas that are not marvelously fertile." During the 1880's settlers poured into the state, and with the turning of the sod, the species was doomed to severe decimation.

During the following 40 years this decline in numbers continued until Norman A. Wood (1923) reported: "On June 4, 1921, Mr. Elmer Judd and I made a long trip by automobile north from Cando [N. Dak.] to Snyder, Rock, and other small lakes. We were in quest of this species, but it was not until passing many of their old haunts that we at last found a male singing by the roadside near St. Johns [N. Dak.]. From here we drove north to the United States boundary line, and there saw our second bird. These were the only two specimens seen by me in life."

For more recent word, Stanley Saugstad of the Minot, N. Dak., district, writes me in 1962: "I have never known Baird's sparrow to be common in this area. There is very little native sod in my home community. I feel the species is less common than it was 15 or 20 years ago." A letter from Mrs. Robert Gammell of Kenmare, N. Dak., adds: "In our area the birds are confined almost entirely to native prairie and are common in that habitat in the Des Lacs and Lostwood National Wildlife Refuges."

Curiously enough, as the population of Baird's sparrow declined in North Dakota, no general exodus seems to have taken place, either to adjoining states or to the prairie provinces to the north. Regarding this, Gale W. Monson of Arizona writes: "There is no question in my mind that the conversion of vast prairie areas to farmland had a profound effect on the numbers of Baird's sparrows in North Dakota. This accounts, in my opinion, for the decline in numbers of this species found wintering in Arizona after 1880."

With the elimination of North Dakota as an important breeding area, it is necessary to go north of the international boundary to find the greatest density of summering *bairdii*, since, at best, Minnesota, South Dakota, and Montana are but fringe areas for this species. Both Alberta and Manitoba have fair numbers of the bird, and more than half the known nests have been found in these two provinces. Here, in southwestern Manitoba, I always know of communities close by, but distribution is very spotty, as it is in all parts of the province where Baird's sparrow summers.

Saskatchewan has been left till last purposely, as there is now strong evidence that the huge areas of suitable habitat in this province probably support a larger population of this species today than any other territory.  Three veteran field naturalists, J. Dewey Soper of Alberta, and C. Stuart Houston and Manley Callin of Saskatchewan, have between them furnished me with a list of over 150 areas in this province where they have found Baird's sparrow.

Manley Callin writes me: "My own observations lead me to believe that Baird's sparrow is not nearly so restricted in distribution in Saskatchewan as has been indicated.  I am inclined to speculate that almost every organized municipality (there are 296 of these) contains some suitable habitat, and that in any specified year, at least half of these and possibly a much higher number are hosts to Baird's sparrows, ranging from a few to a considerable number."

There remains one other ecological change to discuss: Cartwright et al. (1937) thought this was one of the species that would not conform to changing conditions, that it was one of the irreconcilables, but W. Earl Godfrey (1953) gives wheat fields as the habitat of Baird's sparrow at Swan River, Manitoba, in 1937.  Angus H. Shortt of Winnipeg, a member of the field party that gathered these data, writes me: "It was a very dry summer in the Swan River valley, and the wheat fields in question were extremely poor, thin, and with growth not over a foot in height.  I was quite surprised to find the sparrows in this type of habitat, but they definitely seemed established.  There was an adjoining area of upland grass similar to the territory occupied by this species at Deer Lodge, Manitoba, but for some reason the birds preferred the wheat field."

A letter from Manley Callin mentions that he noted several males singing from a wheat field near Moosomin, Saskatchewan, July 16, 1945.  More recently, Margaret Belcher (1961) states that "their breeding habitat in the Regina plains is apparently not restricted to native prairie grasslands.  * * * on July 31, 1960, driving through farmlands north of Rowatt [Saskatchewan] we heard Baird's sparrows singing in weedy grainfields on either side of the road.  At least six separate songs were heard, presumably from birds in separate territories."  In none of these instances were nests located, and Baird's sparrow seldom nests in such terrain unless there is also a great tangle of growth present at ground level.

In July 1965 I found a nest in a field that had been plowed and sown to brome grass (*Bromus inermus*) about 10 years earlier. Because the soil was light and sandy, the annual crop of brome gradually thinned out, and the field had not been harvested for several years.  This allowed a ground cover similar to native prairie

growth to develop, and the hen Baird's sparrow made an excellent
job of hiding her nest in it.

*Spring.*—When spring comes to the midwest grasslands and the
warming world awakes to the joyous minstrelsy of the swarms of
newly returned prairie birds, aerial displays usually form an important
part of courtship activities.    Male prairie horned larks, chestnut-
collared longspurs, western meadowlarks, bobolinks, and Sprague's
pipits all advertise their presence with ecstatic song flights.    These
aerial rhapsodies begin almost as soon as the birds reach the breeding
grounds, and usually last until the nestlings need feeding.    But no
such courting flights aid those who seek the ground-dwelling sparrows.
They who set out, in early May, to learn whether or not Baird's
sparrow has returned do not *look* for the little bird—they *listen* for him.
He may not be there that day, or the next day either, and if any significant change has taken place in his habitat, he will not be there that
May, or that year.

This is a neat little bird, with a prim little bib of radial lines on its
upper breast, buffy patches on its cheek and neck, and an ochraceous
stripe running through its crown.    But identification is difficult, for
none of these marks is clearly definable at any distance.

Though a few winter in the grasslands of Arizona and New Mexico,
and in the counties of El Paso and Midland, Tex., most of these little
finches start their spring migration from the Mexican states of Sonora
(northern), Durango, and Coahuila.

The northward movement begins in late February and lasts a
little more than 2 months.    Mrs. Harold Williams of Midland,
Tex., writes me that the birds may leave El Paso and Midland counties any time from April 9 to April 28.    Richard R. and J. Graber
(1954) took a specimen in Oklahoma on Apr. 23, 1953.    William
Youngworth writes from Sioux City, Iowa, that Kansas, Nebraska,
and South Dakota are all in the migration path, and sends me Harold
Turner's dates for Nebraska as follows: "Arrival, May 4, 1952; May
3, 1953; April 15, 1958; April 12, 1959; May 5, 1960; April 14, 1962."
These dates show that the leading front of the migration wave may
vary from year to year by almost a month.

Few Baird's sparrows are detected in migration because they are
so inconspicuous.    As with many other species of grass-inhabiting
sparrows, they seldom travel in flocks, but usually in small groups, or
even as single individuals, and arrive at their summer home without
fanfare, unheralded, and often unnoticed.    Mrs. Robert Gammell of
Kenmare, N. Dak., writes me: "Birds just appear on the breeding
grounds."

A letter from Clifford V. Davis of Bozeman, Mont., gives late
April or early May as the average arrival time for that state.    Orin

A. Stevens writes from Fargo, N. Dak., that data Perna M. Stine kept from 1929 to 1944 show the average return date for the Minot, N. Dak., area to be May 10.

For the Regina, Saskatchewan, district, Belcher (1961) states: "Usual spring arrival, second week in May; earliest arrival, May 10 (Lahrman)." Cartwright et al. (1937) include a table that shows an average spring arrival date in Manitoba of May 11 and for Alberta, May 10. Stuart Criddle reports the earliest arrival for Manitoba as Apr. 21, 1942. The only other April date for Canada is shown in the Cartwright et al. (1937) table: Apr. 28, 1922, at Belmont, Manitoba, as reported by J. C. Wilson.

*Territory.*—The males arrive first on the summering grounds and immediately establish their territories. I have watched these early arrivals as they disputed possession of a certain breeding area. Rival males leap up from the concealing grass like jack-in-the-boxes, face to face, wings pumping rapidly and claws raking wildly. In a moment they drop back to ground cover again, rest a few seconds, and leap into view once more. Finally one bird flees, the other pursues it a short distance and returns to his domain. Neither bird utters a sound during these contests.

Such struggles persist only for a few days, and soon each male is undisputed master of a sizeable piece of real estate, usually between 1 and 2 acres in extent. With the division of property settled, each male's next action is to select several strategic singing perches within it. These may include a tuft of grass or weeds, a low bush, a post, a strand of fence wire, a boulder, and often he will sing from the ground. But from wherever he sings, the first time he throws back his head and tinkles his silvery little bell-song, he discards the cloak of anonymity that has concealed his identity since he fell silent the previous fall.

*Courtship.*—Cartwright et al. (1937) make the following observations on the courting activities of Baird's sparrow:

One of us (T.M.S.) witnessed the real mating performance * * * on June 3, 1930. A male was observed acting strangely on a patch of matted straw. It was walking slowly along with head drawn in and tail slightly fanned; it vibrated first one and then the other wing rapidly over its back, resembling greatly the wing flutterings of a young bird about to be fed. It never vibrated both wings at once. It bobbed its head to near the ground several times but made no sound during the performance. When it flew its wingbeats were abnormally fast and fluttering. It hardly seemed able to contain itself and had no sooner alighted on another patch before it recommenced the display.

Further examples of courtship performances were observed by one of us (R.H.D.) on June 27, 1931. Two singing males, whose territories adjoined, were frequently observed to invade each other's territory. A tussle then ensued and the invader was then driven back to its own domain. They would sometimes pursue each other about erratically, often alighting, and sometimes fighting. The bird occupying the territory to the north of the other was found to be uttering a curious, soft, complaining whine, "*Meeerr, meeerr, meeerr, meeerr, meeerr,*" and so on. It was uttered either when the bird was on a bush, on the ground, or in low flight over the ground. The note was usually accompanied by wing flutterings when the bird was settled and by abnormally fast wing beats when in flight. Neither of these birds was seen on June 20. After three hours' watching on June 27, a female was seen. Pursued by both males, she flew from the territory of the southern male to that of the northern male. Near the boundary of the two she dropped into the grass, followed by both males. The southern male now returned to his own territory, however, while the other one followed the female as she flew into a patch of mixed wolfberry and silver willow. The female could not be found there. She was seen sometime later, however, again near the boundary of the two territories. Both males came to her and fought for a brief time and then dispersed.

*Nesting.*—Between 1873 and 1930 no more than 21 authenticated nests of this species were reported, 2 each from Minnesota and Montana, the rest from North Dakota and Alberta. Another nest was found in Alberta in 1931, and between 1930 and 1934 Cartwright, Shortt, and Harris (1937) found 15 nests in Manitoba. All but one of these were in two communities of Baird's sparrows that had settled near the city of Winnipeg, perhaps in 1928. No major changes took place in these habitats during that time, and the birds returned each year to at least one of the areas.

Environmental disturbances caused by plowing, burning, brushing, or mowing and raking always result in Baird's sparrow quietly abandoning an area. Nor can it prosper on close-cropped pastureland, and the introduction of grazing animals into a field usually causes the species to desert it. Mrs. Robert Gammell writes me from Kenmare, N. Dak.: "One of our favorite chestnut-collared longspur spots for many years was an over-grazed pasture, an area of about 160 acres west of Kenmare. In 1960 there were no cattle in the field and the grass grew up. Immediately a number of Sprague's pipits and Baird's sparrows joined the longspurs there."

The impression still lingers that these sparrows prefer to nest in damp areas. Audubon (1844) found them hiding in the long grass of wetlands, and Taverner (1919) believed the absence of the species at Shoal Lake, Manitoba, in 1918–19, was due to "the lowering of the lake level and the disappearance of the broad marshes." The opposite view is expressed by Gale Monson, who writes me: "My impression, based on my experiences in both North Dakota and Arizona, is that the density of *bairdii* varies markedly from year to year on both the breeding and wintering grounds. In the damper parts of its breeding range, it is probably more plentiful in dry years, while in the drier parts of the range it is more numerous in wet years."

Monson's findings are supported by W. Ray Salt and A. L. Wilk (1958): "Grassy slough bottoms and alkali flats are favorite haunts in dry years but after a rainy cycle such places become too damp for Baird's sparrow and the species may disappear from a locality which it has occupied for several years."

My observations in Manitoba suggest that Baird's sparrow likes to keep its feet dry and thus prefers well-drained terrain. A field of tangled grass, both old and new growth, mixed with various species of native plants, and with patches of western snowberry, wolfwillow, rose, or low willow perhaps present in the area, is a favorite habitat. This terrain may be close to wetlands, or it may be quite a long way from them. The main concentration near my own city of Brandon, Manitoba, is more than 2 miles from the river, the nearest water.

In selecting her nest site, the female Baird's sparrow prefers longer grass than do some of her neighbors, such as the prairie horned lark, the chestnut-collared longspur, and sometimes the Sprague's pipit. For her home she chooses a tangle of grass interspersed with prairie plants within the ample territory her mate has established. The pair may have the whole field to themselves, but more often a few pairs nest fairly close to one another, forming a small community.

Occasionally, one or more singing males will appear in an area late in July, and it appears that they and their mates are the overflow from a community where there was not enough room for all. Such a situation is described by Cartwright et al. (1937), who also furnish the following on nest types:

The situation of Baird's sparrows' nests varies somewhat but is limited in the one respect of being always placed upon the ground amongst the grass. For convenience of description they can be divided into three general types, although it must be borne in mind that this is an arbitrary classification and that the distinguishing characters may not be strictly adhered to from nest to nest.

First comes the type where the nest is placed in a tuft of grass which is usually held up by a wolfberry or other kind of shrub. The tuft is hollowed out, a floor of grass is added, and the sides are then built up with grass woven in and out sometimes to a height of five inches. In another type, the location is chosen beneath an overhanging often horizontal tuft of dead grass, leaving only a small entrance hole at the side. Frequently there is a slight depression underneath the tuft, but if none exists, a shallow one is made by the bird. In the third type, which seems to be the most common, the nest has no overhead concealment. Nests of this type are quite often situated in cavities—generally hoof marks—that in some cases are so deep as to place the nest two or three inches below ground level. If such a cavity is not utilized, however, a shallow excavation is made so that the nest is sunken to the level of the surrounding recumbent dead grass.

Differences in structure are only slight and depend largely upon the type of situation. In the first and second types the floor is composed of short lengths of dead grass laid down to form a sort of thick mat. This is surmounted by a rim of interwoven grass which varies in height, being high in the first case and low in the second. The entrance in the first type is fairly high up in the tuft, where the side is gradually pressed down by the birds in alighting and departing. In the second type the entrance is at ground level, is small, and is usually the only position from which the interior can be viewed. In the third case, if the nest is sunken in the ground, it is then a more substantial affair, being a bulky, well-woven, cup-like structure.

The average inside dimensions of a nest are: diameter, 2.5 inches; depth, 1.5 inches.

The variety of materials found in the nests is very limited. Dead grass is used almost exclusively, the lining often being of finer strands than the rest. P. B. Peabody in North Dakota and Minnesota, and A. Dawes DuBois in Montana have found that weed stems were sometimes used. No similar observation has been made in our studies. In one nest we have seen bits of a moss that grew sparsely in the vicinity. In the lining of two nests a few strands of horse hair were noticed. Another material often favored where it could be obtained was the red setae of moss, greatly resembling hair and possibly used for the same reason.

The life of the nest is very short, lasting only about three or four weeks. During the course of nesting it suffers greatly from the trampling of both parents and young. Moreover, when the young birds leave, it has been observed by us that the sides are broken down and the material of the nest strewn about so that traces of its existence are obliterated. This must necessarily be done by the parent birds.

The birds are exceedingly close sitters, even on fresh eggs, and will not flush until one is on top of them. One female (on fresh eggs) would even allow a light rope to be dragged over her without flushing. In consequence, the nest is extremely difficult to find. The fact that of the thirty-five nests which are recorded * * *, fifteen of them are ours, the balance being practically all the nests of this species which have been discovered in fifty-eight years, will tell the story of countless hours of searching much more graphically than any words.

There seems to be little variation in nesting habit or situation in any part of the breeding range.

I believe this species delays its nesting activities till late in June because the tough prairie sod is slower to grow the necessary cover. This late start also reduces the probability of a second brood. Normally both parents are caring for their offspring until the end of July, after which a second nesting would not be feasible.

Cartwright et al. (1937) give no nesting records for Saskatchewan, but at least three nests have been found there. The first is recorded by W. E. Clyde Todd (1947) from the Last Mountain Lake area: "Dr. Sutton found a nest here on June 23, [1932]; it held four eggs which closely resemble those of the grasshopper sparrow." Fred G. Bard, of the Saskatchewan Museum of Natural History, collected the second nest with five eggs near Hatfield, Saskatchewan, June 28, 1933. The third, also with five eggs, was found by Manley Callin just east of Percival, Saskatchewan, June 24, 1934. Bearing in mind the vast areas of this province where Baird's sparrow occurs, it probably nests more plentifully here than in all the rest of the breeding range. Once the field naturalists of Saskatchewan become more familiar with it and its habits, they should find many more nests to study.

Much has been said of the long searches necessary to the finding of nests of this species. To point up this fact, an organized search of one 350-acre field which harbored at least 30 singing males during the first three weeks of July 1962, yielded only two nests of Baird's sparrow. Over 100 man-hours of intensive search were spent in this hunt, during which 15 active nests of other species of ground-nesting birds were found, despite the lateness of the season. One nest in 1962 had a life history of just over one month—from a nest-scrape made June 18, until the fledglings left the nest, July 21.

*Eggs.*—Oliver Davie (1898) states: "The eggs are laid in June and July and they range from three to five in number * * *." But Cartwright et al. (1937) found the numbers varied from three to six in the 15 nests they studied, with five eggs the average. They write:

The ground color of the eggs is white, rarely showing a faint tinge of bluish. Reddish-brown spots and blotches showing a decided tendency to form a wreath about the larger end are the commonest markings. Occasionally there are small black spots and lilac or lavender markings, the latter being probably due to the obscuring of reddish-brown pigment by shell layers. The eggs are not easily distinguished from those of the savannah sparrow, which are variable both in ground color and markings, nor from those of the vesper sparrow, which they closely resemble. They are larger than the savannah sparrow's and smaller than the vesper sparrow's as a rule.

Seven of the eight nests I found between 1960 and 1965 contained four eggs as a full set; the eighth held five. The eggs of the first two sets I found in 1962 were wreathed about the larger end; those in the later nests were spotted more irregularly.

W. G. F. Harris writes: "The usual set for the Baird's sparrow consist of three to five eggs. They are ovate and have only a very slight gloss. The ground is grayish white, but this is frequently obscured by the numerous spots, blotches and speckles of 'auburn,' 'hazel,' 'chestnut brown,' or 'russet,' which often cover the entire egg. Underlying spots of 'light Quaker drab' are discernible on many eggs, especially on those which have less brown markings. Occasionally, an egg will have a few spots of black. In many of the sets I have examined, the spots and markings seem to be somewhat dull or clouded. The measurements of 50 eggs average 19.4 by 14.6 millimeters; the eggs showing the four extremes measure *21.8* by 15.2, 20.3 by *16.3, 16.4* by 12.6, and 17.5 by *12.5* millimeters."

*Incubation.*—Cartwright et al. (1937) made the following observations on incubation:

As mentioned in Table III, the duration of incubation has been found in one instance to be eleven days. No other observations on this point are known to exist. Incubation is performed entirely by the female, which leaves the eggs only for brief periods, at nearly all times returning secretively by mousing away through the grass. She is rarely seen during incubation except at the nest.

Eggs, especially large sets, usually lie in the nest in a definite arrangement. A set of six eggs lying in two rows of three each was several times shifted out of that position, and just as frequently it was returned by the bird to its original order.

During the first incubation period, the male passes the time in the vicinity of the nest, singing and feeding. Neither his voice nor his actions give any indication of the location of the nest, and even when it is in immediate danger of discovery his manner does not change.

I made one incubation check on a nest in 1962; the period between the laying and the hatching of the last egg of the clutch was between 11 and 12 days.

*Young.*—Cartwright et al. (1937) describe the nestling as follows:

Newly hatched young of Baird's sparrow are clothed with pale smoky-grey down, this being longest and densest on the head (capital tract). Down also shows along the spinal, humeral, alar (between the elbow and wrist) and femoral tracts. By way of contrast, the down of the savannah sparrow is dull mouse-grey while that of the chestnut-collared longspur is whitish-grey to buffy-grey.

The skin is reddish-flesh color, translucent (paler and less orange than the young savannah sparrow of the same age). The young are blind for the first three days of their lives but the eyelids begin to open on the third day in the case of the strongest and most vigorous of a nestful. Development is rapid, the remiges growing more quickly than any other feathers until about the time the young are ready to leave the nest, when general feather growth appears to be retarded except the scapulars which continue to develop steadily.

* * * Iris—rich dark brown; bill—pinkish-grey suffused along the culmen with brownish which intensifies as the young become older; lower mandible pale pink; tarsi, feet and claws—pale pink, translucent.

* * * For the first day or two they lie prone in the nest with the head turned back toward the body. They are so weak that they can raise their heads to receive food only with difficulty. For two days after hatching the female broods occasionally in the daytime, for a period of about three minutes each time. During the night she appears to cover the young every night until they leave. On the fourth day the young birds begin to utter a faint peeping noise. By the fifth day they have acquired sufficient strength to stand up in the nest when being fed. On this date they begin to use a "taepe" note as a food call.

Young Baird's sparrows depart from the nest on their eighth to tenth day. By then they are well feathered, wide awake, and active, although incapable of flight. They usually leave together, the struggling of the first bird being a sufficient stimulus to urge them all to action. They crawl rapidly away and hide in the grass, where they are lost to view for the next few days.

By about the thirteenth day of their lives they are able to fly for a few yards. One bird at this stage was found lying in a small cup-like hollow almost like a nest. When they are about nineteen days old they have developed to the point where they begin to wander away from their parents' territory. At this time they begin to utter a thin "seeep" which appears to be a flocking note.

My observations show that the mother cares for the hatchlings alone for the first several days. She feeds them, broods them, and removes and eats all excreta. Then her mate usually comes to her aid. At a nest I found in 1965 the father had only one eye. Despite this handicap he proved a model spouse and did his full share of feeding and brooding the young and cleaning the nest. Daytime brooding ceases on the fifth day after hatching.

After the young leave the nest, both parents continue to carry food to them. Though the flightless young never travel more than a few yards from the nest area, for the first day or two the parents seem to have difficulty locating them, and hover on threshing wings until a *tip!* call from a youngster guides them to earth.

*Plumage.*—Cartwright et al. (1937) give the following description of the juvenal plumage:

Loral region and forehead black sparsely tipped with buff; crown black tipped with buff, more buffy in the center, showing an indistinct median line; superciliary line buff; auriculars buff tipped with black; malar region buff, nape and hindneck black edged with buff; back black edged with pale buff, giving a scaly appearance; rump black edged with ochraceous-buff; upper tail coverts and rectrices the same; scapulars black edged with buff, paler at the tips; primary and secondary coverts greyish-black; throat and upper breast black widely edged with buff, the same pattern continuing along the sides; belly white tinged with buff, paler toward the vent; undertail coverts white; crural tracts whitish with black centers. The general coloration of the juvenal is ochraceous buff about the head, a mixture of blackish and ochreish on the back giving a scaly appearance. The colors are more intense than any plumage of the adult and the breast and side markings are heavier.

A thesis by R. R. Graber (1955) compares the juvenal plumages of *Ammodramus* as follows:

The two species of this genus, *savannarum* and *bairdi* are very much more alike as juvenals than as adults. Adult *bairdi* bears a striking resemblance to the savannah sparrow, *Passerculus sandwichensis*, and Ridgway (1901) placed the species in a montypic genus, *Centronyx*, between *Passerculus* and *Coturniculus* (= *Ammodramus*), stating that it was much closer to the latter. He did not mention the juvenal plumage in his discussion of the relationship of the three forms, but the characters of the juvenal support his view that *bairdi* and *savannarum* are close. Certain patterns are common not to juvenal or adult *savannarum* but to juvenal *savannarum* and adult and juvenal *bairdi*. I refer particularly to markings on the chin and side of the head and the conspicuous ventral streaking. Juvenals of both species have a scaled back-pattern. This pattern appears to be an adaptive feature in prairie birds, but juvenal *Passerculus* does not have it, despite the fact that *Passerculus* and *Ammodramus* are prairie associates in the many areas throughout which their ranges overlap.

A striking feature of the juvenal plumage in *Ammodramus* is its firm texture. In this respect, the plumage is like that of the adult. This is particularly true of *bairdi*, in which the juvenal plumage appears to be long-lived. The occurrence of juvenal specimens and worn adults in Arizona has led to speculation concerning a discrete southern breeding range. Among the many *bairdi* records listed by Cartwright, Shortt and Harris (1937) were several southern records of juvenals. In every case these were late August or September records. I have seen three such specimens, worn birds in the early stages of the postjuvenal molt. Such specimens are not reliable evidence of breeding, though stub-tailed juvenals would be. The number of records of juvenals south of the known breeding range of *bairdi* indicates that this species migrates often, and probably regularly, in juvenal plumage. This is also true of Leconte's sparrow, *Ammospiza lecontei*, though the two species are not particularly closely related. *Ammodramus savannarum* appears to complete its molt before migrating, but this is difficult to prove. Because of the much broader range of *savannarum*, migration of juvenals in this species can be proved only through banding.

In both species of *Ammodramus* there is a precocious development of winter plumage in the scapular region of the upper back, but the bulk of the juvenal plumage is retained until well after the first flight feathers are grown. Sutton (1935, 1937) discussed the development of the juvenal plumage and the early stages of the postjuvenal molt in *savannarum*. Dwight (1900) described the molt of this species as complete, and mentioned a partial prenuptial molt (spring) involving mainly feathers of the head and anterior portions of the body. There is a similar spring molt in *A. bairdi*, as indicated by the only adult specimen at hand, but I have found no published data on the molts of this species.

The nearest ally of *Ammodramus* is probably *Passerherbulus henslowi*. The three species are similar in habitat, and all have a scaled back pattern in juvenal plumage. Their molts are similar, so far as I know. The underparts of juvenal *Passerherbulus* are immaculate, of juvenal *Ammodramus*, streaked.

T. M. Shortt (1951) compares the juvenal plumage with that of 2 other species:

A circumstance that struck me forcibly while collecting specimens of juvenile birds in the prairie region of Manitoba was the similarity in juvenal plumage of three species of birds, representing two families, that were closely associated on the nesting grounds. I refer to Sprague's pipit, *Anthus spragueii*, Baird's sparrow, *Ammodramus bairdii*, and chestnut-collared longspur, *Calcarius ornatus*, all of which have a "scaled" pattern on the dorsal area. This was considered somewhat remarkable, especially since the "scaled" juvenal plumage is not common among the Fringillidae and since another species of *Calcarius* (*C. lapponicus*) has the dorsal surface streaked.

The implication seemed to be that there may be some survival value in a "scaled" dorsal plumage for prairie-nesting passerine birds, though why it should be more advantageous than a streaked plumage is not obvious.

T. S. Roberts (1932) gives the following description of the adult plumage:

Top of head and nape a rich, strong buff or brownish-yellow, striped with black, especially on sides of crown and nape; sides of head and neck pale buff, more or less flecked with black; a narrow line of black spots on side of throat; feathers of back dull black centrally, margined with grayish-white or pale buff, producing a streaked appearance; rump lighter, more buffy; underparts white or pale buff on throat and breast; streaked on sides, flanks, and across breast with black, the streaks on breast sharply defined and forming a necklace, those on sides more diffuse and tinged with rufous; wing feathers greyish-brown, the coverts darker centrally, all edged with pale rufous; 2 not very distinct wing-bars; tail dull brown or blackish, the outer feather on each side narrrowly edged with white outer web and pale, dull white terminally, suggesting a white outer tail-feather when seen by transmitted light; the other feathers narrowly tipped with dull white or buffy, bill light flesh color, darker at tip; legs flesh color, feet darker; iris brown. * * * The middle pair of tail-feathers is much narrower and more pointed than the others.

Two female adults, taken at Gardner Wash, Ariz., by R. Johnson and P. J. Gould, Feb. 6, 1960, weighed 17.0 grams and 17.8 grams respectively. Six males taken by a field party from the University of Minnesota in Clay County, Minn., in July 1961, had an average weight of 18.6 grams, an average length of 135.6 millimeters, and an average wingspread of 236.3 millimeters.

*Food.*—The food of this species varies with the seasons. During their winter sojourn in Mexico, weed seeds must form the main diet, as they do in Texas. Mrs. Harold L. Williams writes me from Midland, Tex.: "They are usually seen feeding on the ground in fields of maize stubble. 'Maize,' or 'milo,' in Texas refers to the several varieties of grain sorghum grown as food for cattle. Baird's sparrows have also been seen in patches of tall 'careless weeds,' (*Amaranthus* sp.)."

When Richard and Jean Graber encountered Baird's migrants near Norman, Okla., in April 1953, some of the common plants in the field where the birds occurred were: red three-awn (*Aristida*), little blue-stem (*Andropogon scoparius*), brome (*Bromus*), six weeks' fescue (*Festuca octoflora*), yellow sweet clover (*Melilotus officinalis*), perennial ragweed (*Ambrosia psilostachya*), plantain (*Plantago virginica*), blazing-star (*Liatris*), and evening primrose (*Oenothera laciniata*).

Stuart Criddle writes me that: "The food of our Manitoban sparrows changes sharply with the seasons. In the spring and fall a great variety of seeds are eaten. These include: "Lamb's quarters (*Chenopodium album*), Russian pigweed (*Axyris amaranthoides*), Russian thistle (*Salsola kali*), redroot pigweed (*Amaranthus retroflexus*), false flax (*Camelina microcarpa*), tumbling mustard (*Sisymbrium altissimum*), and green foxtail (*Seraris viridis*). This last-named plant probably produces more food for the sparrows, longspurs, and horned larks than any other weed."

In summer, adult Baird's sparrows take spiders and numerous varieties of insects and their larvae, and Cartwright et al. (1937) show that these are the only food they give the young. Part of their account follows:

Our astonishment was great when we found young birds but two days old being fed with unmodified grasshoppers. * * * Later, specimens of the grasshoppers present in the area were collected and submitted to Mr. Norman Criddle, together with a moth and a cricket which were occasionally fed to the young. We are indebted to Mr. Criddle for the following identifications: *Orthoptera: Chorthippus curtipennis* Harr; *Camnula pellucida* Scud; *Arphia pseudoneitana* Thoms; *Melanoplus dawsoni* Scud; *Melanoplus bivittatus* Say; *Gryllus assimilis* Fab; *Lepidoptera: Caenurgia erechtea* Cram.

Mr. Criddle points out that *C. pellucida* and *M. bivittatus* are pests of economic importance.

It is of interest to note that, while the young are fed almost entirely on large grasshoppers, the food of adults in summer consists mainly of smaller insects. The examination of the stomachs of four adults reveals only one small grasshopper nymph, but many small items such as leaf-hoppers, spiders, moths and small seeds are present. It would seem that the adult, in searching for food for the young, consumes all the small insects it comes across which are not worthy of a trip back to the young. Thus the "by-products" of its search for food for the young are, in effect, a natural economy during the period when the demands on the adult are great.

The foregoing data were gathered during the early 1930's, when severe drought conditions probably curtailed the varieties of food available, but in 1962, small green caterpillars formed the whole diet for the first 5 days of the fledglings' life, and even after the parents began bringing small grasshoppers to the nest on the sixth day, caterpillars and moths still formed a large part of the daily food.

*Behavior.*—The outstanding behavior characteristic of Baird's bunting was noted the day the species was found. Audubon (1844) wrote: "Several times Mr. Bell nearly trod on some of them, before the birds would take to wing, and they almost instantaneously re-alighted within a few steps, and then ran like mice through the grass."

This reluctance to fly is typical of the bird at all seasons. Allan R. Phillips of Arizona, reporting data on four wintering specimens of Baird's sparrows taken in Mexico, Arizona, and New Mexico, writes me: "All of these were lone birds, running mouselike in open grassland."

On the summer territory the male spends the incubation period patroling his home grounds, singing, feeding, and generally enjoying the good life. The appearance of a hunting harrier hawk or short-eared owl will cause him to lapse into silence and prudently take cover in the ground vegetation. Sometimes, when the tinkle-bells are silent, the entrance of humans into a field will immediately result in the males resuming their singing, almost as though the birds wanted to warn the intruders they were violating private property.

The Baird's sparrow has an equable disposition and gets along well with his neighbors. Only once have I seen one act aggressively toward another species. While perched on a fence post singing to his hidden mate, a Baird's male suddenly broke off to pursue a clay-colored sparrow that had alighted on a strand of fence wire close by. He returned shortly and spent five minutes preening his ruffled feathers and regaining his composure. Then he resumed the serenade, his throat pulsing and body quivering from the effort.

On rare occasions a male Baird's sparrow will leave an elevation and coast to the ground, singing as he goes, and continue the serenade from his new position.

He appears to be rather tardy in aiding his mate in the important chore of providing food for the nestlings, for I have heard him still singing his regular matins and vespers several days after the young appeared. However, the sangfroid with which he views the efforts of searchers to find the nest disappears after the young are several days old, and he will then join his mate in their defense. This is corroborated by Gordon Smith, of Winnipeg, Manitoba, who noted at a nest observed July 22, 1961: "Nest holding three fledged young found in grass 8–12 inches high. Both adults present, chipping excitedly."

While brooding the young in hot weather, the parent may start to pant and then lift the back feathers away from the body, apparently to cool itself, starting with the tail coverts and progressing up the back to the nape and crown. This gives the head a spectacular crested appearance, in sharp contrast to the usual low profile. After a few moments the bird settles the feathers into place again by reversing the action, the crown first resuming its normal outline.

*Voice.*—Audubon and his companions, on first hearing the notes of this little bunting, thought they were produced by marsh wrens, and Coues (1873) compared the song to that of the Savannah sparrow. In a later volume he (1903) wrote: "Song peculiar, of two or three tinkling syllables and a trill, like 'zip-zip-zip-zr-r-r-r'."

Actually, of all the so-called "grass sparrows," Baird's sparrow has, to my ears, by far the most pleasing song—much superior to the sibilant gasp of the grasshopper sparrow, to the nearly inaudible hiss of Le Conte's sparrow, to the broken sigh of the Savannah sparrow, or to the guttural ejaculation of Nelson's sharp-tailed sparrow, and infinitely preferable to the hiccups Henslow's sparrow uses for a song. Though neither loud nor impressive, the refrain is still a pleasant combination of opening notes and ending trill.

The song is in two distinct parts, each of which may vary somewhat in duration and composition between individual birds, and no two listeners hear it exactly alike. Though each male has his own idea of just how the song should be given, the "normal" presentation is three or four opening notes followed by a trill of five or six "beats," thus: *Dee-dee-dee l-l-l-l-l*. The last part of the song, the trill, is a half to a full tone lower in pitch.

The first part of the melody, a repetition of the one note, has a breathless, tinkly timbre. The second part is a pulsing trill, almost a warble, and it has a clear, sweet quality that makes it thoroughly entrancing. There is no perceptible break between the two sections of the refrain, other than a connecting half-note, and the entire outpouring is one entity, despite the sudden lowering in pitch. Under favorable conditions the song can be heard 250 yards away, with the ending trill carrying even farther.

When a male has fallen into a pattern of territorial song, he gives his refrain six to eight times a minute. Morning and evening find him in best voice. At other times, his singing is spasmodic and he will often lapse into a silence for an hour or more, unless disturbed.

The female does not sing, but gives a high *chip* and sometimes a low, crooning *tr-r-i-p* note when danger threatens her young. The male's similar note is much deeper. The low, murmuring, *Meeerr-meeerr* sound noted by Cartwright et al. (1937) is apparently an expression of endearment. It may be uttered during copulation, though this has never been proved. Both parents utter it when approaching the nest after the young begin to call for food on their sixth day of life. The nestlings soon give voice to a stronger *tip* note, and when one was lifted from the nest on the eighth day of life, it gave a loud, squalling cry. The species has the usual chipping flock call in migration.

I have noted earlier that familiarity with the song of the Baird's sparrow is the best means of locating the bird in the field. Two recently issued song recordings, "Finches," by Donald J. Borror and William W. H. Gunn (1960), and "Prairie Spring," by W. W. H. Gunn (1962), include excellent reproductions of the variable melodies of the species. Such recordings will prove of great aid to all who wish to become acquainted with this lovely little finch.

*Field marks.*—*A. bairdii* strongly resembles *A. savannarum* and other closely allied genera. Allan R. Phillips tells me by letter that: "In Mexico I once chased a remarkably pale, buffy sparrow for a long time, in September, sure that it was a Leconte's, Baird's, or some other rarity. I finally got it, and it proved to be just a washed-out, freakish Savannah!"

In my experience, the ocherish patches on Baird's sparrow's head and neck are not apparent, even through good glasses, unless the bird is at close range. At greater distances a back view shows a slim, dark bird, and when it turns to face the observer, the shining, grey front resembles that of a pale Savannah sparrow, which as a general rule looks much darker.

Like the grasshopper sparrow, the other member of the genus, Baird's sparrow has a flat-headed silhouette which aids in identification. The low, hurried flight across the grass and sudden pitch to earth is another good mark, though not an infallible one.

Since the sitting hen is invariably flushed from the nest at very close range, it is often possible to note the pale-yellow margin on the two outer tail feathers.

*Enemies.*—Among the dangers confronting the prairie-dwelling species of birds, fire and the plow are the most serious, and the effects of the plow are even more profound and lasting than those of an all-consuming fire. Land eventually recovers from a scourge of flame, but that once turned by the plow is usually lost forever to ground-nesting birds.

Among the mammals, the larger animals such as horses and cattle occasionally trample a nest, but losses from this are negligible.  The smaller animals are the most deadly, and Stuart Criddle writes me that "The mammals known to prey on our ground-dwelling birds can be placed in the following order, the smallest first-named: Baird's white-footed mouse (*Peromyscus maniculatus bairdii*), Drummond's vole (*Microtus pennsylvanicus drummondii*), thirteen-lined ground squirrel (*Citellus t. tridecemlineatus*), short-tailed ermine (*Mustela erminea bangsi*), prairie long-tailed weasel (*Mustela frenata longicauda*), least weasel (*Mustela r. rixosa*), northern plains skunk (*Mephitis mephitis hudsonica*), plains coyote (*Canis l. latrans*)."

Of the above list, the three rodents are frequent raiders of grassland nests, but are often content with just one or two of a brood. However, when raiding nests in tufts of grass above ground level, both voles and white-footed mice often drill holes in the bottom of the nest that allow all the contents to tumble through to their doom. The weasels and largers predators are never satisfied with less than the entire contents of the nest.

Concerning the effect of raptors on the ground birds, Stuart Criddle's letter continues: "While most of our hawks in Manitoba take a few prairie birds, the marsh hawk is the most persistent hunter and captures more young sparrows and other small birds than all the other hawks together.  I have often watched a harrier chase a sparrow, knock it down with a sharp blow of a wing, then turn like a flash and pounce on the half-stunned bird before it could recover and fly again."

James A Munro (1929), reporting on the nest of a marsh hawk, writes: "A beheaded juvenile Baird's sparrow in nestling plumage was the only food at her nest."  Glen A. Fox writes from Saskatchewan that: "I checked an active nest of Richardson's merlin, July 9, 1961.  Thirteen tarsi were removed from the nest, and Donald R. Baldwin of the Royal Ontario Museum of Zoology identified one as that of an immature Baird's sparrow."

*A. bairdii* is fortunate in one respect: nesting as it does in wide, open grasslands, it shares with several neighboring species almost complete immunity from the visits of that parasite, the brown-headed cowbird.  This bird prefers to lay in nests located in brush or tree growth, and I have never found the nest of a prairie horned lark, a Sprague's pipit, or a chestnut-collared longspur victimized by it.  The western meadowlark is usually exempt also, and not until 1962 did I find a nest of this species that had been visited by *Molothrus ater*, two of the six eggs being strangers.  This nest was within a few feet of fairly heavy bush growth, which probably afforded the hen cowbird the opportunity she seldom misses when a nest is near such cover.

Cartwright et al. (1937) report two cases of Baird's sparrow being victimized by the brown-headed cowbird. The first was reported by Roberts (*in* litt.) from North Dakota June 18, 1883. The second was a nest R. D. Harris found at Winnipeg, Manitoba, July 7, 1931 with three Baird's sparrow eggs; the following day a cowbird egg had been added to the clutch, which Harris removed. In addition to citing these two records, H. Friedmann (1963) lists two parasitized *bairdii* nests collected by L. B. Bishop in North Dakota, and two others without definite locality data. In writing me of these he comments: "the fact remains that Baird's sparrow has been recorded but seldom as a host of the cowbird."

*Fall.*—As summer wanes, the tinkle-bell pealings of the males gradually fade away and Baird's sparrow once more assumes its will-o'-the-wisp character. This lapse into silence usually coincides with the appearance of the fledged young.

Where the hatch is late, the young may not be on the wing until mid-August. When leaving their birthplace they are usually accompanied by their parents. They wander about the countryside in little family groups while the juvenile wings strengthen for the fall migration. As dates of latest sightings on the summer range vary from mid-September to late October, the autumn leave-taking extends over a 5- to 6-week period.

In early August, while the main population of Baird's sparrow is still in the north, some juveniles and adults in worn breeding plumage occasionally appear on the fringes of the winter range. This led to speculation at one time on a possible breeding population on the high grassy plateaus of New Mexico and Arizona. However, Richard R. Graber (1955) points out that only the presence of stub-tailed juveniles would lend credence to this suggestion, and that these have never been found in the southwest.

*Winter.*—Baird's sparrows spend the winter months in their usual inconspicuous manner, wandering about alone or rarely in twos or threes. Allan R. Phillips writes me from Mexico that: "The species is never found in flocks, so far as my knowledge goes. Nor have I heard any of them sing."

While most of the population continue their migration until they reach northern Sonora (south of Sasabe), Durango (Ojito), and Coahuila (Saltillo), a few remain in the southwestern United States in western Texas, New Mexico, and Arizona. In Arizona their numbers vary greatly from year to year, according to Gale W. Monson (1960) who states: "Baird's sparrows, usually very rare in Arizona, were almost common in some localities; they were collected at Gardner Canyon on the east side of the Santa Rita Mts., Feb. 6 and April 10 (R. Roy Johnson), 1960; 1 was seen along Rillito Creek near Tucson, Dec. 6, 1959 (Thornburg), and 4 were noted on the Tucson Christmas count, Jan. 2, 1960." Despite these recent records, Monson also writes me that: "The picture of Baird's sparrow in winter is indeed a cloudy one. Many, or even all sight records, are very unsatisfactory and must on the whole be disregarded." A letter from Roger T. Peterson adds: "Obviously there are very few definite records for Mexico."

## DISTRIBUTION

*Range.*—High plains from southern prairie provinces to north central Mexico.

*Breeding range.*—Baird's sparrow breeds from southern Alberta (Castor), southern Saskatchewan (Crane Lake, Kutawagan Lake), and southern Manitoba (Oak Lake, Grand Rapids, Lake St. Martin) south to northwestern Montana (Dutton), northwestern and central South Dakota (Harding County, Eureka), southeastern North Dakota (northern Sargent County), and central western Minnesota (Wheaton).

*Winter range.*—Winters from southeastern Arizona (San Rafael Valley, Sonoita, Chiricahua Mountains) and southern New Mexico (Animas Valley) south to northern Sonora (10 miles south of Sasabe), Durango (Ojito), and Coahuila (Saltillo); in migration to western and south central Kansas (Pendennis, Udall), central Missouri (Columbia), central Oklahoma (Cleveland County), and western and central Texas.

*Casual records.*—Casual in southern California (Joshua Tree National Monument). Accidental in New York (Montauk).

*Migration.*—Early dates of spring arrival are: Arkansas—Winslow, March 23. Missouri—St. Louis, March 17. Ohio—Ottawa County, April 22. Iowa—Grinnell, March 24. Minnesota—White Earth, Becker County, May 5. Oklahoma—Inola Prairie, April 12. Nebraska—Holstein, March 28. North Dakota—Billings County, April 25; Jamestown, May 5; Cass County, May 6 (average, May 17). Manitoba—Treesbank, April 21; Whitewater Lake, average May 9. Saskatchewan—Dinsmore, April 19. New Mexico—Rodeo, April 9. Arizona—Tucson, April 21. Colorado—Fort Lyon, April 1. Wyoming—Torrington, May 2. Montana—Missoula, April 20; Fallon, April 24. Alberta—Castor, May 10.

Late dates of spring departure are: Missouri—St. Joseph, May 25. Texas—Gainesville, April 24. Arizona—Cochise County, May 4; base of Huachuca Mountains, May 3.

Early dates of fall arrival are: Arizona—Ash Flat, August 15. New Mexico—Upper Pecos, August 11. Texas—Gainesville, September 26.

Late dates of fall departure are: California—Joshua Tree National Monument, October 3. Montana—Terry, September 10. Wyoming—Midwest, September 19. Colorado—Colorado Springs, November 26. Arizona—Rincons, October 24. New Mexico—Gila River, October 16. Saskatchewan—Rosetown, September 7. Manitoba—Treesbank, October 5. North Dakota—Billings County, October 21; Union County, October 15. South Dakota—Faulkton, October 15. Nebraska—Holstein, November 8. Oklahoma—Edmond, November 24. Texas—Bonham, November 5. Minnesota—Hallock, September 11. Iowa—Grinnell, October 16. Missouri—St. Louis, October 29.

*Egg dates.*—Alberta: 5 records, June 9 to June 23.

Manitoba: 10 records, June 6 to August 11.

Minnesota: 2 records, June 7 and July 22.

Montana: 2 records, July 18 and July 20.

North Dakota: 9 records, June 5 to July 15.

## PASSERHERBULUS CAUDACUTUS (Latham)

## Le Conte's Sparrow

PLATE 43

### Contributed by LAWRENCE H. WALKINSHAW

### HABITS

Le Conte's sparrow was described by Latham in 1790 from a specimen taken in the interior of Georgia. Apparently the species was not recorded again until May 24, 1843, when Audubon collected one along the upper Missouri and named it "after my young friend Doctor Le Conte," a student of natural history. The third known specimen was taken in Washington County, Tex., by Linceceum in 1872. Then in the summer of 1873 Elliot Coues (1874) encountered the species in North Dakota between the Turtle Mountains and the Souris River and wrote:

"I only noticed the birds on one occasion, August 9th, when a number were found together in the deep green sea of waving grass that rolled over an extensive moist depression of the prairie. Five specimens were secured in the course of an hour, not without difficulty; for the grass being waist-high, the only chance was a snap shot, as the birds, started at random, flitted in sight for a few seconds; while it was quite as hard to find them when killed."

Since then the range and distribution of this unobtrusive and elusive little finch have gradually been worked out, but as yet comparatively little is known about its breeding habits, winter behavior, and migration. The bird is so secretive, so nondescript, and so hard to observe that its presence often passes unnoticed. An inhabitant of the drier borders of the larger marshes of central North America, it lives hidden in the grasses and sedges and is seldom seen in flight. P. B. Peabody (1901) writes of his experiences with it in northwestern Minnesota:

This weird, mouse-like creature I met in the Red River Valley of Kittson County, Minnesota, on May 27, 1896. Two specimens were taken in a timothy field redeemed from marshy meadow, and swarming at the time with Red-winged Blackbirds, Soras, Western Savanna Sparrows, Wilsons Phalaropes, and Bobolinks, along with the water fowl and other larger birds * * *. One might, for example, search its familiar haunts day after day during the daytime, at the beginning of the period of its arrival in the North, without detecting the slightest evidence of its presence. One must learn just what sort of "cover" is favored by the bird or he will fail to flush it even with minutest search, as the bird, save during the early and the late hours of the day, even in the height of its courtship, is conspicuously silent * * *. I have searched a whole day, on favorable ground, without meeting the bird; while at dusk after starting home, I counted fifteen distinct recurrences of its note along the wayside in going two miles through the meadows.

Most of its time is spent in the dense dead grass, though it feeds, in the morning and at sunset, where the living grass is scanty.

Because of its secretive habits and its unimpressive, insectlike song, Le Conte's sparrow has often been and doubtless still is overlooked in many regions where it is fairly common. Of my own early experiences with the species in Chippewa County, Mich., in 1935, I (1937) wrote:

My first impression of Leconte's Sparrow was that it is a very elusive bird. If a male was heard singing and one approached to within fifty to seventy feet, his song would cease. On pacing over the area the bird might be flushed once, when he would fly just over the rushes for about a hundred feet, then drop into the matted masses of dead vegetation where he disappeared completely. But, after several minutes of quiet waiting, the same wheezy song would be heard and the male located in a similar manner. One male was not as wild * * *, but remained within a range of twenty feet. On several occasions he was seen sliding underneath a mass of vegetation only eight or ten feet away, then coming out from the other side, craning his neck to see if I was following. If I did follow his incessant chipping, he soon widened the space between us and finally disappeared. If I returned to the supposed proximity of the nest-site, he was there to repeat the performance; otherwise he would soon begin to sing.

In the Munuscong Bay State Park area where the above notes were made, the species inhabited the drier borders of the rush-grown marshes, "where the most conspicuous plant was *Scirpus validus* (Vahl). During June, the marsh growth consisted almost entirely of this rush; masses of old dead rushes strewed the ground as the past seasons had left them, with new stalks protruding from these masses.

PLATE 43

Munuscong State Park, Mich., June 5, 1935        L. H. Walkinshaw

Munuscong State Park, Mich., June 5, 1935        L. H. Walkinshaw

LECONTE'S SPARROW AND NEST

PLATE 44

Butler County, Pa., June 18, 1945                    H. H. Harrison

EASTERN HENSLOW'S SPARROW WITH YOUNG

Quonochontaug, R. I., June 16, 1907                  H. S. Hathaway

NEST OF EASTERN SHARP-TAILED SPARROW

Intermixed with these were many little willows, mostly about one or two feet in height."

These sites are frequently flooded during periods of heavy rainfall. The Munuscong nest I found in 1935 was inundated twice, but the birds remained in the vicinity to renest when the water receded. For about the next five years the Munuscong nesting grounds stayed free of deep water. Then they flooded again, and the high water has persisted to this day, forcing the Le Conte's sparrows to desert the area.

Elsewhere on the Upper Peninsula of Michigan I found the species summering regularly on certain drier marshes covered with fine sedges and grasses, often where they were completely surrounded by bog in Luce, Chippewa, and Mackinac counties. In 1935 one or two singing males could usually be heard in most of these damp, grass-grown clearings. I also found them on the drier portions of the great Seney Marshes in Schoolcraft County, which has since become the Seney National Wildlife Refuge. After highways were built far out in these marshes I found the species there regularly until 1956. They were there in 1955, but in 1956, though the marshes appeared no different than before, neither C. J. Henry nor I were able to find a single bird.

In central Saskatchewan we found the species fairly abundant in similar grassy areas during the summer of 1947. Here again the nesting sites were subject to flooding, often in completely isolated open marshy spots surrounded by coniferous forest.

*Spring.*—Le Conte's sparrow apparently migrates through the central portion of the United States in a general north-northwestward direction in spring. At this season, as at other times, it frequents damp open fields and marshes covered with thick grasses and sedges. It is just as hard to flush and flies only a short distance before dropping into the tall protecting grasses.

Russell E. Mumford tells me (*in* litt.) that he finds the species each spring and fall on grassy, damp, marshy areas at Willow Slough Game Preserve, Newton County, Ind. Robert Ridgway (1889) writes that in Illinois this elegant little sparrow is, in some localities at least, an abundant spring migrant. He noted a specimen taken May 13, 1875, at Riverdale, Ill., from a depression in the prairie near the Calumet River, where the moisture had caused an early growth of grass about 3 inches high; also that Charles K. Worthen of Warsaw took some 20 specimens from low swampy prairies in the Mississippi bottoms, occasionally from dry bluffs, but generally from wet, marshy ground.

Richard E. Olsen (1935) noted the first arrivals at Munuscong Bay State Park, Mich., on May 11 and 12, 1934. For Minnesota, Thomas S. Roberts (1932) gives the average arrival date as about

April 28, with earliest dates of April 6 (1929) and April 8 (1921). C. Stuart Houston and Maurice G. Street (1959) give the earliest arrival date at Nipawin, Saskatchewan, as Apr. 30, 1943, and the average May 5. Most Saskatchewan observers find May 10 to 26 as the date of first observance. Bernard W. Baker and I (1946) saw the first birds at Fawcett, Alberta, during the spring of 1942 on May 22.

*Nesting.*—The nest of Le Conte's sparrow somewhat resembles that of Henslow's sparrow. It is built on or slightly above the ground in the drier borders of open marshes beneath tangles of old dead rushes, grasses, or sedges. It is so well concealed that it is extremely difficult to find; in fact, probably no more than 50 have ever been found. P. B. Peabody (1901) who probably found more nests than any other single person wrote of it:

Leconte's Sparrow nests where dead grass is thickest. All along the Red River are still wide stretches of prairie, the lowland sections of which abound in lower spots with luxuriant growths of heavier grass and vetch. It is in such places that Leconte's Sparrow breeds. This bird is exceedingly local. Every such bit of meadow as I have described will have its pair of birds; and an expert can repeatedly flush the male, and at times the female, from this patch at almost any time of day. * * *

It [the nest] would seem to be built, in the main, as follows: where dead and fallen grass is thickest, the bird interweaves dead grasses among the standing stems, thus forming a rude nest. Within this is placed the nest proper; this is an exquisitely neat, well-rounded and deeply-cupped structure, composed uniformly of the very finest grasses. In all but two of the nests noted above, there was a more or less thick covering of fallen dead grass; all the nests except these two were in the lowland. The average nest is placed with the base about eight inches above the ground. One of the lowland nests noted barely touched the ground, however, while the two upland nests were half sunk into the earth, being thus, in situation and surroundings, somewhat like nests of the Western Savanna Sparrow, though somewhat smaller and relatively deeper.

Of a nest I found at Munuscong Bay State Park, Mich., I wrote (1937):

The nest was built in a perfectly dry area which on two occasions became flooded during heavy rains, water filling the lower half of the nest the first time, yet the female incubated regardless. The second time, the young had hatched, and although I had raised the nest several inches, they were drowned. Originally this nest was about 30 mm. from the ground under a mass of fallen last year's rushes, through which the new rushes were just beginning to show. A few short willows were scattered throughout the area, two or three of which were very close to the nest. * * * It measured, when fresh, 60 by 60 mm. inside and 90 by 120 mm. in outside dimensions. The floor was 30 mm. below the top and the walls were from 30 to 35 mm. thick. It was a rather bulky affair, yet beautifully constructed.

This nest was built of stems of grass, of *Eleocharis palustris*, and smaller rushes lined with very fine grass. Thomas S. Roberts (1932) reports hair in addition to fine grasses in the lining.

*Eggs.*—Le Conte's sparrow lays three to five, usually four eggs.

They are ovate and only slightly glossy. The ground is grayish white, speckled, spotted, blotched, and clouded with "snuff brown," "Saccardo's umber," "cinnamon brown," or "Mars brown," with undermarkings of "light Quaker drab." These markings are generally more or less evenly dispersed over the entire surface. The measurements of 50 eggs average 18.0 by 13.7 millimeters; those showing the four extremes measure 20.4 by 13.9, 19.7 by 15.0, 16.3 by 13.0, and 18.3 by 12.7 millimeters.

*Young.*—The length of the incubation period is not known accurately. The nest I found in northern Michigan contained five eggs on June 4, 1935, three of which hatched on June 16 and 17, a period of 12 to 13 days. Incubation should not require any more time than this, judging by the requirements of related species of similar size, and might even take less under ideal conditions.

Incubation is performed entirely by the female while the male guards the territory and sings nearby. On June 17, 1935, when the female was brooding and feeding three newly hatched young and incubating one unhatched egg, I watched the nest closely for 225 minutes (11:15 a.m. to 3:00 p.m.). In this time she brooded for 146 minutes (65 percent) and was away for 79 minutes (35 percent). She left the nest 16 times; her periods of brooding averaged 9 minutes with extremes from 1 to 21 minutes; her absences averaged 5 minutes with extremes of ½ to 20 minutes. At no time was I sure that the male fed the young, but they were fed 10 times during this period at an average interval of 21.4 minutes, with extremes of 5 to 41 minutes between feedings.

At hatching these three young weighed 1.7, 1.7, and 1.8 grams respectively. One young at one day of age weighed 2.5 grams, one at two days weighed 3.4 grams, and one at three days 4.5 grams. The skin color of newly hatched Le Conte's sparrows is lighter and pinker than that of Savannah sparrow young. The sparse natal down is wood brown.

*Plumages.*—T. S. Roberts (1932) thus describes the juvenal plumage: "A general suffusion of pale tawny or buffy-yellow above, below, and on sides of head; very little chestnut above; the color on hindneck and median crown-stripe tawny yellow; *streaked more or less thickly across breast* with narrow blackish lines, bend of wing white in four specimens, very pale yellow in two; tail obscurely barred. By September the throat and abdomen are becoming paler (whitish in some specimens), the bird generally less tawny, with chestnut appearing on head and back, and the breast-stripes more sparse; the latter disappear with the completion of the postjuvenal molt."

R. W. Dickerman (1962) adds the following details, which help distinguish the juvenal Le Conte's from the juvenal Nelson's sharp-tailed sparrow, which have occasionally been confused in the literature. The colors in italics are from Ridgway (1912).

1. Underparts pale, band across breast nearest *Cinnamon Buff*, much paler on chin and belly, fading to whitish in older juvenals.
2. Streakings of breast band fine, but usually well developed, comparable to the breast streakings in adult Henslow's Sparrows, occasionally nearly obsolete in the middle of the band; streakings on flanks heavier than those of breast.
3. Dorsally similar to Sharp-tailed young but much paler, nearer *Clay Color* but ranging between *Cinnamon Buff* and *Tawny Olive*.
4. Tertials with broader black shaft-streak bordered narrowly with rust and with pale buff or buffy white edges.
5. Rectrices with sharply demarked shaft-streak bordered by rust colored area paling outwardly to pale greyish brown feather edge.

The subsequent sequence of plumages and molts in this species has not been well worked out. From the limited material available, the first winter plumage apparently is acquired by a complete post-juvenal molt which starts in August and is completed by late September or early October. In this dress the young birds closely resemble the adults.

Le Conte's sparrow undergoes at least a partial spring molt which apparently begins on the wintering grounds in March or April and is completed by the time the birds reach the breeding grounds in May. Chapman (1910) claimed this "spring molt is confined to the head and breast," but H. B. Tordoff and R. M. Mengel (1951) produce evidence that all the body feathers are replaced at this time. They note, however, "We found no positive evidence of molt of remiges other than that involving the tertials. Comparison of birds taken in late winter and early spring with specimens taken in May indicates, in general, greater wear of primaries and secondaries in the May birds." While they found some tail feathers being replaced, the evidence for complete involvement of the tail in this molt is inconclusive, for the feathers being replaced "may, of course, have been lost in some mishap." They continue:

"The spring plumage acquired by the molt here described differs slightly but definitely from fresh fall plumage. The faint necklace of dark streaking on the breast usually characteristic of fresh fall specimens is nearly or totally lacking in the newly molted spring birds we have seen. It might be assumed that these streaks have been lost by wear, but even worn late winter birds usually have some remnant of these markings. The dorsal plumage in spring lacks some of the richness of tone (*i.e.*, abundance of warm browns at the expense of black) present in fall."

*Food.*—Little seems to have been recorded about the food of Le Conte's sparrow. Its diet probably closely parallels those of the closely related grassland sparrows such as Henslow's and the sharp-tails, being largely insectivorous in the breeding season with a higher percentage of vegetable matter, primarily weed seeds, in winter. David A. Easterla (1962) reports that the contents of 15 gizzards of birds collected in the spring and fall near Columbia, Mo., contained 83 percent vegetable matter, mainly seeds of grasses and forbs, and 17 percent animal foods, predominantly leafhoppers, spiders, and stinkbugs. Apparently the young are fed almost entirely on insects. Those I watched in Michigan were being fed small larvae gleaned from the nearby marsh vegetation.

*Voice.*—I (1937) described the song of Le Conte's sparrow from my own notes and the published accounts by others as follows:

The song of the Leconte's Sparrow is very unimpressive, resembling more the song of some insect than that of a bird. It has been described by many authors. Seton, in "The Birds of Manitoba" (1890, p. 596) describes the song as "a tiny, husky, double note *'reese-reese'*, so thin a sound and so creaky that I believe it is usually attributed to a grasshopper." Roberts, in the "Birds of Minnesota" (1932, 2: 393) gives Breckenridge's impression of the song: "The Leconte's song begins with one short, barely audible, squeaky note, followed by a fine, high, insect-like buzz similar to [that of] the Grasshopper Sparrow and about one second in duration: a tiny, hardly audible 'chip' terminates the effort" (Red River Valley, June 23, 1928). Farley in the "Birds of the Battle River Region" (1932, p. 57) says: "Its soft lisping note, *tze*, uttered with monotonous frequency as the bird clings to a tall grass stem, sounds more like an insect than that of a bird."

The song when near at hand to me sounds like *z-z-z-buzzzz*, and lasts by the stop-watch 0.015 of a minute in duration, which is approximately one second as stated by Breckenridge. The first part of the song reaches its shrillest just at the close, when it can be heard for some distance. It is much higher pitched than that of the Savannah Sparrow, heard in the same wet meadows, yet the song of the Savannah lasts nearly three times as long. Often, when in the blind, another song was heard, sometimes alone, again preceding the regular insect-like buzz. This song has been described by Peabody as "a dry, creaky *e'elree-e'elree-e'elree-e'elree.*" He adds: "This note must be rarely indulged in, as I recall having heard it but twice." It is not uttered nearly as often as the other more common song. This song resembles a similar one of the Grasshopper Sparrow (*Ammodramus savannarum australis*), and like the song of the latter, it is more often followed by the regular buzzing song.

Very seldom have I observed the bird utter the song more than a foot from the ground. Once, while crossing near the supposed nesting-site, a male suddenly flew into the air with quivering wings, and while maintaining a stationary position, uttered his regular song, then dropped again to the dead rushes. The procedure was much like the one often given by the Prairie Marsh Wren.

Although I was not awake all of the hours of darkness, the male was heard to sing as early as 3 a.m. and as late as 10:30 p.m., long after dark here in Michigan. From my cabin door I could easily hear it. For a period of fifteen minutes 10 to 10:15 p.m. on June 16, 1935, I timed his songs with a stop-watch and he repeated the song at the rate of ten times per minute, excepting for one minute when it was repeated nine times. At dawn it was repeated at about this same rate. For thirty minutes between 1:45 and 2:15 p.m., on June 17, it was repeated the following number of times per minute: 7,6,6,7,2,0,0,0,0,0,0,0,0,0,5,6,5,0,0,2,1,0,5, 5,0,7,4,0,0 and 0. This was at about the regular rate for the middle of the day * * *. In central Alberta the rate corresponded with that in Michigan but daylight is much longer there during the nesting season.

The alarm note was a *chip*, sometimes single, but more often double, and if one were near the nest, it became a very rapid *chip-chip-chip-chip-chip*, then repeated * * *. Another call heard from the blind as the female approached the nest was a very low, barely audible, *z-z-zz-z*. The male uttered this same call at one time when he circled over the nest and returned to his singing perch. Then there was the song uttered twice on June 17, 1935, by the female on the nest as the male sang nearby. This song was *chit-chit-t-t-t-t* and I have heard the Grasshopper Sparrow, both male and female, utter a song almost identical at the nest in southern Michigan (July, 1935).

*Enemies.*—In some areas Le Conte's sparrow is subject to cowbird parasitism. Peabody (1901) reported that 4 of the 14 nests he found in Kittson County, Minn., in 1897 contained cowbird eggs. Friedmann (1963) lists a few more records for Saskatchewan and Alberta. The extent to which cowbird interference affects reproductive efficiency in this species in unknown.

While Le Conte's sparrow must certainly fall prey to hawks, owls, and other predators, and its nests must surely be ravaged at times by snakes, weasels, skunks, and foxes, no examples have been reported in the literature.

*Field marks.*—This small grassland sparrow of wet, weedy fields and marshes is characterized by its buffy throat and underparts with streaking confined to the sides, its buffy eyestripe, white crownstripe, pinkish-brown nape, and heavily striped back. It may be confused in the field mainly with the Savannah, grasshopper, sharp-tailed, and Henslow's sparrows, which may occupy the same surroundings at various times of the year. The Savannah is markedly larger and lighter, and can be told in flight by its notched tail. The grasshopper sparrow lacks the streaked sides and the sharp-tails the white median crown stripe. The buffy underparts distinguish it from the lighter-bellied Henslow's sparrow, which is also slightly larger and heavier billed.

*Fall.*—Le Conte's sparrow migrates through the central United States in a general south-southeasterly direction in fall. In migration it frequents the same type of habitat it prefers during the remainder of the year. In Michigan the birds stop in the drier marshy areas and at times may be seen sitting on top of grass or sedge spikes, or even on a fence wire. While they may occasionally be found wandering in the longer grasses of dry fields near the marshes, they favor the wetter spots.

While hunting prairie chickens in Richland County, Ill., Oct. 27 and 28, 1882, Robert Ridgway (1883) "was somewhat surprised to see Leconte's Bunting there in great abundance; also Henslow's, which, however, was less numerous. The locality where the Leconte's Buntings were first observed consisted of a patch of 'open' prairie

160 acres in extent, entirely overgrown with iron-weeds (*Vernonia noveboracensis*) mixed with occasional patches of prairie grasses—the only part of the prairie not under cultivation. They were found, however, almost everywhere, grassy places being most affected. In flushing them it was almost necessary to kick them from the grass, and it was very rarely one would start up farther in front than a dozen feet. Their flight, like that of *C. henslowi*, was very irregular making it difficult to shoot them * * * ."

*Winter.*—In winter Le Conte's sparrow is as hard, perhaps even harder to find than at any other season. In Georgia, where the type specimen was taken, T. D. Burleigh (1958) considers it "a scarce winter resident throughout the state" as well as "one of the least-known birds in the state," collected there on fewer than a dozen occasions. He continues:

Few small birds are as secretive and difficult to see as is the Leconte's Sparrow. In Georgia, it seems to prefer old fields overgrown with broom sedge in which to spend the winter months, and to find one in such a spot requires both perseverence and a certain amount of luck. Reluctant at all times to fly, it will, if alarmed, seek safety by running swiftly along the ground, and only when hard pressed will it flush and remain briefly in view. Its flight then appears slow and feeble, and it will go but a short distance before dropping into the concealing vegetation. Instant pursuit may or may not result in another glimpse of this elusive little sparrow, depending largely on whether one has guessed correctly in which direction it ran on reaching the ground again. Considering these circumstances, it is not surprising that it has been so seldom reported in the state, and it is not improbable that it is much more common during the winter than the few records would indicate.

Of its winter status in Florida little has been discovered since A. H. Howell (1932) wrote:

A winter resident, chiefly on the west coast; apparently rare in most sections, though perhaps locally common. * * * Leconte's Sparrows are probably the most elusive of the small sparrows, living in old fields under cover of dense, matted grass and weeds, from which they are flushed only with difficulty. Maynard is apparently the only collector who has found them common in Florida. His notes, made at Rosewood [Levy County] and published by Brewster (1882 * * *), are as follows:

"The first *C. lecontei* was shot November 4. Shortly afterwards they became so abundant that as many as twenty were sometimes seen in a day, but notwithstanding their numbers, it was by no means easy to obtain specimens. The chief difficulty arose from their excessive tameness, for they could rarely be forced to take wing, while in the long grass it was impossible to see them at a greater distance than a few yards. Indeed so fearless were they that on several occasions Mr. Maynard nearly caught them in his insect net."

Maynard was able to collect only 11 specimens in two seasons. Howell lists another half-dozen sight records, most of them in December and January. He collected one at Cape Sable "in short grass on the coastal prairie" Feb. 13, 1918. Since Howell's day the species has been reported only about a dozen times, mainly on Audubon Christmas censuses. H. M. Stevenson lists it on his "Field Card of Florida Birds and their Status in the Tallahassee Region" (undated) as occurring in northwestern Florida from the third week of October to the first week of May.

In Alabama T. A. Imhof (1962) considers Le Conte's sparrow "rare to uncommon in winter and on migration." His earliest fall record is September 23, his latest in spring May 15, both at the Wheeler Refuge in the Tennessee Valley. He reports the bird most commonly from December to March on the lower coastal plain and along the Gulf Coast.

Concerning its habits in Louisiana in winter G. H. Lowery, Jr. (1955) writes:

Leconte and Henslow Sparrow are both commonly called "stink birds" by quail hunters because sometimes even well-trained bird dogs point them or are distracted by them. Both species occur mainly in broom sedge (*Andropogon*) fields where, even though they are often common, they are seldom seen except for the few moments when a bird jumps out of the grass at one's feet, flies twenty yards or so, and then pitches back into the grass.

* * * As a rule its habitat in Louisiana in winter is somewhat drier than that of the Henslow Sparrow, and it is nowhere more numerous than in slightly rolling terrain where there is a dense stand of broom sedge. On the coast of southwestern Louisiana, however, it is also plentiful in the short grass prairies paralleling the Gulf beach, as, for example, along the highway between Cameron and Johnson Bayou.

The Leconte Sparrow arrives in Louisiana in the latter part of October and remains sometimes until after the first of April. The bird is decidedly more numerous in southern Louisiana in midwinter than it is in northern Louisiana.

## DISTRIBUTION

*Range.*—Southern Mackenzie and northern Ontario south to southern Texas and the Gulf Coast.

*Breeding range.*— The Le Conte's sparrow breeds from southern Mackenzie (Little Buffalo River), northeastern Alberta (Fort Chipewyan), central Saskatchewan (Flotten Lake, Churchill River), central Manitoba (Lake Winnepegosis, Lake St. Martin), and northern Ontario (Fort Severn, Attawapiskat Post) south to north central Montana (Glacier Park), southeastern Alberta (Cassils Lake), southern Saskatchewan (Davidson), northern North Dakota (Souris River, Rock Lake), northwestern and eastern Minnesota (Marshall County, St. Paul), northeastern Wisconsin (Oconto County), and northern Michigan (Germfask, Munuscong Bay); casually south to southeastern South Dakota (Miner County), northeastern Illinois (near Chicago), and southern Ontario (near Bradford). Casual in breeding season east to Quebec (St. Fulgence).

*Winter range.*—Winters occasionally from southern Missouri and southern and northeastern Illinois (Glenwood), and more regularly from central western Kansas (Lane County), central Oklahoma (Canadian and Payne counties), northwestern Arkansas (Fayetteville), central Alabama (Elmore County), south central Georgia (Tifton), and central and eastern South Carolina (Savannah River Plant, Georgetown County), south to southeastern New Mexico (Roswell), southern Texas (Corpus Christi), southern Louisiana (Avery Island), southern Mississippi (Gulfport), northwestern Florida (Milton, Rosewood), and southeastern Georgia (Camden County).

*Casual records.*—Casual west to Idaho (Fort Sherman), Utah (Provo), and Colorado (Gunnison); east to Quebec (Beaupré, St. Fulgence), New York (Ithaca) and North Carolina (Raleigh); and south to southern Florida (Cape Sable).

*Migration.*—Early dates of spring arrival are: North Carolina—Raleigh, April 21. Kentucky—Bowling Green, April 12. Missouri—St. Louis, March 15 (median of 5 years, April 5). Illinois—Quincy, March 14; Chicago, March 15 (average of 9 years, April 18). Indiana—Bloomington, April 28. Ohio—Ross Lake, April 5. Michigan—Munuskong Bay State Park, May 11. Ontario—Kenora, April 21. Iowa—Iowa City, March 29. Wisconsin—Mayville, April 1; Sauk County, April 16. Minnesota—Elk River, April 8 (average, April 25). Nebraska—Lincoln, March 17. South Dakota—Yankton, April 11. North Dakota—Jamestown, April 22; Cass County, April 27 (average, May 8). Manitoba—Margaret, April 6. Saskatchewan—Indian Head, April 30.

Late dates of spring departure are: Florida—Manatee, May 3; Wakulla Beach, April 21. Alabama—Wheeler Refuge, Decatur, May 15. Georgia—Athens, April 6. South Carolina—Charleston, May 8. North Carolina, Raleigh, April 21. Louisiana—Lobdell, April 25. Mississippi—Saucier, April 8. Arkansas—Winslow, May 11. Tennessee—Nashville, May 14. Missouri—St. Louis, May 6 (median of 5 years, April 21). Illinois—Chicago, May 23 (average of 9 years, April 24). Ontario—Point Pelee, May 10. Texas—Sinton, April 20. Oklahoma—Cleveland County, April 3. Kansas—Onaga, May 14. Nebraska—Neligh, April 15.

Early dates of fall arrival are: North Dakota—Jamestown, September 29. South Dakota—Forestburg, September 25. Kansas—Lawrence, October 7. Oklahoma—Cleveland County, October, 12. Michigan—Newberry, September 26. Ohio—central Ohio, October 31. Illinois—Chicago, September 9. Missouri—St. Louis, September 25. Louisiana—Baton Rouge, October 31. South Carolina—Charleston, October 25. Alabama—Decatur, September 23. Florida—Tallahassee, October 18.

Late dates of fall departure are: Manitoba—Treesbank, September 18. North Dakota—Cass County, October 18 (average, September 26). South Dakota—Forestburg, October 5. Kansas—Neosho Falls, December 18. Minnesota—Hutchinson, October 26 (average of 6 years for southern Minnesota, October 9). Wisconsin—Iowa County, November 5. Michigan—Newberry, October 10. Ohio—Hebron, November 23. Illinois—Port Byron, October 14; Chicago, October 12. Missouri—St. Louis, November 20.

*Egg dates.*—Alberta: 6 records, June 6 to June 24.

Illinois: 6 records, May 22 to June 12.

Manitoba: 7 records, June 4 to June 21.

Michigan: 1 record, June 4.

Minnesota: 15 records, May 29 to June 24; 13 records, May 29 to June 9.

Ontario: 4 records, June 10 to July 11; 1 record, June 10.

Saskatchewan: 1 record, June 4.

Wisconsin: 6 records, May 23 to June 6.

## PASSERHERBULUS HENSLOWII SUSURRANS Brewster
## Eastern Henslow's Sparrow

### PLATE 44
### Contributed by WENDELL P. SMITH

### HABITS

The Atlantic coastal race of the Henslow's sparrow, described by William Brewster in 1919 from Falls Church, Va., is slightly darker than the nominate western form, has buffier underparts, more yellow at the bend of the wing, and a much stouter bill.

Henslow's sparrow is a shy and retiring little inhabitant of open fields and grasslands, where it associates with the far more obvious and familiar bobolinks, meadowlarks, Savannah and grasshopper sparrows. While occasionally found in dry and in cultivated uplands, it shows a preference for old weedy fields and swales, especially wet or damp ones. In most instances thick vegetation seems a basic requirement of its habitat, which is in keeping with its custom of skulking or running mouselike through the grass at the approach of an intruder. Its scurrying through the undercover is so characteristic that Robert F. Mason, Jr., suggested in a letter to Mr. Bent that "mouse sparrow" might be a more appropriate name for it. It seldom flies when disturbed, and when it does take wing, it is often for only a short distance, so short that N. C. Brown (1879) calls its flights little more than "respectable jumps over the grass."

Because of its secretiveness and of the security afforded by the thick vegetation it prefers to live in, the habits and behavior of the Henslow's sparrow are rather poorly known. Those of the eastern race apparently differ little, if at all, from those of the more fully studied western form, as described in detail in the next account.

## DISTRIBUTION

*Range.*—New York and central New England to Florida.

*Breeding range.*—The eastern Henslow's sparrow breeds from central New York (Jefferson County, intergrading with *P. h. henslowii*), southern Vermont (Bennington), southern New Hampshire (Wonalancet), and northeastern Massachusetts (West Newbury) south to extreme eastern West Virginia (Morgan and Berkeley counties), central and southeastern Virginia (Lynchburg, Princess Anne County), and east central North Carolina (Chapel Hill).

*Winter range.*—Winters on the Atlantic Coastal Plain from South Carolina (Horry County) and Georgia (Sapelo Island, Athens) to south central Florida (Glades County). Casual in New York (Patchogue) and Bermuda.

*Migration.*—The data apply to the species as a whole. Early dates of spring arrival are: Florida—Lake Jackson, March 5. Alabama—Autaugaville, March 11. North Carolina—Raleigh, March 18. Virginia—Blacksburg, April 21. District of Columbia, March 25 (average of 31 years, April 18). Maryland—Baltimore County, March 16; Laurel, March 24 (median of 9 years, April 16). Pennsylvania—Philadelphia and State College, April 20. New Jersey—Salem, April 12; Carney's Point, April 13. New York—Bronx County, April 4; Binghamton, Cayuga, and Oneida Lake basins, April 14 (median of 20 years, April 25). Connecticut—Litchfield, April 27. Rhode Island—Charlestown, April 24. Massachusetts—Huntington, April 28. Vermont—Bennington, May 1. New Hampshire—Tilton, April 17. Arkansas—Monticello, April 8. Tennessee—Nashville, March 26. Kentucky—Bowling Green, March 25. Missouri—Shannon County, March 19. Illinois—Chicago Region, March 16 (average of 14 years for Chicago, April 18); Urbana, April 13 (median of 6 years, April 14). Indiana—Tippecanoe County, April 7; Wayne County, April 11 (median of 12 years, April 23). Ohio—Cleveland, April 5; Buckeye Lake, April 6 (median of 40 years for central Ohio, April 21). Michigan—Battle Creek, April 10 (average of 33 years, April 27). Ontario—London, May 1. Iowa—Grinnell, March 28. Wisconsin—Madison, April 3. Minnesota—Minneapolis and Cambridge, April 25 (average of 8 years for southern Minnesota, May 6). Kansas—northeastern Kansas, April 14. Nebraska—Lincoln, April 22. South Dakota—Vermilion and Sioux

Falls, April 29 (average for Sioux Falls, May 9).  North Dakota—Red River Valley, April 30.  Oregon—Corvallis, April 12.

Late dates of spring departure are: Florida—Tallahassee and St. Marks Light, April 21.  Alabama—Birmingham, May 4.  Georgia—Denton, April 22.  South Carolina—Horry County, April 13.  North Carolina—Raleigh, May 3.  Vermont—Rutland, May 12.  Louisiana—Cameron, May 15.  Tennessee—Nashville, May 21.  Kentucky—Bowling Green, May 16;  Missouri—St. Louis, May 8.  Illinois—Chicago, May 21 (average of 14 years, May 5).  Ontario—London, May 14.  Iowa—Hudson, May 22.  South Dakota—Vermilion, May 6.  North Dakota—McKenzie County, May 27.

Early dates of fall arrival are: South Dakota—Faulkton, September 1.  Illinois—Chicago, October 3.  Missouri—St. Louis, October 5.  Kentucky—Bowling Green, September 21.  Arkansas—Monticello, October 20.  Louisiana—Baton Rouge, October 24.  Georgia—Fitzgerald, October 21.  Alabama—Birmingham, October 31.  Florida—Tallahassee, October 24.

Late dates of fall departure are: North Dakota—McKenzie County, October 29.  South Dakota—Faulkton, November 1.  Nebraska—Papillion, October 9.  Kansas—northeastern Kansas, October 15.  Minnesota—Minneapolis, September 2.  Wisconsin—Racine, November 29; Dane County, November 14.  Iowa—Blakesburg, October 27.  Ontario—Point Pelee, October 15.  Michigan—Birmingham, October 25.  Ohio—central Ohio, October 25 (median, October 3).  Illinois—Chicago region, November 12.  Missouri—St. Louis, November 19.  Kentucky—Bowling Green, November 4.  New Hampshire—New Hampton, October 23.  Massachusetts—Osterville, November 6.  Rhode Island—Charlestown, October 14.  Connecticut—West Haven, October 27.  New York—Shelter Island, November 20; Cayuga and Oneida Lake basins, October 30 (median of 12 years, October 19).  New Jersey—Island Beach, October 13.  Pennsylvania—State College and Centre Furnace, October 8.  Maryland—Baltimore County, November 21; Laurel, October 29.  District of Columbia—November 16 (average of 6 years, October 11).  Virginia—Charlottesville, October 30.

*Egg dates.*—Maryland: 5 records, May 18 to June 26.

New Jersey: 6 records, May 22 to July 7.

PASSERHERBULUS HENSLOWII HENSLOWII (Audubon)

# Western Henslow's Sparrow

## Contributed by JEAN W. GRABER

### HABITS

Henslow's sparrow is a grassland species occupying meadows or marshy openings in the woodlands of central and eastern United States and southern Canada. A shy, unobtrusive, and secretive little bird that tends to run when disturbed instead of flying, it is consequently hard to find and difficult to observe in the field. When Audubon discovered the first specimen in Kentucky just across the Ohio River from Cincinnati in 1820, he painted the bird and named it (1829) for his friend the Reverend John Steven Henslow, professor of botany at Cambridge University, England.

The nominate western subspecies differs from the Atlantic coastal race, *susurrans*, in being generally lighter, with less yellow at the wing bend, heavier black streakings and less chestnut on the back and scapulars, and a thinner bill. The Appalachian mountain chain may have been the isolating mechanism in the formation of the two races, each of which has apparently expanded its range since the opening of North America by man. As A. Sidney Hyde (1939) points out: "The primeval forests which extended almost unbroken from western Indiana to the salt marshes of the Atlantic coast must have originally offered little to induce colonization by this bird. * * * Widespread clearing of the forests has made more habitat available * * *. Recent marked increases in abundance are reported from Ohio, southern Michigan, and Ontario. * * * many of the known breeding colonies are so situated as to lead to the belief that watercourses serve as important migration highways for the species. In the Appalachian highlands the valleys of the Merrimac, Connecticut, Hudson, Delaware and Susquehanna rivers appear to have a more than casual relationship to the locations of colonies reported from northern New England, New York, and Pennsylvania."

Throughout its summer range the western Henslow's sparrow occupies weedy prairies and meadows, and neglected grassy fields and pasturelands, which are often dotted with low shrubs or bushes. The vegetation it inhabits may be rather irregular in height and density, or fairly uniform; the ground cover is usually quite dense and at least a foot or two high. In northeastern Kansas the species occupies the lower, moister depression in upland, mid-grass prairie. Hyde (1939) notes the dominant plants in its southern Michigan habitat to be cord grass (*Spartina pectinata*) and shrubby cinquefoil (*Potentilla fruticosa*). It seems to prefer low-lying, damp situations, but it may also be found in drier upland fields.   Though drainage of lowlands and intensive cultivation appear recently to have reduced its breeding area and numbers in parts of Iowa, Wisconsin, and Illinois, the bird has adapted to man's agricultural practices by occupying unmowed timothy-clover hayfields in Ohio, Illinois, Wisconsin, and possibly elsewhere.   Smith (1963) states that Henslow's sparrows abandon a field when the grass is cut.

Some of the birds commonly found nesting in the same environment with the western Henslow's sparrow are: marsh hawk, ring-necked pheasant, bobolink, meadowlark, red-winged blackbird, dickcissel, and grasshopper and Savannah sparrows.   Other species that frequently nest near by and associate with it occasionally include: greater prairie chicken, upland plover, horned lark, short-billed marsh wren, Traill's flycatcher, yellow warbler, yellowthroat, and song and swamp sparrows.

*Spring.*—The western Henslow's sparrows usually leave their southern wintering grounds in late March or early April.   The latest southern records are: South Carolina, March 28; Georgia, March 29; Florida, April 11; Alabama, May 4; and Louisiana, May 15.   Milton Trautman (1956) observed a mass migratory flight of the species at South Bass Island, Ohio, on April 21–22; the birds were moving in company with juncos, and Savannah, swamp, song, chipping, field, and fox sparrows.

The earliest arrival dates in the north are: Shannon County, Mo., March 19; DuPage County, Ill., March 28; and Sauk, Wis., April 7. The following average arrival dates are given in the literature: Oberlin, Ohio, April 29; Saginaw, Mich., April 22; Dane County, Wis., April 23; Minnesota May 6; and South Dakota May 9.   There are Nebraska first records from April 22 to May 9.   No data are available as to when the bulk of the breeding population arrives in any area.   Lynds Jones (1892) noted that in Iowa "The first arrivals * * * are always found in the underbrush skirting native woods.   Later they move out to their prairie homes."

*Territory.*—Henslow's sparrows tend to live in loosely formed colonies.   They seem to establish territories within these colonies, but the boundaries are not too rigid and may be violated occasionally. Hyde (1939) observed fighting males "bowing to each other beak to beak, like fighting roosters."   He adds: "The fighting was apparently not vicious; one bird flew at the other.   Then they both disappeared in the grass; shortly thereafter both birds separated and began singing—one fifty feet south of blind, the other from a tall weed not more than twenty feet east of it."

He thus described the population density of the colonies he studied in southern Livingston County, Mich.:

In fields inhabited by colonies of Henslow's Sparrows the numbers of birds an acre may run rather high, but over any extensive area, taken as a whole, the population will be low because of the large amount of uninhabited land. In one nine-acre field (Field 3) at Anderson four pairs nested in 1934. In 1936 it was estimated that seven males had their territories in this field, in which four nests (one deserted) were found before June 10. In field 6 there were about 40 acres of habitable territory, which held about thirty to forty singing males in 1934. A similar density is reported from Mahoning County, Ohio, by Vickers (1908: 150–52), who found from nine to twelve males in a fourteen-acre field. Hennessey (1916: 115) found from forty to sixty birds (he does not say pairs) in an area of about 160 acres in southern Michigan, near Albion. A record for density is reported from Iowa by Anderson (1907: 317) on the authority of G. H. Berry, who reported ten pairs breeding in a field of hazel and blackberry of about one-half acre in extent.

Sutton (1928a) found about a dozen pairs in a 10-acre area of dense grass in Pymatuning Swamp in northwestern Pennsylvania.

*Courtship.*—Little has been observed of the courtship of this rather secretive species. Hyde (1939) writes of it as follows:

Aside from the increasing frequency and volume of song, the first courtship behavior was noted on the afternoon of May 9, 1936. A singing bird that had been changing his perch frequently, dropped to the ground and was joined by another individual as the call of intimacy was uttered. Presently the male was seen with a piece of dry grass in his mouth, hopping among the hummocks. He soon dropped the grass and began singing feebly from the ground. The female remained concealed, except at intervals when one bird closely following another flitted above the grass for an instant and then dropped back, the actions being punctuated with frequent renditions of the call of intimacy. No trace of a nest could be found.

Early the next morning at the same place a singing male with a mouthful of dried grass alighted on a hummock near another bird. Dropping the grass and fluttering his wings continually the male proceeded over and among the hummocks. He appeared to be taking the female on a tour of the area, indicating to her each possible nesting site by violently fluttering into it.

A male was seen copulating with a female perching in open view on a bush, and holding dead grass in her bill, on July 23, 1934. After the second union both birds dropped into the grass. The male appeared again, flying with rapid vibrations of the wings characteristic of many birds just subsequent to copulation.

A pair of birds were apparently mating under concealment of the grass on July 11, 1934. The male, at first singing, began to chase the other bird, and both disappeared in the vegetation. Whenever they reappeared their wings were fluttering or vibrating characteristically. Finally the female ate a caterpillar she had been holding all the time, and the male began singing in a subdued voice.

Though the species is essentially monogamous, Hyde observed copulation between a mated female of one territory and the male of an adjacent territory.

*Nesting.*—The well-concealed nest is always placed on or near the ground. A few nests have been found actually sunk into depressions in the ground. Usually it is built at or near the base of a thick clump of grass with its bottom two or three inches above the ground. The grass often arches over the nest so as to form a partial roof. Some nests are attached to vertical stems of grass and herbs from 6 to 20 inches above the ground; these lack the roof of arching vegetation.

Usually the nest is a deep cup, though Hyde (1939) found one that was merely a shallow open saucer and poorly concealed. The nest cup measures about 2 inches in inside diameter, 3 inches in outside diameter, and has a depth of 1 to 2 inches. The nest is made of coarse grasses and dead weed leaves and lined with finer grasses and sometimes with hair.

Nest material is gathered near the nest site, within 50 feet of one nest Hyde watched. The nest building is done chiefly if not entirely by the female. Hyde reports (1939) the male of one pair sang softly nearby while the female was at work; when she stopped working he became more vociferous. The male of a pair observed by J. T. Southard (pers. comm.) was seen carrying blades of grass twice while the female worked at nest building. Hyde watched one female bring nesting material from 9:08 to 9:50 a.m. at the rate of once every 3.3 minutes; she spent 0.7 of a minute arranging it at the nest before leaving for more supplies.

Nest building activity seems to be most intense during early morning, but may occur throughout the day until dusk. The nest is built in 4 to 5 days. Hyde reports that one pair, after its nest was destroyed, chose a new site and completed a new nest in 5 to 6 days.

*Eggs.*—Henslow's sparrow usually lays from 3 to 5 eggs. They are ovate and slightly glossy. The ground is creamy white or pale greenish white, with speckles, spots, and occasional large blotches of reddish browns such as "russet," "hazel," "auburn," "Rood's brown," and "tawny," with undermarkings of "light purplish gray" or "light neutral gray." The eggs of this species are not so heavily marked as those of the sharp-tailed or seaside sparrows, but resemble more the pattern of those of the grasshopper sparrow. The spottings are concentrated toward the large end where they often form a wreath. The spots may be either sharp and distinct or dull and clouded. The measurements of 55 eggs average 18.3 by 14.1 millimeters; the eggs showing the four extremes measure *20.3* by *15.2*, *16.7* by 13.8, and 18.8 by *13.0* millimeters.

The finding of many nests with eggs in Michigan in July and of four eggs laid in one nest between August 12 and 16, and of young still in the nest in Wisconsin in September suggests that some pairs may be double-brooded.

*Young.*—Incubation is entirely by the female. While she incubates the male sings from various perches nearby. She has been observed to respond to his singing by twittering softly from the nest. Hyde (1939) determined that incubation starts with the laying of the last or the next to last egg and takes about 11 days.

Both parents brood and feed the young. Food was brought to one nest Hyde was watching about one hour after the first egg hatched. As he saw no egg shells carried away from the nest, he assumed the parents ate them. During their first day of life the young are fed about once ever 2 hours. Feedings increase as the young grow to as many as 10 per hour at the age of 7 to 8 days. The adults carry away fecal sacs at irregular intervals and sometimes eat them. The young leave the nest on the 9th or 10th day after hatching.

*Plumages.*—The natal down which Dwight (1900) calls smoke gray, Hyde (1939) terms "pale buffy gray." He found it distributed on a bird 4 hours old in "A superciliary patch of about two tufts on each side; a patch on the back of the head; one on the middle of the back; one lateral to the femur; a humero-scapular tract of two tufts; and a patch on the posterior margin of the ulna. * * * At four days of age down was still prominent. At six days the superciliary and alar tracts retained conspicuous tufts." He describes a 6-day-old nestling whose juvenal "feathers were almost completely unsheathed, except on the forehead, the crown, and underneath the eye" as follows:

"Sides of crown black, center of crown and nape all around light olive-brown, contrasting with the pale rufous back feathers, which have black centers; edge of wing sulphur; remiges fuscous, the primaries very narrowly margined along outer edges and tips with pale light brown, the secondaries similarly margined with a slightly deeper brown; tertials black, broadly margined with pale cinnamon; scapulars and wing coverts fuscous margined with pale rufous. Upperparts sulphur yellow, sides strongly washed with vinaceous. The feathers of the anterior part of the sides of the breast have narrow fuscous streaks."

Birds in the completed juvenal plumage also show a characteristic "fused" barring (present also on some adults) on the tail feathers, which are shorter than those of adults. This plumage is replaced in a post-juvenal molt by the first winter plumage, in which the birds are similar to adults but have deeper buff-colored underparts. The post-juvenal molt and the complete post-nuptial molt of the adults appear to be essentially finished on the breeding grounds before migration. Kumlein and Hollister (1951) thus vividly describe the molting adults: "During the latter part of August and September the adults especially are in a condition of such extreme moult as to be almost unable to fly, there being many days when not an individual can boast of even a single tail feather."

Dwight (1900) states that both the first and the adult nuptial plumages are "acquired probably by a partial prenuptial moult confined chiefly to the head and chin." This still needs verification for, as Dwight continues, "In species so much affected by wear it is not easy to be sure of a moult without specimens which actually show it. The freshness of many feathers in spring indicate it."

*Food.*—From 17 stomachs (12 adult, 5 immature) Hyde (1939) collected between April and October, he determined the food to be 82 percent animal matter by bulk and 18 percent vegetable matter. Orthoptera comprised 36.47 percent of the August–September food, Coleoptera 19.3, Heteroptera 12.2, Lepidoptera 3.3, and Hymenoptera 1.8 percent. Additional items of animal matter included Diptera, Neuroptera, spiders, unidentified arachnids, myriapods, and gastropods.

The Orthoptera eaten were crickets (especially *Nemobius* sp.), grasshoppers, and katydids; the Coleoptera were weevils (mostly), chrysomelids, carabids, scarabaeids, and histerids; the Heteroptera were lygaeids, pentatomids, and a few others; the Lepidoptera included caterpillars of cutworms (noctuids); and the Hymenoptera were andrenids (chiefly), ants, ichneumonids, tenthredinids, and chalcids. All the insects were species found on or near the ground in the vegetation in which the bird lives.

Seeds of grasses constituted 6.2 percent of the total food; ragweed 9.2 percent (75 to 85 percent in two specimens taken in October); Pologonaceae 1.6; and sedges less than 0.5 percent. Hyde adds: "It is nearly certain that if fall, winter, and early spring specimens had been examined in proportion to those collected in the summer, the percentage of vegetable matter would have been much higher."

The principal food brought to day-old nestlings was smooth noctuid caterpillars. These and soft abdomens of Orthoptera (katydids, tree crickets, and grasshoppers) were the chief items fed to young birds the first 3 days after hatching. After the third day the parents brought a greater variety of insect food, though caterpillars and Orthoptera still predominated. Other items Hyde saw fed to the nestlings included sawflies (*Cimbex*), a large garden spider (*Argiope*), and a firefly (lampyrid).

*Voice.*—"More often heard than seen" describes Henslow's sparrow. Unless the bird happens to be singing, its presence is easily overlooked. Though its unobtrusive song has been described (Peterson, 1947) as "one of the poorest vocal efforts of any bird, * * * a hiccoughing 'tsi-lick'," it is characteristic and readily identifies the singer. It is sometimes given from concealment in the grass, but more usually from a weed stem or bush just above the level of the surrounding vegetation.

Though the song is generally heard as two short buzzy notes, often described as "*flee-sic*," an audiospectrographic analysis of tape recordings by Borror and Reese (1954) revealed that it actually consists of six separate notes, the last three of which are the ones usually heard and described. The *flee* is the lowest, loudest, and fourth note in the song, while the *sic* is actually two notes, the fifth and sixth, the fifth being slightly higher in pitch than the sixth.

In addition to this characteristic song which the male gives from singing perches atop a weed or stalk of grass, Jouy (1881) described a six-noted flight song, "*sis-r-r-rit-srit-srit*," which Sutton (1928a) thought Jouy may have attributed to the wrong species, as it is an excellent rendition of the flight song of the grasshopper sparrow, and in his studies of Henslow's sparrow Sutton "never once heard the birds utter this song." Nor does Hyde (1939) mention hearing it. However, R. R. Graber tells me he has heard Henslow's sparrow give this flight song in Illinois.

Hyde (1939) describes what he terms the "call of intimacy," heard only during the height of the breeding season, as a series of intense, high-pitched, sibilant, descending whistles. It may be given by birds of either sex in situations of high emotional intensity, as during courtship, combat, or when warning off an intruding male. Hyde continues:

"The hunger call of the young is a nasal whistle, 'kee,' pitched like the monosyllabic 'pee' of the Wood Pewee, but less sharp. The usual alarm note is a sharp 'tsip' similar to that of the Chipping and Savannah Sparrows. A higher pitched, more penetrating 'tsip' is used as a warning when a hawk appears."

George M. Sutton has written me of a variety of calls given by juveniles he kept in captivity. He decribes the food call of the young as "a high, clear *yeee-eee*," a call given by the young to parent birds as "*reee*," a call given when caught in the hand as a loud "jeer" or "djeer," and a "lonely" call as a "thin, very high note, not exactly a cheep," which is hard to hear. He heard well-fed captives singing "little whisper songs" 11 days after leaving the nest, at an age of about 20 days.

The birds are in song when they arrive on the breeding grounds. Their singing increases in vigor and frequency during the courtship period. After the young hatch it decreases noticeably, presumably because the males are then busy helping feed the young. A second period of less intensive singing in late July and early August is terminated when the adults start undergoing their postnuptial molt. They are then heard to sing no more, though they may remain on the breeding grounds into October.

Song begins at dawn and sometimes continues all night. One male Hyde (1939) watched closely for 529 minutes in early July while his mate was incubating spent 80 of them in song. He found that the average interval between individual songs during singing periods increased from 4.19 seconds on June 17 to 8.7 seconds on August 9.

Sutton reported singing peaks at sunrise and early evening, but Hyde found singing lessened toward evening.

W. E. Saunders (MS.) reports that Henslow's sparrows sang intermittently throughout the night of July 20–21, 1935, at Morpeth, Ontario, and that not more than 15 minutes elapsed without a song being heard. Other observers have had similar experiences. The species has also been observed singing incessantly when rain was pouring down. Perhaps lessened light intensity stimulates singing, and in this respect the bird seems crepuscular.

*Behavior.*—This small sparrow spends much of its time concealed in the grass and dense vegetation in which it lives. During the breeding season it does not move far from its nest, which is often hard to locate because it is so well concealed and because the female usually runs some distance from it before flushing, and returns to it on foot as well. When not singing, it is seldom noticed unless it is flushed from the cover. It is difficult to flush, for it apparently places great reliance on its marvelously concealing coloration, and either runs through the grass from the intruder or remains motionless in hiding until almost stepped upon. When it does flush, it seldom flies more than a few yards before dropping back into the vegetation. It evidently has a strong game effluvium, as bird dogs often point it, to the annoyance of their quail-hunting masters.

Sutton (1928a) describes its flight as being more erratic and undulating than that of the grasshopper sparrow. The wing beat usually alters just after the bird takes flight, and the tail and rump are twisted in a peculiar and characteristic manner.

*Field marks.*—The Henslow's is confused mainly with the grasshopper and Le Conte's sparrows, which frequently share its habitat, particularly in winter. The best field marks are its distinctly reddish wings and the olive-green nape (rufous-brown in the Le Conte's). The Henslow's streaked breast and flanks distinguish it from the clear-breasted adult grasshopper sparrow.

*Enemies.*—Although nests of Henslow's sparrow are occasionally victimized by the brown-headed cowbird, the species appears to escape heavy parasitism, possibly because the nests are so well hidden. No data are available on the percentage of nests parasitized (which is apparently low), or as to whether the presence of a cowbird nestling precludes successful fledging of the young Henslow's sparrows in the nest. J. T. Southard writes me of finding nests of this species containing two cowbird eggs in addition to three or four host eggs.

Snakes are probably the foremost predators of the species. In Pennsylvania, Henslow's sparrows and their eggs were found to constitute 12 percent of the diet of specimens of the blue racer (*Coluber constrictor*) examined by Ruthven et al. (1928). Hawks also prey on this sparrow.

Stoddard (1931) found remains of a Henslow's sparrow in a marsh hawk from a winter roost in Leon County, Fla., and Sutton (1928b) reports one from the stomach of a sharp-shinned hawk in Pennsylvania. Skunks, minks, weasels, raccoons, and foxes are all potential predators, and opossums and ground squirrels probably devour eggs when they find them, though no examples are recorded in the literature.

Hyde (1939) reports one nestful of young destroyed by cattle trampling. Mowing of hayfields must also result in some losses.

Ectoparasites reported by Hyde include red mites or chiggers (*Trombicula bisignata*) found on the skin, particularly about the ears and anus, and mallophaga (unidentified). He notes the species "seems to be relatively free from lice." He also notes one nest of three young destroyed by "cool weather and a heavy infestation of nest mites."

*Fall.*—Hyde (1939) comments: "In August * * * there seems to be a tendency for the birds, at least the immature ones, to venture into new territory. * * * From late August on, the birds have a tendency to make longer flights when disturbed. If flushed several times in succession they frequently fly to the edge of a thicket or into a low tree. Such behavior presages the reactions of the birds during the migrating period. Nearly all of the definitely migrating birds seen by me in Kansas, Illinois, and New Jersey were along hedgerows or at the edges of similar shrubby places."

The migratory exodus begins in September and by late October or November the birds have left the breeding grounds.

*Winter.*—Henslow's sparrow winters in the southeastern United States from South Carolina, Georgia, and Florida westward to southeastern Texas. In South Carolina, Alexander Sprunt, Jr., and E. Burnham Chamberlain (1949) consider it a "Fairly common winter resident, October 21 to March 28, probably throughout most of the State" and notes that "The western race of the Henslow's Sparrow seems to be, so far as it is possible to determine from specimens examined, about as numerous in South Carolina as the eastern race." Arthur T. Wayne (1910) says the bird varies greatly in abundance in South Carolina from year to year.

In Georgia, however, Thomas Burleigh (1958) considers the western Henslow's sparrow "A scarce and local resident in the southern part of the state." He lists less than a dozen specimen records assignable to it, and considers the eastern subspecies the predominant form there.

In Florida, Sprunt (1954) again considers "the eastern and western forms about equal in distribution." The specimen record, however, shows the western subspecies predominant in the "Panhandle" and southward along the west coast to the Tampa region. Though Sprunt (1954) states it frequents "old fields, roadsides, and thick, rather wet growth," its principal habitat in Florida is the open longleaf pine flatwoods, where it lives on the damp ground in the wire-grass (*Aristida stricta*), which grows thickly in the wet acid soil in clearings and where the tree growth is sparse, providing the birds ideal cover. Francis Weston wrote Hyde (1939) that "the birds are so difficult to flush in their winter home that it is very hard accurately to judge their abundance."

Imhof (1962) writes: "North of the Fall Line in Alabama, this sparrow is rare in winter and on migration. In the Coastal Plain it is uncommon in winter but undoubtedly more numerous than recorded because it is difficult to flush and identify. * * * The species frequents weedy, rank growths like other sharp-tailed sparrows, but also occurs in open, wet, shrubby areas. On or near the coast, it usually lives in broomsedge or other grasses in boggy places in the pine flats."

In Louisiana, George Lowery (1955) says "it is often found in the same broom sedge situations [as the LeConte's sparrow] but it appears to be less numerous there. It is most common in the grass of the 'pine flats' particularly in the Florida Parishes. * * * Henslow Sparrows arrive in Louisiana in late October. They are usually gone by the end of March."

### DISTRIBUTION

*Range.*—Eastern South Dakota, Wisconsin, and southern Ontario south to Texas and the Gulf Coast.

*Breeding range.*—The western Henslow's sparrow breeds from eastern South Dakota (Moody County), central Minnesota (Grant and Isanti counties), southern and northeastern Wisconsin (Dane and Oconto counties), casually north to central Michigan (Mackinaw City) and southern Ontario (Barrie, Carlsbad Springs) south to central Kansas (Cloud County), northeastern Texas, Central Missouri (Hickory and St. Louis counties), southern Illinois (Richland County), northern Kentucky (Jefferson County), and central southern West Virginia (Monroe County).

*Winter range.*—Winters from north central Texas, Louisiana (Monroe, New Orleans), and southern Mississippi (Saucier) to western and northern Florida (Eau Gallie), southeastern Georgia (Tifton, Sapelo Island), and South Carolina (Chester, Aiken, and Charleston counties); casually in southern Illinois and southern Indiana (Jackson County).

*Casual records.*—Casual in northwestern North Dakota (Kenmare). Accidental in Massachusetts (Osterville).

*Egg dates.*—Illinois: 20 records, May 20 to July 4; 10 records, June 19 to June 26.

Iowa: 9 records, May 18 to June 29.

Michigan: 30 records, May 28 to August 16.

Missouri: 1 record, May 26.

Ontario: 2 records, both August 14.

Wisconsin: 4 records, May 23 to June 12.

AMMOSPIZA CAUDACUTA SUBVIRGATA (Dwight)

## Acadian Sharp-tailed Sparrow
Contributed by NORMAN P. HILL

### HABITS

The Acadian sharp-tailed sparrow (*Ammospiza caudacuta subvirgata*) is the name applied by Jonathan Dwight in 1887 to the pale grayish race of the sharp-tailed sparrow breeding in the maritime provinces of Canada, the type locality being Hillsborough, Albert County, New Brunswick. It breeds from Phippsburg, Maine, northeast along the coastline of New Brunswick, Nova Scotia, Prince Edward Island and the Gaspe Peninsula and west along the south bank of the St. Lawrence to Kamouraska. There is one questionable report from the Magdalen Islands, but none from Anticosti Island, Newfoundland, or Labrador.

*Spring.*—The Acadian sharp-tailed sparrow is one of the latest of spring migrants. The last birds have left South Carolina by May 29 (Sprunt and Chamberlain, 1949). A. D. Cruickshank (1942) reported stragglers as early as April 25 in New York but the main flight is the end of May to June 9. In Massachusetts, Griscom and Snyder (1955) report that the earliest date is May 15 and the latest June 15, the bulk of the birds passing through about June 1. No reliable data on dates of arrival on the breeding grounds are available; the statement of J. Macoun (1900) that they arrive in April must be rejected.

*Territory.*—The breeding habitat of the Acadian sharp-tail shows more variation than that of any other race of the species. In Maine it is found where the glacial moraine landscape gives way to rocky promontories. A. H. Norton (1897) describes it thus: "North of Scarboro', beginning with Cape Elizabeth * * * the coast presents an uneven or hilly face of rocks, indented with coves and bays, studded with dry ledgey islands. Between the hills are innumerable arms of the sea often extending as 'tide rivers' or fjords several miles inland, bordered by narrow swales rather than broad expanses of marsh. Coincident with those features is the low spruce woods, so conspicuous a feature of the Maine coast, so characteristic of the scanty soiled granite ridges, and the fog drenched coast of the north-east."

So small are these marshes that from their centers hermit thrushes and olive-sided flycatchers may be heard singing on the neighboring spruce-covered ridges. These marshes are well drained and subject to daily tidal flooding only to the grass roots. They are occupied by the same plants as farther south, *Spartina alterniflora* on the wetter edges, and *Spartina patens*, *Juncus gerardi*, and *Triglochin maritima*.

On Grand Manan Island, O. S. Pettingill (1936) found the sharp-tails in an "ill smelling marsh at Castalia that is gouged in typical fashion by tidal channels and stagnant sloughs." To the eastward, the marshes become gradually less salt. Near Sackville, New Brunswick (C. S. Robbins and G. F. Boyer, 1953), as in the Petitcodiac valley (J. Dwight, 1896), the meadows are diked for the cultivation of hay. *Spartina pectinata* is the dominant plant and grows luxuriantly, but along the ditches where brackish water occasionally backs up, *Juncus gerardi, Triglochin maritima, Puccinellia maritima*, and a few patches of *Salicornia europea* also occur. The sharp-tails were noted in both fresh and brackish portions of the marsh. Savannah sparrows and bobolinks were in close proximity, but were nesting only along the dikes which supported a different plant community. In the study area at Sackville, the density of *subvirgata* was five pairs in 26.6 acres. Elsewhere in New Brunswick, Dwight (1887) found them "along a swampy brook fully a mile from salt water, fraternizing with Swamp Sparrows and * * * Yellowthroats among the alder bushes." C. W. Townsend (1912a) reported them in the St. John valley in an entirely fresh water environment that included arrowhead and white pond lilies. Moore (*in* Squires, 1952) found them in the same valley breeding on islands above Fredericton, N.S., nearly 100 miles from the sea.

About the area farther north, Jonathan Dwight (1896) says: "Quite different are the salt marshes of Prince Edward Island and of the St. Lawrence * * *. There short grass, bogs and few ditches are the rule, though the birds seem equally at home." Elsewhere on Prince Edward Island, William Brewster (1877) reported them at Tignish in "a wide waste of marsh, dry, and at some distance from the sea, grown up to bushes, with scattered dead pine stubs, remnants of a former forest."

At Corner-of-the-Beach near Percé on the Gaspé Peninsula, L. M. Terrill (in litt.) found them "along the Portage River * * * nearly a mile from the St. Lawrence. This extensive area of marsh * * * was somewhat brackish, being subject to tidal flow up the streams which meander through it. * * * Dense stands of the bulrush, *Scirpus validus*, formed the principal growth in the areas occupied by the Sharp-tail. Nesting associates included several ducks, notably the Pintail, Wilson's Snipe, American Bittern, Virginia Rail, Sora, Yellow Rail, a few Red-winged Blackbirds and numerous Swamp Sparrows." R. C. Clement (in litt.) found them at Kamouraska, the westernmost breeding station, in "a lush meadow of tall grasses (*Calamogrostris* and *Elymus*)" and also "in a higher but still moist meadow of flags (*Iris versicolor* and *I. setosa*) and cinquefoils (*Potentilla palustris*)." This is obviously a completely fresh-water habitat.

*Nesting.*—A. H. Norton (1927) found a nest at Phippsburg, Maine. "The nest was completely covered by the reclining mat of *Spartina patens* and was entered and left by a narrow passage parallel with the direction of the culms of that grass. It was suspended by the sides from the culms of the 'thatch,' *Spartina alterniflora*, with its bottom about two centimeters above the wet soggy ground." This nest externally measured 80 mm. deep, 100 mm. long, and 90 mm. wide. It was constructed of blades of *S. alterniflora* and culms of *S. patens* and lined with fine blades of *S. patens*.

H. F. Lewis (1920) describes a nest found at Yarmouth, Nova Scotia:

The nest proper was a neat, round cup of fine, dry grass, with some horsehair in the lining. Its foundation consisted of some small masses of "eel-grass" and roots. Its dimensions were: inside diameter, 2.5 inches; outside diameter, 4.5 inches; inside depth, 1.5 inches; outside depth, 2.375 inches. It was elevated above the general surface of the marsh by being placed on the top of a low grassy ridge, about 14 inches high, formed from material thrown up when a ditch was dug across the marsh, many years before. During some storm, a mat of dead "eel-grass" had been left on the top of this ridge, and this had been later lifted by the growing marsh grass, leaving several inches between it and the ground. The nest was placed at the northwest edge of this mat, about half the nest being under it, while the other side was sheltered and concealed by grass about 6 inches high. The nest was not sunk in the ground at all.

*Eggs.*—Four to five eggs form the complete set. The appearance of the eggs is identical with those of *A. c. caudacuta*. The measurements of 40 eggs average 19.7 by 14.9 millimeters; the eggs showing the four extremes measure *21.1* by 14.9, 20.0 by *15.9*, *17.9* by 14.3, and 18.6 by *13.6* millimeters.

*Young.*—A. H. Norton (1897) states that incubation is performed by the female alone; the length of incubation is not known. Jonathan Dwight (*in* F. M. Chapman, 1896) and W. La Brie (1931) both comment on the absence of anxiety of the adults over the nest and young, and L. M. Terrill (*in* litt.) thinks that nearby Savannah sparrows showed more concern than the true parents when a sharp-tail's nest was found. Both parents are said to feed the young; this seems unlikely in view of the findings of G. E. Woolfenden (1956) with *A. c. caudacuta*.

*Plumages.*—The pattern of the adult plumage is clearly that of a sharp-tailed sparrow but the colors are paler and grayer and the breast streaking less distinct than in *A. c. caudacuta*. The molts are the same as in that subspecies. R. R. Graber (pers. comm.) has supplied information on other plumages as follows:

"Natal down: The natal down varies from brownish black on the head to mouse gray on the rump. Juvenal plumage: No sexual dimorphism. Crown black, with broad median and superciliary stripes of rich olive-tinged buff. Nape rust-tinged buff, unstreaked. Feathers of back black, broadly edged with rich buff. Rump and upper tail coverts rich buff, obscurely marked with black. Rectrices

olive gray with black shafts. Remiges black, primaries edged with
gray, tertials with rich buff as are coverts. Throughout upperparts,
buff coloration distinctly tinged with olive. Lores and eye-ring buff,
like superciliary. Auriculars brown, partially margined with black
post-ocular stripe. Sub- and post-auriculars rich buff. Underparts
rich orangish buff (lightest on belly). Sides of chest with few obscure
black streaks. Underparts otherwise immaculate."

The identification and field marks of this subspecies are discussed in
the life history of *A. c. caudacuta.*

*Food.*—As in *A. c. caudacuta,* the summer diet contains a high proportion of insect food, which decreases somewhat in winter. O. W.
Knight (1908) describes the contents of five stomachs of *subvirgata* as
"Nemertean worms, beetles, * * * unidentifiable flies, * * * beetle
larvae and sand with a little vegetable matter which was seemingly
extraneous." H. F. Lewis (1920) tells of the birds visiting an upland
hayfield near their marsh to feed.

*Behavior.*—In general, this subspecies behaves similarly to *A. c.
caudacuta.* J. Dwight (1896) says: "They may fly considerable
distances when disturbed, but they are more likely to dive into the
grass and defy all efforts to again flush them." J. Macoun (1900)
mentions that "They feed about the margins of pools of still water
where they seem to procure aquatic insects and grass seeds."

Where its range borders the Bay of Fundy, this subspecies must
adapt to a very large tidal rise and fall. In July 1965 I watched two
broods in the marshes below Truro, Nova Scotia, each brood being fed
by a single parent. The young were able to fly short distances, but
they stayed in the grass on the upper levels where the marsh showed
no evidence of recent flooding, while the parents foraged on mud
banks along the channels 15 or more feet below the marsh. The
rising tide steadily narrowed the foraging area, but the birds did not
forage in the grass until the mud was submerged. Each parent returned with food about every 45 seconds and fed whichever immature
was most vociferous. I could not determine the nature of the food.

Observing the bird on migration at Revere, Mass., William Brewster
(MS.) writes:

"All were seen in tall sedge on the edge of the water, none on the open
marsh or about the salt pools where *caudacutus* breeds * * *. Flight
slightly undulating and beelike, the wings beating rapidly like a
bumble bee.

"We usually started the birds—sometimes singly, frequently in twos,
occasionally three or four together—from the matted sedge. * * *
They would at first fly only a few rods along the bank and then
almost invariably pitch down into the creek and alight on the mud
under the overhanging bank. * * * Frequently, they would dip

beneath the bank at once and perform their flight close over the mud or water. * * * [When pressed] they would either double back past us or fly out into the marsh and drop into the short grass.

"After the first flight * * * the bird would run only a few yards and * * * show himself on the mud or eel grass near the middle of the creek, hopping slowly about and feeding, every now and then standing erect and still to look about him, or, climbing the steep bank, would raise his head and breast among the grass and remain for several minutes perfectly motionless, evidently aware that his buffy head and and cheeks matched the color of the bleached sedges sufficiently closely to make him fairly secure from detection."

*Voice*.—The song of the Acadian sharp-tail is of the same pattern as that of *A. c. caudacuta*, a short hiss preceded or followed by one or more sharper notes. They seem to sing more frequently than the more southern birds; C. W. Townsend (1905) heard one sing "fifteen times in a minute by the watch." The flight song is more elaborate; as O. S. Pettingill (1936) says: "Each began his flight performance by rushing several feet skyward, giving, during the descent, a sugges- tion of a song, though it resembled more the sizzling sound made when a cap is slowly removed from a bottle of ginger ale." A. H. Norton said they may rise as high as thirty feet. Of the perching song, Jonathan Dwight (1887) writes: "Even their song is inaudible at the distance of a few yards, and at its best is suggestive of the bird's being choked in the attempt. * * * It is usually delivered from the top of a weed, where, as the bird sits crouching, he presents an absurd appearance of ill-concealed fright." W. Montagna (1940) reports that they sing mostly in the morning, the frequency was decreasing by noon and stopping altogether by mid-afternoon. There is occa- sional singing in the evening. He heard the song regularly to July 25 and more rarely to August 14.

*Fall*.—R. S. Palmer (1949) mentions that there is some premigra- tion wandering in the fall. This race moves south a little later than *A. c. caudacuta*, the maximum counts in Massachusetts being in the first ten days of October, stragglers remaining into November. In New York, the peak is in the last week of October and stragglers are present into December.

The main migration route of this subspecies is along the coast, but it clings to the coast of the mainland. It is less common on outer Cape Cod (Hill, 1965), Nantucket (Griscom and Folger, 1948), and Martha's Vineyard (Griscom and Emerson, 1959) than in Essex County, inner Cape Cod, or Dartmouth, Mass.

Though the great bulk of migrants of this race move along the coast, some go overland across New England, presumably those occupying the more western colonies along the St. Lawrence. Inland

sight records are unacceptable because of possible confusion with
*altera*. However, W. E. C. Todd (Griscom and Snyder, 1955)
identified a specimen from Wayland, Mass., as *subvirgata* and I
consider that several others in the Museum of Comparative Zoology
from Wayland and from Sing Sing, N.Y., are *subvirgata*, as well as the
specimen from Longmeadow, Mass., taken Oct. 6, 1908 (12157 in the
Springfield Museum), reported by R. O. Morris (1909) and Bagg and
Eliot (1937). I also examined the Clarendon, Vt., specimen taken
Oct. 8, 1917 (12403 in the Boston Museum of Science) originally
reported as *nelsoni* (G. L. Kirk, 1917) and then as *subvirgata* (Bagg
and Eliot, 1937); I consider it a typical *altera*. Farther west, specimens taken at Ithaca, N.Y., have been rechecked for me by K. C.
Parkes who considers them *altera*. It may be suspected that all the
far inland records of this race will turn out similarly.

*Winter.*—This race winters along the coasts of South Carolina,
Georgia, and northern Florida, with individuals of all the other races.
Over a century ago Audubon (1841) noted their grayer appearance,
and remarked that some sharp-tails "were so pale as almost to tempt
one to pronounce them a different species." I have found no reports
of this race on the Gulf Coast. A few scattered birds attempt to
winter along the coast as far north as Massachusetts.

## DISTRIBUTION

*Range.*—Southern Quebec and Maritime Provinces south to
northern Florida.

*Breeding range.*—The Acadian sharp-tailed sparrow breeds locally
in brackish and salt marshes of southern Quebec (southern side of the
lower St. Lawrence Valley, Kamouraska, Riviere du Loup), New
Brunswick (Petitcodiac River, Hampton), Prince Edward Island
(Tignish), Nova Scotia (Cape Breton Island, Barrington), and eastern
Maine (southwest to Popham Beach).

*Winter range.*—Winters in coastal marshes from South Carolina
(Charleston County) southward to northern Florida; casually north to
New York (Long Island); in migration along the Atlantic seaboard.

*Egg dates.*—Nova Scotia: 27 records, June 8 to July 4; 16 records,
June 19 to June 25.

AMMOSPIZA CAUDACUTA CAUDACUTA (Gmelin)

# Eastern Sharp-tailed Sparrow

PLATE 44

Contributed by NORMAN P. HILL

## HABITS

The sharp-tailed sparrows are retiring and wary inhabitants of Atlantic coastal and some inland marshes; however, though common or even locally abundant, they are little known. The casual visitor to the seashore has scant reason to roam through the mud, silt, and grass of their habitat. Hence these birds remain secure and unobserved except by boatmen and hunters who know them as "grass finches." Even when one is accidentally flushed, it quickly drops back into cover and patient field work is needed to provide a satisfactory study of this handsome but mouselike bird.

The sharp-tailed sparrow as a species occupies as its breeding grounds a great, though discontinuous arc in eastern and north-central North America. This extends from Virginia northeastward to the St. Lawrence River, then skipping a gap of unsuitable territory, northwestward to James Bay and, finally skipping another gap, westward to the Canadian prairie provinces. Within this area the A.O.U. Check-List now recognizes five distinct populations or subspecies, each varying slightly from the other morphologically, mainly in color. In their life histories, habits, and behavior the five forms vary but little. Hence most of the available information on the nesting, food, enemies, and other essentials shared by all five are presented here under the nominate race, which also happens to be probably the best known and most thoroughly studied of the five subspecies.

The sharp-tail and the congeneric seaside sparrows are members of the "grassland group" of Emberizine finches. This group, which also includes the genera *Passerculus* (Ipswich and Savannah sparrows), *Ammodramus* (grasshopper and Baird's sparrows), and *Passerherbulus* (Le Conte's and Henslow's sparrows), is fairly well separated from all other finches in habits and morphology as well as in habitat. The sharp-tails and seasides may be considered the salt-marsh representatives of the group, though each is occasionally found in fresh water marsh habitats, the sharp-tails more so than the seasides.

That the sharp-tails and seasides are closely related cannot be questioned. Though each occupies a separate niche in the same marshes as regards nesting sites and feeding habits, they share many similarities in appearance, song, behavior, and food. In 1928 a male seaside sparrow spent the early summer in a sharp-tail colony in

Revere, Mass., and was observed trying to copulate with a female sharp-tail (Ludlow Griscom, pers. comm.). In New Jersey, W. Montagna (1942a) collected a male sharp-tail and a female seaside apparently in copulation. Sage, Bishop, and Bliss (1913) recorded a female hybrid of the sharp-tail and the seaside taken near New Haven, Conn., May 1, 1890; I have examined this specimen in the Museum of Comparative Zoology and agree with their diagnosis. In 1957 in an area occupied by both species in Barnstable, Mass., I studied a bird which appeared identical with this specimen and which I believe was another hybrid. No hybrid of either the sharp-tail or the seaside with any other species has ever been recorded, to the best of my knowledge.

It seems likely that the southern Atlantic coast, where all five subspecies of the sharp-tailed sparrow now winter, was the Pleistocene breeding refuge of the then undifferentiated species. With the retreat of the glacial front, the sharp-tails followed the development of marshes northward along the coast, and eventually responded to the new environments by subspeciating. W. J. Beecher (1955) pointed out that the existence of the now isolated James Bay and Nelson's races may be accounted for by the former occurrence of a marine corridor via the St. Lawrence and either the Ottawa or Saguenay Rivers to James Bay, and thence westward to Lake Winnipeg, this being permitted by the temporary downward warping of the earth's crust by the weight of the ice. There is both geological and botanical evidence for the existence of such a corridor.

*Spring.*—In spring it is impossible to tell when the first sharp-tails leave their wintering grounds on the southern Atlantic coast and difficult to identify the first arriving migrants because of possible confusion with wintering stragglers. Sprunt and Chamberlain (1949) stated that all have left South Carolina by May 16. The latest record for coastal Alabama is May 16, 1911 (Imhof, 1962). Witmer Stone (1937) believed the first migrants appeared at Cape May as early as April 11. A. D. Cruickshank (1942) reported the first on Long Island at about the same time, although the first real wave never comes prior to April 25 and the bulk of the birds arrive in May. In Massachusetts (Griscom and Snyder, 1955) the earliest strays have appeared by May 9, these being scattered single birds, the main arrival being between May 23 and June 1. The date of arrival in Massachusetts seems to be correlated with the new green growth of *Spartina;* when this reaches about six inches, the sharp-tails appear.

The eastern sharp-tailed sparrow migrates along the coast. I have seen only one specimen from a truly inland locality, a bird taken May 30, 1952, in Wayland, Mass. The species migrates at night, and I

have had the experience of finding them one morning in a marsh
where none were present the day before.

*Habitat.*—The breeding range of *A. c. caudacuta* (type locality, New
York) is strictly coastal, extending from near Tuckerton, N.J., where
the population intergrades with *A. c. diversa*, north to Scarboro, Maine,
where it intergrades with *A. c. subvirgata.* The southern limit coincides
roughly with the southern limit of glaciation and the northern with a
shift from morainal to rocky substrate. This section of the eastern
seaboard is characterized by glacial deposits, chiefly moraines, both
terminal and recessional, with their outwash plains.

The sharp-tails dwell in the wide green salt marshes, soft and
meadowlike, that are usually enclosed by low-terraced barrier beaches,
often with a line of sand dunes interposed between the beach and the
marsh. Back of the marshes the uplands rise gradually in more
terraces and low rounded hills, usually of gravel interspersed with
boulders and often supporting a broad-leafed forest. These marshes
are of fine black silt, often seemingly bottomless, with some mixture
of sand along the creeks and tidal channels that interlace them. In
William Brewster's (MS.) words: "Narrow winding creeks intersect
the marsh in every direction. Near their mouths these creeks are
often 15 or 20 feet wide, but they narrow rapidly as one follows them
back and frequently branch into several still smaller ones, which are
lost altogether in subterranean passages or take their rise in little
pools or swampy areas a few yards square. Their depth is very
uniformly about 5 feet, with muddy banks of about 4 feet, and from
the edge of the banks a gentle incline up to the level of the salt marsh.
At high tide these creeks are nearly or quite bank full; at low tide the
water is only a few inches deep with black mud and eel grass exposed
in many places. The banks are always at least perpendicular and
usually more or less overhanging, the water eating them out beneath."

The intricacy of the winding and twisting pattern taken by these
creeks and the rapidity with which they narrow to small channels is
most appreciated when viewed from the air.

The plants of these marshes form a stable climax community.
Regarding them, C. W. Townsend (1905) writes:

From a botanical point of view the salt marshes can be divided into three distinct regions. First, the region of the coarse salt-grass (*Spartina stricta*) [=*S.
alterniflora*] everywhere in Essex County called "thatch," which flourishes on the
edges of the creeks only, washed by every tide. It grows to a height of four or
five feet. * * * The second region is that of the salt-grass or marsh hay (*Puccinellia maritima* and *Spartina patens*), a region reached by tides once or twice a
month at full or new moon. This grass rarely grows more than ten or twelve
inches in height. * * * Among the salt-grass grow patches of samphire (*Salicornia
herbacea*) [=*S. europea*]. The marsh rosemary (*Statice limonium*, var. *caroliniana*)
[=*Limonium caroliniana*] is common, and the grass-like seaside plantain (*Plantago*

*decipiens*). The third region is the upper edge of the marsh where it joins the uplands, a region visited only by the unusual spring and autumn tides. Here grows the "blackgrass," in reality a rush (*Juncus gerardi*) which gives the edges a distinctly dark color, almost black when the rush is in fruit. * * * In the channels of the creeks grows the eel-grass (*Zostera marina*) commonly mistaken for a seaweed but in reality a flowering plant.

In addition to the living grass which tends to lean over and form mats, low windrows of dried and matted thatch torn off by the winter storms are deposited in the upper and middle regions by the tides, mixed with driftwood, seaweed, and all kinds of flotsam and jetsam cast up by the sea. These mats and windrows form an important shelter and hiding place for the sharp-tailed sparrows.

On the Long Island marshes, which are the center of abundance of this subspecies, and in New Jersey, the sharp-tails are found in the drier spots in *Spartina patens*, whereas the seaside sparrows are confined to the coarser, taller, and sparser *Spartina alterniflora* in the wetter areas. I have found the same to be true in Barnstable, Mass., where both birds occur, but elsewhere in Massachusetts where the seaside is absent or at least very rare, the sharp-tails tend to move into the taller grasses. They do not, however, go into the very tall coarse sedge during the breeding season, though numbers of migrants are found there in the spring and particularly in the fall. G. E. Woolfenden (1956) noted that sharp-tailed sparrows seem to be less restricted in type of feeding habitat than seasides in that they feed in the thick grass, along the perimeter of the marsh and on the banks of pools and creeks.

The eastern sharp-tail's range is coastal and essentially linear, seldom more than a mile wide and often interrupted by unsuitable shoreline. The exceptions to this occur where suitable marshes may be found inland along estuaries. Probably the best known of these are the Piermont marshes in New York, 30 miles up the Hudson River from the Narrows, which formerly supported a colony of sharp-tailed sparrows that was apparently extirpated by pollution about 1930. The birds have also followed Narragansett Bay inland and nest there 15 or 20 miles from the sea. These inland marshes, and indeed some marshes around shore ponds, contain practically fresh water, but their vegetation is always that typical of the salt marsh, indicating that the spring tides bring in sufficient sea water to eliminate plants less tolerant of salt.

Regarding its local distribution, Ludlow Griscom (*in* W. Montagna, 1942) noted: "One of the curious things about the Sharp-tailed Sparrow * * * is that as you proceed northward the bird tends to become local. In a good marsh on the south shore of Long Island, for instance, Sharp-tails are ubiquitous and abundant. By the time you reach the coast of Massachusetts north of Boston,* * * for no known reason the Sharp-tail is not ubiquitous. There will be a colony here and there along the bank of some tidal creek when, for all you can see, the Sharp-tails might just as well as not be up and down the entire length of the creek." Counts of such colonies I have made at Plum Island, Barnstable, Monomoy, and Dartmouth, Mass., and Tiverton, R.I., show they may contain 3 to 15 pairs with a density of 1 to 1.5 pairs per acre, and the colonies may be a half mile to a mile apart. At Barnstable the total number, the sum of many such colonies, is about 1,000 pairs (Hill, 1965). Breeding birds with which they are associated include American bittern, black duck, marsh hawk, clapper rail, and seaside sparrow. Savannah sparrow and meadowlark areas fringe on the sharp-tails, and several species each of gulls, terns, and swallows are overhead.

*Territory and courtship.*—The sharp-tailed sparrow apparently does not establish a breeding territory in the usual sense of the term. In his study of banded birds in a New Jersey marsh, Woolfenden (1956) found that "Marking made it evident that the males were not territorial, although they did confine themselves to what might appropriately be called a breeding home range, the area to which an individual confines itself in the course of one nesting attempt. Observations of marked birds also indicated that there was considerable overlap of the breeding home ranges of individual males." He estimated that each male ranged over about four acres, none of which he actually defended, and that the individual females restricted themselves to less than one acre in the vicinity of the nest. This, and the relative reticence and stealthy actions of the nesting females, largely account for the apparent unbalanced sex ratio of three or four males to one female observed by Montagna (1940) in Maine and by my own random collecting in Massachusetts during the nesting season.

Reflecting this comparative lack of territoriality, the species apparently has little if any special courtship behavior. Montagna (1942a) noted occasional fighting between males in Virginia (so determined by collecting the fighting pair), which he assumed were "over a female." In his observations on *subvirgata* in Maine, the same author (1940) noted that "Male birds, as many as three, were seen crowding over one female, perhaps attempting to copulate. * * * Repeatedly birds were seen copulating immediately after the males' descent from the song flight." At Barnstable, Mass., I have several times seen a male simply fly to a female feeding on the mud and copulate without any preliminary display. The female squatted and partially spread her wings as the male mounted her back with fluttering wings for a brief moment and consummated the act. As Woolfenden (1956) remarked, this species is "promiscuous, relations between the sexes being limited to copulation."

*Nesting.*—The nest of the sharp-tailed sparrow is one of the most difficult to discover. Yet, William Brewster (MS.) found no less than seven in one day, June 19, 1890, at Revere, Mass.: "All seven nests were similar in composition but they varied widely in position and surroundings. Two were placed squarely on the ground within 20 yards of one another, one in the middle of a dense matted bed of *Juncus gerardi* well above the reach of the tides on one of the highest points in the marsh, the other near the edge of a tide creek barely above high-water mark among the coarse sedge that grows along these creeks. Both of these nests were perfectly concealed from above and every side, the first by living erect grass which grew almost as densely as fur on an otter's back and to a height of about 20 inches, the second by a broken down bunch of dry sedge under which there was barely room for the bird to enter.

"The other five nests were all raised well above the ground among the upright stems of the coarse sedges, the clear space beneath their bottoms varying from one to three or four inches. Four of them were perfectly concealed from above as well as from all sides, three by the tops of the clustering grasses in which they were placed, the fourth by a mat of drift sedge which had been lodged on the tops of the grasses by an unusually high tide. This last nest was in the middle of a bed of coarse creek sedge. * * * The other nests were among the fine salt grass on the edge of salt ponds. * * * The seventh nest was on the edge of a ditch built in the very top of a clump of fine short dry grass and as open above as the nest of a Red-winged Blackbird."

Of another occasion, on June 25, 1890, at Falmouth, Mass., he writes (MS.): "The nests were all built among the stems of short, upright grasses, their bottoms 2 or 3 inches above the ground, which was wet and shiny but in no instance actually covered with water. One nest was under a broad flake of broken down grass cemented together into a firm mat by dried mud or slime. On one side, however, it was entirely open so that the eggs could be easily seen from a distance of several yards. Another nest was under a similar mat of slime-glued dead grass and leaves, but not trusting to this alone, the bird had bent down the living grass on every side interweaving the tips so as to form a perfect screen as well as a canopy extending out an inch or more over the entrance which was a hole on the side. * * * The third nest was among short wirey grasses, about half green, half dry, the tops of which were bent down and interwoven so as to form a perfect dome-shaped roof nearly as solid and thick as that of a Marsh Wren's nest."

The nests I have found at Barnstable, Mass., have all been in *Spartina patens*, two in the center of pure growth about 10 inches high and one in lower growth near the edge of a tidal channel where *Spartina alterniflora* was beginning to appear. They were raised 2 or 3 inches above the ground, which was very moist, and each was sheltered overhead by a tuft of dead brown grass which was not woven together in any way. These nests were very clean, no excrement in or around them and no parasites found; they contained respectively newly hatched young, a fresh set of eggs, and well fledged young. The adult birds flushed directly from the nest without a sound, there being no runway through the grass as has been described by other observers. Some observers have noted that nests may be placed in depressions in the ground apparently excavated for the purpose.

According to H. O. Greene (1935), the nests are more or less spherical and measure 3½ to 4 inches high by 3½ to 4½ inches in diameter externally, the cavity being 2 to 2½ inches wide and 1½ to 2 inches deep. They are made of coarse dry grasses and seaweed inexpertly woven together with many loose ends protruding tangentially in all directions and are lined with finer similar material. The nest is considered more bulky than that of the seaside sparrow. My observations agree with this description and measurements, the material used being exclusively *Spartina patens*, however. The female alone builds the nest and, as Woolfenden (1956) surmised, the males probably "do not even know where nests are."

*Eggs.*—The usual set of the species is three to five, occasionally six and rarely seven eggs. They are ovate and have a slight gloss. The ground is greenish-white profusely specked and spotted with "snuff brown," "russet," "Brussels brown," or "auburn." The underlying spots are "pale purplish gray." Usually the markings are well scattered over the entire surface. On some the speckles are so thick they are confluent, obscuring the ground and giving the egg a "deep brownish drab" appearance; on others the spots are sharp and distinct. In series the eggs are noticeably smaller than those of the seaside sparrow and the markings tend to be much finer. The measurements of 105 eggs of the species average 19.4 by 14.6 millimeters; the eggs showing the four extremes measure *21.1* by 14.9, *17.8* by 15.2, 20.0 by *15.9*, and 20.8 by *13.2* millimeters. The measurements of 50 eggs of *A. c. caudata* average 19.3 by 14.5 millimeters; those showing the four extremes measure *21.0* by 14.5, *17.8* by *15.2*, and 20.8 by *13.2* millimeters.

Four or five eggs form the usual set in New England (Brewster, MS.), and three are more usual in New Jersey (Woolfenden, 1956). Reportedly the species usually rears two broods each summer in New Jersey but only one in New England. Yet the late hatchings I observed at Barnstable, Mass., on July 19, 1957, suggest a second brood.

*Young.*—My data from Barnstable, Mass., indicate an incubation period of 11 days. A nest under observation completed its set of four eggs on July 9, 1957. On July 22 the nest contained young birds 3 days old (as estimated by Woolfenden's observations and measurements) which probably hatched July 19. The female alone does the incubating (A. H. Norton, 1897; G. E. Woolfenden, 1956). Woolfenden says: "The first indication of hatching is a crack in the side of the egg along the line of greatest circumference. The crack is extended along this line by the egg tooth, and then contraction of muscles of the neck by the embryo separates the shell into two pieces. Extension of the legs frees the bird from the shell. * * * When free from the shell, the young birds rest on their tarsi, abdomen and forehead; their down dries in a few minutes, and their skin becomes noticeably darker." He further notes that by the second day the feather papillae showed through the skin, but the feathers remained sheathed until the seventh day. The eyes began to open on the third day. Gaping began on the day of hatching and continued to the eighth or ninth day; cowering appeared on the seventh. The last egg tooth was shed on the sixth day. The average weight of five nestlings, 1.7 grams at hatching, doubled at 2 days, tripled at 3 days, and reached 14.2 grams on the 10th day when most left the nest. The young were fed in the nest by the female alone, and for about 20 days after leaving the nest.

William Brewster's (MS.) observations at Revere, Mass., also showed the young to be fully feathered and ready to leave the nest in 10 days. He watched these young being fed about once each minute. The adult "uttered the *cŭp cŭp* note almost incessantly on its way to the nest but never while leaving it. On the outward trips it usually carried an excrement sac of the young in its bill, dropping it 50 yards or so from the nest. On the inward trips it brought a little lump of food the character of which we could not ascertain. * * * It alighted directly at the nest and flew directly from it." He noted that the interior of the mouths of the young was "yellow as gold." However, nestlings I have seen have had pinkish mouth linings with a yellow rim around the bill. Young have been reported well feathered and nearly ready to fly as early as June 19 in Massachusetts, and by July 10 I have found the marshes full of newly fledged young, though some broods do not even hatch until much later than this.

*Plumages.*—The adult plumage was succinctly described by F. M. Chapman (1896 ed.): "General color of the upper parts a brownish olive-green; crown olive-brown, with a blue-gray line through its center; gray ear coverts, inclosed by ochraceous-buff lines, one of which passes over the eye and one down the side of the throat; feathers of the back margined with grayish and sometimes whitish; bend of the wing yellow; tail-feathers narrow and sharply pointed, the outer feathers much the shortest; breast and sides washed with buffy, paler in summer, and *distinctly* streaked with black; middle of the throat and belly white or whitish."

The sexes are similar in plumage but E. H. Forbush (1929) says that the female is the smaller. This was confirmed by G. E. Woolfenden (1956), who found the weight of 33 males to average 20.7 grams and of 14 females to average 17.8 grams. J. L. Peters (1942) mentions that there is "a more rufescent type and a less rufescent type" of plumage, although these are not actually two color phases.

Partial albino specimens have been described from Scarboro, Maine, Nantucket, Mass., and Mt. Pleasant, S.C. J. L. Peters (1942) described one partial melanistic specimen which he tentatively assigned to *nelsoni*; curiously enough, this bird was taken at Cape Sable, Fla., far south of the normal wintering range.

The sequence of plumages was described by J. Dwight (1900) as follows:

1. Natal down. Grayish woody brown.

2. Juvenal plumage, acquired by complete post-natal moult. Everywhere rich buff brightest on superciliary and malar stripes and on jugulum; the back broadly, the jugulum and sides narrowly streaked with clove-brown. Crown and wings nearly black, wing coverts and tertiaries broadly edged with ochraceous buff, the secondaries with russet, the primaries and their coverts with greenish tinged olive-gray, the alular with white. Tail olive brown with clove-brown shaft streaks and indistinct barring. Auriculars dusky. Bill and feet pinkish buff the former becoming dusky, the latter sepia brown with age.

3. First winter plumage acquired by partial post-juvenal moult during September and early October which involves almost the entire plumage except the primaries, their coverts and the secondaries, and apparently these also in some vigorous individuals. Unlike the previous plumage; the upper parts resembling *A. maritima*. Above, dull brownish olive-green, an orange tinged patch on the nape, the feathers of the back edged with pearl and cinereous gray, the crown rich sepia faintly streaked with clove-brown, an indistinct median stripe cinereous gray. The tertiaries are edged with buff, the secondaries and greater coverts with russet, the lesser coverts with olive-yellow; the edge of the wings is bright lemon-yellow. The new tail has more olive and is less barred than the old. Below, dull white, washed on the chin, across jugulum and on sides, flanks and crissum with ochraceous buff, superciliary and malar stripes deeper buff; streaked on jugulum, sides and crissum with clove-brown veiled by overlapping feather edgings. Auriculars cinereous. The buff everywhere fades rapidly and abrasion is marked bringing the throat streaking into prominence. Birds become grayer above and much whiter below by fading and by actual loss of the veiling feather tips * * *.

The nuptial plumage is acquired by a complete molt prior to migration in March and April each year, after which the first year birds are indistinguishable from older ones. The birds arrive on the breeding grounds in fresh plumage, although abrasion soon damages the feathers. Subsequent winter plumages acquired by complete molts prior to migration in late August and September are essentially the same as the first winter plumage, though the colors average richer.

The occurrence of two complete molts in the sharp-tailed sparrow can perhaps be correlated with the excessive and rapid abrasion of the feathers by the coarse grasses in which they live. The seaside sparrow, which has only a postnuptial molt, feeds more in the open as do the Savannah, Ipswich, grasshopper, Le Conte's, and Henslow's sparrows, which have a complete postnuptial and a partial prenuptial molt. Certainly the sharp-tails get mud on their plumage as I have watched them bathe from a partially submerged piece of driftwood after extracting a morsel of food from a deeper layer in the mud.

*Food.*—S. D. Judd (1901) reported that 51 stomachs of the sharp-tailed sparrow taken between May and October showed 81 percent animal matter and 19 percent vegetable matter. C. S. Robbins (in litt.) reported that additional birds collected in Delaware in June and September 1938 showed 100 percent animal food. Birds I collected in June and July in Massachusetts varied between 80 percent and 90 percent animal material. My studies of the contents of 250 stomachs representing all five subspecies supplied by the Fish and Wildlife Service further confirm this preponderance of animal food, greater than for any other sparrow, during the warmer months. Proportionately more vegetable matter is taken in the winter. The animal matter has been further broken down to Hymenoptera, 3 percent; Coleoptera, mostly weevils, 6 percent; Orthoptera, 7 percent; Lepidoptera, 14 percent; Hemiptera, especially leaf-hoppers, 12 percent; Diptera, 5 percent; miscellaneous insects, 8 percent; amphipods (sandfleas), Arachnida, and small snails, 26 percent. There is no record of its taking small crabs as does the seaside sparrow. Birds I have watched in late June and early July in Barnstable, Mass., were feeding extensively on a small whitish moth. Salt marsh birds are reported to take grasses and wild rice as vegetable matter, but fresh water birds take a large variety of weed seeds.

The only agricultural crop with which these birds are in contact is "salt hay" and their effect is primarily beneficial. Sage, Bishop, and Bliss (1913) described the food, both animal and vegetable, as 2 percent of beneficial forms, 30 percent harmful, and 68 percent neutral.

*Behavior.*—Sharp-tailed sparrows are retiring and secretive, but not overly shy. C. W. Townsend (1905) says:

Sharp-tailed Sparrows are rather difficult birds to observe, especially if they are vigorously followed, as they then lie close, and when flushed, soon drop into the grass and instantly conceal themselves. If, however, the observer keeps still the birds often become quite tame and display their interesting habits. They run through the grass like mice, with heads low, occasionally pausing to look around, stretching up to almost double their running height. They occasionally alight in bushes or small trees, and I have seen them running about a stone-wall near the marsh like mice.

A. Sprunt and E. B. Chamberlain (1949) write of them on the wintering grounds: "The Sharp-tail responds well to the 'squeak.' One may stop in a patch of marsh which is apparently birdless, make the squeak noise, and suddenly up will pop these inquisitive little birds, peering here and there and balancing and swaying on the marsh grass stems."

In 1890, William Brewster studied several colonies of these birds on the Massachusetts coast, notably one at Revere. He reports (MS.): "They were along ditches (not tide creeks) and the edges of salt ponds bordered by dense, matted, fine and short grass (not coarse sedge such as occurs on the tide creeks).

"When flushed they would fly only a few rods and then drop into a ditch where they would run very swiftly and much like mice as they often took advantage of a shelving piece of bank by skulking well out of sight beneath it.

"Two * * * were sitting. When flushed for the first time they started about six or eight feet ahead of us rising in the usual manner without any preliminary running or tumbling about on the ground. * * * Neither bird chirped or came back about us but both, after flying thirty yards or so, alighted, one in a ditch, the other on a bare mud flat and began running and dodging among the mud lumps and grass in the usual characteristic way.

"These breeding Sharp-tails show themselves on the wing much more freely than do autumn birds. * * * The characteristic flight was short and hovering the bird rising to a height of six or eight feet and often fluttering along for a few yards dropping again into the grass. Sometimes one would go 100 to 200 yards, however, in which case it generally moved swiftly in long, gentle sweeps or undulations resembling closely those of an English Sparrow. * * * We several times saw a bird rise to a height of 15 or 20 feet and fly 100 yards or more in a perfectly straight, level course, moving as slowly and feebly as a Rail and sometimes dropping its feet and legs in a similar manner. A bird feeding young in the nest always flew in this way both going and returning."

F. H. Allen (*in* litt.) writes me: "The bird in flight presents a strange appearance, as if the head end and tail end were about equal in length. The flight is direct and steady, very different from that of the Savannah Sparrow." Thomas Nuttall (1903 ed.) commented on these birds walking on floating weeds as successfully as on land. G. E. Woolfenden (1956) said: "When searching for food, Sharp-tailed Sparrows walk through the dense black grass, deftly brushing stems aside with their bill as they go. Open areas are generally traversed by rapid running. * * * They stop to investigate openings in the matted understory of grass, often sticking their head into the holes."

My own observations have been made mostly in Massachusetts. These birds are easily watched, almost tame if not pursued, and soon forget the presence of a silent observer. They readily show themselves along ditches and on the mud banks where they search for food. The habit of stretching the head and neck upward to survey the neighborhood, described above by Townsend, is their most characteristic gesture. When hunting food, they walk and run, rather than hop, in a zig-zag course in the grass or across the mud, picking up particles of food as they go along. They drink the water in the ditches, usually rather brackish. I have seen them fly to a partially submerged piece of driftwood, scoop up water in the mandible and tip the head backward to swallow it. On one occasion in early June in Dartmouth, Mass., a very high tide had forced the birds into the *Iva* bushes where they were surprisingly clumsy in alighting and in maintaining their balance. Sharp-tails are most active early in the morning and late in the afternoon, but they do not retire completely during the middle of the day. On several occasions, I have found them active through the dusk until it became too dark to see.

F. V. Hebard (*in litt.*) recorded "feigning" in this species observed Aug. 1, 1953, in New Jersey: "Most of the young were out of the nest, but one pair of adults first scurried through the grass like mice and then flew from one bush to another as if injured." He defined "feigning" broadly as any "form of behavior such as rodent-running or impeded flight which tends to divert a predator from eggs or young." I have several times been led away from a presumed nesting site by a bird making short flights with much calling and, after going about a hundred yards, circling back to the starting point.

Little is known of the life span of the sharp-tailed sparrow. G. E. Woolfenden (in litt.) has reported a female banded at Lavallette, N.J., July 3, 1955, and recovered in the same place on the same island Aug. 27, 1957. This bird, originally netted and banded at her nest, was therefore at least 3 years old when retaken, and feathers reappearing on her incubation patch indicated that she had bred in 1957 also.

*Voice.*—The song of the sharp-tailed sparrow is not impressive. William Brewster (MS.) writes: "These sparrows are far from persistent singers. At times fully 15 minutes would pass without a sound. * * * When one began, however, he would usually start others, and for a few minutes there would be general singing all over the marsh. The song is the faintest and carries the poorest of any bird song that I have ever heard. * * * Nonetheless, it is varied and at times decidedly musical and pleasing." It has been described as the plunging of a hot iron in water, which may or may not be preceded or followed by one or more sharp *tics*. Brewster (MS.) adds that "it would not be wide of the mark to say that the Sharp-tail's song seems to combine a part or all of the songs of the Henslow's, and Yellow-winged or Savannah Sparrow's and the Long-billed Marsh Wren's." To this list I would add the seaside sparrow, though the sharp-tail's song is thinner, less liquid in quality, and carries less well.

A. A. Saunders (in litt.) has contributed the following description: "The song of the Sharp-tailed Sparrow is mainly a short fricative buzz, occasionally with a few introductory notes before it. The buzz fades away in intensity, starting comparatively loudly and growing softer till it can barely be heard, and one is not quite sure just when it actually ends. The buzz is fricative, rather than sibilant, that is, it sounds like a series of *f*s or *th*s rather than *s* or *z*. Songs vary from 1.4 to 2.5 seconds, averaging about 1.7 seconds. The pitch varies from F''' to C'''', and the pitch interval from 1 to 2½ tones."

In my own notes, I have recorded several song patterns which may be phoneticized as *ts-ts-sssssss-tsik*, *ts-ts-ts-ts-ts-tsi-lik*, and *tsi-lik tssss-s-s-s--s---s*. I have heard songs lasting up to 5 or 6 seconds. Woolfenden (1956) recorded them to 20 seconds.

The song is given in two manners, from a perch and in flight. William Brewster (MS.) says: "The Sharp-tail usually sings from the top of a cluster of tall grass but sometimes perches on a stake. It sits as erect as a Hawk and quite as motionless. I could not detect any quivering of the wings or tail and was not even sure that the throat swelled perceptibly. * * * The bird has one peculiar habit in connection with its singing, viz. it rarely sings more than twice consecutively and often only once from the same perch, taking numerous short flights from place to place." I have often observed the flight song at Barnstable, Mass., and Tiverton, R.I. The bird springs up from the grass, rises about 20 feet, then flutters in a semi-circle with quivering wings and drooping head and tail while singing three or four times, and finally drops straight downward rapidly and silently. Sometimes the bird makes this flight without uttering a sound. I have not heard singing earlier than May 23, and the latest recorded date is August 9 (A. A. Saunders, 1948). Walter Faxon reported to William Brewster their singing in the Neponset Marshes in Massachusetts on July 8, 1890, when the temperature stood at 92°.

The call note is a soft scolding and chirping, uttered relatively infrequently. It is variously described as *tic, cup, chuck, tchep, tsip chut,* etc.

*Field marks.*—The sharp-tailed sparrow is a handsome and well-marked bird, always identifiable if sufficient care is taken to study it adequately. The ochre-buff facial marking surrounding the gray cheek patch is the essential mark. The crown and nape appear grayish, the breast streakings are variable, and the back brown sometimes with considerable grayish. The sharply pointed tail feathers are sometimes a useful mark as the bird flies away. It can be confused only with the seaside sparrow, which appears appreciably larger, darker, and grayer.

My comments on subspecific identification are based on both field experience and a study of many museum specimens. *A. c. caudacuta* seems to be the "mean of the species," the facial markings being well defined, the breast streaking sharp, and the back brown with contrasting pale edgings to the scapulars. *A. c. diversa* has a darker back with less pale edging on the scapulars, and stronger breast streaking with some buffy wash. *A. c. subvirgata* is the palest and grayest race, the yellow of the face and the gray of the cheek being quite light and the back quite gray; the breast streaking is present but blurred. *A. c. altera* has richer orange and gray facial markings than *subvirgata* but a grayer back than *nelsoni*. *A. c. nelsoni* is slightly smaller and has a strong buffy wash across the breast which is practically devoid of streaking, the facial markings being very rich ochre.

In summary, without the specimen in the hand and without adequate skins for comparison, it is my opinion that *diversa* vs. *caudacuta* are inseparable as are *subvirgata* vs. *altera*, *altera* vs. *nelsoni*, and perhaps *nelsoni* vs. *caudacuta*. Birds from certain marshes on the Maine coast intermediate between *caudacuta* and *subvirgata* are often surprisingly like *altera*.

*Enemies.*—The predation files of the U.S. Fish and Wildlife Service report sharp-tailed sparrows present in only 3 of 617 marsh hawk stomachs, all from Fisher's Island, N.Y., and in only 1 of 1,275 marsh hawk pellets from wintering birds in Florida. Also *nelsoni* was found in one of 281 short-eared owl stomachs from Illinois. In addition, it must be assumed that such ground-dwelling birds are occasionally taken by minks, foxes, rats, and snakes, although specific records are lacking.

H. S. Peters (1937) listed only one external parasite, a louse, *Philopterus subflavescens*, on this bird. I examined 12 specimens, collected at Barnstable, Mass., for parasites: 8 were completely free; 4 showed from 1 to 10 individuals of the above louse, and 1 had a tick, not yet identified. No Mallophaga, hippoboscids, or endoparasites were found. Examination of blood smears proved negative.

Eastern equine encephalitis virus has not yet been reported from this species.

Friedmann (1963) reports no instance of parasitism by the cowbird on this race of the sharp-tailed sparrow. Indeed, he (1929) specifically excludes it because it is "ecologically distinct in [its] breeding grounds from the Cowbird." This distinction apparently applies to all races except *nelsoni* (see under that subspecies).

Unusual storm tides take a toll of sharp-tail nests, built as they are just at the upper limit of normal high tides. O. S. Pettingill (1936) described such destruction in June 1935 on Grand Manan Island, referable of course to *subvirgata*. H. F. Lewis (1920), also referring to *subvirgata* in Nova Scotia, noted an apparent correlation between the height of spring tides and the time of nesting, and he questioned whether the bird may take the expected height of the tide into account in building its nest.

More important are the changes in the habitat produced by man. William Brewster (1906) said of these birds in Cambridge, Mass., "Formerly a common summer resident of one locality which has long since been totally abandoned." At that time, this was a tidal marsh; at present, no vestige remains, the marsh having been filled and densely built up with industry. Witmer Stone (1937) noted a restriction in range in New Jersey caused by drainage. My records show that the marshes of Scusset Creek at Sagamore, Mass., were once satisfactory for sharp-tails and supported a number of pairs, but widening and deepening the Cape Cod Canal partially filled these marshes in and changed the drainage pattern so that they were no longer subject to periodic salt water flooding. As the salt leached out of the soil after four or five years, the *Spartina* disappeared and with it the sharp-tailed sparrows. Now these former marshes are mostly brush-covered and in places growing up to pitch pine and scrub oak.

*Fall.*—Fall migration begins in mid-September and consists of a general withdrawal southward. The largest concentrations of the year are usually seen at this time. Early fall arrivals have been collected in South Carolina and coastal Alabama on September 21, but some birds are seen regularly in Massachusetts and New York, excluding wintering stragglers, to late November. Most observers agree that the sharp-tails are less shy on migration than when nesting, and show themselves more readily, often clinging to tall reeds rather than flying away. In my experience this trait is more marked in the fall than in spring, and probably results from the larger number of individuals present and to the high proportion of inexperienced immature birds.

*Winter.*—The principal wintering grounds of the entire species are along the coasts of South Carolina, Georgia, northern Florida, and

Alabama. They are gregarious in winter and Audubon (1841) said of them in South Carolina: "I have observed thousands * * * in late December, and so numerous are they, that I have seen more than 40 * * * killed with one shot." A. T. Wayne (1910) considered this race the most abundant around Charleston, S.C. Sprunt and Chamberlain (1949) wrote: "They are tidal to the extent that they live in the marsh until forced out by the rising tides; then they congregate along the shoreline, on the back beaches of the islands, on the spoil banks of the Inland Waterway or along the edges of the mainland. An observer walking along the rim of such places at high water will flush them by the score."

A. H. Howell (1932) considered them common in northern Florida south to Mosquito Inlet on the east coast and to Tampa Bay on the west, and commented that they are practically silent in winter. The appearance of this race on the west coast of Florida, substantiated by many specimens I have examined, is the only evidence that it ever makes a regular overland flight. The scarcity of records from southern Florida suggests these individuals cross over 100 or more miles of land to reach the Gulf Coast.

A few straggling individuals attempt to winter in favorable marshes north to Massachusetts and have been recorded regularly in recent years on Christmas counts from Cape Cod southward. It is to be doubted, however, that many of these birds survive until spring, at least in New England, as February and March records are few and far between. I have personally found sharp-tails on Cape Cod in January and then failed in mid-March to locate them in an intensive search of the same marshes.

## Distribution

*Range.*—Coastal marshes from southern Maine to southern and western Florida.

*Breeding range.*—The eastern sharp-tailed sparrow breeds locally in salt marshes of the Atlantic coast from southern Maine (Scarborough) south to coastal New Jersey (south to near Tuckerton); extends to Martha's Vineyard and Nantucket County off the coast of Massachusetts.

*Winter range.*—Winters in coastal marshes from southern New Jersey (Cape May) south to northern and western Florida (Mosquito Inlet, St. Vincent Island, Tampa Bay region) and southern Alabama; casually to Massachusetts (Barnstable) and southern Florida (Cape Sable).

*Migration.*—The data apply to the species as a whole. Early dates of spring arrival are: Pennsylvania—State College, May 6. New Jersey—Cape May, March 31. New York—New York City area, May 26. Connecticut—New Haven, April 30. Rhode Island—Point Judith, April 27. Massachusetts—Revere, May 19; Essex County, May 23. New Hampshire—New Hampton, May 22. Maine—South Harpswell, April 5. New Brunswick—Scotch Lake, April 6 and April 22. Nova Scotia—Wolfville, June 3. Arkansas—Stuttgart, May 14. Missouri—St. Louis, April 18. Illinois—Quincy, April 5; Chicago, May 12. Ohio—Buckeye Lake, April 18. Michigan—Grand Rapids, April 11. Iowa—Mason City, April 20. Wisconsin—Milwaukee, May 3. Minnesota—Isanti County, April 8 (average of 5 years for southern Minnesota, May 22). Kansas—Elmdale, April 4. South Dakota—Vermilion, April 29. North Dakota—Ward County, May 21; Jamestown, May 24.

Late dates of spring departure are: Florida—Tallahassee, May 18; Amelia Island, May 11. Alabama—Bayou La Batre, May 16. Georgia—Chatham County, May 2. Virginia—Blacksburg, May 23. Maryland—Baltimore County, June 3. New York—New York City area, June 8. Connecticut—North Madison, June 9. Massachusetts—Essex County, June 11. Arkansas—Mena, May 24. Missouri—St. Louis, May 15. Illinois—Chicago, May 23; Rantoul, May 16. Ohio—central Ohio, May 27. Wisconsin—Milwaukee, May 21. Minnesota—Duluth, May 15. Texas—Cove, May 20. North Dakota—Jamestown, June 10.

Early dates of fall arrival are: Kansas—Topeka, October 6. Oklahoma—Tulsa, October 17. Texas—High Island, October 31. Minnesota—Minneapolis, September 21. Wisconsin—Milwaukee, September 20. Ontario—Toronto, September 23. Michigan—southeastern Michigan, September 27. Ohio—central Ohio, September 19. Illinois—Addison, August 31; Chicago, September 12 (average of 6 years, September 20). Missouri—St. Louis, September 6. Tennessee—Smyrna, September 24. Mississippi—Gulfport, September 26. New Hampshire—New Hampton, October 8. Massachusetts—Essex County, September 3 (median of 5 years, September 13). Connecticut—New Haven, September 14; Portland, September 21. New York—Syracuse, August 29 (average of 6 years for upstate New York, October 3). Pennsylvania—State College, September 20. Virginia—Cape Henry, August 20. North Carolina—Greensboro, September 29. Georgia—Tybee Island, September 29. Alabama—Orange Beach, September 21. Florida—Amelia Island, October 17; Seven Oaks, October 20.

Late dates of fall departure are: North Dakota—Jamestown, September 14. South Dakota—Sioux Falls, October 20. Minnesota—Minneapolis, October 11 (average of 3 years for southern Minnesota, September 24). Wisconsin—Iowa County, October 8. Iowa—Iowa City, October 12. Ontario—Ottawa, October 16. Michigan—

Grand Rapids, November 21. Ohio—Central Ohio, October 8. Illinois—Chicago, October 21 (average of 6 years, October 3). Missouri—St. Louis, October 23. Tennessee—Memphis, October 25. Louisiana—Shreveport, October 19. Prince Edward Island—Gladstone, September 21. New Brunswick—Grand Manan, October 6. Maine—Scarboro Marsh, November 15. New Hampshire—New Hampton, October 22. Massachusetts—Swampscott, November 9. Connecticut—New Haven, November 12. New York—Moriches Inlet, November 24; Cayuga basin, October 29. New Jersey—Elizabeth, October 28; Cape May, October 25. Pennsylvania—State College, November 2. Virginia—Lexington, October 17.

*Egg dates.*—Connecticut: 60 records, May 24 to July 14; 34 records, June 8 to June 13.

Maryland: 7 records, May 14 to August 21; 5 records, May 25 to June 27.

Massachusetts: 12 records, June 9 to July 2.

New York: May 9 to August 4 (number of records not stated).

Rhode Island: 10 records, June 11 to July 6.

## AMMOSPIZA CAUDACUTA DIVERSA (Bishop)

### Southern Sharp-tailed Sparrow

#### Contributed by NORMAN P. HILL

#### HABITS

The southern sharp-tailed sparrow was described by Louis B. Bishop in 1901, the type locality being Wanchese, Roanoke Island, N.C. Its breeding range as now defined extends from Tuckerton, N.J., south to Chincoteague Island, Va., and includes suitable marshes within the estuary of Chesapeake Bay north to Anne Arundel County on the west shore of Maryland and to Queen Anne County on the east. Though the 1957 A.O.U. Check-List extends the breeding range south to Pea Island, N.C., the marshes south of Chincoteague Island, Va., and those in North Carolina have been vainly searched for breeding colonies of this species by Montagna (1942a,b) and, independently, by me. The specimen reported as this species taken as a nestling at Pea Island, N.C., on which the Check-List range is apparently based, proves actually to be a juvenile seaside sparrow (Wetmore, 1944).

The range of the southern sharp-tailed sparrow lies entirely to the south of the area of Pleistocene glaciation. The marshes occupied by this race are similar to those of the eastern sharp-tail. They are salt or brackish, well-drained, and green with soft thick grass usually less than a foot tall. Again *Spartina patens* is the dominant plant, but also associated are *Spartina glabra, Distichlis spicata, Juncus gerardi,* and several species of *Scirpus.* The marshes themselves vary in size from the extensive ones around Chincoteague, Va., to rather narrow strips flanking estuaries in Maryland, where the sharp-tails may be found breeding within a few yards of grasshopper and Henslow's sparrows. South of the breeding range of *A. c. diversa* the coastal marshes are no longer green and meadowlike, but become coarse, sparse, tall, and brown, with *Juncus roemerianus, Salicornia europea,* and *Eliocharis* sp. the predominant plant growth. While the sharp-tails occupy this plant association commonly in winter, they have never been known to nest in it.

Like the more northern representatives of *A. c. caudacuta,* this subspecies is distinctly colonial, and chooses one section of marsh over another without apparent reason. A census of a colony in Somerset County, Md., showed a density of 17 pairs in 17 acres (P. F. Springer and R. E. Stewart, 1948). Its habits and behavior are not significantly different from those of *A. c. caudacuta.* Nests and eggs described by H. H. Bailey (1913) are similar in location and appearance to those of the nominate race. Nests with full sets of eggs have been found May 22 to August 21.

Montagna (1942a) writes that "The race *diversa* chirps more frequently than *subvirgata* and *caudacuta.* * * * Also the occasional flight songs of *diversa* which I witnessed did not seem as spectacular as those of the other races to the north. The males rose only twenty feet or so in the air, uttering the song repeatedly, in the ascent as well as the descent. The song, too, seemed to be harsher and more varied than that of *caudacuta* and *subvirgata.*"

For comments on identification, see the appropriate section under *A. c. caudacuta.* As far as is known, the plumage sequence and molts are identical with those of that subspecies.

Montagna (1942a) mentions that the diet of this race when he studied them during June and July was almost exclusively small blackish spiders, which they were also feeding to their young.

Migration consists chiefly of withdrawal down the coast to the main wintering grounds along the South Carolina, Georgia, and Florida coasts. Like *A. c. caudacuta,* a few birds cross Florida to the Gulf coast and have been collected as far west as Louisiana (H. C. Oberholser, 1938).

## DISTRIBUTION

*Range.*—Tidal marshes from Chesapeake Bay and southern New Jersey to northern Florida.

*Breeding range.*—The southern sharp-tailed sparrow breeds locally in salt and brackish marshes from upper Chesapeake Bay (Sandy Point, Kent Narrows) and southern New Jersey (Tuckerton, intergrading with *A. c. caudacuta*) south to Virginia (Wallop's Island).

*Winter range.*—Winters from South Carolina (Charleston County) south to east central Florida (Titusville) and along the Gulf coast of northern Florida (Wakulla County, Tarpon Springs); casually north to Virginia (Smith's Island), west to Louisiana (Buras), and south to southern Florida (Cape Sable).

*Egg dates.*—New Jersey: 24 records, May 22 to August 21; 12 records, May 30 to June 22.

## AMMOSPIZA CAUDACUTA ALTERA Todd

### James Bay Sharp-tailed Sparrow

Contributed by NORMAN P. HILL

#### HABITS

The James Bay race of the sharp-tailed sparrow was described as *Ammospiza caudacuta altera* by W. E. C. Todd in 1938, the type locality being East Main, James Bay, Ontario, Canada. The breeding range is restricted to the marshes at the southern end of James Bay. It is separated by 600 miles from the nearest *nelsoni* to the west and by 475 miles from the nearest *subvirgata* to the southeast.

H. F. Lewis (1939) thus describes the marshes this race inhabits:

James Bay, which is about 230 miles long and 140 miles wide, occupies the lowest part of a shallow depression with sides that are very flat and slope very gently. * * * Although the tide rises and falls vertically only 5 to 7 feet, the southern and western shores are so nearly horizontal that in the course of this rise and fall the waters of the bay advance and recede over flats of fairly firm material that are often from two to four miles in width. * * * Above normal high-tide mark, * * * is a border of sedge-grown marsh, usually about a mile wide, with fresh to brackish water. In exceptionally high tides, the bay overflows this marsh for short periods. Back of the marsh are woods, first a profusion of willows, then white spruce and poplar, often 75 or more feet high, then black spruce and tamarack.

The James Bay area has been heavily glaciated and relatively more recently than farther south, so the soil is glacial debris of gravel, boulders, sand, and clay in the process of rearrangement by water activity.

As would be expected, the sharp-tails are found in sedge and grass areas. *Juncus gerardi, Carex maritima, Scirpus rufus*, and *Triglochin* sp. are reported in these marshes. The plants are more separate and upright, so the vegetation gets less matted than in *Spartina patens* areas, and the marshes have a more varied appearance than those farther south.

There are no published data on habits, nest, young, molts, song, food, and so forth, of this race. I see no reason to believe they differ from any of the others. In the field, *altera* cannot be separated from *subvirgata* on one hand or from *nelsoni* on the other; even with the specimen in the hand, the diagnosis is difficult and sometimes impossible. J. A. Hagar was impressed by the extreme buffy color of the young in juvenal plumage.

In migration, this bird moves more or less directly north and south. There are numerous records around Lake Ontario and Lake Erie, and in the Finger Lakes region of New York (see *A. c. subvirgata*). From here the birds apparently move toward the Atlantic coast rather than down the Ohio and Mississippi valleys, though specimens from the interior should be reexamined. They have been collected on the Atlantic coast from Massachusetts south to their wintering grounds in South Carolina, Georgia, northern Florida, and Alabama. This race has also been collected once in Louisiana (H. C. Oberholser, 1938). There are many more fall than spring records along the northern part of the Atlantic coast.

### DISTRIBUTION

*Range.*—James Bay to coast of South Carolina, Georgia, and Florida.

*Breeding range.*—The James Bay sharp-tailed sparrow breeds in marshes bordering James Bay in northern Ontario (Cape Henrietta Maria) and northern Quebec (Eastmain).

*Winter range.*—Winters in coastal marshes from South Carolina (Charleston County) south to eastern Florida (Ft. Pierce); casually west to Louisiana (Buras); recorded in migration west to Michigan (Livingston County) and Ohio (Richmond County) and east to Vermont (Clarendon), Massachusetts (Swampscott, Revere, Scituate), New York (Highland Falls, mouth of Croton River, Westchester County) and Chesapeake Bay, Md. (Cornfield Harbor).

*Egg dates.*—Ontario: 2 records, June 25 and July 12.

### AMMOSPIZA CAUDACUTA NELSONI (Allen)

## Nelson's Sharp-tailed Sparrow

### Contributed by NORMAN P. HILL

#### HABITS

Nelson's sharp-tailed sparrow (*Ammospiza caudacuta nelsoni*) was described by J. A. Allen (1875) from specimens collected by E. W. Nelson at Calumet Lake, now within the boundaries of the city of Chicago, Ill. Though the discoverer believed them to be breeding there, this report is unsubstantiated, and the area is far to the south of the known present breeding range, which covers a wide area of the prairie provinces from western Alberta, southern Mackenzie, central Saskatchewan and Manitoba to northern North Dakota and northwestern Minnesota. At one time, Nelson's sparrow was considered specifically different from the eastern sharp-tail.

*Territory.*—Nelson's sharp-tail is the only race of the species occupying an exclusively fresh-water habitat in the breeding season. In Kittson County in northwestern Minnesota, Breckenridge and Kilgore (1929) describe its habitat as "extensive, swampy lakes bordered here and there with strips of tamarack. Poplar thickets and a few bits of prairie occupy the higher ground. A number of the shallow lakes have been entirely overgrown with a more or less floating layer of sphagnum and on this, wirey sedges are thriving so as to give the uncertain expanse the appearance of a perfectly firm level meadow." T. S. Roberts (1936) adds that they "inhabit wet, boggy swamps where the water is ankle or knee deep." In North Dakota, E. S. Rolfe (1899) finds them in short, scant grass on an alkaline flat, formerly an arm of Devil's Lake.

J. A. Munro (1929) found *nelsoni* at Beaver Hill Lake 50 miles east of Edmonton, Alberta; he described this lake as fairly deep and alkaline, the surrounding country either flat or slightly rolling, mostly unbroken prairie sparsely dotted with clumps of willow and poplar. The shoreline was of two types, a hard sand and a gumbo, the latter covered with short grass and bog rush on the outer portion and sedges on the land side with isolated areas of bulrush. Some of the marshes of tule and bog rush appeared to be a solid expanse but were actually intersected with channels and isolated ponds with some dry grassy islands. The sharp-tails were found in the tule beds.

I visited Beaver Hill Lake in June 1964. The surrounding prairie is now mostly farmland and much of the marshes are gone. Nevertheless I found Nelson's sharp-tails with little difficulty in the remaining tule beds. They were singing steadily, even at mid-day. The song was of the same pattern as that of *A. c. caudacuta* but seemed shorter, more wheezy, and lower pitched.

This race is relatively scattered over a wide geographical range and is generally quite rare and local, so much so that W. J. Beecher (1955) questioned the success of its adaptation to fresh water. He did not describe any characteristic behavior traits, but N. S. Goss (1891) writes: "They are very active, running about and climbing with ease the stalks of grass or reeds, where they sway about, often head downward, in their search for insect life and seeds." T. S. Roberts (1936) describes its food as: "Seeds of various plants; bugs, midges, horseflies, beetles, grasshoppers, etc."

Breckenridge and Kilgore (1929) describe a nest at Twin Lake near Karlstad, Minn., thus: "The meadow itself was covered with about six inches of water but the nest was built just above the water level where the soil though very damp, was free from standing water.

It was constructed of coarse grass lined with finer grasses and rested on the ground, not being in the least sunken. A tiny dead willow a few inches high supported one edge of the nest but no definite clump of vegetation surrounded it."

C. W. Bowman (1904) found a nest at Devil's Lake, N.D., which was "sunken level with the ground, * * * well concealed by its small size and the thick clump of grass." E. S. Rolfe (1899), also at Devil's Lake, found another nest sunken into the wet earth. At Long Lake, Manitoba, J. Macoun (1900) reported a nest in a tuft of marsh grass a few inches above the ground. The Nelson's sharp-tail is said to exhibit more anxiety about its nest than do the other races.

Nelson's sharp-tail migrates in a southerly and a southeasterly direction to both the Gulf and the southern Atlantic coasts. It has been collected widely but sparingly on the Atlantic coast as far north as New England, and is steadily more regular southward. There are many more fall than spring records toward the north. Many of the northeastern reports, however, were made prior to the description of *altera*, so specimens should be reexamined to check the race (cf. the Clarendon, Vt., specimen reported in the life history of *A. c. subvirgata*). Contrary to apparent logic, J. L. Peters (*in* Griscom, 1949, and Griscom and Snyder, 1955) found *nelsoni* to outnumber *altera* in Massachusetts; yet A. D. Cruickshank (1942) found no specimens of *nelsoni* whatsoever for the New York City region. Obviously, more collecting is necessary to determine the status of these races in the northeast. In the Mississippi valley *nelsoni* has been reported widely in small to moderate numbers.

Though it breeds only in fresh water, the Nelson's sparrow is always found in salt marshes in the winter and is common on the South Carolina, Georgia, and northern Florida coasts along with all the other races. It is by far the commonest of the five races on the Gulf coast. It has been collected southwest to Corpus Christi, Tex., and there are sight records on the Laguna Atascosa Wildlife Refuge just north of the Rio Grande. It may be surmised that this race tends to follow its "ancestral" route to the southern Atlantic coast, but that many individuals accompany other migrants down the Mississippi Valley. The dates in South Carolina (Sprunt and Chamberlain, 1949) are September 24 to May 17 and in Louisiana (H. C. Oberholser, 1938) October 24 to May 20. Ridgway (1891) described one specimen collected accidentally in California as the type of the race *becki*, not accepted by the A.O.U. Check-List Committee.

*Eggs.*—The eggs number four or five and are described as marked exactly as those of *A. c. caudacuta* but smaller, averaging 16.5 to 18.3 by 12.7 millimeters.

*Plumages.*—Nelson's sparrow is the smallest of the five races of the sharp-tailed sparrows, the bill in particular being proportionally much smaller. The adult plumage of this race is of a much richer brown with more orange facial markings than the other races, and has a strong buffy wash across the breast which is essentially devoid of streaking. The molts are the same as in the other races. The natal down has apparently never been described. R. R. Graber (pers. comm.) thus describes the juvenal plumage:

"Males exhibit more ventral streaking than do females. Forehead and crown black, with broad superciliaries and broad irregular median stripe of orange-buff. Nape light chestnut. Feathers of back black, broadly edged with orangish buff. Rump orange buff. Upper tail coverts similar but black along feather shafts. Rectrices black along shaft, edged with olive tinged buff. Remiges blackish, primaries and secondaries edged with olive gray, tertials broadly edged with orangish buff. Coverts black, edged with orangish buff. Lores buffy. Side of head rich orangish buff, with post-ocular strip of black. Underparts orangish buff, richer anteriorly. Sides of jugulum and chest with few fine streaks of black. Ventral streaking variable. Leg feathers dusky and buff."

The field identification of this race is discussed in the appropriate section of the life history of *A. c. caudacuta.*

*Enemies.*—Friedmann (1929, 1963) lists *nelsoni* among the hypothetical victims of the brown-headed cowbird on the basis of one hearsay report. The first definite record was made by John Lane, who reported in a letter to Oscar M. Root: "On June 20, 1962 I found a Nelson's sharp-tail nest with 4 eggs plus 1 cowbird egg in a grassy hummock where the yellow rail nests in Dixon's Slough, Gorrie School District, Brandon, Manitoba."

*Voice.*—The Nelson's sharp-tail sings both perched and in flight as do the other races. N. S. Goss (1891) writes the song is "uttered at times as it rises and hovers for a moment, but usually from a perch or as it hops from stalk to stalk of the reeds, rushes and coarse grasses." W. J. Breckenridge (*in* Roberts, 1936) writes that "a low initial note slurs immediately into a high, wheezy, nasal buzz, which terminates in a low, short, grating *ur.*" It sings incessantly and with great effort. Song has been reported to July 22.

## DISTRIBUTION

*Range.*—Southern Mackenzie and prairie provinces southeast to Gulf and Atlantic coasts.

*Breeding range.*—The Nelson's sharp-tailed sparrow breeds in fresh-water prairie marshes from northeastern British Columbia

(Charlie Lake), southern Mackenzie (Great Slave Lake), central Saskatchewan (Emma Lake), and central Manitoba (The Pas, Sturgeon Creek) south to southern Alberta (Red Deer, Beaverhill Lake), southern Saskatchewan (Cypress Lake, Last Mountain Lake), northwestern and southeastern North Dakota (Towner, Ludden, Hankinson), northeastern South Dakota (Rush Lake), and northwestern Minnesota (Kittson and Marshall counties). Recorded in summer in eastern Montana.

*Winter range.*—Winters along the Gulf coast from Texas (Corpus Christi, Galveston County) to western Florida (south to Tampa Bay area); also on the Atlantic coast from South Carolina (Charleston County) to Florida (south to Merritt's Island); in migration to Maine (Cumberland County), Massachusetts (Barnstable), southeastern New York, southern and eastern Maryland (Cornfield Harbor, Ocean City), and eastern Virginia (Cobb Island).

*Casual records.*—Casual in Colorado (Gunnison County). Accidental in California (Milpitas, Morro Bay, Alameda and Imperial Counties) and Baja California (Bahia de San Quintín).

*Egg dates.*—Alberta: 2 records, June 3 and June 20.
Manitoba: 5 records, June 12 to June 20.

## AMMOSPIZA MARITIMA MARITIMA (Wilson)

### Northern Seaside Sparrow

PLATE 45

Contributed by GLEN E. WOOLFENDEN

#### HABITS

This dark-colored little salt marsh dweller was discovered by Alexander Wilson, who collected the first known specimens in 1810 along the New Jersey shore probably near where Ocean City now stands. He called it the "sea-side finch" and in his description (1811) of it writes:

Of this bird I can find no description. It inhabits the low rush-covered sea islands along our Atlantic coast, where I first found it; keeping almost continually within the boundaries of tidewater, except when long and violent east or northeasterly storms, with high tides, compel it to seek the shore. On these occasions it courses along the margin, and among the holes and interstices of the weeds and sea-wrack, with a rapidity equalled only by the nimblest of our sandpipers, and very much in their manner. At these times also it roosts on the ground, and runs about after dusk.

* * * Amidst the recesses of these wet sea marshes, it seeks the rankest growth of grass and sea weed, and climbs along the stalks of the rushes with as much dexterity as it runs along the ground, which is rather a singular circumstance, most of our climbers being rather awkward at running.

Confined as it is to the salt marshes of the Atlantic and Gulf coasts of North America, the seaside sparrow is by far the most maritime in distribution of all our land birds. So rigidly is the species restricted to its marsh habitat that its presence any distance from it is essentially accidental. Practically the only times one ever sees it away from the thick shelter of *Spartina, Juncus,* and other salt marsh grasses is when, as Wilson noted, storm-driven tides inundate the marshes and force it to take temporary refuge on adjoining higher land.

The 1957 A.O.U. Check-List recognizes nine distinct forms of the seaside sparrow, which W. J. Beecher (1955) has postulated were probably encouraged to develop by barriers in the form of drowned rivers created by fluctuations in sea level during late Pleistocene time. The nominate subspecies, breeding from Massachusetts southward to Virginia, is the northernmost race of this interesting complex. In the spring and summer of 1955 I was able to study its nesting habits in Ocean County, N.J., only a few miles north of where Wilson first found it a century and a half ago, and where it breeds side by side with the congeneric sharp-tailed sparrow. Unless otherwise noted, the ensuing data are taken from my published report (1956) of those studies.

*Spring.*—Though a few individuals winter fairly regularly throughout its breeding range, the northern seaside sparrow population is essentially migratory, and most individuals winter to the southward. Nothing is known of their departure from the wintering grounds in spring, but Allan Cruickshank (1942) reports that in the New York City region "while there is sometimes a light flight in mid-April, the first widespread movement seldom comes before the initial week of May. A spring peak is reached during the third week of this month."

At Chadwick, Ocean County, N.J., I saw the first seasides on May 5, 1955, when several appeared on the territories where they eventually nested. As these birds were not in evidence the previous day, they had apparently arrived during the night. During the next two weeks the species was most abundant, as birds continued to arrive and to pass by the territories being defended by the resident males.

*Territory.*—Unlike the closely allied sharp-tailed sparrow, the male seaside sparrow establishes a nesting territory which he advertises and defends against enroachment by other males. This he accomplishes mainly by singing, also by chasing when necessary. The song, given from an exposed perch such as a cattail (*Typha*) stalk or marsh-elder (*Iva frutescens*) bush within the territory, advertises its occupancy and warns that other seaside sparrows will not be tolerated. When the warning is disregarded, the male flies directly toward the intruder, close to the ground and often uttering rapid chipping notes.

PLATE 45

Jones Inlet, Long Island, N.Y.     A. D. Cruickshank

Ocean City, Md., June 8, 1940     B. Meanley

NORTHERN SEASIDE SPARROW AND NEST

PLATE 46

Levy County, Fla., Apr. 28, 1933                    S. A. Grimes

Levy County, Fla., May 10, 1936                    S. A. Grimes

SCOTT'S SEASIDE SPARROW AND NEST

The chase is not vigorous, and fighting is minimal, for occupancy is widely respected and almost invariably the intruder flees.

My study area in New Jersey, a marsh islet approximately 1,400 feet long and 600 feet wide, supported eight pairs of seaside sparrows in 1955. The territory of each pair consisted of a nesting area in the thicker sedges or bushy growth within the marsh, and a feeding area in the more scattered cord-grass (*Spartina*) and open mud at the marsh edge. The two were contiguous in some cases; in others they were separated by several hundred feet of marsh that the birds flew across and seldom alighted in. I never saw the species forage in the interior of the marsh, but each pair fed within a particular segment of shore-line usually not more than 200 feet in length and scarcely 20 feet wide. All parts of the territories of the different pairs were mutually exclusive, and in 6 weeks of close observation of marked birds (June 15 to August 1), I saw no resident seaside sparrow outside its defended area, which in no case extended more than 400 feet in any one direction.

No population density studies of the seaside sparrow have been conducted in large tracts of optimum habitat. In Maryland, Springer and Stewart (1948) found two territorial males in 19.5 acres (10p/100) of a salt marsh bulrush (*Scirpus robustus*)—saltgrass (*Distichlis spicata*) marsh and two territorial males in 22.25 acres (9p/100) of needlerush (*Juncus roemerianus*) marsh. The ditched islet I studied in New Jersey had 8.25 acres of marsh (the remainder was sand fill) domi-nated by smooth cord-grass (*Spartina alterniflora*), black grass (*Juncus gerardi*), and rows of marsh-elder (*Iva frutescens*). Each of the eight occupied territories here contained portions of the open mud shoreline where the birds fed. A larger tract of similar habitat would not have so dense a population (97p/100) because it would possess relatively less open shoreline.

Nothing is known of courtship and pair formation in this species. When I began intensive observations on June 15, all nests already contained eggs. In late June an influx of unbanded birds occurred, apparently individuals that had not yet nested or had perhaps nested unsuccessfully elsewhere. A few of these established territories in marsh unoccupied by the remaining original residents. On July 7 I watched one of these females as she seemed to be searching for a nest site. She crawled about in a marsh-elder bush, apparently testing the various forks in the branches for size. The male followed, remaining a few inches above and behind her. Several times the two birds dis-appeared in the lower branches where they were hidden by the sur-rounding black grass. Finally while the female squatted on a branch the male fluttered his wings, mounted on her back, and continued fluttering his wings during the few seconds of supposed copulation.

*Nesting.*—In contrast to the sharp-tailed sparrow which prefers the higher and drier parts of the marsh, the seaside sparrow almost always nests in the wetter portions (Stone, 1937; Forbush and May, 1939; Cruickshank, 1942). It usually builds just above the normal summer high tide mark where black grass (*Juncus gerardi*) and smooth cord grass (*Spartina alterniflora*) are the dominant plant growth. Most of the salt marshes in New Jersey have been ditched for mosquito control. On the mounds of excavated muck along these narrow ditches grow rows of marsh-elders (*Iva frutescens*) which provide suitable, often preferred nesting sites for the seasides.

Of the eight nests I found in 1955, four were supported by marsh-elders (three of them dead), three were built in black grass tussocks, and the eighth was supported mainly by cord grass stems. All eight nests were simple open cups built entirely of black grass stems and well concealed in the black grass, which grew so thickly around them they could be entered from only one direction. The prevailing southwest winds of spring and summer lean the marsh grass to the northeast, and six of the nests were approached from the easterly quadrant. Two nests, built in marsh-elders that held the surrounding grass stems upright, were entered from the northwest. One nest, built in a small dead marsh-elder, was soon tilted by the growth of the black grass supporting one side. Though this did not spill the contents, the adults shortly deserted the nest.

From the ground to the upper rim the eight nests varied from 9 to 11 (average 9.6) inches. Their outside diameters ranged from 3 to 4.5 (average 3.9) inches, and outside depths from 2 to 3.5 (average 2.7) inches. Inside diameters varied between 2 and 2.5 inches; seven nests had an inside depth of 1.5 inches, the other only 1 inch.

*Eggs.*—The seaside sparrow lays three to six eggs, with four or five comprising the usual set. They are ovate and have only a slight gloss. The ground is white or pale greenish-white, profusely speckled, spotted, and blotched with dark reddish browns such as "Hay's brown," "burnt umber," "Mars brown," "Prout's brown," or "auburn," and with underlying spots of "light purplish gray." The markings are usually well defined and tend to be concentrated toward the large end. On some the undermarkings are quite prominent, on others entirely lacking. In series the eggs are noticeably larger than those of the sharp-tailed sparrow, and their markings are generally larger and bolder. The measurements of 50 eggs of the nominate race average 20.9 by 15.5 millimeters; the eggs showing the four extremes measure *22.9* by 15.8, 20.3 by *16.5*, *18.3* by 15.2, and 22.1 by *14.5* millimeters.

*Incubation.*—The birds I studied in 1955 raised only one brood that summer, and the egg dates suggest that the northern seaside sparrow is normally single-brooded. The literature contains no information on the duration of incubation, which I also was unable to ascertain because I found no nest before it contained its full complement of eggs.

The female seaside sparrow does all the incubating. While she is on the nest the male usually remains a short distance away and sings frequently from some favorite perch. When disturbed he gives alarm notes that bring the female off the nest and both chip at the intruder. When the female leaves for the feeding grounds before the eggs hatch, the male accompanies her, and normally they return together.

*Young.*—At hatching a crack develops around the widest part of the egg where it has been etched on the inside by the egg tooth. Contraction of the chick's neck muscles separates the shell into two pieces, and extending the legs frees the bird from the shell. Each of two young I held in my hand during this process defecated in the shell while freeing itself. When free of the shell the nestling rests on its tarsi, abdomen, and forehead. The down dries in a few minutes, and the skin becomes noticeably darker.

The day they hatch the young start to gape, and as the parents feed them their abdomens distend. During the first 24 hours they frequently utter a soft "peep," and at its end are better able to right themselves, and many feather papillae show distinctly through the skin. On the second day the young are able to move short distances by using their wings and feet. A thick ridge of tissue forms over the eyeball where the eyelids later delaminate. The call now becomes a double version of the "peep" note. When the young are 3 days old the eyelids open slightly. During the next 3 days they become better coordinated and their eyes open fully. The egg tooth is usually lost by the sixth day.

All incoming feathers remain sheathed until the seventh day, when the body feathers start to emerge from the tips of their sheaths. Up to this time disturbing the nest produced only a begging reaction. Now they show the first signs of cowering and utter a squealing distress call when handled. On the eighth day begging is less frequent, cowering is the predominant attitude, and the young try to escape when removed from the nest. The remigial sheaths now turn from dark blue to gray and begin to slough off.

The first young left the Lavallette nests, which it must be remembered were being disturbed daily by my visits, on the ninth day, and none remained in the nest beyond the tenth day. When I parted the grass over a nest on the tenth day, the four young jumped out and scattered in the grass. They were able to run well. One of them gave a chipping note similar to the adult distress call.

Both parents fed the young and maintained nest sanitation by carrying fecal sacs away in their bills. I never saw an adult swallow a fecal sac, and I found several discarded ones on the feeding grounds.

Nice's (1943) observation that devotion of parent passerines to their young typically increases as they grow was exemplified by several incidents. A banded female who lost her mate early in incubation successfully hatched her three eggs, but deserted the young on their second day. A male whose mate disappeared when their four young were 6 days old continued to care for them until they fledged. The death of one of these nestlings on the eighth day and the fouling of the nest with excreta by the ninth day suggest he had difficulties carrying on the parental duties alone.

At another nest I visited daily from the time of hatching until the young fledged, the parents never performed the distraction display until the last day. As I lifted the 9-day-old young from the nest to weigh them they gave the distress call. This brought the parents from the feeding grounds 60 yards away. They ran around on the ground within 10 feet of me uttering the *tsip* notes and fluttering their wings. Several times they flew within a few feet of me buzzing their wings audibly. Although well aware of its purpose, I still found their display distracting.

The Lavallette nestlings were weighed and measured daily. During their first 7 days of nest life they increased in weight from 2.1 to 13.7 grams, or 1.6 grams per day. The remaining 3 days showed an average gain of only 1.5 grams to 15.2 grams. The rectrices and remiges began growing rapidly on the third day and averaged 4.5 and 17.5 millimeters respectively on the ninth. The tarsi, which measured 7.0 millimeters at hatching, were over 22 millimeters, or essentially adult length, when the young left the nest. As running is their only means of locomotion for several more days, it is not surprising that their tarsi mature so quickly.

Comparable weights and measurements were made on 14 adult males and 3 females taken at Chadwick between May 6 and June 27, 1955, as follows: Weight, males 24.2 grams (21.9–27.4), females 22.3 grams (19.8–24.4); wing (chord), males 64.2 millimeters (60–66), females 58.3 millimeters (58–59); tail, males 55.3 millimeters (54–59), females 51.0 millimeters (49–53); tarsus, males 23.0 millimeters (22–25), females 22.2 millimeters (21–23).

*Plumages.*—The color of the plumages of the seaside sparrows matches their natural surroundings. The olive-gray upperparts of the adults resemble the color of the mud on which they forage. The browner streaked plumage of the juveniles, which shows a striking resemblance to that of the sharp-tailed sparrow, doubtless hides them more effectively in the dense grass where they spend most of their time.

The young undergo a complete post-juvenal molt in late August. The resulting first winter plumage is indistinguishable from that which the adults acquire by their complete postnuptial molt at about the same time (Dwight, 1900). In August a high proportion of the seaside sparrows, including adults, have stubby tail feathers. A simultaneous molt of the rectrices may be normal for the species. There is no prenuptial molt, and the spring breeding plumage is acquired entirely by feather wear.

Dwight (1900) expressed surprise that the sharp-tailed sparrow has two complete molts annually while the congeneric seaside sparrow "living in the same environment * * * and suffering equally from abrasion due to coarse marsh grasses and reeds" has but one. My observations show the two species do not occupy precisely the same habitat. The sharp-tails nest and usually forage in the densest stands of grass, while the seasides prefer to feed in more open areas where they suffer less abrasion.

Ridgway (1901) thus describes the adult plumage (sexes alike):

Above alove-grayish, tinged with olive, especially on back, where feathers are somewhat darker with light grayish edges, producing more or less distinct streaks; pileum olive laterally, grayish medially, producing three broad but very indistinct and faintly contrasted stripes; a supraloral streak of yellow, usually passing into whitish posteriorly, succeeded by a broad supra-auricular stripe of olive-grayish; a malar stripe, chine, throat, and abdomen white; submalar stripe and broad streaks on chest grayish; edge of wing yellow. * * *

Some specimens show more or less black streaking on the posterior portion of the pileum, but in the large series examined (40 adults) this is never conspicuous. Autumnal and winter specimens show more or less of a pale buff suffusion on the chest, the white malar stripe also more or less buffy.

Richard R. Graber (1955) thus describes the juvenal plumage: "Feathers above nostrils white. Forehead and crown streaked black, olive, and olive brown. Nape olive brown. Back feathers black, edged with olive brown and buff (pattern: heavy black streaks on olive brown). Rump buffy or buffy brown obscurely marked with black. Upper tail coverts olive brown streaked with black. Rectrices olive brown, black along each shaft. Remiges black, edged with drab, tertials edged with dull rusty brown and tipped with buffy white. Median and greater coverts black, edged with buff. No wing bar pattern. Lores buffy gray. Superciliary (in front of eye) buffy-yellow. Postocular strip buff; feathers around eye gray or buffy gray. Auriculars gray; sub- and postoculars light buff (distinct cheek patch). Chin and throat white with dusky "mustache" marks. Upper chest, sides, and flanks buff, streaked with dark brown or blackish (amount of streaking variable). Belly white, crissum buff, both unmarked. Leg feathers buffy or buffy gray."

*Food.*—Judd (1901) determined the food of the seaside sparrow to be, like that of its congener, the sharp-tailed sparrow, more than 80 percent animal matter. Audubon (1839) noted their food "consists of marine insects, small crabs and snails, as well as the green sand beetle, portions of all of which I have found in their stomach." His added comment "Having one day shot a number of these birds, merely for the sake of practice, I had them made into a pie, which, however, could not be eaten, on account of its fishy savour" is as interesting a reflection on the customs of his day as it is on the seaside sparrow's feeding habits.

The bills of both the *Ammospizas*, more elongated and less conical than those of any other fringillids, are perhaps better adapted for insect eating. In winter they eat some vegetable matter, mainly seeds of marsh grasses, but this is apparently never an important part of their diet. A funnel trap baited with canary seed on the Lavallette marshes during the spring migration of 1955 caught Savannah sparrows (*Passerculus sandwicensis*) in quantity, but not a single *Ammospiza*. The nesting seasides at Lavallette fed extensively on noctuid moths. I counted some 40 wings of these moths in the feeding territories of two pairs along a tide-deposited windrow of eel grass (*Zostera marina*). Often the four wings of a single moth lay as they had on the insect, whose body the sparrows had neatly snipped out. The parent birds seemed to give smaller and softer food items to their nestlings at hatching and larger things as they grew.

*Behavior.*—To quote Audubon (1839) again: "The monotonous chirpings which one hears in almost every part of our maritime salt marshes are produced by this bird. * * * The Seaside Finch may be seen at any hour of the day, during the months of May and June, mounted on the tops of the rankest weeds which grow by the margins of tide-water along the greater portion of our Atlantic coast, where it pours forth with much emphasis the few notes of which its song is composed. When one approaches it, it either seeks refuge amongst the grass, by descending along the stalks and blades of the weeds, or flies off to a short distance, with a continued fluttering of wings, then alights with a rapid descent, and runs off with great nimbleness."

On the species' running ability Stone (1937) remarks: "While making but little show in the air the Seaside Sparrow is very much at home on the muddy bottom of the marsh and its large feet are well adapted for running over the soft ooze while they, as well as the short tail, shape of body, and somewhat elongated bill, all recall the structure of the rails, which are co-tenants of the meadows. The Seaside Sparrow can run very swiftly, threading its way in and out among the coarse stalks of the Spartina grass that grows along the edges of the creeks.  As it runs the legs seem rather long and the body is held well up from the ground while the tail is always pointed downward."

Trotter (1891) explained this species' large strong feet and short, stiff pointed tail as adaptations for clinging to tall reeds being swayed about by the wind.  Stone's suggestion that the feet are enlarged for running over the soft mud seems more plausible.  Short tails are a characteristic of a number of species that dwell in dense grassy habitats, those that do not cling to reeds such as the rails and meadow-larks (*Sturnella*) as well as those that do, such as sparrows of the genera *Ammodramus* and *Passerherbulus*.  The short pointed tails seem more likely an adaptation allowing the birds to dart through and turn quickly in the maze of vertical grass stems.

*Voice.*—The song of which Audubon wrote so disparagingly is uttered only by the male seaside sparrow, who seems to use it primarily to advertise the occupancy of his territory.  It normally lasts just under two seconds, three-fourths of which are taken up by the final buzzing note.  Saunders (1951) describes it as short and buzzlike, beginning with two or three rather faint short notes followed by a higher-pitched, louder, strongly accented buzzy note that drops slightly into the final trill, which starts loud and fades away toward the end.  The song has been variously written *tup tup ZEE reeeeeeeee* and *tup TEE tle reeeeeeeee* (Saunders, 1951), *cutcut, zhé-eeeeeee* (Peterson, 1947) and *che-zheéeege, che-zheé, che-weége, chur-zhée* and *too-szheée* (Stone, 1937).  My field notes contain the following renditions: *CHUR-er eeeee, CHUR eeeee*, and *oka-CHE weeeee*.  These and other variations in syllabization occur not only between individual birds, but individuals also vary their song.  I have heard birds giving a characteristic song suddenly sing a different type for a while, then revert to the original again.

The seasides usually sing from exposed perches on their territories such as tall cattail stems or tall or isolated marsh-elder bushes.  The bill is elevated and opened considerably with each note, and the head bobs with the accented note.  In Tomkins (1941) are excellent photographs of the seaside's typical singing postures.  The birds also perform an extended version of the song in flight, the male fluttering upward 10 or 20 feet and gliding back down into the marsh grass while buzzing.  In the Lavallette and Chadwick populations the flight song was infrequent, of short duration, and seemingly unimportant.  It is probably commoner and of greater significance in populations inhabiting marshes of even growth where prominent exposed perches are scarce, such as occur more plentifully along the coasts to the southward.

The seasides at Lavallette started singing the morning after their nocturnal arrival. Song is then at its maximum intensity among the resident birds, and they maintain it at a high level throughout incubation. After the eggs hatch and the males start helping feed the young song declines sharply. The birds start to sing at daybreak. One male I checked at Chadwick on May 6, 1955, sang 395 times between 6:00 and 7:00 a.m., or 6.6 times per minute. Morning song decreases when the temperature rises markedly by 9 or 10 a.m., but in cloudy weather lasts longer into the day. Singing again increases toward dusk, but not to the frequency of the morning peak.

The species has a soft, lisping call note, probably the one Saunders (1951) refers to as a squeaky *tseep*, which functions as a social call to keep groups together. Migrating birds utter it frequently, and you hear it often from the wintering flocks. In early summer when the marshes are inhabited only by a stable breeding population this note is seldom used.

Both sexes use two types of alarm notes. One, a short *chip* or *tick'* seems to signify apprehension for it is given when an intruder comes onto the territory and near the nest. The other, a high, sharp *tsip* uttered with a downward jerk of the tail, is indicative of a higher degree of excitement, as when a nest with well-grown young is being investigated.

*Field marks.*—In its salt marsh habitat, which it seldom leaves unless driven by storm tides, the seaside sparrow is likely to be confused only with the sharp-tailed, swamp, or Savannah sparrows. The only other passerines apt to be found there are the two little marshes wrens and an occasional red-winged blackbird, which are readily distinguishable. When the birds can be seen clearly, as when the males are on territory and singing from the grass tops, the yellow spot before the eye and the white mustache mark along the jaw are unmistakable and diagnostic.

When not nesting the seaside is often hard to observe, for it is shy, retiring, and likes to stay hidden down among the marsh grass stems from which it can be difficult to flush. One's usual view of it is of a very dark grayish sparrow that rises on fluttering wings, scales away just above the grass tops for perhaps 50 to 100 yards, and then quickly drops out of sight again. The other three sparrows commonly found in the salt marshes in fall and winter act much the same way, but with a little practice and experience are easily differentiated. The swamp sparrow is slightly larger, much ruddier, and has a distinctively longer tail. The Savannah sparrow is slightly smaller and much lighter in color. Both species strike me as flying more strongly, with less fluttering of the wings than the seaside and sharp-tail. The sharp-tail flies very much like the seaside, but can usually be recognized by its smaller size and browner color.

*Enemies.*—A Lavallette nest that contained four 3-day-old nestlings on July 2 was empty when I checked it July 3, robbed by an unknown predator. Both the common crow (*Corvus brachyrhynchos*) and the fish crow (*C. ossifragus*) visited the marshes frequently as might be suspected. A marsh hawk (*Circus cyaneus*) was also in residence nearby, and whenever it appeared the sparrows disappeared quickly and quietly into the grass. I watched it make many passes at what I thought were sparrows, but I never saw it catch anything but microtine rodents.

The seaside sparrow has few natural enemies, for its salt marsh home is comparatively free of the reptile and mammalian predators that harass species inhabiting fresh marshes or upland fields. Perhaps the few raccoons, skunks, or foxes that wander out on the marshes get an occasional nest of eggs or young, and the bird-catching hawks must take an unwary adult or two, but no evidence of either is recorded in the literature. In listing the one known case of cowbird (*Molothrus ater*) parasitism on a seaside sparrow, Friedmann (1949) comments: "The cowbird ordinarily does not penetrate brackish or salt water marshes, and so probably rarely foists any of its eggs on the birds that nest in such places. The seaside sparrow would appear, then, to be an unusual, and rarely imposed upon victim."

The worst threat to the seaside sparrow is the steady shrinking of its habitat as the human population encroaches upon it and alters it. Stone (1937) described how the "draining and 'development' of the marshes" drove out all but a few pairs "of the thousands that once nested about Cape May." He states "this species, the sharp-tail and the Marsh Wrens are actually threatened with extinction so far at least, as most of the New Jersey coast, is concerned."

*Fall and winter.*—After the young have left the nest the adults continue to feed them for approximately 20 days. Young seaside sparrows have a characteristic method of flying and dropping back into the grass when they are flushed which makes them easy to recognize as birds of the year. Stone (1937) saw a young bird still being fed by an adult in Cape May County, N.J., on August 18, but remarks that the date is very unusual and probably due to a delayed nesting. At Lavallette all nesting duties were concluded early in August 1955, and the birds were then beginning to form flocks.

Cruickshank (1942) states that in the New York area "With the first light frost in September a definite southward movement sets in. It reaches a peak during the middle of October and is virtually concluded by the middle of November. A number of birds regularly linger until Christmas, and a few remain on the larger marshes throughout the winter."

Stone (1937) writes that at Cape May "In the autumn we have recorded them as late as October 7, 1923; October 25, 1929; October 19, 1931 and 1934; while birds seen on November 9, 1930, and November 21, 1926, may have been wintering individuals; as was one observed on January 23, 1927." Practically every subsequent Audubon Christmas count has reported from one to a dozen individual seaside sparrows in the Cape May area.

Most of the northern population apparently winters in the Atlantic coastal marshes from Virginia south to northeastern Florida. Howell (1932) called it "A common winter resident on Amelia Island, where Worthington collected numerous specimens between October 18 and March 24." The southernmost record is a bird taken at Fort Pierce, Fla., Jan. 5, 1964, and now in the collections of the Florida State Museum.

## DISTRIBUTION

*Range.*—Tidal marshes from Massachusetts to Florida.

*Breeding range.*—The northern seaside sparrow breeds in salt and brackish marshes from Massachusetts (Plum Island, Cape Cod, Martha's Vineyard) south to extreme northeastern North Carolina (Elizabeth City) and along Chesapeake Bay (north to Idlewilde and Kent Narrows, Maryland).

*Winter range.*—Winters in coastal and bay marshes from New York (Long Island) and Chesapeake Bay (Churchton, Md.) south to eastern Florida (Amelia Island, Ft. Pierce), occasionally north to Connecticut (New Haven) and Massachusetts (Plum Island).

*Casual record.*—Casual in Maine (Shark Rock in outer Muscongus Bay).

*Migration.*—Early dates of spring arrival are: New York—Suffolk County, April 22. Connecticut—New Haven, April 28. Massachusetts—Monomoy Island, April 14.

Late dates of spring departure are: Florida—Taylor County, April 5. Georgia—Chatham, April 18. South Carolina—May 15.

Early dates of fall arrival are: Texas—High Island, October 31. South Carolina—October 23. Georgia—Savannah, October 3. Florida—Worthington Island, October 18.

Late dates of fall departure are: Texas—High Island, November 11. Massachusetts—Martha's Vineyard, September 12 (median of 5 years, September 4). Rhode Island—South Auburn, October 8. Connecticut—New Haven, October 30. New York—Far Rockaway, November 25. New Jersey—Cape May, October 25. Virginia—Cape Henry, November 25.

*Egg dates.*—Connecticut: 77 records, June 3 to July 6; 55 records, June 3 to June 13.

Maryland: 14 records, May 20 to June 29; 8 records, June 6 to June 12.

New Jersey: 63 records, May 18 to July 19; 33 records, June 7 to June 21.

New York: May 23 to July 2 (number of records not stated).

Rhode Island: 4 records, June 8 to July 4.

## AMMOSPIZA MARITIMA MACGILLIVRAII (Audubon)
## MacGillivray's Seaside Sparrow
### Contributed by ALEXANDER SPRUNT, JR.

### HABITS

A resident of the coastal marshes from Dare County, N.C., to southern Georgia, this sparrow, like Bachman's and Swainson's warblers, was discovered near Charleston, S.C., by the Reverend John Bachman in the early 1830's. When Audubon painted and described it, he named it for the English ornithologist, William MacGillivray, for whom he entertained a high regard.

In general appearance there is nothing striking about the seaside sparrows. Rather drab, often ragged-looking olive-gray birds, they give the impression of being definitely dingy and frayed, particularly when in worn breeding plumage. The yellow line before the eye and the white streak along the jaw are diagnostic of the species. *A. m. macgillivraii* is darker above than *A. m. maritima*, the back feathers and central rectrices are distinctly, often broadly streaked with black, and the streaks on the chest and sides are broader and darker.

The predominant growth of the wetter parts of the South Carolina salt marshes and bordering the wet creek edges is cord grass (*Spartina alternifolia*), which is often displaced by wide expanses of black rush (*Juncus roemerianus*). Drier parts of the marsh support shorter grasses such as salt joint-grass (*Paspalum vaginatum*) and a rush-grass (*Sporobolus virginicus*). Still farther back on higher ground grows the groundsel bush (*Baccharis halimifolia*), which the low country negroes for some inscrutable reason call "she-muckle" and which bears beautiful cottony blooms. Along the edges of the marshes and on the occasional small marsh islands or hammocks grows the abundant wax myrtle (*Myrica cerifera*) and other vegetation of the sandhills and dunes.

Sharing this environment with the seaside sparrows and living in closest proximity to them are the long-billed marsh wren (*Telmatodytes palustris*) and the clapper rail (*Rallus longirostris*).

*Nesting.*—Regarding the Georgia birds, Tomkins (1941) states that "the local colonies in the Savannah area begin to be peopled with singing birds by late March, and the first wave appears to be all of males. A week or so later there are females among them." Little appears to be known of the mating and courtship procedures in this form. The writer has never witnessed them or heard from anyone who has. That they differ from those of other subspecies seems unlikely.

In the Savannah, Ga., area, Tomkins (1941) notes the "nests may be built in many different situations * * * from eight inches above the marsh mud in *Sporobolus-Paspalum* to three feet in *Spartina* or *Juncus*, and up to five feet in *Baccharis*." He adds that the top entrance nests "are built of the softer grass blades in the vicinity, and when not covered by the natural foliage, are canopied. This canopy was more nearly complete where there were heavily incubated sets of eggs, so probably it is added to as incubation progresses. The growing grasses are woven into the canopy if available. Those nests naturally sheltered by the foliage in the tops of *Baccharis* are without canopy." On Cabbage Island, Ga., he found the birds "nesting in the head-high tops of the groundsel trees (*Baccharis halimifolia*) that rimmed the sand-shell ridge back of the outer beach. The birds did not feed near the nests at all, but commuted back and forth from the nest locality to the wet banks of the salt creeks some two hundred yards back in the island."

Arthur T. Wayne, the veteran ornithologist of the South Carolina Low Country from 1883 to 1930, knew this sparrow intimately and collected it often, but search as he might and did, he was not able to find its nest. He looked for it where he collected the birds in the salt marshes, and, as the years passed, his puzzlement increased. In 1910 he wrote: "I have been unable to find this form breeding on our coast, yet it is possible that it does, since the young in first plumage occurred during the second week in July, and the adults in worn breeding plumage are to be seen during the third week in July. A distinct northward migration takes place about April 16, and continues until April 27, when all the birds have gone north, and of course to their breeding grounds."

Wayne had simply looked in the wrong place. When these sparrows leave the salt marshes in April, they retire just a few miles inland to nest in brackish or fresh water habitats, where Wayne just never happened to be at the right season. I (1924) described how, accompanied by E. B. Chamberlain, I had the good fortune to find the first nests in South Carolina. Driving down the Ocean Highway (U.S. Route 17) we saw several seaside sparrows fly across the road about 10 miles south of Charleston where it crosses a brackish marsh near Rantowles Creek. The birds flew into the marsh and disappeared into clumps of bulrushes (*Scirpus* sp.) dotting the area. Unable to stop then, we returned at our first opportunity a few days later on

May 16, 1924, and in less than an hour found five nests. We notified Wayne at once, and he came out and had no difficulty finding more nests a mile or so east of where we found ours.

The sparrows nested in a loose colony here in 1925, 1926, and 1927. In 1925 the birds were in the area as early as April 10, but we found no nests until April 29, when they contained fresh eggs. The nests here were all rather deep cups made of dried grasses and attached to the upright stems of the needle-pointed bulrushes. They were from 4 to 6 inches from the ground and, as a rule, toward the outside of the clump. On May 24, 1927, a small colony was found breeding in completely fresh water surroundings near Goose Creek Reservoir, Charleston County, some 12 miles north of the city. Four nests were found, all practically on the ground in short green grass (*Paspalum* sp.) much like Bermuda grass.

Incubation consumes about 12 days. In the Charleston area apparently only one brood is raised, though we found young out of the nest and able to fly about 25 feet as early as May 22, 1924. Tomkins (1941) comments about the Savannah area: "The nesting season here is very long. Incomplete sets of eggs have been found in late April, and young birds partly fledged have been seen in late August. The greatest number of nests have been found in June and nearly as many in May, but not so many visits have been made in July and August. The natural supposition would be that two or more broods are raised each year."

*Eggs.*—The measurements of 27 eggs average 21.1 by 15.3 millimeters; the eggs showing the four extremes measure *23.4* by *16.4*, *19.8* by 15.5, and 21.0 by *14.3* millimeters.

*Food.*—Living as it does so extensively in salt marsh, *macgillivraii's* food appears to be predominantly animal matter, a departure from usual sparrow custom. Small marine life such as various worms, tiny shrimp, and crabs, together with grasshoppers, moths, flies, and spiders compose the bulk of its food. I have watched these birds catch the little moths that flit about the stems and tips of the marsh grass, as well as foraging about on the mud in and out among the stems of the grass. Seeds of the cordgrass and glasswort make up part of the vegetable content.

*Behavior.*—The way of life pursued by *macgillivraii* is in most respects typical of that of the species. It spends much time on the muddy floor of the marshes searching amid the thickly growing stems for its food and usually keeping well out of sight. Its characteristic call note helps to locate it at times. This bird responds to the "squeak" readily, and in a manner surprising to one unfamiliar with this technique. I have often looked over a stretch of marsh apparently void of avian life of any sort. Then, after a few moments of making the squeaking sound, I have seen these birds pop up all about, swinging on the marsh stems and peering excitedly around. Close observation is quite possible if one keeps perfectly still. I have a small dock over a salt creek that makes in from the Inland Waterway. Sitting there quietly I have had these sparrows feed, preen, and search about within a few yards or even feet of me.

Its flight is the usual "family" type, never for long distances, and marked by a precipitate drop into the grass at its termination. Audubon (1839) described it as performed "with apparently slow beats of the wings," but I have always been impressed with quite the reverse; the wings seem to be moved very rapidly, almost as to constitute a blur, and strongly reminiscent of those of some heavy, stout-bodied insect. The bird is often difficult to flush, and even if one marks the exact spot of descent and makes for it immediately, it is by no means certain that the bird will flush again. Upon alighting the bird must often run some distance under the shelter of the grass, and so elude the searcher.

*Voice.*—The notes of the seaside sparrows are notoriously difficult to transcribe into words. Audubon says *macgillivraii's* song impressed him as being "impossible to imitate," and he describes it as "a sort of roll of five or six syllables." My (1924) own description set down when recording the discovery of the bird's nesting in South Carolina was "The song is very peculiar, consisting of a sort of guttural roll, heard only when the observer is very near the bird, then a short trill, ending with a strange rasping buzz." Though the term "roll" is somewhat indefinite, no other word seems to express the effect more adequately. The song is often uttered in flight, the bird rising into the air, then dropping down to just above the grass tops and leveling off for varying distances, singing as it goes, before dropping suddenly into the grass.

The call note might be translated as *chip*, but that gives little idea of the note's distinctive inflection and tonal quality. It is doubtful if the call of this subspecies can be differentiated from that of nominate *maritima*.

*Fall and winter.*—These seasons find *macgillivraii* in the great salt marshes. The best times to observe them are when the full moon forces the tides considerably above normal levels and floods the marshes. The birds then throng along the edges of the highlands and of islands in the marsh where they are easily seen. As Wayne (1910) noted, they first appear back in the Carolina marshes in late July, and they may be found there, usually in loose flocks, until the following spring. Some southward movement takes place, for birds of this race have been collected in winter as far down the coast as the marshes of St. Johns County, Fla.

## DISTRIBUTION

*Range.*—MacGillivray's seaside sparrow is resident in the Atlantic coastal marshes from North Carolina (Dare County) south to Georgia (Camden County); casual in winter southward to Florida (St. John's County).

*Egg dates.*—Georgia: 48 records, May 20 to June 29; 20 records, May 10 to May 30.

### AMMOSPIZA MARITIMA PELONOTA (Oberholser)
## Smyrna Seaside Sparrow
### PLATE 46
### Contributed by OLIVER L. AUSTIN, JR.

### HABITS

This poorly-marked subspecies, which Griscom (1944) regarded as a "barely-recognizable minor population in northeast Florida," is very similar to *macgillivraii*, from which it differs allegedly in averaging slightly smaller and in lacking the broad dark shaft stripes on the middle tail feathers. The 1957 A.O.U. Check-List gives its distribution as "*Resident* locally in salt marshes of northeastern Florida from Amelia Island to New Smyrna."

The marshes at New Smyrna Beach, where Howell collected Oberholser's type in 1925, was apparently then the form's southern limit, for Howell (1932) states: "Search was made for these birds in the marshes of Mosquito Lagoon in May 1925, but none was found there; apparently there are no breeding colonies of Seaside Sparrows south of New Smyrna, except on Merritt Island, where the Dusky Seaside occurs." This was verified by the late Donald J. Nicholson of Orlando, a veteran egg collector who knew the Florida seaside sparrows very well. He (1946) states: "the birds breed within a very limited area in very large numbers, within a radius of four miles of New Smyrna. * * * I have not found the species nesting South of New Smyrna. A few breed as far North as Daytona Beach along the Halifax River. I have not found the birds in apparently suitable spots along the river south of Matanzas Inlet where they again are found in colonies."

A few years later Nicholson (1950) noted an alarming decline in the New Smyrna population:

As recent a date as 1939, hundreds of birds still bred in this marsh, but since that date have become increasingly fewer in numbers, and during the Springs of 1948 and 1949, when repeated searches were made by both Wray H. Nicholson and myself, not a single bird, or even an old nest, was in evidence. They have completely disappeared.

About 15 years ago it was noticed that the birds stopped nesting on the south side of the road that splits this marsh, since this side had become thickly grown up to Mangrove trees, and now on the northern side of the road the same changed condition has also taken place and has driven out these Sparrows which apparently cannot survive in marshes crowded by tree-growth * * *.

A far more likely cause of their disappearance was the heavy sprayings with DDT to which these marshes and those along the Halifax River northward to Daytona and Ormond Beach were repeatedly subjected for mosquito control in the late 1940's and early 1950's. Persistent searching by Charles H. Trost and myself since 1959 has still failed to reveal any seaside sparrows breeding between Matanzas Inlet and the dusky seaside colony on Merritt Island. Currently (1964) the *pelonota* population occupies a spotty distribution scattered in the few suitable marshes remaining from Matanzas Inlet northward some 70 miles to the Georgia–Florida boundary.

*Nesting.*—We are indebted to D. J. Nicholson (1946) for the following account of the nesting of these sparrows at New Smyrna, where he, his brother Wray, and their friend Joseph C. Howell, Jr., often collected together. He writes:

As many as 40 occupied nests and as many old nests have been found in a single day's hunt by the three of us. The nests are by no means easy to locate and one can only imagine the true population of this New Smyrna colony.

Twenty years ago the site in which they bred was mostly grown up to *salicornia* and the scattered patches of salt marsh grass which bordered the edges of meandering streams, dotted with a few very young mangrove bushes. At that time the vast majority of nests were to be found in the matted salicornia or in salt marsh grass, with but an occasional nest being found in the small mangrove bushes. But of recent years the marsh has gradually filled with great numbers of mangrove bushes and trees now having grown to considerable size. * * * This has caused a marked change in the former nesting habits of the seasides, which now seem to prefer mangrove bushes and trees in which to build their neats, placing them from a couple of feet to as high as 14 feet above the mud and water. They still continue to nest in the matted salicornia which well conceals their nests in this expansive marsh. * * * Nests placed in salt marsh grass are frequently arched, but those in salicornia or in mangroves are not.

Usually the nests are placed in a crotch of a young mangrove from two to five feet from the mud. Sometimes they are built near the ends of the lower branches among the ever-present jungle of salicornia which envelops every inch of ground, shady or otherwise in the marsh. Beneath the mangroves, this succulent plant grows luxuriantly and many nests are found in this growth in the shade, and it also affords wonderful concealment.

The nests are made entirely of dead marsh grass blades and stems which are collected in a soggy condition, and the adhering sticky mud aids in binding the nest securely as it dries. These nests are about the size of your closed fist, deeply cupped to receive the three or four eggs * * *.

Nesting usually begins in earnest about the middle of April but sometimes a full set is found by the tenth of April. Nesting continues into August and there is scarcely a day during the nesting period that eggs cannot be found. I have found in different parts of a colony, little areas where most of the nests held young and in others mostly fresh eggs. This only a few hundred yards apart. Generally speaking the height of the first nesting is April 20th; second sets June 1st, and third sets July 10th–15th, on into August. Perhaps a fourth laying is fairly general.

*Eggs.*—D. J. Nicholson (1946) says the three or four eggs are—

white or greenish-white, finely and heavily marked with irregular spots or specks of light or dark brown, grayish, or "lavender" markings. Some are heavily capped or wreathed at the large end and, in addition well sprinkled over the entire surface. Occasionally a specimen is found with a cap or wreath on the small end of the egg. Many have a bluish or greenish ground color, differing in this respect from the eggs of the dusky seaside sparrow whose eggs are usually white of ground color. The shapes of the eggs vary considerably, some being quite roundish, others very long and narrow, but the majority are ovate. As compared in a large series with the eggs of the Dusky, the latter are lighter in color, partly because of the white ground color and also larger areas of the eggs are unspotted. However sets of both species can be matched.

*Young.*—The same author (1946) states: "Usually the incubating does not commence until the last egg is laid, however, in a number of nests incubation *does* vary in eggs of a set several days or more. I have never determined the length of time it takes to hatch the eggs, but about 10 to 11 days should be about correct.

"The newly hatched young are practically naked with the exception of a little smoky grey fuzz along the back and on top of the head. By the time the fledglings are ready to leave the nests the yellow on the bend of the shoulder is present. * * * They remain in the nest about 7 or 8 days."

*Voice.*—To quote Nicholson (1946) again:

Towards the end of March the marshes are fairly buzzing with the purring, wheezing songs of the Smyrna sparrow as the males perch in the concealment of the glossy mangrove leaves. He tires of one perch and seeks another fifty or seventy-five yards away flying low over the rank growth. Every so often he fairly "explodes" with passion leaving his concealment to rise on fluttering wings sixty or seventy feet above the marsh uttering his erratic little song as he goes up and down dropping out of sight in the salicornia. All day long throughout the breeding season many pairs of rivals are seen chasing each other swiftly here and there chippering as they go. Invariably as the female rises and flies from her nest the male leaves his perch and chases her uttering rapid chipperings as they skin the tops of the low growth. The song reminds one strongly of that of redwing blackbirds; the initial part of the song resembles that of the redwing. Their song is unlike that of the dusky.

To this Howell (1932) adds: "The birds are shy, and during the breeding season remain concealed in the dense vegetation of the marsh a good part of the time, and may be heard chirping in these retreats. Every little while one will fly to a small mangrove bush or a weed stalk and deliver his short, weak song, which suggests a faint, distant song of the Redwing. It consists of a sharp, double note, followed by a weak, buzzing trill. Occasionally a bird indulges in a more prolonged and varied flight song. When flushed, the birds frequently fly for 50 yards or more before alighting."

*Food.*—Howell (1932) states: "Examination of 13 stomachs of birds of this subspecies taken on the east coast of Florida showed the bird's food to consist wholly of animal matter—small crabs, amphipods, marine worms, dragon flies, grasshoppers, beetles, bugs, moths, Hymenoptera, and spiders."

*Enemies.*—As a final note, D. J. Nicholson (1946) adds: "It is outstanding the percentages of the nests found with broken eggs or egg shells; fully one fourth of the nests found have been broken up by some unknown agencies which I suspect is mice which infest the marsh. It is almost useless to mark down nests with a view of returning later to find a set of eggs. Nine times out of ten you will find upon your return that the nest has been deserted or torn up. Rarely is the nest occupied. Ants are very numerous and build their nests everywhere in the marsh and doubtless are responsible for part of the damage."

## DISTRIBUTION

*Range.*—The Smyrna seaside sparrow is resident locally in salt marshes of northeastern Florida from Amelia Island to Matanzas Inlet, formerly to New Smyrna.

*Egg dates.*—Florida: 9 records, April 26 to June 19.

### AMMOSPIZA MARITIMA (Wilson)
## Seaside Sparrow: Eastern Gulf Coast Subspecies*

#### PLATE 46
### Contributed by OLIVER L. AUSTIN, JR.

#### HABITS

The extensive marshes of black rush (*Juncus roemerianus*) that rim the Gulf Coast of Florida almost continuously from Tarpon Springs northward and westward to Wakulla and Franklin Counties support resident populations of seaside sparrows distinguishable at a glance from all the Atlantic Coast populations (except *nigrescens*, the blackest of the entire complex) by their darker color above and below. A gradual cline is evident from the smaller, grayer population in the south (*peninsulae*) to the slightly larger, darker, and dorsally browner birds in the northwest corner of the range in the Wakulla area (*juncicola*).

Little has been published on the habits and behavior of these subspecies, which do not seem to differ materially from those described

---

*The following subspecies are discussed in this section: *Ammospiza maritima peninsulae* (Allen) and *A. M. juncicola* (Griscom and Nichols).

for the Atlantic Coast forms.   Howell (1932) tells of his experiences afield with *peninsulae* as follows:

At the mouth of the Suwannee River, on a cold, windy day in January, the birds stuck very close to the dense, matted marsh grass, and it took me an hour and a half to flush three or four individuals, only one of which was collected. During the breeding season, however, the males give frequent vent to their springtime exuberance by ascending to the tops of the tallest rushes and rendering their curious little song, then perhaps making a short flight before dropping into the cover of the marsh. The song, though not loud, has considerable carrying power. Heard at close range it begins with a faint click in the throat, then a low throaty tone, followed by the song proper, which is of about two seconds' duration, and consists of two, or sometimes three, notes slurred into one, ending in a trill, this suggesting the finishing note of a Red-wing's song.

At Port Richey, where we found the birds breeding abundantly, we collected well-grown young on May 28, but failed to find any nests. At Elfers, June 2, 1929, Nicholson observed two nests, 6 and 14 feet above the ground in mangrove trees. On that date the birds had hatched their first broods and only broken egg shells were found in the nests. At the same locality, on May 31, 1931, Oscar Baynard found a nest with 4 fresh eggs, 2½ feet up in a tuft of "needle-grass" (*Juncus*), and on June 2 and 11, several more nests were found in similar situations.

Of his experiences with *juncicola* the same author writes:

This race is very similar in its habits to Scott's Seaside, and inhabits the same type of marsh, one in which there is a very heavy growth of *Juncus*. In some places, as on St. Vincent Island, the birds were shy and difficult to approach, while in other places, as at St. Marks Light and Rock Island, they were less suspicious. At Rock Island they were found in the low growth of *Salicornia* as well as in the tall rushes. At Goose Creek, Wakulla County, in January, the birds were very numerous in the heavy stands of *Juncus*, and on sunny days they gave utterance to numerous little squeaky, chippering songs. Even at that date, a squeaking noise made on the back of the hand would often bring a bird out of the cover, to fly rapidly toward the sound and alight on top of the rushes. A nest noted near St. Mark's lighthouse, May 18, 1926, was placed in a thinly grassed area of marsh, 22 inches above the ground in a small clump of rushes, and contained three naked young and one egg.

Donald J. Nicholson sent me the following notes on *peninsulae:*

"I have found these sparrows breeding in the marshes near Elfers in Pasco County from early April to late June. They nest very much as do all other seasides, usually in small, loose colonies, the nests being at least 50 or more feet apart. They build a neat, open cup of dead *Juncus* stems and grasses lined with either or both. Nests I found concealed under drifts of dead vegetation left by high tides on top of the tall *Juncus* also contained bits of a silvery, ribbon-like white seaweed.

"Most nests are well out in the marsh, only a few hundred feet back from the waters of the Gulf of Mexico, often where the water was two or three feet deep and touched the bottom of the nests at high tide.  I also found nests here in mangroves as high as fourteen feet up. All are remarkably well hidden, and rarely does one ever flush a sitting bird from the nest.

"The usual clutch is 4 eggs, but many lay only 3, and often but 2 eggs complete the set. No sets of 5 have ever been reported. Many of the sets I collected in the Elfers region differed from those of all the other forms in being more finely and densely speckled with reddish-brown markings. However, Charles G. Doe wrote me in 1942 that his collection of about 150 sets from the Cedar Keys area 'show a wide variation from almost spotless to very dark, and some that cannot be told from song sparrow eggs!' "

Of the Wakulla seaside Nicholson writes: "My scant experiences with these sparrows during the nesting season found them exceedingly shy. They remained hidden even when singing in the dense, needle-like *Juncus*. On Apr. 10, 1959, I collected a set of 3 eggs incubated four or five days, from a dense patch of *Juncus* at Wakulla Beach. The next day I collected another set of 3 fresh eggs and a third of 2 fresh eggs. These, so far as I know, are the only eggs of this race in collections. They are similar in both size and shape and markings to those of the other races."

Howell (1932) says of the food of *peninsulae:* "Five stomachs of birds of this race, examined in the Biological Survey, indicated food preferences similar to those of the east-coast birds; spiders, grasshoppers, and beetles formed the bulk of the contents, with some bivalves and gastropods." Of *juncicola* he writes: "The stomachs of six birds of this race examined contained practically the same items in the food as were found in the food of the other subspecies; small crabs, however, were taken in greater quantities, amounting in some cases to more than half of the total food contents."

### DISTRIBUTION

*Range.*—Scott's seaside sparrow is resident in salt marshes of the west coast of Florida from Pepperfish Keys to Old Tampa Bay. The Wakulla seaside sparrow is resident in coastal marshes of the northern Gulf coast of Florida from Escambia Bay to southern Taylor County.

*Egg dates.*—Scott's, Florida: 43 records, April 5 to July 7; 24 records, April 12 to May 10.

Wakulla, Florida: 4 records, May 3 to June 6.

AMMOSPIZA MARITIMA (Wilson)

# Seaside Sparrow: Western Gulf Coast Subspecies*

### Contributed by ROBERT A. NORRIS

#### HABITS

The seaside sparrow populations of the Gulf Coast from extreme western Florida to the marshes of Nueces and Copano Bays in southern Texas represent the races *fisheri* and *sennetti*, the Louisiana and the Texas seaside sparrows. *A. m. fisheri* occupies most of this range, *sennetti* being restricted to the environs of the two Texas bays. Both differ from the nominate race, *maritima*, in the distinct black streaking of their upper parts. Most examples of *sennetti* are relatively pale and have a unique greenish-gray cast to the upper parts; most *fisheri* are darker and browner both above and below. *A. m. fisheri* differs from the races *macgillivraii*, *pelonota*, *peninsulae*, and *juncicola* by its conspicuously buffy chest, sides, and flanks, *sennetti* by its paler and greener coloring above.

Ludlow Griscom (1944) considered *fisheri* the most variable of all the seaside sparrow forms. In a large series of breeding birds he distinguished two color phases, a dark and a light, each "sufficiently distinct so that extreme specimens would be distinguishable in life," and "numerous * * * 'intermediates'" between the two. He also called attention to an apparent correlation between the darker colored seasides and a heavier vegetative cover in their habitats. Further study of this suspected ecological relationship and of the genetic characteristics of the color phases, if any, might well be rewarding.

In many of the gulf coast marshes seaside sparrows, like long-billed marsh wrens (*Telmatodytes palustris*), are common to abundant birds. Both tend, however, to be rather local in their occurrence (Kopman, 1907; Howell, 1928; Burleigh, 1944). Along some stretches of coast the sparrows' spotty distribution is due in part to man's activities. Thus Griscom (1944) notes: "Local observers report it as extirpated at Brownsville, Aransas Pass and Galveston Island by civilization, naval installations, and oil wells." The sparrows are usually strictly coastal in distribution, their range extending inland only where salt marsh is present, such as the pair Simmons (1914) reported nesting in a salt marsh about six miles south of the Houston courthouse, "fully twenty-two miles from Galveston Bay and fifty miles from the Gulf of Mexico."

One of the principal plants of the marshes harboring these birds is salt grass (*Distichlis spicata*), which in some areas may be alive with fiddler crabs and littorine snails. Other monocotyledonous plants

---

*The following subspecies are discussed in this section: *Ammospiza maritima fisheri* (Chapman) and *A. m. sennetti* (Allen).

include black rush or needle grass (*Juncus roemerianus*) and sand rush (*Fimbristylis castanea*).   From a sparrow's-eye view (or a marsh wren's for that matter) a most important component of the salt-meadow vegetation is a small shrub called honey mangrove (*Avicennia nitida*), which provides these marsh-dwelling passerines much-favored cover both in Louisiana and in some parts of the Texas coast (Brooks, 1933). In some areas marsh-elder (*Iva*) bushes are also important (Griscom and Nichols, 1920).   In coastal Mississippi Burleigh (1944) states: "One of its requirements during the breeding season seems to be the presence of clumps of sharp-pointed rushes (*Juncus*) in which to nest. Where this growth is lacking in stretches of salt marsh that are otherwise suitable, the species occurs only in rather limited numbers during the winter months."

Neither the Louisiana nor the Texas seaside sparrow has been the subject of an extensive life history study, but I was able to make some observations on breeding individuals of *fisheri* at the race's type locality, Grand Isle, La., in April 1960.   Consequently the following incomplete life history deals mainly with *fisheri*, with the few squibs of information available on *sennetti* incorporated here and there.

*Territory.*—In the early morning of Apr. 15, 1960, I mist-netted and color-banded a breeding pair of seaside sparrows in a salt grass–honey mangrove association on Grand Isle.   I placed red plastic bands on the male (subsequently called Red) and yellow bands on the female (called Yellow).   The female showed a full-sized vascular-edematous brood patch, the male no sign of such a patch; both appeared to be in the light color phase.   I watched the activities of this pair and of some of their neighbors on April 15-17 and again on April 30 and May 1. A grid of stakes set out in the march at 20-pace intervals allowed me to map individual movements and from these to work out the extent of each bird's territory.

The size of the area the banded pair utilized in the mid-April period was 1.7 acres, most of it grassy.   About 15 to 20 percent was strips or scattered patches of knee- to breast-high mangrove, and about 10 percent consisted of salt-water pools and narrow sloughs.   As some parts of the marsh were apparently little used by seaside sparrows, the over-all population density seemed to be less than one bird per acre.   A transect census I ran later through 3,400 feet of suitable-looking marsh yielded a rough estimate of 68 sparrows per 100 acres.

An unmated male (called UB for unbanded) maintained a territory to the south and west of Red's, and a pair, of which I saw very little, held another tract toward the south and east.   I saw encounters between the color-banded pair and UB a number of times.   On April 16, when Yellow's eggs had begun to hatch, I noted both Red and UB in a mangrove bush near the territory border.   They were hopping from branch to branch rather slowly and deliberately, within one to three feet of each other. Low *chut* notes were given regularly by Red, sparingly by UB. Yellow visited the bush briefly. For a moment she spread her wings slightly, fluffed out her feathers, and then flew to the vicinity of the nest. Red and UB remained in the bush perched about a foot from each other and continued to call. There was no special display. At times, Red, the more agitated bird, assumed what seemed to be an "uncomfortable" position, as when straddled between two separate twigs, one foot stretched out laterally to each. After about five minutes Red flew to a tiny mangrove 12 paces away, and UB promptly sang several times. Red continued to give *chut* notes and once started to sing but "swallowed" the song. Soon he moved farther away, and shortly UB also left the bush and went off in another direction.

Most of the sites marking the approximate boundary of the territory were Red's song posts. Some of the peripheral points to the south the female established as she flew to various spots, mostly in open marsh, to forage for herself and the newly hatched young.

Observations on April 30 and May 1 indicated considerable relaxation of Red's and Yellow's territorial boundaries, for UB had moved in from the south and west and was now frequenting about one-third of the pair's former home range. Red and Yellow were now associating with bob-tailed young, which were able to fly short distances. UB, still apparently unmated, sang frequently, Red much less so. At times, though, the two males sang at about the same rate, the songs tending to alternate. Around midday, April 30, UB began pursuing Red over large parts of the territory. The repeated pursuit flights gave the impression that UB was "taking over." But Red was not being dominated completely.

About 7:20 a.m. the following day I found Red and UB hopping about in salt grass only two or three feet apart. They presently engaged in a brief but apparently inconclusive aerial battle just above the grass tops. Shortly after this scuffle, Red was singing in a mangrove clump close by while UB sang some 60 paces away not far from the former nest site. A little later, about 8:00 a.m., I saw the two males once again close together toward the southern part of the territory in low grass and on the ground. Their mutual attitude was manifestly hostile. Though no particular displays were observed, another brief "upfluttering" battle carried them above the grass tops. Neither seemed to give ground in this encounter. Soon afterward UB left and flew to the vicinity of the old nest. A little later I saw Red chasing UB, again in the southern part of the territory. Two or three times on April 30 I saw Red carrying strands of nest material.

Possibly he was beginning to build a new nest, but I was not able to find one.

*Nesting.*—The nest of Red and Yellow when I found it April 15 contained three eggs and one tiny nestling. Made of interlaced strands of grasses secured to upright stalks of *Distichlis*, it was almost globular with an opening on one side somewhat toward the top. Its bottom was about eight inches above the ground, which was covered by about an inch of water. The same day I found another nest of similar construction, its bottom about nine inches above the barely submerged ground. This nest was fastened between three upright *Avicennia* shoots at the border of a patch of these mangroves 2½ to 3 feet high. It contained four downy young an estimated three days old.

The literature contains few reports of nests. Kopman (1915) mentions finding "a nest on Battledore Island [La.], July 23, 1908, containing four young a few days old. It was built of grass and the opening, on one side, was rather large. It was four feet from the ground in *Avicennia nitida*, a bush that is common along the coast." In a salt marsh south of Houston, Simmons (1915) flushed a seaside sparrow "from a nest on the moist ground in a clump of thick grass. The nest was composed of coarse dry grasses, lined with finer, and contained three well fledged young. The nest was not a domed structure, but was more on the order of nests of the Florida Red-wing (*Agelaius phoeniceus floridanus*) which surrounded it, for some of the nesting material was entwined about the stalks of the grass. Inside, the nest measured two and a fourth inches in diameter by one and a half deep. Both parents were present, and though nervous were not at all shy, for they approached within three or four feet of us, perching for a moment on one reed and then on another." Although little information is available on number of broods or span of breeding season in *fisheri* and *sennetti*, these races probably resemble *pelonota* of the northeastern coast of Florida, which Nicholson (1946) found laid three and perhaps four clutches between April and August.

*Eggs.* Limited data suggest that eggs of *fisheri* and *sennetti* are essentially like those of the nominate form and other races of the seaside sparrow. The clutch size is usually three or, more commonly, four. The length of the incubation period apparently has not been determined.

The measurements of 16 eggs of *fisheri* average 20.4 by 15.4 millimeters; those showing the four extremes measure *21.5* by 15.3, 20.8 by *15.8*, and *18.7* by *14.7*. The measurements of 16 *sennetti* eggs average 20.4 by 15.7 millimeters; those showing the four extremes measure *21.9* by 16.1, *19.0* by *15.0*, and 20.1 by *16.5* millimeters.

*Young.*—On April 15 from 5:15 to 6:04 p.m., I watched Yellow's movements to and from the nest, which then contained three eggs and one tiny nestling. Red sang throughout this period. Yellow's four sessions on the nest, which involved incubating and brooding, ranged from 4 to 10 minutes and averaged 7.2 minutes. Her five recesses for foraging ranged from 1.5 to 6 minutes and averaged 4.1 minutes. On leaving the nest she usually gave a series of sharp, high-pitched flight notes, *jee-jee-jee-jee-jee-jeee'u-jeee'u-jeee'u*, as she flew to grassy spots 35 to 50 yards south of the nest. She exercised caution on each return, which usually consisted of one long flight, a pause in the grass, and then one or more short flights to the nest. She was still active after sunset, which came at 6:20.

The next day between 8:30 and 9:00 a.m., I noted both Yellow and Red near the nest. It was apparent that Red had discovered the young, of which there were now three fluffy ones plus one pipped egg. As I examined the nestlings, Yellow approached but remained in the grass about eight yards away uttering a series of low *chut* notes. Red, too, gave these notes whenever I was near him, even at places away from the nest. It seemed as if the appearance of the young made him more concerned by my presence. He sang intermittently.

The nestlings were well endowed with patches of natal down which I described in my notes as "smoke gray" or "mouse gray." Dense tufts in the coronal and occipital areas were clearly separated, as were those in the spinal and femoral areas. The maximum length of down feathers on the dorsum was approximately eight millimeters. Symmetrical tufts of relatively long down characterized the scapular and alar tracts, and there were two or three tufts of short whitish down in the lower crural tracts. Little strips of short whitish down marked the ventral tracts in the belly region. From the ventral aspect two or three short whitish bits of down, which we might call "inner crural down," could be seen where the inner part of the leg meets the skin of the belly. Young birds found in another nest the same day had down like that of Red's and Yellow's offspring except that the crural tracts, both "inner" and "lower," were lacking.

In late April in another part of the Grand Isle marshes I caught a newly fledged seaside sparrow from which I entered the following description of the fresh juvenal plumage in my notes:

"Bill dusky-horn color, paler at tip. Gape pale whitish-yellow. Iris brown. Crown and back broadly streaked with blackish, with dull ochraceous-brown feather edgings. Rump feathers somewhat lax or fluffy, the feathers with blackish central areas and ochraceous-buff edgings. Rectrices ensheathed for nearly half their length (these being up to 20 millimeters long), blackish centrally with dull, buffy brown edgings. Wing coverts (except primary) blackish, edged and tipped with grayish buff (lesser coverts) to ochraceous buff (middle and greater coverts). Primary coverts dusky with slightly paler edgings. Remiges or flight feathers dusky, becoming edged with brownish buff on inner secondaries and especially on tertials. Remex sheaths five to seven millimeters long. Subterminally on outer web and along border of inner web of tertials the brownish buff becomes pale buff. Alular coverts whitish with a grayish spot in center of each feather, giving juvenile the appearance of having a whitish bend of the wing. Alulae dusky with whitish edges along outer webs. Under wing coverts whitish. Auricular region dark or dusky with some buffy interspersed. Chin whitish. Loral region and trace of superciliary stripe dull buffy. Submalar region and upper breast buffy, with rather heavy, blurry streaking. Streaks largely confined to upper breast but extend, in less well defined fashion, down onto sides and flanks. Sides and flanks also buffy, though paler than on upper breast. Lower breast and upper belly whitish; undersurface becoming buffy on lower belly and crissum. Anterior crural tracts buffy whitish; posterior aspect brownish gray. Feet grayish-horn color."

Lowery (1955) states that "individuals that have passed through the postjuvenal molt resemble full adults but have a stronger wash of buff on the breast and about the face."

As noted previously, Red's and Yellow's nest contained three young and a pipped egg the morning of April 16. In mid-morning I timed one of Yellow's periods away from the nest at 15.5 minutes, while two sessions on the nest were 2 and 5.5 minutes. When she flew from the nest she usually gave a succession of *chut* notes unlike the high-pitched calls she gave the previous afternoon. For the race *pelonota* Nicholson (1946) claims: "Invariably as the female rises and flies from her nest the male leaves his perch and chases her uttering rapid chipperings as they skim the tops of the low growth." I saw no such behavior in my banded pair. Red spent considerable time near the nest, but I did not see him go to it during the morning. Once near the nest he scolded a red-winged blackbird with a rapidly uttered series of notes, *bzzt-bzzt-bzzt-bzzt-bzzt*. He also spent time in other parts of the territory and sang at intervals.

Watching the nest site steadily from 2:15 to 4:33 p.m., I saw the nestlings fed 11 times, 6 times by Yellow and 5 by Red, or about 4.8 feedings per hour, and virtually no time was spent in brooding. My presence may have slowed the birds' feeding rate somewhat. They always approached the nest stealthily. Several times Red made arching flights over the nest before settling down in the grass and then slinking toward it. During this afternoon period Yellow flew from the nest in complete silence. At 4:16 p.m., the neighboring male,

UB, came in with food in his bill as if he intended to feed the young. Apparently he did not succeed, for Yellow chased him away twice for distances of 15 to 20 feet, uttering as she did so a series of subdued husky *tchurt-tchurt-tchurt-tchurt* notes, softer, slightly higher pitched, and more rapidly delivered than her *chut* notes.

When I revisited Red's and Yellow's territory April 29 both parents continued to give *chut* and also higher-pitched *zeet* notes from time to time. The nest was empty, and I saw Yellow feed the short-tailed fledglings in the salt grass at several different places on the territory. I saw neither Red nor UB, who by that time occupied a large part of the territory, feed the young, though either may have done so.

*Food.*—According to Oberholser (1938), "the food of this bird reflects the character of its habitat—marine worms, crustaceans, dragonflies, grasshoppers, moths, beetles, bugs, and spiders, with some mollusks." Howell (1928) provides a not dissimilar list, including also crickets, caterpillars, flies, wasps, small crabs, and some weed and grass seeds.

*Voice.*—Kopman (1915) after stating that the Louisiana seaside sparrow is "an extremely abundant breeder in all tidewater marshes," reports having "seen scores at a time in the rushes and marsh grasses, perched just below the level of the grass tops, delivering in more or less regular concert their strange monotonous songs. The usual song sounds like 'te-dunk-chee-e-e-e.' Sometimes the trill alone is given." Lowery (1955) says: "The notes have been perfectly described by Peterson as *cvtcut, zhe'-eeeeeeee.*" At Grand Isle I jotted down various renditions from *thk-ze-e-e-e-e-e* to *zeee-chrepl-ze-e-e-e-e-e*, there being one, two, or even three not always distinct syllables preceding the buzzy *ze-e-e-e-e*.

Red and other males sang perched in grass, rush, sedge, or mangrove at heights of one to three or more feet. As they utter each song they stretch the head and neck up perceptibly, but point the bill only slightly upward. Usually singing birds stand fairly erect with the feet close together, but occasionally they sing while straddling between two adjoining branches or grass stems. Sometimes they hold the tail drooped, and sometimes erect at a 50- or 60-degree angle from the back. I once recorded 12 songs per minute for Red, and 15, 16, and 18 per minute for UB. Within a given minute-long period an individual's song tended to be a bit irregular. Various circumstances interrupt the males' singing now and then, including the birds' need to forage intermittently.

I heard comparatively elaborate flight songs at irregular intervals and at various times of the day. In a typical one I witnessed about 10 a.m. April 16 Red suddenly flew up from the grass in a steep climb of about 70 to 80 degrees, uttering a very high-pitched *see-see-see-see-see-see* as he rose. When he reached the summit some 15 to 20 feet above the marsh and began to descend, he delivered more emphatic *tcherp-chee'-tcherp-chee'* notes. He then pitched groundward as steeply as he rose, with a series of buzzy *ze-e-e-e-e* notes that could almost be syllabified as *buzz-zz-zz-zz-zz-zz*. The entire performance lasted but a few seconds, yet it took decidedly longer than the regular song. Also the phrases were more clearly separated than those of most songs delivered from perches.

On April 15 the seaside sparrows, and the redwings and marsh wrens as well, sang more or less regularly in the late hours of the day. In almost any given minute, a song from at least one species could be heard. After watching the sun go down at 6:20 p.m., I heard blackbirds singing until about 6:40, marsh wrens until 6:46, and the sparrows Red and UB, respectively, until 6:45 and 6:50, when it was indeed dusk.

*Enemies.*—My limited experiences in Louisiana, together with an examination of the literature, reveals very little regarding predators of the races *fisheri* and *sennetti*. In April 1960, I noted in the Grand Isle marshes a number of ribbon snakes (*Thamnophis sauritus*) and a great many tracks of raccoons (*Procyon lotor*). Either of these animals might prey on marsh passerines to some extent. Stevenson and Meitzen (1946) found the remains of a nestling seaside sparrow in the nest of a white-tailed hawk (*Buteo albicaudatus*) in Texas.

Among other hazards that affect seaside sparrows are storms such as hurricane Audrey, which blasted the southwest coast of Louisiana in late June, 1957. Though such storms doubtless wreak havoc among the seasides and other marshland dwellers, it is both interesting and gratifying to read Newman's (1957) observation: "On Aug. 9 at Grand Chenier, 8 Seaside Sparrow were quickly squeaked up at one spot in the marsh that had been under 10 feet of water 6 weeks before."

*Fall and winter.*—Griscom (1948) states that *"fisheri* is now proved to be a permanent resident at all localities of record in Louisiana and Texas." Among the evidence leading to this conclusion is Lowery's note (*in* Griscom, 1944): "I, too have never been convinced that there is much shifting of populations in the winter. If such was [sic] the case, there would certainly be areas that would be devoid of birds at one season or another. On the contrary I have many colonies in mind that I visit from time to time through the year, and the populations in these colonies never seem to vary numerically in the slightest." Nor is there real proof of migration or vagrancy among members of the race *sennetti*, as Griscom (1944, 1948) has brought out. If these races do make limited migratory movements, they could best be detected through banding studies or by observations of birds moving through or into coastal regions that are not inhabited during the breeding season.

## DISTRIBUTION

*Range.*—The Louisiana seaside sparrow is resident in coastal marshes from eastern Texas (San Antonio Bay, eastward) east to Alabama (Alabama Port, Dauphin Island) and extreme western Florida (Pensacola). Recorded in winter south to Nueces County, Texas. The Texas seaside sparrow is resident in coastal marshes of southern Texas (Nueces and Copano Bays). Recorded in winter south to the mouth of the Rio Grande.

*Egg dates.*—Alabama: April 22 to June 25 (number of records not stated).

Louisiana: 3 records, May 12 to June 11.

Texas: 22 records, April 15 to July 12; 12 records, May 12 to May 25.

## AMMOSPIZA NIGRESCENS (Ridgway)

### Dusky Seaside Sparrow

#### FRONTISPIECE PLATE 47

#### Contributed by CHARLES H. TROST

## HABITS

Limited to the salt and brackish marshes within a 10-mile radius of Titusville, Brevard County, Fla., the dusky seaside sparrow has one of the most restricted ranges of any North American bird. Robert Ridgway described it as a "variety" of the seaside sparrow in 1873 from a specimen sent him from Dummitts Creek, just south of the Haulover Canal between the Indian River and Mosquito Lagoon. Actually the bird was discovered the year before at Salt Lake, a few miles west of Titusville, by Charles J. Maynard (1881), who thus describes the area and his first encounter with the bird he called most fittingly "the black and white shore finch":

Near the sources of the St. Johns River in Florida is a little body of water, only about two miles in circumference, called Salt Lake and, as its name implies, is quite brackish. * * * In fact the vegetation which covers these wide-spread plains is almost exactly like that which grows on the marshes of the Indian River. It is composed mainly of coarse grass and a species of rush, both of which grow to a height of four or five feet, and so thickly together that one can scarcely make his way through them. The margin of the lake is, however, destitute of vegetation as are the beds of numerous small creeks which in the spring and summer are dry, and thus form convenient roads.

I was making my way along one of these novel paths on the seventeenth of March, 1872, keeping a sharp lookout for birds, at the same time carefully watching the ground at my feet in order to detect the presence of the venomous water moccasins which were more numerous here than I had ever seen them elsewhere, when my attention was attracted by a little black bird which rose from the high grass about twenty yards from me, hovered a moment, uttering a feeble sputtering song, then dropped down and disappeared. I saw it but a moment, yet I was convinced that it was something that I had never seen before. I laboriously made my way to the spot, but was unable to start it even after the most vigorous efforts. This was my first sight of the new *Ammodromus,* for I was certain that it belonged to this genus and in a day or two my suspicions were confirmed, for an assistant brought in a specimen which he had taken in the place I had first seen it. We did not find any more near Salt Lake nor did I see a single specimen, but shortly after I found them quite common on the marshes of Indian River. Yet I only took seven specimens there, for the birds are exceedingly difficult to obtain as they are not only very shy, but after once starting will seldom rise a second time, remaining concealed in the thick grass. * * * This species was quite common on the marshes of the Indian River, just below Dummett's Grove, but I never saw a specimen north of Haulover Canal. They were very abundant on the upper end of Merritt's Island where I obtained a few.

The birds still occur today about where Maynard reported finding them almost a century ago. A few small colonies persist in brackish marshes bordering the St. Johns west from Titusville and Indian River City, but the main breeding colonies occupy the salt marshes directly across the Indian River from Titusville along the western shore of the peninsula north of Merritt Island.

Concerning its remarkably restricted range Chapman (1912) commented: "In view of the fact that this species is abundant and that the region it inhabits is in no sense isolated, but that both to the north and south there are marshes apparently similar to those it occupies, the restriction of its range to an area of only a few square miles in extent makes its distribution unique among North American birds." This is not quite accurate, for the adjoining marshes both to the north and south have extensive growths of black mangrove, *Avecennia nitida,* which seem to act as a barrier to the duskies. The barrier to the north is not permanent, for it is near the mangrove's northern limit of growth, and frosts kill the larger shrubs back every 20 to 30 years.

The northern edge of this mangrove growth also marked until a few years ago the southern boundary of the breeding range of the Smyrna seaside sparrow (*A. m. pelonota*), which led George Sutton (1949) to remark:

"There is, apparently, a definite break between the range of *nigrescens* and that of *pelonota* * * * about 30 miles north of Titusville. [Should the mangroves continue to encroach,] *pelonota* might conceivably drift southward into the range of *nigrescens.* We could, perhaps, lay no better plan for ascertaining whether *nigrescens* is a full species. Were the bird not merely a race of *Ammospiza maritima* it would, presumably, find its own peculiar niche within the salt marsh habitat and maintain its specific integrity despite inevitable competition with the structurally and ecologically similar intruder."

PLATE 47

Brevard County, Fla., May 8, 1932        S. A. Grimes
NEST OF DUSKY SEASIDE SPARROW

Monroe County, Fla., Spring 1921        G. R. Wilson
TYPICAL NESTING SITE OF CAPE SABLE SPARROW

PLATE 48

Monroe County, Fla., May 12, 1921                    G. R. Wilson
NEST OF CAPE SABLE SPARROW

That the dusky really merits the specific status the A.O.U. Check-List has always accorded it is questionable. Though its intense black streaking makes it by far the most distinctive of the seaside sparrows, its basic color pattern, habits, and behavior leave no question of its close relationship to the other recognized forms of the seaside complex. Ludlow Griscom (1944) argued: "*A. nigrescens* (Ridgway) is a small local population in an extreme development of the dark phase. It possesses two absolute characters in the heavy black streaking on a white ground below and the loss of the yellow postocular [sic] stripe. It has, consequently, real claims to specific distinctness. A modern school of thought would unhesitatingly reduce it to subspecific rank, on the indisputable grounds that the differences between any Seaside and any Sharp-tailed Sparrow are the real specific criteria with which Nature has supplied us."

Unfortunately neither of Griscom's two "absolute characters" for the dusky's specificity is valid and he (1944) admitted "that the whiter under parts of *mirabilis* deprive *nigrescens* of one of the latter's absolute characters." As black streaks occur in several other populations, notably in *A. m. juncicola*, their presence in *nigrescens* is not a difference of pattern, but of degree. As for the alleged "loss of the yellow postocular stripe," the yellow does not extend behind the eye in any seaside population, and that of the preocular, or supraloral, stripe is every bit as well marked in the dusky as it is in all other adult seasides.

Whether or not the dusky's reproductive isolation has progressed to the point of specificity will probably never be put to the test, as Sutton hoped, by its possible breeding in sympatry with other seasides that might invade its range. Today it is more isolated geographically than it has been since it was discovered. The nearest breeding grounds of *pelonota* are now 75 miles northward beyond Matanzas Inlet; the nearest *peninsulae* are 125 westward across Florida on the gulf coast; from Titusville southward to the range of *mirabilis* beyond Cape Sable lie 250 miles of coastline that offer few suitable marshlands and contain no known breeding seaside sparrows.

Since 1956 the entire breeding range of the dusky on the east side of the Indian River has been impounded for mosquito control purposes by earthen dikes thrown up around the perimeter of the salt marshes, which are now kept covered with from 4 to 12 inches of fresh water. This treatment, though unquestionably superior and preferable to the use of insecticides, is causing marked changes in the salt marsh vegetation. The stands of bunch grass (*Spartina backeri*) and black rush (*Juncus roemarianus*) in which the duskies nest are thinning out and are giving way to cattails (*Typha*). Over the last few years the dusky population appears to have decreased markedly, especially within the impoundments. I began a special study of the bird in 1961, primarily to discover the causes of its decline so that remedial action might be taken to prevent its extinction. Many of the observations presented here have resulted from this study. For information on the status of the duskies during the several decades preceding the impoundments, I have quoted freely and at some length from notes sent to the editor of the *Life Histories* by the late Donald J. Nicholson of Orlando.

*Spring.*—A few birds are present in the marshes all winter, but more seem to appear in late February and early March. The males usually start to sing during the first or second week of March, and at first are heard only in the early morning or at dusk. Their singing increases as the season progresses and soon, especially in calm, cloudy weather, the song may be heard throughout the day. A spring shower increases the males' ardor and activity tremendously. Nicholson (MS.) thus describes the marshes at such a time:

"Upon entering their habitat one sees individuals on all sides. They seem to appear from nowhere, perch a few moments on the tops of the vegetation, and scold continuously. Here and there males chase the females in zigzag courses, flying low and very swiftly just above the grass tops, sometimes for several hundred yards or more. Others from many directions simultaneously sing their rasping, far-carrying songs from prominent perches atop grass or rush stems. Here and there an exuberant male performs his courtship song flight. Bubbling over with his jerky, rasping, erratic song he flutters slowly almost straight upward to a height of 20 or 30 feet, pauses a moment at the apex, and then, still singing, descends just as slowly to perch in the grass tops again."

*Territory.*—The dusky tends, as do other seasides, to nest in rather loose colonies. Each male establishes and defends a definite nesting territory, which seems to vary in size according to its location in the marsh. The region immediately around the nest is most exclusive, and only one pair of birds is ever found inhabiting it. Birds in the center of the marsh seem to defend a roughly circular territory about 100 yards in diameter, depending on the vegetation. When the circle includes one of the dikes, where the birds are often seen feeding, the male defends the entire area, including the dike. Birds with nests well back in the marsh are often seen flying 200 yards or more over unsuitable habitat to feeding areas in the tidal zone. The males sometimes sing in such a feeding area, but do not seem to defend it.

The sizes of individual territories seem to have increased in recent years. Nicholson (MS.) states that in the 1930's he often encountered as many as 20 or 25 sparrows within 100 feet of marsh, and found occupied nests within 40 feet of one another. The birds are certainly not that plentiful today, nor do they nest nearly so close together. Both the thinning of the marsh vegetation and the decrease in population pressure have probably tended to increase territory size.

The male advertises his territory by singing from the tops of the bunch grass or black rush. One male I watched moved about his territory 31 times in an hour and sang an average of 25 seconds at each stop. Intervals between moves ranged from 5 seconds to 4.75 minutes. The advertising is so effective that physical contact is seldom observed between a territorial male and an invader. Once when banded male 733 was feeding on his dike and an unbanded bird flew onto it, he ran at the intruder with wings outspread, feathers ruffled, head back, and bill slightly open. The intruder fled before he was touched, and 733 did not pursue him.

Banding has shown the males return to the same territories year after year. Two males, 703 and 705, that I banded on their territories in 1961, I recaptured defending the same territories the summer of 1963. I have had no returns of adult females in successive years, but fewer were banded originally, and they are harder to observe and to catch than the singing males. Two other males, 711 and 713, and one female, 712, I banded as juveniles the summer of 1962, returned the following year and established territories only some 300 yards from where they were fledged. I have never seen a banded dusky away from the vicinity where I banded it.

The main breeding marsh on the Indian River now contains at least four loose colonies of duskies, each isolated one or two miles from the other by stretches of unsuitable habitat. If no interchange of birds occurs between colonies as the banding data suggest, inbreeding must be the rule rather than the exception. And if inbreeding is as prevalent in other seaside sparrows as it seems to be in the dusky, it is easy to see how so many well-marked forms have developed within the complex.

*Courtship.*—Pair formation has never been observed in the dusky, but presumably it occurs shortly after the males start to sing in March. Nicholson (MS.) notes: "In late March the males begin courting the females with their aerial flight songs. Also we see them vigorously pursuing the females low and rapidly just above the tall grass until both drop from sight into it. In all the years I have watched these birds I have never seen them copulate. This probably occurs on the ground hidden in the thick grass after the chase, for the birds usually are not seen for several minutes afterward. Flight chases may be observed throughout the nesting season from April into August, but one sees very few flight songs after mid-June. Perhaps such arduous courting is not needed for the late renestings."

*Nesting.*—Nicholson (MS.) considered the ideal nesting habitat to be a damp, but not flooded, salt marsh dotted with small open ponds. Formerly the Indian River marshes had dense patches of low, thick salt grass or hay (*Distichlis spicata*), tangled plots of knee-high pickleweed (*Salicornia* and *Batis*), large stretches of waist-high bunch grass (*Spartina backeri*), and various-sized stands of the bayonetlike black rush (*Juncus roemarianus*). In the 1920's the birds built occasionally in the bunch grass and under blown-over black rush, but he found most nests then in the dense patches of succulent pickleweed, placed usually just below the weed tops and from 10 to 20 inches above the damp ground. The small, neat, open cups were made entirely of dry grass blades and stems with a few dead pickleweed stems mixed in. By the late 1930's he found the birds nesting almost exclusively in the low salt hay and seldom more than 3 to 5 inches off the ground.

With the flooding the salt hay and pickleweed have now disappeared from the impoundments, and the birds nest today in the high *Spartina* and *Juncus*, usually from 5 to 15 inches above the water. One nest I measured was 4 inches high and 5 inches in outside diameter; the inside of its cup was 3 inches wide and 2½ inches deep. Until the young hatch and the parents are actively engaged in feeding them, the nests are very hard to find. They are usually well concealed in thick vegetation, and the incubating female rarely flushes directly from her eggs. Hunting nests in the sharp-tipped *Juncus* may aptly be termed searching for a ball of hay in a needlestack, and no prudent man attempts it without wearing glasses or goggles to protect his eyes.

*Eggs.*—The eggs of the dusky seaside sparrow are ovate to short-ovate, have very little gloss, and are practically indistinguishable from those of *A. maritima*. The usual set is three or four, and rarely five. The ground color is dirty-white or very pale bluish-white, speckled and spotted with dark reddish browns such as "sorghum brown," "Mars brown," "russet," "chestnut," or "auburn," occasionally with underlying spots of "light purplish gray," which are often lacking. The spottings are usually sharp and distinct, but at times may be somewhat clouded. Generally the eggs are marked profusely with a tendency to concentrate toward the large end, where the spots may be confluent. The measurements of 65 eggs average 19.9 by 15.0 millimeters; the eggs showing the four extremes measure *21.6* by 16.2, 20.7 by *16.8, 18.5* by 14.5, and 19.3 by *14.2*.

Nicholson (MS.) claims the eggs of the dusky show larger areas of ground color and vary more in spotting then those of the other seaside sparrows. He notes four the commonest clutch size, five having been found only four times, but three eggs also common, and two fairly frequent, especially late in the season. He reports finding nests with young as early as May 2, and with fresh eggs as late as August 20.

From the dates the eggs are apparently laid in two peaks, the first in late April and early May, the second in late June and early July, and the species appears to be two-brooded.

*Incubation.*—One egg is usually laid per day until the clutch is complete, but the hour of laying is not known. Incubation starts when the last egg is laid and takes between 12 and 13 days. As the male has never been seen sitting on the nest, the female apparently does all the incubating and brooding of the young alone. When she leaves the nest her mate often chases her to the edge of the territory where he stops and sings, though he sometimes accompanies her when she goes to feed in the tidal area outside the dike. When she returns he usually follows her back to the nest and he sometimes chases her to it.

*Young.*—At hatching the nestlings are pink and show only sparse patches of gray natal down. The egg tooth is shed the second or third day. On the third day the skin has darkened to almost a bluish-gray, but the feather tracts are not obvious until the fourth day. By the sixth day the eyes are open, and on the seventh the feather shafts start to slough off.

The male helps his mate feed the young, which remain in the nest quietly and are not heard crying for food. They normally remain in the nest about nine days, but by the eighth day are apt to bounce from it at the least disturbance. Upon leaving they can fly only a few feet, but they scramble actively about in the vegetation and are very difficult to find. The high-pitched cheeps they utter probably help the old birds find them for feeding. They usually remain on the territory about 20 more days, following their parents and begging for food.

Toward the end of this period the male starts to ignore them, and when a begging juvenile approaches he flies to another perch and continues singing. There is some indication that the male may drive the juveniles out of the territory when renesting begins. During this second nesting period fewer young are seen in the vicinity. On July 30 I collected one bird in juvenal plumage some three miles from the nearest known breeding colony.

*Plumage.*—The juvenal plumage of the dusky seaside is much like that of the other seasides, but the head and back are considerably darker. The lores and bend of wing are buffy, the throat white, the breast and belly an off-white or buff, and a band of tan streaks extends across the breast. The wings, back, and tail are greyish brown. The post-juvenal molt starts in late August, and by November the birds of the year can be distinguished from adults only by a faint tan remainder of the juvenal chest band.

Adults undergo a complete postnuptial molt which starts in August and may continue into October. During this period many tailless birds are in evidence. One adult captured August 24 had the first five primaries new, and new primary coverts only over the new primaries. The fresh feathers are darker and longer than the old ones. I have seen no evidence of any molt in winter or spring. The white and buffy edges of the contour feathers wear off during the winter to produce the very dark nuptial dress.

*Food.*—Howell (1932) states: "Six stomachs of birds of this species were examined * * *. The food contents consisted largely of insects and spiders, with some vegetable matter. Grasshoppers and crickets composed about 37 percent of the total, and spiders about 25 percent. Other items were beetles, bugs, horse flies, dragon flies, lepidopterous larvae, Hymenoptera, and a praying mantis. The vegetable matter consisted of a few seeds of sedges, one seed of wax myrtle, and a quantity of tubers of a grass or sedge."

In addition I have seen them feeding on small snails and possibly ants. I saw one female carrying a dragonfly larva and another an adult salt marsh butterfly to their nestings. Except for a few redwinged blackbirds, the salt marshes do not harbor many other insectivorous birds, and the seaside sparrows have little competition for their food.

*Behavior.*—During the nonbreeding season the duskies are quite shy, and either remain concealed in the dense vegetation or fly long before one comes near. In the breeding season they become rather tame. Parents with heavily incubated eggs or young in the nest are very bold and will come to within 15 or 20 feet of an intruder at the nest. They perch on the grass tops and nervously twitch their tail and wings, bob up and down, and scold continuously with their metallic *chip-chip, chip-chip* until you leave. For a week or so after the young leave the nest the female will come almost within arm's reach and *chip* incessantly while trying to lead you away.

After a shower the wet males often sit exposed on the top of the vegetation to fluff and preen their feathers. I watched one such male scratch his head three times, twice over and once under the wing, after which he stretched the same wing out over the extended foot, downward and behind the body.

*Voice.*—The dusky male usually gives his territorial song from an exposed perch with his head thrown back, bill open, and neck visibly vibrating. Typically the song has one or two short introductory syllables which do not carry far, followed by a longer buzzing note, which Nicholson (MS.) writes *toodle-raeeeee*. Peterson (1947) calls it "A buzzy *cut-a-zheeeeee* (like *maritima*) vaguely suggestive of Florida Red-wing in pattern, but not in quality."

Howell (1932) writes: "Comparing their song with that of [*A. m.*] *pelonota*, which I had been hearing a few days previously, I noted a similarity but some differences. It begins with a single (rarely double) liquid note, followed by a short, buzzing trill. It is not so long nor so loud as the song of the Smyrna Seaside, and the final 'buzz' is more pronounced."

The song varies considerably between birds, and some variation may be evident in the songs of an individual bird. One extreme was a male who always threw back his head and uttered a single, high-pitched lisp. Another, whose normal song was the usual *e-eedle-reeeee*, trespassed on a neighboring territory momentarily and sang *Tsui-Tsui-tsui-twe-twe-twe*.

The flight song is apparently used only for courting and is seldom heard after mid-June. The bird starts from an exposed perch with a *chip-chip-chip*, then takes off on fluttering wings and climbs 10 to 20 feet in the air, uttering rapid *chips* all the way up. Hovering a moment at the crest of his flight, he descends at an angle to another perch, giving two or three very fast renditions of his normal territorial *chipereeeee-chipereeee*.

I once heard a juvenile give a high-pitched, squeaky call that sounded like *Psi-psi-psi-psivee*, after which it flew into a bush with an adult, and both proceeded to scold me with the *chip-chip* alarm note. Females also utter similar squeaky lisps while tending flying juveniles. I heard one female fly from her nest calling *tu-tu-tu-tu-twi-twi-twi*.

*Field marks.*—Peterson (1947) notes: "About size of Seaside Sparrow, but *upper parts blackish*, and under parts heavily streaked with black. * * * any Seaside Sparrow seen in the Titusville area in summer is this species." In the fall and winter both northern seaside and sharp-tailed sparrows frequent these marshes. The adult dusky is much darker than any of these, and larger than the sharp-tails. The juvenal dusky is more difficult to distinguish, but it is somewhat darker and should be molting into blacker winter dress when the northern birds arrive. From the Savannah and swamp sparrows which also winter in the salt marshes, the seasides may be told by their low, level, and more fluttery flight.

*Enemies.*—The chief enemy of the dusky seems to be man and his works. Nicholson (MS.) writes that from 1942 to about 1953 the coastal marshes were sprayed from aircraft with insecticides, mainly DDT, to control mosquitoes. By 1957 he estimated this had reduced the dusky population by at least 70 percent. Hickey (1961) points out how especially serious the use of insecticides is to bird species of limited distribution. Not only are food chains disrupted, but reproductive failures often result from slight ingestions of DDT. Considering the dusky's dependence on insect and animal food and its extremely limited distribution in an area sprayed heavily for mosquito control over a number of years, it is miraculous that any have survived.

The mosquito control impoundments completed in 1956 have already altered or eliminated much of the vegetation in which the duskies formerly nested. The gradient of the salt marsh is such that the fresh water in the impoundments is deepest near the tidal area of the Indian River and shallows to damp marsh near the high ground. Consequently the vegetation a quarter to a half mile from the river has been relatively unaltered, except for the encroachment of a few cattail stands. Although the higher marsh looks ideal for nesting, it is some distance from the birds' usual feeding grounds in the tidal area. Some duskies have moved into this higher portion of the marsh, but the food supply there may not be large enough to support a dense population.

Present in the marshes are a number of natural predators. The rice rat (*Oryzomys palustris*) is quite common and builds its ball-like nests in the tall *Spartina*. The racoon (*Procyon lotor*) is abundant in the area, and its tracks and trails may be found all through the marshes. Among the commoner snakes are the banded water snake (*Natrix sipidon*), the king snake (*Lampropeltis getulis*), the pigmy rattlesnake (*Sistrurus militarius*), and the water moccasin (*Agkistrodon piscivorus*). All of these probably consume some eggs or young, but they have always been there and their depredations have not affected the dusky population measurably in the past. Several duskies have been noted to desert their nests when large black ants, common in the marsh, built their mud nests in the same clump of *Spartina*.

Possibly more serious may be predation by two new animals that have moved into the marshes since they were freshened. The large pig frogs (*Rana grylio*) which are now abundant within the dikes may not be able to catch adult sparrows, but they could certainly capture nestlings. Boat-tailed grackles (*Cassidix mexicanus*), well known to be fond of the eggs and young of other birds, are now nesting in bushes on the dikes near the dusky colonies. Should either of these suspicions prove correct, the frogs could be easily eliminated by flooding the impoundments temporarily with salt water, and the grackles discouraged by cutting down the bushes in which they nest.

*Fall and winter.*—Shortly after the molt commences in the fall the duskies become very shy and elusive. They no longer respond to a squeak by flying to the top of the grass to watch and scold the intruder. One gets the impression that fewer birds are present in the marshes, which is probably only partially true. Instead of being concentrated in the small nesting colonies, the birds now spread throughout the marshes and remain so through the winter. Perhaps the lower concentration of food available in winter may force them to reduce their density in their habitat. They also disperse to other marshes, both brackish and fresh, up to 20 miles from the breeding grounds. On Sept. 16, 1962, I found an adult in a marsh on Mosquito Lagoon, about 5 miles from the closest colony. Another adult was seen in a fresh water marsh north of Cocoa on Dec. 28, 1962, during the Christmas census. In a limited sense this might be termed a migration, but dispersal is more fitting.

By late February or early March the birds start to move back into their ancestral breeding colonies, and the cycle begins once more.

### DISTRIBUTION

*Range.*—The dusky seaside sparrow is resident in salt marshes of eastern Orange and northern Brevard counties, central eastern Florida (Persimmon Hammock on St. Johns River, near Indian River City, and Titusville, Merritt's Island).

*Egg dates.*—Florida: about 40 records, April 19 to July 23.

### AMMOSPIZA MIRABILIS (Howell)

## Cape Sable Sparrow

### PLATES 47 AND 48

### Contributed by LOUIS A. STIMSON

### HABITS

All seaside sparrows are noted for their secretiveness, but none has proved more elusive and difficult to find than the Cape Sable sparrow, the last avian species to be discovered on the North American continent. None of the great ornithologists who studied Florida birds in the 19th century, from Audubon to Ridgway and Chapman, even suspected its existance. It is small wonder that when Arthur H. Howell (1919) discovered it on the swampy prairies of Flamingo near Cape Sable in 1918, he considered its presence something of a miracle and named the bird *mirabilis*. Now, following its extirpation from those prairies by the disastrous hurricane of 1935, and its possible extermination by fire on much of its remaining southwest coast habitat in 1962, we may be gravely concerned about its future.

Howell (1919) recognized the bird's affinities by calling it the Cape Sable seaside sparrow. The 1957 A.O.U. Check-List accords it full specific standing in its vernacular name, Cape Sable sparrow, as well as in its technical binomial.  Many systematists consider it only a well-marked subspecies of *A. maritima;* among those who have written me to that effect are O. L. Austin, Jr., R. A. Paynter, Jr., and C. G. Sibley.  Beecher (1955) lists it subspecifically as *A. maritima mirabilis.* Griscom (1944) writes: "*A. mirabilis* (Howell) * * * has no real claim to specific distinction, certainly none of equal weight with those of *nigrescens.*"  After discussing the various differences he adds: "These are all differences of degree, none are absolute.  Indeed it could be argued that the whiter underparts of *mirabilis* deprive *nigrescens* of one of the latter's absolute characters."

Although I am not a systematist, it seems to me that the differences in color between *mirabilis* and the races of *maritima*, or even between *mirabilis* and *nigrescens*, are no greater than, for instance, those between certain races of the song sparrow or of the rufous-sided towhee. The similarities between *mirabilis*, *nigrescens*, and the *maritima* subspecies in song, nesting habits, and other behavior are striking, and the differences very slight.  The present complete isolation of the *mirabilis* population from all other seaside sparrows in Florida can be explained by recent geological events (Stimson, 1956).  However, the A.O.U. Check-List still considers it a full species, and until the Check-List Committee rules otherwise, we will have to abide by that decision.

The Cape Sable sparrow's only known remaining habitat today is the marshes lying a few miles inland behind the southwest coast of Florida northwest of Cape Sable.  Along this coast inland from the Gulf of Mexico first lies a belt of mangroves, commonly called the mangrove fringe, from 2 to 17 miles wide and cut by streams, inland bays, and a few salt marshes.  Some of these marshes look from the air as though they might be suitable seaside sparrow habitat, but few have been investigated on the gound.  Over the centuries this fringe has acted as a buffer, protecting the adjoining marshes farther inland from the destructive fury of the hurricanes that periodically sweep the coast.  The marshes at Cape Sable lack such protection.

Inland from the mangrove fringe is a belt of marshes from $\frac{1}{2}$ to 3 miles or so in width.  These marshes vary from salt through brackish to fresh, and contain extensive stretches of cord grass (*Spartina* sp.), which seems to be one of the Cape Sable sparrow's preferred habitats. Bordering the marshes landward are cypress swamps, or strands, and some pine woods interspersed with wet prairie, usually fresh and dry during droughts.  From the Lostmans Pine Islands area southeastward to Broad River and the Shark River Valley, the forest border is absent and the marshes merge directly into the marsh prairie of the southern Everglades.  It was here that the surprising discovery was made, only a decade ago, of Cape Sable sparrows breeding in a fresh water saw-grass (*Mariscus*) habitat (Stimson, 1956, 1961).

Subsequent investigations have shown the entire population of the species today to be scattered in small colonies in the narrow belt of fresh and brackish marshes from the Shark River basin northwestward some 40 miles to the Ochopee–Everglades City area.  Before the Tamiami Trail was opened in 1928, this region was truly a wilderness and extremely difficult to reach.  The highway now traverses parts of the inland marsh between the mangroves and the cypress from Royal Palm Hammock in Collier-Seminole State Park to Ochopee, and has opened up the adjoining land to humans, somewhat to the detriment of the birds.  Swamp-buggies and air-boats now give deeper access into it, but for a man on foot the area is still difficult to penetrate.

*Territory.*—In the coastal marshes at Cape Sable, Howell (1932) found "the birds occur rather sparingly in small, more or less isolated colonies."  This pattern the birds still adhere to in their present range.  Over the years from 1943 to date I have often found from 10 to 16 singing males in areas of a quarter to a half a square mile.  On Apr. 26, 1959, O. L. Austin, Jr., searched the Ochopee marsh and wrote me: "I found a thriving little colony and spent most of the day studying it.  I counted 19 birds, most of them in pairs, and apparently established on territories from 100 to 300 yards apart.  I estimated at least 9 or 10 pairs in that perhaps square mile of marsh."  Aside from singing to advertise their occupancy, I have never observed any defense of territory, nor have I found any mention of it in the published accounts.

*Nesting.*—H. H. Bailey (1925) describes the first nest of the Cape Sable sparrow he found May 12, 1921, as "composed of dry salt marsh grass, and lined with very fine grasses, attached to some upright marsh grass waist-high and growing in a brackish swale, and completely covered with matted-down dead marsh grass."  The second known nest, according to Howell (1932) was taken by E. J. Court on Mar. 29, 1925.  It contained five fresh eggs and was situated on the ground at the base of a clump of grass.  The third man to find nests and eggs of this species was D. J. Nicholson (1928) who thus describes his experiences near Cape Sable on Apr. 10 and 13, 1927:

Coming to several scattered bunches of switch-grass [*Spartina*] near a shallow pond, I thought I would give it a search and in a few minutes was staring down upon my first set of four eggs of this very rare sparrow.

There was no bird in sight nor did I see one leave the nest, and there was no indication that sparrows owned this nest, so quiet and indifferent were the birds. I left the nest for fifteen minutes and returning flushed her off the nest at ten feet. She flew directly from the nest and perched on top of the grass fifteen feet away, giving a weak chirp and no other sound. Soon she disappeared seeming indifferent to the fate of her nest.

This nest was situated sixteen inches above the ground in switch-grass, about midway; and made of dead grass lined with finer blades of grass neatly cupped. Over the top of nest enough grass was placed to conceal it, though it could not be strictly called an arched nest. It gave the impression of a nest just begun. * * *

Again on April 13, 1927, * * * I found three nests * * *. The first nest was built in the short salt-grass [*Salicornia*] several inches above the ground, built of the same material, lined with fine grasses. It was only found by accidentally parting the grass and contained three young about two days old. The parents were quite solicitous, scolding with a loud chipping note, accompanied by jerks of the tail. * * * A second nest was located by observing the parent fly into a dense clump of switch-grass three different times. Twice I searched well but could not find a nest, but the third time was rewarded by finding the nest with three young of the same age as found in the other nest. A deserted nest that had been occupied earlier in the season was found several inches above the ground in [a] dense patch of salt-grass.

*Eggs.*—The Cape Sable sparrow lays three to five ovate and slightly glossy eggs, very similar to those of the other seaside sparrows. The ground color is greenish-white to grayish white, speckled and spotted with such reddish browns as "Mars brown," "Prout's brown," or "auburn." The three sets in the American Museum of Natural History in New York are grayish-white with spotting well scattered over the entire surface with only a slight concentration toward the large end. Some eggs have undermarkings of "pale purplish gray." The measurements of 15 eggs average 19.9 by 15.1 millimeters; those showing the four extremes measure *20.6* by *16.6*, *18.3* by 14.5, and 20.3 by *13.9* millimeters.

Howell (1932) states: "The five eggs collected by Court * * * are pale bluish white, heavily and rather evenly spotted with different sized spots of verona brown and lavender gray. They are very similar to certain eggs of the Smyrna Seaside, but the ground color is more bluish, and the eggs are less pointed than the average egg of that race."

The earliest nesting date known is indicated by J. C. Howell, Jr. (1937), who writes: "On March 30, 1934, near Flamingo in Monroe County, Florida, Messrs. J. Adger Smyth, D. S. Riggs, and the writer observed a young Cape Sable Seaside Sparrow * * *. This bird had not been out of the nest more than a day or two. The set of eggs from which this youngster hatched must have been deposited during the first week in March."

*Plumage.*—Nothing is known of the incubation period in this species, and though several observers have reported seeing young in the nest, no description of the nestlings exists in the literature. Apparently the only juvenal specimen in existence is one I collected June 29, 1952, for the U.S. National Museum. Concerning this bird O. L. Austin, Jr., writes me: "John Aldrich and I just examined together the juvenile you collected. Compared with February and April adults, the upper parts of the young bird lack their distinctive greenish-gray cast. The back feathers have heavier blackish-brown centers edged with buffy-white. The yellow of the lores and the wing edging is also replaced with buffy-white. The entire underparts are suffused with pale yellow; the breast streaks are smaller, more brownish, and less continuous than in the adult plumage. We cannot see any 'pinkish yellow' as you report [*in* Sprunt, 1954], nor would we call the bird any 'lighter'; if anything it is browner." The pinkish tinge I thought I saw in the field could well have been caused by early morning light effects, which only emphasizes the value of a specimen.

*Food.*—The only information on the food of this species is that of Howell (1932): "Stomachs of 15 specimens of this species have been examined in the Biological Survey; the food consisted almost wholly of insects and spiders, with a few small amphipods and mollusks, and about 3 percent of vegetable debris. Beetles of many species composed the largest single item, and spiders were next in importance. Other insects taken were dragon-fly nymphs, moths and their larvae, bugs, parasitic wasps, flies, crickets, and locusts."

*Behavior.*—In my experience and from what little has been written about it, the general behavior of the Cape Sable sparrow differs very little if at all from that of its close relatives. Howell (1932) remarks: "Like the other species of Seaside Sparrows, they are very shy and secretive, spending most of their time on or near the ground, concealed in the vegetation. * * * During the breeding season, late in March and April, the birds flush rather easily from the tall grass, flying with a steady flight for a distance of 100 to 200 yards before dropping into the grass again. They usually run as soon as they alight and are hard to flush a second time." Sometimes they fly considerably farther; one bird I flushed from its singing perch flew in a large half circle for almost half a mile before dropping into the grass.

During the summer I find that the adults, and particularly the young, may be called out of cover by "squeaking." The birds are most easily observed when the males are singing, which may be any time from January to August. J. C. Howell, Jr., in a letter to A. H. Howell, heard "some singing December 26, 1933, 5 miles west of Flamingo." S. A. Grimes wrote me Nov. 20, 1953, saying: "When Roy Hallman, Wayland Shannon and I were at Cape Sable in January, 1932, we found the Cape Sable sparrow quite common and in full song." I have heard the birds singing in the Ochopee marshes as early as March 15 and as late as August 4.

To me the birds seem quite temperamental and sensitive to weather conditions. Although I have heard them sing at all times of the day, they sing more frequently early in the morning and late in the afternoon. When I discovered the Ochopee colony on Apr. 3, 1953, the birds were singing freely early in the morning. The next day I returned at 1:00 p.m. with two companions, and though we searched diligently for an hour and a half, we could not find or flush a single sparrow. Returning at 5:00 p.m., we soon saw two singing males and heard others in the distance. W. B. Robertson, Jr., writes me that "on 16 May 1960 at Ochopee two birds sang until well past sundown."

A rising wind will often cause the birds to stop singing. The heat of midday also seems to be a deterrent. On the other hand, a cloud passing over the sun or the cooling effect of a sudden shower will sometimes cause the birds, silent until then, to pop out of the grass and sing.

*Voice.*—The Cape Sable sparrow has a number of short call or alarm notes which it utters throughout the year. The most common sounds to me like *zup-zup-zup;* another is a high-pitched, twittering *zee-zee-zee.* Best known, however, is the territorial song of the male which he usually gives from a perch on or near the top of a grass stem. Both Howell (1932) and Sutton (*in* Holt and Sutton, 1926) speak of hearing the song "coming apparently from well down in the thick marsh grass," but this is contrary to my own experience and those of other recent observers. W. B. Robertson, Jr., writes me: "All I have seen on four trips to Ochopee sang from conspicuous perches near the top of a tall stem."

Howell (1932) states that "The ordinary song resembles that of the other Seaside Sparrows, but seems to be simpler in character. I wrote it at the time *churr-buz-z-z,* the last syllable accented and prolonged. In this buzzing character it most resembled the song of the Dusky Seaside (*nigrescens*)." Sutton (*in* Holt and Sutton, 1926) transliterates it as "*d'le, d'le, d'le.*" To me the song sounds like *churr-eee-e-e-e.* The final buzzing note may be heard for some distance, a quarter mile or so, and unless one is close enough to hear the rest of the song it may easily be confused with the *e-e-e-e* note of the redwinged blackbird or the call of one of the marsh frogs. When one is extremely close to a singing bird, the song is preceded by two or more noticeable guttural *clicks.* I have heard these same *clicks* from the dusky seaside sparrow.

Compared to the songs of other seaside sparrows, that of *mirabilis* seems to me most like that of *nigrescens,* but not quite as strongly buzzing. W. B. Robertson, Jr., contributes: "H. Teter and I listened to two sing at Ochopee for perhaps 45 minutes on 16 May 1960. We were close enough to hear the introductory *clicks* distinctly. We were impressed by the similarity to the song of the Dusky which we had heard the day before near Titusville." The song of *A. m. maritima* seemed somewhat similar as I heard it in marshes near Holgate, N. J. The song of *A. m. macgillivraii* near Charleston, S.C., seemed to me decidedly weaker, in fact a rather poor effort. I have heard *juncicola* and *fisheri* only once each and can make no comparison. As I listened to the song of *A. m. sennetti* at Copano Bay near Rockport, Tex., it seemed very similar, but appeared to have an extra syllable, which I wrote *churr-ur-eee-e-e-e*.

The Cape Sable sparrow also has a flight song which I have often heard. Howell (1932) describes it as "of longer duration and * * * preceded by a sort of twittering chirrup." My observations have been that the bird springs into the air, gives several rather excited twittering notes in flight, then returns to a grass-top perch and gives the regular song, *churr-eee-e-e-e*.

*Field marks.*—Howell (1932) describes the bird as: "About the size of Scott's Seaside, *upperparts more greenish and underparts more whitish* than in any of the races of *maritima;* hind neck and back yellowish olive, streaked with fuscous; scapulars edged with white; tail fuscous, edged with citrine drab (olive drab); lores yellow; wings fuscous, edged with olive; edge of wings yellow; underparts white, moderately streaked on breast and sides with fuscous or mouse gray."

As no other seaside sparrow has been taken within 150 miles of the Cape Sable's range, the species with which the Cape Sable is most likely to be confused is the sharp-tailed sparrow, which has an identical flight pattern and is only slightly smaller and browner. The Savannah sparrow, swamp sparrow, and grasshopper sparrow also occur commonly in the same marshes during the fall, winter and spring.

For positive field or sight identification I prefer to see a singing bird. The Cape Sable's habit in winter of dropping immediately back into the grass on being flushed makes it extremely hard to identify by sight. Unless the bird flushes very close with the sun shining directly on its back making the greenish cast plainly visible, I simply refuse to identify it as a Cape Sable sparrow.

The difficulty of identifying Cape Sables by sight in winter is attested by the many sight records of the species reported from the Cape Sable marshes since the 1935 hurricane. That these reports were based on misidentifications is strongly suggested by the fact that no Cape Sable sparrow has been reported from that area since then during the period from May 15 to August 1, when no other sparrow would be present and the Cape Sable, if present, would be in song and easily found and recognized.

*Enemies.*—Although a number of natural enemies of ground-nesting birds are plentiful in its habitat—raccoons and several species of snakes for instance, which surely destroy some eggs and nestlings—no preying on the Cape Sable sparrow has been reported. Its chief foes today are hurricanes, droughts, fires, and man's alterations of its habitat, chiefly by drainage.

Hurricanes have been striking southern Florida periodically in the late summer and fall for centuries. Their high winds and flood tides can be extremely destructive to any bird life in their path, as the report of W. B. Robertson, Jr. (1961) on the 1960 hurricane Donna shows. When the rising waters drive the sparrows from their marsh habitat during daylight, the birds have a good chance of reaching and riding out the blow in the protection of vegetation on higher land. This the Cape Sable birds doubtless did during the 1926 hurricane, the center of which passed over Miami, and during a less severe one that passed over Cape Sable by day in 1929. Howell (1932) quotes a letter from J. B. Semple dated Jan. 3, 1930: "The Cape Sable Seaside Sparrow is still in its old haunts in the long grass, notwithstanding that last October five feet of salt water driven by a wind of about 100 miles per hour, passed over the entire range of this little bird."

The birds were not so fortunate when the hurricane of Sept. 2, 1935, one of the most violent storms on record in the western hemisphere, hit Cape Sable. That hurricane struck at night, and the sudden wall of water at least 8 feet deep it drove before it must have caught the birds asleep with their toes locked around their grass stem perches. As I (1956) explained elsewhere: "It seems incredible that any small sparrow could have escaped alive. If any sparrow did manage to get into the air when that eight foot wave struck, it would have been blown to sea towards the center of the storm and would have dropped from exhaustion into the waters of the Gulf * * *. To my knowledge no reliable reports have ever come from that part of the coast of the presence of this species since the storm." And to this day the birds have failed to move back into the area where Howell first found them, which is now completely under the jurisdiction and protection of Everglades National Park.

Most if not all their present range was completely inundated by the floods accompanying hurricane Donna in 1960. Donna passed Cape Sable at daybreak on September 10. Her center proceeded northeastward along the coast and struck Ochopee and Everglades City about noon, ravaging vegetation and damaging property. Yet the birds managed to escape her effects somewhere nearby, because I found them in several places along the Ochopee marshes in 1961 and 1962.

Fires, whether started by man or lightning, are a serious if not a catastrophic threat to the species, as Sutton (*in* Holt and Sutton, 1926) noted long ago: "However, it is well to mention the constant danger of extermination of this colony by fire. * * * It is quite possible that the whole area might be devastated by a single blaze." I (1961) described the destruction by fire of colonies in the Lostmans Pine Islands section in 1957 and in the Ochopee marsh in May 1959. O. L. Austin, Jr., also mentions the Ochopee fire in his previously quoted letter which continues: "Five weeks later, 6 June 1959, I stopped to check on the colony. I was horrified to find the marsh where the birds were had been burned flat, probably several weeks previously. I spent the rest of the day tramping all the unburned marsh I could find in the vicinity, but could not flush a single sparrow."

In May 1962, following the most prolonged and severe drought in recent history, a number of fires broke out in southern Florida. Two that started at almost the same time, one near Cooperstown on the Tamiami Trail, the other in the Lostmans Pine Island area, eventually joined and together burned 77,000 acres within Everglades National Park and some 107,000 acres more outside its borders. They covered much of the territory inhabited by the Cape Sable sparrows, including the area of greatest concentration bordering the Shark River Valley. It would indeed have been a miracle for any sparrow in the path of those fires to have escaped.

However, the fires did miss a tract of about 23,000 acres lying mainly north, west, and southwest of the water gauge (see map, Stimson, 1956). I have found Cape Sable sparrows at several points on the perimeter of this unburned section in years past, but I have never been able to penetrate its interior. This area, together with a few small spots toward Ochopee, may now remain the only possible reservoir for the future perpetuation of the species.

On July 21, 1962, W. G. Atwater and I investigated the marsh at the foot of the Barnes Strand where I had found Cape Sable sparrows on Apr. 16, 1955. The day was ideal for our purpose, but though we reached and had crisscrossed the marsh in ankle- and knee-deep water a number of times before 10:00 a.m., we could not find a single sparrow. We did find clear evidence that the entire marsh had been burned, probably prior to 1962.

A prolonged drought such as occurred from 1961 to June 1962, cannot help but having in itself a decimating effect on the sparrows. The complete dehydration of the land must destroy insect and other invertebrate food of the seaside sparrows that depends on moisture for its existence. On May 30, 1962, I visited the colony where I took the 1952 specimen, and where I could always find at least 10 singing males. Although the area fortunately had not been burned, I could find only three singing males. Three weeks later, on June 20, 1962, H. M. Stevenson and I hunted the same place for more than an hour without finding a bird, though the weather conditions were ideal that morning. At another colony, although a few males were singing, we both thought the actions of the birds suggested they had not nested, even at that late date.

Recently, in the Ochopee area, another threat to the species has developed. Real estate developers have put drag-line dredges and bulldozers to work. They have dredged small lakes out of the marsh and used the fill thus obtained to level up building lots at the very edge of the marshes inhabited by the sparrows. Another drag-line is currently at work in the marsh behind the village. A carelessly thrown cigarette could start a blaze that might destroy all the sparrow colonies from the Immokalee road to the Turner River.

Surely the preceding few paragraphs justify the "grave concern" expressed at the start of this life history. However, with water conservation work now in progress in the Everglades to counteract the effects of drainage over the past 40 years, the Cape Sable sparrow's habitat may yet in time revert to something near its condition in predrainage days. I, for one, pray that the future will disprove my present fear for the continued existence of this species.

## DISTRIBUTION

*Range.*—The Cape Sable sparrow is resident in southwestern Florida from the Ochopee Marshes near Everglades southeast toward the headwaters of Huston River and the mouth of Gum Slough to the Shark River Basin; formerly to Cape Sable.

*Egg dates.*—Florida: 3 records, March 29 to May 21.

### POOECETES GRAMINEUS GRAMINEUS (Gmelin)

## Eastern Vesper Sparrow

### PLATE 49

### Contributed by ANDREW J. BERGER

### HABITS

Early American ornithologists called this species the bay-winged bunting or the grass finch. According to T. S. Roberts (1932): "It was John Burroughs who gave to this bird the inappropriate name of Vesper Sparrow because he felt that its singing was sweeter and more impressive toward evening, but its simple lay is by no means a vesper song as it may be heard at all hours of the day." It is true that the clear, far-carrying song of the vesper sparrow is perhaps more conspicuous in the still of warm summer evenings after most of the song sparrows and field sparrows have stopped singing and when the Henslow's sparrows begin in earnest to give forth with their short and improbable song. But the vesper sparrow sometimes sings just as persistently shortly after dawn on cold April days.

George M. Sutton (MS.) writes: "Singing continues virtually all day long during midsummer, though it is less fervent during the middle of the day in very hot weather; it is especially brilliant on calm evenings or just after a rain. On June 24, 1946, I heard the first

song of the morning at 4:05 a.m. (e.s.t.). Thereafter singing was
almost continuous until about 11:00 o'clock, at which time it subsided
for about two hours. Singing after sunset, even in the gathering dusk,
is a common midsummer phenomenon." The vesper sparrow is,
however, better known to many for its white outer tail feathers, which
provide an excellent field mark when the bird flies away from the
observer, rather than for its song (which some confuse with that of
the song sparrow).

*Spring.*—The first vesper sparrows usually arrive in the northern
states (Massachusetts, New York, Michigan, Minnesota) during the
last week or 10 days of March, and the spring migration is well under
way by the first week of April. In Ohio, M. B. Trautman (1940)
reports that "throughout spring the species principally inhabited the
better-drained and more upland fields and pastures. It was found in
greatest numbers in sparsely vegetated fields, and in close-cropped
pastures and meadows. It never flocked in large numbers in spring,
and seldom more than 15 birds were seen in a well-organized flock, and
then only early in the season. During the last half of the migration it
was always well scattered over fields and pastures. When several
birds were flushed they did not group together, but flew a short
distance by themselves and dropped independently to earth." In his
report on the birds of Lucas County, Ohio, L. W. Campbell (1940)
states that spring flocks of 25 or 30 birds were sometimes seen and
that the greatest number seen in one day was 100 (on Mar. 31, 1932).
Cordelia J. Stanwood (MS.) writes that at Ellsworth, Maine, the
first vesper sparrows were seen "in mid-April, or a few days earlier."
Her earliest record was Apr. 6, 1909; on Apr. 13, 1916, she saw about
30 birds, the first seen that year.

*Territory.*—Although much remains to be learned about the
territorial behavior of the vesper sparrow, we know that this species
uses a much larger home range than do certain other sparrows. On
a 10-acre field near Ypsilanti, Mich., cultivated in part the previous
year and surrounded by woods on three sides, I found 15 pairs of
song sparrows, 8 pairs of field sparrows, and only 3 pairs of vesper
sparrows, all of which had established nesting territories. At the
Edwin S. George Reserve, also in southern Michigan, Francis C.
Evans (MS.) studied a 14-acre uncultivated field for 8 years (1949–56).
He found that the number of breeding territories vesper sparrows
established during this period "has ranged from a minimum of 8 to
a maximum of 12. The entire field seems to be utilized by the birds,
and this would give an average territory size ranging from 1.2 acres
at the highest population density to 1.8 acres at the lowest density.
However, the birds have frequent recourse to the adjacent woods,
penetrating at least 50 or 60 yards, and if territory boundaries are

extended into the woods, the average territory may be somewhat larger than the estimate just given. We have frequently seen the vesper sparrow in territorial combats essentially similar to those described by M. M. Nice (1937: 57–58; 1943: 153–156) for the Song Sparrow." John L. George (MS.) found 9.9, 8.7, and 9.5 pairs of vesper sparrows per 100 acres of cultivated farm land during a 3-year study in southern Michigan.

It seems likely that the number of pairs inhabiting extensive cultivated tracts planted to hay, wheat, or corn is limited by the number of available song perches rather than by actual territorial conflict. The vesper sparrow rarely sings on the ground, and it seems to prefer the highest singing perches available. Favorite song perches in nesting areas bordered by woods are branches 25 or more feet above ground along the woods' edge. Where there are no trees, the song perch may be a fence, a dead weed, a thistle, shrub, or any vegetation or structure higher than the nesting substrate.

G. M. Sutton (MS.) notes: "In areas inhabited by both vesper and grasshopper sparrows I have never witnessed interspecific territorial disputes of any sort. I think it quite possible that nest-territories of these two species may occasionally overlap. As for the vesper and lark sparrows, I have never seen one species chasing, or fighting with, the other."

Rarely I have observed a vesper sparrow chase a song sparrow or a field sparrow, but usually these species nest and feed together without conflict. On May 10, 1946 I found a vesper sparrow nest 14 yards from a killdeer (*Charadrius vociferus*) nest and 21 yards from a field sparrow nest. Ralph A. O'Reilly, Jr., found a nest July 3, 1950 only 10 feet from a killdeer nest.

*Courtship.*—According to E. H. Forbush (1929), "courtship is carried on mostly on the ground. The male walks or runs before or after the female, with wings raised, and both wings and tail widely spread, occasionally rising into the air to give his flight-song." However, the vesper sparrow rarely gives a true flight song.

*Nesting.*—As far as is known the vesper sparrow invariably places its nest on the ground, frequently near small patches of bare ground or where the vegetation is sparse and low. First nests—those built in April or early May—may be built in an excavation in the ground under cover of prostrate dead weed stems; these nests may be very well concealed by a complete matted covering of such weeds. Nests along dirt roads or country lanes, or those placed in last year's alfalfa or corn fields, usually are built at the base of a grass tussock, a thistle, a dandelion, some other plant, or even a clod of dirt. Some nests are nearly completely exposed from above during the egg-laying period, but with the rapid growth of spring vegetation, these nests

PLATE 49

Excelsior, Minn.                                                    A. D. Du Bois

NEST AND EGGS OF VESPER SPARROW

Ronan, Mont.                                                    A. D. Cruickshank

VESPER SPARROW FEEDING YOUNG

PLATE 50

Seward County, Kans. W. Colvin

NEST AND EGGS OF LARK SPARROW

Brownsville, Texas A. D. Cruickshank

LARK SPARROW AT NEST

may be well hidden by the time the eggs hatch. John L. George (MS.) found the preferred habitat on farmland to be a "hay field giving a yield of one ton per acre," but that "each year several pairs established territories in corn stubble of the previous year, which already had a heavy growth of foxtail, *Setaria*."

The vesper sparrow is one of the nesting associates of the Kirtland's warbler (*Dendroica kirtlandii*), both in plantations of jack pine (*Pinus banksiana*) and in areas in which natural growths of jack pines are repopulating burned territory. In Minnesota, T. S. Roberts (1932) writes, "Its favorite haunts are the open, dry uplands, wild or cultivated. In the forests of the north every clearing, old burned-over area, wind-fall, or cut-over region, has its considerable quota of vesper sparrows."

At Buckeye Lake, Ohio, M. B. Trautman (1940) writes: "The species mostly nested in short-grass pastures and meadows, and in better-drained fields of short sparse vegetation that were cultivated or fallow. It appeared to avoid heavy viscous clays and concentrated in lighter soils which contained considerable sand and gravel. Because of its preference it was found in greatest nesting abundance on the gravelly and well-drained slopes and tops of glacial moraines south and east of the lake." Trautman adds that "all nests were built in small depressions made in the earth by the bird previous to actual nest building," and that "the nests of rootlets and fine grasses were in some instances lined sparingly with cattle or horse hair." E. H. Eaton (1914) also mentions that the nest is "rather loosely constructed of coarse grass and weed stalks, lined with finer grasses, rootlets, and long hair." T. S. Roberts (1932) says that the nest is in some areas "a depression in the ground lined with grasses, and in the north with pine needles."

Writing of this species at Ellsworth, Maine, Cordelia J. Stanwood (MS.) says that "in my immediate vicinity, the vesper sparrow nests in a meadow that has been under cultivation or used for pasturage for more than a century, and it breeds in old fields where hay is sparse, fine, and weedy and the ground in many places is covered with sphagnum moss, birdwheat moss, and reindeer lichen; such fields often are grown over in spots with highland cranberries and blueberries."

Francis H. Allen (MS.) observes that "one who is familiar with the open fields and pastures with short grass which always seem to be the normal habitat of this species may be surprised to find that it is a common breeding bird in the wide stretches of beachgrass on the seashore, where the Savannah sparrow also breeds."

The nesting season of the vesper sparrow is a long one, extending from about the third week of April to about the middle of August in Michigan, New York, and Ohio, and probably also in Minnesota.

In southern Michigan, I have found nests with eggs as early as Apr. 21, 1946; Mrs. Alice D. Miller found an adult building a nest on July 14, 1952; George M. Sutton found a nest with three eggs on July 31, 1935—the nest and eggs were destroyed August 6 or 7. Young out of the nest have been found as early as May 11, in 1946 and 1949, and young have been observed to leave nests as late as Aug. 3, 1942 and Aug. 5, 1948. In Ohio, M. B. Trautman reports that "the first young out of the nest were observed May 17 (1930, at least 2 young), and the last August 13 (1925, 1 young)." Cordelia J. Stanwood (MS.) mentions a nest in Maine in which the first egg hatched on Aug. 13, 1909.

T. S. Roberts (1932) gives a good description of the behavior of the vesper sparrow when flushed from its nest: "When it slips from the nest, almost at one's feet, it frequently feigns injury * * * fluttering along the ground with wide-spread tail and dragging a wing or leg, as though badly crippled. More commonly it flies directly away, low over the ground * * *." Some female vesper sparrows consistently leave a nest with eggs without feigning injury or giving alarm notes and fly 50 or 60 yards to a tree, but their behavior may change completely after the eggs hatch. Then the bird may run along the ground with tail widely spread, so that the white feathers are conspicuous, and with both wings held over the back and fluttering slightly, much as some song sparrows are prone to do.

*Eggs.*—The vesper sparrow usually lays from three to five eggs, and sometimes six. They are ovate and have a slight gloss. The ground color is creamy white or pale greenish white, with spots, blotches, scrawls, and cloudings of "sorghum brown," "Verona brown," "russet," or "Mars brown," and black, with undermarkings of "pale mouse gray." The eggs of this species show considerable variation in both type and amount of markings. Some have spots, blotches, and scrawls about equally distributed over the entire surface; others may have a few very dark brown or even black scrawls at the large end with only a few fine spots over the rest of the egg. The markings may be all in one shade of brown, or in two or three shades of brown mixed with the "pale mouse gray." The measurements of 50 eggs of the nominate race average 20.7 by 15.2 millimeters; the eggs showing the four extremes measure *22.9* by 16.3, 21.8 by *16.8*, *18.3* by 14.7, and 18.8 by *13.1* millimeters.

While four eggs seem to constitute the usual clutch for spring nests, a few five-egg clutches have been reported (Baillie and Harrington, 1937). M. B. Trautman (1940) found five nests with five eggs or young and one nest that held one cowbird egg and six sparrow eggs. Francis C. Evans (MS.) found the number of eggs in 96 complete clutches to be: 2 eggs, 4 sets; 3 eggs, 25 sets; 4 eggs, 67 sets; the mean clutch size was 3.7 eggs. He adds that there is "a distinct seasonal decline in clutch size: most of the clutches produced in May contain 4 eggs, most of those produced in late June and July contain 3." There are exceptions, however, and I have found July nests with four eggs, both in southern Michigan and in Oscoda County; Douglas S. Middleton found a nest with four eggs on July 12, 1947 (Oakland County, Mich.); G. M. Sutton found a nest at the Edwin S. George Reserve in which three of the four eggs hatched on July 24, 1942; and Lawrence H. Walkinshaw found a nest with five eggs on July 15, 1945. Mr. Bent (MS.) mentioned two nests, each with four eggs, found in Massachusetts on July 1, 1886 and July 9, 1887.

*Young.*—The incubation period is reported by John L. George (MS.), Francis C. Evans (MS.), and L. H. Walkinshaw (MS.) to vary between 12 and 13 days; some authors have given the period as 11 to 13 days. Incubation is performed chiefly by the female, but E. H. Forbush (1929) comments that both sexes "have been seen on the nest," and Evans has recorded four instances in which the male was flushed from a nest containing eggs. Both adults have been observed to eat the egg shells. E. M. and W. A. Perry (1918) watched one parent "take a shell some few feet away from the nest before eating it."

The female usually and the male occasionally brood the young. The amount of time the young are brooded depends in part on the time of the year, that is, they are brooded more in early May than in June and July. During hot summer days the young also are shielded from the sun, usually by the female. Both adults feed the nestlings and both eat or carry away the fecal sacs.

As with many ground nesting passerines, the nestling period varies considerably from nest to nest. John L. George (MS.) found that in two vesper sparrow nests "the young fledged 9 days after hatching; in a third, 10 days; in a fourth, 13 days; and in a fifth, 14 days." If they are disturbed—by banding, weighing, or by a predator—the young will leave the nest at 7 or 8 days of age. Francis C. Evans found the nestling period to vary from 7 to 12 days, and found the mean period to be 9.1 days. The young are unable to maintain flight when they leave the nest, but they are very quick and agile in moving through the vegetation. Once the young have left the nest, they remain quietly hidden, except when being fed, and they are extremely difficult to find.

The male apparently takes over most of the feeding of the first brood while the female begins a second nest. The fledglings appear to be semi-dependent on the adults until about 30 to 35 days of age. Evans found adults feeding banded young "which had left the nest 18 to 22 days previously."

Although the long nesting season has led many ornithologists to assume that the vesper sparrow is double-brooded ("probably even three sometimes," Forbush, 1929), two recent investigators, working with color-banded birds, have proved that the vesper sparrow is indeed double-brooded, at least in southern Michigan. John L. George (MS.) reports that "a banded pair that raised two broods successfully hatched the second brood 29 days after the hatching of the first." Francis C. Evans found one female that successfully raised three broods in one season and states: "Of the remaining 28 records, 13 raised two broods and 15 raised only one brood. I cannot definitely say of any pair that it failed to raise even a single brood, and I believe that almost every pair succeeds in raising at least one brood."

On May 17, 1946 I observed copulation by a pair of vesper sparrows on the ground in whose nest the first egg (cowbird) had hatched that day; the male then flew to a tree some 50 yards away and the female returned to the nest. That this species undoubtedly is double-brooded in New York is suggested by E. H. Eaton's (1914) statement that fresh eggs may be found "from the 28th of April to the 20th of May," and that "later sets are frequently observed from the 20th of June to the 25th of July." Theoretically there is time in the period mentioned above for a pair of vesper sparrows to raise four broods during a single season. In view of the frequent destruction of nests, however, such a possibility is unlikely. Evans found 52 percent of 137 nests to be successful in fledging at least one young sparrow.

*Plumages.*—G. M. Sutton (1935) made a careful study of the juvenal plumage of the eastern vesper sparrow, which he describes as follows:

The natal down of this species is grayish brown. With the molting of this down a heavily streaked, strongly black-and-white nestling-stage of the juvenal plumage appears. Individuals from eight to twelve or fifteen days old are in this dark plumage-stage, which appears to be as nearly a complete juvenal plumage as the species ever wears. The scapulars are very dark, the dark areas in the middle of each feather being broad and the margins comparatively narrow. Feathers of the back, neck, and crown also have broad black medial streaks and narrow margins; and the underparts, except for the middle of the belly, are more heavily and more definitely streaked with black than in any subsequent plumage or plumage-stage. The fact that many feathers of the loral, superciliary, mental, and malar regions are still partly sheathed gives the face a strongly black-and-white appearance that it does not have a few days later.

In a later paper, G. M. Sutton (1941) adds: "Each of my three captive birds began its postjuvenal molt when approximately eighteen days old. * * * As for the time at which the postjuvenal molt begins in the young of first broods, until we have more facts it is unwise to make further assertions. * * * It is quite possible, therefore, that the young of first broods molt more slowly than do the young of

second (and third) broods or that, quite independently of age, all
young birds of a given summer begin their postjuvenal molt more or
less simultaneously." He found that the postjuvenal molt usually
involves "only the body plumage," but that it "occasionally involves
the outermost primary, but not the other remiges or the rectrices."

J. Dwight (1900) comments that the "sexes are practically alike in
all plumages, although the colors will average duller in the female, and
the moults are the same." He adds that the first nuptial plumage is
"acquired by wear which is marked and produces a brown-streaked
plumage. The buffs and browns are largely lost. A few new feathers
may be assumed about the chin in spring, but there is no evidence of a
moult." The adult winter plumage is "acquired by a complete postnuptial moult beginning in mid-August. Practically indistinguishable
from first winter dress, sometimes paler below, the tertiary edgings
rather darker."

*Food.*—E. H. Forbush (1929) writes that the food of the vesper
sparrow "consists of nearly one-third animal matter, chiefly insects, * * * including many first-class pests such as weevils, click
beetles, grasshoppers, locusts, cut-worms, army-worms and moths of
destructive species." T. S. Roberts (1932) states that "Among the
seeds taken (about one-third the entire food) are ragweed, purslane,
wild sunflower, lamb's quarters, pigeon- and crab-grass, knotweeds,
and grain (mostly waste)."

*Behavior.*—Field ornithologists often observe the vesper sparrow's
propensity for taking dust baths. This behavior is well described by
G. M. Sutton (MS.) who writes:

"The most distinctive attribute of the vesper sparrow is, perhaps,
its liking for dust baths. Young vesper sparrows which I reared in
captivity in 1935 and 1940 bathed in dust almost daily (Sutton, 1943:
4), whereas young field sparrows, Henslow's sparrows, indigo buntings,
and cardinals never did. Noncaptive vesper sparrows, both young
and adult, take dust baths frequently. A common phenomenon of
the Edwin S. George Reserve in midsummer is dust puffing out from
the plumage of vesper sparrows surprised into sudden flight along a
road; another is vesper sparrow tracks leading up and down the ruts
to and from little basins of dust in which the birds have bathed.

"A favorite haunt of the vesper sparrow in midsummer is a flat
stretch of road in the very middle of the Reserve. The birds do not
flock here—they fly up singly or in twos or threes—but the place is
obviously attractive to them. Food is abundant in the form of seeds
and insects. The habitat is open, the only trees being widely scattered
elms, oaks, and small cedars. Mullein is fairly common. Under the
broad leaves of this plant the birds find shade when the sun is very hot.
Best of all is the road itself, with its clear-cut, dust-filled ruts, some of

which are deep enough to furnish shade.   I have never walked along
this road in summer without flushing several vesper sparrows.   I make
this statement advisedly, for I have found the birds there at all hours.
Early in the morning I have found them feeding.   Later in the morning
I have seen young birds at play, chasing each other up and down the
ruts or squatting on the bare ground, nibbling at grassblades.   At noon
on hot days, I have watched both young and old birds seek shady spots.
At night I have flushed them between the ruts and returned the following morning to discover little piles of droppings marking the roosting
places, as well as the footprints of a fox in the dusty ruts only a few
inches away."

G. M. Sutton comments further that the vesper sparrow "does not,
apparently, depend upon a regular water supply either for drinking or
for bathing.   During the very dry summer of 1936 many species came
daily to the spring just south of Colonel George's house—but neither
the vesper sparrow nor the grasshopper sparrow was among them."

*Voice.*—Aretas A. Saunders sent the following information to Mr.
Bent: "The song of the vesper sparrow is sweet and musical.   It
suggests that of the song sparrow, but has a more definite form.   The
song in the east rises in pitch and then falls, the notes when the song
rises being rather long and slow, but when the pitch falls the notes are
shorter and more rapid.   The rising notes are commonly in two pairs,
the second pair being higher in pitch than the first.   The short notes
usually begin on the highest pitch of the song and are commonly in
groups of three to five notes, each group lower in pitch than the
preceding.   The paired notes at the beginning are often downward
slurs.   My records seem to show that birds of central and western
New York begin songs with slurs more frequently than those of
Connecticut.

"The length of songs varies from 2.4 to 4.2 seconds, the average
being 3.25.   Pitch varies from B'' to D''''.   The pitch interval varies
from two to six tones, the latter being exactly an octave.

"Two records from North Dakota and two from South Dakota seem
to indicate a difference in the song.   The long notes at the beginning
are the highest pitch of the song, and the whole song trend is downward in pitch, not up and then down.   This may be the song of the
western subspecies (*confinis*), but the Check-List range is rather
indefinite about this."

*Enemies.*—One is rarely fortunate enough to observe the destruction of a bird's nest or to account for the disappearance of eggs or
young.   However, E. M. and W. A. Perry (1918) describe finding a
garter snake that had caught a fledgling vesper sparrow.   Nicholas L.
Cuthbert sent the following eye-witness account of the destruction of a
nest:

"At about 4:20 p.m. on July 13, 1956, in a field one mile west of Mount Pleasant, Mich., Frank Gardner and I flushed a vesper sparrow from its nest at the base of a small mullein plant. The bird feigned injury, fluttered along the ground, and disappeared in the vegetation about 20 feet from the nest. After checking the nest, which contained two eggs, we left the area, but returned at 4:50 p.m., again flushing the bird from the nest. Again it fluttered away. We then withdrew to a small weed-covered mound 60 feet from the nest and, while hiding somewhat in the weeds, watched the nest with 8-power binoculars. At 4:52 p.m. we realized that a 13-lined ground squirrel (*Citellus tridecemlineatus*) had quickly approached the nest and had taken one of the eggs. The ground squirrel sat on its haunches about 4 inches from the nest, holding the egg in its forepaws, and rolled the egg over and over as it ate the contents. After a few minutes, the squirrel dropped the apparently empty shell and took up a crouched position over the nest, as if eating the other egg. At 4:57 p.m. a vesper sparrow appeared and instantly pounced upon the ground squirrel and pecked it from above as it dashed away into some grass. The sparrow immediately returned to the nest, hesitated a moment to eat the shell, which the ground squirrel had discarded, and then settled on the nest. At 5:03 p.m. the ground squirrel again approached within a foot of the nest and the sparrow left the nest, attacked the squirrel, and drove it into the grass. The sparrow returned, stood by the nest for a moment, then departed. We went to the nest and found it empty; only a small fragment of an egg shell lay on the ground beside the nest."

F. N. Hamerstrom, Jr., and F. Hamerstrom (1951) report finding the remains of vesper sparrows at nests of the Cooper's hawk.

Reports in the literature on cowbird parasitism of vesper sparrow nests are conflicting. H. Friedmann (1929) considered the species "a common victim," but added that there was just one record from Ithaca, N.Y. E. H. Eaton (1914) considered the vesper sparrow among the "commonest" of hosts in New York State. Francis C. Evans found only one out of 85 nests parasitized at the Edwin S. George Reserve in southern Michigan, and G. M. Sutton found no parasitism of 11 June and July nests at the Reserve, although he saw a vesper sparrow feeding a fledgling cowbird, July 25, 1936. In southwestern Michigan, James F. Ponshair found four nests parasitized out of a total of 25 nests; in Ohio, M. B. Trautman found 3 of 14 nests parasitized.

The available evidence suggests that the degree of parasitism of vesper sparrow nests varies both with the nesting habitat and with the time of the breeding season. Because relatively few species are nesting at the start of the cowbird's laying season, April and early

May vesper sparrow nests are more apt to be parasitized than later nests. H. W. Hann (1937), M. M. Nice (1937a), J. Van Tyne (*in* Bent, 1953), and others have described the cowbird's habit of watching host species in the process of building nests. A. J. Berger (1951a) states: "I believe that there is a correlation between parasitism and proximity to higher vegetation. In general, parasitized nests in fields were near bordering woodlots or thickets, whereas non-parasitized nests were not near such vegetation. Thickets and trees apparently provide perches and cover for female cowbirds on the alert for nest building activity."

*Banding.*—John L. George (MS.), writing of his study of the vesper sparrow in southern Michigan, reports that "of eight adults banded in 1948, six (75 percent) returned * * * the following year; and of 16 banded adults present in 1949, 5 (31 percent) returned in 1950." One pair remained mated for two years, but none of 45 banded nestlings was seen in subsequent breeding seasons. L. H. Walkinshaw (MS.) studied a male vesper sparrow that returned to the same nesting territory for 4 consecutive years; for the first 2 years this male had the same banded mate.

## DISTRIBUTION

*Range.*—Northern Minnesota, central Ontario, southern Quebec and Nova Scotia south to northern Tamaulipas and the Gulf coast.

*Breeding range.*—The eastern vesper sparrow breeds from northern Minnesota (eastern Marshall County), central and northeastern Ontario (Rossport, Moose Factory, Lowbush), southern Quebec (Blue Sea Lake), Prince Edward Island, and northern Nova Scotia south to central Missouri (Appleton City, St. Louis), southern Illinois (Murphysboro, Mount Carmel), central Kentucky (Lexington), northeastern Tennessee (Tate Spring, Johnson City), western and central North Carolina (Weaverville, Greensboro), and south central Virginia (western Amelia County, Richmond).

*Winter range.*—Winters from central Texas (Ingram, Waco), Arkansas (Rogers), southern Illinois (Murphysboro), central southern Kentucky (Mammoth Cave), West Virginia (French Creek), southeastern Pennsylvania (Edge Hill), central New Jersey (Princeton), and Connecticut (Guilford) south to northeastern Tamaulipas (Matamoros), the Gulf coast, and central Florida (Seven Oaks, Micco); occasionally north to Ontario (Point Pelee, Toronto) and Nova Scotia (Wolfville); in migration west to eastern Nebraska, eastern Kansas, and eastern Oklahoma.

*Casual records.*—Casual in Yucatán (Chichén Itzá), southern Florida (Key West), and Bermuda.

*Migration.*—The data deal with the species as a whole. Early dates of spring arrival are: Virginia—Richmond, March 10. West Virginia—Licking County, March 4. Maryland—Caroline County, March 1; Laurel, March 5 (median of 7 years, March 22). Pennsylvania—Wilkinsburg, February 26; Somerset County, March 16. New Jersey—Moorestown, March 5. New York—Cayuga and Oneida lake basins, March 11 (median of 21 years, April 2). Connecticut—Hartford, March 12; Bridgeport, March 14. Rhode Island—Pawtucket, March 12. Massachusetts—Martha's Vineyard, March 18 (median of 5 years, April 11); Concord, March 22. Vermont—Bennington, March 25 (median of 23 years, April 10). New Hampshire—New Hampton, March 27 (median of 21 years, April 13). Maine—Orono and Farmington, April 2. Quebec—Montreal, March 27. New Brunswick—Fredericton, April 8; Scotch Lake, April 9. Nova Scotia—Bridgetown, April 12 (average of 28 years for Nova Scotia, April 22). Prince Edward Island—North River, April 17. Arkansas—Fayetteville, March 14. Tennessee—Nashville, March 1 (median of 15 years, March 22); Knox County, March 6. Kentucky—Eubank, February 23. Missouri—St. Louis, March 8 (median of 13 years, March 21). Illinois—Urbana, March 5 (median of 19 years, March 28); Chicago, April 1 (average of 14 years, April 7). Indiana—Wayne County, March 15 (median of 18 years, March 27). Ohio—Canton and Hillsboro, March 5; Buckeye Lake, March 8 (median of 40 years for central Ohio, March 25). Michigan—Detroit area, March 16; Battle Creek, March 22 (median of 40 years, April 1). Ontario—London, March 22; Ottawa, April 1 (average of 17 years, April 13). Iowa—Sioux City, April 8 (median of 38 years, April 25). Wisconsin—Dane County, March 19. Minnesota—McLeod County, March 23; St. Paul, March 31 (average of 18 years for southern Minnesota, April 5). Texas—Valley, March 30. Oklahoma—Cleveland County, March 14. Kansas—northeastern Kansas, March 21 (median of 17 years, March 31). Nebraska—Red Cloud, March 14. South Dakota—Rapid City, March 9. North Dakota—Jamestown, April 19. Manitoba—Margaret, March 30; Treesbank, April 12 (average of 25 years, April 18). Saskatchewan—Conquest, April 2. Mackenzie—Fort Simpson, April 24. New Mexico—Mesilla Park, March 2. Arizona—Flagstaff, February 28; Camp Grant, March 1. Colorado—Boulder, April 2. Utah—Kanab, March 5; Washington County, March 8. Wyoming—Yellowstone Park, March 31. Idaho—Lewiston, March 24 (median of 11 years, April 10). Montana—Billings, April 4; Moiese, April 14. Alberta—Buffalo Lake, April 12. California—Inyo County, April 4. Nevada—Mercury, March 13; Carson City, April 2. Oregon—Klamath County, March 23. Washington—Yakima, March 14; Grant County, April 10. British Columbia—Okanagan Landing, April 4.

Late dates of spring departure are: Florida—Tallahassee, April 22; Old Town, April 15. Alabama—Birmingham, April 20; Jackson, April 15. Georgia—Atlanta, May 5. South Carolina—Charleston, May 11; Clemson College, April 23. North Carolina—Raleigh, May 11. Virginia—Richmond, April 24. District of Columbia— April 15. Maryland—Baltimore County, May 23; Worcester County, May 16. Louisiana—Baton Rouge, March 26. Mississippi—Gulfport, March 31. Arkansas—Fayetteville, April 10. Tennessee— Knox County, May 7. Kentucky—Eubank and Bowling Green, May 6. Missouri—St. Louis, April 15 (median of 13 years, April 2). Illinois—Chicago, May 3 (average of 14 years, April 28). Texas— Sinton, May 7 (median of 5 years, April 30). Oklahoma—Cleveland County, April 28. California—Parker Dam, May 20.

Early dates of fall arrival are: California—Fresno, September 12. Oklahoma—Payne County, September 27. Texas—Sinton, September 17. Illinois—Chicago, September 18 (average of 13 years, September 30). Missouri—St. Louis, September 11 (median of 13 years, October 2). Kentucky—Bardstown, September 12. Tennessee—Nashville, October 5; Knox County, October 9. Mississippi—Saucier, October 27. Louisiana—Baton Rouge, November 18. New Jersey—Island Beach, October 7; Cape May, October 12. Maryland—Talbot County, September 2; Prince Georges County, September 9. District of Columbia—September 1. Virginia— Richmond, October 10. North Carolina—Raleigh, October 11. South Carolina—Charleston, September 22 (median of 6 years, October 12); Summerton, September 24. Georgia—Fitzgerald, October 1. Alabama—Camden, October 13; Booth, October 17. Florida—DeFuniak Springs, October 5; Tallahassee, October 13.

Late dates of fall departure are: British Columbia—Okanagan Landing, October 16. Washington—Grant County, November 10; Yakima, November 8. Oregon—Yamhill County, October 9. Alberta—Calgary, October 11. Montana—Big Sandy, October 30. Idaho—Moscow, September 27 (median of 11 years, September 13). Wyoming—Yellowstone Park, October 23. Utah— Spectacle Lake, October 25. Colorado—Fort Morgan, November 25. Arizona— Springerville, November 12. New Mexico—Las Cruces, November 28. Saskatchewan—Eastend, October 29. Manitoba—Killarney, November 9; Treesbank, October 15 (average of 23 years, October 10). North Dakota—Jamestown, November 2. South Dakota—Mettette, November 20. Nebraska—Lincoln County, November 14. Kansas—northeastern Kansas, November 22 (median of 14 years, October 15). Oklahoma—Oklahoma City, November 12. Minnesota—Minneapolis–St. Paul, October 14 (average of 9 years, October 4). Wisconsin—Rock County, November 11. Iowa—Sioux City, November 8 (median of 38 years, October 15). Ontario—Reaboro and Toronto, October 21; Ottawa, October 17 (average of 17 years, October 7). Michigan—Battle Creek, November 8 (median of 21 years, October 4). Ohio—Buckeye Lake, November 30 (median, October 29). Indiana—Wayne County, October 27 (median of 7 years, October 16). Illinois—Chicago, November 21 (average of 13 years, October 28). Missouri—St. Louis, November 30 (median of 13 years, November 10). Kentucky—Bardstown, November 18. Tennessee—Nashville and Knox County, November 11. Arkansas—Saline County, November 10. Prince Edward Island—North River, October 7. Nova Scotia—Yarmouth, October 25. New Brunswick—Scotch Lake, November 27. Quebec—Montreal, October 17. Maine—South Portland, November 15. New Hampshire—Concord, October 24; New Hampton, November 19 (median of 21 years, October 20). Vermont—Clarendon, November 2. Massachusetts—Martha's Vineyard, December 6; Concord, November 28. Rhode Island—Block Island, October 27. Connecticut—New Britain, November 14. New York—Cayuga and Oneida lake basins, December 10 (median of 19 years, November 5); New York City, November 20. Pennsylvania—Pittsburgh, November 21; State College and Renovo, November 17. Maryland—Prince Georges County, November 16. District of Columbia—November 21. West Virginia—Bluefield, November 16. Virginia—Richmond, November 9.

*Egg dates.*—Alberta: 9 records, May 20 to June 7.

British Columbia: 22 records, May 20 to July 11; 11 records, June 2 to June 21.

California: 15 records, April 28 to July 8; 9 records, May 22 to June 9.

Illinois: 35 records, May 7 to July 14; 20 records, May 13 to May 28.

Maryland: 31 records, May 5 to August 1; 16 records, May 26 to July 5.

Michigan: 51 records, April 21 to July 31; 16+ records, June 15 to June 27.

New Brunswick: June 3 to August 15 (number of records not stated).

New York: 16 records, April 30 to July 9; 10 records, May 2 to May 26.

Nova Scotia: 4 records, May 19 to July 6.

Ontario: 63 records, April 23 to July 30; 32 records, May 16 to June 11.

Oregon: 34 records, May 6 to July 18; 18 records, May 24 to June 14.

Quebec: 9 records, May 2 to July 11.

Wyoming: 14 records, May 30 to July 4.

## POOECETES GRAMINEUS CONFINIS Baird

# Western Vesper Sparrow

### Contributed by JAMES R. KING

#### HABITS

The adults of this race of the vesper sparrow are characterized as slightly larger than those of the nominate race, with a more slender bill, and paler, grayer coloration. The streaks on the breast are not so distinct or dark as in *P. gramineus.* The comparative coloration of the juvenal plumages in *P. gramineus* sp. is analyzed in detail by R. R. Graber (1955). The principal differences are encountered in the back and crown: *confinis*—feathers of the back black, broadly edged with buffy white, crown and back streaked with light brown or buff and black, tertials edged rusty and tipped white; *gramineus*—similar to *confinis* but dorsum much darker (no white), crown and back streaked with brown (not buff or light brown) and black, tertials edged with brown, not buff.

The ecology and life history of the vesper sparrows of the West have been studied very infrequently, and the published reports yield only a fragmentary picture. During the breeding season *P. g. confinis* is found in open habitats east of the Sierra Nevada–Cascade mountains system from southern Mackenzie south to eastern California, northern Arizona, and northern New Mexico. The breeding range extends eastward to central western Ontario, western Nebraska, and presumably the Dakotas. The western vesper sparrow occupies an extensive altitudinal range within this area, and is typically absent only from the lower dry areas corresponding to the traditional descriptions of the Lower Sonoran Zone and arid Upper Sonoran Zone. This is demonstrated especially well in eastern Washington, where the race is distributed throughout suitable open grassland and sagebrush areas except for the arid (annual rainfall less than 10 inches) artemisia–agropyron association of the south central Columbia Basin (Daubenmire, 1942; Dumas, 1950; Jewett et al., 1953).

In eastern California J. Grinnell and A. H. Miller (1944) describe the preferred habitat as "artemisia association in which the sagebrush is well spaced * * * or of no more than moderate height. Much open or sparsely grass-covered ground is required, and this usually is level or gently sloping." In Utah, W. H. Behle (1958) and

W. H. Behle, J. B. Bushman, and C. M. Greenhalgh (1958) also emphasize the artemisia association as a major habitat of the western vesper sparrow, but note also that the race occurs in the pinon-juniper association and in the low grass of alpine and subalpine meadows. For the southern Rocky Mountains, F. M. Bailey (1904, 1928) reports breeding populations commonly in meadows as high as 9,000 feet, and occasionally as high as 12,000 feet. S. G. Jewett et al. (1953) mention breeding populations at 5,000 feet in the Blue Mountains of eastern Washington.

The wintering grounds of the western vesper sparrow extend from southeastern California, southern Arizona, New Mexico, and Texas, south through Baja California and west central Mexico to Oaxaca (casually east to Vera Cruz, Louisiana, and Mississippi). The migration between wintering and breeding grounds is very sparsely documented. N. Criddle (1921) reports the mean date of arrival of vesper sparrows at Aweme, Manitoba (lat. 49°42′N.) as April 18, based on 25 years' observation; the earliest recorded arrival date is April 12. Records for migrants and summer residents in eastern Washington (Jewett et al., 1953; Hudson and Yocom, 1954) extend from March 10 to September 19. W. B. Davis (1935) reports autumn migrants on November 4 at Rupert, Idaho, but this is exceptionally late. Migrating western vesper sparrows may be observed as far east as western Kansas.

Nests with fresh eggs have been found from April 5 to June 3 in eastern Washington (J. H. Bowles, 1921) and from May 24 to June 20 in eastern Oregon (Gabrielson and Jewett, 1940). In New Mexico (Santa Fe County; Jensen, 1923) fresh eggs have been reported from May 15 to July 15. W. Weydemeyer (1936) mentions two "unusually late" clutches hatched in Montana on July 19 and 25. Other fresh egg dates from Idaho (Davis, 1935) and Utah (Behle, 1958) fall within the above spans. In certain parts of the breeding range, at least, two annual broods are reared. R. B. Rockwell and A. Wetmore (1914) mention a first brood in May and a second one in July near Golden, Colorado.

The nest of *P. g. confinis* (and *P. g. affinis*) is described by B. R. Headstrom (1951) as "rather bulky, thick-rimmed, well-cupped but not tightly woven; of dried grass, rootlets, and hair." Mean dimensions: outer diameter, 4.5 inches; outer height, 1.8 inches; inner diameter, 2.2 inches; inner depth, 1.4 inches. F. M. Bailey (1928) describes the eggs as greenish or brownish white, and often blotched and streaked with reddish brown and lavender. She mentions clutches of four to six eggs in New Mexico. J. K. Jensen (1923), also reporting from New Mexico, cites only clutches of three to four eggs. R. Hoffmann (1927) and E. Stevenson (1942), probably referring also to *P. g.*

*affinis*, describe the eggs as white, speckled and clouded with reddish brown, and report clutches of four to five eggs.

The measurements of 40 eggs average 20.9 by 15.2 millimeters; the eggs showing the four extremes measure *22.4* by 15.8, 21.8 by *16.8, 18.3* by 14.7, and 19.3 by *14.2* millimeters.

The food habits of the western vesper sparrow in relation to agriculture were studied by G. F. Knowlton (1937a,b) and by G. F. Knowlton and W. P. Nye (1948). The insects recognized in stomach analyses were principally injurious forms; the vesper sparrow is cited particularly as a significant predator on the beet leafhopper, *Eutettix tenellus* (Baker).

## DISTRIBUTION

*Range.*—British Columbia, the prairie provinces, and western Ontario south, east of the Cascades and Sierra Nevada to southern Mexico.

*Breeding range.*—The western vesper sparrow breeds from central and northeastern British Columbia (François Lake, Pouce Coupe), southwestern Mackenzie (below Norman, Fort Smith), central Saskatchewan (Dorintosh, Prince Albert), central Manitoba (The Pas, Lake St. Martin, Hillside Beach), and central western Ontario (Wabigoon, Rainy River) south, east of the Cascade Range and the Sierra Nevada, to central eastern California (eastern Tulare County, Inyo Mountains), central Nevada (Toiyabe Mountains), southwestern Utah, central northern and central eastern Arizona (Williams, White Mountains), central western and central northern New Mexico (Zuni Mountains, Santa Fe), eastern Colorado, and western Nebraska; casually north in summer to northwestern Ontario (Favourable Lake).

*Winter range.*—Winters from central California (Fresno, Owens Valley), southern Nevada (St. Thomas), central and southeastern Arizona (Camp Verde, San Carlos), southern New Mexico (Fort Webster, Carlsbad), and southern Texas south to southern Baja California (La Paz), Guerrero (Chilpancingo), and Oaxaca (Tamazulapam), casually east to Veracruz (Zacualpilla), Louisiana (Natchitoches), and Mississippi (Saucier); in migration to western Kansas.

## POOECETES GRAMINEUS AFFINIS Miller

## Oregon Vesper Sparrow

### Contributed by JAMES R. KING

## HABITS

G. S. Miller, Jr. (1888), describes the adults of this Pacific coastal form of the vesper sparrow as "similar to *P. g. confinis* with respect to slender bill and narrow dark dorsal streakings, but differing in being smaller and having the ground color above buffy brown rather than grayish brown. All the lighter areas of the plumage * * * suffused with pinkish buff." In the juvenal plumage, according to R. R. Graber (1955), *P. g. affinis* closely resembles *P. g. gramineus*, but with the black back feathers "only narrowly margined with whitish." The superciliary line is more distinct and complete than in *P. g. confinis.*

The breeding range of *P. g. affinis* is restricted to the lower valleys and plains west of the Cascade Range in Washington and Oregon. I. N. Gabrielson and S. G. Jewett (1940) report it to be an abundant summer resident in the Willamette Valley of Oregon, but less common in other coastal valleys. It is an inhabitant of "open meadow and farm lands where it frequents the fence rows and pasture lands" (Gabrielson and Jewett, 1940), and of "cultivated land and open pastures" (Jewett et al., 1953). In western Washington, summer residents and migrants have been reported from April 4 to September 8 (Jewett et al., 1953). J. H. Bowles (1921) reports nests with fresh eggs in Washington from May 9 to June 2. Plural broods are not reported for *P. g. affinis.*

The measurements of 40 eggs average 20.7 by 15.2 millimeters; the eggs showing the four extremes measure *22.9* by 16.3, 21.8 by *16.8*, *19.3* by 14.7, and 20.3 by *14.2* millimeters.

The wintering range of the Oregon vesper sparrow lies west of the Sierra Nevada from central California south to northwestern Baja California, where it overlaps the winter range of *P. g. confinis.* Migrants are found occasionally as far east as western Utah (Behle and Selander, 1952). The winter habitat in California is described by J. Grinnell and A. H. Miller (1944) as "Open ground with little vegetation or else areas grown to short grass and low annuals. Bushes and taller grass may be used as retreats or for shelter. Often seen in stubble fields and meadows and along road edges where they forage in a skulking manner." These authors report that the winter residency extends from October to early April; migrants are seen in April and in late August and early October.

## DISTRIBUTION

*Range.*—Western Washington to northwestern Baja California.

*Breeding range.*—The Oregon vesper sparrow breeds in western Washington (Dungeness, San Juan Islands) and western Oregon (Willamette Valley, Coos Bay).

*Winter range.*—Winters from central California west of the Sierra Nevada (Fulton, Lagrange) south to northwestern Baja California (Santo Domingo).

*Casual records.*—Casual east to southern Utah (St. George, Henry Mountains).

## CHONDESTES GRAMMACUS (Say)

## Lark Sparrow*

PLATE 50

Contributed by DONALD HENRY BAEPLER

### HABITS

The lark sparrow is easily recognized in the field. Its white outer tail markings, its white underparts with dark spots on the breast, the bold chestnut and black markings of its head, its habits of walking, of singing in flight, and of drooping its wings and spreading its tail during courtship, make it a distinctive bird. Alexander Sprunt, Jr. (1954) writes: "Seen from the front, back, or side it is a very attractive bird, and even where it is very abundant, as in central Texas, one never tires of its sprightly appearance and animated ways."

The bird is at home in parklike areas, in abandoned fields, in brush-lined pasture lands, and in completely treeless plains. It does not fear man and in the heart of its range nests abundantly near farmhouses, in city parks, and on the edges of towns. In the eastern and northern parts of its range where it is not common, it prefers open areas where bare ground or short grass is much in evidence. In southeastern Michigan where scattered pairs nest irregularly, its habitat is characterized by poorness of soil, by a scattering of saplings, and by such ground-hugging vegetation as thin grasses, foliose lichens, and by earthstar fungi (*Geaster* spp.).

The lark sparrow is widely distributed throughout the United States and its range extends into southern Canada. It is, however, typically a bird of the west and it is in parts of the southwest that it is truly common as a nesting bird. Two races are recognized; the eastern and nominate subspecies breeds as far west as central Minnesota, eastern Kansas, and northeastern Texas; west of these points the western race, *C. g. strigatus* Swainson, occurs. In the western race the chestnut head markings and the upperparts in general are paler and the back streaking is narrower. The races are much alike in color and, so far as I can determine, they are identical in behavior. L. Nelson Nichols (1936) states: "There is * * * no practical difference in the habits, song, and beauty of eastern and western birds."

Much of the following account is based on studies I made of the lark sparrow at the University of Oklahoma Biological Station at

---

*The following subspecies are discussed in this section: *Chondestes grammacus grammacus* (Say), and *C. g. strigatus* Swainson.

Lake Texoma, Okla., where the birds were abundant during the summer of 1957. David F. Parmelee of Kansas State Teachers College, Emporia, Kans., helped with much of the field work. George M. Sutton of the University of Oklahoma contributed many valuable suggestions. The work was financed by a National Science Foundation grant.

*Spring.*—The series of specimens in the University of Oklahoma collections shows the males return from the wintering grounds considerably in advance of the females. The earliest female was collected May 19; 2 March specimens and 19 taken in April are all males. G. M. Sutton recorded in his notes the arrival of a flock of about 30 singing males near Norman, Okla., on April 6. When I began my study at Lake Texoma on June 2, both sexes were plentiful in the study area.

*Courtship.*—The male lark sparrow's courtship involves much strutting, singing, chasing, and fighting. E. S. Cameron (1908) writes of Montana birds, "Lark Sparrows arrive early in May, and are the most pugnacious little birds I have ever seen. The cocks fight on the ground or in the air indifferently, and are then so oblivious to their surroundings that five or six fighting on the wing have nearly hit me in the face."

T. S. Roberts (1936) remarks from Minnesota:

During the mating- and early nesting-season the male is a perfect little turkey-cock, spending much time parading around on the ground with his tail fully spread and wings trailing, bubbling over with fragments of song, and seeming at times fairly bursting with emotion as he displays his charms before his mate or, vibrating with rage, dashes after some intruding male. Combats are frequent often in mid-air, when little can be made out except a whirling mass of three or four infuriated Finches darting and dashing at one another with white tail-feathers flashing on all sides and angry bits of song coming from the contestants now and again. In one such battle * * * four males were engaged, and, after a fierce and lengthy bout in the air, they all came to the ground in a perfect whirl of confused motion, and in an instant the tiny maelstrom was over.

Anne L. LeSassier writes (*in* litt.) of lark sparrows courting near Midland, Texas: "On April 29 nine males were alternately singing and disputing in the cemetery. The disputes usually started when one of of the more aggressive birds attacked another who wandered into his territory by flying at him on the ground from a tombstone or low limb. Both then flew around the low bushes in the cemetery, often joined by other lark sparrows until as many as five might be chasing one another round and round. At the end of the chase the contestants paraded up and down the tombstones and cement curbs with heads and tails held very erect and occasionally spreading their tails to show the white outer feathers. The parading and posturing dwindled as one and another sparrow began feeding."

At Lake Texoma the males exhibit their strongest sense of territoriality early in the courtship phase of the reproductive cycle. Each male on territory challenges any other lark sparrow that approaches, advances toward it until the two are only inches apart, then raising his head and pointing his bill skyward. If the second bird is a male it responds by raising its head and elevating its bill in like manner. The two then fly at one another and rise high into the air together, frequently striking their wings against each other. They may repeat this performance several times before one of the two retires. I once watched two males repeat the fighting flight six times in 3 minutes before one bird gave in.

If the second bird is a female it does not posture in any way, and either ignores the advancing male or retreats. If the male is not mated, he will probably court her by strutting about on the ground before her with bill pointed upward, tail fanned, and fluttering his half-opened wings. Or he may fly some 30 yards or more with rapidly beating wings, singing and spreading his tail. He sings frequently during courtship (see *Voice*) from the ground, in flight, or perched in trees or on wires. He sometimes sings his flight song while flying from one perch to another, but often he flies high into the air, singing the entire time, and alights again in the same spot, still singing. He is not a treetop singer like the painted bunting, for instance, and does not choose a favorite perch to sing from throughout the day, but sings from a variety of perches within his territory.

Copulation is attempted soon after the birds are paired and is performed frequently during courtship and throughout the periods of site selection and nest building. As J. C. Barlow (1960) describes it in Kansas, "the female crouches in a precopulatory or solicitation posture; the male, meanwhile having picked up a small twig, then mounts the back of the female. Copulation ensues, lasting for approximaely two seconds. Within this short passage of time the male passes the twig to the female, which turns its head slightly to facilitate the transfer to its beak. Upon completion of copulation the pair, the female still carrying the twig, flew to a distant part of the nursery and the two birds were lost from sight."

I never observed the twig-transfer in the Oklahoma birds, but during the nest-building stage the female often held a straw in her bill while copulating. This might take place either on the ground or while she perched on a wire or branch. Apparently either sex may initiate the procedure. Several times when a pair sat side by side on a wire or branch the female suddenly fluttered her wings and raised her tail, which evidently stimulated the male, for copulation ensued immediately. Or the male may start the action by flying toward the female and hovering above her for a few seconds until she becomes receptive to him. I watched one pair make 20 attempts at copulation within 3½ minutes before it was consummated.

E. H. M. Knowles (1938) presents an interesting account of polygamy in this species near Regina, Saskatchewan. "On May 24, 1937, I again located a nest and on May 28, 1937, a second nest at least one hundred yards distant from it. On the latter date I saw the male and female copulating about twenty feet from nest no. 1, and was surprised to see a second female with wings quivering, fly close to the pair. The male then commenced to copulate alternately with the two females. This was accomplished several times and one of the females then flew to nest no. 1, while the other, when disturbed, flew immediately to nest no. 2, the site of which was clearly visible from where I was standing." Perhaps the scarcity of birds at the edge of the species' range encourages polygamy, which I never observed where the sparrows are plentiful in southern Oklahoma.

*Nesting.*—Both the male and the female share in selecting the nest site. The two birds fly about examining likely spots on the ground or in small shrubs and trees. The male usually picks up a small twig or straw, carries it for a short time, and then deposits it at a suitable site. Often he drops material at a number of different places before the female selects the actual spot where she will build. As she gathers material the male either perches nearby and sings, or flies with her. Sometimes he carries a straw back and forth in his bill for a number of trips before he discards it. I never saw a male add material to the nest.

The nest site varies considerably. Florence M. Bailey (1928) states that in New Mexico the birds usually nest on the ground, but "sometimes in bushes, mesquite, or mistletoe." Merritt Cary (1901) found nests only on the ground in Wyoming. J. M. Markle (1946) reports finding 28 nests in crevices of cliffs in California at heights of 5 to 10 feet above the ground. At the Biological Station in southern Oklahoma, the birds often built in the ornamental evergreens near the buildings, placing their nests surprisingly close together. Two were 23 yards apart, a third was 26 yards from them, and within 60 yards of these, there were four more occupied nests. Several nests were on the lawn, in small depressions hollowed out in bare spots free of grass, usually in the shade of a broad-leafed plant such as a mullein.

At Lake Texoma the birds nested in low trees and shrubs or on the ground in pastures, lawns, abandoned fields, and active cotton fields. Among the favorite trees were red cedar (*Juniperus virginianus*), post oak (*Quercus stellata*), winged elm (*Ulmus alata*), chittamwood (*Bumelia lanuginosa*), persimmon (*Diospyros virginiana*), and osage orange (*Maclura pomifera*). Most nests were within 7 feet of the ground; the highest I found was 25 feet up in a post oak. The ground nests were usually shaded by a lone broad-leafed plant or by a grass tuft, but occasional ones were out in the open with no shade whatever.

In the short-grass prairies of the Oklahoma panhandle, where there are trees, the nest is usually on the ground in a bare or eroded place. G. M. Sutton informs me that on the Edwin S. George Reserve in southeastern Michigan, where the bird was not common from 1933 to 1950, it nested on the ground in open, sandy, sapling-dotted areas with a decidedly "western" appearance known locally as "blow-sands."

Ground nests are often merely hollow depressions lined with fine grasses, but those built above the ground can be quite bulky. The cup-shaped structure has a wall of stout grasses and weed stems placed on a foundation of small twigs. Newly cut clover is a favorite building material at Lake Texoma. The nest lining is usually of fine grasses with occasional fine rootlets added. H. T. Gier (1949) reports a nest in Ohio lined with rootlets and hair.

Nest building at Texoma is not limited to any particular time of day, but activity is at its highest peak early in the morning. On June 26 I watched a female carry material to her nest nine times from 5:00 to 5:20 a.m. The nesting material, especially the lining, was gathered from a distance and the birds often flew through the territories of other lark sparrows in their search. One female gathered lining material from a point 200 yards from her nest.

Territoriality, never strongly marked in this species in Oklahoma, seems to wane as the breeding cycle progresses. During the time of nest building and egg laying both sexes drive other lark sparrows away from the site itself and furiously attack any stuffed lark sparrows placed near the nest. Once incubation is well under way, they tolerate dummies and show no resentment when other lark sparrows wander in the vicinity. Throughout the nesting season the birds gather in small bands as they feed on the lawn and in nearby deserted fields.

They tolerate other bird species on their territories at all times. One lark sparrow started building only 14 inches from an active mockingbird's nest. The lark sparrow was apparently satisfied with the situation, but the mockingbird finally succeeded in driving it from the shrub. I found four examples of lark sparrows and orchard orioles nesting in the same small tree; in one case, in a persimmon, the two nests were only 5 feet apart. One small tree simultaneously contained active nests of a lark sparrow, an orchard oriole, and a scissor-tailed flycatcher. The flycatcher built first, then the sparrow placed her nest 6 feet from the flycatcher's, and finally the oriole built 7 feet above the sparrow's nest. No fighting was observed between these birds.

Building the first nest of the season usually takes the female 3 to 4 days, and a full day or more elapses after the nest is finished before the first egg is laid. On June 10, however, I found an egg laid after only 2 days of nest building. The nest was far from complete, and the female added the lining after laying the egg.

*Eggs.*—The lark sparrow usually lays four or five eggs, but sometimes only three, and more rarely six. They are ovate and have a slight gloss. The ground is creamy or grayish white, with scribblings, scrawls, and spots of black or very dark browns such as "Mars brown," "carob brown," or "mummy brown," with underlying spots of "light neutral gray." The scribblings, most of which are black, are the predominant markings. These tend to concentrate toward the large end where they are often continuous and form a wreath around the egg, frequently leaving the lower part free of markings except for a few scattered spots. Occasional eggs will have a few scrawls of "light neutral gray" mingled with the dark brown or black scribblings. The measurements of 50 eggs of the nominate race average 20.1 by 15.9 millimeters; the eggs showing the four extremes measure *23.9* by *17.3*, *18.0* by 15.0, and 18.8 by *14.7* millimeters. The measurements of 40 eggs of *C. g. strigatus* average 20.4 by 16.1 millimeters; the eggs showing the four extremes measure *22.9* by *17.8* and *16.8* by *14.0* millimeters.

At Lake Texoma the eggs were usually laid between 5:00 and 7:00 a.m. Before laying, the female sits quietly on the nest and can be approached closely without her showing alarm. As she lays the egg she rises slightly on the nest; after depositing it she settles rather deeply back into the nest and often shuts her eyes and sleeps for a short time. The newly laid egg is slightly moist and sticky, but it dries in a matter of minutes.

*Incubation.*—Incubation is by the female alone. In the early nesting season she does not start incubating until the clutch is complete but may return during the day to shade the nest from the sun by sitting rather high on it. In July, females at Lake Texoma, whose earlier nesting attempts were frustrated by snakes or other predators, often started incubating with the first or second egg.

The female lark sparrow incubates so diligently that she can frequently be approached quite closely before she takes flight. She is particularly reluctant to leave her nest when the sun is shining on it, and on one unshaded nest in an abandoned field I caught the incubating bird several times by hand. She spends night hours on the nest, and as incubation progresses, leaves it less frequently during the day. At the start of incubation she may leave it for as much as an hour; toward the end she seldom stays away more than half an hour at a time, and I have watched several that stayed on the nest continually for more than 3 hours.

On a number of occasions I saw the male come near the nest with food in his bill and chirp in plain sight of the female for several minutes until she left the nest and joined him.   He then ate the food himself and the pair flew off to a feeding area.   This performance seemed to occur more frequently toward the end of incubation, and never did I see the male feed or offer food to the female when she left the nest.

When the female is flushed from a ground nest she usually feigns injury and runs along the ground with her tail spread, fluttering one or both wings and chirping softly.   If her nest is in a shrub or tree she is less likely to feign injury, but perches near by and utters sharp alarm notes that soon summon the male.

E. S. Cameron (1908) states that the female incubates about 12 days.   At four Texoma nests I timed, marking each egg with pencil the morning it was laid, the maximum possible elapsed times from the laying of the last egg until it hatched were 11 days 13 hours, 11 days 10½ hours, 11 days 10 minutes, and 10 days 23½ hours.   The fourth nest with the shortest incubation time was in an open cotton field. Since it was only partly shaded by a lone broad-leaved plant, the female spent long stretches on the nest throughout the incubation period.

Eggs often pipped a full 24 hours before they actually hatched.   In each of the several eggs I watched hatch the process appeared identical—the young bird cut through the shell in a straight line around the widest part of the egg, then pushed the two halves apart.

*Young.*—Both parents care for the young from the moment they hatch.   On July 15 I saw a male with food in his bill return to a nest that contained two eggs and one young bird 2 hours old.   After perching near the nest and chirping for about 5 minutes, the male flew to the nest and presented the food to the female, who fed it to the young bird.   Later in the day he returned to the nest during the female's absence and fed the nestling.   Both these adults were color-banded, which facilitated recognizing them as they cared for the young.

At another nest where the adults were color-banded, the male fed the young four times on the day they hatched and the female fed them three times in a 2½-hour period.   In addition, during 45 minutes of this period the female brooded the young and the male brought food to the nest three times and presented it to the female, who in turn fed the young; thus, they were fed 10 times in 2½ hours.

At a nest with young in Michigan, F. N. Wilson (1931) pressed down the surrounding vegetation to allow sunlight to reach the nest for photography.   When the birds returned, the female stayed at the nest to shade the nestlings.   The male brought food to her, some of which she fed to the young; the rest she ate herself.

As the young grow, the adults increase the tempo of their feeding until toward the end of the fledging period they may feed the young every few minutes. On June 4 the parents brought food 28 times in an hour to a nest with four 5-day-old young. The female made 19 trips, the male only 9, but he seemed to bring more each time than his mate did. Both parents carried fecal sacs away and dropped them from 20 to 80 feet from the nest. I never saw an adult lark sparrow eat a fecal sac.

Young lark sparrows normally remain in the nest until they are able to fly short distances on the 9th or 10th day after hatching. They can be handled and placed back in the nest until they are 6 days old; when disturbed or handled after 6 days, they usually desert the nest and scramble about on the ground or hide in low vegetation where they can be difficult to find. By surrounding a nest in an Austrian pine on the Biological Station lawn with a half-inch mesh hardware cloth 30 inches high, I was able to confine its three young where I could find them and still permit the parents free access.

One of these young I marked and weighed daily at 7 a.m. from the time it hatched until it fledged. Weighing 2.2 grams at hatching, its gram weights at successive 24-hour intervals were: 3.9, 5.8, 8.7, 11.0, 12.9, 14.0, 12.5, 11.8, 12.5. When it reached its greatest weight, at the end of the 6th day, it would no longer stay in the nest. Its weight losses the 7th and 8th days probably reflect its increased activity, for the parents continued to feed it as before. Shortly after it was weighed on the 9th day, showing an increase, it flew over the fence with its siblings to a shrubby area near by, where the parents continued to care for the brood. All were flying too well to be caught.

Largely because of its long nesting season, lasting in Oklahoma from early May to late July, the lark sparrow generally has been assumed to be double brooded. G. S. Agersborg (1885) states that in North Dakota: "The first brood is raised from nests placed in unplowed fields; the second or third are generally built among potato vines or vegetables with heavy foliage. Have no doubt that three broods are often raised." E. S. Cameron (1908) writes from Montana: "I have also seen eggs in July, but these were doubtless for a second brood." M. G. Brooks (1938) concludes on the basis of finding a nest on July 8 that the species raises two broods in West Virginia. These and other similar assumptions in the literature are questionable, because none is based on definite evidence from observations of marked birds.

While my observations on double-broodedness at Lake Texoma were perhaps inconclusive, I obtained no definite proof of its occurrence and considerable evidence against it. The nesting attempts, successes, and failures of a number of color-banded females in the study area showed those that built nests in July had had one or more unsuccessful nests earlier in the season. The tendency of most pairs after fledging young was to join with other families in flocks in the nearby fields. A pair that successfully fledged a brood June 7 remained with one surviving young in the vicinity of the station throughout the summer and made no attempt to build another nest.

On July 17 I found a pair of lark sparrows about 15 miles from the station feeding three fledglings only a day or two old. They were also feeding two young lark sparrows about a month old perched in a tree close by. That these represented an earlier brood cannot be assumed, for they may have been "adopted." One color-banded female whose brood fledged in early July started to build another nest on July 18, but she deserted it after 2 days' work, and 3 days later joined, with her mate and young, a large flock of lark sparrows that had gathered near by.

*Plumages.*—At hatching, the young bird is sparsely covered with brownish-gray down. When the nestling is 2 days old, primaries and secondaries appear, but they are entirely sheathed. On the 3rd day the chick can partly open its eyes. On the 4th day the eyes are open wide, the remiges have lengthened but are still mostly sheathed, the rectrices have begun to appear, and the feathers on the breast to develop. During the 5th day the terminal third of each primary and secondary is out of the sheath, the rectrices are still very short and entirely sheathed, and the underparts begin to look white with brown streaks. During the 6th day the rectrices begin to break out of their sheaths, and by the 7th day the chick looks well-feathered, although considerable down still clings to the feathers, especially those on the head and neck. The feathers continue to grow on the 8th day, and on the 9th, when the bird can usually fly, he is well feathered, although the wing feathers are not quite fully developed and the tail is still very short.

R. R. Graber (1955) describes the juvenal plumages as follows: "Lores dusky in stub-tailed birds (superciliary not complete). Supra- and post-ocular stripe buffy white. Median crown stripe white or buffy white. Otherwise, forehead and crown brown, streaked with dark brown or blackish. Feathers of hind-neck and back black edged with buff or buffy white. (Pattern heavy streaking of black and buff.) Rump and upper tail coverts buffy or buffy brown, obscurely streaked with black. Rectrices black, outer four (at least) marked white terminally. Remiges black, outer primary edged with white. Tertials edged with light buffy. Greaters edged with cinnamon, tipped with buffy white (two wing-bars). Eye-ring and feathers about eye white. Auriculars light brown, dark-margined. Post- and subauriculars white (definite cheek-patch). Underparts white, more or less buffy tinged on chest, sides, flanks, and crissum. Chest, sides, and flanks profusely streaked with black. Belly (lower) and crissum immaculate. Leg feathers white."

The first winter plumage is similar to the juvenal plumage, except that it is not streaked below and shows a dark brown central chest spot. The head pattern is very distinct—crown light brown, a well-defined buffy superciliary stripe, rictal and loral streaks black, auriculars chestnut. No specimens examined showed any molt of the juvenal remiges; although some rectrices were replaced in a few specimens, first winter birds are easily recognized by the presence of a light brown spot at the tip of the four outer rectrices. This spot is lost by feather wear and is not present on spring specimens.

The nuptial plumage resembles the first winter plumage, but a partial molt of feathers on the head, chin, and throat makes these areas appear somewhat brighter; the rectrices and remiges are usually badly worn and frayed.

The adult winter plumage, acquired by a complete postnuptial molt, and occurring in Oklahoma during July and August, resembles the first winter plumage, but its colors are slightly more intense and the markings on the outer tail feathers are solid white.

The sexes are similar in appearance in all plumages throughout the year.

*Food.*—Few detailed studies of the lark sparrow's food habits have been made. F. M. Bailey (1928) writes that in New Mexico its diet consists of:

Insects 27 per cent and seeds 73 per cent. The lark sparrow, with the exception of the grasshopper sparrow * * * is the most valuable grasshopper destroyer of our native sparrows. More than half its animal food is grasshoppers. On the prairies and plains it also does much good in helping to check the invasions of the Rocky Mountain locust. In an outbreak of locusts, they made up over 91 per cent of its diet. It also eats great numbers of alfalfa weevils. One half of its vegetable food consists of seeds of grain and grass. Pigeon grass and Johnson grass are both eaten freely. The weed seed, including pigweed, destroyed, more than twice outweighs the grain consumed, and the grain is doubtless largely waste; beneficial insects are less than 1 per cent while injurious insects, including the alfalfa weevil, constitute 25 per cent of the food.

T. S. Roberts (1936) adds from the U.S. Biological Survey report: "Grass-seeds (including pigeon- and panic-grasses), and waste grain; seeds of ragweed, knot-weed, wild sunflower, purslane, etc. More than 14 per cent of its total diet consists of grasshoppers; other animal matter taken consists of weevils, caterpillars, and other insects."

At Lake Texoma adults gathered food for their young from an unmowed section of the lawn where the grass grew some 15 inches tall. Here they captured small grasshoppers and the larvae of other insects, each adult returning to the nest with several insects in its bill at a time.   They also fed their young fruits of the grass *Bromus catharticus.*

*Voice.*—T. S. Roberts (1932) gives the following account:

The song of the lark sparrow is long and varied, full of life and animation, and is poured forth with great fervor.   It consists of a series of runs and trills, liquid and clear, broken here and there by fine aspirate notes which, however, do not detract from its beauty.   Mr. Robert Ridgway, in his *Birds of Illinois* (1889), after expressing surprise that the vocal capabilities of the lark sparrow have been so generally neglected by authors and stating that in sprightliness and continuity the song "has few, if any, rivals among North American Fringillidae," goes on to describe it in the following glowing terms, which coincide perfectly with the writer's experience:

"As the bird perches upon the summit of a small tree, a fence post, or a telegraph wire, his notes may be heard throughout the day—in the morning before those of any other, and late in the evening when all else but this unweary songster are silent; indeed, often have we been awakened at midnight by a sudden outburst of silvery warblings from one of this species.   This song is composed of a series of chants, each syllable rich, loud, and clear, interspersed with emotional trills. * * * Though seemingly hurried, it is one continuous gush of sprightly music; now gay, now melodious, and then tender beyond description,—the very expression of emotion.   At intervals the singer falters, as if exhausted by exertion, and his voice becomes scarcely audible; but suddenly reviving in his joy, it is resumed in all its vigor, until he appears to be really overcome by the effort."

The performer usually sings from the spreading limb of a tree, but at times from a more lowly perch, changing his position frequently.   Snatches of the song may be given on the wing while the bird is passing from one place to another, and rarely he indulges in a brief flight song; he then arises a little way above the perch and with upturned head pours out the sweetly liquid notes in an ecstasy of fervent feeling.

At Lake Texoma singing was rather sporadic.   So far as I could determine, only the male lark sparrow sings.   Instead of establishing a favorite singing perch or perches, he may sing almost anywhere within or near his territory, from the ground or from various vantage points in shrubs or trees, or in flight.   The flight song is particularly characteristic of the courtship period.   During combats a series of high trilling notes is often heard, which is also uttered during copulation, apparently by both sexes.

The alarm note is a rather sharp *chirp* used by both sexes.   When disturbed they also may utter low guttural notes.   Nestlings use a soft trilling note when begging for food.   After leaving the nest their frequent soft chirps enable the parents to locate them.

Birds continued to sing throughout the summer, even while they were molting and had gathered in large flocks.   In early August I heard individuals singing from telephone wires late in the evening and well after dark.   J. G. Tyler (1913) noted of the species in California: "Aside from the inimitable Western Mockingbird, I know of no other bird that sings so often at night."

*Behavior.*—Where it is plentiful, as on its Oklahoma breeding grounds, the lark sparrow is markedly gregarious. Even at the height of the nesting season one sees them feeding together in small flocks. In such flocks at Lake Texoma I frequently identified color-banded individuals from active nests. While pairs defend their nest and its immediate environs, they do not establish or defend a feeding territory. Birds may fly some distance from the nest for both nesting material and food.

The flocks increase in size as summer wanes and become rather noisy, with much chirping and occasional outbursts of song. Individuals in the flocks quarrel with one another fairly frequently; the fights do not seem to be governed by sex or age, for males may combat with other males and with females, and adults with juveniles. Other species sometimes join the flocks. In one flock of 40 lark and 10 field sparrows, interspecific fighting occurred occasionally. In late summer the flocks become very wary and difficult to approach, and will leave the field where they are feeding at the first sight of an intruder.

Strangely, in my study area that bordered Lake Texoma, I never saw the birds drink from or bathe in the lake. They often did both, however, in a small pond near by. On July 17 I recorded in my notes that "At least six different birds came to the pond to drink this morning. Each flew to within 3 feet of the water's edge and then walked up until it almost stood in the water. Each bird drank at least a half dozen times by dipping its bill in the water and then lifting it to an angle of 45°."

Early in the summer the birds usually came to the pond to bathe individually, but by mid-July they came in small flocks and bathed together. After bathing they generally stood around for perhaps a half hour preening themselves. L. M. Whitaker (1957a) describes how her captive lark sparrow habitually oiled its tarsi after bathing and before preening:

After briefly touching the [uropygial] gland [with its bill], the Lark Sparrow deliberately places one foot firmly forward on the cage top and rather quickly runs its opened bill down upon the front of that tarsus, from bend of heel to the toes. It pulls itself upright, places the other foot forward, and treats this other tarsus in like manner. Only *after* both tarsi have been oiled does the bird begin to preen, usually starting by pulling at mid-breast feathers and then stripping remiges of either wing. Preening and drying actions, continuing until the bird is dry, sometimes require 35 minutes. Once preening has started, the bird neither utilizes the oil gland nor employs the bill upon its tarsi.

*Field marks.*—R. T. Peterson (1941) points out that " *The best mark* [on this open-country sparrow] *is the rounded tail with much white in the outside corners* (somewhat as in Towhee—not as in Vesper Sparrow)." It also has "*chestnut* ear-patches, striped crown, and white breast with single dark central spot. * * * Young birds are finely streaked on the breast and lack the central spot, but are otherwise quite recognizable."

*Enemies.*—H. Friedmann (1929) notes that "Both the eastern and western forms of the Lark Sparrow are known to be victims of the Cowbird." He considers the eastern race "an uncommon host," for which he then had only three records, one from Oklahoma. Later he (1934) records nine parasitized nests in Decatur County, Kans., and for the western race notes that "Mrs. Nice (*Birds of Oklahoma,* rev. ed., 1931, p. 183) records five parasitized nests (out of 23) in Oklahoma."

During the summer of 1957 at the Lake Texoma Biological Station, several life history studies of birds were in progress. As it was felt that fewer nests would be deserted if the cowbird population was thinned out, a number of cowbirds were collected in the vicinity of the station early in the season. During the summer I recorded only three cases of cowbird parasitism near the station. On June 7 a cowbird laid in a lark sparrow's nest containing one egg; the parents promptly deserted. On June 14 a cowbird laid in another lark sparrow's nest containing three fresh eggs, probably an incomplete clutch as the female had not yet started to incubate; she also deserted. On July 6 I found a female lark sparrow incubating four of her own eggs and one cowbird egg. The four lark sparrow eggs hatched July 10, the cowbird egg on July 13. This suggests the lark sparrow may be more apt to accept a cowbird egg after she has started to incubate her own clutch. Later that month I saw a number of young cowbirds out of the nest being fed by lark sparrows away from the station. The lateness of these records also suggests that the lark sparrows may accept cowbird eggs more readily late in the season, after experiencing several nesting failures.

## DISTRIBUTION

### Eastern Lark Sparrow (*C. g. grammacus*)

*Range.*—Minnesota, southern Michigan, southern Ontario, and western New York south to southern Mexico and southern Florida.

*Breeding range.*—The eastern lark sparrow breeds from northwestern and central Minnesota (Warren, Isanti County), north central Wisconsin (Dunn County, Kelley Brook), southern Michigan (Kent and St. Clair counties), southern Ontario (Hyde Park, Toronto), western New York (Monroe County), and central Pennsylvania (Beaver, State College) south through eastern Nebraska (West Point), eastern Kansas and Oklahoma to northeastern Texas, Louisiana (Bienville), central western Alabama (Greensboro), western and central North Carolina (Cranberry, rarely to Raleigh), and north central Virginia (Dale Enterprise, University).

*Winter range.*—Winters from central Texas (Austin), southern Louisiana (Diamond), and central Florida (Seven Oaks) south to Guerrero (Chilpancingo), Oaxaca (Santa Efigenia), and southern Florida (Key West); occasionally north along the Atlantic coast to Delaware (Lewes) and northern New Jersey (Bergen County). In fall migration stray birds regularly reach the Atlantic coast, Nova Scotia to Florida.

*Casual records.*—Casual north to northern Michigan (Copper Harbor), central Ontario (Chapleau), and east central Quebec (Aguanish) and south to Cuba (Guantánamo).

*Migration.*—Early dates of spring arrival are: Florida—Flamingo, April 5. Alabama—Birmingham, April 7; Livingston, April 10. South Carolina—Alto, April 15. Virginia—Cape Charles, April 24. West Virginia—Waverly, April 16. Pennsylvania, Linesville, May 2; Sewickly, May 4. New Jersey—Riverhead, April 11. New York—Jay, April 7; Riverdale, April 11. Massachusetts—Framingham, April 29. New Hampshire—Dover, May 2. Louisiana—Curtis, April 20. Mississippi—Tishomingo County, April 17. Arkansas—Garland County, April 6. Tennessee—Nashville, March 29 (median of 8 years, April 17). Kentucky—Bowling Green, March 20. Missouri—Concordia, April 4; St. Louis, April 20 (median of 14 years, April 28). Illinois—Peoria, March 25; Urbana, March 27 (median of 17 years, April 22). Indiana—Frankfort, March 11. Ohio—central Ohio, April 18 (median, May 12); Oberlin (median of 10 years, April 28). Michigan—Three Rivers, April 19. Ontario—Windsor, April 20. Iowa—Sioux City, April 15 (median of 38 years, May 1). Wisconsin—Lafayette County, April 15. Minnesota—Rochester, April 5; Minneapolis, April 6 (average of 25 years for southern Minnesota, April 25). Texas—Denton, March 1; Commerce, March 9; Tyler, March 15. Oklahoma—Norman, March 22; Moore, March 24; Milburn, March 16, Mill Creek, March 18; Tulsa, April 11. Kansas—northeastern Kansas, March 29 (median of 23 years, April 18). Nebraksa—Omaha, March 25. South Dakota—Faulkton, March 15. North Dakota—Bismarck, April 20. Manitoba—Margaret, April 28; Treesbank, May 6 (average of 19 years, May 14). Saskatchewan—Wiseton, April 17. New Mexico—State College, April 8; Rio Grande Valley, April 27 (median of 8 years, May 10). Arizona—Fort Apache, April 15; Flagstaff, April 16. Colorado—Durango, April 6. Utah—Salt Lake City, April 4. Wyoming—Jay Em, May 1; Careyhurst, May 2. Idaho—Castleford, April 17 (median of 11 years, May 3). Montana—Billings, April 19; Terry, April 27 (average of 6 years, May 7). Alberta—Flagstaff, May 3. California—Yosemite Valley,

April 12. Nevada—Mercury, April 9. Oregon—Coorvallis, April 1. Washington—Spokane, March 27. British Columbia—Okanagan Landing, May 10.

Late dates of spring departure are: Florida—Tallahassee, April 29. Georgia—Chickamauga Park, May 10. South Carolina—Alto, April 26. Virginia—Charlottesville, May 1. New York—Montauk, June 12, New Hampshire—Concord, May 30. Tennessee—Nashville, May 3. Kentucky—Bowling Green, May 1. Indiana—West Lafayette, May 25. Ohio—central Ohio, May 27. Michigan—Three Rivers, May 27. Texas—Cove, April 20. South Dakota—Faulkton, May 1. North Dakota—Jamestown, May 13. Manitoba—Margaret, May 27. New Mexico—Apache, May 30. Arizona—Tucson, June 16 and June 9. California—Inyo County, April 29. Nevada—Pyramid Lake, May 5. British Columbia—Okanagan Landing, May 25.

Early dates of fall arrival are: Nevada—Quinn Crossing, August 29. Montana—Heath, August 11. Arizona—Globe, July 5; Tucson, July 9. Texas—El Paso, August 5. Indiana—Sedan, August 26. Illinois—Chicago, September 6. Tennessee—Knox County, August 11. Mississippi—Gulfport, August 16. Louisiana—Baton Rouge, August 24. New Brunswick—Grand Manan, August 13. Massachusetts—Newburyport, August 2; Martha's Vineyard, August 19 (median of 7 years, September 6). New Hampshire—Star Island, Isle of Shoals, August 12. Connecticut—Guilford, August 27. New York—Shelter Island, July 7. Maryland—Laurel, July 17. District of Columbia—August 8. Virginia—Charlottesville, July 4. North Carolina—Greensboro, July 30. South Carolina—Charleston, August 1. Georgia—Camden County, August 11. Alabama—Dauphin Island, August 22. Florida—northwest Florida, July 25; St. Marks Light, July 29.

Late dates of fall departure are: British Columbia—Okanagan Landing, September 15. Washington—Yakima, September 27. Oregon—Rogue River Valley, December 14 and November 9. California—Berkeley, November 27. Idaho—Lewiston, October 13 (median of 11 years, September 12). Wyoming—Careyhurst, October 15. Utah—Willard, October 12. Colorado—Fort Morgan, November 17. New Mexico—Mesilla, October 27. Manitoba—Treesbank, September 11. North Dakota—Charlson, September 9. South Dakota—Faulkton, November 15. Nebraska—Valentine, November 1. Kansas—northeastern Kansas, October 16 (median of 7 years, October 12). Oklahoma—Norman, September 25; Fort Sill, November 26; Lake Texoma, October 10; Payne County, October 7. Texas—Tyler, December 11. Minnesota—Minneapolis, October 16; Fillmore County, September 9 (average of 7 years for southern Minnesota, July 27). Wisconsin—Adams County, September 16. Iowa—Sioux City, August 16. Michigan—Plymouth, September 20. Ohio—Lucas and Ottawa counties, October 18; central Ohio, September 28 (average, August 30). Indiana—Indianapolis, November 20. Illinois—Odin, October 24. Missouri—St. Louis, October 10 (median of 14 years, September 14). Kentucky—Bowling Green, October 18. Tennessee—Nashville, September 18. Arkansas—Garland County, September 29. Mississippi—Bay St. Louis, October 14. Louisiana—Baton Rouge, October 14. New Brunswick—Grand Manan, October 3. Maine—Kokadjo, October 5. New Hampshire—Hampton, October 20. Massachusetts—Newtonville, November 25. Rhode Island—Block Island, October 5. New York—Miller Place, November 27. Maryland—Worcester County, October 21. Alabama—Foley, November 1. Florida—Arcadia, December 5.

*Egg dates.*—Arizona: 9 records, May 17 to June 27.

California: 132 records, April 4 to July 16; 72 records, May 1 to June 1.

Colorado: 6 records, June 2 to June 30.

Illinois: 32 records, May 5 to July 4; 22 records, May 20 to June 12.

Oklahoma: 61 records, May 14 to July 20; 42 records, June 1 to June 30.

Texas: 63 records, April 10 to July 14; 35 records, May 1 to May 23.

## Western Lark Sparrow (*C. g. strigatus*)

*Range.*—British Columbia and southern portions of prairie provinces south to southern Mexico and El Salvador.

*Breeding range.*—The western lark sparrow breeds from western Oregon (Corvallis), central interior British Columbia (Savona, Cascade), central Idaho (Payette Lake), southeastern Alberta (Medicine Hat), southern Saskatchewan (Cypress Hills, Regina), and southern Manitoba (Treesbank, Winnipeg) south to southern California (Vallecito), central Nevada (Reno), south central Arizona (Quitobaquito eastward), northeastern Sonora, Zacatecas (Cerro Gordo), Coahuila (Sierra del Carmen), southern Texas (Raymondville), and east to western Kansas; summer records north to central British Columbia (140 mile on Cariboo Road, Puntchesakut Lake), south central Alberta (Red Deer), and central Manitoba (Lake St. Martin).

*Winter range.*—Winters from central and southern California (Nicasio, Colfax), southern Arizona (Yuma, Phoenix, Camp Verde), western and southern central Texas, and Louisiana (Cameron, New Orleans) south to southern Baja California (Cape San Lucas), Guerrero (Chilpancingo), Chiapas (San Benito), El Salvador (La Aldea), and Veracruz (El Conejo).

*Casual records.*—Casual in migration east to New Brunswick (Grand Manan), Massachusetts (Ipswich), North Carolina (Stumpy Point), and Florida (Key West).

## AIMOPHILA CARPALIS CARPALIS (Coues)

### Rufous-winged Sparrow

#### Contributed by ALLAN R. PHILLIPS

#### HABITS

One of the several confusing, obscure species of southern Arizona and Mexico, the rufous-winged sparrow, like most of its close relatives, looks like "just a sparrow." It sports no striking black tail nor cravat, no showy pattern on crown or tail. It has no brilliant song nor striking call. It is just a trim little bird, much like a chipping sparrow in general appearance, but with different striping on the head. It does not gather into prominent flocks. The casual observer would probably vote it among our birds least likely to be of any interest, especially if he were aware that it is sedentary and presents no problems of migration.

How wrong he would be! The rufous-winged sparrow is far more than "just a sparrow." It is a bird of exceptional interest, particularly for its history and the strange interrelations of its life cycle and molts. Besides, it can well claim the title of the most misunderstood bird in the United States. As R. T. Moore (1946) aptly says: "few species have suffered so much from conjecture and inspired guessing." Moore himself, unfortunately, here adds his share of inaccuracies.

Historically, the last two really distinct species of United States birds to be discovered (except for the nocturnal *Caprimulgus ridgwayi*) were found by the redoubtable Charles E. Bendire on the Rillito near Tucson, Ariz., in 1872: Bendire's thrasher and the rufous-winged sparrow. To be sure, a few other local and well-marked races of birds were yet to be discovered, but probably none deserves the rank of a full species. When the now historic Fort Lowell was removed from Tucson to the Rillito, both C. E. Bendire and Henry W. Henshaw promptly found the rufous-winged sparrow abundant there; yet within a few years it vanished completely. Herbert Brown took a specimen at or near Tucson early in 1886; thereafter not a single *Aimophila carpalis* was found in the Tucson area for half a century. Finally E. C. Jacot secured a pair in 1936 well away from the original points of discovery, and some time later took a third specimen. Unaware of these details, I found the birds late in 1938. In the late 1930s most or all of the birds in the Tucson area were in grassy swales on the desert east and southeast of town. Later I found others in

brushy bottomlands south of town.   About 1951 the species began to
spread out in the valley, and in 1956 an extraordinary expansion of
range carried the species into areas of almost solid grassland and even
into one wooded mountain canyon to the south, well above its usual
desert or Lower Sonoran Zone haunts.   Few species have shown such
drastic fluctuations in habitat and numbers.   It is small wonder that
*A. carpalis* was considered extinct in the United States by some
authors, including the American Ornithologists' Union (1931) especially as no one understood the bird's requirements and everyone
looked for it in the wrong places (Swarth, 1929; van Rossem, 1931,
1936b; Phillips, Marshall, and Monson, 1964).

The genus *Aimophila*, with certain close allies, forms a large group
of sparrows centered in the southern half of Mexico.   A few species
extend northward well into the United States, but only one, *A. aestivalis*, is limited to this country.   In their life histories, most or all of
these sparrows react markedly to factors other than the calendar and
the photoperiod.   Thus, the customary way of presenting life histories must, in these cases, be modified to obtain a clear understanding.

*Habitat and phenological background.*—The essential parts of the
normal habitat of the rufous-winged sparrow, as already stated
(Phillips, 1955), are grass and brush (thorny, dense, or preferably
both).   The grasses favored in Arizona are of bunching types, not
plain low *Bouteloua*, though in recent years areas with very sparse
grass and low weeds have been inhabited.   The brush–grass combination and the birds are common and widespread over much of
Sonora; they give way southward to taller, denser thorn forest in
Sinaloa, and northward to deserts devoid of grass and to unbroken,
brushless desert grasslands in Arizona.   In both Sinaloa and Arizona
the birds thus seem to be in rather restricted, isolated colonies.   Even
these, however, are not uniform ecologically, at least near Tucson
(the only point whence we have detailed data on the life history).   To
discuss these data, we must distinguish at least five types of habitat:

SWALE HABITAT: Areas where flood waters seep into desert soils,
not yet badly gullied, producing wide stands of grass in the bottom,
chiefly tobosa (*Hilaria mutica*).   Around these stands the better
drained edges support leguminous brush and low trees, and usually
desert hackberry (*Celtis tala* var. *pallida*) bushes which may be of
considerable density and circumference, and over 2 meters tall, when
the soil is still healthy.   Moisture comes entirely from rains over the
local drainage area; no underground water is within reach of the roots.

DESERT WASH HABITAT: Similar, but gently sloping, without seepage
or the consequent stands of tobosa; the bottom is plain sand, completely drained and usually gullied shallowly.   Dominant trees are
usually palo verde and mesquite, and there is an understory of brush,

cacti, weeds, and what little grass escapes the inevitable cattle. This is marginal habitat for *Aimophila*, but it was definitely occupied in 1958.

RIPARIAN HABITAT: Here water still flows more or less throughout the year. High waters flood the bottomlands occasionally, producing originally "bunches of tall rye [=sacaton] and mesquite grasses" (Bendire, 1882). These habitats were soon grazed to destruction in Arizona, but many remain in Sonora, where they have not been studied. The closest approach in Arizona now (in the range of our sparrow) is lower Sabino Creek, leaving the Santa Catalina Mountains. Near its rocky bed, this creek has some broad-leafed riparian trees (willow, cottonwood, ash, etc.); farther back, lower mesquite trees dominate, with considerable tangles of weeds and grass in ungrazed spots.

Originally, C. E. Bendire (1882) found his new sparrow "particularly partial to a strip of country . . . then covered with good sized mesquite trees interspersed with sage and thorn bushes, small undergrowth," and grasses. They were "seldom any great distance" from these woods "in the dry and arid cactus covered plains."

FARMLAND HABITAT: Back from the now-dry bed of the erstwhile Santa Cruz River, Papago Indians have for years farmed fields in what was once, centuries ago, a dense thicket of mesquite woods. Irrigation ditches border the fields; along them grows a profusion of weeds, grass, and often a hedgerow of mesquite trees, elderberries, and brush, chiefly *Condalia lycioides*. The principal study area here is that of Joe T. Marshall, Jr., near the silted-over Indian Dam (see map, fig. 1*b*, *in* Marshall, 1960). Here the birds inhabit the edges of the brushy and cleared parts. After the early 1950s, with the illness and death of the owners, these fields were not irrigated and received only normal rainfall. The nearby river, not visited by the sparrows, ceased trickling regularly in the late 1940s and is now dry.

DEEP-SOIL HABITAT: This is very near the farms just mentioned, but on the east rather than the west bank of the river and perhaps 200 meters farther north, below the dam site. The mesquite trees are somewhat more cut over and spaced apart, though rather taller; often they are overgrown with vines or have weedy tangles below. Many clumps of tall sacaton grass, in the openings between trees, are a sad remnant of the day when the river slowly sank into the soil here, to reappear below. With the subsequent deep channeling, this is now the driest of the occupied habitats, the most dependent on day-to-day rainfall.

Because the time of nesting may vary widely from year to year at the same spot owing to ecological factors, most or all of which depend on rainfall, we must understand both the normal climate and the rainfall pattern of the abnormal years when the birds reacted differently. Usually almost no rain falls between March and the end of June. Tradition has the rains starting on San Juan's day, June 24, but they seldom do. Early July is a more usual time for rains to start. These, in summer, tend to be very local—a downpour here today, another there later, and mere drizzles elsewhere. Accurate measurements of water available to plants in each area are obviously impossible, and were not attempted. Even for the University of Arizona campus, I cannot consider the figures given (see below) as strictly accurate, but they show the trends of rainfall.

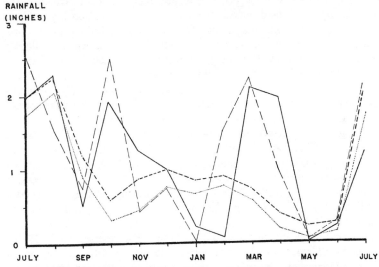

Rainfall at Tucson, Arizona (University of Arizona station)

Fine dots=normal (median)
Short dashes=calculated arithmetic mean, all years
Solid line=1951–1952
Longer dashes=1957–1958

The climatic picture of the fall, winter, and spring of 1951–52, though quite similar to that of 1957–58, was strikingly different from normal. The weather remained hot through Oct. 20, 1951, then cooled off. Storms at the end of each fall month brought less rain in September than later, but added up to a very wet fall in southwestern and central Arizona. It stayed cool and rainy through Christmas, but 1952 opened with a long spell of warm, dry weather from January 10 through February 29. This gave way abruptly to a cold, rainy period from March 1 to 17; intermittent rains continued through at least April 28, though the weather warmed to normal after March 25.

Thus, since the start of weather recording at Tucson in 1868, only two previous years (1905 and 1926) approached 1952 in the quantity of rain that fell in March and April, and only 1870, 1924, and 1925 were drier in January and February. The total rainfall was normal or greater from July 11 to December 25, 1951, except in the period August 29 to October 24; but only 7 millimeters (0.27 inch) fell from Dec. 26, 1951, through Feb. 29, 1952, which is normally the winter rainy season.

Naturally, this abnormal weather produced an unusual reaction in the habitat. Most obvious, though probably not important to our sparrow, was a veritable plague of greasy cutworm moths and other adult Noctuidae at the end of March and later. Robert H. Crandall (*in* litt.) noted several other unusual features near Tucson; the usually dry- and dead-looking "burro-brush," (*Hymenoclea pentalepis* and perhaps also *H. salsola* and *H. monogyra*), a thin wiry next-to-nothing, was green and succulent about the first of April; evidently it was well supplied with minute inchworms (Microlepidoptera), whose pupae he found about April 20. In late April he saw some big caterpillars of a sphinx moth which usually appear only after the summer rains start; and from early to mid-May (approximately) many inchworms appeared on the native palo verde trees.

The rainfall pattern of 1957–58 was generally similar to that of 1951–52. After Sept. 1, 1957, no rain fell until October, which was very wet. Light rains continued to December 7, but from December 16 through February 3 no measurable rain fell. Then a succession of storms wet the valley from February 4 through April 9, with later sprinkles on April 16 and May 11. The summer rains began on June 20 and 26.

I have little information on the ecological picture of 1957–58, for Robert Crandall had moved away. A plague of big grasshoppers, *Trimerotropis pallidipennis*, occurred in and near Tucson from May 5 to about May 10 (and later?); at the same season Floyd G. Werner noted a plague of false chinch-bugs, *Nysius raphanus*. A lesser infestation of the same (?) grasshopper invaded the city later, on June 28–29. We may probably safely conclude that small insects were present in unusual quantities in both springs, but that the species were different. (Westward, in the California deserts, at least one butterfly was exceptionally common from November 1957 to May 1958—C. H. Abbott, 1959.) From late March through April the swale habitat was quite well covered with herbs, even on the desert away from the bottoms; most of those flowering in late March were Compositae. Notable among these was a purple-rayed *Erigeron* which was rare or absent in the desert wash habitat. Also scarce in the latter habitat were grass clumps and weedy *Aplopappus*-sized shrubs; otherwise, the vegetation there was rather similar to that of the outer part of the swale habitat, dominants being palo verde and *Opuntia fulgida*, with considerable mistletoe, desert hackberry (most of which had been partly killed back earlier), whitethorn, and low composite herbage, but somewhat less mesquite.

In the bottom of the swale habitat, the thriving tobosa grass nearly excludes other plants. There on May 20, 1952, I saw little else than a few flowering *Erigeron divergens* and the crucifer *Descurainia pinnata*.

*Factors that induce nesting.*—It does not seem, however, that mere abundance of plants or insects or a given amount of rain will *per se* cause the rufous-winged sparrow to nest. Nesting depends on the readiness of the female, because in most if not all years the male seems to be in breeding condition long before actual nesting occurs. (A reverse situation, with the male in full breeding condition away from the usual breeding grounds long *after* nesting, occurs in the same region in *A. cassini*—A. R. Phillips, 1944.) Nesting by the female is apparently triggered by additional factors which, at present, we can only guess. Thus in 1959–60, rainfall was again above normal in December and January; this was followed, April 10 to 20 and later, by a plague of army cut-worm moths, *Chorizagrotis auxiliaris* (fide William X. Foerster). The weather, of course, always becomes very warm by May and June at Tucson. Neither Robert Crandall nor I was there in 1960, but several friends kindly looked in vain for evidence of unusually early nesting of *A. carpalis*. Some factor, apparently, was missing.

Certainly a most important aspect of the rufous-winged sparrow's nesting is the lack of concordance between different areas, and prob- ably even between close neighbors within the same little colonies, in the breeding activities of the females. A proper understanding of the factors that trigger nesting will thus require the amassing of more de- tailed data over long periods of time. Based on data as of 1963, the only reasonable conclusion is that nesting depends on certain unclear ecological conditions within the pair's territory. Obviously no fashionable all-inclusive theory can possibly explain the strange facts about to be presented; these do not coincide with dates, photoperiods, amounts of cloud cover, darkness or sunshine, cyclonic or anticyclonic weather, temperature variations, or other current phenomena.

The rufous-winged sparrow responds, instead, to the most potent of several perhaps conflicting environmental factors, like the responses of certain nesting passerine birds in Latvia (Vilks, 1958), and its individual variability parallels that of some Australian ducks (Frith, 1957). Both it and other *Aimophilae* (*ruficeps* herein; see H. Wagner, 1955), as well as *all* the birds of the arid parts of Australia (Keast, 1960), afford overwhelming evidence against the automatic photo- period hypothesis expounded by A. Wolfson (1960), A. H. Miller (1960) and D. S. Farner and A. Oksche (1964). (For an excellent review of this subject see A. J. Marshall, 1951.)

A particularly interesting problem, which would require far more time to investigate than I could devote to it, is whether nests built when conditions first begin to look favorable are abandoned if the weather turns hot and dry again, as Paul Schwartz and E. T. Gilliard believe may occur normally with Venezuelan birds (Gilliard, 1959).

*Spring.*—As the rufous-winged sparrow neither migrates nor often gathers into flocks that are obviously larger than family size, the changes in its behavior and local distribution in spring are not striking. By mid- or late March most of the birds seem to be in pairs, but this is not universal. For one thing, the apparent pairs may not be true pairs. Thus on Mar. 24, 1940, I collected one bird from an apparent pair which on skinning later, I found to be a male (testes somewhat enlarged, left 2.8×1.8, right 1.7×1.7 millimeters); yet while I was preparing it to take home its supposed "mate" sang. Therefore, either the female may sing or (more likely) some apparent pairs are not of opposite sexes, a condition that was proved, also in March, in the case of a wren, *Uropsila leucogaster brachyurus* in Yucatán (Chapman, 1896b).

For another thing, even in wet springs some birds remain in small flocks through March. On Mar. 29, 1958, my ornithology students saw two groups of three birds each near Tucson in the swale habitat. More exceptional was a flock of about five or six sparrows that I saw in the desert wash habitat on Apr. 27, 1958; at least four birds, if not the whole flock, were rufous-winged sparrows; yet, in the same area, some pairs already had eggs in the nests. Farther south in southern Sonora according to A. J. van Rossem (1945a) the birds were not yet paired in late May and even up to June 22 ,1937; while Joe T. Marshall, Jr. (MS.) could find no nests there from May 8 to 12, 1958, on which dates some pairs near Tucson had young nearly ready to leave the nest (in desert wash) or actually on the wing (in riparian habitat). In northwestern and central western Sonora I found at least some birds paired,. though not yet nesting, Apr. 20 and 28, 1947.

*Territory.*—As might be expected, the size of the territory evidently varies inversely to the desirability of the habitat. In the farmland habitat Patrick J. Gould (MS.) found a pair holding about ⅘ hectare (2 acres); most of this was not contiguous to the territories of other pairs. The favored swale habitat may support as many as 8 to 10 pairs per ⅘ kilometer (½ mile), the swale being perhaps 50–100 meters wide on an average (A. R. Phillips, 1955); probably most territories here do not greatly exceed ½ hectare. On Mar. 29, 1958, flights here seldom exceeded 15 meters; and in a cholla cactus flat I saw two "pairs" perched in chollas not over 10 meters apart with no apparent friction. Whether these birds had yet established territories at that date, however, is uncertain.

In the original riparian habitat, their density must have been rather spectacular. In 1872 in a strip of mesquite trees, brush, and grass measuring about 1500×400 meters, C. E. Bendire (1882) "found not less than forty-three of their nests with eggs and a still larger number of those of the Black-throated Sparrow * * * besides a number of nests containing young."

*Courtship.*—Twice I have seen billing or possibly courtship feeding. On Mar. 12, 1952, in the Coyote Mountains (eastern edge of Papago Indian Reservation, southwest of Tucson), I saw a pair billing, but could not see whether any food was actually passed; collecting the birds, I found them to be male and female with gonads slightly enlarged: testes averaged 2.4×1.8 millimeters, the largest ovum was about 0.6 millimeter in diameter. The other occasion was on Mar. 29, 1958, in the swale habitat near Tucson. After one of the two pairs in nearby chollas had flown, the remaining pair then billed several times; the upper bird reached down and slightly to its left, while the lower one seemed to reach up, to the right, and a bit forward. I feel sure that they were only billing, for I saw nothing *in* their bills and no swallowing actions, nor had they apparently been feeding just before. Neither this one pair nor the other in the chollas was collected.

*Nesting season.*—Customarily we confine our main discussion of nesting to the location and construction of nests, relegating the dates to a few lines at the very end, after the migration dates and casual records. To do so with the rufous-winged sparrow, however, would be to pass over one of the most fascinating aspects of its life history, which sets it (and most of the other *Aimophila* sparrows) off from the general run of birds of northern latitudes.

The nesting season corresponds in all cases with a season of rainfall and warm to hot temperatures. In normal years, though the testes of males enlarge greatly in late April or May, no eggs are laid near Tucson until the end of June or early July, and perhaps later in years and areas of delayed rains. Gale Monson and I found nests with one and four eggs (incubation of the latter just starting) on June 30, 1940.

On June 29, 1954, 4½ days after the big rains began, Joe T. Marshall, Jr. (MS.) found two nests in the same state of construction in swale habitat. "Herbaceous vegetation is now very definitely sprouting— tiny cotyledons are up everywhere, and green is starting to appear on the perennials." One of these nests seemed ready for eggs on July 2, but was unlined. Similarly, Herbert Brandt (1951) never found nests in his years in Arizona, for he usually left about the end of June.

Thus it came as a tremendous surprise when Eliot F. Porter discovered rufous-winged sparrows with large young on the wing on May 19, 1952. This occurred in a swalelike habitat 6½ kilometers north of Vail, after heavy March and April rains. He also found apparently full-grown young in a weedy desert wash on May 24, 1952, more than a month before the first eggs are usually laid.

On May 20, 1952, E. F. Porter and I took a census of ⅛ kilometer (½ mile) of a broad swale. We found three or four families of young

on the wing, which had recently left the nest or were somewhat larger
(two juvenal females had the tail 21 and 37 millimeters long); one pair
with two eggs (incubating); another pair at an apparently completed
but empty nest; and at least three other males were heard singing
near by, but their mates (if any) were not found.

Three days later I checked the deep-soil habitat. Here three or
four males were singing, but I found no nests or young. To verify
this surprising difference between two localities about 25 kilometers
(15 miles) apart, I revisited the deep-soil habitat on July 13. Again
no young were found, and it seemed that nesting had started normally
in late June; for the most advanced birds detected were a pair with
the male singing and the female carrying small grasshoppers, presumably to young in the nest. Another nest was found with one
broken egg.

In 1958 unseasonal nestings occurred in the swale habitat, though
apparently less commonly or successfully. Arthur Twomey, Jr.,
and I could find no active nest on April 20, though one looked completed. (A cracked egg was later found just below, but the nest
was apparently abandoned.) Some early nests did succeed, however,
for I took a female just out of the nest (tail 11.2 millimeters) on
May 10, and Robert W. Dickerman and I took grown young, possibly
from two different families, on June 12, well into the post-juvenal
molt.

More conspicuous, however, were the unseasonal nestings discovered in the marginal desert wash habitat by James M. and Eugenia
W. Gates (MS.). On Apr. 20, 1958, they found a nest with four
eggs, subsequently deserted, plus two possibly new nests; and on
revisiting the area on April 27, we found more nests with and without
eggs. One nest the Gates followed up later had three very small
young and one egg on May 3; another was apparently successful, the
young presumably leaving on May 15 or 16. At this time rufous-
winged sparrows were also nesting in other places. In the riparian
habitat I found a nest with four eggs (later deserted?) on April 30, and
Eliot F. Porter (MS.) found another which four young left, prematurely in his judgment, on May 7, 1958. In the farmland habitat Joe
T. Marshall, Jr. (MS.) found two nests, with two and three eggs,
respectively, on May 2. The former had an apparently newly hatched
chick on May 17, when the latter's young appeared to be about 6 days
old. These were still being brooded on the 18th.

Another exceptionally wet year was 1940–41. In the Wilson C.
Hanna collection (*fide* W. G. F. Harris) is a set of eggs Oscar F. Clark
took on May 4, 1941, at Sells on the Papago Indian Reservation,
Arizona, where the desert wash is the principal habitat.

Nesting continues in Arizona into September. C. E. Bendire
(1882) "found fresh eggs as late as Sept. 1, 1872." These are presumably the same eggs reported (Baird, Brewer, and Ridgway, 1874)

as taken September 11 and still preserved in the U.S. National Museum (*fide* W. G. F. Harris). Nevertheless Elliott Coues (1873b) does not include this species among birds C. E. Bendire found "still laying September 13," 1872. Farther south in Sonora, a family of three young was "at most two or three days out of the nest" on Nov. 1, 1946 (Pitelka, 1951); and even near the Arizona border a "small juvenile" was taken September 29 (Miller et al., 1957). Likewise R. T. Moore (1946) reported heavily incubated eggs found by C. C. Lamb in Sinaloa, Oct. 2, 1933.

There is, unfortunately, no sure evidence of just when the birds in the old Tucson riparian habitat normally nested. We know only that C. E. Bendire (1882) found the first eggs "about June 14, 1872, although I believe these birds commence to breed about a month earlier, their nests having been previously overlooked by me"—an understandable possibility, as the species itself was undescribed. Also, Frank Stephens (Brewster, 1882a) found a nest with three eggs May 25, 1881, a year of better-than-average March and April rainfall. So all this is very inconclusive.

Charles E. Bendire (1882) thought that two or three broods were raised in the riparian habitat in 1872. Likewise in 1958, some pairs probably raised two broods in the desert wash habitat. Here the Gates (MS.) found two new nests with eggs on July 6; one of these, with one egg, was only about 7 or 8 meters from the site of the apparently successful nesting in May.

*Nesting.*—The nest site preferred in the swale habitat is the edge of a thick, tall desert hackberry bush (*Celtis tala*, var. *pallida*), 0.6 to 2 meters above the ground. In the desert wash habitat where most of these bushes were partly bare due to the increasing desiccation of the country, the birds showed a marked preference for the edges of or open parts within palo verde trees (*Cercidium*) 1.3 to 2.5 meters above the ground. Sometimes the nests were in the less dense clumps of mistletoe on the palo verde trees, or in cholla cacti (*Opuntia fulgida*)—in one case in a cholla growing within the shelter of a palo verde. In the farmland habitat, where none of these plants grows, the favored site is 1 to 1.3 meters up in a thorny *Condalia lycioides* bush. In the old riparian habitat nests were "firmly fixed into a fork, or crotch" 0.15 to 1.5 meters up "in low bushes, preferably small mesquite bushes" (Bendire, 1882).

The building of two nests in swale habitat on June 29, 1954, was accomplished as follows (Marshall, MS.): "The male gets up and sings a bit while the female brings a big bundle of the pale, curly, basal leaves of tobosa grass. She comes down to the nest from above, enters, and works there 15–30 seconds; then she climbs out, hops up higher, and both birds fly down to feed 30–40 meters away."

The nest itself is a conspicuous, solid, deep cup of old, dead (usually gray) plant stems, lined with fine grass and usually (at least on the bottom) with horsehair. In the swale habitat, as in the old riparian habitat, the shell is made of coarse grasses (sometimes mixed with weeds), chiefly the stems but including leaves and the fine stalks of inflorescences. Elsewhere the outer shell is built of similar material (much of it is not grass)—weed-stems, at times with the top of the root or with what seem to be strips of some thin, gray plant cortex such as fine bark. Except for this last and the leaf-blades, most of this outer material is largely from ½ to 1 millimeter thick, and more often below than above these limits. The use of a fine thorny twig (*Acacia constricta*?) seems unusual in the swale habitat, though twigs are the common component of nests in farmland habitat. A conspicuous component at times, because it is easily identifiable, is the stalk of an *Eriogonum*.

Over-all outside dimensions of the shell are usually 8.5 to 12 centimeters in diameter, and 6 to 8 centimeters in depth; sometimes larger in nests of tobosa grass (swale habitat), or with grasses straggling beneath. The inner cup is usually 4 to 5.5 centimeters in diameter and 5 to 6.5 centimeters deep. C. E. Bendire (1882) describes the nest in the old riparian habitat as "three inches [7.5 centimeters] deep in the inside, so deep in fact that nothing but the tip of the tail of the bird is visible when setting."

*Eggs.*—The set usually comprises four eggs. Recent extremes show a bird incubating two eggs, May 1958 (Marshall, MS.), and a nest with five fresh eggs (one a cowbird's) taken on Aug. 8, 1959 (Patrick J. Gould), both in farmland habitat. But in C. E. Bendire's time, sets of five were not unusual, and three eggs were rare or unknown. The eggs are slightly glossy, ovate, very pale bluish white, and unmarked. W. G. F. Harris' measurements of 50 eggs average 19.1 by 13.9 millimeters; the eggs showing the four extremes measure *20.3* by 14.7, 18.8 by *15.0*, *17.8* by 14.0, and 18.8 by *13.0* millimeters. C. E. Bendire (1882) gives somewhat larger figures, while my own attempts give smaller ones; doubtless this reflects differences in individual techniques and measuring equipment.

*Incubation.*—The female is a close sitter, even when the eggs are fresh. One whose eggs were hatching on September 1 refused to fly when I was less than a meter away. The male on such occasions of danger seems usually to be singing near by. One bird in the desert wash habitat came onto the nest so secretively that I never saw her, though I was watching for her, until she was incubating. While I have never captured incubating birds, I have no reason to suppose that males incubate. The length of the incubation period is unknown.

*Young.*—A young bird I thought to be newly hatched on May 17, 1958, had sparse dark down. Young seem to remain in the nest 9 or 10 days. A nest found with two eggs and two newly hatched but dry young on Sept. 1, 1939, was empty on September 12, but two of the four young were caught and banded near by. This nest was also found independently by A. H. Anderson on September 10, when it appeared to contain only two large young. On September 6 when I rustled the bottom of the nest, the young with eyes open popped their head up to be fed, but their voices were still hardly audible.

Both parents attend and doubtless feed the young. They do not regularly clean the nest, which becomes filthy. Only once did I see an adult carrying a fecal sac, which it deposited on a branch.

The young, or at least the last brood, remain with or near their parents through the fall, if not the winter. One of the young banded Sept. 12, 1939 was seen not far from its native bush 2½ months later on November 25.

*Plumages.*—There seem to be no specimens of the natal down. The juvenal plumage is of the usual streaky sparrow type, but the dusky streaks below are unusually coarse. Robert Ridgway (1901) describes it as: "Upper parts, including pileum, light grayish brown, broadly streaked with blackish; lesser wing-coverts dusky centrally, broadly margined with pale brownish buff; under parts whitish, the chest and sides streaked with dusky." The head markings are at first all dusky on a brownish-buff background, but rufous soon appears behind the eye in the postocular streak. The iris is a grayer brown, less rusty or reddish than the tan or rufous eye of adults and the lower mandible is almost wholly dusky, like the upper and not pinkish. The mouth varies from flesh color to whitish; the gape is pale buffy to creamy whitish. The feet are somewhat more lavender and purplish-tinged than those of adults, and are sometimes even grayish. The adult's feet are more pinkish or yellowish.

The first prebasic or postjuvenal molt may occur at any time from June to October or even November, depending on the date of hatching. It starts to replace the short-lived juvenal plumage early on the anterior parts and the wing coverts. Two young taken in swale habitat on June 12, 1958, were already largely in first basic (first winter) plumage, especially the male taken by Robert W. Dickerman. Normally the juvenal flight feathers (except the tertials) are retained as are the primary coverts and alula. It would be interesting to trace the molt in early hatched birds that molt in June to see whether they molt again in September or October, and if so how fully. One September immature was found to be molting primaries and rectrices (A. R. Phillips, 1951b). This molt produces a definitive, adultlike plumage, though the sides of the head are usually a more buffy and less grayish brown. The best distinguishing marks are the broader, less pointed tip to the alula and the usually browner, less dusky and whitish primary coverts.

A. R. Phillips (1951b) discusses the normal (dry year) molt sequence in some detail. Briefly, a prealternate (or prenuptial) molt in May and June renews the body plumage, tertials, and central rectrices, even if these are juvenal rectrices. In Arizona the later prebasic (postnuptial) molts occur mainly from mid-September into October; they are notable for the apparently aimless, disorganized order of the tail feather molting. Females seemingly lag behind males in all molts. (Molt of juvenal feathers in birds in spring is unusual, according to Humphrey and Parkes, 1959.)

Molt between November and May seems to be a most exceptional event in Arizona. I have seen but one molting specimen—the male of a pair taken in swale habitat by J. A. Munro on Jan. 31, 1952. It was molting on the throat and on the middle (median) part of the breast and especially of the belly.

Farther south in Sonora, a smaller race was still in worn alternate plumage at the end of October 1946, with the males only just starting the prebasic molt (Pitelka, 1951). Nesting here is apparently later than in Arizona. If R. T. Moore (1946) is correct in saying that "some July and August birds are in the midst of molt," the prealternate molt must often be correspondingly late in Sinaloa. But Moore's statement that the species molts at any time of year in the Tropical Zone is not supported by the material I have examined. Nor can I believe that "many March individuals have completed their prenuptial [=prealternate] molt" there, as Moore states.

Just as the timing of the prebasic (postnuptial) molt is evidently affected by the timing of the nesting period, so also is the extent, timing, or perhaps even the very occurrence of the prealternate (prenuptial) molt. In years of unusually early nestings in Arizona, the latter is often curtailed or postponed until after the young leave the nest. I know of no clearer illustration of the undesirability of tying the names of plumages and molts to the breeding cycle in the classic Dwightian tradition.

Particularly instructive is a small family group taken on June 12, 1958, in swale habitat. The young one, a female, was fully grown, with the tail 65.2 millimeters and not sheathed at base; she was well into the first prebasic (postjuvenal) molt. The parents were both adults more than a year old. Except for one of the outer, longer tertials in each wing, the prenuptial molt of the father had been postponed and was just starting, chiefly on the back but also on the breast and belly. The mother, on the other hand, had molted normally, or nearly so, even while incubating, and was now well into the prealternate or prenuptial molt. Her oviduct was now small, and the brood patch no longer vascular; her largest ova were 1.5 and 1.8 millimeter in diameter. That the molt is a prenuptial one seems certain. The primaries and secondaries show no molt, though that of the tertials is near completion, and the only short rectrices are the central pair, now 34.5 and 44.6 millimeters long. One outer rectrix is missing, and the other appears fresh. All other tail feathers are old, and the longer ones are more or less worn and frayed. Curiously the secondaries, longest tertial, and innermost two primaries are all new in the right wing, though old in the left. Molt of the greater and especially middle wing coverts is also markedly asymmetrical.

Most of the few specimens taken in years of atypical nestings point to a partial or complete suppression of the prealternate (prenuptial) molt by the developing ecological conditions that ultimately induced nesting. Thus parents of small young taken in swale habitat on May 20, 1952 (adults, male and female, of different families) and June 21, 1952 (first-year female) are not molting and have not replaced many feathers. The male has lost several flight feathers, chiefly secondaries, but shows few new feathers (inner right scapulars; left central and next-to-central tail feathers). The females are even more worn, but the first-year one has started to molt on the breast, lower chest, and back. On the other hand, an adult male of the *same date* (June 21), but whose nest had fresh eggs, has molted almost normally, is largely in fresh feather, and still shows some molt, mostly on the breast and lower chest.

In the deep-soil habitat no early nestings were observed. In the most advanced nesting noted, an adult female was carrying grasshoppers to young on July 13, 1952; she had molted parts of the wing coverts, most of the forecrown, back, and chest, and some remiges in the right wing (tertials and innermost primary); she also had some new feathers in the rump, and perhaps elsewhere, but she retained the old nape, upper and under tail coverts, rectrices (except the outer pair), flanks, sides of the neck, and part or all of the throat, malar area, and lores. An adult male was seemingly in an earlier part of the breeding cycle; he was singing near a nest containing an egg shell. Some molt was still in progress, and he retained some old plumage, including the greater wing coverts and part of the crissum; but the prealternate molt was nearly complete. In fact, even the two innermost pairs of primaries had been replaced. Thus molt in this population had been less affected by the unusual weather and ecological conditions.

Aside from the scanty data provided by Frank A. Pitelka (1951), no information is available which would suggest whether or not rainfall also affects the timing and extent of the molts of the more southern races in Mexico.

*Food.*—Field observations show that during the nesting season a good deal of the food consists of small green caterpillars of the inchworm type. Other blackish caterpillars and small grasshoppers 7 to 10 millimeters long are also taken. The adults feed largely in the desert hackberry bushes at this time. Earlier in the summer the birds catch low-flying insects in short sallies while on the wing and glean others from the stems of small plants such as burroweed,

*Haplopappus tenuisectus.* The young soon start to eat seeds; one female in first prebasic molt as early as June 12, 1958, had chiefly small seeds and gravel in her stomach and only one or two small insects. Food at other seasons presumably consists largely of grass and weed seeds. Henry W. Henshaw (1875) found them in September "hopping about in search of small seeds and insects." C. E. Bendire (1882), possibly referring to the winter food, wrote that it "seems to feed principally on various kinds of small seeds."

The strangely molting female of June 12, 1958, however, had fed largely on small ants, determined by Floyd G. Werner to be workers of *Solenopsis (xyloni?).* Her stomach also held some small seeds, a little gravel (and bits of glass?), and one large, blackish mandible which probably came from a grasshopper.

*Behavior.*—In its favorite haunts the rufous-winged sparrow is a bird of modest habits and is easily observed. When disturbed, it flies up into a bush or low tree from which it watches the observer's approach. Only once have I seen it run like a mouse through the grass in the exasperating manner of its relatives, such as *A. cassini.* On the other hand I have never seen it burst into a flight song as *cassini* commonly does in summer, though C. E. Bendire (1882) mentions it singing "while hovering a few feet in the air, generally in close proximity to" its nest, in the crowded population of the old riparian habitat.

On one occasion, early in June 1951, I did see a rufous-winged sparrow several meters above the ground. This bird was singing from a telephone wire by a road that separated homes with lawns and citrus and Eucalyptus trees from the desert mesa. At that moment a Harris' hawk was sitting in a tree not far off, and I suspected that the hawk's presence may have accounted for the unusually high perch the rufous-winged sparrow chose.

For a small bird, the species shows much courage at nesting time. While I was examining a replacement nest with two fresh eggs, a bird came very near me in the lower part of the same bush and "chipped," with its wings somewhat spread as if trying to drive me away. It is not so approachable at other times, but (like Scott, 1886) I have always found it less shy than others of its genus. Both C. E. Bendire (1882) and H. W. Henshaw (1875) liken it to the black-throated and chipping sparrows in behavior.

In marginal, overgrazed areas it may be less confiding. Near Sells, Ariz., in June W. L. Dawson (MS.) writes that "the birds themselves are very shy, and [C. I.] Clay spent half an hour securing a pair." R. T. Moore (1946) also called them "extremely shy" at Fresnal, east of Sells, but seemingly had no difficulty in collecting specimens. Doubtless the birds tend to retreat farther when they can do so without entering the territory of another pair. Even where fairly common, however, most rufous-winged sparrows seem unusually secretive when laying and incubating.

*Voice.*—The rufous-winged sparrow has a wide variety of calls and songs. The characteristic "location note" is a shrill, piercing *seep*, or as C. E. Bendire puts it, "a lisping 'tzip,' 'tzip,' frequently repeated." It differs from those of such *Spizellae* as the chipping sparrow and of most other sparrows in its somewhat higher pitch and loudness, and its firmer, more metallic quality. The song is variable, one frequent type being a monotone. More often the opening notes, commonly three in number, vary in pitch from the closing series, and generally among themselves as well. In any event, the song ends in a rapid, almost trilled series of notes identical with the call and on a single pitch. The opening notes are more widely spaced and seem to be held a bit longer, but are scarcely more musical. The usual song is thus much like that of a canyon brown towhee, but sometimes the second of the opening notes is lower-pitched and sounds rather different. One such song is rendered in my notes as *chip burr chee-he-he-he-he-he*; another as *tee yoor tee te-te-te-te-te* the *yoor* being reminiscent of the call of Say's phoebe. There are other variations, too.

Altogether I consider the song pleasing, if hardly pretentious, but I cannot scold C. E. Bendire for calling it "rather weak and monotonous." While I admit that the bird is no musician, I think Dawson (MS.) uses some poetic license in stating that "its sharp iterative staccato notes" are "utterly destitute of musical quality." He continues: "The song * * * is curiously like that of the Abert or California [brown] towhee, lightened, quickened, and continued, *tsip, tsip, tsip, tsip, tsip, tsip, tsip, tsip, tsip*." A less common chattering note, much like a brown towhee's or a black-throated sparrow's, of a tinkling quality, is possibly used only when the birds are excited.

The main season of song in normal (dry) years is from June or July to mid-September. Singing may be heard at almost any time, though I have not specifically noted hearing it in December. When singing, the bird prefers a perch several feet up on top of a medium-sized cactus or thorny bush.

*Field marks.*—The rufous-winged sparrow resembles the chipping sparrow on its upper parts, with its rufous crown and black-striped back. The white malar area, however, is bordered above and below by thin black stripes, separating it from the throat and cheeks; and the line through the eye is rufous rather than black. Thus the head-stripings resemble more closely those of the rufous-crowned sparrow, which is found at higher altitudes, but the back and mustache-cheek markings are more pronounced, and the whole bird is more slender and trim. The ground color of the side of the head is somewhat paler, so that there is no obvious whitish ring around the eye. In fresh plumage, a hint of white at the outer corners of the dark tail when spread, will help distinguish it from both the rufous-crowned and the chipping sparrow. The rufous bend of the wing can be seen only under favorable circumstances. Voice and habitat are the best clues, especially in early summer when chipping sparrows are not apt to be present in the Lower Sonoran Zone.

*Enemies.*—Little is known of those enemies of the rufous-winged sparrow that man conventionally (or conveniently) discusses. In the old mesquite thickets, C. E. Bendire (1882) found that its "nest appears to be one of the most favored by" the brown-headed cowbird; about one-half of the nests were parasitized, and in a number of these the owner's (but not the parasite's) eggs were "minutely punctured in one or more places," presumably by the cowbird. In the swale habitat, however, I have found little parasitism by cowbirds, which are scarce there.

Undoubtedly the most important enemy of the rufous-winged sparrow is the unscrupulous cattleman. The distribution of the bird in the Tucson Valley during the 1930s and 1940s made this clear. Those areas where colonies survived were never heavily grazed; furthermore, they were in places where the grass derived its water from rainfall in the immediate vicinity and was not dependent on a healthy range above. The late J. J. Thornber of the University of Arizona informed me that light grazing in the opening decades of the century had largely replaced the once-dominant grama grass (*Bouteloua Rothrocki*) with *Aristida* in these areas. But there was always some sort of grass cover. The most flourishing colonies were around meadows of tobosa (*Hilaria mutica*). This is good evidence that the general abuse of the country by overgrazing exterminated the bird about Fort Lowell and Oracle and sadly reduced its numbers along the Santa Cruz River, so that the once marginal colonies became the species' only strongholds in this region.

*Fall and winter.*—After the young are grown, small (probably family) groups of rufous-winged sparrows are generally found associating with such other sparrows as the black-throated, chipping, and Brewer's. Where it was densely congregated in the mesquite thickets, C. E. Bendire (1882) found the species "sociable and gregarious at all times," especially in winter, when "it is found in small flocks." W. E. D. Scott (1887) found winter flocks of 4 to 20 individuals, but some of these would seem to be exceptionally large. Recent observers usually find only family-sized groups, which may associate with other sparrows such as *Spizellae*.

Occasionally this sparrow may show signs of some sexual activity in fall. On Oct. 9, 1938 I watched one snuggle down into an old nest in a desert hackberry, but I am not sure that this nest was originally of a rufous-winged rather than a black-throated sparrow. J. T. Marshall, Jr. (MS.) saw one enter a cactus wren's nest in farmland where it remained for 15 seconds on Nov. 16, 1956. Such actions have not been noticed in winter.

### DISTRIBUTION

*Range.*—Southern Arizona south to central Sinaloa; nonmigratory. The rufous-winged sparrow ranges north to Pinal County, Arizona (Oracle Junction and Oracle); east to central southern Arizona (Oracle and Tucson regions, sporadically near Sonoita), eastern Sonora (Rio Bavispe, Santa Rosa, and Guirocoba), and northeastern Sinaloa (Colmoa, Rancho El Padre, Tabalá on Rio San Lorenzo); south to central Sinaloa (Elota); west to the coasts of Sinaloa and Sonora (north to Estero de Tasiota and Rancho Costa Rica, and west of Caborca), and Arizona (western part of Papago Indian Reservation at Menager's Dam and Ventana Ranch).

The entire species as outlined has been divided into three subspecies, of which only one (*A. c. carpalis*) enters the United States.

*Egg dates.*—Arizona: 25 records, April 20 to September 11. Sinaloa: September 11, October 2.

### AIMOPHILA RUFICEPS EREMOECA (Brown)

## Rock Rufous-crowned Sparrow

### Contributed by ALLAN R. PHILLIPS

### HABITS

This race inhabiting the southern Great Plains south to northeastern Mexico differs from *scottii* of the northwestern Mexican plateau and interior southwestern United States, according to Robert Ridgway (1901), by being "much grayer above and paler below; the back and scapulars smoke gray or olive-gray (sometimes almost ash gray) narrowly streaked with brown, these streaks often inclosing more or less distinct shaft-lines of black or dusky; chin, throat, and abdomen almost white (often quite so in summer plumage)." The slight average differences in size include a stouter bill. There is, however, considerable variation in color within both races. In fact R. B. Sharpe (1888) divided his series from the Santa Catalina Mountains, Ariz., into two subspecies.

With *eremoeca* the American Ornithologists' Union includes *A. r. tenuirostra* Burleigh and Lowery (1939) of extreme western Texas, although A. H. Miller (1941c) considered this "rather distinctive," differing from *eremoeca* by its "dark coloration and slender, less conical bill."

On the Great Plains there is no shortage of grass; thus rocky glades and edges of mesas become the limiting factor to *eremoeca*, as its old name "rock sparrow" told us. Farther west its habitat is like that of *scottii*—"boulder-strewn hillsides" in Brewster County, Texas (Van Tyne and Sutton, 1937). Its general habits (Simmons, 1925) hardly differ from those of *A. r. scottii*, save perhaps for the male's "singing from a conspicuous perch atop a small tree near the nest." A. P. Smith (1916) mentions a similar habit somewhat farther west.

*Nesting season.*—The generally better moisture conditions in early spring on the plains of Oklahoma, enable *eremoeca* to nest earlier there than is usual for *scottii*. Thus in the Arbuckle Mountains G. M. Sutton (MS.) took a female with a well defined brood patch and males with large testes on Apr. 17, 1954 at which time he also observed "several pairs" carrying food. Similarly in Quartz Mountains State Park, Greer County, he notes "several adults seen feeding young out of nests" May 4 to 6, 1956. Nesting continues through May, but apparently not all the birds nest at this time. Thus in the Wichita Mountains, June 4 and 5, 1929, Margaret M. Nice (1929) writes that "None of the many birds I had seen had been carrying food, nor had they objected in any way to my presence * * *" (though evidently singing was common), except for a single pair carrying food to young. No young on the wing are mentioned. Juvenal-plumaged young are apparently rare in eastern and central Oklahoma after July (Sutton, MS.), though in the west they were taken with molting adults in late September 1933 (Sutton, 1934). Of special interest is the finding (Sutton, MS.) that "great enlargement of the testes of a singing male in worn breeding feather taken in Arbuckle Mountains on Sept. 11, 1953, after an exceedingly dry summer, suggests that species may occasionally breed in fall when precipitation at that season assures a supply of insect food for young."

Nesting in central Texas is, curiously, somewhat later. Pairing apparently occurs in April, or earlier; the song was first heard at Boerne, near San Antonio, on Feb. 25, 1880 (N. C. Brown, 1882). Eggs have been found from Apr. 9 (1882, Comal County—Doe collection, Florida State Museum, *fide* W. G. F. Harris) to June 2 (1952, near Kerrville; "apparently nearly fresh"; L. R. Wolfe, MS.). In Bexar County it "nests in the latter part of May and in June" (Quillin and Holleman, 1918). While Simmons (1925) and Wolfe (MS) both suggest that two broods may be raised, this cannot yet be considered as an established fact. Interestingly, L. R. Wolfe writes me that "I don't believe that rains here have anything to do with their nesting." This would seem to be a worth-while subject for research.

PLATE 51

California                                    D. Bleitz

RUFOUS-CROWNED SPARROW

Whittier, Calif., April 12, 1942                R. Quigley, Jr.

NEST OF RUFOUS-CROWNED SPARROW

In western Texas the nesting season is probably the same as for *scottii*. Males taken here by Van Tyne Mar. 22, 1937 and Apr. 1, 1935 had small testes (data received by courtesy of H. B. Tordoff); while three specimens from the Chisos Mountains in July 1928 were in breeding condition—the females were carrying nesting material on July 9 and 18, and juvenal-plumaged specimens were also taken in July (Van Tyne and Sutton, 1937). In Presidio County H. W. Phillips and W. A. Thornton (1949) found nests "near the middle of June, [1948] some of which contained two eggs." In the Davis Mountains males sang vigorously to mid-September, 1916, and four young with "eyes not yet opened" were found on September 26; by then other young "retained only traces of the spotting on the breast" (A. P. Smith, 1917).

*Nesting.*—In the Austin region, Texas, George F. Simmons (1925) records some nests above ground, though always within 2 feet of ground level. These were "wedged in among thickly-sprouting, upward-growing branches of low bush or scrubby cedar tree." More usually nests were "under 12-inch ledge running horizontally along side of terraced slope near hill top." Contrary to Scott's description of nests of *A. r. scottii*, the Austin region nest is usually a "very pretty, compact, neat, deeply-cupped structure of fine cedar twigs, fine grass stems, a few narrow cedar bark strips, with considerable Indian tobacco or muslin weed in base; neatly and compactly lined with fine soft cedar bark fiber and other plant fibers, shredded and packed into a smooth-surface lining, into which a few fine grass seed stems have been woven; * * * sometimes containing horsehairs."

"Outside, diameter 3.30 by 3, height 2.65. Inside of cup, rim diameter 1.76 by 1.38, inside diameter 2.08 by 2.12, depth 1.80 [inches]."

From the Kerrville, Texas, area, L. R. Wolfe writes me that his experience is similar except that nests average higher, "most commonly in thick shin-oak bushes (*Quercus pungens Vaseyana*) about 12 to 18 inches from the ground. Another location is on or close to the ground in a spreading prickly pear cactus (*Opuntia Engelmanni*). * * * I have never seen a nest under a rock or any other overhang." Their nest is compact and well built of grasses and lined with soft grass. The nest differs from that of the Cassin sparrow in that the latter is often loosely built with many grass stems sticking out and appears straggly." This distinction evidently does not hold true in other regions, however. Nests in the shin-oaks varied from ground level (concealed by the branches) up to 60 centimeters above ground. A nest in the Chisos Mountains was "under soto[1], bulky, made of grass and lined with fine plant fibers" (F. M. Bailey, 1902). One near San Antonio was "on the ground in a tuft of grass near a running stream, and was composed of fine grass and lined with a few horse-hairs" (Attwater, 1892).

*Eggs.*—Clutches of four are listed from the Chisos Mountains, Texas, about June 1901 (F. M. Bailey, 1902); the Arbuckle Mountains, Okla., May 16, 1926 (Nice, 1931); and the Austin region, Texas, May 6, 1892, and May 1919 (Simmons, 1925). In the Kerrville, Texas, region, L. R. Wolfe finds "normally three or four, pure white." G. F. Simmons gives the variation as "three to five", and describes the egg as "plain white, with faint bluish tinge," 20 by 15.5 millimeters.

*Behavior.*—H. W. Phillips and W. A. Thornton (1949) flushed a bird that "fluttered about 10 feet from the nest feigning an injury in an attempt to distract us." Unfortunately the contents of the nest are not mentioned.

*Voice.*—The song of this sparrow seems to vary geographically. Florence M. Bailey (1928) describes one heard in northeastern New Mexico (presumably this race) as *"tchee-dle, tchee-dle, tchee-dle, tchee-dle, tchee-dle."* Margaret M. Nice (1929) says that in the Wichita Mountains, Okla., "The usual song is a chippering of six to nine notes, the first two-thirds ascending very slightly, the rest descending in a more marked degree. Its length was 1.2 to 1.5 seconds. When a bird was singing steadily, the number of songs per minute ranged from seven to nine, while the intervals from the beginning of one song to the beginning of the next varied from 4.5 to 10.7 seconds, the average of thirty-one being 7.3 seconds. The song is not loud, and to my mind not at all musical." She also describes a number of other songs, calls, and scolding notes, as does Simmons (1925). The latter gives the season of song near Austin, Texas, as Mar. 17, 1905 to July 18, 1915.

*Fall and winter.*—Most of the "proof" of migration in the rufous-crowned sparrow rests on this race. Long ago Robert Ridgway (1901) identified two grayish specimens from Veracruz and Puebla as migrants of *eremoeca*. I have not seen these specimens, but as Pierce Brodkorb (1948) records a grayish specimen taken in Veracruz in May, this evidence needs to be reviewed.

At its northern limit, in southernmost Kansas, the only two records for the species are in summer, but little work has been done there in winter, when small populations of *Aimophilae* easily escape detection. In adjacent Oklahoma, G. M. Sutton (MS.) finds "no evidence that species descends to lower elevations or changes habitat in any way in winter." He lists winter records for Cimarron, Jackson, Kiowa, Greer, Comanche, Murray, and Latimer counties. In northeastern Texas (Fort Worth–Dallas region) and the Kerrville region, Warren M. Pulich, Sr. (MS.) and L. R. Wolfe (MS.) have no records for migration or winter at any point far from the nesting areas. In northeastern New Mexico, however, some movement is suspected. On the plains 5 kilometers north of Estancia, Gloria Jean Penwell (MS.) saw a flock of about four to six birds in or about September 1954; and her cat brought in another bird about the same time, as well as one on May 6, 1954. Unfortunately, unaware of the problems, she failed to preserve the specimens. The subspecies would in any case be doubtful here.

There is, to be sure, a published report of the rufous-crowned sparrow's presence in "an invasion of western birds" at Corpus Christi, on the Gulf coast of Texas, on Apr. 30, 1946 (Williams, 1950), but as no specimens are mentioned of any of the species listed, most of which are hard to identify, these records cannot be considered unquestionably reliable. Curiously, all the records to date for the species in Utah (Zion National Park) are for the winter.

### DISTRIBUTION

*Range.*—Southeastern Colorado and central Oklahoma south to Puebla and northern Veracruz.

*Breeding range.*—The rock rufous-crowned sparrow breeds from southeastern Colorado (Regnier, Baca County; probably Trinidad) and northwestern and central Oklahoma (Cimarron County, Arnett, Arbuckle Mountains) south through eastern New Mexico (Carlsbad) and western Texas (Frijole) to central Coahuila (50 miles south of Monclova) and southern Texas (San Antonio).

*Winter range.*—Winters north to northern Texas (Palo Duro Canyon) and central southern Oklahoma (Arbuckle Mountains), south to Puebla (Chachapa) and central western Veracruz (Maltrata).

*Casual record.*—Casual in southwestern Kansas (Comanche County).

*Migration.*—Data on migration are sadly lacking. Late dates of spring departure are: Hidalgo—Jacala, April 11. Texas—Taylor County, May 1.

*Egg dates.*—Texas: 28 records, April 4 to June 19; 14 records, May 1 to May 31.

### AIMOPHILA RUFICEPS SCOTTII (Sennett)

## Scott's Rufous-crowned Sparrow
### Contributed by ALLAN R. PHILLIPS

### HABITS

The rufous-crowned is an unobtrusive sparrow. Squeak or imitate an owl and it may fly up onto a rock to inspect you, but soon it will retire to the grass, low *Agave* masses, or behind a bush again, for this is its home—rocky, open slopes in the oak belt or just below it in or near the Upper Sonoran Zone. Occasionally one flies up onto a bush or a low oak limb when danger threatens his family or to sing, but most of its life is spent on the ground, except perhaps at night. In Mexico the species' habitat is more variable locally (Phillips, 1962).

In the Huachuca Mountains, Ariz., Frank C. Willard (1912b) found the species "most common on the scantily covered lower ridges and foothills, where scattering oaks, madrona, and scrubby mountain mahogany are the only trees, together with plenty of bear grass and mescal plants. They much prefer slopes with a southerly exposure," which of course are the less heavily vegetated slopes. The same preference for grassy, south-facing slopes is mentioned by F. M. Bailey (1923).

The haunts of *scottii* are not those generally favored by man. Only W. E. D. Scott has actually lived among them. Thus it is not surprising that information is still scanty on a species that keeps well hidden behind grass, brush, or rocks most of the time. In the un-spoiled Arizona of 1876 Aiken (1937) found it "one of the most common and characteristic birds" at Seven-mile Hill, near Fort Apache. "The true home is in a secluded little ravine opening into a larger ravine or cañon, and if the latter contains a stream, so much the better. I have found them breeding, however, several miles from any water. I have never found them anywhere there was not the coarse mountain bunch grass of the country growing. A few low bushes and perhaps an old dead fallen tree are usually present in this sparrow's home."

In this species we find to a lesser extent the same problem of year-to-year variation in breeding season that so complicates the study of the related *A. carpalis*, the rufous-winged sparrow. But luckily *A. ruficeps* has a higher, more uniform environment and normally nests earlier, so the contrast between normal and abnormal years is less striking. On the other hand, interpretation is correspondingly more difficult.

Few if any climatic data are available for the haunts of the rufous-crowned sparrow. The reader must refer to the chart given for Tucson rainfall under *A. carpalis carpalis*. This chart, of course, is less exact when applied to the home of *A. ruficeps* in the surrounding mountains, where rainfall is greater, but the trends should be roughly parallel. (The year 1936, not shown on the chart, was marked by heavy snowfall at Flagstaff in late March.)

*Spring.*—W. E. D. Scott (1886) saw rufous-crowned sparrows most commonly from the last of February to mid-October in the Santa Catalina Mountains, Ariz. He apparently thought this was due to emigration of part of the population in winter, but it seems more likely that March to October is the period of sexual and family activity so the birds are less inconspicuous. He "noted the birds as beginning to sing and mate [i.e., pair?] as early as the middle of March," which made him think (mistakenly?) that "The species raises three broods at this point, and * * * the breeding season extends over a period of five months." While this seems unlikely, detailed observations of what rufous-crowned sparrows actually do in late March, April, and May of both normal and wet years are still lacking and most urgently needed.

*Nesting season.*—In Arizona during normal, dry springs the first eggs are laid about the end of May or in early June. In the Huachuca Mountains F. C. Willard (1912b) found eggs with "incubation advanced" May 24, 1907, and "newly hatched young May 25," which he considered exceptional. Unfortunately he failed to specify the year in the latter case. He states that "fresh eggs may be looked for after May 20," with the first week of June being the "height of the nesting season." Later he (Willard, 1913) found them "nesting regularly during August" 1913, having taken his last set of "nearly fresh" eggs on August 15.

My own observations agree with the above to a great extent. Thus, I have heard singing east of Tucson as early as Mar. 18, 1939, and the abundance of young in early fall shows that the July and August nests reported by W. E. D. Scott and F. C. Willard were perfectly normal. In fact Seymour H. Levy (MS.) found birds incubating eggs (two and three, respectively) near Arivaca, southern Pima County, on Sept. 5, 1960. Farther south, in Nayarit, Mexico, I have taken young (of a darker race) still not fully grown (tail 46.8 millimeters) on Oct. 24, 1957; and in Oaxaca (grown, but not far into the postjuvenal or first prebasic molt) on Nov. 23, 1958.

In wet years in Arizona, the story is different. Thus it is unfortunate that Scott did not give further details on why he thought breeding commenced in mid-March; for my wet year studies yield dates exactly between this period and F. C. Willard's. While agreeing with Willard that even newly hatched young are unusual on May 25, nevertheless I took full-grown young May 26, 1952 in the Santa Catalina Mountains—a young male from each of two different families which differed in the amount and heaviness of streaking. Both showed some apparent first-basic plumage beside the lower back; probably this area produces no juvenal plumage, for neither was molting there. Both had pin feathers on the breast and in different parts of the upper surface; one also had some on the legs but was not in obvious first prebasic molt. The other had begun this molt, and its testes were already 1½ by 1 millimeters.

The 1958 rains had much less effect in the same place; my companions and I found no young on May 25 and only one family on

June 10. A female from the latter group had a tail measuring 30½ millimeters.

Other early breeding records in Arizona are as follows: a juvenal female, tail 65 millimeters (nearly fully grown), was taken in the Santa Rita Mountains, May 23, 1940 (Sutton, 1943; tail condition *fide* Richard R. Graber, MS.); at Aravaipa Creek near Klondyke, Graham County, J. S. Rowley (MS.) took a juvenal (tail 18 millimeters) on May 30, 1936; and Seymour H. Levy (MS.) found a nest with three eggs in the southeastern corner of the state May 13, 1960.

The total rainfall in years when early singing or nesting was recorded was not necessarily exceptional. Thus in the winters of 1938–39 and 1939–40, rainfall at Tucson was below the mean (calculated arithmetical average) in every month from October to April, except February; rainfall was particularly low in 1939–40, when the total October-through-January rainfall barely exceeded the February total of 36 millimeters and March and April yielded only 9 millimeters.

The winters of 1906–07 and 1935–36 followed a different pattern. Rainfall was well above normal in December and January (1906–07) and November and December (1935), dropping gradually to below mean figures in February 1907 and March 1936, but never seriously below the median rainfall after October. Thus proper, moist ecological conditions in February or March seem to produce the occasional April nests, regardless of the preceding rainfall.

In Mexico the unusually early nests in some years are obviously attributable to the early start of the summer rains, as most of the country has no winter rainy season. Thus W. J. Schaldach, Jr., took a female with a greatly enlarged ovary in Jalisco on May 10, 1959, a year when the rains began 2 months early (in mid-April), and I took another on May 15, 1959, which had apparently started an unsuccessful nest as its oviduct was swollen and its ovary contained what appeared to be a corpus luteum.

*Nesting.*—The rufous-crowned sparrow commonly nests on the ground, usually near or under a clump of grass, sometimes at the foot of a sotol or a sapling. W. E. D. Scott (1886) describes the nest as "very bulky for so small a bird * * * loosely and carelessly put together * * * of coarse, dried grasses throughout * * * no attempt at lining with any finer material. The interior diameter is two and three-quarters inches, and the interior depth one inch and a half. The walls are about one inch thick, but in places the grasses are allowed to straggle about in so careless a manner that the walls seem at least two inches in thickness." G. M. Sutton and A. R. Phillips (1942) report a nest lined with deer hair. I know of no nests of *scottii* found above ground level (see *A. r. eremoeca*, above).

*Eggs.*—The eggs, usually three in number in Arizona, vary (for the species as a whole) from two to five. They are ovate, slightly glossy, very pale bluish-white, and unmarked. The measurements of 71 eggs average 20.0 by 15.6 millimeters; the eggs showing the four extremes measure *22.8* by *16.8*, *17.9* by 15.7, and 19.1 by *14.2* millimeters.

*Incubation.*—The rufous-crowned sparrow is a very close sitter. The incubating bird usually does not fly until nearly stepped on, and thus betrays the whereabouts of the nest. No detailed studies of incubation or care of the young have been made.

*Plumages.*—The juvenal plumage is rather variable. Usually it is heavily streaked with dusky on the chest, sides, crown, and back; these streaks are sometimes so faint that they are hardly noticeable until in the hand. The streaks are never conspicuous on the dark brown background of the upperparts. This background color varies considerably in hue and depth, but is never pale and sandy as in *A. carpalis*. The variation is especially conspicuous on the upper tail coverts. Similarly, the whiskermark is often obscure, and the deep grayish median crown stripe is hardly visible except in the most dusky-crowned individuals. Below the pale superciliary is a hint of an eyeline of the same color as the dark crown; this becomes a rufous eye stripe, as in adults, about as soon as the bird is fully grown. Before then the white eye ring is about the only conspicuous head marking. Very young birds have narrow, dull buffy wing bars.

The first prebasic or postjuvenal molt varies somewhat, probably according to when the bird was hatched. In Arizona and Sonora it rarely involves the tail or the primary coverts, and perhaps never the inner ones. The body, tertials, and lesser and secondary coverts are regularly molted; the primaries and alula are molted less frequently. This molting time varies but molting is probably completed in most cases by November 1, at which stage young and old look alike.

I have detected no prenuptial or prealternate molt. Adults molt late—in Arizona the molt is completed about early November. To the south in Oaxaca, a female *A. r. australis* was in heavy molt, but still not far advanced into it, on Nov. 23, 1958.

It should be mentioned that young males I took in Arizona Apr. 20 and 27, 1958 still had the occipital part of the skull partly or wholly unossified; yet they were in breeding condition. Under favorable weather conditions, therefore, they may breed when less than a year old. Also the rate of ossification of the skull may sometimes lag, being far slower than in most small songbirds; for these males could hardly be less than 7½ months old; one still had frontal windows as well in the skull. Further, the apparently breeding female from Jalisco, May 15, 1959, still shows indications of windows laterally in the occipital region.

*Food.*—The food of the rufous-crowned sparrow apparently varies considerably according to season and locality—depending largely on its availability and condition. Probably the young are fed largely or wholly on insects and insect larvae, as in *A. r. eremoeca* (Nice, 1929), though no data are available. Later the food varies greatly. Patrick J. Gould took stomachs with about 80 percent animal matter on Oct. 23 and Nov. 4, 1960; but others he examined November 12 and February 13 and 17 held 95 to 100 percent plant material, aside, of course, from the inevitable gravel.

The above data suggest a simple seasonal change of diet, but the stomachs of Mexican specimens, kindly examined for me by Leonila Vásquez and others of the Instituto de Biología, Universidad Nacional Autónoma de México, do not bear this out. The above-mentioned female of May 15, 1959 and another of Oct. 4, 1961 had eaten largely seeds; while a male from arid southwestern Oaxaca (May 7, 1962) was feeding mostly on insects.

The plant material ingested was largely small, unidentified seeds. But the November 12 female (an adult from the Graham or Pinaleno Mountains, Ariz.) held "95+ percent short lengths of fresh grass stems" (P. J. Gould, MS.); and the February 17 female had eaten "many tender plant shoots and a lot of unidentifiable bulk" besides, of course, seeds. Animals eaten include arthropods of many kinds, mostly small beetles and orthopterans; Coccinellidae and grasshoppers are the only important groups identified. Others ingested occasionally were spiders, ants, mosquito, Anthomyiid fly, cockroach, mantis, wasp, aphid, leafhopper, and an adult butterfly or moth.

*Behavior.*—When we make occasional visits to its haunts, the rufous-crowned sparrow seems almost a will-o'-the-wisp. It flushes from the roadside or low brush and dives into the grass, *Agave* mats, or rocks, never to reappear. Only singing males or anxious parents let us really see them. But when accustomed to man, they evidently lose this shyness. Living among them, W. E. D. Scott (1887) found them "quite tame and familiar, coming to feed on grain and crumbs daily about my house."

Aiken (1937) writes:

If I am walking near where one is feeding in the grass it mounts upon a log or the under branches of a tree to see what is going on, where he remains silent and motionless except [for] perhaps a jerking of the tail. If excited he hops around uneasily with the tail raised at an angle of 45 degrees and if frightened it dives in the long grass. It is almost useless to pursue them after they are once aroused. * * * I sometimes find them among the thick low bushes of the creek bottom, but think they have only resorted to such places for water or food.

Nowadays they seldom have to get up into trees to see above the pitiful remnants of grass.

*Voice.*—The characteristic location note of the rufous-crowned sparrow is a clear, thin, descending *teew*, usually given in a series of three. The song is hardly as musical as this call, being a staccato chittering that usually changes its pitch two or three times in the course of the outpouring. Aiken (1937) likens it to a softened house wren's song. There are also the usual short sparrow alarm notes. As befits a bird usually well hidden, the calls and song carry well, and may often be heard across a small canyon or barranca. The song is usually delivered from atop a rock or bush, or from low in a small tree. It is often introduced by three longer, somewhat more distinct and spaced out *chips*. In Nayarit I heard a faint, rising *seep*, like that of a green-tailed or rufous-sided towhee, which I attribute to this species. Presumably some fathers of small young give the extraordinary performances of *A. r. eremoeca* also (Nice, 1929).

*Field marks.*—Besides the voice, the principal field mark is a complete white eye ring, set off against solidly dark cheeks and sides of the neck. The pale malar area is bordered by a sharp black line below, but not above. Otherwise the bird is very plain, adults having no dark or pale streaks, wing bars, tail patches, or central crown stripe. The pale gray superciliary in adults is bordered by rufous above (whole crown) and below (line back from eye); it passes into white at and before the eye.

*Enemies.*—Presumably the rufous-crowned sparrow is not immune to the enemies of most sparrows, but little is known of the subject. Its habitat is not generally attractive to either *Accipiter* hawks or cowbirds, and its principal losses might thus be attributed to snakes and mammalian predators. H. Friedmann (1963) lists no record of cowbird parasitism. Very likely, however, the old report of a brown-headed cowbird parasitizing a rufous-winged sparrow at San Antonio, Texas, really refers to this species; *A. carpalis* does not occur in Texas.

*Fall and winter.*—There can be no doubt that most rufous-crowned sparrows remain on or near their breeding grounds in winter, in singles or pairs. They evidently descend from higher altitudes to the adjacent high Lower Sonoran Zone during times of deep snow. They do not form flocks.

The question of whether some individuals migrate remains open. I have received several reports of rufous-crowned sparrows at points well away from any breeding haunts in migration or winter; but in no case was the identity proved by a specimen; nor was the bird even trapped in the cases of the Arizona reports. The one valid published record of a migrant probably of this race is from Sulphur Springs Valley (presumably), Ariz., Apr. 18, 1895 (Osgood, 1903).

The reports of Visher (1910) on this, *A. carpalis*, and other birds are obviously erroneous.

## DISTRIBUTION

*Range.*—Scott's rufous-crowned sparrow is resident from central northern and eastern Arizona (Grand Canyon, Fort Apache) and southwestern New Mexico (Catron County) south to central southern Arizona (Ajo and Baboquívari mountains), northeastern Sonora (Rancho La Arizona; La Chumata), and northwestern Chihuahua (Babícora).

*Egg dates.*—Arizona: 4 records, June 14 to August 15.

### AIMOPHILA RUFICEPS RUPICOLA van Rossem
# Harquahala Rufous-crowned Sparrow
## Contributed by ALLAN R. PHILLIPS

### HABITS

This race was described from the Harquahala Mountains, Ariz.; van Rossem (1946b) says it is:

Similar in size and proportions to *Aimophila ruficeps scottii* * * * but coloration everywhere grayer and darker. Dorsal edgings, together with rump, "Deep Grayish Olive" instead of "Light Grayish Olive"; chest, sides, and flanks, "Olive-Gray" instead of "Smoke Gray"; chin, throat, and median under parts darker, grayer (less buffy white), and in distinctly less contrast to the pectoral region and sides; crown and reddish brown areas of feathers of the upper parts darker; dorsal streaking narrower with gray edgings correspondingly broader.

A. R. Phillips and W. M. Pulich (1948) referred 10 specimens from the Ajo Mountains, also in western Arizona, to *rupicola*. In fact, all of the material that I have seen from western Arizona, and some from western Sonora (the Sierra San Antonio–Sierra Aconchi area) seems to be dark. In any case, *rupicola* is not a strongly marked race; it is doubtful that its life history differs significantly from that of *scottii*.

### DISTRIBUTION

*Range.*—The Harquahala rufous-crowned sparrow is resident in the Harquahala Mountains of western Arizona.

AIMOPHILA RUFICEPS RUFICEPS (Cassin)

## California Rufous-crowned Sparrow

PLATE 51

Contributed by HOWARD L. COGSWELL

### HABITS

John Cassin (1852) described the bird now known as the rufous-crowned sparrow from specimens A. L. Heermann collected on the Calaveras River, California, presumably in foothills east of Stockton and thus in the northern part of the range of the nominate race as it is now designated. Four years later, and presumably from the same specimens, J. Cassin (1856) illustrated the species nicely in color. However he still gave it the most inappropriate vernacular name of "western swamp sparrow," stating that the birds "live in the vicinity of the shores of the ocean and the margins of streams of fresh water." How he obtained such a completely erroneous idea of the habitat of this predominantly dry hill country bird is not clear. Apparently all he had to base it on were A. L. Heermann's skimpy notes, which he quotes as follows: "In the fall of 1851, I met with a single specimen of this bird, in company with a flock of sparrows of various kinds. In the spring of 1852, I found it quite abundant on the Calaveras River, where I procured several specimens. Its flight appeared feeble, and when raised from the ground, from which it would not start until almost trodden upon, it would fly a short distance, and immediately drop again into the grass."

Its shy nature and inconspicuous song, coupled with the discomfort attending any pursuit or wait for such a bird in its typical habitat of dry hillside grass with scattered or open brush or rocks, are doubtless partly responsible for the scant attention given this species since the 1850s. In the San Francisco Bay region Joseph Grinnell and Margaret W. Wythe (1927) refer to it as being "closely restricted to open sunny hillsides clothed sparsely with chaparral particularly California sage." In that region this plant (*Artemisia californica*) is widespread on steep, south- or west-facing slopes with poor or little soil (Grinnell, 1914b). William Brewster (1879) states, based upon information from C. A. Allen of Marin County, that:

"They * * * are found in considerable numbers every season on all the mountains about Nicasio. Black Mountain, however, seems to be their stronghold. It is destitute of forests and the exceedingly steep, rocky sides are abundantly clothed with 'wild oats' and a bush very like the sweet-scented southern-wood. Another shrub, called by hunters the 'spit-bush' is also characteristic of the locality, which is otherwise dry, and barren to a degree. The males sing from the tops of these low bushes."

While we might wish for a more detailed description of this area where the nests of the species were first found and described, it is obviously typical rufous-crowned sparrow habitat. Joseph Grinnell and A. H. Miller (1944) summarize most succinctly the habitats the race *ruficeps* prefers as follows: "Hillsides that are grass covered and grown to sparse low bushes, scarcely dense enough to constitute true chaparral. Rarely bushes may be absent if rock outcrops are present. Slopes frequented are sunny and well drained. Marked preference is shown for California sage (*Artemisia californica*). This in its typical open growth, associated with grass tussocks, is adhered to exclusively by these sparrows in many areas."

The mixture of low shrubs and grass they emphasize as this sparrow's prime habitat often includes other plants that they probably use. On the outer coastal mountains Hubert O. Jenkins (1906) found the species at Big Sur and at Mount Mars, Monterey County, where I have seen them in April and December of recent years on the steep slope just above a high sea cliff where golden yarrow (*Eriophyllum staechadifolium*), mock-heather (*Haplopappus ericoides*), low-growing coyote brush (*Baccharis pilularis*), poison oak (*Rhus diversiloba*), and many broad-leaved herbs grow amid the sagebrush and grass. However, where the shrubs are too dense in this coastal area rufous-crowned sparrows are absent.

In the inner coast ranges and presumably the western foothills of the Sierra Nevada, black sage (*Salvia mellifera*) and other low shrubs mix with or replace the *Artemisia*, and the grass and other herbs between the shrubs are often much sparser in this area, which is occupied by rufous-crowns, than near the coast. J. Grinnell and T. I. Storer (1924) emphasize that scattered low bushes on the driest slopes form this race's habitat at El Portal and Pleasant Valley near the eastern limit of its range in the Sierra Nevada foothills. In both the coastal and inner foothill areas the open spacing of these types of short shrubs, as well as their soft, often woolly leaves and relatively thin, flexuous twigs characterize the vegetation types known as coastal scrub or coastal sage scrub, as distinct from the taller, stiffer, harsher-leaved chaparral.

The rufous-crowned sparrow is, in fact, one of the most characteristic birds of the coastal scrub and undoubtedly reaches its highest population levels in that type of vegetation, whether on the foggy coast itself or in the sunny interior foothills. This race is also reported occasionally where true chaparral is regrowing after fires and is consequently still low and sparse. J. Grinnell (1905d) found them daily from Aug. 29 to Sept. 4, 1904 in a ravine near the base of Black Mountain, Santa Clara County, "only on a southern hillside covered with a low growth of greasewood brush (*Adenostoma*)." In the Poso

Range of Kern County H. Sheldon (1909a) found the species "quite plentiful * * * inhabiting the wild gooseberry thickets in the canyons and in such patches growing among rock piles on the hills." Scattered trees, usually oaks, may also be present in some areas where rufous-crowned sparrows breed, but as J. R. Pemberton (1910) notes in the hills of southern Alameda County, "The birds seldom leave the bushes for the oaks, their favorite perches being the tops of the sage."

Harry S. Swarth (1917) notes this race in shrubless foothill areas east of Fresno: "As many as ten or twelve might be observed in the course of half an hour. The hills they frequented are devoid of brush or trees of any sort, and the sparrows resorted for shelter to the numerous rock piles and outcroppings. Here, in company with a large Rock Wren population, they seemed to find congenial surroundings despite the lack of vegetation of a size to afford shelter."

*Spring and courtship.*—Despite references to it in the early literature as a summer resident, the rufous-crowned sparrow is apparently essentially a permanent resident wherever it occurs in California. The onset of regular singing in March was probably the feature that called this otherwise obscure bird to Charles Allen's attention in Marin County at that season (Brewster, 1879). Near Milpitas, Santa Clara County, Barlow (1902) found them present in pairs in a nesting area as early as March 23, but apparently not yet nesting; the males were singing despite a cold north wind.

No notes on the courtship of the race *ruficeps* seem to have been published, and the literature contains no precise account of the behavior of adults of the species during this phase of the breeding cycle; presumably it differs little from that of *A. r. canescens* which will be described farther on.

*Nesting.*—Nearly all authors who have reported finding nests of this species have commented on the difficulty of locating them. Nests are apparently almost always on the ground, and usually sunk into a small hollow so the nest rim is flush with the ground surface (Grinnell and Wythe, 1927). Charles G. Sibley (MS.) reports them "rarely in bushes close to the ground."

Brewster (1877) describes the first nest Charles A. Allen found on Black Mountain near Nicasio, Marin County, July 10, 1875, as: "very loosely put together, and the original shape is so nearly destroyed that measurements are almost impracticable. An approximation would, however, be nearly as follows: External diameter, 4 inches; internal, 2.25 inches. External depth, 2 inches; internal, 1.25 inches. * * * The locality was an open heathy tract on the mountain-side, and the nest was placed on the ground under a bush."

Writing of a nest he found in the hills beyond Hayward, Livermore, and Mount Hamilton July 8, 1908, Pemberton (1910) says it "was a poor affair—simply a few dry grasses * * * arranged on one side and part of the bottom of an irregular hole on the edge of a bank along the side of a small gully. The eggs rested upon the earth with a few grasses crost between * * *." The photographs accompanying the account show several oaks along the draw near the bottom of which the nest site is shown.

The most detailed account of the nest and associated behavior of this race is that of Chester Barlow (1902) based on his observations of "a colony" near Milpitas, Santa Clara County. He does not mention the locality in his account, but it is on his specimen labels of the same dates in the collections of the Museum of Vertebrate Zoology at Berkeley. He writes: "This particular hill possesses a decidedly scraggly growth of sage, and why it was chosen in preference to some heavily covered hill which might afford secure protection, is best known to the birds themselves. Perhaps the stone wall * * * and the adjacent road afford a generous food supply. It should be mentioned also that a small country schoolhouse lies just across the road * * *." After a considerable search back and forth over the hill, J. Grinnell found a nest. Chester Barlow (1902) continues:

The nest was sunk flush in the ground, being built partly under a sage root, and contained four eggs with a very perceptible light bluish tinge. * * * We sat down at a distance but not a sound came from the female, who had flushed and disappeared. After perhaps 10 minutes of quiet watching the bird appeared up the hill but was extremely wary. She flew past the bush and alighted, but would not go to the nest. Then she flew up the hill again, when I collected her. Dissection showed the set to be complete [and the eggs slightly incubated].

The nest mentioned was substantially built * * *. It was composed outwardly of grass, grass roots, a few small twigs and fibers. The lining was almost entirely of horsehair. The outside diameter was six inches, the inside three inches. Depth inside, 1½ inches; outside three inches. The front or exposed rim of the nest was much thicker than the back.

The clumped distribution of breeding pairs Barlow noted was also reported by J. R. Pemberton (1910) who says: "Colonies are the rule, and the writer found usually a dozen pairs in the confines of a two or three acre hillside." It is doubtful that *breeding* pairs ever attain this density, even in optimum habitat, but no accurate censuses of such areas have been reported for this race. I have often encountered isolated pairs in the small patches of coastal scrub containing sagebrush that border the woodland tongues or occupy small steep slopes away from the trees in the hills from Berkeley to Hayward, east of San Francisco Bay.

Joseph Grinnell and Margaret W. Wythe (1927) give the nesting season in the San Francisco Bay region as "the last of April to well into July"; their extreme dates for fresh eggs of April 27 and July 8 apparently refer to the two nests described above. J. Grinnell and T. I. Storer (1924) obtained a fully fledged juvenile in the Yosemite foothills May 25, 1915 and concluded that nesting evidently began there in April. C. G. Sibley (MS.) cites records near Milpitas for newly hatched young ranging from March 22 to August 1, indicating that the earliest nesting attempts begin at least by early March. The great span of dates involved led William Brewster (1879) and William L. Dawson (1923) to believe two broods might sometimes be raised, but no evidence shows the later ones are not renestings after failures.

*Eggs.*—The eggs are usually four in number in California, but vary from two to five for the species as a whole. They are ovate, slightly glossy, very pale bluish-white, and unmarked. For measurements see the section on *A. r. scottii*. Chester Barlow (1902) notes that some sets are pure white.

*Incubation.*—It seems incredible that the length of the incubation period has never been determined for this species, but I can find no mention of it in the literature. The early oologists attributed the small number of nests found of this common species to the closeness with which the incubating female sits. W. Brewster (1879) wrote that the sitting bird steals away silently under cover of the surrounding vegetation and is likely to be mistaken for a startled mouse. Whether this performance is the stereotyped "rodent run" distraction display described for other ground nesting birds by E. Duffey and N. Creasey (1950), A. H. Miller (1951c), and others is not certain.

*Young.*—Published data on the nestlings and their length of stay in the nest also appear to be lacking for this race. Nor, apparently, has anyone recorded the length of parental care of the young after leaving the nest. Most young out of the nest are found from May to August, though extreme dates (Sibley, MS.) are much earlier. Hubert O. Jenkins (1906) reports seeing many "immatures" between June 16 and July 18 in the coast ranges of Monterey County. I have noted juveniles, apparently independent of parents, in the hills east of Oakland from July 1 to September 1.

Roger Simpson (1925) caught and photographed four fledglings apparently just out of a nest in the Berkeley Hills May 4, 1924. Both adults appeared and scolded his intrusion; the one which was "of a quieter disposition and was much less concerned" he assumed was the male. When he placed the fledglings on a stump, the presumed female was there with food for them within a few seconds.

*Plumages.*—The only reference given by David K. Wetherbee (1957) on the downy plumage of this species is from a statement by Harriet W. Myers (1909) that "the orange-skinned nestlings were partially covered with tufts of black down." The young begin in the nest to acquire the juvenal plumage which they wear for several months.

Most young leave the nest before they are completely covered by a coat of feathers, with the wings and tail only partly grown.

The juvenal plumage of this species, according to Robert Ridgway (1901), is "Much like [the] adults, but pileum dull brown, obsoletely streaked with darker; back more narrowly streaked with darker brown; chest narrowly streaked with dusky brown, and submalar streak indistinct or obsolete." The greater secondary coverts are margined with buffy in the juvenile and with grayish in the adult. Often the tail feathers are more acute than in the adult birds, but this character is variable and not a completely reliable one for aging individuals.

Probably some young begin the postjuvenal molt within 6 to 8 weeks after leaving the nest. The earliest records of individuals in the initial stages of the postjuvenal molt are in mid-June. Young hatched later may not begin the molt until late August or early September. The many young birds found later in the year in the early stages of the molt that have not completed growth of the tail feathers suggests that late-hatched young begin the postjuvenal molt at a younger age than those hatched earlier.

The postjuvenal molt usually begins on the mid-back and scapular regions. From there it spreads both anteriorly and posteriorly along the back at the same time as the breast and sides are beginning to molt. Some individuals may begin the breast and side molt simultaneously with or even before the back molt. Usually the forehead begins to show new feathers as the breast feathers are replaced. The last areas to molt are the lower parts of the back and abdomen, the under tail coverts, and the sides of the head and neck.

Molt of the flight feathers occurs as the body molt is nearing completion. While the body molt is invariably complete, the wing feathers are replaced to different degrees in different individuals. Most individuals replace one or more of the primaries and secondaries. If only a few are changed, they are the outer feathers on the primary tract and the secondaries closest to the body. Presumably this partial replacement includes those feathers that are most subject to wear in this sparrow's rather harsh environment. Usually all the tail feathers are molted; occasional birds may retain all the juvenal tail feathers until after the first breeding season.

The only regular normal molt after the postjuvenal molt is the postnuptial, which takes place annually after the breeding effort. This molt renews the complete feather coat. The new feathers are identical in color to those being replaced in all birds 2 years of age and older. The species has no prenuptial molt, and in the breeding season the birds are attired in their most worn plumage.

The adult plumage of *ruficeps* has the forehead and crown rusty with grayish margins on the feathers in fresh plumage. The lores and a small median forehead stripe are whitish; the superciliary is gray. The back is reddish-brown, the feathers margined broadly with grayish brown; the rump and upper tail coverts are brown, the coverts tipped with grayish. Ventrally the adult has a whitish throat with a black "whisker" mark; the mid-abdomen is also whitish. The breast and sides are grayish brown and the flanks buffy brown. The wings are dark brown edged with reddish-brown which shades to whitish on the outer primaries. The secondary coverts and primary coverts are dark brown edged with grayish. The tail is dark rusty.

Compared with other races of *A. ruficeps:*

ADULT PLUMAGE:

*A. r. obscura*—like *ruficeps* but colors darker. Back feathers with darker centers.

*A. r. canescens*—like *ruficeps* but reds and grays darker. . Approaches *obscura* in darkness.

*A. r. sororia*—like *ruficeps* but averages lighter, especially ventrally, and red of head and back not as dark.

JUVENAL PLUMAGE:

*A. r. obscura* and *A. r. canescens* average darker than *A. r. ruficeps*, especially the breast streaks. *A. r. sororia* seems to retain all its juvenal primaries through the postjuvenal molt more often than the other races do.—Larry Wolf

*Food.*—In Chester Barlow's (1902) detailed account of the food habits of the species, most of the data probably refer to this race:

In two stomachs collected [locality unnamed] by Prof. Beal on June 27, 1901, the average of vegetable matter was 97% and of animal matter 3%. In eighteen stomachs collected by Mr. Grinnell and myself on Sept. 22, 1901 [doubtless near Milpitas], the average of vegetable matter is 88.4% and of animal matter 11.6%; one stomach collected March 16, 1902, vegetable and animal matter each 50%; one stomach collected April 27, 1902, vegetable matter 6% and animal matter 94%. The food of the June specimens consisted of small oats, Erodium, grass seeds and Hymenoptera. Those taken in September had a more varied bill of fare, consisting of crickets, carabid beetles, ants, grasshoppers, Hymenoptera and one olive scale, chickweed, Polygonum, Amaranthus, Erodium and oats. Grasshoppers in the animal and wild oats in the vegetable food seem to largely predominate. One March stomach contained Hymenoptera and Hemiptera and unidentified seeds, while the April specimen showed Chrysomelid and Lampyrid beetles, Jassids, Arachnids, oats and Erodium.

Thus a decided shift from seeds to insects is manifest during the nesting season in spring. W. Brewster (1879) remarks that the food "consists largely of grubs and a certain green worm" which C. A. Allen saw the parents carrying to the young. The food brought to the fledglings Roger Simpson (1925) posed to photograph "consisted mostly of white grubs and small caterpillars, with an occasional black insect or tiny butterfly."

Foraging rufous-crowned sparrows usually keep on or close to the ground, hopping slowly about over or through the herbaceous layer and low shrubs. On several occasions I have seen birds of the race *ruficeps* apparently foraging in taller shrubs and low oak trees.

*Behavior.*—Ever since John Cassin's (1856) first account of the habits of this species, observers have remarked upon the bird's tendency to remain hidden when approached. Still it is not so skulking when approached carefully as, for instance, a grasshopper sparrow. J. Grinnell and A. H. Miller (1944) summarize the many earlier comments: "Within the grass and beneath the bushes the birds forage and find retreats from disturbance, staying on or close to the ground most of the time and out of sight in the cover. Flights over the bush tops are rapid and short and usually down hill. Occasionally when alarmed or curious, and when singing, bush tops and rocks are mounted in order to survey the terrain."

Though usually not a door-yard bird, the rufous-crowned sparrow may become so where houses have been built on its favored hillside haunts. J. Grinnell (1914a) describes how, at a hillside home in Berkeley, "this ordinarily reclusive species has come to be a familair door-yard bird, even entering the house regularly, when allowed to, to be fed. The parent birds have brought their young there from the adjacent hill-slope for several successive seasons."

Ordinarily such small family groups of five or six are the largest "flocks" of rufous-crowned sparrows one encounters, for it is quite nongregarious, at least throughout most of California. Some of the earlier reports of compact flocks (such as that by Esterly, 1920) feeding on open garden plots and in trees are almost certainly based on misidentifications.

*Voice.*—In my experience rufous-crowned sparrows have three main call notes. First, and most like that of other emberizids, is a soft, high-pitched *sssssp* of 1 to 1½ seconds duration, which both sexes use throughout the year, apparently as a location or contact note. Second, but heard less frequently than either the first or the third, is a sharp *tsip* note, the significance of which is not clear, unless it is the same as the short, sharp scolding note "given as rapidly as possible" to which Harriet W. Myers (1922) refers. This brief note also has some resemblance to the louder, more piercing alarm notes of the towhee and other fringillids. The third call which is most characteristic of the species, at least in California, is a nasal *dew, dew-dew* or *tew-tew-tew*, with a slight rise and then fall in pitch usually evident in each short note. The notes may be given singly or run on into a long series on occasion. W. L. Dawson (1923) renders the call by the same syllables, and J. Grinnell and T. I. Storer (1924) very similarly write them *kiew, kiew, kew-kew-kew*. Harriet W. Myers (1922) implies an *r* quality with *dear, dear, dear,* as does Margaret M. Nice (1929) in describing an apparently homologous vocalization in *A. r. eremoeca* in Oklahoma as "a queer nasal *pur-pur-pur*" and at another point *peer*. C. Barlow (1902) spells what is evidently the same note as *quirk, quirk*.

Given singly or in short series, the *dew-dew* note seems to convey mild alarm or alertness to danger. Hence it is often the first note a person hears when entering a rufous-crowned sparrow's domain. At Oakland on Feb. 19, 1955, a previously silent bird gave this call from the brush when a sparrow hawk flew low over the hillside. At times this or a similar note is uttered in a longer, stuttering series. R. Simpson (1925) writes that the most characteristic call of a pair with fledglings at Berkeley "was a very loud, clear *r-r-rup, chur, chur chur chur*" which "had good carrying qualities and could be heard for quite a distance."

To me the full song of this race does not differ noticeably from that of *canescens* described farther on. C. Barlow (1902) describes the song of one or two males he heard near Milpitas on March 23 as a weak *te-a-te-tree-e-e*, which differs from the songs heard there later in the season.

*Fall and Winter.*—When the singing of the males has dwindled away, by late July in the San Francisco Bay region, and the juveniles have become independent of their parents, the birds' secretiveness again makes them difficult to study. They can be found throughout the winter, however, still in their typical breeding habitat, as C. Barlow (1902) first suggested. Some wandering into nearby habitats not used for breeding has been recorded. In Marin County, for example, Joseph Mailliard (1900) notes that in late summer this race "may be observed among poison oak bushes and blackberry vines on grassy hillsides far away from the sage." His assumption that August–September birds in the area were southbound migrants now seems quite unwarranted.

A slight altitudinal shift may occur, particularly in the interior. Lyman Belding (1890) lists the species as "rare" at 3,000 feet altitude in Calaveras County in December, and reports "one specimen, several seen" Nov. 19, 1884 at Colfax, Placer County (2,400 feet); he also states that he saw it occasionally at lower altitudes in winter. It is possible that some individuals of the Sierra Nevada rufous-crowned populations move upward when their foothill breeding grounds become very hot and dry in late summer. Such movements are well known among more conspicuous species in California, and have been suggested for rufous-crowned sparrows in the arid southwest by A. R. Phillips (1951a), but confirmatory data for California have not been obtained.

## DISTRIBUTION

*Range.*—The California rufous-crowned sparrow is resident in the coast ranges and on the western slopes of the Sierra Nevada in central California (Clearlake Park, Sutter Buttes, McChesney Mountain, Onyx).

*Egg dates.*—California: 24 records, March 22 to July 10; 13 records, April 17 to May 13.

### AIMOPHILA RUFICEPS OBSCURA Dickey and van Rossem

## Santa Cruz Rufous-crowned Sparrow

### Contributed by HOWARD L. COGSWELL

#### HABITS

In 1863 James G. Cooper collected two rufous-crowned sparrows on Santa Catalina Island off the southern California coast; the specimens were eventually deposited in the Museum of Vertebrate Zoology at Berkeley where, according to D. R. Dickey and A. J. van Rossem (1923) "they are too faded and worn to be of use for color comparison." This comment on these, the only specimens of the species ever taken on Catalina Island, was with respect to the status there of the new subspecies *A. r. obscura* which these same authors described as "Darker and less rufescent than either *Aimophila ruficeps ruficeps* or *A. r. canescens* of the neighboring mainland; central streaking of the dorsal feathers much darker and less rusty; maxillary streaks heavier; bill heavier and more swollen at base; tarsi and feet averaging slightly longer and heavier." Hinting that it was doubtful the species still occurred on Catalina Island, they state it was "Common in suitable localities on Santa Cruz Island." J. Grinnell and A. H. Miller (1944) list its range as "Santa Rosa, Santa Cruz, Anacapa, and Santa Catalina islands; but not reported from the latter since 1863!" The same authors give the habitat of this race as "Grassy hill slopes and canyon walls where there are scattered bushes or clumps of cactus."

James G. Cooper (1870) writes: "I have only met with this species on Catalina Island in June, a few keeping about the low bushes, feeding on the ground, and very difficult to get a sight of. I heard them sing a few musical notes that reminded me of those of the *Cyanospiza* [lazuli and related buntings]. They flew short distances only, and in habits seemed more like the *Melospiza*. Their favorite resort, like that of the Eastern species, may, perhaps, be pine woods." Although his last surmise was quite wrong, in this earliest reference to the habits of what is most probably the race *obscura*, J. G. Cooper thus briefly mentions the secretive behavior and the similarity of song to that of the lazuli bunting which the accounts of *ruficeps* and *canescens* here emphasize.

In addition to the disappearance of rufous-crowned sparrows some-time after 1863 from Santa Catalina Island, where song sparrows (*Melospiza melodia*) are also unexpectedly absent as breeding birds, there seems to be considerable question as to the presence of rufous-crowned sparrows on Santa Rosa Island, separated from the still larger Santa Cruz Island by only about 6 miles. A. H. Miller (1951b) gives a thorough comparison of the avifaunas of these two neighboring islands, both of which "have grassland, chaparral (both tall and open, and low and wind-cropped), oak woodland, and an artemisia-opuntia(cactus)-grass association. * * * [The last] is perhaps roughly of equal amount on the two." These and the neighboring islands to the east and west, Anacapa and San Miguel, A. H. Miller points out, "almost certainly * * * have been connected with the mainland at periods in the Pleistocene time." Miller's own visit to Santa Cruz and Santa Rosa extended from Mar. 5 to 13, 1950, and included extensive collecting of specimens in various parts of each island. Of the rufous-crowned sparrow he writes:

With respect to resident sparrows, it was at once evident that the artemisia-opuntia-grass association on Santa Cruz was well and exclusively populated by the Rufous-crown (*Aimophila ruficeps*) whereas across the channel in identical vegetation and on the same type of sloping terrain on Santa Rosa nothing but Song Sparrows (*Melospiza melodia*) occurred. This habitat is a normal one, in terms of mainland conditions, for Rufous-crowned Sparrows. But, the island population of the endemic race *A. r. obscura* is, I think, somewhat more dense in it than is the population of the southern Californian coast. On Santa Rosa the Song Sparrows of the race *M. m. clementae* occupy this cover without limitation to stream courses or canyon bottoms in a way not done by the mainland race of southern California even on slopes facing the ocean. Song Sparrows have spread out ecologically, so to speak, to occupy the habitat of *Aimophila* and at times situations remindful of that of the resident White-crowned Sparrows (*Zonotrichia leucophrys nuttalli*) of the coast of San Luis Obispo County. It is rather clear that with lack of competition from somewhat similar kinds of sparrows and with a range of adaptability, quite possibly enhanced by inherent adaptive changes, *Melospiza* has come to dominate an unusual range of vegetative conditions on Santa Rosa. The foggy climate of the island doubtless is an aiding factor, enabling the moisture-seeking Song Sparrows to occupy brushlands near the sea as do other races much farther north in an even more humid belt. Yet it should not be forgotten that on the adjoining point of Santa Cruz Island in equally fog-swept cover Song Sparrows are absent.

After reviewing the few records of song sparrows on Santa Cruz Island, A. H. Miller concludes that they "make it clear that the Song Sparrow is not a dominant species on the island and indeed is apparently lacking in the artemisia-opuntia-grass and chaparral habitats." He then continues:

Concerning the presence of *Aimophila ruficeps* on Santa Rosa Island, we have only the report by Pemberton (Condor, 30, 1928:148) that O. W. Howard noted a pair on April 2, 1927. No record specimen was taken and there is a chance of misidentification. After my failure to note these sparrows on my first day ashore on Santa Rosa, I searched specially, exploring the most suitable places and squeaking for them, as I had done successfully on Santa Cruz. Not one could be found. I am led to think that if Howard was not actually mistaken, they are rare and certainly not a dominant resident on Santa Rosa, in spite of the presence of suitable habitat.

Immediately subsequent to A. H. Miller's visit to Santa Rosa Island, Egmont Z. Rett (1953) stayed there from Mar. 15 to 28, 1951 and especially searched areas up to 4 miles inland for *Aimophila ruficeps* but found none. Some sort of competitive interaction between the song sparrows and rufous-crowned sparrows on these two islands is thus rather strongly suggested. William Leon Dawson (1923) found rufous-crowns abundant on Santa Cruz Island in the spring of 1915 but writes "prickly pears are very abundant on Santa Cruz Island, and * * * the birds frequent the thickest patches. They are really very ungetatable, if you please."

*Nesting.*—James G. Cooper (1887) long ago indicated for Ventura County that rufous-crowned sparrows were found "on some islands, where they doubtless breed." Despite their abundance on Santa Cruz, however, no one seems to have published anything about the nesting of this race. Alfred B. Howell and A. J. van Rossem (1911) reporting on their visit to Santa Cruz Island April 24 to May 2, 1911, write of the rufous-crown: "Rather common in suitable places. One of the females of two pairs within fifty yards of camp, was incubating when shot April 26, as the absence of feathers upon her belly indicated."

*Young.*—The only information I have been able to find for the young of *A. r. obscura* is the comment by Frank A. Pitelka (1950) that he found on Santa Cruz Island, Aug. 29, 1949, a "pair with at least two bob-tailed fledglings no more than two or three days out of the nest."

*Plumages.*—Larry Wolf (MS.) reports no significant differences in postjuvenal or annual adult molt in this race as compared with his description herein of *A. r. ruficeps*. The juvenal plumage of *A. r. obscura* averages darker than that of *A. r. ruficeps*, especially the breast streaks; and the adult plumage is distinguished from the nominate race by a generally darker coloration, the back feathers having darker centers.

*Voice.*—In his description of the song of this race, the only such I have found, William Leon Dawson (1923) suggests a possible difference from that of birds of the nearby mainland, *A. r. canescens*. He writes: "On Santa Cruz Island, where I found the birds abundant in the spring of 1915, I was deceived repeatedly by the chattering, vivacious, and wren-like qualities of the Rufous-crown's song. *Wee chee chit i wit*

*chit i wit chit it,* the bird said, all at a breath; and it may be that there
is an average shade of difference in the insular song."

*Winter.*—Clarence B. Linton (1908b) seems to have published the
only note on this race at this season: "Mr. Willett and I each secured
a specimen in the brushy canyon near the south coast [of Santa Cruz
Island]. In the early evening of December 16 I observed a flock of 40
or 50 birds feeding on a grassy hillside near Prisoners' [Harbor],
securing two specimens." This also seems to be the largest actual
estimate of numbers in one "flock" reliably recorded for the species
anywhere in California, although one is left without information as
to whether real gregarious behavior was involved or merely aggregation
in a good feeding area.

### DISTRIBUTION

*Range.*—The Santa Cruz rufous-crowned sparrow is resident on
Santa Cruz, Anacapa, and (formerly) Santa Catalina islands off
southwestern California.

### AIMOPHILA RUFICEPS CANESCENS Todd
## Ashy Rufous-crowned Sparrow
### Contributed by HOWARD L. COGSWELL

### HABITS

This race of the rufous-crowned sparrow as now defined by the
A.O.U. Check-list includes all the mainland populations from Santa
Barbara, Ventura, and northern Los Angeles counties southward well
into Baja California—the area where the "coastal sage" plant association (Epling and Lewis, 1942) the species favors was originally most
widespread. The general color tone of many of the shrubby plants in
this association is gray-green—white sage (*Salvia apiana*), California
sagebrush (*Artemisia californica*), and California buckwheat (*Eriogonum fasciculatum* var. *foliolosum*); many others among the herbaceous
plant components are bright green in winter and turn brown early in
the rainless summer season. Somewhere in relation to this complex
of environmental colors there is probably an adaptive significance in
the coloration of *A. r. canescens* which W. E. Clyde Todd (1922)
characterizes as: "Similar to *Aimophila ruficeps ruficeps* (Cassin),
but wing and tail longer and under parts less buffy, more grayish in
tone. Similar also to *Aimophila ruficeps sororia* Ridgway, but darker
above, and darker, more grayish, below. * * * *A. ruficeps canescens*
is really intermediate * * * between *A. ruficeps ruficeps* and *A.
ruficeps sororia*, but is grayer than either * * *."

This subspecies occupies the same general type of habitat as that described for *A. r. ruficeps* in an earlier section, composed of openly spaced low shrubs with grasses or other herbs, or more rarely bare ground between the woody plants. As its range extends from moist coastal scrub areas near Santa Barbara to the borders of desert scrub vegetation in the low mountain passes of interior southern California and Baja California, the variety of shrubs it utilizes is probably greater. George Willett (1933) considers this form to be "partial to grass-covered hillsides," but Joseph Grinnell and Alden Holmes Miller (1944) list its habitat as "Sparse low brush on grassy hill slopes [with] preference * * * shown for tracts of California sage (*Artemisia californica*)."

In northwestern Baja California these birds are apparently abundant. George Willett (1913) writes that the species "was more plentiful in the hills near Point Banda, below Ensenada, than I have ever seen it anywhere else." Near the mouth of the Santo Thomas River in the same general area, Laurence M. Huey (1941) also found greater numbers than he ever observed elsewhere, "both on the hillsides facing the sea, and in the grassy, brushless areas, which were beginning to recover from incendiary fires." Joseph Grinnell (1926b) in describing the race *lambi*, now synonymized with *canescens* from northwestern Baja California, says, "As usual they kept to a low, sparse, dry-hillside type of chaparral * * * ."

Where I have studied them in the southern San Gabriel Mountains of Los Angeles and western San Bernardino counties, Calif., rufous-crowned sparrows are moderately numerous both in the coastal sage scrub of the lower foothills where this has not been pre-empted by cultivated or urban areas, and higher up in suitable places within the lower half or so of the true chaparral belt, at least to 3,000 feet. In the chaparral they are found only where steepness of slope or recent fires have kept the shrubs low and open. Near Pasadena one foothill plot of 41 acres of chamise chaparral that had regrown 7 years after a fire to an average height of 4½ feet with many openings between the shrubs was estimated to hold five territories (12 per 100 acres) in one season (Murdock and Cogswell, 1942). Re-evaluation of the original data, however, indicates that this was probably an overestimate, as only two definite territories were wholly within the plot and two, possibly three others partly in it. Comparable censuses of the birds of a mature chaparral plot of 50 acres north of Arcadia (Cogswell, 1946, 1947, and 1948) included only 1 or 2 territories per year for an average of 2.7 per 100 acres. Furthermore the birds were restricted to a steep rocky slope and to the lower altitude portion of a gentler south-facing slope where the shrubs were shorter and of more open arrangement than elsewhere in the plot.

Studies of the breeding birds of six plots farther east in the San Gabriels included mapping territorial activities and computing populations on both a space and time basis in units of "full season territories," each unit equal to a territory wholly within the plot occupied throughout the period of mapping, usually about 10 weeks (Cogswell, MS.). The plot in this series with the sparsest shrubs was studied 3 to 5 years after a fire, when about 44 percent of the ground was covered by shrub canopies and the regrowing chamise, scrub oak, manzanita, and *Ceanothus* were still far overshadowed by vigorous black sage (*Salvia mellifera*), deerweed (*Lotus scoparius*), and several other subshrubs. On this 43-acre plot near Glendora, the rufous-crowned sparrow populations had 2.5, 3.4, and 5.8 "full season territories" per 100 acres in 1950, 1951, and 1952 respectively.

In the one plot of the six that lay below the main chaparral belt, on a low foothill near San Dimas where the vegetation was typical coastal sage scrub with only a few patches of chamise and of poison oak, about 55 percent of the ground was covered by shrub canopies, mostly California sagebrush, California buckwheat, white sage, and a prickly pear cactus (*Opuntia occidentalis*), with scattered taller *Yucca whipplei* and the laxly branched laurel sumac (*Rhus laurina*). Here the populations of rufous-crowned sparrows in the same 3 years had 6.9, 5.7, and 3.9 territories per 100 acres, the decline being due in the last year to the disappearance of several territory holders during the spring.

In view of the roughly similar population densities of rufous-crowned sparrows in these two plots despite the strong differences in shrub species composition and other differences in the herb cover, the factors favoring occupancy of "scrub" types of vegetation in this area are not so much dependent upon any particular species of shrubs as on their general low form and interspersion with lower, non-woody plants. This may even apply to the species' supposed preference for *Artemisia californica* cited by Joseph Grinnell and Alden Holmes Miller (1944) and other authors, for that shrub was almost entirely absent from the recently burned area near Glendora.

*Spring, territory and courtship.*—In the foothills of the San Gabriel Mountains I have noted a few rufous-crowned sparrows in obvious pairs as early as February 1. Indeed some may remain in pairs through the winter, as advertising song by many of the males does not begin until mid-March or later, a considerable length of time after many pairs are found foraging together and keeping in touch by call notes. Of 45 territories in 5 of the study plots I examined from 1946 through 1952, in 10 no rufous-crowned sparrow other than the singing male was detected; most of these birds were presumably unmated, though some females were probably missed. In quite a number more, the pair records begin much later than the singing, despite the early occurrence of pairs in adjacent territories. Hence pair formation apparently may take place at any time from very early spring to perhaps as late as the latter part of may.

The male proclaims the territory he and his mate occupy by his song in typical emberizine fashion. In my experience it nearly always lies on a moderately steep slope or across the two slopes of a gully or small canyon, more rarely astride a ridge. Harry L. Heaton (1928) reports, "It is true the bird prefers a slope or hillside but * * * I have found them nesting on comparatively level land some distance from the hills and always quite removed from the abode of man. The rim about an arroyo seems to appeal to them, probably because it offers an easy disappearance into the depth below and reduces the chances of enemy approach."

The tendency for breeding pairs of rufous-crowns to be clumped, discussed earlier for *A. r. ruficeps*, does not seem to have been mentioned in the literature for *A. r. canescens*. In the plots I studied in the San Gabriel Mountains from 1950 to 1952 which were largely composed of habitat suitable for the species, most rufous-crown territories were relatively close to each other, leaving large unoccupied areas near by. In some cases this may have been due to mutual attraction to the more open ground along a road cut or head of an eroding draw, but other grouped territories lacked such features. Without a more thorough behavioral analysis, the question of a possible social attraction seems unanswerable, even though the evidence suggests it exists.

Territory sizes were measured by planimeter from my mapped records of the three plots in the San Gabriel Mountains in which rufous-crowns occurred from 1950–52. In the 43.5-acre plot of regrowth "chaparral" above Glendora at altitudes of 2,100 to 2,900 feet, 13 territories averaged 2.2 acres apiece, with extremes of 0.96 acres and 3.78 acres. In the 54.3-acre plot of coastal sage scrub in the lower foothills, 14 territories ranged from 1.21 to 3.15 acres, with an average of 1.9 acres.

No description of the courtship in California races of *Aimophila ruficeps* has been published. One display, however, seems to function in much the same way in this species as does the similar one J. T. Marshall (1960) described as a "squeal duet" or "pair reinforcement duet" for the brown and Abert's towhees, or which was later described (Marshall, 1964) as a "pair reunion duet." In the rufous-crowned sparrow I saw the best display Apr. 3, 1952, in a canyon in the plot above Glendora. From 9:26 to 9:35 a.m. one bird sang and gave its typical *dew, dew* call from four locations on the west-facing slope within 150 feet of a possible nest site, to which it went twice in this time. At 9:36 a.m. a single *dew* call came from another bird about 100 feet away. The singer, presumably the male, stopped singing and gave two *dew* notes. He then flew to a bush top above the presumed female where he gave soft, light *sst* notes and, with the tail slightly above horizontal, turned his body to right and left in quick succession. After several seconds the "female" flew up to a perch close to the displaying bird. Almost immediately, at 9:37, the pair flew some 75 feet across the canyon where they perched in low shrubs and gave light "skitter" calls. I could not see whether postures of the same or another sort accompanied the calls, as they typically do in the towhees. After this the two birds moved near each other to forage in a more open area 40 feet away, and then gave only *dew* calls.

The "skitter" call is similar to the *squeee-squee-chee-chee-churrrr of* the California races of the brown towhee (written *see see crrrrrr* by Marshall, 1964) but is higher in pitch, of decidedly less volume, and seems to run its course more rapidly. Crudely represented as *skee-ske-ti-ti-tititi*, it seems to be given during or at the conclusion of a "greeting" ceremony when paired rufous-crowned sparrows rejoin after having been apart. I have heard it from pairs or presumed pairs of rufous-crowns as early as February 12 and commonly through early June, which was usually the end of my breeding season visits to the San Gabriel Mountain plots. On Sept. 1, 1951, however, I saw and heard several pairs giving this call in each plot where I had mapped territories in the spring.

*Nesting.*—L. Percy Williams (1897) described the first nest of this race—one with four fresh eggs he found in the Crafton Hills east of Redlands Apr. 23, 1893. It was under a bunch of grass where "a slight hollow had been scratched for the nest, and was lined with coarse grasses and had an inner lining of fine, dry grass stems and a few horse hairs woven loosely together. It was rather deep but not much larger in diameter than was necessary to accommodate the bird's body." Six nests he subsequently took were more or less similar, although usually the nest was flabby. Three contained no horse hair. All were positioned to catch the morning sun.

Nelson K. Carpenter (1907b) describes a nest of three eggs he found near San Diego on May 29 as follows:

The nest was placed at the foot of a bank which was about a foot high. A small bush which had grown on top of the ledge had died and fallen over making a miniature brush pile. Into this the birds had broken their way using the fine twigs of the bush as a foundation for the nest. This mat of twigs was nearly two inches wide on the front side of the nest and entirely lacking where the nest touched the bank. The nest itself was made of very fine dry yellow grass with considerable black horse hair in the lining. The inside dimensions of the nest are one and a half inches deep by two and three-quarter inches across. The mat of twigs around the exposed edges was so interwoven with the surrounding bush that if was hard to tell exactly where the nest began.

He also reports other nests near San Diego, one of them made entirely of grass.

Generalizing for various nests near San Diego, Harry L. Heaton (1928) writes that an area "medium to sparsely covered [with shrubs] is usually selected although one nest was discovered in rather thick sagebrush three feet in height. The nest, always on the ground, is exceedingly well concealed and made of slender stems, grass, and rootlets with a lining of hair. * * * One nest was in an old, rusty tin can, the extended top of which lent additional protection. There was so little room left in the can that we wondered how the bird managed her tail so as to feel comfortable while sitting."

Apparently the only detailed watching of a relatively undisturbed nesting of this race was begun on April 10 by Harriet W. Myers (1909) on an uncultivated hill "just outside the Los Angeles city limits, overlooking the Arroyo Seco, and * * * overgrown with the usual vegetation—clumps of sage brush, wild oats, clover, grasses, and many varieties of wild flowers. The nest was placed directly on the ground under a clump of grass over which white convolvulus was twining; owl clover, brodiaeas, and lupines were blooming in the same clump. The nest itself resembled in shape and size the Song Sparrow's nest, being made of brown grasses, lined with finer fibers and a few horse hairs." Other details of this nesting are given in subsequent sections.

As to nesting season, George Willett (1933) cites records of 15 southwestern California nests with eggs that range in date from March 11 to June 2, and L. Percy Williams (1897) mentions a nest with fresh eggs taken in the middle of June. The March 11 nest, originally reported by Sharp (1907) near Escondido, seems truly exceptional for it must have been begun in late February. In my San Gabriel Mountain studies, none of which was particularly directed toward this species, I noted rufous-crowns carrying nest material Mar. 2, 1940, almost as early as Sharp's Escondido nest was built. In the coastal sage scrub near San Dimas I also found one nest with four eggs May 5, 1950, located near a ridge top at the east edge of a territory that encompassed an eroding south-facing draw. The actual site and nest were much like those cited by earlier authors. By May 16 this nest was empty and abandoned. On June 1 the following year a bird was noted leaving a nest under construction on a lower, gentler slope at the opposite side of a larger territory that included the same draw. Unfortunately this was my last visit to the area that season and the progress on the nest was not followed up.

Despite the great span of some 15 weeks between the earliest and latest dates, no definite evidence of a pair renesting after successfully fledging a brood has been published. William Leon Dawson (1923) merely makes the unsupported statement "one or two broods" for the species.

*Eggs.*—The eggs of this race apparently do not differ materially from those of the nominate subspecies.

*Incubation.*—No one seems to have determined the incubation period for this sparrow. The nest that Harriet W. Myers (1909) observed so carefully near Los Angeles held three eggs when first found on April 10, the female "brooding" and allowing approach to within 3 feet before flying away. As these eggs all hatched between late afternoon of April 15 and the morning of April 16, incubation evidently does not start until the last egg is laid.

Mrs. Myers' notes on the behavior of these birds on April 11 and 13 are the most accurately pinpointed of any I have seen on the breeding cycle. At 10 a.m. April 11, when observations began, there was no adult seen, but one appeared at 10:23 a.m. and gave a high-pitched scolding note. This bird went onto the nest at 10:49 a.m. and gave a low *sit* call from the nest in answer to the high-pitched alarm call from a second bird upslope, presumably the male of the pair. The sitting bird left at 11:33 a.m., called *dear dear*, preened momentarily near by, and then flew uphill out of sight. At 11:55 a.m. she returned and perched on a pole back of the nest. After the observer moved back she went onto the nest again at 11:59 a.m. and remained there steadily for at least the next hour and 31 minutes. On April 13, when observations began at 1:12 p.m. the bird was "brooding," in the next hour and 46 minutes "not once turning or moving. When she left the nest she did so quietly, slipping through the grass, then onto a bush, and from there flying directly up the hillside, a route she invariably took." Upon the bird's return 29 minutes later, she again went to the nest only after the observer moved more than 10 feet away.

*Young.*—Mrs. Myers (1909) watched the nest described above after the young hatched on April 16 until the morning of April 23 when the nest was found robbed. No other account of this phase of the breeding cycle seems to have been published, and the excerpts below are entirely from Mrs. Myers' (1909) article. April 17, late afternoon:

In ten minutes an old bird came to a nearby bush, an inch-long green worm dangling from its bill. I was about ten feet from the nest. After giving the plaintive call-note twice the bird carried the worm to the nest. From where I stood I could not see just how this worm was fed and in my effort to get a better view the bird flew out, a small part of the worm still in the bill. The mate had almost immediately followed the first bird to the nest and when the first one flew out this other one went at once to the nest with his bill filled with a small dark-looking substance. This was fed to each nestling, not with the pumping motion of regurgitation, but rather as tho emptying the bill and mouth.

April 19, morning:

At 9:27, I found a bird brooding. The morning was cloudy, with cool wind. The brooding bird lookt [sic] browner and I thought had more stripes on its back than the bird that had brooded the eggs. The dark stripe leading from the eye was also more pronounced and led me to wonder if this bird was not the male. * * *

At 10:15 I heard the note of [a] Rufous-crowned Sparrow up the hillside. At 10:23 * * * the brooding bird left the nest, slipping thru the grass and making his way to a weed stalk where he preened himself and gave a sharp note, a sort of "sit" that I have heard given by a number of species nesting near the ground.

Then a camera was set up and the old birds disappeared. Some 22 minutes later one called on the hillside and soon one appeared with something in its mouth. One of the pair that was shyer than the other was thought to be the female. The shyer bird would not go to the nest while the camera was there but flew about giving the call note. When at 11:25 the other bird, which I believe was the male, came, the first bird swallowed the food she carried and flew away. This last arrival carried a long green worm in his bill. This he took to the nest and fed to one young bird. I could see the green sticking up in the youngster's throat as he still kept his mouth open * * * . Finally he gave a little swallow, the worm disappeared and he closed his mouth, satisfied. The old bird rested on the edge of the nest about three minutes * * * [then] flew up the hillside. Fifteen minutes later both birds came with worms. One went to the nest and fed, but one, as before, would not go to the nest while the camera was there.

At 12:25 p.m. the presumed male appeared "with an immense wasplike fly dangling from his bill, the body down and head held in mouth. This was fed to more than one young."

I noted fledglings being fed by adults, or with adults in close attendance, in at least six territories within my plots near Glendora and San Dimas on various dates ranging from April 21 to June 7, and also in the chaparral plot censused above Arcadia, on May 18, 1947. Nothing seems to be known of the duration of parental care of fledglings.

*Plumages.*—Mrs. Myers (1909) remarks of the 1- to 1½-day-old young in the nest she watched at Los Angeles: "The orange-skinned nestlings were partially covered with tufts of black down." These same young two days later "were still quite naked—the only indication that they would ever be otherwise being that the wing quills were just pricking thru."

Larry Wolf (MS.) reports that the juvenal plumage of *canescens*, when fully acquired, averages darker than that of *A. r. ruficeps*, especially the breast streaks, and that he can find no significant differences in the postjuvenal molt of this race and that which he described under *A. r. ruficeps*, earlier.

In adult plumage, *canescens* is like *ruficeps* but with reds and grays darker, approaching *obscura* in darkness (Wolf, MS); and as originally described by W. E. Clyde Todd (1922) with "underparts less buffy, more grayish in tone."

*Food.*—Other than the comments of Mrs. Myers on the insects fed to young noted above, little has been reported on the diet of *A. r. canescens*. L. P. Williams (1897) writes that "The food contained in the stomachs of two females shot during May [near Redlands] consisted of alfileria seeds and some small pieces of some grass stem, and also coarse grains of sand and small particles of gravel." The foraging habits of this race do not differ in any obvious way from those of *A. r. ruficeps*, and presumably the adults take similar foods. The damage to garden plants attributed to this species at his home in the Eagle Rock portion of Los Angeles by C. O. Esterly (1920) was almost certainly due instead to sparrows of the genus *Zonotrichia*, for his description of the "flock of *ruficeps*" feeding on the open lawn and in the fruit trees does not fit what has since been learned of rufous-crowns.

*Behavior.*—No significant differences in movements, responses to intrusion, or defense of nest or young, have been reported for *canescens* from those described above for *A. r. ruficeps*. Birds of the southern race are perhaps less often seen in trees, which may only reflect the comparative scarcity of trees within their favored coastal scrub habitat.

In my San Gabriel Mountains study areas relatively rapid movements of pairs or male rufous-crowned sparrows through and between the low shrubs were mapped on several occasions, covering total distances of up to 700 or so feet. The longest flight I noted was one of 550 feet, about the usual maximum length of territory, although one probable territory was nearly 950 feet long. I noted rufous-crowns chasing each other through and between the shrubbery only a few times; one chase, May 22, 1951, involved a pair apparently intruding some 100 feet within the territory of a neighbor across a small draw and being forced out. Another on May 24, 1952, involved three birds, one pair plus a supposed intruder. Other chases noted on April 26 and May 12 in the plot above Upland, where possibly only one pair was in residence, and a slow flight of two birds in an apparent chase through a horizontal arc 100 feet long just above the shrub canopy on May 12 in the plot near San Dimas, may have been instances of courtship behavior, for no pairs had been observed earlier in either territory. Whenever a known pair was involved in a chase with neighbors, it usually gave the "skitter" call in its own territory after the conflict.

*Voice.*—The various call notes of this race seem identical with those described under *A. r. ruficeps*. The "skitter" call of the pair-reunion duet is described above under the section on courtship. The full song, used for advertising purposes in the territory by the male, is a jumble of listless and spirited notes resembling in general pattern the song of a lazuli (or an indigo) bunting but lower in volume and with less musical tone. One I heard Mar. 27, 1941 in South Pasadena I syllabified as *chi-chi-chew, CHU, tsi-tsi- ti -tsi -ti, tweeee.* The pitch varied somewhat throughout, but only the *ti* notes and the final, unemphatic short trill were distinctly lower. In general the song has less tendency toward a see-saw rhythm or doubled note sequence than that of the bunting. It is of comparable length, usually about 2 seconds.

The resemblance of the rufous-crown's song to that of the lazuli bunting has impressed so many acquainted with both birds in the field, beginning with William Brewster (1879), that one wonders why Ralph Hoffmann (1927) wrote that "the song of the Rufous-crowned Sparrow is short, with little carrying power, and is not given freely; it suggests a somewhat feeble Song Sparrow." In my experience the songs of both *A. r. canescens* and *A. r. ruficeps* lack the typical introductory notes and sharply distinct timbres of the remainder of the song sparrow's performance. Perhaps some of the birds on the offshore islands or in other local situations have developed other patterns. William Leon Dawson (1923) writes most extensively of this aspect of the voice:

The song of the Rufous-crown is one of the freshest, most vivacious and engaging, as well as varied, of all that may be heard upon our southern hillsides. Its vivacity is wren-like. * * * [It] has the spontaneity of a Winter Wren's, but its volume, duration, and cadence are rather those of the Lazuli Bunting. My attention was once caught by a spirited passage-at-arms and pursuit between a Lazuli Bunting and a Brown Towhee, and I passed on, musing upon the ways of Lazulis, when a song burst forth at my elbow near the roadside. *Sult sult zul eb stutz tuzzuzzu wei,* said the voice, and I should have let it pass for the song of the Lazuli if curiosity had not been provoked by its nearness. There in a brush-clump not ten feet away sat a Rufous-crowned Sparrow vigorously delivering himself of the stolen (?) song. Fortunately, the Lazuli returned presently to defend his honors, and I had ample opportunity to make a critical comparison of their songs. The resemblance is, after all, superficial, due rather to the accidental characters before enumerated than to quality. The Sparrow's song is more sprightly, more varied, and of a sharper, more penetrating quality. It is rather less musical, and it lacks altogether that caressing drawl which marks the Finch's effort. A few moments later the Rufous-crown took a station well up in a eucalyptus tree and burst forth with great regularity at intervals of ten seconds, with each "performance" lasting about one and a half seconds. The song is so little stereotyped that it contains hints now of Vesper, now of Lark Sparrow (in the *killy killy* opening notes), now of Willow Goldfinch (for vivacity), but always, most of all, of Lazuli Bunting.

The male rufous-crowned sparrow often sings for some time from perches within the canopy of low shrubs, but when undisturbed for long periods, and especially early in the day, may select a perch on the very top of a bush for his announcements. Even then, however, it is often not the tallest bush of the vicinity. The use of a tree canopy as a song perch, as noted by William L. Dawson, is rather exceptional.

The main season of advertising song in the San Gabriel Mountains extends from late March into July. A few birds were noted in song as early as February, and singing seems to increase in persistence from mid-April through mid-May. In Griffith Park, Los Angeles, I found one rufous-crown giving a full song repeatedly Dec. 27, 1945, the only instance I know of fall or winter singing.

*Enemies.*—No doubt the destruction of much of the original coastal scrub vegetation, to which *A. r. canescens* is partial, by the mushrooming urbanization of southern California has greatly reduced the populations of this race. Little is on record of other agents of mortality, except that a number of the nests found have been later discovered robbed or abandoned, as is common among many small birds. Mrs. Myers (1909) attributed such loss of the brood of young she was watching to "a skulking feline." The lists of host species of the brown-headed cowbird contains no record of *Aimophila ruficeps* serving in this capacity, although probably it does so occasionally.

*Fall and winter.*—Information on activities of these resident birds through most of the hot late summer postbreeding period is lacking. On the one round of visits I made to my San Gabriel Mountains plots at that season, Aug. 31 to Sept. 3, 1951, individuals or pairs were present in or near most of the 12 territories mapped the previous spring. The "skitter" calls described under *Courtship*, were heard in all three plots, once coming from a group of four birds apparently made up of two pairs or potential pairs in conflict. No songs were heard at this season, nor on a round of visits to these same plots in late December 1951. At this winter period the birds were much more silent; I heard only the *dew* and *tssp* calls, and these in only five territories. I heard one bird in another plot where the species was not encountered the previous or subsequent springs—deep within the chaparral belt and surrounded by dense chaparral but on an eroding slope in a canyon where shrubs were shorter and sparser. This record suggests that dispersal, at least of young, takes place some time during fall or early winter. When the young take up their first territory is unknown, but some occupancy of good feeding areas may take place first, perhaps accounting for the approximately 15 rufous-crowns I found within a half-mile of trail in good habitat just within the mouth of Fish Canyon, near Azusa, Sept. 27, 1942.

## DISTRIBUTION

*Range.*—The ashy rufous-crowned sparrow is resident in southwestern California (Gaviota, Redlands) and northwestern Baja California (south to lat. 30°30′N.; San Martín Island; east to east base of Sierra San Pedro Mártir).

*Egg dates.*—California: 18 records, March 11 to June 15.

### AIMOPHILA RUFICEPS SANCTORUM van Rossem

## Todos Santos Rufous-crowned Sparrow

### Contributed by HOWARD L. COGSWELL

## HABITS

In his description of this insular subspecies of extremely limited range, Adriaan J. van Rossem (1947b), writes: "Ventrally, the darkest and grayest (most plumbeous) of the races of *Aimophila ruficeps*. Dorsally, most nearly similar to the darker and grayer examples of *Aimophila ruficeps canescens* of southwestern California and northwestern Baja California but averaging still darker, the general color of the dorsum and crown close to 'Mars Brown' rather than grayish 'Kaiser Brown,' and with the grayish edgings narrower, darker, and less in evidence. Size somewhat smaller than *canescens*, particularly in length of tail."

Van Rossem then comments on the extreme darkness of the Todos Santos birds, although the islands are only 3 miles offshore and hence of similar or identical climate to that experienced by *A. r. "lambi"* of the nearby mainland (now included in *A. r. canescens*). He expresses the opinion that isolation in the limited area of the islands and consequent inbreeding has "fixed and accentuated tendencies [toward slaty color] already present in mainland populations." The evolutionary differences in morphology thus attributed to what is now usually called genetic drift, a well known phenomenon in small populations, have in this case unfortunately not as yet been accompanied by any comparison of the habitat or behavior of the birds with those of the nearby mainland populations.

The only other reference to this race in the literature is in Henry B. Kaeding's (1905) report of his visit to its home in 1897. He remarks only "Noted on Todos Santos Islands, March 10th * * *." On San Martín Island, 90 miles farther south and much farther offshore, Henry B. Kaeding found the species present but "not common" on Mar. 12, 1897. The fifth edition of the A.O.U. Check-List (1957) includes the population on this larger island within the range of the mainland race, *A. r. canescens.*

## DISTRIBUTION

*Range.*—The Todos Santos rufous-crowned sparrow is resident on the Todos Santos Islands off northwestern Baja California.

### AIMOPHILA RUFICEPS SORORIA Ridgway

## Laguna Rufous-crowned Sparrow

### Contributed by HOWARD L. COGSWELL

## HABITS

Robert Ridgway (1898a) describes this subspecies of the Cape district of Baja California as "Similar to *A. ruficeps* [presumably=*A. r. ruficeps* and *A. r. canescens* as now recognized] in coloration of upper parts, but chestnut of pileum somewhat lighter or clearer, supraloral line whiter, and supra-auricular stripe lighter and grayer; smaller than *A. ruficeps scottii*, with back, etc., less ashy with chestnut streaks darker and much narrower, and the under parts much more strongly tinged with buff; differing from *all* the other northern forms of the species in much thicker and relatively shorter bill." Robert Ridgway gives the range as "Southern portion of Lower California, in mountains (Laguna; Victoria Mountains)." Joseph Grinnell (1928) gives its status as "Common resident locally in the mountains of the Cape district."

Discussing the probable evolutionary origin of this isolated population of the rufous-crowned sparrow, John Davis (1959) indicates that it "differs considerably [in morphology] from the nearest population to the northwest, *canescens* * * * . In the general pallor of its coloration and in the much greater development of ventral white *sororia* is much more nearly similar to *scottii* of Arizona, New Mexico, northeastern Sonora, and northwestern Chihuahua, and to *simulans*, which ranges in México from southern Sonora to Nayarit and from southern Chihuahua south through Durango and Zacatecas to Guanajuato."

The emphasis Adriaan J. van Rossem (1934a) placed in his description of *simulans* on its similarity to *sororia*, which is distinguishable chiefly by its larger bill, is also cited by John Davis (1959) in support of his statement that "The affinities of *sororia* are clearly with the populations to its northeast and east, and not with the populations of the Pacific coast to its north."

For 14 of the 17 endemic forms in the Cape district avifauna John Davis (1959) says that "The available evidence, then, suggests strongly that most of the highland endemics of the Cape district colonized that region from the mainland of México and the adjacent inland United States. When one considers the habits of the species concerned, it does not seem likely that such sedentary forms as * * * Rufous-crowned Sparrows * * * would have invaded the Cape region by an overwater, or even island-hopping route from the Mexican mainland." After citing geological and paleobotanical evidence that no significantly greater land connection between the Cape area and the Mexican mainland to the east than now exists has existed since the Miocene, John Davis (1959) concludes:

It seems most likely that most of the avian endemics of the Cape highlands [including *A. r. sororia*, as he makes clear elsewhere] have their closest affinities with forms to their northeast and east because the habitat in which these Cape endemics occur today has become relatively little modified from the habitat with which the ancestral stocks of these species were associated in México. In northwestern Baja California, the western foothills of the Sierra Juárez and the Sierra San Pedro Mártir support a vegetation that is clearly related to the flora of southern California. As might be expected, the highland avian endemics of northwestern Baja California show clear relationships with the populations of the Pacific coast to their north.

Thus the similarity of *Aimophila ruficeps sororia* to *A. r. simulans* is of long standing, the form *A. r. canescens* now interposed between them along the apparent route followed by the species into Baja California being a later evolutionary product.

Larry Wolf (MS.) notes that this form "may more often retain all the juvenal primaries than the other races. (Based on small sample to date.)" Nothing more has been published on this form.

### DISTRIBUTION

*Range.*—The Laguna rufous-crowned sparrow is resident in southern Baja California (Triunfo, Sierra Laguna).

### AIMOPHILA AESTIVALIS BACHMANI (Audubon)

## Bachman's Sparrow

### Contributed by FRANCIS MARION WESTON

### HABITS

This sparrow was first named *Fringilla Bachmani* by John James Audubon (1833) in the folio edition of his *Birds of America*. In his *Ornithological Biography* the following year (1834), he described it under the name *Fringilla Bachmanii*. The earlier spelling has been accepted by the A.O.U. Committee on Nomenclature (A.O.U. Check-List, 1957) as given in the heading of this account.

In his description John Audubon (1834) writes: "In honouring so humble an object as this Finch with the name of BACHMAN, my aim is to testify the high regard in which I hold that learned and most estimable individual * * * ."   John Bachman discovered this species and obtained the first specimens on the Edisto River, about 30 miles west of Charleston, S.C., at Parker's Ferry (erroneously cited by some later writers as Harper's Ferry), but Audubon himself took the specimens, upon which he based his description, within 6 miles of Charleston and later found others in clearings at various points along the main highway north of the city.

To anyone familiar with the present-day pine woods of coastal South Carolina, where Bachman's sparrows may be heard singing in every sizable patch of pines, it is inexplicable that so keen an observer as John Bachman had to go far afield to discover them.   Perhaps, as by his own admission he had mistaken the song for that of the towhee (*Pipilo erythrophthalmus*), he had consistently overlooked them nearer to home.   It is certain, though, that Bachman's sparrow was not nearly as numerous in the 1830s as it had become by 1905 when this writer first roamed the woods of the Charleston area.   It is not difficult to account for the increase in its numbers.

In John Audubon's time virgin pine forest covered coastal South Carolina except immediately around the cities and towns.   So close and dense was this growth that there was little or no underbrush and the ground was bare except for a clean mat of pine needles.   The only cover or food available for ground-ranging birds was along the infrequent edges.   I can well remember in the middle 1890s, before the great lumber companies had completed their desolation of the virgin forests of the South, that the railroads out of Charleston ran for miles at a stretch through unbroken pine forests.   But the destruction of the great pineries and the subsequent springing up of a fairly open second growth with a ground cover of grasses and underbrush gave Bachman's sparrow an almost unlimited territory favorable to its expansion.   The increase in its numbers may well have paralleled that of the chimney swift (*Chaetura pelagica*) when the building up of the eastern part of the nation provided an abundance of chimney nesting sites to replace the comparatively few hollow trees that had, until then, held the numbers of that species severely in check.

There can be no doubt of the almost explosive increase in numbers because, before the close of the nineteenth century, Bachman's sparrow had become so common throughout the southeast that it had to expand into areas that had never known it before—Tennessee, Kentucky, West Virginia, and even southern Ohio and southwestern Pennsylvania.   Maurice Brooks (1938) gives a detailed account of this "invasion," and I have drawn upon it freely in writing the following pages. He states that, from a first appearance in Ohio and West Virginia in the last few years of the nineteenth and the first few years of the twentieth century, the species reached its maximum abundance in those states between 1915 and 1922. After 1922 a distinct recession in numbers over much of the region was recorded, but he advances no explanation to account for it.

Perhaps the most striking feature of the bird's range in West Virginia is in the altitudes it attained, which contrast sharply with the low elevations in its ancestral range in the southeast. Maurice Brooks (1938) writes that in

Upshur County * * * the species was positively common at elevations of 1700 feet. In Webster County a number of individuals were observed at altitudes around 2500 feet.* * * The altitudinal record for the State, so far as I am aware, was made near Pickens, Randolph County. Here, on Turkeybone Mountain, at elevations around 3000 feet, the birds were found in 1920, and perhaps in other years. The territory thereabout lies within the "Spruce Belt," the natural growth of Red Spruce (*Picea rubens*) which followed the higher Allegheny summits. At the time the Bachman's Sparrows were found, the area had, of course, been cleared, but Winter Wrens, Veerys, Magnolia and Cairns's Warblers, Juncos, and Red-breasted Nuthatches all nested nearby.

In a later article, Maurice Brooks (1952b) repeats his theory that the earlier movement into the region came from Kentucky, crossed the Ohio River into unglaciated Ohio, spread eastward along the river into West Virginia and thence northward down the Monongahela Valley into southwestern Pennsylvania "until they reached the first high Allegheny ridges. Here their invasion was checked * * *. In more recent years Bachman's Pine Woods Sparrows have seemingly made another invasion and extended their range northward through the Shenandoah Valley to the east of the Alleghenies. They are now locally common in portions of northwestern Virginia and the Eastern Panhandle of West Virginia."

In the breeding season in the southeast, I have found Bachman's sparrow only in areas of pine. The preferred habitat seems to be rather open pine woods with an understory of various species of scrub oaks and a ground cover of grasses and scattered low bushes. Here its nearest neighbors are red-cockaded woodpeckers, wood pewees, brown-headed nuthatches, pine warblers, and summer tanagers. Herbert L. Stoddard (*in* Burleigh, 1958) states that, in extreme southern Georgia in the area of intergradation between this and the Florida race, Bachman's sparrow "is a highly adaptable species, however, and finds life more attractive in present day tung-oil [*Aleurites fordi*] groves or around borders of cultivated fields."

How different is the habitat of Bachman's sparrow near the northern edge of its more recently occupied range. Maurice Brooks (1938)

cites data supplied to him by Lawrence E. Hicks on nesting habitat in Ohio, and he finds similar conditions prevailing in West Virginia. Both observers state that the typical habitat is an abandoned field, usually fallow for 4 years or more, which is well grown up with golden-rods and asters, various grasses, and the miscellaneous composites and weeds typical of dry, eroded slopes. The presence or absence of pine seedlings seems to have no bearing on the desirability of the site. The cutting of the forest growth and soil erosion are the factors favoring the selection of a nesting site. Also, this species is practically confined to hill country, almost never appearing in the valleys or even on the lower slopes of the hills. A typical territory is near the top of a slope where eroded gullies have been healed and are covered with shrubs, particularly blackberry bushes.

*Spring.*—The coming of spring is heralded in the Deep South, even as early as the last week of February, by the addition of the song of Bachman's sparrow to the late winter chorus of Carolina wren, mockingbird, brown thrasher, pine warbler and cardinal. Even severe, temperatures are no deterrent for, as Arthur T. Wayne (1910) writes from Mt. Pleasant, S.C., under date Feb. 26, 1901: "Heard a Bach-man's Finch sing beautifully at night. He sang as sweetly as if it were May, although the night was very cold and the ground partly covered with snow and ice." Although there must be many more Bachman's sparrows in the South in winter than in summer, only the most persistent searcher is aware of their presence prior to the beginning of the song period.

It is probably at this time that the northern breeding birds commence their withdrawal from winter quarters, but the movement is so unob-trusive that observers in the South are not aware of it. But the arrival of singing birds in territory unoccupied in winter is readily observed and recorded. Maurice Brooks (1938) cites the earliest arrival date as March 27 in Upshur County, W. Va., with a median date of April 11; an early arrival date of April 10 in Ohio, with a median date of April 22; and an early date of April 15 near Waynesburg, Pa.

*Courtship and nesting.*—I can find nothing in the literature on the courtship of this race of the Bachman's sparrow, and very little on either of the other two races. In my own field work, I have never seen anything in the behavior of this species that could be construed as courtship activity. Actually, this is one of the most elusive of the sparrows and all its actions except the attention-compelling song are shrouded in secrecy.

On the other hand, the subject of nesting bulks large in the literature and many excellent descriptions of nests are available. However, and unfortunately, some of the widely accepted statements about nest con-struction are very misleading. Charles E. Bendire (1888) makes the positive statement that *all* nests of *A. a. bachmani* are domed and cylindrical, while the nests of the Florida race (*A. a. aestivalis*) are "not arched over * * * in any way, perfectly round, with the sides and rims everywhere of equal height * * *." But writers throughout the range of Bachman's sparrow describe both open nests and domed nests and sometimes an open nest with one edge noticeably higher than the other. The open nests described far outnumber those of the domed type. In my own experience, of the very few nests that I have found some were open and some domed, and I cannot now recall a preponderance of either type. The one point on which all writers agree is that the nest is invariably built on the ground, usually concealed under a low bush or against a tussock of grass.

Nests are constructed of weed stems and various grasses, which are coarse in the body and fine in the lining. Several observers mention having found a few horse hairs in the nest lining, one mentions cattle hair, and one a few strands of corn silk, but in most nests the lining is of fine grasses only.

The actual process of nest building has been witnessed by very few observers. Fred M. Jones (1940), writing from southwestern Virginia, describes a domed nest that he saw under construction in his yard only 50 feet from his dwelling. Incidentally, he states that this was the only domed nest of a dozen or more that he had found in the neighborhood, and even this "was not in the same class as Ovenbirds' nests." His attention was first attracted by seeing a Bachman's sparrow with a mouthful of grass fly to a spot under a walnut tree. A search of the place revealed only a typical field sparrow nest, located some 6 inches off the ground. Later, after having seen the Bachman's sparrow make a number of trips to the same spot, he succeeded in finding her nest. It was on the ground under a small limb that had fallen from the tree and was situated only 12 inches from the field sparrow's nest.

The foregoing account well illustrates the difficulty of finding a nest of this species, even though this one had been almost "pin-pointed" by the building bird. Most writers on the subject agree that the nest of the Bachman's sparrow is in the same category (so far as difficulty of detection is concerned) as the nests of grasshopper and Savannah sparrows. Neither John J. Audubon nor John Bachman ever succeeded in finding a nest.

William G. Fargo (1934) quotes Walter Hoxie in a statement that is, in the experience of all other observers, at least open to question: "In the summer he [the Bachman's sparrow] and the Pine-woods have the same habit of singing to the brooding mate from some elevated perch and looking down at her where she is on the nest. So, to the initiated it is a dead 'give away' of the situation of their home on the ground among the dense cover which otherwise it is almost impossible to locate." Clearly, I am not one of the initiated or else am particularly inept at nest finding, for I have found fewer than a dozen nests in more than 50 years, and those few purely by chance, never as a result of crawling around on the ground below habitual singing perches. Maurice Brooks (1938) states that "One male whose nest was discovered had a favorite singing perch * * * about fifty yards from the nest. The birds were not crowded in their territory, and we found some points from which habitual singing was carried on at distances of seventy-five to one hundred yards from the nest."

As would be expected of a species whose nesting range spans a 10° latitude, dates of nesting at or near the upper and lower extremes of the range differ materially. A. H. Howell (1924) cites April 30 and July 14 as inclusive dates on which full sets of eggs were found in southern Alabama. A. Sprunt and E. B. Chamberlain (1949) state that the average date of first nests in the Charleston, S.C., area is from April 28 to May 4 but that, in forward seasons, nests have been found early in April. They also state that three broods are reared in a season, with the third brood hatching in August. Maurice Brooks (1938) cites the extreme dates at French Creek, W. Va., as May 27 and July 2, and concludes that two broods may be reared in a season. With only five nests to my credit in the Pensacola, Fla., area, my inclusive dates are of but little significance; but it seems probable that, from the greatly protracted length of the song period which goes well into August, at least two broods are reared.

Several observers agree that the female alone does all the nest building and all the incubation of the eggs, but only one writer goes into any detail. B. J. Blincoe (1921) of Bardstown, Ky., states that: "The male generally accompanied the female as she carried the nesting material, and, frequently, he sang while she searched over the ground for the piece of dead grass suited to her needs."

The only nest measurements that I can find in the literature are given by Charles E. Bendire (1888), when describing a series of six nests taken by William C. Avery near Greensboro, Ala. The measurements are presumably the average of the six nests, for he states that "These measurements vary somewhat in different specimens. All six nests were distinctly roofed over or domed * * *. They are cylindrical in shape, about seven or eight inches in height, and four and one half inches wide. The inner cavity is from three to four inches in length, about two inches wide, and one and three quarters inches high. The rear wall of the nest is about one and three quarters inches thick, the sides about an inch, and the roof a little over half an inch in thickness. * * * the roof projects somewhat over the entrance in all cases. * * * the entrance is invariably canted upwards, at an angle of about 15° * * *. The entrance to the majority of the nests found faced the west."

*Eggs.*—Bachman's sparrow (*A. aestivalis*) lays from three to five eggs. They are ovate, slightly glossy, white and unspotted. The measurements of 71 eggs average 19.3 by 15.3 millimeters; the eggs showing the four extremes measure *20.9* by *16.3*, *17.8* by 15.2 and 18.0 by *14.0* millimeters.

For *A. a. bachmani* the measurements of 50 eggs average 19.4 by 15.3 millimeters; the eggs showing the four extremes measure *20.9* by *16.3*, and *18.0* by *14.0* millimeters.

*Young.*—Bachman's sparrow is so secretive in all its actions, except singing, that little can be found in the literature on the various phases of nesting and the rearing of the young. Even the exact period of incubation of the present race is not stated by any writer, though I have found mention of this point for one of the other two races. Several observers agree that both parents attend to the feeding of the young.

Incubating or brooding birds are particularly difficult to see actually on the nest. In the few cases in my experience, the adult bird ran from the nest while I was still several feet away, no matter how cautiously I approached. In only one instance did I see the adult fly directly from the nest. Maurice Brooks (1938) writes: "Brooding birds were found to sit very close, allowing themselves to be approached within a few feet before flushing. When flushed, the bird would frequently drag its wing, flutter along the ground, and, in general, go through a performance that we have come to think of as 'injury-feigning' * * * much like the performance of a Killdeer * * * leaving her nest." Albert F. Ganier (1921) cites a similar experience near Nashville, Tenn., as follows: "I flushed a Bachman's sparrow which feigned crippledness as it fluttered off through the grass. A search revealed two young birds just learning to fly and which were captured. The one parent bird present remained near and most persistently endeavored to lure me away by fluttering through the grass * * *." Charles E. Bendire (1888) quotes William C. Avery, of Greensboro, Ala., stating that the flushed bird invariably runs (not flies) away from the nest, and that it imitates the movements of a snake, even giving at this time a distinct hissing note.

The actions of adult birds, even when not disturbed by intrusion, are secretive in the extreme. Maurice Brooks (1938) writes: "Parent birds do not fly directly to the nest, but * * * drop inconspicuously into the grass and weeds from low perches at some distance from the nest, making their approach in such a manner that it is very difficult to follow them. In one case where we found a nest by watching the birds the habitual approach was from an old rail fence about thirty feet from the nest. * * * Both parents were carrying insects to the young birds, and they were shy and secretive. When the nest was located (it contained four young birds) both parents nervously flew from low perches in weeds and grass to the ground, remaining within sight for very brief intervals."

William C. Avery (*in* Bendire, 1888) had an interesting experience in flushing four juvenile birds, presumably from the nest. They flew like a miniature covey of bobwhites, rising with an audible whir of wings. An additional instance of the actions of fledglings is given in the account of one of the other two races of this species.

*Plumages.*—Juvenal plumage: Forehead and crown feathers black, edged (in varying amounts) with buffy brown or reddish brown; pattern irregular streaking. Youngest specimen with least light feather edging (nearly uniform black crown). Nape similar but more light edging. Back similar, feathers broader. Rump with black much reduced, light color predominating. Upper tail coverts like back. Rectrices blackish with faint suggestion of "herring-bone" pattern. Remiges blackfish, primaries edged with buffy, tertials with rich cinnamon. Tertials margined with cinnamon and buff. Coverts black, lessers edged with rich cinnamon, medians and greaters narrowly edged with buff or cinnamon buff. Wing bar pattern not prominent. Lores buffy. No distinctive face pattern. Auriculars tinged with buff, spotted with black. Under parts whitish or cream, tinged with buff on flanks and crissum. Chin finely spotted with black; throat, breast, sides, and flanks streaked and spotted with black (most heavily on breast). Leg feathers black and cream.

Herbert L. Stoddard (*in* Burleigh, 1958) writes from Grady County, in extreme southern Georgia, in an area where *A. a. bachmani* intergrades with *A. a. aestivalis:* "This species seems to be forever in moult, bob-tailed ragged adults and young being the rule throughout the summer and fall months, while they seem to be replacing lost feathers much of the time during the winter months."

*Food.*—A. H. Howell (1924) sums up the food of Bachman's sparrow in the southern part of its range as follows: "The food of this sparrow, as indicated by examination of 10 stomachs from Alabama, consisted of 58 percent animal matter, and 42 percent vegetable. The animal food includes leaf-beetles, 9.3 percent; other beetles, including weevils and longicorns, 23.1 percent. Bugs constituted 12 percent and the other food items were grasshoppers and crickets (5.7 percent) with some snails, spiders, and millipeds. The vegetable food consisted principally of grass seed and the seeds of sedges; wood sorrel and Indian strawberry made up the remainder."

I can find in the literature no other results of stomach examinations. Sight observations, including my own, add nothing of significance to

Howell's list quoted above. The few observers who mention food were probably unable to get near enough to these secretive little sparrows to identify any item but an occasional large insect—a grasshopper or a cricket.

We may reasonably expect the food habits of Bachman's sparrow in the northern parts of its range not to differ materially from those of the southern birds in the proportions of animal and vegetable food taken, though an actual analysis would doubtless show variations in the species' consumption.

*Behavior.*—Most observers who have had experience with Bachman's sparrow will agree, I believe, that were it not for the unmistakable ringing song, this secretive little bird could be overlooked in any given territory for a long time and its presence never suspected. That is actually the case in winter in the South when the birds are not in song. When it comes to elusiveness, I class Bachman's sparrow with the notoriously secretive Henslow's and LeConte's.

Observers in the northern parts of the breeding range of this species designate its singing perches as fences and tall weeds and seldom mention a higher perch. In the pineries of the South, however, the usual singing perch is in a tree, and I do not now recall ever having noted any other. The favorite perch is within 20 feet of the ground on the stub of a broken branch of a pine tree or on one of the dead twigs one often sees halfway up the trunk of a mature long-leaf pine. The bird seldom goes as high as the crown branches.

Early morning and late afternoon seem to be the preferred singing periods, but even the heat of a summer day is no deterrent to this indefatigable singer as I have often heard his song ringing out through the shimmering noontime heat in the southern pineries.

Singing persists until late in the summer in all parts of the range. Maurice Brooks (1938) mentions having heard the song a few times in August in West Virginia. In the Pensacola, Fla., area, I have heard it as late as the last week of August. Alexander Sprunt and E. Burnham Chamberlain (1949) note that the song can sometimes be heard in coastal South Carolina in early September. They also record sporadic singing "late in December."

Maurice Brooks (1938) records the unusual, perhaps unique, experience of having had Bachman's sparrows come to a feeding shelf on his farm in Upshur County, W. Va., where they learned to relish "exotic" foods that they certainly never found in nature. He writes:

Much to our surprise, a pair of the birds, evidently nesting in a nearby brushy field, frequenting one of our window feeding shelves. No similar circumstance had come to our attention, and we tried a variety of foods with the birds. They took raisins freely, but, like so many birds which we have fed, seemed to prefer the kernels of black walnuts to any other food which we could offer them. They also took coarse corn meal, cornbread, particles of cracked corn in ordinary poultry feed, and "cracklings" left from the "trying-out" of lard.

Both birds fed at the small shelf at the same time, and once they had come, manifested little fear. They would sometimes remain for periods of five minutes or more, feeding both on the low shelf and on the ground where particles of food had been scattered. * * * We did not see them at the shelf very early in the morning or late in the evening, the times when singing was most in evidence.

Evidently this sparrow gives off an emanation or scent that the keen senses of hunting dogs can detect. Many a hunter has had occasion to swear at his dog for having come to a "false point" at a "d—d ground sparrow." However, this is not a peculiarity of the Bachman's sparrow, for I have known dogs to point Henslow's and grasshopper sparrows and perhaps other ground sparrows that occur in the winter habitat of the bobwhite.

*Voice.*—Of all the observed activities of the Bachman's sparrow, the song easily ranks first. Writers compare its sweetness and ethereal quality to the famous song of the Hermit thrush (*Hylocichla guttata*) and some even claim superiority for the sparrow.

First, technical description follows. Aretas A. Saunders (1951) writes that the song "consists of a series of phrases, sung one after another in varied order, with pauses between them, so that the whole performance may be considered one long-continued song.

"Each phrase consists of a long, sweet note, followed by a trill or series of rapid notes on a different pitch. The pitch intervals between the long notes and the trills are quite perfect, being minor or major thirds, fourths, fifths, or even octaves.

"Each individual sings from five to twelve different phrases, averaging about seven. The long note introducing each phrase and the change in pitch from one phrase to another suggest the singing of the Hermit Thrush."

R. M. Strong (1918) records that "the duration of the song, which was very variable, was about two or three seconds. Usually, the song started with a single long note followed by a group of short notes in a tempo so fast that we could not be sure of our count. So far as we could determine, the bird had seven to twelve notes in this group, usually about ten. As a rule, they were of essentially uniform pitch, but not of the same pitch as the long opening note. The pitch was sometimes lower than that of the first note and sometimes higher. A few performances had two or three opening notes not so long as the usual single one. On one occasion, the song was repeated or rather one song followed another with no interruption or pause, both being a little shorter than usual."

Many writers have set down transliterations of the song (an example is *theeeeee-thut, lut, lut, lut*), but all these are meaningless to one who has never heard it and grossly inadequate to anyone familiar with its ethereal quality. Some writers have even become sentimental in their attempts to describe this quality, but I have yet to find a description that does it justice. One must actually hear the song in all its purity and sweetness before he can appreciate or even understand the high place that the singer has attained among our native birds. Attendant circumstances have much to do with the charm of this song. My memory goes back to a warm spring morning in the pine woods, the fragrance of the pine and a faint tang of wood smoke in the air: it is in such a setting that the mellow notes of Bachman's sparrow leave an unforgettable impression on the hearer.

In addition to the usual song, Maurice Brooks (1938) describes a variation from West Virginia that I have never been fortunate enough to hear: "The louder songs are not uncommonly interspersed with 'whisper songs,' so low that they are inaudible to a person at a little distance. Frequently there are broken twitterings between the more ordered songs as well." He also quotes A. B. Brooks, who, after following a singing bird through a weedy field, states that: "When I approached a little nearer he discovered me and changed his song into a fine, mixed-up combination of slurs, whistles, and trills."

Robert M. Mengel (1951) describes an evening flight song that he heard near Bowling Green, Ky., which seems to have been missed by observers in general: "Shortly after sundown I saw a small fringillid in flight about 150 feet above the ground. It was ascending in an erratic, fluttering manner, signing a song which was completely unfamiliar to me. The song was bubbling and exuberant and, though distinctive, was difficult to describe. According to my notes, it reminded me of a much speeded-up Indigo Bunting (*Passerina cyanea*) song of wren-like quality." On another occasion, when he heard the same song again, he succeeded in collecting the singer, which proved to be a Bachman's sparrow.

A peculiar sound, which I cannot find mentioned anywhere in the literature, is a prolonged, monotone trill that I have heard uttered only after sunset on winter afternoons. It seems to be some kind of roosting assembly note. It is much longer than the long opening note of the song and is pitched much higher. I have called it a trill rather than a single, sustained note, but if it is a trill it is so exceedingly fine and rapid that I cannot be sure of my term for it. Often at the close of a Christmas bird count, and after I had failed to flush a single Bachman's sparrow in its usual daytime haunts, I have gone to a known roosting spot on the edge of the pine woods and, sitting quietly, have heard this note come from several widely scattered locations in the underbrush.

Aside from its song, this species has few other sounds. As already mentioned in the section *Young*, a bird flushed from the nest has been known to utter a note, which C. E. Bendire (1888) characterizes as "*chäy, chäy*," a sound more like the hissing of a snake than the scolding of a bird." A sharp, rather prolonged *pseet* of alarm or remonstrance is sometimes given by a parent bird when a nest with young is disturbed. The common call note of the species is a typical sparrow-like *chip*, which is not distinctive in any way.

*Field marks.*—This is one of the most nondescript of birds. Even when seen to good advantage, it has no prominent or conspicuous mark that makes for easy identification. In general it is just a plain, rather reddish sparrow with an unstreaked, slightly buffy breast. The grayish superciliary line is not well marked. The unstreaked crown and much longer tail distinguish it from the grasshopper sparrow, another species with a plain breast sometimes found in the same habitat. The dark bill, noticeably larger than that of the small-billed chipping and field sparrows, gives the whole head a fairly distinctive outline that I have found at times to be a good field mark. Perhaps the bird is best identified by its habitat—the only reddish-backed sparrow of overgrown fields and pine woods.

The juvenal plumage has a noticeable eye ring and the breast and sides streaked with dark gray.

*Enemies.*—H. S. Peters (1936) lists only two ectoparasites on the Bachman's sparrow: a mite (*Analgopsis* sp.) taken from birds collected in Ohio, and a tick (*Haemaphysalis leporis-palustris*) from some birds in Georgia.

Herbert Friedmann (1943) cites only three instances of finding eggs of the brown-headed cowbird in the nests of this species. Several writers consider that this comparative immunity is because domed nests are difficult for the cowbirds to find, but this point is not well taken because, as has been stated earlier in this account, the great majority of the nests within the breeding range of the cowbird are not domed. It seems more likely that this immunity is achieved by the sparrows in their expert concealment of all nests, whether domed or not, and that the cowbird has as much difficulty in finding nests as the ornithologist.

Undoubtedly, Bachman's sparrow, in common with all other small ground-nesting birds, is at the mercy of a number of predators—stray dogs and semiferal cats, in addition to the native mammals. Several observers specifically name the "blacksnake" (though whether it is *Elaphe* sp. or *Coluber* sp. is not indicated) as a known destroyer of nests, and undoubtedly other species of snakes are equally guilty. Fred M. Jones (1940) states that, in southwestern Virginia, of "a dozen or more" nests that he had found, "the crows accounted for all of them" except the two in his yard.

Such a high percentage of nest failure must be exceptional, however, because Lawrence E. Hicks (*in* Brooks, 1938), when accounting for the 26 nests he had under observation in Ohio, states that "the percentage of success is distinctly higher than that which Mrs. Nice has found for the Song Sparrow, and which I have found for the Field Sparrow and the Vesper Sparrow," but he does not give an actual percentage figure.

*Disease-carrying potentialities.*—In a letter from the Communicable Disease Center, Atlanta, Ga., to Oscar M. Root, of North Andover, Mass., in reply to his request for "information regarding the public health importance of * * * Fringillids," the writer states that "to our knowledge, encephalitis is the only human disease in which these birds are incriminated. * * * the following Fringillids have been found to carry antibodies to one or more of the American arthropod-borne encephalitides." In the list of 12 species cited, the pine-woods (=Bachman's) sparrow is included as a carrier of antibodies of western equine encephalitis, but this species does not appear again in a further list of three sparrows in which virus has been actually isolated.

*Fall.*—Bachman's sparrow begins to withdraw from the northern part of its range before the end of August. Maurice Brooks (1938) quotes Lawrence E. Hicks in citing September 2 as the latest date on which he has ever found this species in southern Ohio. In West Virginia, Brooks gives September 1 as the latest date in his field notes.

Thomas D. Burleigh (1958), writing of the northern part of Georgia, states that "it doubtless lingers * * * through September and possibly into October * * * but there are very few fall records later than the end of August."

*Winter.*—In winter, Bachman's sparrow occupies the territory south and east of a line drawn from extreme southeastern North Carolina, about along the fall line across South Carolina and Georgia, through middle Alabama, thence to the coast of Mississippi. In Florida, it invades the eastern part of the state and penetrates almost halfway down the peninsula, well into the range of the Florida race.

At this season it spreads out from its summer breeding habitat in the pineries into open broomsedge fields and areas of scrub oak. In the Pensacola, Fla., area, I have found it along the wet upland edges of creek and river swamps where I had never seen it in summer. It comes down, too, almost to the salt water shores of the coastal woods into areas which, although apparently optimum for nesting, were not occupied in summer. The spot that I mentioned in the section *Voice*, where I could always hear the evening trills of roosting birds, is within 100 yards of a salt water beach. Herbert L. Stoddard (*in* Burleigh, 1958) says that it is often found "even in the fence corners with other sparrows" where it "always seems to be out of character."

A source of continual amazement to us as observers in the Deep South is that, although there must be many more Bachman's sparrows present in winter than in summer, now that they are silent it is seldom that any can be found except by purposeful search, and few are seen even then.

## DISTRIBUTION

*Range.*—Ohio, southwestern Pennsylvania, and Maryland south to southern Mississippi and central Florida.

*Breeding range.*—The eastern Bachman's sparrow breeds from central northern Kentucky (Jefferson County), southwestern and north central Ohio (Montgomery and Wayne counties), southwestern Pennsylvania (Beaver, Fairchance), eastern West Virginia (Berkeley County), western and central Maryland (Green Ridge Mountain, Beltsville) south to southern Mississippi (Gulfport), southern Alabama (Mobile, Dothan), southern Georgia (Newton, Tifton), and south central South Carolina (Aiken, Charleston).

*Winter range.*—Winters from central Alabama (Greensboro, Coosada), northern Georgia (Athens), South Carolina (Camden), and central North Carolina (New Bern) south to southern Mississippi (Gulfport) and central Florida (St. Petersburg, Welaka); casually eastern Maryland (Princess Anne).

*Casual records.*—Casual in Michigan (Monroe and Wayne counties), southern Ontario (Point Pelee, Long Point), New York (Mendon Ponds Park), and New Jersey (Fort Lee, Atsion).

*Migration.*—The data deal with the species as a whole. Early dates of spring arrival are: Florida—Leon County, March 1. Alabama—Huntsville, March 7. Georgia—Atlanta, February 28; Macon, February 29. Virginia—Richmond, April 3. District of Columbia—April 11. Maryland—Kensington, April 29. Pennsylvania—Waynesburg, April 15; Beaver, April 29. New Jersey—Fort Lee, May 9. Arkansas—Delight, April 5. Tennessee—Nashville, March 17; Knox County, March 29. Kentucky—Bardstown, March 18. Missouri—St. Louis, April 14 (median of 5 years, May 3). Illinois—Urbana, March 19 (median of 13 years, April 6). Indiana—Bicknell, March 19; Wayne County, April 26 (median of 5 years, May 1). Ohio—central Ohio, April 10 (average, April 24). Michigan—North Cape, April 29. Ontario—Point Pelee, April 16.

Late dates of spring departure are: Florida—Leon County, April 5. Maryland—Cabin John, May 9. Mississippi—Gulfport, April 25. Tennessee—Nashville, April 25 (median of 24 years, April 6).

Early dates of fall arrival are: Mississippi—Deer Island, October 21. Georgia—Grady County, September 27. Florida—Leon County, September 24.

Late dates of fall departure are: Ohio—central Ohio, September 17 (average, August 27). Indiana—Bicknell, August 26. Illinois—La Grange, August 13. Kentucky—Eubank, September 26. Tennessee—Nashville, October 17; Knox County, September 27. Maryland—Prince Georges County, August 15. Virginia—Richmond, September 3. Florida—Leon County, October 30.

*Egg dates.*—(*Aimophila aestivalis*) Alabama: 8 records, April 13 to June 28. Arkansas: 12 records, April 26 to July 4. Florida: 19 records, April 14 to July 28; 11 records, April 22 to May 10. Georgia: 12 records, April 26 to June 19. Illinois: 2 records, May 31 and June 1.

(*A. a. bachmani*)—Alabama: 18 records, April 30 to July 14; 9 records, May 7 to June 10.

Florida: 5 records, April 20 to July 27.

Georgia: 8 records, May 9 to June 25.

Kentucky: 4 records, May 2 to June 18.

North Carolina: 4 records, May 2 to June 15.

Tennessee: 6 records, May 11 to July 20.

## AIMOPHILA AESTIVALIS AESTIVALIS (Lichtenstein)

### Pine-woods Bachman's Sparrow

#### PLATE 52

#### Contributed by FRANCIS MARION WESTON

#### HABITS

This southern race of the Bachman's sparrow, formerly known as the pine-woods sparrow, is slightly larger and darker, less rufescent above and more grayish (less buffy) below than *A. a. bachmani*.

It occupies a range from the extreme southern corner of South Carolina, southward through coastal Georgia and westward along the southern edge of that state at least to Grady County, and all of the Florida peninsula down to Lake Okeechobee and Immokalee.

In its habits, haunts, food, nesting, and behavior, it so closely resembles its near relative to the north that, in general, the account of that race applies equally well to this. However, a few notes of interest in the literature should be cited.

Robert F. Mason, Jr., of Orange County, Fla., in a letter to Mr. Bent describes a nest he found in the process of construction Apr. 26, 1953: "The nest was complete and the first egg deposited April 30, prior to 8:30 a.m. Eggs were laid on succeeding days, all prior to 8:30 a.m., until the fourth and last egg was deposited on May 3." The nest was "beneath and partially roofed over by a clump of grass. It was almost perfectly round and its inside diameter was 2½ inches by

2 inches inside depth. In addition to the tentlike covering of grass, it was definitely domed in its construction by the birds themselves. An opening in the grass clump provided entrance, but so well concealed was the nest that had I not seen the bird go to it I would not have found it." The finding of a domed nest of the Florida race is directly at variance with a statement of C. E. Bendire's (1888), cited in the section *Nesting* in the account of *A. a. bachmani*, that the nests of *A. a. aestivalis* are "not arched over in any way, perfectly round, with the sides everywhere of equal height."

Much of the ground cover in the pine woods of Florida consists of saw palmetto (*Serenoa serrulata*). Many nests of this sparrow are located beneath low-growing palmetto fronds that lie in a plane parallel to the ground. They are thus not only well protected, but are also completely concealed and are very difficult to find.

Samuel A. Grimes (1931), of Jacksonville, Fla., cites an example of a remarkably short interval between successive nestings: "On May 11 a nest with three small young was noted, on the ground under a palmetto frond. These young were successfully reared, and on May 23 this pair was found making a new nest a hundred feet from the first. Seven days later this second nest held five eggs."

The measurements of 21 eggs average 19.2 by 15.4 millimeters; the eggs showing the four extremes measure *20.5* by 15.7, 20.3 by *15.8*, *17.8* by 15.2, and 17.9 by *14.8* millimeters.

A note on the food of this race is given by A. H. Howell (1932): "Examination of the stomachs of 8 specimens of this species taken in Florida showed the bird's food to consist mainly of insects and spiders, with smaller proportions of seeds of grasses and other plants. The insects most frequently taken were grasshoppers and crickets and their allies, these composing the major portion of the food in four of the stomachs and being present in all but one. Other insects eaten were beetles, moths, leaf hoppers, caterpillars and Hymenoptera. Seeds taken included blueberry seeds, pine seeds, and seeds of various grasses and sedges."

A unique instance of the extremes to which this secretive sparrow will go to escape detection is given by James A. Pittman, Jr. (1960). In the pine woods near Orlando, Fla., a party of observers saw a sparrow disappear into a small isolated clump of saw palmetto. After an unsuccessful attempt to flush the bird again, it was discovered that the palmetto clump concealed the entrance to a burrow of the gopher tortoise (*Gopherus polyphemus*), and one member of the party glimpsed a small bird at the limit of visibility down the burrow. By opening the burrow, the bird was finally caught at a point almost 4 feet back from the entrance and 2 feet below the surface of the ground. It was identified as a Bachman's (pine-woods) sparrow.

Aretas A. Saunders (1951) has this comment on the song: "Farther south, chiefly in Florida, the bird is sub-specifically distinct, and known as the Pine-woods Sparrow. Its song is essentially the same [as *A. a. bachmani*], but it is my impression that the song there is not quite so rich and fine in quality as that of the more northern form."

H. S. Peters (1936) lists a louse (*Ricinus* sp.) as an ectoparasite found on some specimens of this sparrow taken in Florida.

In winter, this race withdraws from the northern part of its breeding range and is then found from extreme southern Georgia through almost the whole of the Florida peninsula.

### DISTRIBUTION

*Range.*—South Carolina to Florida.

*Breeding range.*—The pine-woods Bachman's sparrow breeds on the coastal plain of southern South Carolina (Allendale, Jasper, and Beaufort counties), southeastern Georgia (Savannah, Folkston), and peninsular Florida (south to Fort Pierce and Immokalee).

*Winter range.*—Winters chiefly in peninsular Florida; casually north to Grady County, Georgia.

### AIMOPHILA AESTIVALIS ILLINOENSIS (Ridgway)

## Illinois Bachman's Sparrow

### Contributed by FRANCIS MARION WESTON

### HABITS

Robert Ridgway (1879) described the oak-woods sparrow (*Peucaea illinoensis*) from specimens he collected at Mount Carmel, Ill. He considered it a distinct species because "a very wide area exists between the habitat of *P. aestivalis* and *P. illinoensis* in which no *Peucaea* is known to exist * * *." He knew that his new sparrow ranged southward into central Texas, but certainly he did not know that its winter range extended as far east as southern Mississippi, where it met that of *A. a. bachmani*. Nor could he foresee, of course, the "invasion" of Bachman's sparrow 20 years later into southern Ohio, where it occupies territory almost contiguous to that of *illinoensis*.

It was not until may years later that the A.O.U. Committee on Nomenclature (1944) accepted Ridgway's *illinoensis* as a race of *A. aestivalis*, giving it the name that appears at the head of this account.

Robert Ridgway, in his description, states of this race that "the upper parts are much paler and more 'sandy' in hue, and the black mesial streaks which in *aestivalis* mark all the feathers (except those of the nape and wings) are either entirely wanting or confined to the

PLATE 52

Duval Co., Fla., June 10, 1930          S. A. Grimes

NEST AND EGGS OF PINE-WOODS BACHMAN'S SPARROW

Duval Co., Fla., May 1939          S. A. Grimes

PINE-WOODS BACHMAN'S SPARROW FEEDING YOUNG

interscapular region; the breast and sides are very distinctly ochraceous-buff, these parts in *aestivalis* being buffy grayish.   The proportions
are much the same in the two species, but *illinoensis* has a longer wing
and thicker bill."   Apparently, then, *illinoensis* is the most rufescent
of the three races of *A. aestivalis*.

In its habits, haunts, nesting, food, and behavior, this race so
closely resembles its near relative to the eastward that, in general,
the account of that race applies equally well to this.   A few notes of
interest in the literature, however, may be included here.

The habitat of this race in south central Indiana, near the northern
limit of its breeding range, is similar to that favored by *A. a. bachmani*
in Ohio.   Russell E. Mumford writes in a letter to Mr. Bent: "In
these haunts, pine-woods [=*illinoensis*] sparrows are nesting associates of the blue-winged and prairie warblers.   At times, I have been
able to call up all three species by squeaking on the back of my
hand * * *.   Evidently, these three find their optimum nesting
requirements in the many similar areas present.   On many of the old
fields, broom grass, locally called broomsedge, is present and forms a
considerable portion of the ground cover.   Other ground cover is
likely to be dewberry, cinquefoil, aster, and similar plants."

Near the southern limit of the range, the preference for pineland is
again similar to that of *A. a. bachmani* in the same latitude.   Brooke
Meanley (1959) writes from central Louisiana:

Natural vegetation is predominantly Longleaf Pine with an interspersion of small
stands of hardwoods along drainage systems.   * * *

Forest management studies in progress in this area indicate that manipulation
of the habitat greatly favors Bachman's [=*illinoensis*] Sparrow.   The cycle of clear
or partial cutting followed by direct seeding or planting provides, apparently,
optimum habitat.   A scattering of seed pine trees, clumps of shrubs and brush
piles are left from these operations; these provide singing perches, escape cover
and appropriate sites for nesting.   The opening of the forest and burning of the
ground cover results in an abundance and variety of foods, especially grasses and
legumes * * *.   Selective cutting or thinning of overcrowded stands produces an
open park-like aspect approximating the optimum habitat of Bachman's Sparrow.

The only mention that can be found in the literature on courtship
activity of any of the three races of *A. aestivalis* comes in a letter to
Mr. Bent from Val Nolan, of Bloomington, Ind.: "On May 6 I heard
for the first time a vocal performance that circumstances suggest was
connected with courtship.   At 4:00 p.m. a male (assumed) burst out
with a succession of ringing, bubbling notes in pattern and variety not
unlike those of the Indigo Bunting's typical song.   These notes continued rapidly for 3 or 4 seconds, then abruptly switched to the usual
song of the subspecies; this concluded the effort.   I did not see the
position of the male during this utterance, but a second or two after

it ended two pine-woods sparrows flew up from the ground in the direction from which the song had come.

"On May 7 at 8:00 a.m. at the same place a bird repeated the song just described several times, once singing in mid-air. The flight of the singer was slow, the wings fluttering rapidly. At the moment of utterance the back was arched and the head thrown up at an angle of 45° from the body, which was more or less parallel to the ground. I failed to see the other member of the pair, if it was present. This ecstatic song was never heard again."

The only record that can be found in the literature of the exact period of incubation of any of the three races of *A. aestivalis* is cited for this race by Brooke Meanley (1959). Writing of a nest he found in central Louisiana Apr. 16, 1956, he states that the nest "was virtually complete by this date and the first egg was laid April 17. An additional egg was deposited each day through the 20th, completing the clutch of four eggs. The four eggs were marked and on May 2, the first three eggs laid had hatched; the fourth egg laid hatched the next day." This seems to indicate that incubation commenced after the laying of the third egg, and that the period of incubation was 14 days.

Val Nolan gives an interesting account of the behavior of a brood of nestlings from the day of hatching: "On my inspection of the nest during the ensuing few days I was impressed by the absence of any behavior indicative of fear in the nestlings. Until June 4 they did not even shrink from my hand as I parted the grass around them. On June 4 at 4:30 the situation changed. The young birds, now well feathered, sat silently as I bent over to look at them; then they suddenly burst squawking from the nest and scattered in flight. The distances of the flights were at least 10 yards. On landing the fledglings became silent and concealed themselves so well that I was unable to find them. Although my attentions were clearly the immediate cause of this departure from the nest, on the 10th day after hatching, the flight of the birds was so steady that it seems safe to say that the fledging was only slightly premature."

Val Nolan adds a note on the behavior of an adult sparrow at a nest of newly hatched young, when he writes that it "had flown up and perched 2 feet high on a little limb at a few yards' distance. Calling the sharp *pseet* note repeatedly, it also engaged in several other actions of interest. At intervals it bobbed its body up and down vertically in the manner of the wrens, suddenly flexing and then extending the legs and tarsi. At other times its tail switched and its body jerked from side to side, i.e., the sparrow quickly rotated its body horizontally within an angle of some 40° without moving its feet."

Although pine seed forms only a minor item in the food of any of the races of *A. aestivalis*, Brooke Meanley (1959) goes into some detail of its consumption in the pine forest management areas of Central Louisiana: "During years of a bumper pine seed crop (about every fifth year) pine mast is available in great quantities from October to January. Artificial or direct seeding * * * in February and March supplements the native food supply. But in the artificial or direct seeding of cut-over lands Bachman's Sparrow is not an important depredating species. Damage to pine seed is inconsequential because of the relatively small numbers of this sparrow (one pair per two acres in optimum nesting habitat), non-flocking habits, and absence from large open grasslands."

In winter this race withdraws from the northern part of its breeding range and is confined within a territory south of a line drawn from northeastern Texas to central western Mississippi, south to southeastern Texas and the coasts of Louisiana and Mississippi.

### DISTRIBUTION

*Range.*—Missouri, Illinois, and Indiana south to the Gulf of Mexico.

*Breeding range.*—The Illinois Bachman's sparrow breeds from southeastern Missouri (Ink), northeastern Illinois (Philo, La Grange), and central Indiana (Crawfordsville) south to southeastern Oklahoma (Bethel), central Texas (Giddings, Buffalo Bayou), and south central Louisiana (Baton Rouge).

*Winter range.*—Winters from northeastern Texas (Dallas), southeastern Oklahoma (McCurtain County Game Refuge), and central western Mississippi (Edwards) south to southeastern Texas (Silsbee), south central Louisiana (Baton Rouge), and southern Mississippi (Gulfport).

*Casual records.*—Casual in northeastern Kansas (Wyandotte County) and central northern Oklahoma (Alva).

### AIMOPHILA BOTTERII (Sclater)

## Botteri's Sparrow

### Contributed by GALE MONSON

### HABITS

Botteri's sparrow is a Mexican bird whose distribution barely reaches into the United States in extreme southern Texas and southeastern Arizona. It was first described by P. L. Sclater in 1857 in the Proceedings of the Zoological Society of London, from a specimen supposedly taken near the Mexican city of Orizaba, state of Veracruz, by Matteo Botteri, a Dalmatian botanist and traveler. Although C. B. R. Kennerly collected a specimen in 1855 at Nogales, presumably in the Mexican state of Sonora close to the border of Arizona, the species was not admitted to the United States list until 1873 and 1874, when the noted pioneer ornithologist H. W. Henshaw collected 14 specimens in the vicinities of Camp (Fort) Grant, Camp Crittenden (near Sonoita), and Cienega (near Tucson) in the Territory of Arizona. Since these early times Botteri's sparrow has claimed little attention and, until just a few years ago, little was known of of its occurrence in Arizona and Texas, to say nothing of its range in Mexico. Present knowledge of the species' range, both as to season and locality, still is fragmentary at best. At least in Arizona and Texas it is known to be migratory.

According to the A. O. U. Check-List (1957) the Arizona and Texas populations of Botteri's sparrow consist of different subspecies, *botterii* and *texana*. Additional subspecies occur in Mexico. Some students, notably J. Dan Webster (1959), regard the so-called Péten or yellow-carpalled sparrow (*Aimophila petenica*) as being conspecific with Botteri's sparrow. Webster classifies the form of Arizona and Northwestern Mexico as *Aimophila botterii arizonae* (Ridgway). To avoid confusion, the present discussion disregards those forms assigned by some authors to *A. petenica*, or those subspecies formerly regarded as belonging to *A. petenica*, whichever the case may be. It might fittingly be added that the differences of opinion arising from the problems of classifying Botteri's sparrow are typical of other perplexities encountered in studying the species. Much of this, naturally, is due to its secretiveness and from the difficulty of identifying it either in the field or in the hand.

There is nearly universal agreement that Botteri's sparrow throughout its range requires grassland, with at least a scattering of brush or small trees. In Arizona it favors giant sacaton or other tall grasses with mesquite and catclaw (Monson, 1947). In Texas the birds like salt grass (*Spartina*) with some yucca, prickly pear, and mesquite (Harper, 1930). In its Mexican territory, Botteri's sparrow prefers open grassland with live oak, as in the Aribabi Hills of Sonora (Marshall, MS.); almost pure grass, grazed moderately to heavily, with an occasional acacia, stone wall, or prickly pear, as in Zacatecas, Durango, and northern Jalisco (Webster, MS.); and palm-dotted savannah, as in coastal Nayarit (Phillips, MS.). Although heavy grass stands are more typical habitat, the species also occurs in heavily grazed grassland near Oaxaca City (Webster, 1959), and in the Sierra de Tamaulipas it has been found in a burned over section (Martin, Robins, and Heed, 1954). Quite a number were noted in Zacatecas in spots where irrigation ditches, grassy pastures, cultivated fields, and acacia-mesquite-cactus scrub were in close proximity (Webster, MS.).

Botteri's sparrow is a terrestrial bird, spending most of its time on the ground where it feeds. It flushes rather readily, and then flies to the nearest bush, fence post, wall or, more rarely, tree. Frequently it drops back into the grass after flying a short distance. In Arizona its associate birds are mainly scaled quails, western kingbirds, ash-throated flycatchers, mockingbirds, eastern meadowlarks, Cassin's sparrows, and black-throated sparrows; and, in some localities, yellow-throats and blue grosbeaks. Francis Harper (1930) lists its Texas associates as Cassin's sparrows (especially), long-billed curlews, up-land plover, horned larks, eastern meadowlarks, and black-throated sparrows. In Zacatecas, Jalisco, and Durango its commonest asso-ciates are: in short-grass plains—red-tailed hawks, prairie falcons, sparrow hawks, horned larks, eastern meadowlarks, and grasshopper sparrows; in open grassland with mesquite-cactus-acacia scrub—Cassin's kingbirds, horned larks, mockingbirds, curve-billed thrashers, loggerhead shrikes, eastern meadowlarks, brown towhees, and black-chinned sparrows (Webster, MS.). In Nayarit common associates are bobwhites, ground chats, and eastern meadowlarks (Phillips, MS.).

*Nesting.*—Information on the nesting of Botteri's sparrow is singularly lacking. Gale Monson (1947) pointed out the absence of positive nesting evidence for Arizona, despite the species' presence in the state from mid-May to early October. The sexual condition of birds collected in the state, even in August, plus two September and October specimens in mostly juvenal plumage suggest that they do nest there.

In Texas the species nests mainly in June, with a nesting density of one nest to each 10 acres on the Laguna Atascosa National Wildlife Refuge (Davis and Gill, 1948).

The few nesting dates I have for Mexico, in regions not adjacent to Arizona and Texas, fall in May, June, and July; none of these appears to be a positive record, however. Birds still partly in juvenal plumage have been taken in Nayarit in November.

No exact information on the type of nest location preferred or on the type of materials used in construction is available. The nest is said to be placed on the ground.

*Eggs.*—Authentic egg data are almost lacking. The species re-portedly lays from two to five, usually four unspotted white eggs. They are ovate and have only a slight gloss. The measurements of 28 eggs average 19.8 by 15.2 millimeters; the eggs showing the four extremes measure *21.4* by *16.5*, *18.3* by 14.7, and 19.3 by *13.9* millimeters.

*Plumages.*—Adult male: above reddish-brown, the feathers edged with gray; black shaft streaks on the forehead and back; tail dusky with broad brown edgings and tips; bend of wing light yellow; sides of head (including superciliary stripe) and neck dull ash gray; a narrow reddish postocular stripe; chin, throat, and belly whitish; chest, sides, and flanks grayish-buff; maxilla dusky, mandible paler; iris brown; legs and feet very pale brownish buffy or dull straw color.

Adult female: similar to male but with much more extensive black shaft streaking, including the hindneck and crown. Even the flanks are narrowly streaked with blackish.

The following description of the juvenal plumage is quoted from R. R. Graber's (1955) thesis on the juvenal plumages of Fringillidae:

"Fleshy parts: Bill yellow-flesh color, iris dark brown, feet flesh color; lower mandible yellowish pink, feet yellowish-flesh. Natal down: Pale buffy gray on crown and nape; lighter (whitish) on back, wings, and sides of rump.

"Plumage: Feathers of forehead and crown and back blackish, edged with buffy gray. Nape buffy gray, much less black than crown. Rump mottled buffy and black. Upper tail coverts and median rectrices black, broadly edged with Brussels brown. Other rectrices black. Remiges slate gray (tertials black), primaries edged with gray, tertials with rusty. Tertials margined with buff. Wing coverts black, lessers and medians edged with creamy buff, greaters edged with cinnamon, tipped with buff. Two wingbars. Lores light gray. Superciliary line cream, and most prominent anterior to eye. Eye-ring cream colored. Side of head uniform buffy gray. Chin and throat cream, with bare suggestion of 'mustache' marks. Other under parts cream, belly most richly colored. Chest and flanks tinged with pinkish buff. Jugulum, chest, sides, and flanks streaked with dusky. Belly and crissum unmarked. Leg feathers cream, marked with dusky. Coverts black, medians and greaters broadly tipped with creamy white (two distinct wingbars). Greater coverts narrowly edged with light cinnamon. Lores black. Cream-colored line between bill and eye. Eye ring white. Patch below eye black. Superciliary line obscure except anterior to eye. Auriculars gray. Pattern in malar region as in adult, cream-colored malar stripe outlined in black (subocular region and sides of chin). Chin and throat white, flecked with dusky. Other under parts (except crissum) white, tinged with buff on breast. Breast and sides heavily streaked with dusky. Belly and flanks largely white. Crissum rich orangish buff."

*Food.*—Little is known of the food habits of Botteri's sparrow. Clarence Cottam and Phoebe Knappen (1939) analyzed the stomach contents of 2 birds taken in Arizona and 12 from Texas, finding them to be about 86 percent insects, mainly Orthoptera, and about

14 percent seeds of weedy plants and grasses. Joe T. Marshall, Jr. (MS.) found mixed insects and vegetable matter in two stomachs from Sonora and Chiapas, and wholly vegetable matter in a stomach from Chiapas.

*Voice.*—The usual call note is a typical sparrow "chip." The song, although really distinctive once it has been heard a few times, is rather faint and unmusical. Various interpretations of it have been given, all of them subject to individual auditory impressions. L. Irby Davis (1939) describes it as follows:

It is seldom very musical and consists of such a jumble of notes that it seems almost impossible to fit words to it. It begins with some low, rather disjointed, chipping notes and ends with a series that is rather like that of the Chipping Sparrow, or possibly more like the Texas Sparrow. In the middle there are, characteristically, two louder and clearer notes, reminding one of the middle notes of the Sharpe's Seedeater's song. The two words representing these last-mentioned notes will be indicated in quotation marks in the following attempts at describing the song. The usual song may be given as *wit-wit-cheeup-cheeup-"cheer, cheer", chee chee che ee e e e.* Different individuals have slightly different tones and there are a great variety of slight variations such as, *chip-chip-twitter-twitter-chitter-"cheep cheep," we we ee e e e,* or *wit-chee ee-chee ee-chip-chip-ip-ip-"chee chee," wit wit we e e e e.* At times the halting preliminary notes will be continued for some time and the latter part of the song (which is the musical part) left off altogether: *wit-wit-chee-wit-wit-cheeit-wit-wit-chee-wit.*

Allan R. Phillips (MS.) gives the following interpretation:

"Song of Botteri's sparrow, typically, starts with two faint '*tsips*," then gives two '*che-licks*' very like a horned lark, and goes into a metallic trill (monotone, unmusical, speeding up, very like the end of a rufous-winged or black-chinned sparrow's song). But the elaborate opening is sometimes not given."

Henry W. Henshaw (1875) says:

"The song begins with a faint trill, followed by a succession of disjointed syllables, which may be expressed by the syllables *cha, chewee, wee, wee, wee, wir*, the whole delivered in a rather monotonous, listless manner, and remarkable for little else save its extreme oddity, it being entirely different from any song I have ever heard."

Francis Harper (1930) describes the song of Texas birds thus: "The song is composed of clear, sweet notes, slightly canarylike in quality. It is exceedingly variable, and seems to be given scarcely twice alike in succession. It begins in a somewhat halting fashion, gradually increases to a trill, and often winds up with a few notes as slow as those at the beginning. One rendering that I put down goes as follows: *psit, psit, psitta, psitta, tseeoo, tseeoo, wit-wit-wit-wit-wit-wit-t-t-t-t-t, tseeoo, wit, wit.* The distance at which the song can be heard is probably at least 100, and possibly 200, yards."

The foregoing descriptions show little agreement, and not only indicate how different the song sounds to different listeners, but also points to a considerable variation in the song itself.

Joe T. Marshall, Jr., records in his field notes from the Aribabi Hills, Sonora, the following song that may be atypical:

"July 13 at the mesa camp this was the most conspicuous species, with at least two males constantly singing, not only in the dawn chorus, but all day at intervals. The song is terrifically loud. When I first heard them at dawn, I thought they were *A. carpalis* near camp. Later I found that they were loud-mouthed birds at least ¼ mile off or more—down in the gully bottom or far up on the next rise. The song contains as a middle portion the entire trill of *carpalis*, which sounds actually like a field sparrow. It is preceded by some shrill upward inflected *sooeeps*, and then some faltering *pliticks* like an *Empidonax fulvifrons*. Then, after the long trill, there is another *sooeep* (or *seeep*). The singing all took place from the top of oaks, usually on small dead twigs, where the bird is in plain view but is so upright and motionless that the bird was actually seen only three times."

The song is invariably delivered from the top of a tree, bush, or post—never from the ground—and is repeated at leisurely intervals. Both Davis (MS.) and Francis Harper (1930) mention hearing the song given by low-flying birds, but there is no instance of a true flight song being delivered. In the United States the song seems to be given from its arrival until August.

*Field marks.*—This sparrow is very difficult to identify in the field, for it lacks distinctive plumage features. One seeing it for the first time can easily confuse it with other sparrows, particularly Cassin's, and possibly the rufous-crowned or even the shorter-tailed grasshopper and Henslow's sparrows. It generally does not associate with any of these but Cassin's, with which it often shares its nesting range. When in song the males can be separated readily. Otherwise the two species can be distinguished only with difficulty, even in the hand.

*Seasonal occurrence.*—In Texas, Botteri's sparrows begin to arrive, presumably, in late April and most if not all the breeding birds are on hand by May 15. By the end of September, presumably, most are gone again. Authentic records are almost lacking. In Arizona the birds do not appear until the latter part of May, and depart by September (extreme dates May 17 and October 7). Virtually nothing is known of its breeding occurrence in Mexico. Two August specimens in full juvenal plumage were taken in Michoacan and Guerrero, and a July specimen in the same plumage came from Oaxaca.

Central and southern Mexico are presumed to be the species' winter home. However, confirmatory specimens to enable one to depict the species' winter and migration ranges even vaguely are woefully few in number, and until more specimens with adequate data are available any delineation is mostly guesswork.

## DISTRIBUTION

*Range.*—Southeastern Arizona, southern Chihuahua (?), and extreme southern Texas south to southern Mexico. Breeding range and winter range imperfectly known and await clarification by further study.

*Migration.*—Early dates of spring arrival are: Arizona—Huachuca Mountains, May 17; Santa Cruz County, May 23. Texas—Lower Rio Grande Valley, April 9.

Late date of fall departure is: Arizona—Sulphur Springs Valley, October 7.

*Egg dates.*—Authentic egg dates are practically lacking.

### AIMOPHILA CASSINII (Woodhouse)
## Cassin's Sparrow
#### PLATES 53 AND 54
### Contributed by FRANCES C. WILLIAMS and ANNE L. LeSASSIER

## HABITS

Cassin's sparrows are small, nondescript, ground-dwelling birds. Unless they are singing they are rarely seen, as their plumage blends perfectly with the dry grasses among which they spend their lives.

This species is most abundant in the short grass plains of western Texas and Oklahoma, eastern New Mexico, and Colorado. Although open, grassy areas with a few scattered shrubs are preferred habitat, in western Texas these fringillids also occur in mesquite grassland areas if the mesquites are small with open areas among them. When found near draws where trees and thick brush grow, Cassin's sparrows remain on the open slopes, rarely going into the brushy areas at the bottom of the draw. They are almost never found in chaparral thickets.

J. Van Tyne and G. M. Sutton (1937) observe that this species shows a marked preference for open, grassy country in Brewster County, Texas, but found it occurs also in less open, more brushy sections. They state that it is abundant in the yucca-dotted grasslands north of Marathon, where the concentration of singing males gives somewhat the effect of a colony.

In New Mexico, Florence M. Bailey (1928) notes that "Although found sometimes in the tall grass and in meadowy tracts around springs, colonies of the sandy Cassin Sparrow are most numerous on dry plains with a growth of short grass interspersed with small shrubs and bushes. They are also seen on the mesquite plains in yucca patches * * *.

In the only record of Cassin's sparrow occurring in a cultivated area, Margaret M. and Leonard B. Nice (1922) observed four birds "in alfalfa fields about Kenton, Oklahoma," May 30 to June 2, 1922. John C. Johnson, Jr. (1956) encountered three singing males along a fence row and among abandoned oil well equipment in an area of approximately two acres in the moderately overgrazed open prairie two miles north of Norman, Okla. N. S. Goss (1891) reports that in Kansas this sparrow "frequents the barren spots and sandy lands, dotted here and there with low, stunted bushes, bunch grass or cactus."

Cassin's sparrow occasionally occurs in or near mountainous areas. The southern slopes of the Davis Mountains in Trans-Pecos, Texas, are treeless, grassy plains, with a few scattered yuccas of various species. A road traverses these plains for about 15 miles. Along this road 27 singing Cassin's sparrows were counted one July day. About a mile high in the Davis Mountains are open meadows with oaks on the surrounding slopes; this species occurs in the open meadows. It has been found as high as 4,000 feet on the mesa that surrounds the Chisos Mountains. J. Van Tyne and G. M. Sutton (1937) collected it in the foothills of the Santiago Mountains, as well as in the Glass Mountains of western Texas. The vegetation in all these areas consists of widely spaced bushes interspersed with grass. Florence M. Bailey (1928) found it "in the foothills of Mount Capitan to the lower edge of the juniper belt at about 5,500 feet * * * .

"A single specimen was taken in the fall of 1883 near Willis [New Mexico] at 7,800 feet (Henshaw), where it was, of course, a straggler."

All these descriptions of the Cassin's sparrow's habitat have one thing other than "open grasslands" in common; each mentions the presence of small shrubs, bushes, or yuccas. The birds use these as singing perches. The species does not usually inhabit areas that are entirely grass, unless the field is surrounded by a fence where the birds may perch. Although these fringillids are noted for their flight songs, they do not rise from the ground to sing, but rather launch themselves into the air from the highest perch available.

J. Stokley Ligon (1961) and Allan R. Phillips (1944) report that in New Mexico and Arizona these sparrows are more common in wet seasons than in dry ones. The reverse is true in the Panhandle and southern plains of western Texas.

PLATE 53

A. D. Cruickshank

CASSIN'S SPARROW FEEDING YOUNG

Brownsville, Texas

PLATE 54

Seward County, Kans.             W. Colvin

NEST AND EGGS OF CASSIN'S SPARROW

Mohave Desert, Calif., May 30, 1916        W. M. Pierce

NEST AND EGGS OF TEXAS BLACK-THROATED SPARROW

*Spring and courtship.*—Although a few Cassin's sparrows remain in southern and western Texas throughout the winter, they are not conspicuous until the last two weeks of March when they begin singing. It is assumed there is a movement of migrating birds into the area at this time, though possibly the birds may be present several weeks before they begin singing. The first songs are very soft, and are usually given from an inconspicuous perch. As the season progresses, the males sing loudly from the highest perch available.

Territorial defense is carried on by song duels between males. If only one male is in the area, he usually sings from the top of a bush. As soon as another male arrives, the first male begins singing in flight and the second male replies. On one occasion, as male "A" was singing, male "B" began singing about 1,500 feet away. "A" rose into the air to the height at which he usually sang, then flew steadily in the direction of "B." As he flew, he twice rose slightly in his flight and sang. When he was about 50 feet away from "B," he lit on the top of the tallest bush, where he sang three times. "B" flew up twice, singing, but did not approach "A." "A" then flew back until he was again in his own territory.

On another occasion, two males were singing only twenty feet apart. Each was singing in flight—first one, then the other, flying up. Then, as male "X" was floating down to his perch, male "Y" flew rapidly toward him, calling *tzee, tzee, tzee, tzee*. When "Y" was about five feet away, "X" retreated to a more distant perch and "Y" turned abruptly back to his own perch. Behavior like that of "A" and "B" is more common, while active defense of territory such as that shown by "Y" is rare. To date no actual physical contact between two males has been observed.

Several authors have commented on "colonies" of Cassin's sparrows, including Mrs. Bailey (1928) and J. Van Tyne and G. M. Sutton (1937). It is true that this species concentrates in favorable areas. But on the south plains of western Texas, *cassinii* is plentiful everywhere in uncultivated areas and gives no impression of colonialism.

The extent of territory one male defends varies considerably. In a census of a 50-acre tract north of Midland, Texas, three pairs were found to have territories wholly within the tract, and four additional pairs had territory partly within the area. Another 20-acre tract contained only one pair, and both members of the pair ranged over most of the territory.

During courtship pairs of Cassin's sparrows spend much time flying about their territories, just above the tops of the bushes. Both the male and female give rapid "tzee-tzee-tzee" calls as they chase each other around. Occasionally after a male has flown up as if to give his flight song, he instead gives the "tzee-tzee" call for as long as it takes him to float to his perch. When the pair desists briefly from the chasing routine, the male may assume a display posture. He elevates and fans his tail, holds his head down, his wings outward, then flutters his wings and tail. The female may perch low in the same bush during the display. (The male and female are distinguished only by identifying the male as he sings, then keeping him steadily in view as he goes about his activities.)

The following behavior of a courting pair was somewhat unusual: A male sang steadily in one small area for 30 minutes. He sang both perched and in flight. Suddenly a second bird flew up from the ground, sat on top of a mesquite, hung its head, held its tail erect, fluttered its wings rapidly, all the while uttering "tzee-tzee-tzee-tzee." The singing bird was at the peak of his flight, and sailed downward to light about 3 feet from the displaying bird. They immediately took off together, flying about 2 feet apart, to a height at least twice as high as the singing bird had been flying. They floated down, landed in the grass some distance away, and were lost to view. Neither sang nor called during this flight.

In many hours of watching the behavior of Cassin's sparrows, the authors observed copulation only once. The female was not displaying or calling, but was perched on top of a mesquite bush near where the male was singing. The male flew to her from a perch, not from his song flight. Probably the birds usually copulate while on the ground where they are hidden from view in the grass.

*Nesting*—The nest is situated on the ground at the foot of a small shrubby plant or low bush; in a bunch of grass; among grass growing in a brush heap. Or it may be in a low bush, seldom over 12 inches from the ground. Often the nest is in the midst of a tangled patch of the slender branching cactus *Opuntia leptocaulis*, where the nest may be either on the ground or within the branches of the cactus. Descriptions in the literature of nests of this species are about equally divided between nests on the ground and nests above ground.

L. J. Hersey and R. R. Rockwell (1907) found a nest near Barr, Colo., in a Gutierrezia, or small rabbit-brush. "The nest was built among the closely interwoven stems and branches of the plant, the bottom of the nest resting on the ground but not sunken into it." Henry Nehrling (1896) wrote of this species in Texas, "The nests which I had an opportunity to examine, were all placed on the ground, near a tuft of grass or on the side of a low spiny cactus. A typical nest found May 3, 1882, was built under the overhanging leaves of the *Yucca filamentosa* in a mesquit prairie." George Finlay Simmons (1925) writes of the nest sites he found near Austin, Texas: "On ground among roots at foot of small, slender-stemmed rat-tail or needle cactus (*Opuntia leptocaulis* P.D.C.), small evergreen shrub or bush, or in bunch of grass; rarely up to one foot in low bushes." A nest we found near Midland, Texas was in an *Opuntia leptocaulis* growing in the middle of a small mesquite bush. The bottom of this nest was 6 inches from the ground, and the rim was 8½ inches from the ground.

The cup-shaped nest is composed of weedstems, dead grass, and rarely, flowers. It is lined with fine grass, rootlets, grasstops, and sometimes a little horsehair. A nest near Midland, Texas was constructed entirely of grass with the thicker stems on the outside and finer grass on the inside. The outside diameter at the rim was 4 inches, the inside diameter 2½ inches. The inside depth was 2 inches.

A nest Herbert Brandt (1940) found was "Deep in the heart of [a] * * * cactus * * * a tiny, well-concealed nest that could be found only by taking apart the protecting pad. * * * It was rather bulky, and composed of grass, with a lining of finer grasses, horsehair, and some red cattle hair."

The nest described by L. J. Hersey and R. R. Rockwell (1907) near Barr, Colo.,

was a neat structure when supported by the numerous stems, but when removed proved to be rather flimsy in construction and very fragile. It was composed entirely of dry grass blades and stems, weed stems and barks, and vegetable fibers, lined with fine grass blades and a very few fine grass stems. The nest was unusually deeply cupped, with the sides built perpendicularly and slightly rimmed in. It measured as follows: outside, 3½ inches in height, 4 inches in long diameter, and 3½ inches in short diameter; inside, depth of nest cavity from rim of nest 2½ inches, short diameter 2 inches, and long diameter 2½ inches. The circumference of the inside of the rim was slightly less than that of the cavity where the eggs lay. The rim of the nest was not symmetrical but varied in height and thickness to conform to the branches among which it was placed, and altho built near the outer edge of the bush was supported and concealed on all sides by the spreading branches of the plant, which was about 10 inches high and 18 inches in diameter.

*Eggs.*—Cassin's sparrow lays usually four, but sometimes three or five eggs. The eggs are nearly oval, but somewhat elongated. They are white, unspotted, slightly glossy. The measurements of 44 eggs average 19.0 by 14.6 millimeters; the eggs showing the four extremes measure *20.9* by 15.4, 18.9 by *15.6*, and *17.8* by *13.0* millimeters.

*Young.*—The incubation period for Cassin's sparrow is unknown. The parent birds forsake their nest for the slightest cause. Many observers returning to a previously discovered nest have found it deserted and the eggs gone.

Both parents feed the nestlings. At a nest near Midland, Texas the young were fed small moths and caterpillars up to 2 inches in length. In one hour, the parents made five trips to the nest, making a "chittering" noise as they approached the nest. Whether or not this was an alarm reaction to the observer's presence is not known.

J. C. Johnson, Jr., (1956) describes the behavior of a pair of Cassin's sparrows at the nest:

For an hour * * * both remained most of the time along an approximately 100-yard stretch of fence. The male sang from posts and wire, never during flight, with silent periods of up to 20 minutes; its mate spent much of her time on the ground near the fence, occasionally flying for brief visits to a growth of small wild plums about 75 yards to the south. No young birds were in evidence, nor did either adult appear to be visiting a nest. Within half an hour after moving into my car, using it as a "blind," I twice saw the male, with food in its beak, fly directly from one fence post to a particular small area of ground nearby; During the next half hour the female also visited this spot twice with food, though she arrived by a much more devious route. The nest held five nearly-fledged young * * *.

*Plumages.*—The natal down is sparse, and very dark. The gape is a dull orange-yellow. Richard R. Graber (1955) describes the juvenal plumage as follows: "Feathers of forehead and crown blackish brown, edged with light buff (pattern irregular streaking). Nape cream, streaked with dark brown. Back feathers blackish, edged with cream (scaled pattern). Rump similar but lighter. Longest upper tail coverts black along shaft, edged with light reddish brown. Deck retrices vary from dull gray to light rusty brown (color phases?); suggestion of barring from black herringbone pattern along shaft. Other retrices largely black, narrowly light edged, and marked (ventrally) with dull white, terminally. Primaries edged with white, secondaries and tertials with cinnamon buff. Secondaries edged terminally with white, tertials margined with white. Coverts, like remiges, black. Lessers and greaters edged with cinnamon buff, medians and greaters tipped with white (two narrow wing bars). Lores and eyering whitish. Obscure superciliary line, white streaked with black. Side of head tinged with buffy, flecked with dark brown. Under parts light cream-colored; chin, throat, breast, sides, and flanks conspicuously streaked with black. Belly and crissum unmarked. Crissum more richly colored than other under parts. Leg feathers brown and cream."

The postjuvenal molt occurs in late fall (Graber, 1953; A. R. Phillips, 1951b). The breast streakings sometimes persist through the first winter to as late as March.

Robert Ridgway (1901) gives the following description of the adult Cassin's sparrow:

*Adults (sexes alike).*—Above light brown, broadly streaked with light gray, the pileum streaked also with black or dusky; scapulars and interscapulars marked with dusky subterminal spots or bars in a light brown field, the margins of the feathers light ash gray; upper tail-coverts with roundish, cordate, or transverse subterminal spots of blackish, and margined terminally with pale grayish; middle rectrices light brownish gray, with a narrow, pointed median stripe of dusky, this more or less irregular or serrated along edges, the points throwing off more or less distinct indications of darker bars across the gray on either side; edge of wing pale yellow; under parts with chest, sides, and flanks very pale brownish gray, the flanks sometimes distinctly (often broadly) streaked with brown or dusky; else-where beneath dull white (under tail-coverts sometimes pale buffy); sides of throat sometimes marked with a dusky submalar streak.

The bill is dusky, moderate in size, but somewhat broad at the base. The wings are short and rounded, the tail long and rounded. Legs and feet are flesh-colored. The iris is brown.

*Food.*—Food of the Cassin's sparrow consists of insects during the nesting season and seeds the remainder of the year. Joe T. Marshall, Jr., writes that the stomachs of two specimens taken July 27, 1951. in the Santa Rita mountains of Arizona were full of green caterpillars and shiny small beetles. In Midland, Texas, Cassin's sparrows eat caterpillars during the spring months. In the winter they eat what-ever small weed and grass seeds are available. Milo (a grain sorghum) was eaten by the species at a feeding station, and a Cassin's sparrow was caught in a trap baited with fine "chick chow" consisting of ground corn and milo. Flower buds of the blackthorn bush (*Condalia spathulata*) are eaten in season.

Cassin's sparrows seem to exist very well without drinking water. In 20 years in west Texas, where the species is abundant, the authors have seen *cassinii* drink water only four times. Nesting areas of these fringillids are often some distance from water, and the birds rarely leave their territories.

*Behavior.*—George M. Sutton and Thomas D. Burleigh (1941) comment that the Cassin's sparrow "is an exceeding inconspicuous bird when not singing." N. S. Goss (1891) says, "It is very shy and retiring in its habits, and when approached darts from bush to bush, or runs, skulks and hides like mice, and it is no easy matter to flush it from its hiding place."

Both male and female are conspicuous during the courtship chases, but after courtship ceases, only the males are visible until late summer, when the mesquite-covered pastures are suddenly full of streaked young *cassinii*. The young chase the adults, calling "tze, tze, tze" all the while. The young are not so reluctant to show themselves as the adults, and as many as a dozen may perch in plain sight in a small area.

Throughout the remainder of the year it is difficult to find a Cassin's sparrow, even in an area where the species is plentiful, for they spend their lives on the ground, amidst tall grasses. After a cold winter night, when the sun comes up and begins warming the air Cassin's sparrows may fly to the top of a yucca stalk or a bare mesquite shrub and sit warming themselves for half an hour or more. One cold January morning, just after sun-up, eight Cassin's sparrows were seen sitting on yucca stalks in a 20-acre grassy field near Midland, Texas. In the afternoon, when the temperature had risen to 50°, not a *cassinii* could be found in that same field.

Probably because of its secretive habits, the species has never been seen dust bathing. Only once was one noted in a water bath—an immature bathed briefly in a puddle left by a lawn sprinkler. It sat low in a shrub and preened briefly after its bath.

*Voice.*—Cassin's sparrow is known for its exquisitely sweet, haunting song. The song begins with two low, soft notes (seldom heard), followed by a long, loud, high, liquid trill and two shorter descending notes. When the male is defending his territory he gives the song in flight. He flies directly upward for about 20 feet, giving the two low notes as he rises. Then he sets his wings and sings as he floats downward, uttering the two descending notes just before he lights. As he descends, he holds his head up, his tail outspread, and his legs stretched downward. He rarely begins and ends his flight song at the same perch, usually traveling 15 to 30 feet during the downward sail.

Birds that winter in the Midland, Texas area may sing on warm days in early February. First-year birds sometimes begin singing in March before they lose the breast streakings of their first winter plumage. The species does not begin singing regularly until late March. A single male in an area does not begin to sing in flight until a second male enters the area. From April through July their songs are heard incessantly, night and day. H. W. Henshaw (1875) gives a graphic account of Cassin's sparrow's song. "It * * * possesses an indescribable sweetness and pathos, especially when heard, as is often the case, during the still hours of the night. During a night's march from Camp Grant to Camp Bowie, I do not think an interval of five minutes passed unbroken by the song of one of these sparrows. Ere fairly out of hearing of the notes of one performer, the same plaintive strain was taken up by another invisible musician a little farther on, and so it continued till just before dawn."

Territorial songs are usually not sung from the middle of July to the middle of September. September songs are not always typical, and are delivered more quietly and less frequently than earlier in the summer. During the late summer, a "whisper" song may be heard. It is very soft, and consists of a few preliminary notes and an assortment of trills. The song may continue several minutes, but each phrase is slightly different. The bird seems to be singing to itself, and the song seems to come from a great distance. Several birds in the same locality may sing this song, none of them paying any attention to any other one.

The call note is a loud "tsip." Another common call is a rapid "tzee, tzee, tzee." The latter call is used by both male and female during courtship chases, by the young when chasing the parents, and by any wintering bird when it flushes unexpectedly and darts rapidly away from the observer.

*Field marks.*—Cassin's sparrow is one of the most nondescript of all sparrows. It has no wing bars, eye rings, or tail markings, and the head streakings are so fine as to be almost invisible. Its back is dull gray, and the lighter under parts are unmarked in adults. The long, rounded tail and flat-headed appearance are good field marks. The flat head, combined with the thick bill, gives the bird a sloping profile unusual in the Fringillidae.

*Enemies.*—Herbert Friedmann (1934) lists six records of Cassin's sparrow victimized by the dwarf cowbird. Margaret M. and Leonard B. Nice (1924) reported "one bird killed accidently by prairie dog poison." J. Van Tyne and G. M. Sutton (1937) found the remains of a Cassin's sparrow a shrike had killed and impaled on a yucca leaf. As with most ground nesters, snakes probably are responsible for some loss of eggs and young. The young in a nest near Midland, Texas were found dead and almost completely eaten by large red ants from an ant hill under the nest bush. Whether the ants killed them or started eating them after they were dead from some other cause we could not determine.

*Fall and winter.*—Cassin's sparrows withdraw from the northern parts of their range in late October and November. A few winter from southwestern Texas to southeastern Arizona.

Allan R. Phillips (1944) describes the unusual behavior of this species in Arizona in the fall: "The Cassin's Sparrow appears in Arizona in mid-July as an abundant fall transient, having migrated west from the southern Great Plains. Most of the birds are adults. They are in full song, with testes greatly enlarged, and may go so far as to build nests, but so far as is known they do not complete their nests nor lay any eggs. They decrease sharply in numbers at the beginning of September, but some remain through the winter and leave in early May."

A. W. Anthony (1892) described this same post-breeding wandering in southwestern New Mexico. He reported that the species appeared in the extreme southwestern portion of Grant County after the August rains and then remained common there until late fall.

*Range.*—Arizona, Colorado and Kansas to central Mexico.

*Breeding range.*—The Cassin's sparrow breeds from southeastern Arizona (Santa Catalina Mountains), southwestern New Mexico (Apache, Deming), central Colorado (Barr Lake), central western Kansas (Wallace, Hays), central Oklahoma (Norman), and central and western Texas (Gainesville) south to northern Chihuahua (45 miles south of Villa Ahumada), southern Coahuila (10 miles east of Saltillo), and northern Tamaulipas (Matamoros).

*Winter range.*—Winters from southeastern Arizona (Tucson, Chiricahua Mountains) and western and south central Texas (Frijole, San Antonio) south to southern Sinaloa (Rosario), Guanajuato (Irapuato), and central Nuevo León (Linares).

*Casual records.*—Casual in southwestern Arizona (Cabeza Prieta Game Range), southern Nevada (Timpahute Valley) and northeastern Texas (Dallas).

Accidental in New Jersey (Island Beach).

*Migration.*—Early dates of spring arrival are: Texas—Rockport, February 24; Midland, April 5. New Mexico—Clayton, May 27. Nevada—Lincoln County, May 26.

Late date of spring departure is: Texas—Lower Rio Grande Valley, April 20.

Early date of fall arrival is: Arizona—Camp Verde, July 21.

Late dates of fall departure are: Oklahoma—Kenton, September 2. Texas—Rockport, October 4.

*Egg dates.*—Colorado: 1 record, July 14.

New Mexico: 1 record, July 3.

Texas: 85 records, April 12 to July 23; 44 records, May 2 to May 29.

AMPHISPIZA BILINEATA BILINEATA (Cassin)

## Texas Black-throated Sparrow

PLATE 54

### Contributed by RICHARD C. BANKS

#### HABITS

This is a common bird in the open country of central and southern Texas. A summer resident in the northern part of its breeding range, it is a permanent resident in southern Texas and the Mexican part of its range.

Referring to an area some 200 miles west of Dallas, V. P. McLaughlin (1948) says: "This secretive bird arrived unheralded, and it did not sing until May 3, when it was first seen. No nests were ever found, although the birds were locally common all summer until

July 29, when many immatures were seen, apparently migrating southward. There were no further records after August 1."

Farther to the south, in the vicinity of San Antonio, Roy W. Quillin and Ridley Holleman (1918) remark that the black-throated sparrow was "Fairly common over the entire county, but nesting only where an abundance of prickly pear offers its favorite nesting site." From observations made in the winter, Ludlow Griscom (1920) found that the species disappeared with the first cold weather in that area.

Ludlow Griscom and Maunsell S. Crosby (1926) consider the black-throated sparrow a common permanent resident in the Brownsville region of southern Texas, where it prefers the most arid habitat. Herbert Friedmann (1925) elaborates that "This is a bird of the open country, nesting in low, but very dense bushes. Its song is very reminiscent of that of the Song Sparrow, and is quite remarkable in its volume for the size of the bird. The black-throated sparrow is an early nester . . . ." S. Dillon Ripley (1949) reports that the species "was singing and in breeding condition at Port Isabel as early as March 11," 1946. H. Friedmann (1925, 1963) also notes that this sparrow is parasitized by the brown-headed cowbird, *Molothrus ater obscurus*, in this area.

In northeastern Mexico the breeding season seems to be somewhat extended. George M. Sutton, Olin S. Pettingill, and Robert B. Lea (1942) found stub-tailed juveniles in early May near Monterrey, Nuevo León, and Dean Amadon and Allan R. Phillips (1947) observed adults feeding fledged young near Saltillo, Coahuila, as late as August 28.

## DISTRIBUTION

*Range.*—The Texas black-throated sparrow breeds, and is largely resident, from central and central northern Texas (east of Pecos River, San Angelo, Wayland) south to eastern Coahuila (Saltillo), south central Nuevo León (Linares), southern Tamaulipas (Magiscatzín), and southern Texas (Rockport).

*Migration.*—The data deal with the species as a whole. Early dates of spring arrival are: New Mexico—Rio Grande Valley, April 27. Arizona—Camp Verde, March 2. Utah—Kanab, April 15. Wyoming—Laramie, April 27. Nevada—Mercury, March 18.

Late dates of spring departure are: Texas—San Antonio, April 14; Corpus Christi, April 5.

Early date of fall arrival is: Texas—Austin, October 5.

Late dates of fall departure are: Oregon—Harney County, July 15. Nevada—Mercury, August 22. Utah—Kanab, August 24. Arizona—Huachuca Mountains, September 30.

*Egg dates.*—Texas: 101 records, March 20 to August 13; 51 records, April 14 to May 20.

AMPHISPIZA BILINEATA OPUNTIA Burleigh and Lowery

# Guadalupe Black-throated Sparrow
## Contributed by RICHARD C. BANKS

### HABITS

In 1939 Thomas D. Burleigh and George H. Lowery, Jr., described this form of the black-throated sparrow from the Guadalupe Mountain region of western Texas, as being decidedly larger and slightly grayer than the more eastern *A. b. bilineata*, with a smaller white spot on the tip of the outer tail feather, and as grayer and larger than the more western *A. b. deserticola*. This subspecies also occurs in western Oklahoma, southeastern Colorado, eastern New Mexico, and northern Coahuila.

Of the status of the black-throated sparrow in the Guadalupe Mountains, T. D. Burleigh and G. H. Lowery (1940) say:

We found the desert sparrow to be a common bird here throughout the larger part of the year, occurring both in the open desert and in the canyons to an altitude of approximately 6,500 feet. Its distribution during the summer months, however, was limited by the presence of the cane cactus (*Opuntia arborescens*), and in spots where this characteristic plant was scarce or wanting, none of these sparrows was encountered. This partiality was eventually explained by the fact that so far as we could determine the nest was always placed in this cactus. It is apparently the middle of May before nesting activities are well under way and a month later before the young are fully fledged. * * * During the winter months these birds desert entirely that portion of their breeding range lying above an altitude of 4,800 feet, and even at this lower altitude are rather scarce at this season of the year. In early January only an occasional small flock was noted in the open desert * * *.

Elsewhere in the range of the subspecies the restriction to a particular plant for nesting may not be as extreme. Oliver Davie (1898) was apparently referring to birds that would later be called *opuntia:* "Mr. Wm. Lloyd found it breeding in Western Texas, nesting in the cat-claw or chapparal bushes. Nests were found May 6 and 13, June 12, and July 13 containing fresh eggs, indicating that the bird rears at least two broods in a season." Thomas H. Montgomery, Jr., (1905) found it common among the mesquite in Brewster County, Texas.

At the southern extent of the range, where some intergradation with the neighboring races *A. b. grisea* and *A. b. bilineata* occurs in the Sierra del Carmen of northern Coahuila, nesting apparently begins somewhat earlier. A. H. Miller (1955a) states that "This sparrow was moderately common in the open desert scrub at the base of the mountains below 4800 feet. Females taken on April 22 and 26 had brood patches and had recently laid."

*Range.*—Colorado and Oklahoma to central northern Mexico.

*Breeding range.*—The Guadalupe black-throated sparrow breeds from southeastern Colorado (Baca County) and northwestern Oklahoma (Kenton) south through eastern New Mexico and western Texas to northeastern Chihuahua and northwestern Coahuila (Sierra del Carmen).

*Winter range.* Winters in southern part of breeding range.

## AMPHISPIZA BILINEATA DESERTICOLA Ridgway

## Desert Black-throated Sparrow

PLATE 55

Contributed by RICHARD C. BANKS

### HABITS

This attractive little sparrow is a common dweller of the arid southwest. As much as the currently accepted name refers to its most prominent field mark, the often used alternate "desert sparrow" refers to its most characteristic habitat. Herbert Brandt (1951) combined these two features quite well when he referred to this species as a "handsome, black-bibbed obligate of the hot, little-watered areas."

Joseph Grinnell, Joseph Dixon, and Jean M. Linsdale (1930), in their report on the Lassen Peak Region of northern California, emphasize the truly desert character of this bird which "seemed to live in the driest, and apparently the hottest, areas in each neighborhood." J. Grinnell (1932) observed this sparrow in Death Valley and collected a specimen "from the ground beneath a desert holly bush at about −280 feet, less than 50 yards from the very edge of the lowest part of the sink. . . . This last was the lowest occurrence of any bird in Death Valley." In summarizing more recent records from the Death Valley area, Roland H. Wauer (1962) mentioned that "The average annual precipitation, since 1910, is 2.3 inches." Joseph Grinnell (1914) further commented that "This is a bird of the upland deserts; not one was seen in the riparian belt" along the lower Colorado River Valley between southern California and Arizona. In the Lake Mead region of southern Nevada, Gordon W. Gullion, Warren M. Pulich and Fred G. Evenden (1959) characterize it as "one of the ubiquitous birds of the creosote bush and desert scrub environments, being distributed generally independently of available drinking water."

The summary of the habitat Joseph Grinnell and A. H. Miller (1944) give for this species in California applies as well to most of its range elsewhere: "Sparsely vegetated, strongly insolated desert terrain, either steeply sloping or essentially flat, but not ordinarily the floors of sinks or riparian borders. Most favored are desert uplands—alluvial fans and hill slopes, usually with much exposed rock or gravel pavement. Plants associated include a wide variety but especially favored are cholla cactus and creosote bush, at least where mixed with some other shrubs. Catclaw, small mesquites, artemisia, sages, rabbit-brush, and purshia are other plants which the birds often live in and about."

In southern California Smyth and Bartholomew (1966) find that "generally black-throated sparrows prefer hillsides to the flatter areas. We never saw them in the floor of the Coachella Valley, but they could be found from the alluvial fans at the foot of the mountains which support little vegetation but creosote bush, up to at least 4,500 feet in the San Jacinto Mountains where pinon pine and juniper predominate."

A. M. Woodbury and C. Cottam (1962) associate the black-throated sparrow mainly with blackbrush (*Coleogyne*) in much of its range in Utah. William H. Behle (1943) found it "in the creosote bush–Joshua tree association" in the Beaver Dam Mountains of southwestern Utah, however, and mentioned that Merriam had earlier found it ranging up into the junipers in that region. In the Kanab area of southern Utah, W. H. Behle, J. B. Bushman, and C. M. Greenhalgh (1958) found black-throated sparrows in sage and greasewood along Kanab Creek, but "at Cave Lakes Canyon they occupied a sage-juniper habitat." Edward R. Warren (1913) found the species on "a mesa with scattering cedars and pinons" in Mesa County, Colo.

*Nesting.*—W. E. D. Scott (1887), speaking of the Tucson, Ariz., area, gives the breeding season as March through mid-August. This old information still stands for nesting in the southwestern United States, although apparently the extreme months are seldom utilized. Most recorded nesting dates fall in April, May, and June. The protraction of the nesting season into August is probably the result of late renestings or perhaps third broods. J. Grinnell and H. S. Swarth (1913) mention finding a nest on June 1 in the San Jacinto area of southern California and go on to say "This may have been a second set, full-grown juvenals being seen on the same date. As young birds at about the same stage of development were secured in this locality late in the summer, August 23 to 27, the nesting season appears to be rather protracted."

From their studies of the species on the desert slopes of the Santa Rosa and San Jacinto Mountains and in San Gorgonio Pass in southern California in 1964–65, M. Smyth and G. A. Bartholomew (1966) find that song and pair formation usually begin there in February.

PLATE 55

A. D. Cruickshank

DESERT BLACK-THROATED SPARROW AND YOUNG

Brownsville, Texas

PLATE 56

Azusa, Calif., May 18, 1927                                     J. S. Rowley

NEST AND EGGS OF BELL'S SAGE SPARROW

California                                                      D. Bleitz

BELL'S SAGE SPARROW

In 1965 the spring was about a month later than usual, and the first young had left the nest by early June. "We did not find any late nests that would indicate a second brood, but begging young were still being fed by adults as late as early August, so either the nesting season is extended well into the hot months of the year, or else fledglings are attended to for some weeks after they leave the nest."

At the southern limit of the range of this form in central Baja California, Griffing Bancroft (1930) reports finding nests in the latter part of May. In the vicinity of Punta Eugenia, in western Baja California, and on nearby Cedros and Natividad islands, both A. J. van Rossem (1945b) and R. C. Banks (1964a) found that nesting took place as early as February. This part of the range of this subspecies differs from the rest of its range in that it is subject to heavy fogs in the winter, and possibly the earlier nesting here reflects the relative abundance of moisture.

Nests are usually well concealed, not far above the ground in small bushes. Florence M. Bailey (1928) records nesting sites for New Mexico as being "in catsclaw, yucca, cactus, sagebrush, creosote, other bushes, mesquite, and low junipers." Herbert Brandt (1951) reports finding a nest "situated 18 inches up in a well concealed position near center of a dense blackbrush" in Cochise County, Arizona. In southern California, J. Grinnell and H. S. Swarth (1913) found a nest near the brink of Deep Canyon: "It was in a little gully, about a quarter of a mile from water, and placed in a clump of *Dalea johnsonii*, about one foot from the ground. It was loosely fastened among the forking branches, being held in place more by the general thorniness of the shrub than by any evident forethought in its construction."

D. H. Johnson, M. D. Bryant, and A. H. Miller (1948) report several nests found in the Providence Mountains of California between May 13 and 24. One of these "was near the center of a small, dense, cholla cactus that grew among bushes in a side wash. * * * The needle-sharp thorns of the cactus surrounded the nest so closely that the parent seemed to have difficulty in avoiding them. Each time it approached or left, the bird paused to snip off the tips of some of the thorns. When disturbed only enough to cause it to stand on the edge of the nest, it had difficulty in turning around to sit on the eggs again."

Another nest the above authors described in a *Purshia* bush "had a diameter of about 110 mm.; height to rim about 60 mm.; nest cavity 50 mm. in diameter and 40 mm. deep. The outer framework was principally of stiff, dry bundles of dead Joshua tree leaf fibers, with a few grass and weed stems woven in. The lining was of softer material, including individual Joshua tree leaf fibers, cowhairs, and seeds of composites. The last were apparently selected because of the soft, plumelike pappus." A nest in Nevada Jean M. Linsdale (1938) describes "measured 55 mm. inside and 95 mm. outside. The structure was made of whitish material and was lined partly with black horsehair." J. M. Linsdale also reports on two other nests. One "was composed of fine material—grass blades and stems, Eriogonum, and small twigs. The lining was whitish. The exposure was mainly to the east, but slightly to the south, and the nest was partly in the shade." The third nest "was composed of twigs and fibers of sage brush, and it was lined with light colored rabbit fur." Cowhair is a component of nests described by Taylor (1912) in Nevada and Griffing Bancroft (1930) in Baja California. Mrs. Bailey (1928) reports "A nest partly lined with wool, as is the custom in the sheep country." Apparently black-throated sparrows like hair, and are not too particular as to the kind; H. Brandt (1951) mentions a nest with a "lining of finer grasses, plant down, and a few porcupine hairs."

*Eggs.*—Three or four eggs constitute the normal clutch for the black-throated sparrow. The relatively few published reports of what may be taken as complete clutches seem to indicate a tendency toward larger clutches to the west and north. Nests in New Mexico (Bailey, 1928) and Arizona (Osgood, 1903; Brandt, 1951) are usually reported with three eggs or young, whereas those in Nevada (Linsdale, 1938) and California (Johnson, Bryant, and Miller, 1948) more often have four eggs. A family of four young was observed near San Felipe, Baja California (Huey, 1927), but a nest farther south, on Angel de la Guarda Island, contained three eggs (Mailliard, 1923). At the southern edge of the range, in central Baja California, Griffing Bancroft (1930) found two nests with two eggs each.

Little information is available on the color or size of the eggs of this race of the black-throated sparrow. Of those in central Baja California, G. Bancroft (1930) says: "The two eggs we collected are light blue, unspotted, and averaged 17.3 x 13.8 mm." J. G. Cooper (1870) spoke of a nest in the Providence Mountains of California containing white eggs. William L. Dawson (1923) describes the eggs as "3 to 5; bluish white, unmarked; av. size 17.2 x 13.3 (.67 x .52)." Oliver Davie (1886) does not refer to a particular subspecies in his book; he gives the color as "pure white, with a slight tinge of blue" and the size as ".70 to .75 (inch) length, .55 to .60 breadth." In speaking of the more eastern form, *A. b. bilineata*, William Lloyd (1887) mentions that "The eggs have a bluish tinge until blown, when they become pure white." This probably holds true for the entire species.

*Young.*—Jean M. Linsdale (1936b) writes that in 1927 "my attention was attracted to the strikingly whitish linings in several nests of Black-throated Sparrows. * * * Next I noticed that the down of nestlings of this species exhibited a similar whitish appearance, and this aroused the idea that both these peculiarities might be responses to some single item in the environment of the bird." Both nest lining and down of this sparrow fall into the lightest of the categories established to study this relationship in 15 species of desert birds. J. M. Linsdale concludes birds that nest in exposed situations in hot regions "have pale or pallid nestling plumages and nest linings which reflect and counteract the harmful effects of sun rays."

*Plumages.*—J. M. Linsdale (1936b) states that "Down on the young birds was white, slightly grayish, and very buffy". J. A. Allen (in Scott, 1887) describes the juvenal birds thus: "The young in first plumage have the feathers of the breast and flanks narrowly streaked with dusky, the streaks being most distinct on the breast. The general color of the lower parts differs little from that of the adult." The head and cheek patch are gray to grayish-brown, and there is a prominent superciliary stripe. William Brewster (1882a) adds "back faded brown with shaft-stripes of a darker shade on most of the feathers; wing-coverts and outer webs of inner secondaries, reddish-buff." The outer secondaries are dark, edged with buff; the primaries are dark brown. The tail is like that of the adult. Black may begin to appear on the throats of the young birds as early as July, but most of the molt into the adult plumage occurs in the fall.

In the adult the throat patch and lores are black, and the cheek patch is black shading to gray posteriorly. The white superciliary stripes nearly meet over the bill. A white malar stripe does not quite reach the bill, but is continuous with the white breast. Flanks are gray, tinged with buff in some specimens. The fore part of the crown is gray, this blending into grayish-brown on the hind crown, neck and back. The upper tail coverts are gray. The wing feathers are dark, the secondaries lined with buff. The tail feathers are black; there is a white stripe on the outer edge of the lateral rectrix, which is white-tipped. There is a trace of white at the tips of the second and sometimes other rectrices, but this is quickly worn off. The coloration of the sexes is alike.

*Food.*—Joe T. Marshall, Jr., writes me that he obtained seeds and "rocks" from the stomach of a specimen taken in Arizona in the fall. Seeds and gravel were similarly found in a bird taken in New Mexico in November. A specimen taken in Janaury in northern Sonora had been eating small seeds. Marshall considers that the species probably eats seeds in the winter and insects during the nesting period. I have often seen adults carrying insect matter toward their nests. Free water is apparently not necessary for these birds when insects are available.

Smyth and Bartholomew (1966) comment: "The black-throated sparrow's use of drinking water in the field seems to depend on its diet. During the late spring and early fall, stomachs contain almost exclusively seeds and gravel and the birds regularly drink at water-holes even when maximum temperatures are as low as 9° C. But as soon as green grass and herbs appear after the first rains—in 1964 these fell in mid-November—the sparrows are no longer seen at water holes and can be found in small, widely scattered flocks far from the water holes. At this time their stomachs contain green material as well as seeds and gravel, their bills are stained green, and they can be seen often pecking at green vegetation. Then when day-flying insects become more abundant in February these are eaten, sometimes almost exclusively, and this diet allows the sparrows to be independent of drinking water throughout the breeding season. A few adults can be seen coming to drink in June, and the numbers of birds visiting water and the number of visits to water per bird then increase until by August each bird visits, on the average, about twice daily. The young are fed insects, particularly grasshopper abdomens.

"The foraging habits of black-throated sparrows are, of course, reflected in their diet. They spend much of their time on the ground picking seeds or pecking at seed-husks or green grass and herbs, but in the spring and early summer they often fly up, either from the ground or a low shrub, after some flying insect. At this time, too, they often forage in such trees as mesquite, catclaw, and desert willow, obviously for insects."

*Voice.*—The song of the black-throated sparrow is pleasant and distinctive, but also complex and difficult to describe. M. H. and J. B. Swenk (1928) met the bird in the deserts of Arizona: " * * * as soon as we entered the edge of the desert north of Tucson we heard a new bird voice in the tinkling, canary-like song of this bird. Soon we saw several of them * * * and had the opportunity of listening to several males in full, ecstatic song. The song was rapidly given and sustained and frequently included triplets of what sounded like double-toned notes."

W. P. Taylor (1912) reports that "The song is imperfectly represented by the following syllables, 'queet! queet! toodle-oodle-oodle-oodle!' with a rising inflection on the 'queets.' In a variation of the song a note is apparent resembling somewhat a call of the western lark sparrow." This resemblance was also noted by Mrs. Bailey (1928) in New Mexico, where a song "heard frequently on the Pecos, given with a burr like that of the Lark Sparrow was *'tra-ree-rah, ree-rah-ree.'* "

My impression of the voice, heard mostly in Baja California, Mexico, is of a longer, more warbling song, and agrees best with Mrs. Florence M. Bailey's (1923) description from the Santa Rita Mountains of Arizona. In this area, she states, "The song may be rendered as *chee-whee, whit, wher'r'r'r'r, cha, cha, cha,* and also *chee cha cher'r'r'r'r chee.*"

Notes other than the song are rarely mentioned in accounts of this bird. W. P. Taylor (1912) states that "Low 'chips' were heard which were finally traced to a desert sparrow which had its beak full of insects and was perching on a rock."

*Field marks.*—The combination of white facial strips and jet-black throat will serve to identify this small sparrow. The white tips to the outer tail feathers may be helpful in identification at times, but are seldom seen, even when the bird is in flight. The sexes are similar.

*Enemies.*—In the Providence Mountains of California (Johnson, Bryant, and Miller, 1948) "The nests were seldom more than two feet above the ground, and thus were within the reach of most ground-dwelling predators. Near Cima on May 13, 1938, a red racer (*Coluber flagellum*) was found just after it had swallowed three half-grown young from a nest in a low bush."

Florence M. Bailey (1906) recorded a mammalian predator at a nest: "One June morning in New Mexico as I was going thru a grove of small round junipers, with spirits lifted by the bright song from the top of one of the trees, my steps were arrested and I gazed with dismay upon a beautiful little nest rudely torn from its place in the juniper, and the ground below strewn with feathers of the brooding mother bird. The horrid tragedy was probably no older than the night for the wind had not had time to blow away the feathers, and tracks tho blurred by the night's rain were fresh enough to fix the blame upon the marauder—a coyote or lynx."

Cowbirds sometimes parasitize nests of black-throated sparrows. Herbert Friedmann (1963) refers to two instances of such parasitism by *Molothrus ater obscurus* near Tucson, Ariz.

Where both the black-throated sparrow and its relative the Bell or sage sparrow (*Amphispiza belli*) nest in the same area, the two species may compete for territory. J. M. Linsdale (1938) reports an incident in Nevada where "a few minutes earlier an individual thought to be the male of the pair had driven a sage sparrow from a sage bush 20 feet from the nest site." W. P. Taylor (1912) also reports that "a desert sparrow was on at least one occasion seen fighting with a sage sparrow." A. W. Anthony (1895) implies that such conflicts may have some bearing on the distribution of the two species, at least near San Fernando in northern Baja California. He states that "*A. belli* takes the place, to a large extent, of *bilineata* on the coast, crowding it further inland to the north until at San Quintin I very seldom saw it within ten miles of the beach."

*Winter.*—The black-throated sparrow is only partly migratory; many birds are found in the southern part of the breeding range throughout the winter. In California they leave the regions north of the Mohave Desert and are presumed to be partly migratory elsewhere, as the populations in the southern part of the state are smaller and less widely dispersed in winter than in summer (Grinnell and Miller, 1944). The species has been observed in southern Nevada in every month except January, and is (Gullion, Pulich, and Evenden, 1959) "absent from Nevada's deserts for not over two months in midwinter, if that long." In Arizona the species "remains through the winter in some of the warmer southern valleys" (Swarth, 1914b), and in New Mexico "a few winter on the cactus-covered plains" (Hunn, 1906).

In reference to winter activities in California, D. H. Johnson, M. D. Bryant and A. H. Miller (1948) state that "At that season they were frequently in mixed flocks with Brewer sparrows, and tended to stay more in canyons and about the bases of rimrock cliffs. A flock of eight watched near Mitchell's on December 26, 1937, was foraging in the rain. They were very active, hopping about and apparently picking up seeds from the bare ground beneath bushes." In the Organ Pipe National Monument in Arizona, Laurence Huey (1942) reports that "During winter there was a great influx from the north, which bunched up with Brewer and Chipping Sparrows and wandered over the flats in large flocks." Mrs. Bailey (1923) mentions for the Santa Rita Mountains of Arizona that in winter the black-throated sparrow is mainly in small flocks, often with cactus wrens, verdins, or white-crowned sparrows.

Michael Smyth and George A. Bartholomew (1966) note that in the southern California deserts: "From June to September the sparrows move about in pairs or small groups of up to five or six. Later larger flocks of up to a dozen or more birds are not uncommon, and black-throated sparrows often keep company with sage and white-crowned sparrows."

Grinnell (1904) found the birds common in mid-winter at Palm Springs, California, "occurring in scattering flocks of from six to twenty or more. These companies were usually in motion and hard to follow, as the birds had a way of flying off one at a time in rapid succession, retreating over a hill or behind thickets; so that the whole flock seemed to vanish."

## Distribution

*Range.*—California, Nevada and Wyoming to Baja California and Sonora.

*Breeding range.*—The desert black-throated sparrow breeds from northeastern California (Alturas), northern Nevada (Virgin Valley in Humboldt County, Wells), northern Utah (Salt Lake City), southwestern Wyoming (Rock Creek, Big Canyon), and western Colorado (Little Snake River, Cortez) south through desert areas to central Baja California (south to lat. 27°N.; Cedros, Natividad, and Ángel de la Guarda Islands), northern Sonora (south to lat. 30°N.), and northwestern Chihuahua (Casas Grandes, Samalayuca).

*Winter range.*—Winters from southeastern California (Providence Mountains), southern Nevada (Lake Mead), central Arizona (Salt River Valley, Safford), and southwestern New Mexico south to central Baja California (San Ignacio Lagoon, San Lucas) and central Sonora (Guaymas).

*Casual records.*—Casual in British Columbia (Wells Gray Park), Oregon (Depoe Bay, Beaverton, Milwaukie; Silver Lake and Wright's Point in Harney County), Idaho (Pahsimeroi Valley), and Kansas (near Garden City). Photographed (subspecies not determined) in Illinois (Rockton) and New Jersey (New Brunswick); sight records in Wisconsin, Ohio, and Massachusetts.

*Egg dates.*—Arizona: 25 records, April 20 to August 10; 6 records, April 24 to May 21.

California: 10 records, April 15 to June 6.

Nevada: 15 records, May 4 to July 29.

New Mexico: 9 records, May 20 to July 30.

### AMPHISPIZA BILINEATA BANGSI Grinnell
### AMPHISPIZA BILINEATA BELVEDEREI Banks

# Bangs' and Cerralvo Black-throated Sparrows

## Contributed by RICHARD C. BANKS

## Habits

Joseph Grinnell named the subspecies *bangsi* in 1927 in tribute to the ornithological work of Outram Bangs. He described it as similar to the form *deserticola*, but with a slightly shorter wing and tail, a slightly larger bill, and paler on the upper surface. Adriaan J. van Rossem (1930) indicates that this is the smallest of the (then known) races of the species, and claims that it is darker than *deserticola*, the original description having been based on material which had turned paler with age.

J. Grinnell (1928b) gives the range of this subspecies as the southern portion of Baja California, north to about latitude 26°, with intergradation with *A. b. deserticola* taking place to about 27° N. This includes most of the southern islands in the Gulf of California and Magdalena and Santa Margarita islands on the Pacific side of the peninsula. The population on Cerralvo Island has recently been described as *A. b. belvederei* (Banks, 1963a).

Walter E. Bryant (1889) says that "On Santa Margarita and Magdalena Islands they were the most common and generally distributed species. Breeding far from any water, nests were found in bushes from one to five feet above the ground." In the Cape region, I have found this species in fairly open desert, but not where the underbrush is thick nor in the thorn forest.

A nest containing three eggs was found on Cerralvo Island (Banks, 1963b). Several other persons have mentioned finding nests, but have not recorded the number of eggs.

The data relating to the time of nesting of this subspecies are confusing and contradictory. A. J. van Rossem (1945b) indicates a February breeding season on Magdalena and Santa Margarita islands, but presents evidence to show that elsewhere in the Cape region on the mainland the birds nest in October. On the islands in the Gulf of California he mentions March as the breeding month. More recent data from Magdalena Island (Banks, 1964a) contradict the February date without clearly indicating an alternative. While there is some evidence of nesting near La Paz in the fall, other evidence also suggests a spring breeding season.

It seems that the population of each island in the Gulf of California has adjusted its breeding cycle to its own peculiar circumstances. Thus, Richard C. Banks (1963c) found evidence that breeding was in progress or about to begin on San Marcos, Coronados, and Santa Catalina islands in late March and early April of 1962, but not on Monserrate Island. The birds on Espiritu Santo, Monserrate, and Danzante islands were in breeding condition in early May 1963 (Banks, 1964a), and nesting began on Cerralvo Island in mid-May 1962, perhaps continuing throughout the summer (Banks, 1963b).

These birds have been noted feeding at cacti of the genera *Mammillaria* and *Pachycereus*. Several seen foraging on Ocotillo (*Fouquieria*) on Coronados Island were apparently taking aphids from the leaves. On Cerralvo Island most foraging took place among annual plants in washes, but a bird was observed feeding at the flower of a cactus (Banks, 1963b, 1963c).

## DISTRIBUTION

### Bangs' Black-throated Sparrow (*A. b. bangsi*)

*Range.*—The Bangs' black-throated sparrow is resident in southern Baja California from lat. 26°N. southward, including most of the adjacent islands.

### Cerralvo Black-throated Sparrow (*A. b. belvederei*)

*Range.*—The Cerralvo black-throated sparrow is resident on Cerralvo Island, Baja California.

### AMPHISPIZA BILINEATA TORTUGAE van Rossem

## Tortuga Black-throated Sparrow

### Contributed by RICHARD C. BANKS

#### HABITS

Adriaan J. van Rossem (1930) describes this subspecies of the black-throated sparrow as the darkest of the known races, the back being more slaty and less brown, and the under parts being more extensively and deeply colored. It is resident on Tortuga Island in the Gulf of California, an island only a little more than 2 square miles in area.

A. J. van Rossem (1945b) comments on the density of the population of black-throated sparrows on Tortuga Island as follows: "Through some cause now obscure, but which most likely is connected in some way with an abundant, year-round food supply, the density of the population on Tortuga surpasses anything in my experience with the species."

In 1930 A. J. van Rossem (*op. cit.*) visited the island in late March and early April and found that the breeding season was under way. When I visited Tortuga Island on Mar. 30, 1962, breeding had not yet begun (Banks, 1963c); apparently there is some variation in the annual cycle on this island.

#### DISTRIBUTION

*Range.*—The Tortuga black-throated sparrow is resident on Tortuga Island off central eastern Baja California.

AMPHISPIZA BILINEATA CARMENAE van Rossem

## Carmen Black-throated Sparrow

Contributed by RICHARD C. BANKS

### HABITS

This subspecies of the black-throated sparrow is found only on Carmen Island in the Gulf of California. C. H. Townsend (1923) and Joseph Grinnell (1927, 1928b) referred to specimens from this island, but under other subspecific names. It was not until 1945 that Adriaan J. van Rossem separated the birds of Carmen Island from *A. b. bangsi* of the southern part of the peninsula of Baja California on the basis of their slightly grayer color and different wing and tail proportions. Some authorities do not yet accept the race, but I agree with A. J. van Rossem that it can be separated on the basis of color.

Very little information is available for this subspecies. A. J. van Rossem (1945b) indicated that the breeding season began in March, but R. C. Banks (1964a) thought that date was too early, breeding not being well under way until the middle or latter part of April.

### DISTRIBUTION

*Range.*—The Carmen black-throated sparrow is resident on Carmen Island off central eastern Baja California.

AMPHISPIZA BELLI NEVADENSIS (Ridgway)

## Northern Sage Sparrow

Contributed by ALDEN H. MILLER

### HABITS

The sage sparrow is typical of the sagebrush country of the Great Basin where it nests. Inconspicuous in its somewhat concealing color, and neither bold in actions nor in song, it may be overlooked on first exploration of its semidesert environment. The race *nevadensis* is the most wide ranging and the most migratory of the several forms of sage sparrow. The coastal races, sharply demarked in range and in their darker color, are often referred to as Bell's sparrows in contrast to the inland sage sparrows.

All the sage sparrows are ground dwellers, spending most of their time on sand, gravel pavement, and alkali hardpan between and beneath bushes, or if the ground they range over is not bare, it is not more than slightly grown to grass or littered with fallen leaves and twigs. When alarmed they mount to the bush tops briefly, only to drop out of sight again, skulking and running behind or among the bushes. Song posts invariably are on the bush tops.

The breeding range of the race *nevadensis* lies west of the Rocky Mountains and east of the Cascade Range and the Sierra Nevada, some 850 miles in its east-west dimension. It extends from the inner Columbia River basin of eastern Washington southeast to northwestern New Mexico for about 1,200 miles. In all this area the vegetation used chiefly by the sage sparrows is the dominant sagebrush (*Artemisia tridentata*). This widespread plant occurs generally in the areas classed as upper Sonoran and Transition life zones, ranging higher in places among open conifers. R. E. Snodgrass (1903) describes the habitat in Washington as "most refreshing 'scab-land' country. Such areas alternate with the wheat deserts * * * and occupy also a large space along the eastern edge of the Grand Coulee. On them there is scarcely any soil, only enough for sage-brush to grow. The surface is cut by erosion into irregular hollows, low hills, abrupt walls, ridges, and tower-like buttes." Jean M. Linsdale (1938) states that in the Toiyabe Mountains area of central Nevada the sage sparrow occurs "throughout the bush-covered desert well up to the base of the mountains. * * * Sagebrush is a conspicuous feature in the habitat * * * but other bushes were occupied sometimes." In one area of nesting beside the sagebrush there were "a few *Chrysothamnus* and about an equal number of *Sarcobatus*. The soil was sandy but hard and cracked slightly. There was some cover of grass."

Near Prineville in central Oregon I camped on a desert flat among sage sparrows from June 19 to 21, 1938. Here, at an altitude of 3,300 feet, breeding pairs were in *Artemisia* and *Chrysothamnus* cover around the margins of a low area free of junipers. The soil was fairly loose, and in places it was distinctly sandy. Males at times sang from the tops of small juniper bushes but none was seen in the juniper woodland itself.

Indicative of some extension beyond the typical sagebrush cover is Arthur C. Twomey's (1942) report of nesting southeast of Vernal, Utah "in a hot, dry, sandy valley dominated by an Atriplex-Tetradymia Community." In Colorado W. W. Cooke (1897) states that Henshaw found the sage sparrow ranging up to 8,000 feet at San Luis Park, but this would be within the normal upper reaches of sagebrush growth.

*Spring.*—The migration of this race of sage sparrow, although more definite than that of others, is neither conspicuous nor extensive. Not all parts of its breeding range are vacated by all individuals. Thus Ira N. Gabrielson and Stanley Jewett (1940) report a winter record on January 14 at Umatilla, Oreg., and sage sparrows occur in January in the Reno area of Nevada. They probably are resident generally in the southern parts of the breeding range, as in southwestern Utah. Nevertheless, there is a distinct influx of birds in spring to the nesting grounds.

Spring migratory movements are early. Stanley Jewett et al. (1953) comment on the early arrival of this sparrow in eastern Washington and state that nesting begins by late March; they note the presence of sage sparrows within the breeding range by February 28 and March 2 in different years. Gabrielson and Jewett (1940) state that sage sparrows arrive in March in eastern Oregon. Ross Hardy (1947) found them abundant in spring migration at Price, Utah, from March 17 until April 7.

Settlement on breeding territories obviously is later at high elevations than in the lower desert valleys. In some places the higher elevations apparently are not reached until April and early May.

*Nesting.*—In keeping with the sage sparrow's adherence to low bush cover, nests are usually concealed in *Artemisia* shrubs. Some are placed in a depression on the ground as Robert Ridgway (1877) reported, but this is a less usual although not rare situation. Most nests are 6 to 18 inches above the ground as Walter P. Taylor (1912) reported for Humboldt County, Nev. Data on eight other nests in the records of the Museum of Vertebrate Zoology reveal only one other ground nest; the heights above ground of the others range from 3 to 40 inches (average 16½). All but one (in an *Atriplex* bush) were placed in or under *Artemisia*.

Gabrielson and Jewett (1940) state for Oregon that "dates on which nests containing fresh eggs have been found vary from April 5 to May 23, depending somewhat on the elevation. The earliest dates are for the sage areas along the Columbia River near Boardman, and the later nests are found on the high sage plateaus of the southeastern part of the State." But a nest with five young found near Boardman on March 29, following a mild winter, must represent eggs laid no later than mid-March. Jewett et al. (1953) report that in Washington many nests of this species have eggs by late March. Near Prineville, Oreg., I found a nest with three fresh eggs on June 19, a set completed to four eggs on or before June 21. This probably represented a replacement nest as other sage sparrows in the vicinity had fledged young at that time.

On the other hand what apparently are first layings occur in the higher sagebrush areas in parts of Nevada in early June, as attested to by data from Stewart, Ormsby County, 4,600 feet altitude, obtained by Milton S. Ray and by reports (Taylor, 1912) of nests and eggs as late as June 16 at Big Creek, 6,000 feet altitude, at the base of the Pine Forest Mountains in Humboldt County. A very late nest, doubtless a second effort, was recorded by E. R. Hall 13 miles north of Montello, 5,000 feet altitude, Elko County, Nev., on July 17; the nest held 3 eggs.

Walter P. Taylor (1912) writes that the nests above ground level were "variously supported, as a rule being built into the body of the bush so that the foundation was firm, although in some cases the attachment was not so secure. Materials worked into the several nests included dry sage twigs and sticks; in the linings, wool, dried grass, weed stalks, weed seeds, cowhair, and rabbit fur." The nest I found near Prineville was not well concealed in the bush, but it was partly screened from the sun. It was made of grass and bark shreds, with some wool in the lining. The whole nest was larger and thicker-walled than those of Brewer's sparrows and contained none of the coarse hair found in the nest lining of the latter species.

James B. Dixon writes me that a nest found at June lake, Mono County, Calif., on June 17 was in a bitter bush clipped down by feeding sheep, and was composed outwardly of bark strips from the bitter bushes and sagebrush and inwardly of fine bark with a few tufts of sheeps' wool—a favorite lining.

A representative nest from Nye County, Nev., in the collection of the Museum of Vertebrate Zoology has a scant outer frame of ⅛ inch *Artemisia* sticks and dry flowering stalks of annual plants, a core structure of grass stems and shredded bark, finer toward the interior, and a lining of rabbit fur and fine shreds of bark. The nest cups of five nests are 2½ inches across and 1 inch deep; outside dimensions are 4 to 7 inches across and 2 to 2½ inches deep, varying in accordance with the amount of outside framework developed for a particular place in the supporting bush.

Russell W. Hendee (1929) reporting on sage sparrows in Moffat County, Colo., says that "Most of the nests were in sage bushes about a foot from the ground, but many were on the ground under the bushes. The nests were made of grass and lined with feathers and in some cases wool. The last set of fresh eggs was found on June 25." The first eggs were found there on May 20.

Jean M. Linsdale (1938) discovered the nest he reported on in the Smoky Valley of Nevada on May 26 when a parent flushed at 4 feet. The bird "fluttered slightly and moved off, close to the ground, half running for 10 feet and then running for another 10 feet. It stayed within 25 feet of the nest for 3 or 4 minutes and then flew off. * * * During this interval the bird was quiet most of the time. It began to feed as it walked over the ground, part of the time picking off objects from the lower leaves of sage bushes." On May 27 the third egg of the set in this nest had been laid and the incubating sparrow then sat very closely. Thus on May 28 it "would not leave the nest when the bush was hit with a stick." Finally the bird was forced off and it then ran 25 feet over the ground with the tail elevated. Again on June 6 he "had to shake the bush violently before the bird would leave." On the last visit to this nest at 9:00 a.m. on June 9, the young were hatching; one gaped for food; one was still lying in part of the shell and the third egg was unhatched. The incubation period was thus about 13 days, assuming that incubation started on May 26 when the sparrow was flushed from two eggs.

James B. Dixon wrote me also of a sage sparrow that would not flush until the nest bush was struck. All observers emphasize that the incubating bird normally flushes by dropping to the ground and running off. I noted in Oregon that the female ran quietly within 25 feet of us, holding the tail up, thrasherlike. Usually the parent is silent, or it utters the rather faint *tsip* alarm note, and then finally may alternate running on the ground and calling from bush tops, jerking the tail up periodically.

*Eggs.*—The sage sparrow lays three or four eggs, rarely five. Specific records in the literature and data in the Museum of Vertebrate Zoology for what are apparently completed clutches show 12 sets of three and 10 sets of four. There are two records of five, one by William Leon Dawson (1909) and the other by Gabrielson and Jewett (1940).

The eggs are ovate. The ground color is pale blue or bluish white and the surface is speckled, spotted, and often blotched with "Verona brown," "rood brown," or "wood brown"; occasionally black dots and lines occur; undermarkings are "light neutral gray." Spottings may be scattered over the entire surface or concentrated toward the large end, sometimes forming a crude wreath. On some the brown markings are sharply defined, whereas on others they are clouded and confluent. Thus there is considerable variation; frequently the undermarkings are lacking while in others they may be dominant and the brown spots pale and few.

The measurements of 70 eggs average 19.47 by 14.56 millimeters. The eggs showing the four extremes measure *21.2* by 14.9, 19.6 by *15.2*, *18.2* by 15.1, and 18.8 by *13.7* millimeters.

*Young.*—The sage sparrow's young have pale natal down in general correlation with the prevailing paleness of the nest lining and the somewhat exposed nest location, as pointed out by Jean M. Linsdale (1936b). Young are fed insects by the adults, as generally is true in sparrows of the subfamily Emberizinae. J. M. Linsdale (1938) watched an adult feeding a bob-tailed young on the ground, the fledgling being able to fly distances of but 3 feet. "The parent moved about, jerking its tail upward slightly, as it picked up insects, within 10 feet of the young one" that was skulking under an *Atriplex* bush. Another adult, evidently the male of the pair, sang near by.

Near Prineville, Oreg., I found a short-tailed juvenile on June 19. It dodged under an *Artemisia* bush and as I approached began a vigorous flirting of wings and tail that made a distinct drumming sound. It kept this up for at least two minutes until I drove it from the bush. The adults came within 10 yards of me frequently, scolding with their high-pitched *tsips*.

*Plumages.*—In the juvenal plumage the forehead and crown are gray, conspicuously streaked with black; on the nape and neck the streaks are less heavy but become broad and sharp again on the back and rump; the ground color of the latter areas is buffy gray. The streaked upper tail coverts are brown. The rectrices are black, the outer pair with light buff outer webs. The remiges are dull black, the primaries lightly edged and the inner secondaries broadly edged with dull cinnamon. The lesser wing coverts are light brown, the middle coverts blackish tipped with buffy white, and the greater coverts are blackish with broad buff edges and tips of buffy white; thus two light wing bars are formed. The eye ring is white, the lores and feathers below the eye dark. The feathers above the lores are whitish, the superciliary area gray. The chin and throat are white, faintly streaked, and with poorly defined black mustache marks separating the white subauricular area. The breast, sides, and flanks are whitish, conspicuously streaked with black. The lower belly and crissum are unstreaked, white to buff white; the leg feathers are brown and white.

The postjuvenal molt entails replacement of the body plumage and wing coverts but not the rectrices and remiges. It typically is completed early, by late August or early September, and the resulting plumage of the first winter is like that of adults; the sexes are the same in coloration.

In the adults the upper surface is gray, slightly buff-tipped in fresh plumage, the back and rump drab gray. The back is lightly streaked with black. The wings and tail are blackish, edged with clay to dull cinnamon color, the outer web and the tip of the inner web of the lateral tail feathers are white. The wing coverts are light brown, tipped with clay color to buff to form two wing bars. The bend of the wing is pale yellow. A supraloral spot, the eye ring, and the malar stripes are white; the lores, subocular area, the mustache mark, and the breast spot are black. The chin, breast and belly are white; the sides and flanks buffy and faintly streaked with dusky; the maxilla blackish; mandible blue gray; feet dark brown; iris brown.

*Food.*—George F. Knowlton (1937a) reporting on this species in Utah found that fifteen stomachs held the following: "4 grasshoppers; 18 Hemiptera, 13 being false chinch bugs; 68 Homoptera, made up of 64 nymphal and 4 adult beet leafhoppers in 3 birds;

6 Coleoptera in 4 stomachs; 1 lepidopterous caterpillar; 14 Hymenoptera, 9 being ants; 2 spiders; 301 weed seeds; plant fragments." Such food could be obtained from the ground or low in bushes, especially in the summer season. Insects are probably taken rarely, or not at all in winter. In New Mexico, on December 2 and 3, N. S. Goss (1881) found that the stomachs of four birds contained only small seeds and coarse gravel.

James B. Dixon writes me that he has often seen these sparrows "on the ground * * * scratching and apparently securing food from the litter left in the dropped leaves of desert plants." In general, however, the foraging is done by gleaning and not through scratching in the litter. In thus foraging they run swiftly, stopping now and then to pick up food particles. Jean M. Linsdale (1938), as noted earlier, saw a bird picking off objects from the lower leaves of sage bushes.

*Behavior.*—Gabrielson and Jewett (1940) write that this sparrow is "difficult to detect so long as it remains motionless. Its habit of mounting the topmost twig of a sagebrush, however, to sing its tinkling little refrain, twitching its long black tail all the while, offers an opportunity to view this * * * desert dweller to good advantage. * * * It has an almost uncanny ability to slip from one bush to another, keeping out of sight of an intruder as it does so." H. W. Henshaw (1875) states that fall birds are very shy and are most often seen running with great agility among the bushes, their motions being so quick that they might readily be mistaken for mice. In running, their long tails are carried in a perpendicular position suggesting wrens. Ralph Hoffman (1927) states that even on the ground the bird jerks its tail from time to time, and N. S. Goss (1881) describes the birds as "very active, running about with tail steadily erected at an angle of 45°, in an odd, easy, graceful manner." Grinnell and Miller (1944) say that these sparrows "forage from the ground surface and parts of the bushes within reach of it and run swiftly from the base of one bush to another, seeking concealment. Flight is resorted to when the bird is close pressed and at times when moving between lookout posts on bush tops or to and from nest sites in the bushes." Jewett et al. (1953) stress the point that when an observer rushes to the spot where the bird disappears, he finds that it has run along the ground for several yards. "Each time it rises the sage sparrow follows a new course, so that one cannot be sure even of its general direction."

There is little doubt that the long tail of this species and the upright position in which it is held serves as a balancer in the agile running actions. Also, the enlarged auditory bullae of the skull are probably related to this as they seem to occur in many running and hopping animals.

*Voice.*—The song is a rather weak, high-pitched tinkling series of notes. Hoffman (1927) suggests the syllables *tsit tsit, tsi you, tee a-tee*, the third note being high and accentuated. The flocking or contact note is similar to that of the flocking note of juncos, but is weaker. The alarm note *tsip* is only slightly louder. I do not know of other vocalizations that occur with any regularity, but Linsdale (1938) mentions once hearing a long series of harsh notes, the meaning of which is uncertain.

*Field marks.*—Sage sparrows are identified by the dark narrow moustache marks and small black spot in the center of the breast, as well as by the white frontal spot and eye ring, coupled with the gray back and contrasting black tail. The tail flipping and its elevated position while on the ground are also good field characteristics and immediately distinguish the bird from the larger lark sparrow which has large white tail spots, though it shows a somewhat similar black breast spot.

*Enemies and parasites.*—Richard M. Bond (1940) recorded the remains of a sage sparrow in the pellet of a horned owl in Nevada.

R. O. Malcomson (1960) in a study of mallophaga mentions *Bruelia lautiuscula* as a parasite of the sage sparrow.

Henry J. Rust (1917) discovered and photographed a nest in Idaho that contained one egg of the sage sparrow and two of the brown-headed cowbird; this was on July 7. H. Friedmann (1963) comments that as this is the only record in his files, the sage sparrow is a "very uncommon victim" of the cowbird.

*Fall and winter.*—Sage sparrows congregate in late summer in loose flocks immediately after nesting and while they are carrying on the postnuptial or annual molt. The flocks wander in the fall and of course, as indicated earlier, not all of them migrate outside the breeding range. However, this race appears in late September and October on the more southerly wintering grounds. Harry S. Swarth (1924b) found them first arriving on September 25 in the San Francisco Mountain area of Arizona. "Ten days later a few more appeared and by October 17 they were present in fair abundance. At the end of the month * * * [they] had disappeared again," possibly driven to lower levels by a storm. In Joshua Tree National Monument of southeastern California, Miller and Stebbins (1964) report that clear cut examples of this race were taken no earlier than October 22 and November 1. A. J. van Rossem (1911) found the species wintering abundantly in the Salton Sea area of California from December 1 to January 14, represented by both this race and *canescens*. In the lowlands of southern Nevada, near the breeding range, winter flocks are present by October 6, according to van Rossem (1936a). Wilfred H. Osgood (1903) reports that in Cochise County, Ariz., they are "very common during the winter months" and are "seen in flocks about the leafless mesquites till about the middle of March."

The habitat frequented in winter is more varied than in summer and consists of sparse desert scrub in the main with a variety of plants, including tree yuccas, *Atriplex*, *Sarcobatus*, mesquites, and *Chrysothamnus*. Johnson, Bryant, and Miller (1948) found these sparrows frequenting areas of open bunch grass as well as the creosote bush association in the Providence Mountains in the Mohave Desert in winter.

### DISTRIBUTION

*Range.*—Eastern Washington, Idaho, and Montana to northwestern Mexico and western Texas.

*Breeding range.*—The northern sage sparrow breeds from central eastern Washington (Waterville, Wilbur), southern Idaho (Deer Flat, Spencer), southwestern Wyoming (23 miles southwest of Bitter Creek), and northwestern Colorado (Moffat County) south to northeastern California (Sierra Valley, Mono Lake), south central and southeastern Nevada (Toiyabe and Charleston mountains) southwestern Utah (Pine Valley), northeastern Arizona (Hopi Buttes), and northwestern New Mexico (Gallina).

*Winter range.*—Winters from central California (Los Baños, Raisin), central Nevada (Reno), southwestern Utah (St. George), northern Arizona (Tonalea), central New Mexico (Carlsbad), and southwestern Kansas (Morton and Seward counties), south to northern Baja California (San Andrés, Puerto de Calamajué), northern Sonora (Kino Bay), northwestern Chihuahua (Casas Grandes), and western Texas (Fort Davis). Occasionally remains north up to Oregon (Umatilla).

*Casual records.*—West of the Cascade Range it has occurred in British Columbia (Lulu Island), Washington (Dupont), and Oregon (Portland) and east of the Rocky Mountains in Montana (Sedan) and Wyoming (Wheatland, Cheyenne). Migrates along the east base of the Rocky Mountains in Colorado.

*Migration.*—The data deal with the species as a whole. Early dates of spring arrival: Utah—March 2. Wyoming—Superior, April 2. Idaho—Pocatello, March 18. Oregon—Lake County, March 17. Washington—Pierce County, February 27.

Late dates of spring departure are: New Mexico—Organ Mountains, April 25. Arizona—Mercury, April 27.

Early dates of fall arrival are: Arizona—Mercury, October 1. New Mexico—Ojo Caliente, September 21.

Late dates of fall departure are: Washington—Grant County, November 4. Oregon—Malheur National Wildlife Refuge, October 1. Idaho—Rupert, September 16. Wyoming—Rock Creek, October 25. Utah—Book Cliffs, October 10.

*Egg dates.*—(The data concern the species as a whole.) California: 17 records, March 29 to July 6; 9 records, May 7 to June 6.

Colorado: 2 records, May 20 and June 25.

Idaho: 2 records, June 25 and July 7.

Nevada: 7 records, April 1 to June 14.

Oregon: 7 records, May 9 to June 18.

Washington: 3 records, March 25 to April 13.

## AMPHISPIZA BELLI CANESCENS Grinnell

## California Sage Sparrow

### Contributed by ALDEN H. MILLER

#### HABITS

This race is closest in color and size to *Amphispiza belli nevadensis* with which it intergrades in the northern part of the Inyo district of California. Compared with *nevadensis*, it is smaller and slightly darker; the back streaking is reduced or lacking and the moustache marks and streakings of the flanks are somewhat more prominent. The best distinguishing feature is size, and this, as expressed in wing length averages, is about 10 percent less as Grinnell's original table (1905b) of measurements showed.

The subspecies *canescens* ranges from the Inyo area of California and bordering Nevada south to the southern San Joaquin Valley and the adjacent brushlands of the inner and upper levels of the coastal mountains; its range also encircles the Mohave Desert basins on the north, west and south, from which this form is absent in the breeding season.

Like the northern sage sparrow, *canescens* thrives in the *Artemisia* brush in the upper elevations of its range, but it extends beyond this extensively into the *Atriplex* of the floor of the southern end of the San Joaquin Valley. Here it nests at low elevations, such as 200 feet near Tulare Lake. On the east side of the Sierra Nevada it nests up to 8,000 feet (Grinnell and Miller, 1944). On the Grapevine Mountains of western Nevada I found that *canescens* "filtered up through openings in the [piñon] trees from * * * centers of abundance at lower levels" (Miller, 1946). It did not use piñons, in fact avoided them, yet within the piñon belt it found well isolated tracts of brush up to 7,500 feet which it occupied for nesting.

Along the southwestern border of its range I have found this sub-species entering the edge of the heavier brushlands of *Adenostoma* and scrub oak, as on San Benito Mountain, California. Yet in the main this habitat is occupied immediately to the westward by the very distinctive race *Amphispiza belli belli*. Here near this junction the form *canescens* occurs regularly in the rather open *Artemisia californica*, in *Atriplex* and *Haplopappus* bushes, and in *Eriodictyon*.

In August following the nesting season, molting birds and those in new autumnal plumage gather in loose flocks about water sources, from which they drink frequently. On August 23, two miles south and five miles east of Shandon, San Luis Obispo County, these sparrows were coming to drink, flying in from the *Artemisia californica* one to three at a time. They sometimes perched close together favoring the tall open shrubs or the junipers and a single elderberry. Others alighted on open ground beyond the water and ran about before fluttering in among the short sedges. On September 11, among *Atriplex* bushes near McKittrick in Kern County, they were again coming to water in the 100°-weather. Many were heard singing, at times giving as many as 10 full-voiced songs in sequence. These birds were in fresh new plumage and were far past the nesting season.

On Mount Pinos to the south Grinnell (1905c) noted bands of full grown young that had moved upslope from the nesting areas in late June. They were among gooseberry bushes on the very summit at 8,826 feet, about 2,000 feet above the growths of *Artemisia tridentata* where they nest on this mountain.

*Nesting.*—Dates for nesting of this race recorded in the literature and those attested to by the collections of the Museum of Vertebrate Zoology range from March 29 to June 6, with most of them in April and May. Nests are placed low in bushes from 1 to 2 feet up; there are no records of ground nests such as occur on the race *nevadensis*. Three nests I have examined show the same wool lining found in those of *nevadensis*, but fewer bark shreds and more grass and flowering stalks of annual plants. One has some feathers in the lining.

*Eggs.*—Sets of eggs consist of 3 in four instances, and of 4 eggs in eight instances; there is one set of 5 eggs recorded by George Willett (1911). The eggs are indistinguishable in color from those of the northern sage sparrow, but they are, on the average, significantly shorter. Thus the length of 55 eggs averages 18.98 millimeters as against 19.47 millimeters for 70 eggs of *nevadensis*. The width in *canescens* averages 14.46 millimeters which is essentially the same as in *nevadensis*.

*Winter.*—This subspecies of sage sparrow is partly resident in nearly all sections of its breeding range, or at most it moves locally or retreats from the higher nesting areas. But it also migrates south and east of the summer range into lowland areas. Mailliard and Grinnell (1905) state that "sage sparrows were fairly common out on the desert and on the sage flats near" the Mohave River in midwinter; half of the specimens they took there were of the race *canescens*. This is only a short distance from the breeding grounds, as are also the wintering areas in the Joshua Tree National Monument. There Miller and Stebbins (1964) found them appearing as early as August 27, "moving about over sand among dead twig debris at the base of chrysothamnus bushes." After wintering in this general area fairly commonly, the last sage sparrows depart by the first week in April.

## DISTRIBUTION

*Range.*—Interior California to northeastern Baja California and southwestern Arizona.

*Breeding range.*—The California sage sparrow breeds in central interior California, in the southern San Joaquin Valley, including the bordering mountains, from southwestern Merced and southeastern San Benito counties to Tulare County, interior San Luis Obispo, and northern Ventura, northern Los Angeles, and Kern counties; also in the Inyo district (Benton southward) and adjoining central western Nevada (Esmeralda County; Grapevine Mountains) and the western and southern borders of the Mohave Desert (east to the San Bernardino Mountains).

*Winter range.*—Winters in the breeding range and extends south to southwestern California (Riverside), northeastern Baja California (Las Palmas Canyon), and southwestern Arizona (Arlington, Quitobaquito).

### AMPHISPIZA BELLI BELLI (Cassin)

## Bell's Sage Sparrow

### PLATE 56

### Contributed by ALDEN H. MILLER

## HABITS

In the chaparral of the coastal slopes of California the sage sparrows are represented by the strikingly dark and distinctive, small race *Amphispiza belli belli*. The brush to which this form adheres is much denser than that occupied by the desert races of the species and most often consists of relatively compact stands of chamise. Grinnell and Miller (1944) summarize the characteristics of the habitat as follows:

Chaparral of arid, or "hard" type, usually fairly dense or continuous and 2 to 5 feet in height. Marked preference is shown for tracts of chamise (*Adenostoma*) which in many sections is the only plant association occupied. [It] * * * occurs sparingly in baccharis and artemisia [*californica*] brush to northward and also is found in brush growing on sand dunes and mesas near seacoast, and in mixed brush and cactus patches in arid washes. Within the brush cover the birds find all requirements for existence: forage beat on the ground and low in the bushes, nest sites at low levels in concealing twigs, and avenues of escape by running through the bushes or by flight through or over their tops; this form is less given to running long distances than are *A. b. canescens* and *A. b. nevadensis*, perhaps because of the denser brushland habitat it selects.

Because of the dense habitat and the general tendency of the species to run behind and beneath bushes, this race is even more difficult to detect than those occurring inland. Except when singing, most of the time the birds stay below the tops of the brush, but they may occasionally be flushed as one breaks through the cover or they may be seen by squeaking them up, whereupon they briefly occupy lookout posts on the tips of the chamise.

Although the song and notes of this race do not differ from those of the other sage sparrows, its darker coloration and smaller size make it recognizable in the field. In mixed postbreeding groups along the eastern border of the range of *A. b. belli* in San Benito County, I have been able to distinguish it readily from *canescens* in the same flocks. The back is deep brown, contrasting but slightly with the black tail, and the moustache marks and breast spot are black and thick and large; also the sides are conspicuously striped.

Grinnell and Swarth (1913) studied this sage sparrow in spring and summer at the eastern edge of its range in the San Jacinto Mountains of southern California. Here it was first noted at an altitude of 3,000 feet on the west side. At Kenworthy, 4,500 feet, "the birds frequented the denser growth of sagebrush on the floor of the valley. During the first week in June flocks of five or six individuals were occasionally encountered, possibly non-breeding birds, for the majority of the species were in pairs and scattered through the brush at fairly regular intervals. The birds forming flocks were silent, usually feeding on the ground, while of the paired birds the male spent a large portion of the time perched upon a projecting limb of a bush, and uttering his song at frequent intervals."

On the north side of the mountains these sparrows were fairly common in the chamise of the hills above Cabezon.

In late summer upslope movement was conspicuous and juveniles were taken as high as 9,000 feet at Round Valley. As in other races of sage sparrows, the annual molt starts early; in this case adults were in midmolt in the latter part of June. Near the northern end of the range of *A. b. belli* in western Tehama County, Calif., on June 12, I found pairs closely spaced in *Adenostoma* 3 feet in height. The brush was recovering from a burn and one could move about easily in it in the alleyways, along which the sparrows were seen to run. Pairs averaged about 50 yards apart, from the center of one territory to the next. When excited or disturbed, two or three pairs would come in sight at once but they could always be distinguished as pairs. Some pairs obviously had active nests, but others had young out of the nest.

*Nesting.*—C. S. Sharp (1906) found a nest with eggs in a wild rose patch in an opening in a willow grove near Escondido, Calif. This is a very unusual situation and habitat. In this same area, James B. Dixon writes me of sage sparrows occupying comparatively dry, low brush cover. He says that at times the brush is sparse with rocks intermixed. He found a nest in rather dense brush, waist high, on a south-facing hillside about 600 feet above sea level near Lake Hodges, San Diego County, on May 19. The nest was carefully concealed and was discovered only by watching the female from a distance. This nest, in the forks of a heavy bush at practically ground level, was well made of weed stalks and inwardly lined with fine weed stems and soft weed fibers. Both adults "made quite a fuss and would come to within eight feet of us."

Another nest that Dixon found near Paso Robles, San Luis Obispo County, and which I judge belongs to this race, was placed low in a scrubby bush in a dry wash. It was composed entirely of grayish weed fibers, outwardly coarse and inwardly fine. It held three slightly incubated eggs on April 12. Nests of this race that have been reported were all above ground at heights from 6 to 24 inches. Nest materials are generally similar to those used by other sage sparrows, but wool or fine hair occurs less consistently in the lining. I have seen several nests in which seed heads of plants alone constituted the soft lining layer.

Nests with eggs are to be found chiefly in April and May. George Willett (1912) gives earliest and latest dates for fresh or slightly incubated eggs in southern California as April 6 and June 25. Additionally we have records of eight nests with eggs from April 10 to May 19, and in Tehama County, near Beegum, on June 12, I took a female that was laying, but the set she was producing may have been a replacement nest; I could not be certain that it was a true second nesting although there were grown young in the vicinity that may have been hers.

*Eggs.*—Clutches of Bell's sage sparrow usually consist of four eggs. We have records of seven such sets. Two sets of three are reported but one of these at least was fresh and may have been incomplete. James B. Dixon in reporting the nest near Lake Hodges, San Diego County, commented on the unusually large clutch of five eggs that it held.

Measurements of 40 eggs show an average of 18.93 millimeters in length and 14.48 millimeters in width. These dimensions are not significantly different from those for the race *canescens*, but, again, the eggs are significantly shorter than in the large-sized race *nevadensis*.

*Plumages.*—The pattern of markings is similar to that in the northern sage sparrow, except that the dorsal striping is obsolete and the flank striping is augmented; the moustache markings and breast spot are broader, larger, and more solidly black. Coloration is much darker as follows: above, deep brownish slate-gray, becoming browner on back; wings and tail dull blackish, with light brown edgings, the middle and greater coverts indistinctly tipped with pale brownish buffy or pale wood brown; outer web and small tip area of outer tail feathers buff; the sides and flanks are buff to light brown streaked with dusky.

The juvenal plumage of *A. b. belli* is of the same pattern as in *nevadensis*, but the coloration is darker, corresponding to the darker colors to be seen in the adult plumage.

*Food.*—On May 26, near Beegum, Tehama County, I took a female that was carrying four green caterpillars crosswise in her bill. These were ¾ inch long and were of a species prevalent in the *Adenostoma* brush at that time. This food was obviously intended for young birds, but in an adult taken at the same place on June 12, I found a similar caterpillar in its stomach as well as sand and some fragments of seeds.

In the summer and fall periods of warmth and drought, Bell's sage sparrows come to water as do the related races of this species. John Davis writes of the "Bell Sparrows" at Hastings Reservation in the Carmel Valley, Calif., coming to water traps on November 5. This is a time when available water is about at the low point for the year. He has seen the species in fall at water sources well removed from its normal habitat, and apparently the birds must range some distance for water at this dry season.

*Voice.*—The notes of this race are like those of the northern sage sparrow, although the song may be variously described. Grinnell and Storer (1924) write one variation of it as *tweesitity-slip*, *tweesitity-slip*, *swer*. Near Coulterville, Calif., on May 12, they recorded a bird singing every 9 or 10 seconds, each song lasting 2½ seconds. The song would be repeated for several minutes from one perch and then the bird would change to another location. "It would perch on the topmost shoot of a greasewood [*Adenostoma*] bush, facing away from the wind, its feathers blown outward somewhat, and would rock back and forth in keeping its balance on the swaying twig." This bird centered its attention on a particular section of a hillslope and "circled about within a radius of not over 150 feet, singing from one perch, then changing to another. Between song periods he would disappear, presumably to forage, within the mantle of brush * * *."

*Winter.*—Bell's sage sparrow is nonmigratory and remains on the breeding grounds in winter and in the same habitat, usually foregoing even local movements. Thus in winter near Beegum in Tehama County at the northern end of its range, I found sage sparrows on February 7 in the same brush patch in which they had nested; they seemingly were paired. Once I heard one give a subsong.

Hill and Wiggins (1948) state that at lat. 30°21′ N. in Baja California "Bell Sparrows" were singing vigorously on October 22.

One notable exception to permanent residency is recorded by Miller and Stebbins (1964) who found *A. b. belli* ranging eastward at least 25 miles from breeding areas in the San Bernardino Mountains, and occurring on August 24 at Lower Covington Flat and at Black Rock Spring on September 3 and 4, both locations in the Joshua Tree National Monument in high desert brushlands.

### DISTRIBUTION

Bell's sage sparrow is resident in the coastal ranges of California (Hayfork and French Gulch southward; extends to coast from Marin County southward), on the western slope of the central Sierra Nevada of California (Eldorado County to Mariposa County), and in northwestern Baja California (south to lat. 29°30′ N.; Santa Catarina Landing, intergrades with *A. b. cinerea*). Occurs casually east of the southern California mountains in Joshua Tree National Monument.

### AMPHISPIZA BELLI CLEMENTEAE Ridgway

## San Clemente Sage Sparrow

### Contributed by ALDEN H. MILLER

### HABITS

This is a weakly differentiated race of sage sparrow, characterized in comparison with *Amphispiza belli belli* by "longer bill and lighter juvenal plumage" (Grinnell and Miller, 1944); in fresh plumage the adults possibly are lighter also (van Rossem, 1932b).

The race *clementeae* is known only from San Clemente Island off the coast of southern California. The earlier record for sage sparrows for Santa Rosa Island has been thrown in doubt (Miller, 1951b) and there has been no recent confirmation of the occurrence of the species on San Nicolas Island and never any indication of the presence of the race *clementeae* there.

On San Clemente Island, A. B. Howell (1917) reports that this sage sparrow "is common on the mesa lands back from the shore" and he and Laurence M. Huey "found several nests with pipped eggs and young the latter part of March, 1915.    They were situated in scrubby brush a few inches above the ground."

Joseph Grinnell (1897c) writes that these sparrows were "quite common on the hillsides and lower mesas where there is a low thorny bush growing in clumps and patches interspersed with cactus." At the time of his visit, from March 28 to April 3, "the males were in full song, and dissection of females showed that eggs in most instances had already been laid. * * * The notes and habits of this bird were substantially the same as those [of *A. b. belli*] about Pasadena."    Full grown juveniles were plentiful there on a later visit from May 28 to June 7.

### DISTRIBUTION

The San Clemente sage sparrow is resident on San Clemente Island off southern California.

## AMPHISPIZA BELLI CINEREA Townsend

## Gray Sage Sparrow

### Contributed by ALDEN H. MILLER

### HABITS

The race *Amphispiza belli cinerea* is the southernmost representative of the sage sparrows.    It occupies the midsection of Baja California along the Pacific Coast between 29° and 26° north latitude where it is a common resident of the Lower Sonoran Zone.

Ridgway (1901) says it is "Similar in size and proportions to *A. b. belli*, but coloration conspicuously paler; above pale smoke gray or pale ashy gray, the back more decidedly tinged with buffy and obsoletely streaked with darker; lateral throat-stripes narrower, more interrupted, and dull grayish instead of blackish; spot in center of chest smaller and dusky grayish instead of blackish."    The coloration parallels that of the subspecies *canescens* but is a more brownish gray and the black markings are paler.    The lesser coverts are yellowish brown.

Laurence M. Huey (1930b) in commenting on this form and the intergrades between it and *A. b. belli*, which he designated as the race *xerophilus*, reports that *cinerea* occurs in proximity to the sea. He says that it is "not cactus tolerant and * * * [is] not to be found beyond the range of certain types of coastal Lower Sonoran brush." This consists chiefly of plants "of the genus *Lycium*, commonly called *Frutilla* * * *."

Chester C. Lamb met the gray sage sparrow in late May 1927 near the south end of Santa Rosalia Bay.    The birds were found in the coastal sand dunes in low brush where ocotillo, yucca, agave, and cactus also occurred. On May 30 he saw them feeding under bushes in the sand dunes and in open places among ice plants. The birds would come to a bush top when alarmed by a squeak. Juveniles were common and these young birds banded together in flocks of as many as a dozen individuals.

## DISTRIBUTION

The gray sage sparrow is resident on the Pacific shores of middle Baja California from latitude 29° N., south to Ballenas Bay, lat. 26°40′ N.

### JUNCO AIKENI Ridgway

# White-winged Junco

## Contributed by NATHANIEL RUGGLES WHITNEY, JR.

## HABITS

In the northern Great Plains, in western South Dakota and northeastern Wyoming, lies a mountain mass about 100 miles long and 75 miles wide, ranging in elevation from 3,500 feet to a few peaks over 7,200 feet. These mountains, the Black Hills and Bear Lodge Mountains, are the home of the white-winged junco, one of the most numerous and conspicuous species of birds here and, during the breeding season, practically limited to this region.

The white-winged junco is the only bird species whose breeding range is essentially limited to the Black Hills. It has, however, close relatives to the west, north, and east. In Minnesota and across Canada the slate-colored junco breeds in the spruce forest, and in Wyoming various races of the Oregon junco breed in the Big Horn Mountains and the main ranges of the Rockies. The Black Hills are virtually an island of coniferous forest surrounded on all sides by prairies, and this fact may account for the distinctness of its junco population.

All the other characteristic breeding birds of the Black Hills pine forests have fairly wide breeding ranges. Among them are such Rocky Mountain species as Audubon's warbler and the western tanager, which here reach the eastern limits of their breeding ranges, and boreal forest species such as the gray jay and red-breasted nuthatch, which reach the southern edge of their breeding range in the Black Hills. Species of broad ecological tolerance such as robin and chipping sparrow are also numerous here.

Though the white-winged juncos are most numerous in the Black Hills pine forests, they are not limited to them. They may also be found in spruce forests and in aspen stands. In winter they often frequent brushy stream bottomlands, but they usually avoid open grasslands.

*Spring.*—Most white-winged juncos winter in the lower elevations of the Black Hills or farther south in the foothills of the Rocky Mountains. With the first warm weather of early spring, they begin moving back to their breeding grounds. At banding stations in the Rapid City region, this movement is evident early in March. The following two observations are probably evidence of migration. On Mar. 18, 1956, a color-banded individual that had been part of a flock wintering at 3,500 feet elevation on the west edge of Rapid City was observed at another feeding station 13 miles northwest of the point of banding and at an elevation of 4,500 feet. In January 1963, I banded 19 juncos, retrapping 9 of them later the same month but only 2 after the first of March. Meanwhile, an apparently different group moved through during March, and in the third week of March I banded 10 new individuals, some of which remained for a few days and were trapped again.

R. B. Rockwell and A. Wetmore (1914) collected two specimens near Golden, Colo., on April 11.

*Territory.*—Each male white-winged junco apparently establishes and defends a breeding territory of a few acres, which it advertises by a well-developed spring song. Although some winter flocks tend to remain together well into April, two males were noted in full song on Mar. 4, 1956. One of these sang from several perches in pines, covering a territory at least 200 yards in diameter. I am uncertain whether the size of the territory is limited chiefly by the pressure of other males on neighboring territories, or by the maximum distance the male wants to move away from the nest, but suspect that it is the latter, as I have never observed a singing male driving another from his territory.

*Courtship.*—During many hours of watching white-winged juncos in the spring, I have never seen behavior I would consider of definite courtship pattern. Territorial singing is of course conspicuous at this time, and pairs of birds frequently can be seen feeding together. No specific activities, however, appear to precede pairing and copulation.

*Nesting.*—W. H. Over and G. M. Clement (1930) found 29 nests during several seasons of field work in the central Black Hills. Of these six were under logs, four under exposed tree roots, three under rock ledges, and several had used artificial nesting sites. One location, used several seasons, was the roof plate of a busy blacksmith shop, 9 feet above ground, approached from under the eaves; one nest was in an old gallon syrup can and another in an old tomato can, both discarded in the pine forest. Several nests were found in and around a sawmill, where nesting was apparently successful despite the bustle of human activity.

In the summer of 1956 I found a nest built into a depression in the ground under a projecting slab of limestone. The nest construction was an outer framework of coarse grasses and an inner lining of fine grasses. Of the five nests I found in 1958, one was under projecting limestone, two were under the root network of grass or shrubs, and two were in small niches in limestone cliffs. Measurements of these nests showed the following variations: outside diameter–10.0 to 15.0 centimeters; inside diameter–6.0 to 9.0 centimeters; inside depth–3.0 to 5.0 centimeters. The nest studied in 1959 contained 9.0 grams of nesting materials (dry weight).

Summarizing the above observations, I think that white-winged juncos usually select a cave-like situation, with a roof not far above the nest. Exceptions are known, but do not seem to negate the rule.

*Eggs.*—The white-winged junco usually lays three or four slightly glossy ovate eggs. They are white or creamy white, speckled and spotted with "auburn," "Brussels brown," "hazel," "sayal brown," or "cinnamon brown," with undermarkings of "pale mouse gray." In most cases the rather fine markings are concentrated toward the large end, although some may have them well scattered. There is always a considerable amount of ground showing, and the spottings are often somewhat dull and weak. The measurements of 30 eggs average 20.1 by 15.4 millimeters; the eggs showing the four extremes measure *21.7* by 15.2, 20.6 by *15.6*, and *17.8* by *14.7* millimeters.

*Incubation.*—Activities observed at a nest in Palmer Gulch in the central Black Hills, elevation 5,000 feet, in June 1959, were as follows:

June 2 —parents carrying nesting materials
June 4 —nest lining completed
June 6 —one egg in the nest
June 7 —two eggs in the nest, both of which I marked with ink
June 11—four eggs in the nest
June 20—four eggs still present in the nest at 4:00 p.m.
June 21—one young hatched before noon
June 22—four young in the nest at 9:30 a.m.
July 2 —two young still in the nest, one on the ground beside it

From the above observations, one egg proved to have been in the the nest for 15 days between laying and hatching, and all four eggs were known to be under incubation for a minimum of 10 days. A reasonable assumption is that one egg was laid each day, and that incubation began on June 9, immediately after the fourth egg was laid. Another assumption which cannot be proved is that all four young hatched on June 21. If these two assumptions are correct, the incubation period is 12 days. Intensive observations of the critical periods of laying and hatching would be necessary to measure the incubation period with greater precision.

*Young.*—In the nest I watched in 1956 the young hatched some time after 9:30 a.m., June 16, and before 5:00 a.m., June 19. When I visited the nest on June 19, the young were very small and black-skinned with some gray down. They held their heads straight up, begging for food, and one gaped as I leaned over the nest. On June 21 they gaped in response to my tapping the edge of the nest, but not to my blowing on them or shading them with my hand. At that time they showed down on top of their heads and the feather tracts on wings and bodies were appearing.

On June 23 I arrived at the nest at 6:00 a.m. and tapped the edge of the nest. The young closest to me responded by gaping but the others did not, and I presumed that they had just been fed. Thirty minutes later, during which time they were not fed, tapping the nest produced an immediate gaping response in all four young.

On June 24, 1956, I banded and weighed the young and collected the following data (weights in grams):

| Band number | June 24 | June 25 | June 26 | June 27 (at fledging) |
|---|---|---|---|---|
| 24–76557 | 13.0 | 14.0 | 16.0 | 15.0 |
| 24–76558 | 11.0 | 12.0 | 13.0 | 15.0 |
| 24–76559 | 11.0 | 10.5 | 11.0 | |
| 24–76561 | 14.5 | 15.0 | 18.0 | |

When I replaced them in the nest, they all gaped at me, pushing so hard that I had trouble finding room for the last one. At this age their wing and tail feathers are beginning to break through the sheaths.

After being weighed on June 25, all the young were able to scramble back into the nest. They then had a single distinctive call note unlike that of the adults. The wing and tail feathers were well developed by that time, but the white wing bars were not yet evident.

The young left the nest between 6:00 p.m., June 26, and 9:00 a.m., June 27. On the latter day two of the young, still flightless, were found in the vicinity of the nest. One was hiding in a clump of grass, and one under a yucca. On subsequent visits to the nest during the next few days I was unable to find any of the family.

Dennis Carter reports (*in* litt.) the following observations from Jewel Cave National Monument, Custer County South Dakota, in 1958. "White-winged junco is one of the most numerous species here and, on July 1, I found a pair with young birds. The adults were very agitated by my presence and uttered sharp alarm notes. When I finally discovered a juvenile bird, one of the adults swooped down over my head. I found three young birds, and although they could not fly, they moved along the ground at a surprisingly rapid rate and attempted to climb into brushpiles and shrubs."

*Plumages.*—The scant natal down is slate-gray in color. The skin of the newly-hatched bird is black.

Richard Graber (1955), in a comparative study of immature plumages of sparrows, describes the juvenal plumage as follows: "Forehead and crown gray, streaked profusely with black. Nape similar, tinged with brown. Back brown-tinged gray, streaked with black. Rump and upper tail coverts grayish, obscurely streaked with black. Outer three rectrices largely white; others black, edged gray (fourth from outside with white mark). Remiges black, primaries and secondaries edged light gray. Tertials edged with pinkish-buff, tipped with buffy-white. Lesser coverts grayish, medians black, narrowly white-tipped. Greaters edged with buff, ripped buffy white. Two narrow wing bars. Lores gray, eye ring white. Auriculars gray. Post auriculars white, sparsely spotted with dusky (cheek patch partially outlining auriculars). Chin and throat grayish white (lateral black streaks), obscurely flecked with dusky. Sides of chest gray. Chest, sides, and flanks tinged with buff, streaked with black. Belly white, crissum buffy white, both unmarked. Leg feathers gray and white. Much like *J. hyemalis,* though clearly distinguishable."

Robert Ridgway (1901) describes *Junco aikeni* as follows:

*Adult male.*—Head, neck, chest, sides, flanks, and upper parts plain slate-gray, darker (slate color) on the head; middle and greater wing-coverts usually tipped with white, forming two distinct bands; three outermost tail-feathers wholly white, the third sometimes with a little dusky, the fourth with more or less of white * * * .

*Adult female.*—Similar to adult male, but rather paler gray, the upper parts (especially back) tinged more or less with light grayish brown, the wing-bands usually less distinct, frequently obsolete, and the third tail-feather more often with a little dusky * * * .

Winter birds, especially young, are more or less tinged with light grayish brown, especially on the back. In some adult males the tertials are edged with white.

*Food.*—No stomach analyses have yet been made. Insects appear to constitute all the food of the nestlings, and are probably the chief food of adults during the summer. In winter the white-wing's diet is primarily weed and grass seeds picked up from the ground.

*Behavior.*—The white-winged junco is essentially a ground bird. Nesting takes place primarily on the ground, and most feeding does also. Trees are used for singing perches during the breeding season, as resting places throughout the year, and probably as roosting sites in winter. The most obvious behavior patterns can be observed in fall and winter flocks. In one such flock 20 birds observed Oct. 4, 1956, were feeding in a gravel drive at 4,500 feet altitude. They repeatedly flew down to the ground one at a time, but after feeding a few minutes they all flew up into the nearby pines together. While on the ground, they all moved slowly in the same direction, hopping, picking up two or three bites, and then hopping again.

White-winged juncos have often been noted around feeding stations well after sundown. Mrs. Grace McIntyre (pers. comm.) comments that they have fed around her banding station at Devil's Tower, Wyo., long after twilight. Individuals I have banded and released after full darkness have, in contrast, seemed unable to find their way to suitable roosts. I have not yet exactly determined the minimum intensity of light juncos require for feeding.

Alden H. Miller has pointed out (pers. comm.) that the white-winged junco seems less active than smaller juncos, but that basically its habits are similar to theirs.

The general impression of winter flocks is that the birds tend to act as a compact unit. Close watching, however, shows that a definite pecking order exists, and that when two individuals are within pecking distance the dominant one lunges at the other without moving from his place. I have noted this often at banding traps, where one individual invariably defends the entry platform from all the others.

My observations concerning tolerance of other species are limited. Oregon and slate-colored juncos are the most intimate associates of white-wings in the winter flocks of the Black Hills. Oregon juncos, though smaller, may drive white-wings away from a feeding station. Other wintering passerines, such as black-capped chickadees and white-breasted nuthatches, often feed with junco flocks, but seldom so closely that one tried to drive another away. Juncos usually scatter when flocks of piñon jays arrive at the feeding station.

When removed from a banding trap, most white-wings are passive, but some will attempt to peck the bander's fingers if they are held directly in front of the bird's bill. Their reactions are intermediate between those of the very passive piñon jays and the very pugnacious black-capped chickadees.

*Voice.*—White-winged juncos in flocks seem to communicate with each other by a high musical squeak consisting of a single note. I heard this note used frequently by a flock of 10 juncos foraging around my banding trap during a heavy snowstorm.

Another frequent winter call is a single chip, similar to that of the slate-colored junco, but more musical. It seems to be more of an alarm note, while the squeaking note seems to be used in proclaiming intra-flock dominance.

True singing is apparently confined to spring and early summer. Peterson (1961) describes the song as "a loose musical trill, similar to the songs of other juncos." To me, it sounds very much like the song of the chipping sparrow, but somewhat more musical and variable.

*Field marks.*—The traveler in the Black Hills and Bear Lodge Mountains during the summer can recognize white-winged juncos as the small gray birds that fly up from the roadside or the forest floor showing prominent white outer tail feathers. Closer observation shows that actually the plumage is predominantly a uniform pearl gray, except for the white wing bars and the white belly. In winter when the white-wing often associates with slate-colored, Oregon, and gray-headed juncos, it can be distinguished from the Oregon and gray-headed juncos by the absence of contrasting reddish-brown on the back and sides, and from the slate-colored junco by the lighter gray plumage and the presence of more white in the tail. The white wing bars are good confirmatory points, but are not striking field marks in most individuals. White-winged juncos are also somewhat larger than the other juncos with which they may be associated. White-wings average 24 to 27 grams, while slate-colored, Oregon, and gray-headed juncos weigh 18 to 20 grams.

*Enemies.*—The only reported cowbird parasitism on the white-winged junco was found by A. H. Miller (1948) in southeastern Montana. The cowbird (*Molothrus ater*) is not a common breeding bird within the range of the white-winged junco, and many other species of small birds nest in situations much more accessible to the cowbird.

K. C. Emerson (pers. comm.) has sent me the following list of species of Mallophaga (chewing lice) known from the white-winged junco: *Bruelia vulgata* (Kellogg); *Philopterus mirinotatus* (Kellogg and Chapman); *Ricinus pallidus* (Kellogg); *Machaerilaemus* sp.; *Menacanthus* sp. R. O. Malcomson (1960) mentions finding two species of lice, *Ricinus hastatus* and *Ricinus pallidus*.

*Fall.*—Fall flocking begins on the breeding grounds in mid-July. Harry Behrens tells me that he saw several flocks in the central Black Hills about July 15, 1956. For the most part, however, juncos are seen singly or in small groups until early September. Later in the autumn flocks ranging in size from 10 to 30 individuals are usual. At this time, too, juncos begin to move down from the higher elevations of the Black Hills to the foothills. At elevations of 5,000 feet and over, much of the ground is snow covered from early November until mid-April, but below 4,000 feet much ground is bare. R. B. Rockwell and A. Wetmore (1914) note that white-winged juncos arrived in the region of Golden, Colo., on October 24 and reached maximum abundance on November 7.

*Winter.*—The flocking of white-winged juncos in winter seems similar to that of the better known species of the genus. Juncos frequent feeding tables during periods of heavy snow cover, but when the ground is clear they sometimes disappear entirely from artificial feeding grounds. I have yet to determine the exact foraging area a flock of juncos uses during the winter season. One individual Harry Behrens banded in November in a brushy hollow near the center of Rapid City, S.D., was retrapped 11 days later in the pine woods 3 miles northwest of the point of banding. This is unusual; later I started a banding station ¾ mile south of Behrens' station. I banded 100 juncos there, while Behrens had banded 30 at his home. While we each had several retraps of our own birds, we did not catch any of each other's.

For 3 years I made a population study of an area of ponderosa pine forest on the edge of Rapid City. My estimates of the winter population were 61 white-winged juncos per 100 acres the first year, 45 the second year, and 35 the third. The cause of this variation was not clear, although it could be correlated with the persistence of snow cover, juncos being more numerous when the ground was bare, and I could not evaluate its significance.

### DISTRIBUTION

*Range.*—Southeastern Montana and western South Dakota south to New Mexico and western Oklahoma.

*Breeding range.*—The white-winged junco breeds from southeastern Montana (Rosebud Mountains, Long Pine Hills) and western South Dakota (Short Pine Hills in Harding County; Custer) south to northeastern Wyoming (near Newcastle) and northwestern Nebraska (Hat Creek).

*Winter range.*—Winters in the vicinity of the breeding grounds (chiefly lower elevations in the Black Hills) and south to southwestern Colorado (Plateau Valley, La Plata County), north central New Mexico (Sante Fe), western Oklahoma (Cimarron and Texas counties), and western Kansas; sporadically to northern Arizona (Flagstaff, White Mountains), and central Oklahoma (Fort Reno, Norman).

*Casual records.*—Casual in eastern Nebraska (Omaha) and Ontario (Scarborough).

*Migration.*—Early dates of spring arrival are: Wyoming—Laramie, March 10. Montana—Missoula, April 15.

Late dates of spring departure are: New Mexico—Los Alamos, April 4. Wyoming—Laramie, April 16.

Early dates of fall arrival are: Wyoming—Laramie, October 13. Arizona—White Mountains, November 21. New Mexico—Los Alamos, November 16; Taos County, November 19. Oklahoma—Cimarron County, October 19.

Late date of fall departure is: Montana—Carter County, December 5.

*Egg dates.*—South Dakota: 17 records, May 23 to June 29; 8 records, May 27 to June 3.

Wyoming: 2 records, June 8 and June 17.

## JUNCO HYEMALIS HYEMALIS (Linnaeus)

# Northern Slate-colored Junco

### PLATES 57 AND 58

## Contributed by STEPHEN W. EATON

### HABITS

The northern slate-colored junco, or "common snowbird" as persons who know it only in winter often call it, is one of the most distinctive of our common sparrows. With its uniform pale gray upperparts sharply defined against its white belly, aptly described as "leaden skies above, snow below," it is not likely to be confused with anything but other closely related juncos, and then only in the western parts of its wintering range. A friendly little bird that breeds across the continent from Alaska to Labrador and Newfoundland and from the limit of trees southward into the northern United States, it is the summer companion of the canoeist in the Canadian forests and of the mountain hiker of Appalachia. In winter it retreats southward throughout most of the United States in small, congenial flocks of 15 to 25 individuals. These sometimes forage over the snow-covered fields with the tree sparrows searching for the seeds of weeds that escaped the cultivator, and they commonly frequent the yards of homes where food has been put out for them, which they much prefer to scratch from the ground than to pick from an elevated feeder.

Essentially an inhabitant of the more open northern woodlands and forest edges, it is generally common throughout its breeding range in the Hudsonian and Canadian life zones, except in the deeper woods, but tends to dwindle in numbers toward the north. Typical is E. A. Preble's (1908) comment: "This common species, sometimes called 'tomtit' in the North, is the sole representative of its genus throughout most of the wooded parts of the Athabaska-Mackenzie country. Over this vast region it is a common summer resident, being one of the earliest of the smaller migrants to arrive in spring and a rather late lingerer in autumn."

Francis Harper (1953) notes that "Apparently the numbers of this species diminish rather decidedly toward the tree limit in most parts of northwestern Canada although Porsild (1943: 43) reports it well beyond the tree limit at the Mackenzie Delta." Lawrence Walkinshaw writes Mr. Bent of finding the males singing from the tree tops 20 to 25 feet above the ground in the spruce bog areas along the Kuskukwim River in Alaska, and adds: "Where the tree line disappeared, so did the juncos."

*Spring.*—The migrating juncos rush across most of the eastern and midwestern United States about mid-April passing, as they go, their southern relatives already singing on their territories. In Illinois M. C. Shank (1959) reports they build up fat reserves before migrating, but D. W. Johnston (1962) finds the wintering populations leave Wake Forest, N.C., before they deposit any fat. The birds are restless and hyperphagic, and move northward rapidly in flocks of up to 100 individuals. In the East they are often accompanied in the earlier part of the migration by fox and tree sparrows; later along the Saskatchewan River they may be accompanied by tree and clay-colored sparrows (Houston and Street, 1959).

*Territory.*—The males usually arrive on the breeding grounds well in advance of the start of nesting. During 10 years of observation near Olean in southwestern New York State (Eaton, 1965) I heard the average first territorial singing on March 12, but most males here do not start their territorial song in earnest until about March 21. Some 300 miles farther north Mrs. L. de K. Lawrence writes (*in litt.*) the juncos arrive at her home in Rutherglen, Ontario in late March or early April, with a mean arrival date of April 2 for 13 years.

The male proclaims his territory by singing from the top of the tallest trees within it, which may be 50 to 75 feet above the ground. Nero (1963) writes from the Lake Athabasca, Saskatchewan region: "On May 18 I found two males apparently engaged in a territorial dispute. The aggressor approached with its breast feathers raised and spread, forming a broad front, and with its tail widely spread and alternately depressed and elevated. Its pinkish bill was very conspicuous against the dark feathers of the head."

Individual territories appear to vary greatly in size, probably because of the scarcity of choice nest sites. The area a male defends vigorously has never been determined experimentally with models and recorded songs, but casual observations of the location of song perches near Olean suggest it is about 2 or 3 acres. Where ideal nest sites are more plentiful, the territories are probably smaller. Each usually seems to include some sort of opening in the forest canopy surrounding a rock outcrop or an exposed soil bank. The species' tendency to build in or near some sort of vertical wall probably helps to explain many unusually placed nests.

*Courtship.*—The male may continue to sing for some days before a female enters his territory. Mrs. Lawrence (1956) thus describes

PLATE 57

Sevier County, Tenn., June 25, 1950          S. A. Grimes

CAROLINA SLATE-COLORED JUNCO ON NEST

Cook Forest, Pa., June 18, 1946          H. H. Harrison

NEST AND EGGS OF NORTHERN SLATE-COLORED JUNCO

PLATE 58

NORTHERN SLATE-COLORED JUNCO FEEDING YOUNG

Cook Forest, Pa., June 5, 1946

the early courtship between one of her banded male juncos and a female who appeared 11 days after he arrived in 1953:

Her behavior indicated plainly that her sexual drive had not yet reached high intensity. She faced him as he pursued her, showing him her breast, or hopped aside or away to evade his approach, thus displaying her urge to escape to the point of aggression.

The male pursued her doggedly with wings drooped and tail lifted. Every time when the female withstood him, he stooped and with great intensity pecked at the ground and *at his aluminum band* on the right tarsus.

Obviously, this pecking at the ground and at the aluminum band, both irrelevant actions in the present situation, were displacement activities, a "substitute behavior" * * * as his sexual drive was denied by the female's condition of unreceptiveness.

Generally the first one or two days seem to be spent in establishing and strengthening the pair bond. The male follows his mate about as she feeds within the territory and the two birds remain close together, seldom more than 50 feet apart. Both birds, and particularly the male, display by hopping about the other on the ground with the wings drooping and the tail fanned laterally so that the white outer rectrices are conspicuous. The male now sings much less frequently, but he still leaves his mate occasionally to proclaim his occupancy of the property by song from one of his favorite perches.

*Nesting.* —The junco's ground nest is built by the female, but the male often helps by bringing material for it. Cordelia J. Stanwood, who studied this species extensively at her home in Ellsworth, Maine, wrote Mr. Bent about the activities of a pair building their nest one wet May "under a mass of brush and leaves and sheltered by a small spruce. Both birds brought some of the damp materials and they appeared to care little how wet they were, but the female seemed to do the greater amount of the molding." She continues:

"The nest site varies according to its situation. I have seen the juncos brooding amongst the roots of a growing clump of gray birches, partially under stumps and rocks, below a tuft of leaves, in a brush heap shaded by small evergreens, beneath bracken, and many within the side of a bank or knoll. The wall of a knoll covered with bird-wheat moss [*Polytrichum*] or the side of a steep bank just under the overhanging sod seems to be the most typical site for a junco nest. A depression is made or enlarged in the side of the bank or knoll, and the moss or overhanging sod form a natural roof. On a pasture hillside the abode of the junco may be a little cup-shaped structure of straw in the midst of a blueberry patch; in a damp wood it will be a deeper structure with thick walls of moss, twigs, and hay with a substantial lining of fine hay or hair. The brooding female often draws her tail into the nest as the ovenbird does, so that it is well nigh impossible to distinguish the bird or the cradle when looking directly into the nesting cavity."

In wooded country the junco typically nests at the edges of openings in the forest canopy, such as those made by a stream, a logging road, or a clearing.   Preble (1908) describes an Athabasca nest that "was built on the steep side of the river bank, and was quite bulky, the outer portion being constructed of fine twigs, strips of bark, and feathers.  This foundation inclosed a cup-shaped nest of dry grass, thickly lined with gray dog's hair."   E. W. Jameson, Jr. (*in* litt. to Mr. Bent) describes a nest he found on the Gaspé Peninsula in 1940 "on an east-facing slope of birches and alders.  The ground was covered with grass, dead leaves, and bunchberries.  The nest itself was in a cavity four inches in underneath a dead stump, the opening protected by a clump of club moss (*Lycopodium*).  Both parents were feeding insects to the four half-grown young."

B. P. Bole, Jr. (1941–1942) describes the nesting of a small colony of juncos on Little Mountain, just east of Cleveland, Ohio, and in a nearby hemlock-studded ravine known as Stebbens Gulch, which is typical for the species in western Pennsylvania and southwestern New York where similar Paleozoic rocks outcrop:

> Every one of the junco nests found on Little Mountain was in exactly the same type of place.   On this sandstone mesa the brows of the ledges and rocky outlying chunks of puddingstone have curling forelocks of Polypody fern, and it is under the overhanging fronds of these that the Juncos place their nests.   As the ferns are on the very edges of the cliffs, it is frequently a matter of some danger to get into positions from which the nests can easily be seen or discovered.
>
> The nests themselves are made of rootlets of various ferns, that of the Polypody being especially favored.   There is a thin lining of dry sedges and grass.   The whole structure is very compact, and is placed well down in the roots and hanging dead fronds of Polypody.   When danger threatens, the female bird tumbles out and downwards into the crevasse facing her; in this she flies for twenty feet or more before rising into the low yellow birches and hemlocks lining the ledges.

The junco often builds in rather unusual situations.  Forbush (1929) cites a junco nest on a ledge beneath the gable of a house in Nova Scotia.   Wendell P. Smith (1936) writes of a nest of dried grasses and fern stalks and other vegetation 8 feet above the ground in a trellis overgrown with woodbine (*Psedera vitacea*).  Houston and Street (1959) describe a nest in Saskatchewan built in a half-pound tobacco can lying on its side and which contained three junco eggs and three cowbird eggs.   Basil J. Wilkinson showed me a nest near Olean, New York, from which young were successfully fledged, in a wind-vane bird-feeder mounted on an 8-foot iron pipe.  The base of the tri-angular feeder was open, and the two sides were glass.  The nest was jammed into the apex angle, just as it might have been into a niche in a rock ledge.

Throughout the eastern parts of its range the species is apparently double-brooded. In southwestern New York, I (1965) found two laying peaks, the first at the end of April, the second the first of July. In Maine where Palmer (1949) notes first sets from the first week in May to the first week in June, he states: "A second brood is raised, the eggs being laid from late June to late July." Peters and Burleigh (1951a) found flying young near St. Johns June 9 and add: "Perhaps two broods are raised in Newfoundland for Arnold found a nest with three eggs in the Humber River valley on July 18, 1911."

*Eggs.*—The northern slate-colored junco usually lays from three to five and rarely six slightly glossy eggs. They are generally ovate, although some may tend to be either elongated or short ovate. The ground is grayish or very pale bluish-white with speckles, spots, and occasional blotches of reddish-browns such as "Verona brown," "russet," "chestnut," or "Brussels brown," with undermarkings of "pale mouse gray." In most cases the markings are concentrated toward the large end where they frequently form a wreath. There is considerable variation, some being only very faintly speckled, others quite heavily spotted and with a few blotches, but in all considerable groundcolor shows. Often the spottings are quite dull, and the gray speckles may sometimes predominate. One set of eggs in the MCZ is all white and unspotted. The measurements of 50 eggs of the nominate race average 19.4 by 14.4 millimeters; the eggs showing the four extremes measure *21.1* by 14.2, 20.9 by *16.2*, *17.8* by 14.2, and 19.3 by *13.2* millimeters.

*Young.*—Incubation is apparently by the female alone and usually lasts 12 to 13 days. V. A. Greulach (1934) reports a 12-day incubation period for a nest in Allegany State Park in southwestern New York. In two nests I recently (1965) timed in the same region the elapsed times from the last egg laid to the last to hatch were 12 and 13 days, respectively.

Both parents feed the young and attend to nest sanitation. During the first few days they eat the nestlings' fecal sacs, but on the fourth or fifth day start to carry them away instead, usually flying to a perch not far distant and wiping the sac off on a limb. At one of my nests the male always flew to a nearby telephone wire to wipe the sac from his bill; the wire was soon speckled white for a considerable distance before a shower cleaned it up.

V. A. Greulach (1934) comments: "The male removed 27 fecal sacs to the female's 14 during the periods of observation. In all cases where the disposition of the sacs was noted they were wiped off on tree branches. The brooding was apparently all done by the female, and she was not observed brooding after the young were seven days old."

Mrs. Standwood wrote Mr. Bent as follows about a nest she watched from a blind at Ellsworth, Maine:

"In the early stages of nursery life the parent birds fed the nestlings 'regurgitated' or partly digested food, together with a few tender moths and caterpillars. Later I saw them feed yellow grubs, millers, many spruce bud-moths, caterpillars, and crane flies. During one period of many hours of watching, the parents fed the young nothing but great numbers of smooth, green caterpillars.

"The youngsters begin to open their eyes at the end of the second day and, as in other sparrows, their feathers begin to show about the seventh day. At this time the active youngsters begin to show fear by snuggling down in the nest when a person approaches it. I have seen young birds still in the nest on the 11th and 12th days, but know they could leave earlier if danger threatened them."

Greulach's (1934) young left the nest when 12 days old. In two nests near houses the young I (1965) followed left the nest in 9 days, and I know that a number of these were raised to independence. After leaving the nest the young remain at least partially dependent on their parents for about 3 weeks.

One brood I banded Aug. 3, 1959, just before they left the nest, I was able to follow for an extended period. I saw the father, a crippled bird readily identified, feeding them on August 24 and 27. On August 30, however, one of the young perched on the feeder next to its father and crouched in the begging posture with vibrating wings, but without giving the usual begging call. The old bird stretched upward into the aggressive posture a few times, and when the youngster continued to beg, the father flew at it and chased it a short distance without feeding it. The banded young and their father were still visiting the feeder daily on September 19, about 46 days after leaving the nest. At this time the old bird had almost completed his postnuptial molt; the young still had a few juvenal feathers in the head and their undertail coverts had not quite completed their full growth.

*Plumages.*—Mrs. Stanwood noted in a letter to Mr. Bent that "When they first peck their way from the shell, young juncos are a reddish, burnt-orange color, and well covered with burnt-umber down." Dwight (1900) on the other hand calls the natal down "slate-gray." He notes the juvenal plumage is acquired by a complete postnatal molt, and describes it as:

"Above, drab, plumbeous on crown; sides of head and nape streaked with dull black, the feathers especially of the back edged with bistre. Wings and tail slaty black edged with olive-gray, the tertiaries and and wing coverts with dull cinnamon, the greater coverts tipped with buff. Two outer rectrices pure white. Feet pinkish buff, dusky when older.  Bill dusky pinkish buff, flesh-color when older and in dried specimens becoming dull ochre-yellow."

He describes the first winter plumage as "acquired by a partial postjuvenal moult in August and September, which involves the body plumage and the wing coverts, but not the rest of the wings nor the tail.

"Above, including wing coverts, sides of head, throat, breast and sides slaty gray, darkest on the crown and veiled with bistre edgings, especially on the back, more faintly with paler brown or ashy gray on the throat.  Abdomen and crissum pure white, sometimes faintly washed with vinaceous cinnamon."

The first nuptial plumage is "acquired by wear through which the brown and ashy edgings are finally lost, birds becoming ragged but not much faded by the end of the breeding season.  A few new feathers are acquired on the chin early in April, but no regular moult is indicated."

The adult winter plumage is "acquired by a complete postnuptial moult beginning the middle of August.  Practically indistinguishable from first winter, but the tertiaries usually edged with gray instead of faded cinnamon, the wings and tail blacker and showing everywhere fewer brown edgings."  The adult nuptial plumage is acquired by wear as is the first nuptial, from which it is practically indistinguishable.

The sexes are indistinguishable in the natal down and juvenal plumages.  In first winter and subsequent plumages the female is similar to the male, but the gray is much paler and the plumage everywhere more veiled with brown.

Wood (1951) throws new light on the amount of white in the junco's three outer tail feathers.  The outer pair are always pure white, but the amount of white on the inner two, most notably on the third pair, increases greatly in the first adult postnuptial molt. Feathers lost or plucked during the first winter are replaced by feathers having the design of those of the succeeding molt, with more white.

*Food.*—Martin, Zim, and Nelson (1951) say "Juncos, like many other members of the sparrow family, are primarily ground-feeding seed eaters.  They are partial to seeds of common weeds.  In summer, insects constitute about half or more of their diet."  For the northern slate-colored junco "Caterpillars, beetles, and ants seem to be the choice items of the animal diet, the balance being made up of wasps, bugs, grasshoppers, other insects, and spiders."  Heading a long list of mostly weed plants whose seeds the junco is known to eat, they list those most frequently identified in their stomach contents as ragweed, bristlegrass, dropseedgrass, crabgrass, pigweed, and goosefoot.

In southwestern New York I have watched them feeding on the fall cankerworm, *Alsophila pometaria*, in late autumn. During the winter I once saw them eating the seeds of the wild black cherry, and they often eat the seeds of hemlock and yellow birch from the snow surface. Though they usually eat hemlock seeds from the ground, they can and do extract them from the cones on the trees. They feed avidly on the springtails (*Collembola*) that swarm abundantly about the bases of the trees in February, and they will go out of their way to capture, either on the snow surface or in the air, a small species of gnat that hatches out of the small streams about this time. They also join the early phoebes and bluebirds in preying on the late March or early April hatch of the stonefly, *Pteniopteryx nivalis*. Francis H. Allen wrote Mr. Bent of a large flock he watched at Cohasset Nov. 2, 1935, whose members "frequently flew into the air to catch flies. The flight was usually, if not always, from trees or bushes and not from the ground. They continued this off and on for nearly an hour."

*Voice.*—Of the song with which the junco proclaims his territory, F. H. Allen wrote Mr. Bent: "The jingling trill of this junco is well known. It is usually a simple trill, but, as with some other birds whose normal song is a single trill, one will occasionally be heard singing two or even three trills on different pitches but joined together to form a single song." In southwestern New York this song is given mainly in February, March, and April before pair formation and egg laying. After incubation begins it is heard much less frequently, though there is a noticeable recrudescence during late June and early July, and an occasional autumnal upsurge of it in October. As Aretas A. Saunders (MS.) describes it:

"The normal song of the northern slate-colored junco is a simple trill, all on one pitch, or a series of rapid notes, sometimes barely slow enough to count. It resembles that of the chipping sparrow, but is rather more musical in quality. When the notes of the song are slow enough to count they vary, in my records, from 7 to 23 notes, averaging about 12. The length of the songs varies from 1.4 to 2.8 seconds, averaging about 1.9. The pitch varies from E''' to G''''.

"There is a considerable amount of variation in junco songs from the simple trill that is all on one pitch. Some songs vary a bit up or down in pitch, and some vary in time. I believe this bird shows as great a tendency to vary fron the normal type of singing as does the towhee. In the Adirondacks I heard a bird singing a song of three prolonged whistles. I chased it about for parts of three days and finally identified it as a junco. Possibly this bird got its song from a white-throated sparrow, but if so it did not sound enough like that bird for me to think it was such."

In notes she sent Mr. Bent, Mrs. Lawrence comments on "the lovely tinkling chorus by the juncos in early spring, as if a myriad of woodland sprites were shaking little bells in an intensive competition," and she syllabizes three variations of the junco song as follows: *tililililili, tililili-tililili,* and *tuituituitililili.* She also describes a "conversational subsong" between members of a pair heard before and during the egg-laying period as "a rough *zreet, zreet, zreet* followed by a lengthy sotto-voce warbling." E. H. Eaton (1914) quotes Bicknell's description of this as "a whispering warble usually much broken but not without sweetness and sometimes continuing intermittently for many minutes," and which Florence Merriam calls "low, sweet, and as unpretentious and cheery as the friendly bird himself."

Mrs. Lawrence also sent Mr. Bent the following variations she detected in the junco's call notes in different situations:

| | |
|---|---|
| Location: | a simple *tit-tit-tit* |
| Alarm 1: | an explosive *tchet, tchet* |
| Alarm 2: | *bzzz, bzzzz* |
| Scolding: | a smacking *tack, tack, tack* |
| Fighting: | *tuit, tuit,* interspersed with a twanging note and a variety of smacking and buzzing notes |
| Feeding: | A throaty *tulut, tulut* seems to serve as a call to come together. |

*Behavior.*—Juncos usually progress on the ground by hopping in fall and winter, but occasionally run in short spurts when chasing a rival or to capture moving food. During the nesting season they may also hop, but more often one sees them walking with short, mincing steps, moving along not unlike a mouse.

F. H. Allen wrote Mr. Bent: "The juncos scratch for food, though not so often nor as vigorously as the fox sparrows do. They scratch by hopping forward and then back with both feet at once. When a thin layer of snow lies on the ground, a bird will scratch away a roughly circular hole 3 or 4 inches in diameter to get at the grain underneath.

"On the whole they are rather scrappy when feeding together and with other birds. Individuals vary in pugnacity, and sometimes females at a winter feeding station will drive off males. On Mar. 3, 1942 in West Roxbury, Mass., a male junco feeding on our lawn with a few other juncos and a number of English sparrows kept his white outer tail-feathers showing conspicuously for at least 5 minutes. He held the tail motionless without flicking. As the crowd thinned the white on one side was concealed for a time, and then when he was left alone that of the other side disappeared too. It looked as though the white rectrices where used as a threat on this occasion, a display I had never before seen except in momentary flashes."

Forbush (1929) describes how juncos he watched near the top of Mt. Washington in early August "drank from 'the Stream of a Thousand Falls,' which is formed by the melting of the snow, and then bathed in the frigid waters with much fluttering and splashing of spray, reminding me of other Juncos which I have watched in midwinter, similarly engaged in bathing, but in light dry snow, just as other sparrows take dust baths in hot weather."

W. S. Sabine (1957) comments on the flight behavior of a flock of juncos on their visits to a feeder in Ithaca, N.Y., on late winter afternoons. She found the birds, at what was probably their last feeding of the day, always departed in a regular pattern. As each bird finished feeding it perched quietly for a minute or so at the station, then joined others assembled in an arbor vitae clump about 40 feet away where they "made small movements" for about 5 minutes. The whole flock then left the arbor vitae together, closely following one another to an adjacent leafless deciduous tree, climbed high in it, and then flew from tree top to tree top along a ridge to the northeast, always in the same direction. She concludes "It seems a reasonable conjecture that the flock had a common goal, and this in turn suggests the hypothesis that a common roost may be a feature of the integration of junco flocks."

Hamilton (1940), also at Ithaca, found juncos roosting at night in winter "on the ground at the base of a Taxus thicket." While nightbanding robins near Olean on April 13 I flushed four juncos from roosts 3 to 8 feet from the ground in thick Norway spruces. On Dec. 28, 1960 I flushed a junco after dark from a nest 2 feet from the ground in a hemlock hedge near my house, and on Jan. 25, 1961 I again flushed a bird from the same nest at night. Thus, old nests occasionally function as winter roosting sites.

*Field marks.*—A slate-colored bird slightly smaller and more slender than a house sparrow, with uniform gray head, back, breast, and sides contrasted sharply against the white belly, this junco is seldom confused with any other species except some of its western relatives, such as the Oregon junco, which has a much darker head contrasting with a browner back. The pale bill is conspicuous in the field, and the white outer tail feathers are especially prominent in flight.

*Enemies.*—Essentially birds of open woodlands and forest edges, the juncos are subject to attack by accipitrine hawks and other predators. Red squirrels, chipmunks, weasels, and martens must take some eggs and young from the nests. Northern shrikes harry the wintering flocks fairly frequently. Cowbird parasitism is apparently not of great moment to the species' reproduction. Friedmann (1963) states:

> The slate-colored junco is an infrequently reported host; probably it is molested very slightly by the brown-headed cowbird. Eighteen instances have come to my attention. Three races have been recorded as victims: *cismontanus* in British Columbia; *carolinensis* in Virginia and West Virginia; *hyemalis* in Alberta, Saskatchewan, Ontario, Quebec, Nova Scotia, New York, Pennsylvania, and Ohio. * * * Both *cismontanus* and *hyemalis* have been known to rear young cowbirds.

> In the Peace River District of British Columbia, Cowan (1939, p. 59) found that no fewer than four out of five junco nests which were observed were parasitized—evidence which suggests that in this region the bird is a commoner host than it has been found to be elsewhere.

The Communicable Disease Center of the Public Health Service at Atlanta, Ga. has reported finding antibodies of the St. Louis strain of encephalitis in the northern slate-colored junco. Allen McIntosh of the Animal Disease and Parasite Research Division at Beltsville, Md. writes (*in* litt.): "There are 61 references to parasites from this host; the following genera of parasites having been reported: Haemoproteus, Leucocytozoon, Plasmodium, Trypanosoma, Eurytrema, Zonorchis, Diplotraema, Taenia, Filaria, Strongyloides, Syngamus, Amblyomma, Analges, Analgopsis, Bruelia Degeriella, Docophorus, Haemaphysalis, Ixodes, Machaerillaemus, Nirmus, Ornithoica, Ornithomyia, Philopterus, Physostomum, Ricinus, and Trombicula.

*Fall and winter.*—About the time the first wintry blasts begin to blow across the great coniferous forests of the North, the juncos start moving southward. E. A. Preble (1908) last noted them along the Mackenzie River 50 miles below Fort Simpson on October 16. Houston and Street (1959) say the fall migration along the Saskatchewan River usually ends in late October, but some years the birds are common until mid-November. At Pimisi Bay, Ontario, Mrs. Lawrence reports in a letter to Mr. Bent that most of the juncos leave in October, a few late stragglers occasionally remaining into November. E. H. Eaton (1914) writes that in New York State:

"In the fall, migrants begin to appear from the 11th to the 28th of September, in the southernmost parts of the State sometimes not before the 4th to the 12th of October. Among the members of the sparrow family, this species rivals the Song sparrow, Vesper sparrow, Savannah sparrow and Chipping sparrow for the place of greatest abundance during the spring and fall migration, probably being as abundant as the Song sparrow in most localities * * * ."

In her studies of the wintering flocks of this junco at Ithaca, N.Y., Winifred S. Sabine (1956) found "that although the migrant individuals which are to become winter residents arrive irregularly over a period of several weeks, they somehow manage to form themselves into distinct, stable winter flocks with mutually exclusive foraging territories." She continues:

> The junco flock is an association of birds which is firm in the identity of the individuals associated. * * * In a given small area a single group will be seen and no other. The formation of firm associations and the occupation of definite foraging areas take place at once among the earliest arrivals; it becomes obvious as soon as the first migrants are marked. The late comers are integrated into existing groups. The flock thus formed does not fly about as a unit, however. There appears to be no limit to the size of a foraging group. It may include the whole flock or it may consist of a single bird. The entire flocking procedure is marked by the continual forming and dissolving of groups of unpredictable size consisting of individuals that consort together and are daily visitors at the feeding sites.

## DISTRIBUTION

*Range.*—Western and northern Alaska, Mackenzie, northern Ontario and Labrador south to northern Mexico and the Gulf coast.

*Breeding range.*—The northern slate-colored junco breeds from western and northern Alaska (Brooks Range, Kobuk River, Yukon Delta), central Yukon (Ogilvie Range), northwestern and central Mackenzie (Mackenzie River Delta, Fort Anderson, Fort Reliance), northern Manitoba (Churchill), northern Ontario (Shagamu River), northern Quebec (Richmond Gulf), Labrador (Tikkoatokuk Bay), and Newfoundland south to south central Alaska (Lake Clark, Seldovia, Prince William Sound), southern Yukon (Lake Marsh), northeastern British Columbia (Muncho Pass), central Alberta (Edmonton district), central Saskatchewan (McLean), southern Manitoba (Treesbank), central Minnesota (eastern Marshall County, Minneapolis), southeastern Wisconson (Jefferson, Burlington), central Michigan (rarely south to Ingham County), southern Ontario (London), northeastern Ohio (Geauga and Trumbull counties), northern and western Pennsylvania (Pocono Mountains; intergrades with *J. h. carolinensis* in Appalachian Mountains), southeastern New York (Hardenburg, Bald Mountain near Dover), Connecticut (Union; rarely to Hadlyme), and Massachusetts.

*Winter range.*—Winters chiefly south of the breeding range and east of the Rocky Mountains, but sparsely to the westward, from southeastern Alaska (Juneau), southern British Columbia (North Vancouver, Okanagan Landing), northwestern Montana (Fortine), southern Saskatchewan (Eastend, McLean), southern Manitoba (Brandon, Winnipeg), northern Minnesota (Bagley, Duluth), western Ontario (rarely north to Port Arthur), northern Michigan (rarely north to Munising and Sault Ste Marie), central Ontario (Algonquin Park, Ottawa), southern Quebec (Montreal; Anticosti Island, rarely), and Newfoundland (Avalon, Tompkins) south to northern Baja

California (Cocopah Mountains), northern Sonora (Sonoyta), central Chihuahua (Chihuahua), southern Texas (Presidio, Rockport, Port Arthur), southern Louisiana (New Orleans), southern Mississippi (Cat Island), southern Alabama (Mobile), and northern Florida (Pensacola, New Smyrna).

*Casual records.*—Casual in eastern Siberia, the islands of the Bering Sea (Little Diomede Island, St. Lawrence, Sledge, Nunivak, and Pribilof islands, and South Bight of the Aleutian Islands), the arctic coast of Alaska (Cairn, Wales, Point Barrow), Banks, Southampton and Baffin islands, southern Florida (Chokoloskee), Bermuda, and the Bahamas (New Providence).

Accidental in Ireland and Italy.

*Migration.*—Data deal with the species as a whole. Early dates of spring arrival are: Maryland—Laurel, February 25. New Hampshire—New Hampton, March 7 (median of 21 years, March 28); Concord, March 10. Maine—Lake Umbagog, March 21. Quebec—Montreal area, March 10. Illinois—Chicago, February 26 (average of 16 years, March 12). Wisconson—northern Wisconson, March 25. Minnesota—Cannon Falls, March 1 (average of 21 years for southern Minnesota, March 11). South Dakota—Sioux Falls, March 24 (average of 4 years, April 4). North Dakota—Cass county, March 15 (average, March 21). Manitoba—Treesbank, March 17 (average of 25 years, March 30). Montana—Libby, March 20. British Columbia—North Vancouver, April 8. Yukon—Sheldon Lake, April 20. Alaska—Forty Mile, April 22.

Late dates of spring departure are: Florida—northwestern Florida, April 19; Tallahassee, April 11. Alabama—Birmingham, April 21; Russellville, April 18. Georgia—Atlanta, April 24. South Carolina—Charleston, May 2 (median of 5 years, April 11). North Carolina—Raleigh, May 4 (average of 13 years, April 12). District of Columbia—May 17 (average of 36 years, April 30). Maryland—Baltimore County, May 30; Montgomery County, May 24; Laurel, May 14 (median of 6 years, May 2). Pennsylvania—State College, May 15; Beaver, May 10. New Jersey—Plainfield, May 13. New York—Westchester County, June 5. Connecticut—Fairfield, May 12. Massachusetts—Martha's Vineyard, June 7; Concord, May 22. New Hampshire—Concord, May 7. Louisiana—Baton Rouge, March 29. Arkansas—Fayetteville, April 25; Little Rock, April 23. Tennessee—Nashville, May 13. Missouri—St. Louis, May 14 (median of 14 years, April 20). Illinois—Chicago, May 24 (average of 16 years, May 10); Urbana, May 23 (median of 20 years, May 4). Indiana—Wayne County, May 10. Ohio—central Ohio, May 30; Oberlin, May 20 (median of 18 years, May 1). Michigan—Detroit area, May 30 (mean of 10 years, May 24). Iowa—Decorah, May 16;

Sioux City, May 15. Wisconsin—northern Wisconsin, May 5. Minnesota—Minneapolis, May 24 (average of 7 years for Minneapolis, May 14). Texas—Amarillo, April 13. Oklahoma—Cleveland County, April 25. Kansas—northeastern Kansas, May 2 (median of 14 years, April 20). Nebraska—Plattsmouth, May 1. South Dakota—Sioux Falls, May 8 (average of 5 years, April 22). North Dakota—Cass County, May 27 (average, May 16). New Mexico—Los Alamos, April 17. Arizona—Tucson, May 1. Utah—Ashley Creek Marsh, May 6. Wyoming—Laramie, May 8 (average of 9 years, April 17). Idaho—Moscow, April 22 (median of 11 years, April 1). Montana—Fairview, April 20; Gallatin County, April 2. California—Berkeley, April 11. Oregon—Wasco County, April 12. Washington—Lake Crescent, April 14.

Early dates of fall arrival are: Washington—King County, September 30. Oregon—Lake County, September 16. California—Yermo, September 22. Idaho—Potlatch, October 2 (median of 11 years, October 21). Wyoming—Laramie Mountains, September 14 (average of 5 years, October 7). Utah—October 6. Arizona—Prescott, September 8; Wikieup, October 7. New Mexico—northern New Mexico, October 26. North Dakota—Cass County, September 5 (average, September 13). South Dakota—Sioux Falls, September 24. Nebraska—Santee, September 20. Kansas—northeastern Kansas, September 23 (median of 19 years, October 10). Oklahoma—Oklahoma City, September 1. Texas—Amarillo, October 9. Minnesota—Minneapolis, August 18 (average of 14 years, September 19). Wisconsin—northern Wisconsin, September 20. Iowa—Decorah, September 16; Sioux City, September 21. Michigan—Detroit area, September 13 (mean of 10 years, September 18). Ohio—central Ohio, September 15 (average, September 26); Buckeye Lake, September 23 (median, October 2). Indiana—Wayne County, September 15 (median of 17 years, October 1). Illinois—Chicago, September 5 (average of 16 years, September 16). Missouri—St. Louis, September 15 (median of 14 years, October 2). Tennessee—Knox County, October 17. Arkansas—Fayetteville, October 12; Little Rock, October 15. Mississippi—Oxford, October 23. Louisiana—New Orleans, October 5; Baton Rouge, October 12. New Hampshire—Concord, September 23. Massachusetts—Belmont, September 4; Martha's Vineyard, September 19 (median of 5 years, September 30). Connecticut—West Hartford, August 18; Portland, September 15. New York—Long Island, August 15; Oneonta, September 5. New Jersey—Englewood, September 17. Pennsylvania—Hawk Mountain, September 3; Pittsburgh, September 11. Maryland—Talbot County and Laurel, September 5 (median of 7 years, September 29). District of Columbia—September 14 (average of 31 years, October 7). North Carolina—Durham, October 18; Raleigh, October 23 (average of 15 years, October 31). South Carolina—Clemson, October 3. Georgia—Atlanta, October 17. Alabama—Gadsden, October 7; Coffee County, October 20. Florida—Melbourne, October 6; Chokoloskee, October 11.

Late dates of fall departure are: Alaska—Chena River, October 17. Yukon—MacMillan Pass, September 3. British Columbia—Okanagan Landing, November 26. New Mexico—Los Alamos, November 9. Manitoba—Treesbank, November 12 (average of 24 years, November 4). North Dakota—Cass County, November 15 (average, November 11). South Dakota—Sioux Falls, November 15 (average of 3 years, October 28). Minnesota—Minneapolis, November 30 (average of 10 years, November 23). Wisconsin—northern Wisconsin, November 30. Ohio—Buckeye Lake, median, November 28. Illinois—Chicago, December 12 (average of 16 years, November 27). Quebec—Montreal area, November 18. Maine—Lake Umbagog, November 9. New Hampshire—New Hampton, December 18 (median of 21 years, November 18); Concord, November 29. Maryland—Laurel, December 5.

*Egg dates.*—Alaska: 47 records, May 4 to July 13; 30 records, May 30 to June 23.

Maine: 22 records, May 23 to July 23; 14 records, May 29 to June 10.

Maryland: 5 records, May 18 to July 9.

New Brunswick: 73 records, May 6 to August 9; 40 records, May 29 to June 12.

Nova Scotia: 49 records, May 4 to July 30; 23 records, May 30 to July 18.

Ontario: 26 records, April 28 to July 19; 13 records, June 11 to June 28.

Quebec: 15 records, June 3 to June 27.

## JUNCO HYEMALIS CAROLINENSIS Brewster

### Carolina Slate-colored Junco

PLATE 57

Contributed by ALEXANDER SPRUNT, JR.

#### HABITS

The early morning mist hung in a heavy gray curtain over the balsams, drifted in ragged wisps among the huckleberry bushes and stood shroud-like over the lichen-covered rocks. Suddenly atop one of these age-old formations a small gray and white bird took shape, wraith-like against its somber background. Tilting its head upward, the bird opened its beak and poured forth a simple but musical trill which echoed sweetly amid the swirling banners of mountain fog. A Carolina slate-colored junco greeted the advent of another day.

If any one bird could be said to typify a region essentially, this race of the slate-colored junco deserves that accolade for the Blue Ridge Mountains of eastern United States. From the 3,000-foot level to the highest point in eastern North America at Mount Mitchell (6,684 feet), it is *the* characteristic avian form. When William Brewster (1886) described it as "Differing from *J. hyemalis* in being larger, with lighter, bluer, and more uniform coloration, and a horn-colored, instead of pinkish-white or yellowish bill," he placed its type locality at Black Mountain in Buncombe County, N.C.

For some 20 summers I lived much of the time within 3 miles of Black Mountain and had intimate contact with the bird from the Shenandoah Valley of Virginia to the Great Smoky Mountains at the North Carolina–Tennessee line. During that time I learned something of the bird's way of life at first hand. Certainly, anyone interested in ornithology who has ever visited that region will agree that this junco cannot fail to attract attention. Preeminently a mountain dweller, it is as characteristic of the area as the very rocks, the rhododendron "hells," the "balds" and steep ravines, and the the vegetation itself.

*Spring.*—The Carolina slate-colored junco is one of the few examples of eastern American birdlife that can be considered to indulge in vertical migration. Some birds do not leave the mountains at all throughout the winter; those that do usually return at the first marked indications of the change of season, which varies somewhat from year to year. As spring comes on, the birds that descended from the high country to winter at lower levels return to their mountain haunts. This is often only a short distance measured in miles, but it takes them into a completely different environment because of the elevation.

James T. Tanner (1958) comments "The 'migration' of Juncos from the valleys to the mountains in spring is gradual and indefinite. On March 19, 1952, for example, there were very few Juncos in their nesting areas at Mt. LeConte. By April 3 Juncos were common and many were singing there. It appears that March 25 is approximately the time at which the males, at least, move into their nesting territories. Yet some individuals may stay in the valleys around Gatlinburg, at the foot of the mountains, as late as April 20."

*Courtship.*—As my earliest visits to the high country were always about the time nest building was in progress, I have never witnessed the courtship activities of this junco. Tanner (1958) describes the onset of breeding activities as follows:

Each male claims and defends a territory, but the resulting combats and chases are tame and brief, and the territories are not extensive. Early in the season I have frequently seen two pairs feeding side by side, and later birds of different pairs have met with no sign of fight. This behavior suggests that the defended territories are relatively small and leave unclaimed area, and "anyman's land", outside of and around them which may be used for feeding by any Junco.

The male Junco has a display, presumably a courtship display, which is not well known because it is inconspicuous and observed only by those who make a point of watching these birds. It is usually performed on a perch near the ground when the female is nearby. He spreads and droops his tail, droops his wings, and frequently sings a quiet, Goldfinch-like warble which carries only a short distance, very different from the regular song. He displays most frequently in the early part of the nesting season, less frequently later, and has almost entirely ceased before the second brood is started.

However, D. Ralph Hostetter (1961) has the following to say regarding it: "I believe the behavior that I recognize as courtship plays a more prominent part in the life of the birds after pairing than before pairing. * * * If it precedes pairing, it certainly is continued throughout nest building." He continues:

Courtship display on the part of the male begins shortly after the song is in its prime. * * * The male flew about repeatedly from limb to limb on a small tree. He uttered a series of short whistles, "chee-eps," and "tsips", sometimes followed by a short trill. This series of whistles, etc., was continued for about five minutes. The female on the ground seemed to pay no attention to him whatever. During this vocal demonstration the male was about six feet above the ground and the female almost directly beneath him. There was no spreading of wings and tail feathers. Finally he flew into the brush and was lost, followed by the female.

On other occasions there is a pretty feather display accompanying the song. * * * Usually this performance * * * is as follows. The male perches on a small limb above the female who may be feeding or even carrying nesting materials. He sings softly the simple junco phrase or enriches it with various whistles and trills, lowers his wings, and spreads his tail so that the white marginal feathers show beautifully. His head may be thrown back slightly with bill pointed upward, or he may watch the female.

During all this he is nervously changing his position on the limb or changing limbs. The lowering of the wings and the spreading of the tail is one act of short duration, but is frequently repeated. * * * As the wings are dropped from their dorsolateral position, they are slightly turned out away from the body, and sometimes spread open, just a little, like a fan

*Nesting.*—Tanner (1958) describes nest building as follows:

The building of the first nest is a desultory business. The female, which does all the building, will work at it a while, cease for a period of feeding, return again, and so off and on for several days. Her mate may accompany her as she works, but cooperates not at all. The nest is built of moss, rootlets, and stems, and its deep cup is lined frequently with the slender bristles that support the fruiting capsules of mosses. The typical location of a nest is on the ground or in the mosses and ferns growing on rocks. It is usually well hidden by ferns or other low plants, and placed on a bank or rock with a clear space before it, except for the immediate covering, so that an incubating bird can fly outward and downward from the nest when disturbed. Of 84 nests that I found, 74 were located on the ground or rocks as described. One was in an upturned tree root, four were located from one to three feet above the ground in shrubs, and five were placed on the branches of spruce trees, where spreading twigs formed a platform, from five to forty feet above the ground.

The nesting site varies rather considerably indeed for a generally low nesting bird. The conventional site is under a clod, on the sides of a bank, or amid roots of a windfall, but these by no means exhaust the bird's choice. I have found nests directly on, or rather in the ground, depressed into the soil of open meadows until the rim of the nest is even with the ground. Some are concealed from above by grass tufts, some are not. Though I have found several nests in bushes and young evergreens, such have not been over 5 feet from the ground. D. J. Nicholson wrote me, however, of finding one 17 feet from the ground in the tall sprouts of a locust tree at an elevation of 4,750 feet in the Mt. Pisgah area of North Carolina, and another 16 feet up and out on a limb from the trunk of a balsam on Clingman's Dome in the Great Smokies.

An unusual nest site that vividly illustrates the bird's disregard of people was a nest started in a swinging fern basket on our front porch July 7, 1930. The basket hung about a foot from the entrance door that the family used continuously. The bird used a good deal of the coarse threads from a floor mat just to one side of the basket, and often worked at detaching them while people were on the porch a few feet away. The next four consecutive summers juncos built and occupied nests on the rafters of our open-front garage.

The nest is a well made structure, deeply cupped and substantial. It averages 4.5 inches in width, 2.5 inches in inside diameter, and 1.1 inches in depth. The materials used in its construction are consistently uniform, largely grasses, bark strippings, rootlets, and moss. The lining is quite often horsehair and I have found both gray and white used. At times hair of other animals is used, and now and then evergreen needles.

Two and occasionally three broods, I believe, are raised in the North Carolina Blue Ridge. Eggs of the first clutch number four rarely five; later clutches are smaller, usually three in number. On the time of laying Tanner (1958) comments as follows:

The laying of the first egg * * * depends on both the advance of the season and the altitude of the nest in the mountains, and there is also variation between different females or pairs in the same area. The earliest first egg date which I know definitely, April 20, was in a warm spring and at a low altitude. The average date of laying the first egg is about eleven days later for each thousand feet increase in altitude. The latest date for the laying of the first egg, of what I am sure was the season's first nest of the pair, was May 31.

The remaining eggs of the clutch are laid one each day, usually in the morning, until the set is complete. Four eggs is the usual number in the early nests. The female begins incubating with the laying of the next to last egg. While incubating she sits still with little or no turning, and will flush from the nest only when closely approached; I have had my face within a foot of an incubating bird before she left. This, and the fact that the nests are usually well hidden, makes it difficult to find nests during this stage. The male does not incubate, but he stays in the vicinity, foraging for himself and occasionally singing. When the female leaves the nest for food, she frequently flies directly to the male and then moves off to search for food. She forages industriously with the male usually following her, behind and a little above. He may perform the courtship display. The female usually moves in a circle back to the nest, which she frequently approaches by hopping along the ground. During the incubation period she spends about three times as much time on the nest during the day as she does off for feeding, but the periods on and off are irregular. She passes the night on the nest.

The average incubation period is about twelve days, and since incubation begins with the next to the last egg, the eggs of a four egg set begin to hatch fourteen days after the first egg is laid. They do not hatch simultaneously, partly because the last egg is not laid until after incubation has started.

*Eggs.*—Those of this subspecies do not differ in color from those of the nominate race. The measurements of 40 eggs average 20.1 by 15.2 millimeters; the eggs showing the four extremes measure *21.2* by 14.7, 21.1 by *16.0*, and *18.8* by *14.5* millimeters.

*Young.*—Again according to Tanner (1958):

"Both parents bring food to the young, working hard and steadily. Whenever one gets a billful of food, it flies directly to the nest and remains there very briefly, except when the female settles to brood for a short time, which she does more frequently when the young are small. The food brought consists of insects; moths and small caterpillars are common. The size of the insects increase with the size of the nestlings. Because of the feeding activity of the parents, and also because they are likely to scold persistently if a person comes near, nests are most easily found at this stage.

When hatched, the nestlings are naked except for a little down. Two days after hatching the sheaths of the body feathers appear as dark "pinfeathers". Five days after hatching the eyes open, and a day later the primary feathers of the wing begin to break out of the tips of their sheaths. Nine days after hatching the tail feathers begin to break out at the tip and the body is fairly well covered with feathers. The young may leave on the tenth or eleventh day if the nest is disturbed, but normally they will leave on the twelfth or thirteenth day. By this time the wings are well developed, the tail is almost an inch long, and they can fly clumsily but surprisingly well.

Young out of the nest are fed by the parents at least until the former are full grown. The length of care seems to depend on whether or not a second nest is started, in which case the young are earlier left by themselves. The majority of Juncos in the Smokies will nest a second time; the exceptions are some pairs at the very lowest elevations which appear to nest only once. The behavior during the second nesting is the same as during the first.

*Plumages.*—Richard R. Graber (1955) comments that this race is very much like *J. h. hyemalis* in all plumages, but slightly grayer and less brown throughout. He describes the juvenal plumage of *carolinensis* as follows:

"Crown and nape dull gray, uniformly streaked with black. Back tinged slightly with brown, rather sparsely streaked with black.

Rump gray brown, mottled with blackish. Upper tail coverts drab gray brown, obscurely streaked with blackish. Outer two pairs of rectrices largely white, third from outside with some white, others black. Remiges black; primaries and secondaries edged with whitish, tertials with buff or buffy gray. Coverts edged with buff. Lores, eye ring, and sides of head rather flat gray (uniform, except auriculars, lightly flecked with dusky). Chin and throat light gray or whitish, streaked and spotted (obscurely in some specimens) with blackish. Chest buff-tinted gray, or buff; sides and flanks buffy. Chest and sides streaked rather heavily with blackish. Belly and crissum unmarked white. Legs gray."

*Food.*—Though not extensively studied so far as I am aware, the food of this race parallels that of *J. h. hyemalis*. Seeds form much of it, those of both grasses and weeds, particularly in the colder months. During the warmer seasons it eats a higher proportion of insects, and it feeds the nestlings exclusively on animal food. It forages in the usual junco manner, scratching among leaves and ground debris beneath thickets and brush, and it often visits feeding stations immediately adjacent to human dwellings.

*Voice.*—The song of this junco is very similar, practically identical in fact, to that of *hyemalis*. It is a melodious trill, often uttered for considerable periods and frequently from an elevated perch. The call note can hardly be described as anything but a sharp "chip," easily recognized when once learned.

*Behavior.*—The outstanding characteristic of this junco is its tameness. About such heavily populated resort towns as Blowing Rock, Linville, and Highlands, as well as along the Skyline Drive in Virginia, southward along the Blue Ridge Parkway, and in America's most visited national park, Great Smoky Mountain National Park, the bird is almost underfoot everywhere. Along roadsides, trails, and streets, in yards and gardens, the familiar "chip," trilling song, and flash of white outer tail feathers are conmon sights. The bird is omnipresent on manicured estates as well on remote summits and peaks. Its universal local name is "snowbird."

*Fall and winter.*—As fall comes and the first frosts occur, *carolinensis* begins to drift to lower levels. At an elevation of 2,800 feet near Black Mountain where the bird is *not* present during the summer I saw the first ones on Sept. 30, 1931, after four days of frost with day time temperatures ranging from 37° to 42° F. As winter comes on, the birds drop farther into the valleys and along the Piedmont, where they may join the flocks of migrant *hyemalis*. Generally they stay close to the foothills and move only casually southward or out onto the coastal plain. That this junco can and does remain at high altitudes through the winter is attested to by T. D. Burleigh's (1941) record of "small flocks * * * feeding contentedly in the shelter of fir thickets" with a foot of snow on the ground, with the temperature zero near the summit of Mt. Mitchell on Dec. 23, 1930.

## DISTRIBUTION

*Range.*—Chiefly Appalachian Mountains from Maryland and West Virginia to Georgia.

*Breeding range.*—The Carolina slate-colored junco breeds in mountains from northeastern West Virginia (Terra Alta) and western Maryland (Accident, Finzel) south through extreme eastern Kentucky (Black Mountain), western Virginia, and western North Carolina to eastern Tennessee (Unicoi Mountains), northern Georgia (Ellijay), and northwestern South Carolina (Sassafras Mountain).

*Winter range.*—Winters chiefly on breeding grounds, descending in part to lower elevations in the mountains and the adjacent valleys; casually to central Maryland (Howard County), central Virginia (Amelia), central North Carolina (Raleigh), coastal South Carolina (Mount Pleasant), and central Georgia (Augusta).

*Egg dates.*—North Carolina: 42 records, April 20 to August 11, 15 records, May 15 to June 9; 13 records, July 8 to July 22.

Virginia: 6 records, May 6 to June 6.

## JUNCO HYEMALIS CISMONTANUS Dwight

## Cassiar Slate-colored Junco

### Contributed by OLIVER L. AUSTIN, JR.

### HABITS

This name denotes the junco population breeding in the basin country east of the western coastal ranges from south central Yukon southeastward to east central British Columbia and west central Alberta, which A. H. Miller (1941b) characterizes as "a group of hybrid origin, now stabilized, which occupies a geographical area in the breeding season to the exclusion of other forms." Males differ from nominate *hyemalis* in having the head darker than the back and the edge of the slate color on the chest convex instead of concave; females have the sides washed with brown or pinkish rather than gray. The form ostensibly intergrades with the several others whose nesting territories its breeding range adjoins, and individuals taken on the wintering grounds to the southward cannot always be identified with certainty. And, as Miller adds, "In other regions birds of identical appearance may be produced by hybridization."

Practically nothing has been published on this population's habits, which are not likely to differ essentially from those of the adjoining populations described in detail elsewhere in this volume.

The measurements of 34 eggs in the MCZ assigned to this race average 19.3 by 14.7 millimeters; the eggs showing the four extremes measure *21.1* by 14.2, 19.3 by *15.5*, *17.8* by 14.8, and 19.8 by *13.2* millimeters.

## DISTRIBUTION

*Range.*—South central Yukon and British Columbia south to northern Baja California, southern Arizona, and central Texas.

*Breeding range.*—The Cassiar slate-colored junco breeds from south central Yukon (Carcross) south to central interior British Columbia (Hazelton district, Sinkut Mountain, Tupper Creek) and west central Alberta (140 miles west of Edmonton).   (Some hybridization between this form and *J. o. montanus* occurs at the western and southern borders of breeding range.)

*Winter range.*—Winters from southern British Columbia (Vancouver, Okanagan Landing, Cranbrook), Nebraska (Long Pine, Lincoln), Minnesota (Minneapolis), and Wisconsin (Beaver Dam) south to northern Baja California (Laguna Hanson), southern Nevada (Charleston Mountains), southern Arizona (Yuma, Chiricahua Mountains), New Mexico (Las Vegas), central Texas (Waring), and southern Michigan (Kalamazoo, Washtenaw, and Monroe counties); casually east to southern Ontario (Toronto), eastern New York (Hastings), Massachusetts (Wellesley), Kentucky (Graves and Jefferson counties), Virginia (Herndon, Arlington), Tennessee (Germantown), Georgia (Athens, Decatur, and Chatham County), Mississippi (Saucier), Arkansas (Delight), and Louisiana (Catahoula Lake).

### JUNCO OREGANUS (Townsend)

## Oregon Junco *

### PLATE 59

#### Contributed by JAMES H. PHELPS, JR.

### HABITS

To me, Oregon juncos belong to the forest "edge," particularly the edge of the coniferous forest.   An "edge" is that irregular meandering border between a mountain meadow and the timber; a fading woods road no longer used and now crowded with new second growth; an opening in the forest surrounding a pond or along a stream; or an

---

*The following subspecies are discussed in this section: *Junco oreganus montanus* Ridgway, *J. o. shufeldti* Coale, *J. o. thurberi* Anthony.

old burn, full of snags, fallen logs, stumps, and a tangle of shrubs and other low growth. Juncos are everywhere in such situations. When disturbed, their white outer tail feathers flash attention as they scatter from the ground to nearby conifers; at certain seasons one may think juncos are the only birds in existence.

Aspen (*Populus tremuloides*) forests, which often grow much interrupted as subclimax within the true forest, are well liked by nesting juncos. Open park-like stands of yellow pine (*Pinus ponderosa*) and lodgepole pine (*P. contorta*) of the interior west have much suitable and attractive edge. High mountains of Baja California, with similar but perhaps drier forest cover, have juncos. The dry forests of the California interior and southern mountains differ greatly from the forests of the humid coast, but Oregon juncos are found in all of them. Compact low fir growth at timberline attracts nesting juncos.

The northwest "rain coast" has forest and forest understory of such density that it must be seen to be appreciated. Here juncos find the necessary openings in the forest are scattered and infrequent; the sea shore becomes edge. In the humid country west of the Cascade Mountains, Oregon juncos are city and country dooryard birds, sometimes permanent residents. Juncos are common in city parks and on college campuses in many parts of the West; the natural and planted vegetation, including various conifers, has the edge effect they favor.

The many races of the Oregon junco tolerate variable conditions of moisture, forest vegetation, heat and humidity, from sea level to timberline. Adequate ground cover in the way of grasses or flowering broad-leafed herbs and the like that continues green or at least somewhat succulent is necessary during the nesting season. Philip Dumas (1950) says: "A scattered shrub layer may or may not be present. The herb layer, however, is prominent and made up of many grasses and herbs."

Apart from nesting, juncos are not closely dependent upon edge, yet the attraction continues. The forest growth provides shelter and protection; the open spaces and bare ground provide opportunities to forage.

Oregon juncos are as well known to westerners as slate-colored juncos (*J. hyemalis*) are to easterners. A. A. Saunders (1936b), having had field experience with the slate-colored, white-winged (*J. aikeni*), pink-sided (now *J. o. mearnsi*), and Oregon juncos, remarks: "[They] differ from each other in coloration only. Their calls, songs, and nesting habits, so far as I have observed them, are all alike."

As defined in the 1957 edition of the A. O. U. Check-List, which we are following, *Junco oreganus* is divided into eight races: *montanus*,

*mearnsi, oreganus, shufeldti, thurberi, pinosus, pontilis,* and *townsendi.*
J. K. Townsend (1837), who described *Fringilla oregana,* spelled "Ore-gon" with an "a," in common use at that time, and this spelling is retained. Life histories of the races *montanus, shufeldti,* and *thurberi* are given in this account; the other races are given in subsidiary accounts following. The race *montanus* is known to many as the Montana junco and many references in the literature are cited ac-cordingly; similarly the race *shufeldti* is known as Shufeldt's junco and the race *thurberi* is known as the Sierra junco or Thurber's junco.

In July 1911, J. H. Riley (1912) found slate-colored juncos and Oregon juncos nesting together without hybridizing. A. H. Miller (1941b), with more complete knowledge of distribution of the juncos at his disposal than Riley had, indicates *montanus* is the race in-volved; Riley says: "*Junco h. hyemalis* is the common junco east of the main divide, and *Junco o. shufeldti* west of it, but we found them both breeding together at Henry House, Alberta, Yellowhead Pass, B. C., and at the foot of Moose Pass, B. C.; all of these localities are just over the main divide, either east or west. This convinces me that both belong to distinct species as no intermediates were taken."

Nevertheless, Oregon juncos do hybridize with other junco species, and different races of the Oregon junco intergrade with one another where their ranges meet. In some parts of the West as many as 10 forms of juncos may occur during migration and the winter season. Hence it is not surprising that their nomenclature has suffered much change and confusion. For a full account of the relationships of the different juncos, see A. H. Miller (1941b).

*Spring.*—Of the three races discussed in this account, *montanus* mi-grates more or less completely, the race *shufeldti* less so, and the race *thurberi* partially and, in some cases, not at all.

A short dispersal to nearby second growth or cutover timber lands suffices for some juncos wintering in the mild Pacific climate; others make a vertical migration from coastal or interior valleys to the higher mountains. Migratory Oregon juncos wintering on the low moun-tains of New Mexico or in the deserts of Arizona have hundreds of miles to go to reach chosen summer homes.

Where spring migration is noticeable, Oregon juncos appear first at lower elevations and move higher as the season advances. This sug-gests that spring migration follows natural pathways such as river val-leys and mountain passes, pausing if inclement weather occurs. In our intermountain country, with its interesting mixture of isolated mountain ranges and intervening valleys, I have noticed this pattern. On May 10, 1959 several inches of wet, clinging snow covered the low country in our part of Idaho; snow had melted from roadsides and trails only; higher elevations had more snow. Blaine Lyon and I saw juncos

PLATE 59

Mono County, Calif., July 6, 1953                    R. Quigley, Jr.
THURBER'S OREGON JUNCO ON NEST

Pinehurst, Oreg., May 1923                          J. E. Patterson
NEST AND EGGS OF NORTHWESTERN OREGON JUNCO

everywhere as we hiked into the foothills. Juncos flew from beneath roadside cuts, from under shrubs covered and bent with snow, and from the path ahead of us. It seemed to us as though the birds were marking time until they could continue migration.

We could easily recognize more than one race. Included in the many small irregular sized flocks, besides our local breeding race *mearnsi*, were other Oregon juncos with darker heads, more brownish sides, or more brownish backs than *mearnsi*. Two or three slate-colored juncos were seen this day, too, confirming that migratory juncos were indeed present. Two weeks later juncos were gone from the low country and only our local breeding birds were seen in the mountains.

Migration dates in spring, as given by A. A. Saunders (1912a) for western Montana near Butte, are March 10 to April 5. L. R. Dice (1918), at Prescott in southeastern Washington, for the years 1905 to 1913, gives April 13 and May 1 as last spring observations, indicating migration had taken place from the low country. In the Lahontan Valley, Churchill County, Nev., an irrigated farming area, J. R. Alcorn (1946) says: "Juncos (of all races) were seen frequently each month from September to April, inclusive." The status of the different races for California as summarized in Grinnell and Miller (1944) indicates spring migration takes place in March and April. R. B. Rockwell (1908) and others say that the bulk of migration northward in Colorado is about April 1.

T. T. and Elinor McCabe (1927), at their banding station in interior British Columbia, report that during the 1927 spring migration "the great rush began on the 10th [of April]." They comment also on the excess of males over females, about four to one. At Coeur d'Alene, Idaho, Henry J. Rust (1915) writes: "Arriving as early as February 22, becoming common by first week in April." A. R. Phillips (1933) says wintering Oregon juncos were seen in the Baboquivari Mountains, Ariz., until Mar. 16 and Apr. 1, 1932.

The experiments of Albert Wolfson (1942) with resident and migratory races of Oregon junco deserve mention. Wolfson says that internal and external factors were found to regulate the spring migration of the Oregon junco. The external factor is the length of day. "As the days increase in length the birds are awake for longer periods." Longer periods of being awake stimulate an increase in production or release of the production from various glands, which in turn causes physiological changes in the bird such as recrudescence of the gonads and the deposition of large amounts of fat. The internal stimulus triggers the actual migration by releasing the nervous mechanism that controls the migratory behavior. Resident birds show no deposition of fat, says Wolfson. On the other hand, the testes of the residents become active and increase in size at a faster rate than those of the migrants.

*Courtship.*—References in the literature to courtship are sparse and fragmentary.   Perhaps this is because courtship often begins in the flock, and unless an observer has long acquaintance with a particular flock he hesitates to record the actions of a lively group of small birds that look quite alike superficially.

A. H. Miller (1941b) describes a male junco courting a female with young, replacing a male that had been collected.   While the particular reference pertains to the race *mearnsi*, I can find nothing to indicate the other Oregon junco races act differently.   Miller writes: "A new male was on hand, singing, following her with tail fanned, and twittering in characteristic mating behavior."   Miller also had some pairs of juncos in an aviary, and in an additional comment, he writes (pers. comm.): "What was observed there, of course, may have been more a matter of pair formation than actual courtship prior to copulation.   However, the tail spreading and twittering certainly comes in at that early stage of pair relations.   In the cage I saw copulation at least once, and there was no conspicuous behavior preceding it—that is, no special notes or performance."

Just when the mating process began in the flock Winifred S. Sabine (1955) studied was not learned; but she did notice an increasing tendency for the two mated birds to arrive and depart from the feeding station together, and that as spring approached the dominant male showed an increasing intolerance towards juncos other than his mate.   Mrs. Sabine (1952) suggests that though she observed no courtship gestures as such, probably her observations were incomplete for she "has seen them in a different pair of the species and also has seen elaborate displays in a migratory flock of *J. hyemalis.*"

Among spring flocks of foraging juncos, an individual bird may detach itself, fly a more or less brief circle, and alight not far from whence it started.   More often than not another junco will give chase, as it were, flying the same course.   A person observing the the flight is immediately aware of the flashing white outer tail feathers.   Whether or not this behavior should be interpreted as courtship needs further study.

*Nesting.*—I have never found nesting pairs at any great distance from water.   The water may be a small seep or a minute trickle from a melting snow bank, but it is water.

Junco nests are usually on the ground in a cup-shaped depression.   Typically they are made of grasses or fine stems and placed at the base of a shrub or plant.   Animal hairs are often incorporated into the nest structure or used for lining.   Chester Barlow (1901) writes of nests in the California Sierras built on the ground in the sides of shallow ditches and concealed by the vegetation. One nest and its surroundings were composed entirely of pine needles. H. T. Bohlman (1903) tells about two nests found in sides of "railroad cuts" near Portland, Oreg. He writes: "Both were constructed of an outer layer of coarse grasses, then a thick layer of finer grasses, and a lining of cow hair. The inner cavity measures two and one-fourth inches across and one and one-fourth inches deep, while the outer measurements are two, and two and one-half inches in depth respectively." Bohlman comments that one nest was lined with white cow hair, the other with black.

To T. D. Burleigh (1930), juncos are one of the characteristic birds of the scattered stretches of open fir woods of the Puget Sound country: "Here birds were frequently flushed from nests that almost invariably were sunken in the green moss that covered the ground, and protected and concealed by a dead fir limb or, rarely a clump of dead ferns. They were substantially built of weed stems and fine grasses, in one case with green moss intermixed, and lined, sparingly at times, with horse hair."

Burleigh (1930) found one nest "snugly built in an old rusty tin can lying at the edge of an open field, and twenty feet from the nearest underbrush." Milton S. Ray (1903), F. S. Hanford (1913), and D. I. Shephardson (1917) report similar tin can nests. Joseph Ewan (1936) reports a nest on a rafter in an old hay-filled barn; D. S. DeGroot (1934) and others tell of nests in crevices of rock ledges; Ray (1918) reports a nest built in the corner of an empty box in full view of hotel guests passing to and fro; and W. E. Griffee (1944) tells of nests built on stringers between the joists of wooden barracks with no enclosed foundation.

S. G. Jewett (1928) found two Oregon junco nests in trees. His unique observations were made on the same day; the nests were about a mile from each other, both in lodgepole pines each about 8 feet from the ground. He describes them as "loosely built." W. E. Griffee (1947) describes a junco nest he discovered in his own back yard in Portland, Oreg. He writes he "was amazed to find it fully 20 feet above ground and 8 or 9 feet out from the trunk on a thick brushy lower branch of a Douglas fir." H. B. Kaeding (1899) notes most nests are built on the ground, but nests in trees and deserted woodpecker holes have been recorded.

Concerning the actual nest construction May R. Thayer (1912) writes: "Our first intimation that they were building in our immediate vicinity came to us on June 8 [1908], when I noticed the female picking up hairs that Donald, the collie, had scattered on the walk. * * * For two or three days, they busied themselves with the completion of the nest. The actual construction of the nest seemed to fall-to the share of the female, while the male watched over her, encouraging her by his presence and his music. They always came together for the dog hairs. Often he would perch on a tall stump beside the walk, and watch her while she worked, singing with the greatest energy."

A. H. Miller (pers. comm.) tells me the female "builds the nest although, as in so many cases where this is true, it is not unheard of that the male may toy a bit with material; but I have no evidence that he gathers up a substantial amount of material and goes and puts it in the nest."

Nesting begins early along the Pacific coast and at lower elevations. Birds farther north, or at higher elevations and in the interior nest at later dates. H. B. Kaeding (1899) writes: "During the summer juncos may be found up as high as 10,000 feet in the Sierras, but not as a rule lower than 3,000 feet, breeding. The breeding dates vary with the altitude and eggs may be found at 4,000 feet in May and as late as July 15 fresh eggs have been taken at 9,000 feet altitude."

In the vicinity of Portland, Oreg., Griffee and Rapraeger (1937) give April 22 as the earliest date, June 8 as the latest date, and the height of nesting season, when about 50 percent of the birds start incubating, as April 28 to May 3. The earliest date Burleigh (1930) recorded for the lowland Puget Sound area was May 9—a nest with four fresh eggs. At Coeur d'Alene, northern Idaho, Henry J. Rust (1915) cites the following examples: "Pair noted gathering nest material March 27; five nests, each containing five eggs, examined May 8; young able to fly, May 19; nest with five newly hatched young, June 18; nest with five fresh eggs, June 27."

The variation in dates suggests that Oregon juncos raise two broods in a season. In this regard D. S. DeGroot (1934) writes:

Early in July [1933] a pair of Juncos * * * was located feeding four half-grown young in a beautifully hidden nest in a crevice in a rock. These birds were watched daily and the parents quite definitely identified by certain peculiar markings and actions. On July 15 the young of this nest were out learning to fly and three days later they had disappeared in so far as I could ascertain. Two days later the female was seen carrying nesting material and on July 29 she was flushed from her new nest which at that time contained two fresh eggs. This nest was located not twenty-five feet from the first one and was similar in many respects although it was placed in a patch of skunk cabbage instead of a rock crevice, as in the first case. On August 3, the nest contained four eggs and the female was sitting. On the 16th the eggs had hatched and at this writing [August 26, 1933] the young are about ready to fly. Another nest of this species was located in the same area at about the same time and similar observations were made, thus confirming my suspicion that this species is one which nests rather commonly twice each season.

I have not been able to find other confirmation in the literature of A. W. Anthony's (1886) claim that in Washington County, Oreg., the species "breeds everywhere, raising three and often four broods."

*Eggs.*—Usually four eggs are a set, sometimes three, occasionally five, and an authentic set of one is known. Milton S. Ray (1919) describes 75 sets totaling 300 eggs of *thurberi* he collected over a period of nearly 20 years. He says the eggs are: "Usually ovate or rounded ovate, sometimes short ovate, rarely elongate ovate" with a "slight, very slight, or scarcely perceptible gloss. * * * Ground color white, faintly tinged with lichen green * * * spotted and blotched or splashed with hazel, * * * chestnut, * * * and light vinaceous gray * * *."

Wilson C. Hanna (1924) gives the weight of a set of four Oregon junco eggs. The set averaged 2.08 grams, the largest egg weighed 2.15 grams and the smallest 2.00 grams.

W. G. F. Harris (MS.) thus describes the eggs of the species as a whole: The Oregon junco lays from three to five and most commonly four eggs. They are slightly glossy, and ovate, sometimes tending toward short ovate. The ground is white or very pale bluish-white, speckled, spotted, and sometimes blotched with reddish-browns such as "snuff brown," "russet," "cinnamon brown," "Brussels brown," and "chestnut," with undermarkings of "pale mouse gray." The spottings are generally concentrated toward the large end where they frequently form a wreath. There is considerable variation, some eggs are only sparsely marked while others may be quite heavily spotted or even blotched. The eggs of this species are indistinguishable from those of *Junco hyemalis*. The measurements of 142 eggs average 19.3 by 14.6 millimeters; the eggs showing the four extremes measure *21.6* by 15.3, 18.3 by *15.8*, *17.1* by 14.9, and 19.3 by *13.2* millimeters.

*Young.*—D. S. DeGroot (1934) gives dates that indicate incubation lasts about 13 days. So far as I can determine incubation is entirely by the female. A. H. Miller (pers. comm.) tells me "in the aviary, as also in the field, I find that the female alone incubates."

A. D. DuBois, quoted by A. A. Saunders (1921), tells about a nest in which the eggs hatched May 30 and the young left the nest June 12. These dates suggest the young need 13 to 14 days to fledge. The young left the nest 11 days after hatching in a nest Winton Weydemeyer (1936) reports upon.

Irene G. Wheelock (1905) writes that on the day of hatching in a nest she was observing the young were fed 15 times during a 3-hour period in the morning. During the second day feedings were more frequent. She writes: "In two hours, from 9 to 11 a.m., the male came to the nest six and the female eight times. From 1 to 2 p.m. there were 11 feedings." The young were fed both vegetable matter consisting of seeds which she could not identify further and animal food consisting of insects. Large insects had the wings and legs carefully removed by the parents before being given to the young.

*Plumages.*—A composite description of the three races discussed in this account is as follows: The head and breast including the chin and nape are collectively called a hood; the margin of the hood is convex posteriorly. The hood is somewhat darker on the top and sides of the head and is sharply defined from the back and side plumage. Depending upon the race, the hood may be deep to dark neutral gray, sooty gray, and black in some birds. Females average lighter in hood color than males, but this is a relative and not an absolute comparison. The back and scapulars are confluent and are a shade of brown, grayer or brighter depending on the race. Sides may be yellowish, buff, or light ruddy brown; the belly is white. The outer three pairs of tail feathers are white, varying slightly in amount in the three races. In all races the feet are red-brown, the bill flesh color, and the iris some shade of brown.

According to A. H. Miller (1941b) the race *montanus* averages larger than *shufeldti* and about 80 percent can be separated by measurement. Also, about 80 percent of the races *shufeldti* and *thurberi* can be separated by their back color; in fresh plumage *shufeldti* is bister, contrasting with Verona in *thurberi*. At best, however, the races are difficult to separate in the field, and the literature and observations of the many workers over the years are thoroughly intermingled.

No descriptions of the juvenal plumages of the races *montanus*, *shufeldti*, or *thurberi* are available. An unpublished thesis by Richard R. Graber describing the juvenal plumages of *oreganus* and *mearnsi* is quoted in the respective accounts of those races. Oregon juncos do not keep the juvenal plumage for any length of time. I rather suppose that all races are like the race *mearnsi*. Young of this race that I saw in the Centennial Mountains of the Idaho-Montana border country (Clark County, Idaho) were already beginning to get their dark hoods in early August 1960, although their bodies were still streaked.

Gordon W. Gullion wrote to Mr. Bent: "Members of the Oregon junco species breed abundantly in the Yakima Park area in the northeastern part of Mount Rainier National Park in Washington state. While conducting banding operations in that area during the summer of 1947 I had the opportunity to trap a larger number of juvenal birds, often still retaining some of their natal down. Since these juncos remain in the area until late fall, it was possible to obtain three records on the time required for attaining adult plumage.

"One streaked immature bird banded (47–64082) on July 24 had the full adult male plumage 37 days later on August 30. Another

(46–23936) banded in immature plumage on August 1 had the black-headed adult plumage in 28 days on August 28. The third bird, banded as an immature (46–23945) on August 14, had most of its adult plumage in just 22 days on September 5. From these data it seems probable that juncos attain their adult plumage in 2 or 3 months after hatching."

A. H. Miller (1941b) writes:

The annual molt of juncos is the only one of any importance. The prenuptial molt is nearly obsolete and effects no material change in appearance. The post-juvenal, or first fall molt, is incomplete; primaries, secondaries, and greater primary coverts are not replaced, and the tail usually is not molted at this time. Juvenal wing and tail feathers carried through the first year are indistinguishable from those of birds a year or more old. The body plumage of the fall immatures in a number of races is different in average coloration from that of adults. But no absolute differentiation has been revealed—a situation also true of sexual dimorphism.

As stated above, on the average females have the hood lighter in color. In the three races being discussed here, the difference is usually apparent. Brownish overcast of the head is common in all races (somewhat less so in *thurberi* than in the other two); it is to be looked for most often in young and females. Miller agrees with E. Mayr (1933) that the brownish overcast can be "properly viewed as a retarded phase of plumage." White wing spotting is a rare variant. Other odd color patterns occur, especially about the hood, and Miller says of this in *montanus:* "They appear to be due to incomplete molts with retention of some feathers of a previous retarded plumage."

A number of albino Oregon juncos are on record. Louis B. Bishop (1905) writes:

A beautiful, albinistic, male junco was collected at Witch Creek [California] on Nov. 10, 1904, in company with a typical female Thurber's junco * * *. The bill, tarsi, toes, and nails are pinkish white; forehead, lores, infra-orbital region, chin, lower breast, abdomen, wings and tail, white; the wings and tail slightly mottled with ashy; a slight pinkish suffusion on the sides and the greater wing-coverts; and the rest of the plumage, including the throat, and entire upper parts, blackish slate or slate-color, edged with grayish white. In coloring, therefore, this bird is nearer *hyemalis* than to *thurberi.*

Bishop also took a female at Witch Creek, Dec. 14, 1903, that had the chin and part of the throat grayish white.

S. G. Jewett and Ira N. Gabrielson (1929) write: "On December 8, 1924, a perfect albino junco was killed on Sauvies Island [near Portland, Oregon] and brought to the State Game Commission."
R. C. McGregor (1900b) collected an Oregon junco having a narrow collar of white about the neck at Saint Helena, Calif., January 1899 which he classified as *Junco hyemalis oregonus*, though to just what race it would now be referred cannot be determined. A. W. Anthony (1886)

collected an almost pure male albino, mated to a normal female, near Beaverton, Oreg., some time in May 1885. Anthony had noticed the bird the year before but was unable to secure it; local residents told him the albino had been present at least two breeding seasons before Anthony first saw it.

*Hybridization and intergradation.*—The races *montanus* and *mearnsi,* the latter at one time separated specifically as the pink-sided junco, intergrade. The races *montanus, shufeldti,* and *oreganus* intergrade; *shufeldti* and *thurberi* intergrade; *thurberi* surrounds in range and intergrades with *pinosus.* The resident races of Baja California, *pontilis* and *townsendi,* are not known to intergrade or hybridize with other juncos.

The race *thurberi* hybridizes with the gray-headed junco (*Junco caniceps*) as does the race *mearnsi.* This is discussed in the species account of the gray-headed junco.

Hybridization between the slate-colored junco (*Junco hyemalis*) and the Oregon junco (*Junco oreganus*) is likely whenever a junco of one species in breeding condition finds itself surrounded only by juncos of the other species, also receptive. As individuals of each species may be found well within the range of the other, it follows that a wide scattering of hybrids does occur. When the two interbreed the color areas of the side, back, and head are modified, and every degree of mixture in plumage can be found. For a full discussion of the relationships between the different juncos, see A. H. Miller (1941b).

*Food.*—G. W. Salt (1953) aptly classifies the junco as a "ground-seed forager." Seeds of many plants are the main food of the Oregon junco. Weed seeds and waste grain are important during fall and winter. Insects are eaten when available and are important food during the nesting season. A. C. Martin, H. S. Zim, and A. L. Nelson (1951) say: "Beetles (especially weevils), ants, caterpillars, grasshoppers, leafhoppers, together with some spiders, wasps, and flies are the chief items in the animal diet of this junco."

F. E. L. Beal (1910) analyzed the contents of 269 Oregon junco stomachs, most of them taken in fall and winter. His first analysis "gives 24 percent of animal matter to 76 of vegetable." His statement about animal food, mostly insects, agrees well with the statement of Martin, Zim, and Nelson. Beal adds: "Caterpillars are apparently the favorite insect food, forming 9.4 percent of the diet." Weed seeds are eaten in every month and on a yearly basis amount to 61.8 percent of the food, in September nearly 95 percent.

G. F. Knowlton (1937b) reports the contents of 25 stomachs from Oregon juncos as follows: "180 *Homoptera* in 18 stomachs, composed entirely of 13 adult and 167 nymphal beet leafhoppers in 12 stomachs;

3 *Hemipteria* in 3 stomachs; 9 adult and 11 larval *Coleoptera* in 4 stomachs; 2 adult and 36 larval *Lepidoptera*; 1 *Diptera*; 4 *Hymenoptera*, all being ants; 1 spider; 134 weed seeds, a number of which were from sunflowers; numerous plant fragments."

Martin, Zim, and Nelson (1951) report the analysis of 265 Oregon junco stomachs, most of them collected in winter in California. They say that in California cultivated (*Avena sativa*) and wild oats (*A. fatus* and *A. barbata*) make up 10 to 25 percent of the fall and winter food, with common chickweed (*Stellaria media*) being equally important. Cultivated and wild barley (*Hordeum vulgare*) amount to 5 to 10 percent of fall and winter food, as do the small, shiny seeds of various pigweeds (*Amaranthus* sp.). The black shiny seeds of both redmaid (*Calandrinia caulescens*) and minerslettuce (*Montia perfoliata*) are prominent spring foods; also eaten in season are cryptantha (*Cryptantha* sp.), goosefoot (*Eleusine* sp.), knotweed (*Polygonum* sp.), filaree (*Erodium* sp.), and melicgrass (*Melica* sp.); with lesser amounts of pine (*Pinus* sp.), silene (*Silene* sp.), wheat (*Triticum* sp.), eriogonum (*Eriogonum* sp.), annual bluegrass (*Poa annua*), star-thistle (for the most part *Centaurea melitensis*), mayweed (*Anthemis cotula*), scarlet pimpernel (*Anagallis* sp.), sheepsorrel (*Rumex acetosella* for the most part, also called sour grass or red sorrel), woodsorrel (the most abundant being *Oxalis stricta*), tarweeds (*Madia* and *Hemizona* sp.), Pacific poisonoak (*Toxicodendrum diversilobum*), and plant galls.

Of 39 Oregon juncos Lowell Adams (1947) trapped as a part of a study of damage caused to seeds of forest trees, the stomachs of six contained Douglas fir (*Pseudotsuga taxifolia*) seeds. Lincoln Ellison (1934) says that at the Priest River Forest Experiment Station in northern Idaho juncos became active about the seedbeds soon after they were uncovered in the spring, and they ate "In order of preference, the seeds [of]: Western white pine, *Pinus monticola*; Douglas fir, *Pseudotsuga taxifolia*; western larch, *Larix occidentalis* * * * .

"From the appearance of the nipped cotyledons of some young white pine and Douglas fir seedlings, it was surmised that the juncos had picked off the attached seeds which still contained some nutrient matter."

Mrs. H. J. Taylor (1920) watched a red-breasted sapsucker (*Sphyrapicus varius* subsp.) working and feeding in an old pepper tree (*Schinus molle*). Sap exuded from the holes the sapsucker made and attracted insects. If the sapsucker was absent, other birds including the Oregon junco fed from the holes, whether on the sap or on insects, Mrs. Taylor was unable to tell.

S. G. Jewett (1938) notes Oregon juncos among the small birds drinking and bathing in the highly mineralized water flowing from small springs near Paulina Lake, Deschutes County, Oreg. The water is unpleasant to human taste.

John M. Robertson (1931) says juncos are among the many birds in California that utilize the small black seeds produced in great abundance by the imported blue gum tree (*Eucalyptus globulus*). L. L. Hargrave (1939) reports Oregon juncos wintering in Arizona eat the exposed seed pulp of fully ripened pomegranates that remain hanging upon the bush. E. D. Clabaugh (1930) suggests that to trap Oregon juncos for banding "Chick-feed, cracked corn, bread crumbs and bird-seed are all good baits."

*Behavior.*—The Oregon junco is a social bird. Except during the breeding phase of the life cycle the species gathers in irregular-sized flocks. I. N. Gabrielson and S. G. Jewett (1940) say: "After the nesting season the birds roam the country in small family flocks that gradually merge into larger groups that sometimes number into the hundreds."

J. Eugene Law (1924) observes the following of the August flocks in the San Bernardino mountains of California: "The personnel of these flocks of Juncos must be purely fortuitous at this season. Family ties seemed to be entirely broken except for an occasional late-born youngster. The groups, if they can be called groups, were constantly milling about over any part of the meadow, and they did not leave a spot in the same order or numbers in which they arrived. From numbers feeding on open ground scattering individuals frequently left without disturbing many which remained."

Of the wintering flocks Mrs. Winifred S. Sabine (1956) writes: "There appears to be no limit to the size of a foraging group. * * * The entire flocking procedure is marked by the continual forming and dissolving of groups of unpredictable size consisting of individuals that consort together and are daily visitors at the feeding sites."

The "purely fortuitous" composition of the flock remarked upon by Law is questioned by Mrs. Sabine (1959) who finds that Oregon juncos have a definite pecking order which she charts as she determined it among winter flocks. Mrs. Sabine's work suggests this intolerance serves as a spacing device which allows each bird of this social species a necessary area of privacy, maintained by the dominant bird of the pecking order and by each subordinate bird, thereby avoiding conflict with all others dominant over it. The increased intolerance that begins with spring serves to disperse the species for the breeding phase of the life cycle.

James G. Peterson (1942b) fed Oregon juncos cornmeal spread upon the snow at his feeding station at Cuyamaca Peak, elevation 5,000 feet, in San Diego County, Calif. He reports: "As an individual junco came to feed, the tail would be spread each time a morsel of food was picked up. Succeeding birds would not alight on the feeding area at random, but would perch on a shrub or some other elevated point in order to view the flock. Careful appraisal would soon reveal that at one or two points the feeding birds were flashing their tail marks very rapidly. Invariably it was to one of these points that the new and hungry bird would fly, and in alighting force the feeding bird to vacate the spot where the cornmeal was piled. The failure of the feeding bird to obtain food was a sign for the flock to break up."

Oregon juncos often forage in mixed flocks and otherwise associate with other small birds, such as chickadees (*Parus* sp.), common bush-tits (*Psaltriparus minimus*), varied thrushes (*Ixoreus naevius*), ruby-crowned kinglets (*Regulus calendula*), chipping sparrows (*Spizella passerina*), white-crowned sparrows (*Zonotrichia leucophrys*), and others. M. S. Ray (1911a) writes about large numbers of green-tailed towhees (*Chlorura chlorura*) and Oregon juncos associating together among the dry meadowlands of late summer near the southern end of Lake Tahoe, Calif. J. A. Allen and William Brewster (1883) mention collecting an "Oregon Snow-bird" near Colorado Springs, Colo., Apr. 26, 1882, and collecting another the following day, both in the company of white-crowned sparrows.

In the lowland Puget Sound country of western Washington I have seen juncos and varied thrushes foraging in the same leaf litter and debris, but whether the larger thrushes ignored or merely tolerated the smaller juncos was not learned. The shyer thrushes always flushed before the juncos did.

Howard Twining (1940) says that in the high Sierra Nevada the juncos are the birds most commonly associated with the gray-crowned rosy finches (*Leucosticte tephrocotis dawsoni*). He writes:

On July 21, 1936, a male rosy finch was catching mayflies in the air above the north shore of Leuco Lake. A junco in juvenal plumage was performing almost identical actions. The two would leave the rocks at about the same time and head for the same insect. As the rosy finch caught the insect, the junco would feint at it, then both would return to the rocks. This performance continued for about half an hour before the rosy finch left for the opposite side of the lake. It may be that the young juncos learn this method of catching insects from the rosy finches. On other occasions I saw flocks of young juncos mixed with rosy finches on the lake shore, catching insects in a similar way.

Lincoln Ellison (1934) saw juncos active about the seed beds of a forest tree nursery, and in cutover or partly cutover areas, but insofar as he could tell never bothered nearby seed beds in the dense virgin timber. He says: "The birds took seeds from all surfaces: duff (the layer of litter which covers the soil under the forest, in this case 1 to 2 inches thick and composed of dead leaves and twigs * * * ), mineral soil, and burnt mineral soil; but they scratched for seeds below the surface only on those beds covered with duff. They never scratched in a mineral soil bed, although there was invariably a wealth of seeds less than a quarter of an inch below the surface."

Seeds of western white pine were planted in the northwest corner of the different seed beds, and the certainty which the birds showed in flying from one northwest corner to another for their favorite seed indicated to Ellison "a surprisingly exact memory for places." Ellison concludes:

Apparently [the juncos' intelligence] functions expertly within the limits of ordinary circumstances, as illustrated by their returning so accurately to the food source, and scratching among leaf-litter. Such stimuli and reactions are within the realm of the birds' experience. But when extraordinary conditions obtain—and the presence of forest seed buried in exposed soil is probably extraordinary, compared to its common presence on the soil surface or buried in duff—their intelligence does not turn those conditions to advantage.

Moreover, that they did not show any interest in the soil surfaces after the surface seed had been picked off (although they returned for the attached seeds once the seedlings had broken ground), makes it seem probable that juncos do not detect such seed by smell, but by sight alone.

To study the winter society of the Oregon junco, Mrs. Winifred S. Sabine (1955) marked individual juncos by rubber cementing different combinations of trout-fly feathers to the top pair of the birds' tail feathers close to the body. Some members of the flock could not be caught, but enough were marked to simplify the problem and reduce the number of possible errors. She observed the juncos over a prolonged period as they frequented different feeding stations.

Her studies suggest the social activities of the winter society involve an orderly but rather complex type of flocking. She says (1956): "Although the migrant individuals which are to become permanent residents arrive irregularly over a period of several weeks they somehow manage to form themselves into distinct, stable winter flocks with mutually exclusive foraging territories."

Juncos in winter become birds with a definite routine. Each becomes a member of a flock, defined as an association of a group of juncos. The structure of the flock is formed with the earliest arrivals and with the use and occupancy of the foraging areas. Mrs. Sabine says this became obvious to the observer as soon as the first migrants were marked. New arrivals to the flock are integrated into the existing groups without difficulty. Individual birds of an established flock may visit or become temporarily attached to another established flock and are tolerated. Whether birds already established in the flock are dominant over new arrivals was not learned.

*Voice.*—R. T. Peterson (1961) says, concisely: "Song, a loose musical trill on the same pitch. Note, a light smack; twittering note."

To my ear, the usual note between birds of a flock or between the two of a pair is a quiet "tsip." To others, the sound is like a "sharp, metallic, kissing click," as T. G. Pearson (1939) describes the slate-colored junco call note. A. A. Saunders (1936b) says to him the calls and songs of the slate-colored junco and the Oregon junco are alike.

The call note, once a person learns it, draws attention to a flock before the flock is seen. As an intruder, human or otherwise, gets closer to the flock and the members become alarmed, the call notes come more quickly, erratically, and are obvious expressions of the birds' alarm. Other birds or animals may be affected, according to Thane Riney (1951) who notes: "Sounds such as * * * erratic 'thup' notes of the Oregon Junco elicit alarm reactions in deer."

H. H. Sheldon (1907) and Richard Hunt (1920) mention the Anna hummingbird (*Calypte anna*) having a sharp note like the junco; Hunt is more specific than Sheldon, calling it "a sharp smacking *tip*-note."

Peter Marler, Marcia Kreith, and Miwako Tamura (1962) made a series of experiments on song development in hand-raised Oregon juncos. They write: "The song of wild Oregon Juncos has several distinctive properties. It consists, with rare exceptions, of a trill of similar, repeated syllables. The length of the song, the number of constituent syllables, and the duration of those syllables vary relatively little. The fine structure of the syllables themselves shows great individual variability. Each individual has several song types, one of which may be given for long periods without interruption by another type."

None of the hand-raised juncos had the opportunity to hear any songs or calls of wild juncos after being taken from the nest. They were exposed to songs of other species. Marler and his associates describe their experiments, which cannot be detailed in this account. In summary, they say:

Eight male Oregon Juncos were taken from the nest and raised by hand in varying degrees of acoustic isolation. Each developed several song types. In comparison with wild juncos, the songs of the experimental birds were somewhat longer, with fewer, longer syllables. They were more variable. However, there was appreciable overlap, so that each male had at least one "wild-type" song. Some abnormal songs developed from imitations of other species. In addition, the birds raised in a rich auditory environment had more song types and a more more elaborate syllable structure, derived not from imitations but from unspecific stimulation to improvise. Vocal inventiveness is established as a significant factor in the development of song in Oregon Juncos.

*Field marks.*—Oregon juncos are sparrows with a dark-colored head, throat, and breast, called a "hood," and pinkish, yellowish, or light brown sides definitely separated from the "hood." The back is a shade of brown, never slate color. The outer tail feathers and underparts are white. This description includes the races *montanus*, *shufeldti*, *thurberi*, *oreganus*, and *mearnsi*.

The tone of brown on the back, the yellow, buff or pink on the sides, the tone of black on the head varying from gray to black, and their dimensions help the museum worker distinguish one race from another, but normally these characteristics are not to be relied upon for field identification. A. H. Miller (1936) says: "I know of no one who dares claim ability to identify as to subspecies a living, fidgeting Oregon Junco that he may be banding. Identified specimens readily available for comparison can increase a person's accuracy in such a situation, but, even then, many errors will be made. * * * The most detailed study of specimens of some of these races enables one to identify with accuracy only about eighty per cent of wintering birds. Obviously, birds of all these races should be designated merely as Oregon Juncos (*J. oreganus*) in field and banding work."

The exception is the race *mearnsi*, formerly separated as the pink-sided junco. Its sides are a rich pinkish cinnamon that often almost meets across the breast, and its hood is a clear gray.

*Enemies.*—The survival rate of juncos in the wild tells us that its enemies are many. J. M. Linsdale (1949) and coworkers banded 233 Oregon juncos during an 11-year period beginning in the fall of 1937. After 1 year 20 were again trapped, 19 were trapped after 2 years, and retrapping success decreased until in the 8th year 1 bird living for that length of time was retrapped. Thus one junco lived at least 8 years after it was banded.

Loye Miller's (1952) imitations of pigmy owl (*Glaucidium gnoma*) calls at Saragossa Springs, San Bernardino Mountains, Calif., June 25, 1930, brought a quick response from a number of small birds including Oregon juncos. Charles Michael (1927) writes that after a pigmy owl robbed a downy woodpecker nest of a practically full-grown nestling, a pair of juncos and other small birds gave distress cries and scolded the owl with no effect. All efforts by G. B. Castle (1937) failed to make a pigmy owl drop a junco from its talons.

Loye Miller (1952) observes that small passerine species do not react to the larger owls, either by sight or by sound. H. S. Fitch (1947) found the remains of a single Oregon junco among the 1,471 prey items he identified from 654 horned owl (*Bubo virginianus*) pellets.

A pair of Oregon juncos and several pairs of other small birds had nests in the vicinity of a goshawk's (*Accipiter gentilis*) nest being studied by James B. and Ralph E. Dixon (1938). The Dixons write: "All of these birds had fear of the hawks * * * as shown by the fact that the only way we could tell the old hawk was approaching the nest was by the alarm notes these various birds sounded before the hawk appeared upon the nest."

Stomach analyses and personal observations of J. A. Munro (1929b) in British Columbia record the Oregon junco as being prey to the sharp-shinned hawk (*Accipiter velox*) and the black pigeon hawk (*Falco c. suckleyi*).

Cowbirds rarely parasitize the Oregon junco, for they seldom invade its usual nesting habitat. Ian McTaggart Cowan (1939) records one instance of the brown-headed cowbird (*Molothrus ater obscurus*) parasitizing the nest of an Oregon junco (*J. o. montanus*) at Tupper Lake, Peace River, British Columbia, May 20, 1938. The nest was later deserted. Friedmann (1963) reports another from the files of the British Columbia Nest Records Scheme, "a nest with 4 eggs of the junco and 1 of the cowbird, found 35 miles south of Vernon, Okanagan Lake, June 17, 1959."

Allen McIntosh (pers. comm. to Oscar M. Root) lists the following genera of parasites of the Oregon junco: *Isospera*, *Dasypsyllus*, *Euschongastia*, *Ornithomyia*, *Ricinus* and *Physostomum*. R. O. Malcomson (1960) specifically lists: *Penenirmus mirinotatus*, *Ricinus hastatus*, and *R. pallidus*. Oregon juncos were among the birds Don Bleitz (1958) found infected with foot pox, a viral infection called avian lymphomatosis.

John J. Williams (1900) tells of young juncos just out of the nest preyed upon by a "medium-sized chipmunk," not otherwise identified. From the efforts passerine birds make to drive chipmunks from the vicinity of nests, Williams assumes predation by chipmunks to be significant. Lyman Belding (1901), early day California ornithologist, did not agree, saying: "I have seen at least a hundred nests of the junco and can only remember one that was disturbed by bird or animal, the exception being a nest that contained four young which were killed by a gopher snake." Carl Sharsmith (1936) accuses the Belding ground squirrel (*Citellus b. beldingi*) of a carnivorous diet on occasion, and mentions it killing the junco.

J. M. Linsdale (1931) cites an example of the Oregon junco being poisoned by grain placed for rodents, in this instance hulled barley treated with thallium.

Certainly the environment must also be considered. Juncos nesting at high elevations in the mountains suffer from sudden or late season storms. A. M. Ingersoll (1913) tells of severe June storms in the Sierra Navada of California. He writes: "All new snow that fell on June 23 [1912] melted away within forty-eight hours. Two nests that held eggs when discovered were later found to contain dead nestlings. Two nests held dented and cracked eggs after the snow. One nest and five young were destroyed by some mammal

\* \* \*." He adds that severe weather at a critical period in the life cycle increases chances of predation.

*Fall.*—With family cares behind them, as fall approaches the juncos start gathering in flocks to forage together on the matured seeds that are plentiful and readily available in most of the countryside. I believe Oregon juncos that summer in the high mountains of our western states stay in the mountains until fall storms drive them down. With the first hard snow, which can come in early October in the high country, the juncos quickly move to lower elevations or leave altogether. The fall migration may involve long flights for many *shufeldti* and *montanus*. For many *thurberi* the fall migration is merely a withdrawal from the high Sierra to adjacent foothills and valleys.

Migrating juncos may be found in a wide variety of habitat: edges of chaparral, fence rows bordering farm and ranch lands, juniper (*Juniperus utahensis* or *J. scopulorum*) and piñon (*Pinus edulis*) woodland, sagebrush (*Artemisia tridentata*), city cemeteries, brush tangles, riparian plant growth along streams, suburban yards, orchards, and country roads with weed- or brush-covered rights-of-way. Here again, the "edge" effect appears to be overwhelmingly attractive to migrating juncos. They prefer habitats consisting of some tree or bush cover adjoining patches of open ground. Presence or absence of snow affects their movements. Juncos usually desert parts of the country subject to heavy or prolonged snowfall, except for a few individuals held by artificial feeding or those able to peck out a living around a barnyard.

*Winter.*—Oregon juncos of the three races discussed in this account commonly occur in winter in the lower mountains of Colorado, New Mexico, and Arizona, on the great plains adjacent to the Rocky Mountains, the coastal and lowlands of Oregon, Washington, and California, the interior valleys and foothills of California, suitable places in the Nevada and Arizona deserts, similar locations in other western states, and at lower elevations within the breeding ranges of some of the forms as far north as British Columbia. Oregon juncos of different races become thoroughly intermingled in the winter flocks, and according to Winifred S. Sabine (1955) the same winter flock may contain both local and migrant individuals.

C. F. Batchelder (1885) writes about wintering juncos he saw near Las Vegas Hot Springs, San Miguel County, N. Mex., in December 1882:

Passing the various hot springs that come boiling to the surface at numerous points along the stream, a short walk up the cañon brings you to one of the openings where the retreating hills leave a level stretch of a few acres. Among the thick clumps of low scrub oaks that are scattered over it, or in the large patches of tall dead weeds, I was sure to find companies of Juncos (*Junco oregonus* and *J. caniceps*) busily searching the ground for fallen seeds. Of all the species that I met with, the Juncos were decidedly the most abundant. They were to be seen everywhere; it was hard to find a spot they did not like; but these were their favorite haunts. Among the pines on the hills, or in the thickets of willows down the river, they were in small parties, but here they were in large flocks. They moved about a good deal, straggling along one or two at a time, though occasionally a number would fly in a tolerably compact flock. They were shyer and more restless than *J. hyemalis*, and quicker in their motions.

Batchelder noticed no difference in the habits of the Oregon and gray-headed juncos. "They were always together in the same flocks, and seemed on the best of terms." Undoubtedly most of the wintering Oregon juncos he saw belonged to the race *montanus*, which Miller (1941b) considers the predominant "dark-headed" Oregon junco wintering in this region.

Grinnell and Wythe (1927) say of the race *thurberi*: "Abundant winter visitant throughout the whole [San Francisco] Bay region. * * * Inhabit tree-covered areas, showing preference for conifers, but also affecting oaks and eucalyptus, where they forage in scattering companies either in the foliage or on the ground beneath or adjacently."

Jean M. Linsdale (1929) writes: "Some birds, for example juncos, regularly roost at night in crevices in road-cuts. The dark bare soil of roads and their banks is often freed of snow sooner in winter than vegetation-covered adjacent ground. Birds seek out such places." Many of the migratory Oregon juncos Linsdale (1949) and coworkers banded at the Hastings Reservation, Calif., were retrapped again in succeeding winters which suggests that individuals tend to winter in the same place year after year.

### DISTRIBUTION

#### Montana Oregon Junco (*J. o. montanus*)

*Range.*—British Columbia and Alberta south to northern Mexico and central Texas.

*Breeding range.*—The Montana Oregon junco breeds from central interior British Columbia (Hazelton district, near Takla Lake, McGregor River) and extreme western Alberta (Yellowhead Pass, Banff, Didsbury) south through interior British Columbia (east from crests of coast ranges) and eastern Washington (east of Cascade Range) to central and northeastern Oregon (Maury Mountains, Home), central western Idaho (Heath, Lardo), and northwestern Montana (near Florence, St. Marys Lake). (Breeds and hybridizes, sporadically, in parts of the breeding ranges of *J. h. cismontanus* and *J. h. hyemalis*, north to Circle, Alaska, and Fort McMurray, northern Alberta.)

*Winter range.*—Winters from southern British Columbia (Boundary Bay, Arrow Lake), western Montana (Fortine), Wyoming (Thermopolis, Guernsey), and South Dakota (Faulkton, Yankton) south to northern Baja California (latitude 32° N.), northern Sonora (Caborca), Chihuahua (30 miles west of Miñaca; Chihuahua), central Texas (Fort Clark, Austin, Gainesville), and eastern Kansas (Lawrence).

*Casual records.*—Casual in winter or in migration to Banks Island (Sach's Harbour), Manitoba, (Aweme), Michigan (Marquette and Washtenaw counties), Illinois (Waukegan, Ipswich), New Jersey (East Orange), Maryland (Laurel), North Carolina (Wake County), Arkansas (Winslow), Louisiana (Grand Isle), and southern Texas (San Antonio, Galveston Island).

*Migration.*—Data deal with the species as a whole. Early dates of spring arrival are: Montana—Libby, February 27 (median of 9 years, March 1). British Columbia—Departure Bay, March 4. Alaska—Sitka, March 6.

Late dates of spring departure are: New Mexico—Los Alamos, May 9 (median of 6 years, April 24). Arizona—Camp Verde, April 11; White River, April 8. Utah—Mexican Hat, May 1. Wyoming—Laramie, May 9 (average of 6 years, April 29). Nevada—Mercury, April 14. Washington—Tacoma, June 2.

Early dates of fall arrival are: Washington—Stevens Pass, August 23. Nevada—Mercury, October 7. California—Siskiyou and Yolo counties, September 27. Wyoming—Laramie, August 31 (average of 8 years, September 22). Utah—September 9. Arizona—near Prescott, September 8; south rim of Grand Canyon, September 22. New Mexico—Los Alamos, October 10 (median of 5 years, November 8).

Late dates of fall departure are: Alaska—Petersburg, October 8. British Columbia—Sumas Prairie, October 29. Montana—Libby, October 21 (median of 9 years, September 18).

*Egg dates.*—(Refer to the entire species) Alaska: 1 record, June 28. Alberta: 70 records, May 16 to July 10; 36 records, May 25 to June 8. Baja California: 9 records, May 14 to June 12.

British Columbia: 16 records, May 7 to July 8; 8 records, June 8 to June 23.

California: 164 records, March 20 to August 3; 82 records, May 20 to June 12.

Montana: 6 records, May 5 to July 16.

Oregon: 26 records, April 12 to July 15; 14 records, May 9 to June 1.

## Shufeldt's Oregon Junco (*J. o. shufeldti*)

*Range.*—Southwestern British Columbia to southern California, chiefly west of crest of Cascades.

*Breeding range.*—The Shufeldt's Oregon junco breeds from southwestern British Columbia (western slopes of coast ranges; intergrades with *J. o. oreganus* on Vancouver Island) south, from the forests of the Cascade Range to the coast, through western Washington and western Oregon (to latitude 43° N.; intergrades with *J. o. thurberi* in Crater Lake area and the Rogue River Basin).

*Winter range.*—Winters at low elevations throughout the breeding range, south through California (south to Witch Creek, chiefly on coastal drainages), and southeast, sparsely, through eastern Washington, northern Idaho (Fort Sherman), Utah, and Colorado (Wray; northwest Baca County) to southern Arizona (Huachuca Mountains), southern New Mexico (Ancho, Las Cruces), central Chihuahua (Chihuahua), and western Texas (Brewster County).

## Thurber's Oregon Junco (*J. o. thurberi*)

*Range.*—Southern Oregon south to northern Baja California.

*Breeding range.*—The Thurber's Oregon junco breeds from southern Oregon (east to Hart Mountain) south through northern coastal California (Sonoma and Napa counties; intergrades with *J. o. pinosus* in Marin County) and the interior mountains of California to Santa Barbara and San Diego counties (Laguna Mountains), and east to extreme west central Nevada (Galena Creek). (Hybridizes occasionally with *J. c. caniceps* in eastern Mono, Inyo, and San Bernardino counties, California, and along the southwestern border of Nevada.)

*Winter range.*—Winters at low elevations on or near the breeding grounds north to Rogue River, Oregon, and south throughout coastal, southern, and insular California to northern Baja California (latitude 30° N.); sparsely east to northern Sonora (Saric), eastern Arizona (Flagstaff, Fort Apache, Chiricahua Mountains), and southwestern New Mexico (Big Burro Mountains).

### JUNCO OREGANUS MEARNSI Ridgway

## Pink-sided Oregon Junco

### Contributed by JAMES H. PHELPS, JR.

#### HABITS

Yellowstone National Park is a vast volcanic plateau, broken here and there by meadows, streams or lakes, and forested for the most part with lodgepole pine (*Pinus contorta*). The world famous geysers and related scenic phenomona sprinkle the landscape and attract most of the attention, but a naturalist soon becomes aware of the abundant bird and animal life here, unafraid of man. Of course one soon notices the pink-sided Oregon juncos, so named for the rich pink-ish cinnamon of their sides.  I believe they are the most common birds in Yellowstone.

Yellowstone is indeed junco country.  The mixture of meadow and pine affords much of the "edge" that all juncos favor.  Most of the undergrowth is not dense, but is open and grass-covered beneath the pines.

I have seen pink-sided Oregon juncos equally at home in the iso-lated mountain ranges of southern Idaho, the high country near Mount Borah which is the highest peak in Idaho, the dense forests of aspen (*Populus tremuloides*) and Douglas fir (*Pseudotsuga taxifolia*) near Grand Teton National Park, Wyo., and the high mountains of the Continental Divide along the Idaho–Montana border.  Westward through the Sawtooth Mountains *mearnsi* intergrades with *montanus* and southward toward Utah and southern Wyoming this race hybrid-izes with *J. c. caniceps*, the gray-headed junco.  In its habits I detect no significant differences from those of other related Oregon juncos.

A. H. Miller (1941b) says that *mearnsi* tolerates drier forests than *shufeldti* or *montanus*.  Nevertheless an adequate ground cover of grasses and small flowering plants must be available during the nest-ing season.  Wherever the ground cover is suitable, one is almost almost certain to find nesting juncos, especially if there is water nearby.  In the Bannock Range, Bannock County, Idaho, for instance, the slopes have much aspen interspersed with big-tooth sage (*Artemesia tridentata*) and here and there a Douglas fir; each opening in the aspen or "edge" not too far from water supports a pair of nesting juncos.

On the other hand, L. B. McQueen (pers. comm.) found juncos nesting abundantly in the Lost River Range, Custer County, Idaho, and not necessarily near water.  The forest growth of this arid range is open and park-like, with many "edge" situations, and a thick ground cover of grasses under the trees.  The forest is Douglas fir and at higher elevations Engelmann spruce (*Picea engelmanni*) and some limber pine (*Pinus flexilis*).  Mountain mahogany (*Cercocarpus ledifolius*) is quite common on terraces and ridges not otherwise occu-pied by the conifers, and McQueen observed juncos nesting in this cover.  The use of mountain mahogany by *mearnsi* is not reported previously, although *caniceps* uses it often.  McQueen found chipping sparrows abundant in the same habitat as the juncos.  In 1960 in the Caribou Range, Bonneville County, Idaho, near the Wyoming border, I found chipping sparrows more common than juncos in the drier places in the forest, and seldom found juncos at any distance from water, nor far from the "edge" of the denser growth.

*Spring.*—M. P. Skinner (1920) says of the juncos in Yellowstone:

When the juncos first arrive in the spring they appear at low elevations but soon move higher. Even so, they are often so early that they have to seek shelter about barns and other buildings. In March they are seen generally on the bare spots of ground under limber pines and Douglas firs. * * * The late storms of spring catch the Juncos, but they are adept at seeking shelter about the barns, under sheds, and in potato cellars * * *. At other times they take refuge in lodgepole pines under bunches of foliage covered by a canopy of snow, behind the snow caught on an overturned root, under firs, and even under sage bushes if nothing better offers. * * * The first arrivals appear suddenly in March, and they gradually increase in number until June 1.

The pink-sided juncos, as remarked previously, associate with other juncos in migration. In Idaho we first notice the junco flocks of mixed races in such places as cemeteries where plantings of conifers alternate with bare roadways and plots of grass, and along country roadsides, foothill trails, and the outskirts of towns. Our Idaho weather is notoriously unpredictable; winter may linger into May one year, and the next year spring comes in Feburary. Juncos accommodate themselves accordingly and forage or take shelter where opportunity offers.

When we find pink-sided juncos in late May among the aspens and Douglas firs of the mountains, all seem to be in separate pairs and no flocks are in evidence. On May 23, 1959 in the Bannock Mountains at 6,000 to 7,000 feet elevation Blaine Lyon and I saw upwards of 15 pairs in the scrub aspen groves and along a small brook edging open mature Douglas fir growth. The birds were either foraging quietly in the litter or sitting quietly on aspen branches, and we saw no flocks, lone individuals, or conflicts between pairs. Each pair stayed in a certain vicinity that I took to be its territory and could not be flushed away. If one bird of a pair flew the other followed; neither flew far, perhaps no more than 60 feet, nor deserted the general area. One bird, presumed to be a female, was seen carrying several weed stems and a bit of dandelion in her bill; perhaps nest building had begun. M. P. Skinner (1925) says: "The Juncos pair off late in May, and by the middle of June have made their nests. * * *"

*Nesting.*—J. C. Merrill (1881) writes: "A nest taken June 13 was near the top of a ridge connecting two peaks, at an elevation of 8,000 feet. The nest was under a shelving stone, one of many exposed by a land slide, and was in a little hollow dug out by the parents. The nest was rather large, but well and compactly built, composed externally of coarse dry grasses, with an inner lining of fine yellow straws and hairs of the mountain sheep." Edson Fichter (pers. comm.) tells me of a nest he found July 22, 1959, on the ground at the base of a lupine, made mostly of dried grasses. The nest was 2¼ by 2½ inches, outside diameter. M. P. Skinner (1920) describes several nests.  One was made of pine needles and vegetable stems placed under a little bunch of blueberries; another similar nest was more in the open under a tall cluster of lupines.  Skinner also tells about a nest "built of grasses and lined with fine material, placed seven feet from the ground on the back wall of a shallow formation cave at Mammoth (Hot Springs, Yellowstone National Park)."

I have found no proof that the pink-sided race raises more than one brood each year.  M. P. Skinner (1920) says: "Young birds have been seen to fly as early as the end of June at the lower elevations; and as late as August 12 I have found them in the same stage at higher altitudes.  I have not been able to determine whether the mountaineers are second broods or not."

Late nestings sometimes occur.  Eliot Blackwelder (1916) found a junco nest in the mountains of western Wyoming Sept. 1, 1912 "on the ground among flowers and grasses in a straggling grove of spruce trees and at an elevation of 9700 feet above sea.  It contained four newly hatched young birds."  As 3 inches of snow fell that night and another snowstorm came 5 days later, Blackwelder doubted that the late nesting succeeded at this high elevation.

*Eggs.*—Four eggs compose the normal set.  J. C. Merrill (1881) collected a set of five.  He gives the measurements of four in inches as 0.81 by 0.60, 0.80 by 0.59, 0.84 by 0.60, and 0.83 by 0.60; the fifth he broke in blowing.  He describes them as follows: "The ground color of three of these eggs is a dull yellowish-white, marked with spots and blotches of light reddish-brown and with a few blotches of lavender.  The spots are scattered over the entire surface of the eggs, but are largest and most numerous at the larger end.  The ground color of the fourth egg, the largest one, is a rather greenish-white."

*Young.*—Edson Fichter (pers. comm.) watched both adults feed the four young in a nest he discovered July 22, 1959.  The average time between visits was 4 minutes 12 seconds, and one parent or the other or both averaged 32 seconds at the nest during 10 visits.  He adds that the adults removed the fecal sacs; they apparently ate some of the smaller ones, others they carried away and dropped at a distance.

The adults brought food each time by the same route; alighting in the same small conifer about 8 feet from the nest, they dropped to the ground 2 or 3 feet from the nest and approached it by essentially the same path.  When Fichter returned to the nest the next day he found the herbaceous vegetation surrounding and above the nest had been disturbed, apparently by cattle, and the approach route was not as consistent as before.  Fichter watched the birds on two occasions for more than an hour at a distance of 3½ feet from the nest. The adults were unafraid and continued to feed their young in the nest.

A. A. Saunders (1910b) tells about hunting for junco nests in Jefferson County, Mont. He says "a pair of Pink-sided juncos * * * appeared, scolded me, flew about my hed and finally followed me out of the swamp where I had searcht in vain for nest or young. Later I found another spot where a pair of Juncos evidently had a nest or young and where I past several evenings in succession. I searcht this spot for three evenings before I finally found a single young bird. This bird was well feathered but unable to fly and I almost steppt on it before I found it. When I caught it and it called in distress the parents became fairly frantic and flew at my hed, and fluttered in front of me almost within reach."

M. P. Skinner (1920) reports a female fluttering away with a pretended broken wing when he discovered her nest with newly hatched young.

*Plumages.*—Richard R. Graber (1955) describes the juvenal plumage of *J. o. mearnsi* as follows: "Forehead, crown, and nape gray, profusely streaked with black. Back cinnamon brown, marked with heavy black streaks. Rump and upper tail coverts buffy gray, obscurely streaked with black. Outer pair of rectrices white, second from outer largely white. Others black, narrowly edged with gray. Remiges black, primaries and secondaries light gray-edged. Tertials edged broadly with dull pink. Lesser coverts gray, medians (black-tipped) buffy white. Greater coverts edged with buff, tipped with buffy white. Two obscure buffy white wing bars. Lores black. Sides of head gray, rather obscurely spotted with black. Chin and throat grayish-white spotted and streaked with black. Chest, sides, and flanks tinged with buff, streaked with black. Belly and crissum white, unmarked. Leg feathers gray and white."

Iris is brown; bill, flesh colored; feet, red-brown.

*Hybridization and intergradation.*—The pink-sided Oregon junco, now the race *mearnsi*, and the race *montanus*, formerly called Montana junco, meet and intergrade along a more or less north–south line from the Sawtooth Mountains of Idaho northward. Miller (1941b) says: "The meeting * * * occurs in a region where there are no barriers to distribution. At least in Idaho and in parts of Montana they meet in areas of nearly continuous forest habitat. There is more discontinuity within the range of *mearnsi* in northeastern Idaho than in the region of principal intergradation."

Hybridization between the pink-sided race of the Oregon junco and the white-winged junco (*Junco aikeni*) is rare although known. A. H. Miller (1941b) says "occasional *mearnsi* wander eastward from their breeding range in the Big Horn Mountains of Montana and Wyoming

to breed with *aikeni*." Breeding ranges of the two species are quite
possibly separated by no more than 20 miles in this area and Miller
considers it remarkable that more hybridization does not occur. He
says: "Here are two forms, each representative of an extreme modi-
fication of a distinct rassenkreis, that remain peculiarly apart, considering their migratory habit, when in close proximity geographically
in the breeding season."

Hybridization between *J. o. mearnsi* and *J. c. caniceps* is discussed
under the gray-headed junco, p. 1120.

*Food.*—The food of this race is apparently similar to that of other
juncos. One sees them picking up weed seeds or plant seeds, or one
presumes so from watching the birds feeding along roadsides or
borders of trails, in neglected mountain cabin gardens, cemeteries, and
the like. During breeding season I have seen pairs with young
bring various small worms or insects, but have not identified the food
further.

M. P. Skinner (1920) says that in the spring in Yellowstone the
pink-sided Oregon juncos pick up grain and weed seed on bare slopes
and go about barns with Cassin's finches for dropped oats. As the
automobile has not eliminated the horse from Yellowstone and numbers of them are kept for packing into roadless areas or to rent as
saddle horses, this observation of Skinner's should still be true.

*Behavior.*—M. P. Skinner (1920) writes:

Our Juncos are very quick, sprightly and restless in their ways, hopping about
on the ground and keeping up an almost continual cheeping in loud tones, except
when busy with parential duties or flitting through the pines with a flash of the
white feathers in their tails. On the ground they move along with quick little
jerks of the wings and tail at each hop. Sometimes they scuttle out of the road
and under the nearby trees at one's approach. Usually, though, they are very
tame and can be observed at close range * * *. They are quite fearless of the
Red-tail and Swainson hawks, even when those big birds are screaming in the
same tree within a few feet of them.

Pink-sided Juncos are very sociable little birds, associating in spring and fall
with Mountain Chickadees, Nuthatches, Tree Sparrows, and with their cousins,
the Intermediate [now called *J. o. montanus*] Juncos, in the evergreens. At
other times they may be seen with Pine Siskins, White-crowned Sparrows, Chipping Sparrows, Kinglets, Audubon Warblers and Townsend Solitaires. They
are often with the Robins and Bluebirds, with Vesper Sparrows in spring on the
sage flats, and even with Horned Larks and Leucostictes on the bare spots. * * *
The Pink-sided Junco usually progresses by a series of short flights from tree to
tree, or from bush to bush. The flight has a peculiar, halting catch to it, due,
no doubt, to the short and fast moving wings.

Hawking for insects has been observed in this race. M. French
Gilman (1935) saw a pink-sided Oregon junco, at Death Valley, Inyo
County, Calif., "jump several times into the air and catch insects."
This behavior has also been observed in *oreganus* and *thurberi*.

*Voice.*—I do not know whether I should say a junco may sometimes sing for the pure joy of hearing his own voice. But a male I heard singing from the top of a chokecherry near Palisades Dam, Bonneville County, Idaho, one midsummer afternoon almost caused me to think so. The bird was wet, as wet as he could be, from a bath in a nearby backwater pool of a brook. He was perched, his head thrown back, vigorously shaking and fluffing his feathers dry, singing rapidly and repeatedly all the while. He paused only now and then to pick at a feather, and then sang again as I watched from an adjacent path for more than 10 minutes. His song was a whistling "ting-ing-ing-ing-ing" repeated rapidly in series. The calls and notes of *mearnsi* are the same as those of others of the species insofar as I can determine.

*Field marks.*—The pink-sided race may be distinguished in the field from the other Oregon junco races.

The description given by A. H. Miller (1936) is excellent: "The species has broad areas of rich pinkish cinnamon on the sides. The sides are never brownish or vinaceous as in many Shufeldt's Juncos. Pink-sided Juncos have gray, not sooty or blackish heads; sometimes the feathers are tipped with buff. The back is dull brown. No one of these charactors can be relied on solely, but the combination of rich side color and clear gray head is highly dependable."

*Enemies.*—Concerning survival in the wild, John N. and Eleanor Hough (pers. comm.) at Boulder, Colo., banded a total of 3,101 pink-sided Oregon juncos from 1946 to 1958. These yielded 63 returns to their station after 1 year, 21 returns after 2 years, 14 returns after 3 years, 4 returns after 4 years, 2 returns after 5 years, and 1 return after 6 years.

Juncos in Yellowstone are attracted to the warmth of caves, which often become death traps from gases. Edgar A. Mearns (1903) notes: "In any hollow capable of holding the heavy gas (supposed to be carbon dioxide) fatal to animal life, dead birds were liable to be found, provided that the usual accompaniment of heat and moisture (from steam), and sulphurous odors (from emanating gases) were found. Most of the dead creatures were birds * * *. The effect on bird bodies was to cause rapid decay, the flesh quickly disappearing, then the bones, and lastly, the feathers."

Mearns visited the "Stygian Cave" at Mammoth Hot Springs and other similar formations near by. Pink-sided Oregon juncos were always found, usually numbering more than other species. During the September 1902 autumn migration, Mearns says an unusually large number of birds perished and although he kept no records, "The largest number were pink-sided juncos."

*Fall and winter.*—About the first week in August the pink-sided juncos may be found in small flocks—usually birds of a single family, the parents with their offspring. As one hikes through the high country little groups of juncos fly ahead, alighting now and then in a Douglas fir, limber pine or aspen, then fly again as the hiking party disturbs them. But they do not fly far and do not really seem disturbed by human intrusion. I have a suspicion that after leaving the nest young juncos with their parents may make an upward migration among the mountains. Where earlier in the season I found nesting pairs the birds were gone, but in the higher country they seemed more plentiful than before.

Toward the latter part of August the flocks become larger as family joins family. In August 1960 near the Continental Divide in Clark County, Idaho, I encountered flocks of juncos in quantities beyond counting. Juncos were everywhere, in the open places between the scattered conifers of the hillsides, and among the upturned snags and brush of the shore of a small lake which shall remain nameless because of the huge trout my brother and I have taken there and want to take again.

Streaked young predominate in the late summer flocks, but the young juncos get their adult plumage within 2 or 3 months after hatching, and the October flocks are nearly all in adult plumage.

While many remain in the high country as long as possible, even as late as October and November, so far as is known birds of this race migrate completely, and none stays in its snow-covered mountain breeding home through the winter.

Fall migration is irregular as there are records of juncos migrating or at their winter homes while others are still in the vicinity of the breeding grounds. E. R. Warren (1916) says for the Elk Mountain region, Gunnison County, Colo., that the junco arrives "as early as September 24, and remains throughout October." H. S. Swarth (1908) says "first seen on October 18" in the Huachuca Mountains of Arizona.

Pink-sided Oregon juncos winter commonly on the lower mountains and foothills of Colorado, New Mexico and Arizona. At Boulder, Boulder County, Colo., John N. and Eleanor Hough (pers. comm.) report October 11 as their earliest date in the fall and May 1 as their latest date for the years 1946 to 1958. In their opinion "it is certainly the most common winter junco" at Boulder.

Open or scattered woodland or forest, if that is the term, covers many of the mountains that are winter range for this junco. In southern Pima County, Ariz., A. R. Phillips (1933) says: "Found from the crests of the ridges to the canyon bottoms (of the Baboquívari Mountains), but commonest in the live oak belt."

Pink-sided Oregon juncos are found associating in winter flocks with gray-headed juncos, white-winged juncos, and other Oregon junco races, principally *montanus*.

## DISTRIBUTION

*Range.*—Southeastern Alberta and southwestern Saskatchewan south to northern Sonora, central Chihuahua, and western Texas.

*Breeding range.*—The pink-sided Oregon junco breeds from southeastern Alberta (Eagle Butte) and southwestern Saskatchewan (Cypress Hills) south through central Montana (west to Belt River Canyon and Madison County, east to Big Horn Mountains), eastern Idaho (head of Pahsimeroi River, 20 miles northeast of Preston) and northwestern Wyoming (Teton and Wind River mountains). (Hybridization with *J. c. caniceps* occurs to southward in southern Idaho (Cassia County; Swan Lake), northern Utah (to Summit County and Uinta Mountains), and southern Wyoming (Rattlesnake and Casper mountains).)

*Winter range.*—Winters from northern Utah (Salt Lake Valley), northeastern Wyoming (Newcastle), and western and central Nebraska (Crawford, Johnstown, Red Cloud) south to northern Sonora (Sierra Carrizal), central Chihuahua (Bustillos), and western Texas (Hemphill and Brewster counties); casually west to southern California (Potholes, Ramona) and east to eastern Nebraska (Omaha).

## JUNCO OREGANUS OREGANUS (Townsend)

# Northwestern Oregon Junco

### PLATE 59

### Contributed by JAMES H. PHELPS, JR.

## HABITS

This race breeds in the coastal islands and adjacent mainland of southeastern Alaska and British Columbia south to Princess Royal Island and Calvert Island. It is truly a coastal bird, and the pure form does not appear to go inland beyond the tidal inlets and lower river valleys. A number of other species have developed local races in this region of dense forest and heavy rainfall, with attendant pecularities in their life histories.

As the nominate race Townsend (1837) described originally, *oreganus* might be known as *the* Oregon junco, but Grinnell and Miller (1944) use the name northwestern Oregon junco. Theed Pearse of Vancouver Island (pers. comm.) who courteously allowed me to use his field notes, refers to it as the "red" junco. And indeed the backs of *oreganus* are markedly ruddier than those of the neighboring *shufeldti* or *montanus*, and in some individuals are a bright, rich red-brown. Heads are black, darker on the average than in the adjacent races. The impression is that of an intensely colored junco, new looking, as though freshly washed from constant exposure to the incessant rains.

S. G. Jewett (1942), who visited different islands and the mainland of southeastern Alaska in the summer of 1941, comments on the irregular distribution of the race:

Common locally, but entirely or almost lacking in other apparently suitable areas. At Hobart Bay on June 23, during a half-day's hunt, only two adults were seen; and on June 25 several hours spent ashore revealed only one adult male, seen and heard singing. On June 28 at Olive Cove, Etolin Island, and June 28 and 29 at Wrangell the species was very common, many adults and striped young being seen. Almost an entire day spent ashore at Anan Creek revealed just one young junco. At Kake, Kupreanof Island, both young and adults were common in the Indians' garden patches along the beach on July 4.

A. H. Miller (1941b) says:

Juncos in much of this area are sparsely distributed, probably because of the prevailing density of the forest and undergrowth. They occur chiefly along the borders of muskegs, meadows, streams, and beaches and in the occasional tracts of parklike timber, especially on the outer islands. Cedar (*Thuja*), Sitka Spruce (*Picea sitchensis*), and western Hemlock (*Tsuga heterophylla*) dominate the forest. There is an abundance of epiphytic growth. No other junco experiences more overcast weather and precipitation during the breeding season. The sun may be obscured from view for many days in succession. Nearly all the occupied region is below 2000 feet in elevation. Some of the higher mountains of the islands may afford suitable junco habitat at timber line.

From Comox, Vancouver Island, Theed Pearse writes me: "Here the Oregon junco is practically a winter bird and nests at the higher levels."

*Spring.*—The earliest arrival at Windfall Harbor, Admiralty Island, in 1907 according to Grinnell (1909a), was April 19. A. M. Bailey (1927) says the birds are seen "the year round" in southeastern Alaska, but intimates they are less plentiful in winter and become more common with the arrival of spring: "A few were noted during January near Juneau * * * . My notes read 'Wrangell February 27, Kupreanof March 4, Craig the 12th,—few noted.' A few were seen in Hooniah Sound throughout our stay May 7–24, but not daily. By May 31, however, the Juncos were common about Juneau and a female was seen building her nest * * * ."

Theed Pearse (MS.) records juncos of this race singing at Courtenay and Comox, Vancouver Island, Feb. 9, 1928, Feb. 11, 1922, Feb. 24, 1917, and notes on Mar. 30, 1919, that "white outer tail feathers play a prominent part in display."

*Nesting.*—A. M. Bailey (1927) writes: "Saw a female Junco carrying nesting material and watched her for some time. She made several trips, always to one spot which seemed to possess material to her liking. The male did not appear for some time, and then came hopping nonchalantly along. On the appearance of the little female, he promptly pursued her, she protesting vigorously. I noticed, however, that she was very careful not to drop a wisp of the nest lining." The nest, Bailey says, was on the ground, in a thick clump of hemlocks, and tucked back under a carpet of moss, and had four eggs. He tells about another nest completed by a pair, then abandoned, and a second nest built in the moss a few feet away. The nest had five eggs as did another he observed. I have been unable to learn whether sets of five eggs are more common for this race than for others, where the usual number is four.

Bailey mentions one female building her nest with little if any assistance from the male, and a pair that built two nests together. The young in one of the nests he observed "were nearly ready to leave the nest July 4." No information indicates that incubation or fledgling periods differ from those of the other races, nor that *oreganus* rears more than one brood annually.

*Plumages.*—Richard R. Graber (1955) gives the juvenal plumage for this race as follows: "Forehead and crown streaked profusely, brown and dark brown without great contrast. Nape concolor with crown medially, grayer laterally. Back russet, streaked with blackish brown. Rump gray brown, upper tail coverts dark brown, both obscurely streaked with darker brown. Tail largely blackish brown, outer two pairs of rectrices white. Remiges blackish; outer primaries edged with white, secondaries and tertials with rust. Coverts edged with rusty brown, greater coverts tipped with whitish or buffy white (two narrow wing bars). Lores dusky. Auriculars drab gray brown Post-auriculars like nape. Sub-auriculars, chin, and throat heavily streaked, blackish and buffy white. Chest and sides strongly tinged with buffy, other underparts white or buffy white. Chest, sides, and flanks heavily streaked with dark (blackish) brown. Leg feathers brown. Crissum unstreaked."

Of the adult plumage Miller (1941b) notes:

Buff feather tips are less prevalent than in *montanus* and *shufeldti*, yet some extremes occur. * * * The buff tippings of the nape are usually more ruddy in this race. * * * There are no instances of white on the wings or of red on the pileum deeper than the feather tips.

The only aspect of wear that is different from that in other Oregon juncos relates to the back; there the darker red brightens very materially from the Prout's brown of fresh feathers, but never becomes yellowish or whitish along the edges of the feathers as in *shufeldti*, *thurberi*, and *montanus*.

*Hybridization and intergradation.*—Miller (1941b) states that "in south-central Yukon Territory, south of Lake Marsh, *oreganus* characters in the *hyemalis* population become frequent." He also notes that *montanus* and *oreganus* intergrade in the sector of the coastal region from Queen Charlotte Sound to the Portland Canal, British Columbia. Apparently the *oreganus* juncos of the mainland tidewater and coast intergrade with *montanus* juncos of the mountains and valleys of the interior and higher elevations whenever their habitats adjoin.

*Food.*—In his field notes for Oct. 13, 1940, Theed Pearse records: "Juncos are omnivorous; some cooked salmon put out for jays and not attracting them was eaten by the juncos."

*Behavior.*—A. M. Bailey (1927) mentions juncos jumping in the air "like so many flycatchers" to take insects on the wing. A similar observation is recorded for the race *thurberi* in the main species account.

George Willett (1921a) notes that Oregon juncos on the forested coastal islands of southeastern Alaska apparently move after nesting during the latter part of August, up the sides of the mountains and away from sea level, together with the varied thrush (*Ixoreus naevius*) and fox sparrow (*Passerella iliaca*): "the three species being frequently found in close proximity in the woods on the mountain sides from about 1000 feet altitude to timber line. As the weather becomes cooler they work back down the mountains to the shore."

*Field marks.*—The general impression is that of a very intensely colored Oregon junco, with black head, red-brown or ruddy back, and white outer tail feathers. This race cannot be separated with certainty in the field from adjacent races of the Oregon junco that it may associate with in winter or when migrating.

*Fall and winter.*—The race is only partially migratory. Because little snow falls under ordinary circumstances at the lower elevations of its breeding range, juncos can forage successfully all winter. Nevertheless many migrate southward and winter in western Oregon, western Washington, and northern coastal California. While there are sufficient records inland to indicate that some migrate elsewhere, it is rare outside of these limits.

Grinnell and Miller (1944) say of this race in winter in California: "*Habitat*—Open forest understory, woodlands, edges of chaparral, and fence rows. As with all wintering juncos, this race may be found in a wide varity of habitats; but there must always be some tree or bush cover and some patches of open ground. *J. o. oreganus* seems to favor the humid forests, shaded ground and denser brushland more than do related subspecies of juncos; this preference is reflected in the concentration of the winter population in the northern coastal district of the State."

## DISTRIBUTION

*Range.*—Southeastern Alaska and British Columbia to central and coastal California.

*Breeding range.*—The northwestern Oregon junco breeds in coastal districts of southeastern Alaska (Yakutat Bay, Dall Island, Ketchikan) and British Columbia (Queen Charlotte Islands, Fort Simpson, south to Calvert Island).

*Winter range.*—Winters from southeastern Alaska (from Juneau) south through coastal British Columbia (east to Okanagan Lake), western Washington, and western Oregon to central California (Monterey County); sparsely through coastal California to northern Baja California (Santa Eulalia); casually southeast to southern Idaho (Nampa), Nevada (Carson City, Ruby Lake), central Colorado (Denver), southern Arizona (Huachuca Mountains), and western New Mexico (Fort Bayard).

## JUNCO OREGANUS PINOSUS Loomis

## Point Pinos Oregon Junco

### Contributed by JAMES H. PHELPS, JR

### HABITS

The unique central coast of California from San Francisco southward through Santa Cruz and Monterey, with its marked boreal climatic influences, has a local race of the Oregon junco. L. M. Loomis (1893), who described it, comments: "The fact that a Junco should be found breeding at the sea level so far south in California is very significant and in itself is enough to suggest the existence at least of a local race."

The region is characterized by moderate temperatures, frequent fogs, high humidity, and high winds along the ocean shore and exposed headlands. Grinnell and Linsdale (1936) note: "The concentration of rain in the mid-winter months and its almost complete absence in summer are major factors in the composition of the fauna and in the seasonal behavior of the animals." Concerning the fog they add: "At inland localities it contains so little moisture that objects moving through it often remain dry, but at Point Lobos even stationary objects, the trees, bushes, grass and even the ground, are often dripping wet."

Loomis named the race for Point Pinos where he first saw his birds and recognized that they were different. Conditions at Point Pinos are much like those at Point Lobos.   He (1894) writes: "The mean temperature (according to local information) is about 60° F. during each of the summer months.   Heavy fogs, that almost amount to rain, are also frequent during summer."

It is now known of course that Point Pinos juncos are not confined to the coastal forest, the "humid coast belt," but inhabit a great variety of situations, more so than other races of Oregon junco.   They nest in a number of plant associations, not all coniferous.   Grinnell and Miller (1944) say:

Almost any forest or woodland, including plantings of eucalyptus, suffices if it affords shade and ground cover that remains green throughout the summer.   Usually, perhaps always, water may be obtained, either from surface streams or from fog-drenched foliage.   In summer, this race is more tolerant of low zonal conditions than is *thurberi*.   Yet in its typical ground-foraging activity, presence of shade is just as much an essential factor.   Usage of trees for nesting is more prevalent in this race than in others, but the bird is nevertheless predominantly a ground nester.

Summarizing information from both A. H. Miller (1941b) and Grinnell and Miller (1944), the following plant associations meet the requirements of these juncos for nesting: moist redwood (*Sequoia sempervirens*) forests in canyons; dense, though comparatively arid, California live oak (*Quercus agrifolia*) woodland; Monterey pine (*Pinus radiata*), pricklecone pine (*P. muricata*), and Monterey cypress (*Cypressus macrocarpa*) forests; yellow pine (*P. ponderosa*) and Douglas fir (*Pseudotsuga taxifolia*) forests; black oak (*Q. kelloggii*), goldencup oak (*Q. chrysolepis*), and madroño (*Arbutus menziesii*) woodlands; and arid digger pine (*P. sabiniana*) and Coulter pine (*P. coulteri*) "forests."

Point Pinos juncos do not migrate, although as H. B. Kaeding (1899) comments "as soon as the young are fledged the birds wander." There are no records at other seasons more than a few miles from the breeding range.   However in recent years the Point Pinos juncos have extended their range and now breed in city parks and suitable residential areas of San Francisco Bay cities.   Amelia S. Allen (1933) believes that extensive plantings of Monterey pines and other changes in the landscape, all done by man, are responsible.   She (1943) also writes:

It has been interesting to follow the spread of this junco in Berkeley.   Before 1914 I had worked out the earliest dates of arrival for the Oregon Junco as October 17 and the latest date of departure as April 10.   Between 1914 and the date of the finding of the first nest, I had several records of single birds found singing later than April 10 * * *.   On May 15, 1917, on the grounds of the Claremont Country Club, I found the first nest reported in the San Francisco Bay region. By 1918 the local Berkeley birds had spread from their center on the campus to our hillside.   This junco is now one of the common breeding birds of the area.

Another possible extension is reported by A. H. Miller (1945), who writes concerning the collections of the late O. P. Silliman: "Two juncos * * * taken on July 7 and 8, 1937, at San Ardo, 450 feet, Monterey County, seem to indicate a breeding station for the race *pinosus* in the floor of the middle section of the Salinas Valley; one of the birds was molting. This is an unexpected local extension of the breeding range of this race which nests commonly at higher elevations in the mountains on either side of the valley."

*Spring.*—In the mild climate of this part of California the breeding activities of the resident juncos are much advanced over those of the migrants present as winter visitants. The migratory races face spring flights of varying lengths; the resident juncos are near or actually on their breeding territories, and they behave accordingly.

Grinnell and Linsdale (1936) say: "We soon noticed on our winter trips that the resident birds seemed to be paired and the flocks seemed to be made up mainly of winter visitants and transients. The pairs were stationed on the type of ground where the birds later nested and they behaved often as if they were defending the sites against invasion. This situation was detected as early as December [1934] and it was plainly evident by the middle of February [1935]."

In the experiments Albert Wolfson (1942) made on resident and migrant Oregon juncos, mentioned in the main species account (page 1053), the resident juncos he used were *pinosus*. He found that although the different races flock together in winter in the same environment, the residents and migrants show marked differences in their gonadal cycles: "The testes of the residents recrudesce earlier and at a faster rate than those of the migrants." Because of the energy migrants need for their spring flights: "In the migrants there is a heavy deposition of subcutaneous and intraperitoneal fat at the time of migration. The residents show no such deposition of fat."

Grinnell and Linsdale (1936) write: "Definite evidence of the beginning of the nesting season was seen on March 20 [1935], a cold, cloudy day when a pair in copulation was seen in a patch of monkey flower on the floor of the pine woods." They continue: "On March 24 [1935] nearly all of the juncos seen were definitely in pairs and scattered mainly through the pine woods. The birds spent most of the time sitting quietly on perches in the trees. They fed largely in the trees, but about one-third of the time on the ground. Occasionally one or both birds of a pair would indicate excitement by spreading the tail and trilling, but this was followed by another quiet period. There was some singing—often 3 or 4 birds could be heard at once in different directions, but the locations of singing birds were hard to determine."

*Nesting.*—Though they are primarily ground nesters, as are the other races of Oregon junco, the Point Pinos Oregon juncos occasionally build their nests elsewhere. Grinnell and Wythe (1927) say: "Nests may be situated not only on the ground but on branches of cypress trees, and occasionally in appropriate recesses about the eaves of buildings."

H. O. Jenkins (1906) describes a typical nest with four eggs, incubation partial, he found June 26, 1905 at Big Creek, Monterey County; it was placed on the ground in the redwood forest partially hidden by trailing roots, grasses, and blackberry vines. Joseph Dixon (1924) discovered a junco nest on the ground well concealed in a dense mat of ivy on the University of California campus at Berkeley, Mar. 16, 1923.

Milton S. Ray (1911b) writes:

Our first nest [Mar. 27, 1910, San Mateo County] * * * was a strange departure from all previously recorded nest situations being placed 8 feet up in a Monterey cypress where it was well hidden in a thick clump of foliage. The nest, a well built structure consisting almost entirely of pine needles, contained four eggs in which incubation had begun. A second nest of the junco was found 16 feet up in the Monterey cypress in an open situation well out on the limb, and contained fresh eggs. This nest is even a better built structure than the first one found. It is a *very* compact affair of pine needles, roots, grasses and weed stems and well lined with various animal hair.

Ray (1919) quotes Chase Littlejohn's observations for the 1918 season at Redwood City, a suburban town south of San Francisco: "I know of three junco nests being found about Redwood City last summer. These were built about the eaves of occupied dwellings and in one case inside the attic and all of them were of *pinosus.*"

Grinnell and Linsdale (1936) give data on 24 nests they discovered at Point Lobos. Six of the 24 were built in trees, either pine (*Pinus radiata*) or cypress (*Cupressus macrocarpa*). They write: "The first nest was one foot north of the base of one of four small live oak trees. It was at the north margin of an opening in the pines. Both birds of the pair were carrying material to the nest, on March 24 [1935], when it was nearly ready for the lining." This is one of the few reports of both birds of a pair working on a nest. In other races the female usually does the bulk of the nest building. Their first nest with eggs was found Apr. 8, 1935 as was the first nest with small young. The last nest of the season with eggs not yet deposited was found May 20 "7 feet up in pine" and "nearly complete." They remark "young about to leave on June 20."

The dates of nesting for San Francisco and vicinity are about the same. Grinnell and Wythe (1927) say: "Nesting begins by the last of March and continues through May."

The only suggestion that Point Pinos Oregon juncos have more than one brood is the remark by Grinnell and Linsdale (1936) that: "In one instance a nest was built in a tree, apparently by the same pair which had just brought off a brood from a nest on the ground."

*Eggs.*—H. B. Kaeding (1899) writes that the nest and eggs of the Point Pinos Oregon junco apparently do not differ from those of the Sierra or Thurber juncos. The normal clutch of eggs is four, but one of the 24 nests found by Grinnell and Linsdale (1936) at Point Lobos had a set of five. Another had three normal-sized eggs and one not more than half the normal size; at a later date three young were seen in the nest.

*Young.*—Joseph Dixon (1924) writes that the nest he found was completed and the first egg laid on Mar. 23, 1923: "At 6 o'clock on the evening of March 26 the nest contained four eggs which the female had begun to incubate.

"At 9 A.M. on April 9 the nest contained two eggs and two young which had hatched since the previous evening. Only two out of the four eggs hatched. The fledglings left the nest on April 16 when only seven days old. They were not at that time able to fly, but scrambled about readily beneath the tangled ivy and eluded my grasp easily." Dixon's dates indicate about 13 days were needed for incubation. He attributed the early departure of the young to numerous "Argentine ants" in the nest.

*Plumages.*—In his original description Loomis (1893) gives the following characteristics: "Most nearly like * * * *thurberi*, but throat, jugulum, and fore breast slate-gray, varying to dark slate-gray, and upper portions of head and neck slate-gray, varying to blackish slate; bill averaging broader and longer."

*Hybridization and intergradation.*—Grinnell and Miller (1944) say this race: "Intergrades with *J. o. thurberi* in Marin and San Luis Obispo * * * counties." Miller (1941b) notes the Marin woodlands, across the Golden Gate north of San Francisco, are separated from the southern limits of *thurberi* breeding range along the Russian River in Sonoma County by about 20 miles of countryside not suitable for breeding juncos, and: "A similar gap separates the breeding areas north and south of San Francisco Bay. The isolation afforded does not appear great, but in resident populations it means much more than in migratory races."

The intergrades between *pinosus* and *thurberi* show mixing or blending of head, side and back color, and intermediacy in tail pattern and measurements.

*Food.*—The remarks in the main species account quoting the work of F. E. L. Beal (1910) on food habits of juncos in California apply in great part to this race. Beal writes: "It would be better to treat the * * * races separately, but as many of the stomachs were collected before the races were recognized, their exact identity is unknown."

*Behavior.*—Apart from the nesting season when the birds are in pairs, Point Pinos Oregon juncos associate together in small flocks. These are quite possibly family groups. Grinnell and Linsdale (1936) note the juncos on the Point Lobos reserve in small flocks or groups of four or five, six or more, 12 or more, and other such numbers. While they mention a "flock of about 25" and a "scattered flock of 50," most of their references are to small flocks. They cite examples of small flocks or groups feeding at the margin of a roadway or meadow, scattered on moist ground covered with fine litter in shade beneath cypresses, or feeding on ground close to and beneath a pile of brush at the edge of the pine woods. They add: "From these and other records it was apparent that factors prominently important in accounting for the occurrence of juncos [at Point Lobos] were the open nature of the ground, the large proportion of the area in which shade was afforded, and the trees and tall shrubs which provided refuge, roosting places, and singing perches." In the San Francisco Bay region, Grinnell and Wythe (1927) state this form: "Forages and nests in groves of planted evergreen trees and native redwoods; comes familiarly about dwellings." A. H. Miller (pers. comm.) writes me: "*Pinosus* does tend to stay on or very close to its nesting territory, and I have never seen it form very large flocks, but it will mix in with wintering flocks of other races of Oregon juncos here locally and certainly is not as solitary and non-flocking as is *Junco phaeonotus.*"

Concerning the habit of the Point Pinos Oregon juncos of nesting in trees Grinnell and Linsdale (1936) remark: "It was noted at nearly all the nests in trees that the adults showed less concern and less reluctance to go to the nest when a person stood near the site than did most of the ground-nesting pairs." Regarding interspecific behavior, they report an instance of a junco pursuing two pileoated warblers (*Wilsonia pusilla pileolata*) and of a male junco driving a green-backed goldfinch (*Spinus psaltria hesperophilus*) from the bough holding a nest with young.

Reports of juncos catching insects in the air or flycatching have been reported for other races. Grinnell and Linsdale (1936) write: "A junco was seen several times on May 1, catching insects in the air. Again on October 12, in the evening, several were flycatching for large termites."

W. Otto Emerson (1905) had to have a large eucalyptus tree removed that had grown on his place for many years. At dusk he noticed many small birds, among them Point Pinos Oregon juncos, Audubon warblers (*Dendroica auduboni*), and white-crowned sparrows

(*Zonotrichia l. nuttalli*) flying about the barn, near the place the tree had grown before being cut, in great confusion. He writes: "They were coming in from all directions and would fly to where they had been used to roosting, but their lodging house was gone. They came by fours and more, hovering in mid-air, and fluttered about in circles, then alighted on the barn * * *. Many dodged down into the cypress hedge in front of the barn, keeping up short flights to the fallen tree as it lay in the road."

*Voice.*—Calls and notes of *pinosus* are no different from those of others of the species insofar as I can determine.

*Field marks.*—During the breeding season when no other Oregon juncos are present, field identification of the race *pinosus* is no problem. During the winter when other races of Oregon junco and Point Pinos juncos associate together, separating them is most difficult. Mrs. Amelia S. Allen (1933) says the Sierra junco, the race *thurberi*, is "not accurately distinguishable from the resident Point Pinos junco in the field." The numerous citations in the literature for both races in the San Francisco Bay region indicate some of the confusion. While the Point Pinos juncos have ruddier backs than the Sierra race and paler sides and heads, there is so much overlapping that only the most experienced field observers can state with any accuracy whether or not *pinosus* is present in a mixed winter flock.

*Enemies.*—R. F. Johnston (1960) records this race as host to the brown-headed cowbird. On Aug. 14, 1958, on the University of California campus at Berkeley, he watched for one-half hour an adult female Oregon junco "repeatedly feed an almost fully grown, juvenal-plumaged" cowbird.

*Fall and winter.*—Miller (1941b) writes: "There are no records of *pinosus* in the fall or winter for localities more than a few miles from the habitats occupied in the breeding season. Definition of breeding areas thus indicates geographic distribution throughout the year."

He explains the absence of migration by the fact that few places in its range have a severe winter climate or any snowfall. He notes: "In winter, flocks may wander into open country where there is limited cover in the form of isolated clumps of trees. They occur often in orchards in the open valleys. Many are known to stay on the breeding territory in small flocks, possibly family groups."

## DISTRIBUTION

*Range.*—The Point Pinos Oregon junco is resident in the coastal hills and mountains of central California from Golden Gate and Carquinez Straits to southern San Benito and Monterey counties (intergrades with *J. o. thurberi* in San Luis Obispo County).

JUNCO OREGANUS PONTILIS Oberholser

## Hanson Laguna Oregon Junco

### Contributed by JAMES H. PHELPS, JR.

#### HABITS

A man, identified only as an American named Hanson and subsequently murdered, once "tried his hand" at ranching high in the mountains of an obscure corner of Mexico. His name came to be associated, not always with accuracy, with the mountains, the ranch, a shallow lake, and a race of Oregon junco.

Harry C. Oberholser (1919a) named the race *pontilis* from juncos E. W. Nelson and E. A. Goldman collected in the Sierra Juárez (or Hanson Laguna Mountains) in 1905, noting: "It has the very pale pinkish sides of *Junco oreganus townsendi*, but in the color of both head and back is almost exactly intermediate between" *thurberi* and *townsendi*.

Contrary to Dwight's (1918) opinion that *townsendi* was a subspecies of *Junco mearnsi*, at that time considered a separate species, Oberholser proposed: "The study of these specimens and their relationships with the two contiguous forms shows clearly that *Junco oreganus pontilis* directly connects *Junco townsendi* with *Junco oreganus thurberi*, and that, therefore, the former must be a subspecies of the latter."

The race is resident and isolated in the nesting season from other juncos, in a single mountain range in the northern part of the Sierra Juárez-San Pedro Mártir mountain group of northern Lower California, Mexico. According to E. W. Nelson (1922) the Sierra Juárez is a single main ridge about 4,000 feet in elevation at the United States–Mexican border, rising to about 6,000 feet near Hanson Laguna (or Hanson's Lagoon), and decreasing to 4,000 or 5,000 feet at the southern end. The top of the northern part of the Sierra near the type locality of the race at El Rayo (formerly Hanson's Ranch) is no more than three or four miles across. The summit is a long, narrow, rolling plateau, broken by many knolls, ridges of granite, and piled masses of huge, smooth granite boulders, 50 to 300 feet high, between which are small mountain basins or parks and flats. The east face is quite abrupt; the west slope is rolling or undulating.

According to Nelson's (1922) estimate of the area of suitable commercial timber, the available junco habitat along the crest of the Sierra Juárez is no more than 37 miles long by 3 miles wide. A. H. Miller (1941b) says: "Mr. Laurence M. Huey estimates that there is about 20 to 25 miles of scattered Transition Zone forest along this section of the Sierra at elevations between 5000 and 6000 feet.

Granitic outcrops are frequent and, in combination with exposure, are causes of the interdigitation of tracts of Upper Sonoran forest. The junco habitat in summer is the parklike yellow pine forest."

The *pontilis* population is separated in the nesting season from the nearest *thurberi* to the north in San Diego County, Calif., by possibly 40 miles of unsuitable territory; the mountains are not high enough for pine forest from 15 or 20 miles north of the boundary to 15 or 20 miles south. Similarly the decrease in height of the mountains north and south of San Matias pass separates *pontilis* from *townsendi* in San Pedro Mártir Mountain, the gap being 40 miles or perhaps less.

I have found nothing in the literature or by correspondence to indicate any differences between *pontilis* and other Oregon juncos in habits, behavior, nesting, eggs, or other phases of life history.

Joseph Grinnell (1928b) remarks that these juncos are "apparently not very common." Perhaps the explanation comes from E. W. Nelson (1922), who says: "Water is scarce all along the summit of the Sierra Juárez. The Hanson Lagoon (or Laguna Hanson), about half a mile across, is the largest of several small shallow lakelets lying on the highest part of the range northeast of Ensenada. A few very small streams rise at the heads of gulches near the top of the west slope and flow down to the lower border of the foothills * * *. Water is still scarcer on the higher parts of the east slope than on the west * * *."

*Fall and winter.*—Other races of Oregon junco, particularly *thurberi* and to a lesser extent *shufeldti*, winter within the range of *pontilis*. Miller (1941b) says: "The fall-taken specimens all come from these [Sierra Juárez] mountains. One bird was taken at an elevation of 4200 feet at Los Pozos about 30 miles north of Laguna Hanson, October 31. There is no evidence of migration, therefore. There may be some tendency, as in *townsendi*, to descend to lower levels in winter."

### DISTRIBUTION

*Range.*—The Hanson Laguna Oregon junco is resident in the Sierra Juárez (Los Pozos, Laguna Hanson) in northern Baja California.

### JUNCO OREGANUS TOWNSENDI Anthony

## Townsend's Oregon Junco

### Contributed by JAMES H. PHELPS, JR.

### HABITS

The isolated, even to this day, Sierra San Pedro Mártir of Baja California, Mexico, is the home of the southernmost member of the

Oregon junco complex. The San Pedro Mártir is the main and highest mountain mass in the northern section of the peninsula, lying between lat. 30°36' and 31°10' N. Alfred W. Anthony (1889), who described the race, says: "The region embraces a series of small ranges which rise from an elevated *mesa*, having a mean elevation of about 8,000 feet, and an extent of 60 by 20 miles. In these mountains are born the only streams that this part of the peninsula affords, and an abundance of pine timber is found throughout the region." Anthony adds: "*J. townsendi* is probably the most abundant bird to be found in the timbered parts of the San Pedro Mountain, and is, I think, resident * * *."

*Nesting.*—All the information we have about nesting of this race comes from A. W. Anthony (1890, 1893). All the nests he (1890) found were made of soft, dry grasses and lined with finer grass stems and the hair of the mule deer. One nest was "very artfully concealed behind a thick bunch of grass and under the overhanging edge of a large granite boulder." Another "was sunken to the level of the ground, apparently in a cow track, and well hidden in the tall grass on the edge of a running stream." In another year he (1893) states the juncos were building nests upon his arrival in the pines May 5, but he found no eggs until May 10. One "nest was in an old woodpecker's hole in a large pine that had been blown down, with its top resting on a big boulder. The hole which was about six feet from the ground was on the under side of the trunk and the nest about on a level with the opening; it was composed of dry grasses and lined with deer hair. A nest * * * was found on May 26 in a hole in a rotten stub about ten feet from the ground * * *." He mentions a number of nests, under logs, boulders, and other locations, that he left in the hope of collecting full sets, but which he found destroyed when he returned. Apparently the open nature of the forest without much ground vegetation partly explains the numbers of junco nests he found in locations not considered usual for the species elsewhere.

*Eggs.*—Three eggs, without exception, constitute a set according to A. W. Anthony (1890). The three sets he reports upon in detail vary widely in their markings. A set he collected May 1, 1889, has a faint bluish-white ground color, profusely and variously spotted with lilac and raw umber; the eggs measure 20 by 15; 19 by 15; and 18 by 15, in millimeters. In another set taken May 5, 1889, the eggs "are uniformly bluish-white with a few of the faintest minute specks of burnt umber, on the large end, which are not at first noticeable. * * * Measurements 20×15; 19×15; 20×15 mm." In the third set taken May 6, 1889, two eggs "are marked with small spots of pale fawn color, with a few small spots and lines of burnt umber collected about the large end." The third egg shows a faint greenish wash and is also the most heavily marked of the set, being heavily blotched on the larger end with pale lilac, the lilac extending in small flecks over the entire shell. Measurements in millimeters are 19 by 15, 19 by 15 and 19 by 14.

*Plumages.*—Anthony (1889) describes the plumage of his type male as: "Head, neck and breast all around, clear, slatey, gray, much darker than *J. annectens*, but paler than *J. hyemalis oregonus*. Lores and crown, blackish. Dorsal and interscapular region, ashy brown, in some specimens scarcely differing from the head and neck. Rump and upper tail coverts ashy, first two lateral rectrices pure white, the rest blackish with ashy edges. Wings, blackish, primaries and secondaries with grey edges. Sides, pink. Belly and under tail coverts, white. Mandibles and feet, flesh color. Iris, hazle."

Of a female cotype he writes: "Head, neck and chest all around, uniform dark gray, lighter than male. Lores, blackish. Dorsal patch, very faintly defined. Rump, clear ashy. Pink of sides, paler and less extensive than male. Lower parts white. Outer three rectrices white, third edged with dusky. Iris, hazle."

*Field marks.*—Townsend's Oregon junco is a gray-headed junco with narrow "pink" sides resident in the San Pedro Mártir of Lower California. It shows some resemblance to the pink-sided junco, the race *mearnsi* of the Rocky Mountains, but the color area in the sides of *towsendi* is narrower. There are no records of *mearnsi* taken within the range of *townsendi*, although other Oregon junco races, *thurberi* and to some extent *shufeldti*, winter that far south and mixed flocks may be expected.

*Fall and winter.*—Joseph Grinnell (1928b) says: "Common resident on the Sierra San Pedro Mártir. * * * A slight scattering in the fall carries a few individuals to somewhat lower levels close by." Weather conditions must play a part in flights to lower levels when such occur. E. W. Nelson (1922) writes: "The summits of these mountains are never covered with snow during the entire winter but usually only for periods of from two to four weeks. In midwinter snow falls far below the lower border of the pine timber. Anthony writes that it falls down to about 2,500 feet above sea level on the west base of the mountains and it sometimes reaches as far as Valladares."

## DISTRIBUTION

*Range.*—Townsend's Oregon junco is resident in the Sierra San Pedro Mártir (lat. 31°10′N. to 30°36′N.) in northern Baja California. In winter, some movement to lower altitudes, sporadically to San Agustín, latitude 30° N.

JUNCO INSULARIS Ridgway

# Guadalupe Junco

## Contributed by THOMAS RAYMOND HOWELL

### HABITS

This junco is a permanent resident on Guadalupe Island, Baja California, Mexico. The island lies about 135 miles due west of the Baja California coast and about 250 miles south southwest of San Diego, Calif., at lat. 29°10′N. and long. 118°18′W. It is a true oceanic island, volcanic in origin, that has never been connected with the mainland. Its dimensions are approximately as follows: length, 22 miles; width, 4 to 7 miles, broadest at north central portion; maximum elevation, at north central portion, 4,500 feet. The junco is one of a number of endemic land birds found presently or formerly on Guadalupe Island, and like most of the others its ancestors probably reached the island from the mainland to the northeast. A. H. Miller (1941b) discusses the possible origin and relationships of *insularis* in considerable detail in his famous monograph of the genus *Junco*. He concludes that the affinities of *insularis* are with the *Junco oreganus* group. Although some authors consider the Guadalupe junco to be a subspecies of *oreganus*, Miller retains specific status for *insularis* and suggests that this form was derived from vagrants of a migratory junco population inhabiting the California coast in Pleistocene or pre-Pleistocene times.

The Guadalupe junco is distinguished principally by its relatively long bill and short wing and tail, the reduced size of the sternum (F. A. Lucas, 1891), and a virtual absence of sexual dimorphism in color. Both sexes of *insularis* resemble somewhat the females of *Junco oreganus pinosus*. The streaked juvenal plumage of *insularis* also resembles that of *oreganus* juveniles.

The flora and fauna of Guadalupe Island have a sad history of destruction by introduced house mice, house cats, goats, and overzealous collectors. Successive stages of change in the avifauna may be traced through the papers of R. Ridgway (1876), W. E. Bryant (1887), J. E. Thayer and O. Bangs (1908), and T. R. Howell and T. J. Cade (1954). The first biologist to visit Guadalupe Island was the botanist Edward Palmer, and he collected specimens of birds in the spring of 1875 that were subsequently described as new by Ridgway (1876). Palmer's notes on the junco, as quoted by Ridgway, are as follows:

These are the most abundant birds of the island, and are so tame that they may be killed with a stick or captured in a butterfly-net. While I was looking for insects under stones and logs, these birds would sometimes join in the search, and hop almost into my hands. They gathered chiefly ants and their eggs. At times, they even enter the houses, picking up anything edible they can find. Numbers boarded the schooner as we neared the island, and made themselves perfectly at home, roaming over every part of the vessel in search of food. * * * A nest with eggs was found April 12 on * * * the highest point of the island * * *. It was placed in a small crevice in the face of a rock.

Before the introduction of terrestrial mammals the island had well developed flora including many endemic forms (S. Watson, 1875), and the junco undoubtedly became established and differentiated under conditions that were originally very favorable. Within a few years after Palmer's visit, however, the introduced goats had destroyed most of the native flora; by 1906, barren conditions similar to those of the present day had already been reached (Thayer and Bangs, 1908). Nevertheless, despite the extensive destruction of habitat and the depredations of house cats, the Guadalupe junco is still plentiful and very tame. It is found on the northern half of the island from the summit down to the shores. The birds inhabit the remaining groves of pine (*Pinus radiata*), oak (*Quercus tomentella*), and cypress (*Cupressus guadalupensis*) at the higher elevations, and also the now numerous stands of wild tobacco (*Nicotiana glauca*) in the canyons and along parts of the shore. This latter plant, which the goats do not eat, became established some time after 1932 and has spread rapidly. It now provides food and cover for the resident small birds and for the frequent stragglers that reach the island at various times of year. Virtually all other shrubs, undergrowth, and seedlings have long since disappeared or are eaten as soon as they are large enough to provide a mouthful for the innumerable goats.

The extensive ecological changes that have taken place on Guadalupe Island in the past 90 years have probably resulted in some changes in the habits of the junco, and it is perhaps less tame now than it was in the 19th century. Palmer's account has already been quoted, and H. A. Gaylord (1897) mentions an attempt by a junco to alight on the end of a gun that was pointed at it by a collector. Howell and Cade (1954) found that in June 1953 the juncos showed no alarm unless approached within about 6 feet, but the birds moved away at closer range and could not have been caught in a butterfly net or struck by a stick. Apart from this relative tameness, their habits appear to be much like those of other juncos. The birds stay on or near the ground most of the time, but they may be found in the lower parts of the trees or, less abundantly, up in the tops.

W. E. Bryant (1887) is the only ornithologist who has stayed on Guadalupe Island during the early part of the breeding season of the resident passerine birds. He arrived on Dec. 16, 1885, and remained for 3½ months. The biota of the island had already suffered from the activities of man and his introductions, but no birds were yet extinct and Bryant's notes provide the best account of the avifauna as it once existed.

Bryant found the juncos inhabiting primarily the pine and cypress groves, remaining for the most part on the ground among fallen trees, or in the lower branches. He reported that the juncos were paired soon after the beginning of the year and were setting by Jan. 26, 1886, despite almost continuous cold fogs and winds. No courtship behavior has been described.

Bryant collected a male Jan. 2, 1886, with "testes large"; males taken Jan. 26 and Feb. 4, 1886 had "testes very large." Of two adult males and one adult female that we collected buring the second week of June 1953, one male had enlarged testes (6 by 6 millimeters) and the others did not have enlarged gonads. These data and the records of nests and young cited below indicate that *insularis* has a long breeding season, beginning in January and ending in June.

*Nesting.*—Palmer (*in* Ridgway, 1876) reports a nest in a rock crevice, and Bryant (1887) states that the ground beneath a fallen pine was most often used as a nesting place. He describes one nest as being "in a depression, flush with the surface of the ground, and so carefully hidden beneath a covering of brush that it was found with difficulty * * *." Another nest Bryant described was 6 feet above ground in a narrow cleft between two conjoined pine trees. It was constructed of "a few pieces of bark-moss, light-colored dry grass blades, and a tail feather of a petrel, all surrounding a quantity of grass blades, lined within with goat hair. It measures externally about 120 mm. in diameter by 80 mm. in height, with a receptacle 60 mm. in diameter and only 28 mm. in depth."

Brown and Marsden (*in* Thayer and Bangs, 1908) describe a nest found in May or June of 1906 "placed on the lower branch of a pine * * * bulky and made mostly of dried grass stems."

*Eggs.*—W. E. Bryant (1887) describes a clutch of three fresh eggs taken on Mar. 10, 1886, as follows: "In color the eggs are a pale greenish white, marked with fine dots of reddish brown clustered around the larger end. They measure 19.5 x 15; 20 x 15.5; 20 x 16 millimeters."

Bryant believed that these eggs were a second clutch as he noted young birds already present in other nests at that date. H. B. Kaeding (1905) found both fresh eggs and fledged young on Mar. 22, 1903. Palmer (*in* Ridgway, 1887a) reports a nest with eggs on Apr. 12, 1875. Bryant, and Brown and Marsden mention nests containing four young, and it seems likely that three or four eggs is the usual clutch.

According to W. G. F. Harris (MS.) the eggs of the Guadalupe junco are very pale greenish white, speckled and spotted with reddish browns such as "sayal brown" and "chestnut." The two sets of eggs in the National Museum were collected on Guadalupe Island, Baja California April 5 and 12 respectively. The measurements of these six eggs average 20.4 by 14.9 millimeters.

*Young.*—Bryant (1887) noted birds a few days old on Mar. 10, 1886, and he collected fully fledged juveniles on March 16. Kaeding (1905) mentions fully fledged young on Mar. 22, 1903. Brown and Marsden (*in* Thayer and Bangs, 1908) found full grown juveniles on May 1, 1906, but they also found young still in a nest in May or early June of 1906. I found many full grown juveniles in streaked plumage in the second week of June 1953. I estimate that 10 percent of the juncos in the *Nicotiana* thickets were juveniles but that in the cypress grove the proportion was as high as 40 to 50 percent of the total.

*Plumages.*—The Guadalupe junco appears to have the same sequence of plumages as do other juncos. The early nestling stages have not been described, but the juvenal plumage closely resembles that of *J. oreganus*—streaked with dark brown on the entire head, breast, back, and flanks, with the wings, tail, and abdomen essentially like those of an adult. This juvenal plumage is presumably lost in the late summer or fall in the first prebasic (postjuvenal) molt, and the basic plumage thus acquired has the same aspect as that worn by adults. There is a prebasic (annual) molt by adults following the nesting season, but no change in the aspect of the plumage. Two out of three adult birds we collected in June 1953 were undergoing this molt, and many other molting adults were seen at that time. Considering the early beginning of nesting in the Guadalupe junco, it is likely that adult birds have completed their molt by midsummer. As mentioned previously, there is no evident difference in coloration between the sexes.

*Food.*—The Guadalupe junco subsists on both insects and seeds. Palmer (*in* Ridgway, 1876) mentioned that the birds gathered ants and their eggs as he turned over logs. In June 1953 we found most insects rather scarce and ants particularly rare; no other observers have mentioned the latter in the junco's diet. We noted that juncos foraged in loose soil in the cypress grove and that they probed into crevices in logs for moths and possibly other insects. The juncos also fed on the calyces and ovaries of the *Nicotiana* flowers, which were abundant in June 1953. No doubt many other kinds of plant and insect food were utilized when the island was in its primordial condition. Bryant (1887) states that "their food was principally of seeds, a partiality being shown for the green seeds of the 'wild lettuce.'" Whatever plant this may have been, it probably no longer exists on the island.

*Voice.*—The call notes of the Guadalupe junco are similar to those of *Junco oreganus.* Bryant (1887) states that he heard the song only twice, delivered from the top of tall cypress trees, and that it resembled the trill of the chipping sparrow. I did not hear any song approximating a trill, and describe the songs I heard as "wheep-whit-whit-whit-wheep." Bryant (1887) also mentions that the juncos gave a sharp chipping note when alarmed. No other accounts of the vocalizations of *insularis* have been published.

*Field marks.*—As *insularis* is strictly resident on Guadalupe Island, and as no other juncos are to be found there other than accidentally, there is no problem in field recognition. The Guadalupe junco has a gray hood, black lores, a dark brown iris, brownish (not rufous) back and flanks, no wing bars, and a white-edged tail. The long bill is quite noticeable in the field and would probably serve to distinguish *insularis* from any other forms in the same genus.

## DISTRIBUTION

*Range.*—The Guadalupe junco is resident on Guadalupe Island, Baja California.

*Egg dates.*—Baja California: 3 records, March 10 to April 12.

## JUNCO CANICEPS (Woodhouse)
## Gray-headed Junco*

### PLATE 60
### Contributed by DONALD M. THATCHER

## HABITS

One of the most frequently observed and relatively least known avian species of the coniferous forests of the southern Rocky Mountains and the Great Basin is the gray-headed junco. Two races are recognized: the northern *Junco caniceps caniceps* and the southern *Junco caniceps dorsalis.*

According to present taxonomy the genus *Junco* includes 10 species, 4 of which are subdivided, making a total of 21 recognized forms. The over-all range of these 21 forms resembles a chain, double and interlocking in the West, extending from Panama and southern Baja California north to Alaska and northern Canada, thence east to Labrador and Newfoundland, and from there south to Georgia, wherever suitable habitat occurs. From southern Arizona and northern Baja California northward and eastward, junco habitat is essentially continuous or its "islands" not too widely separated, so the chain

---

*The following subspecies are discussed in this section: *Junco caniceps caniceps* (Woodhouse) and *J. c. dorsalis* Henry.

is practically unbroken—in a sense a "cline." Each form occupies its own separate and distinct range, but each mixes freely and hybridizes with its neighbors within a narrow belt, much as though all the dark-eyed, northern members of the genus *Junco* were one species, as some taxonomists consider them. The southern forms, whose chief difference from the northern is their yellow eye color, also form somewhat of a cline, but without mixing, except within *Junco phaeonotus*, as their "island" ranges are more widely separated and no migration encourages mixing. Presumably because all juncos are ecological equivalents and occupy the same niche in essentially similar habitat, there is no sympatry of two or more species such as those in *Dendroica, Sitta, Parus,* and several other avian genera. The gray-headed junco is especially interesting as its two races and their intergrades appear to form a three-stage transitional link near the center of the "chain" between the yellow-eyed juncos southward and the dark-eyed ones northward, combining some of the characteristics of each group.

The two subspecies of the gray-headed junco have had an interesting and confusing taxonomic history, probably equaled by few other birds. S. W. Woodhouse (1853) described the northern form as a full species, *Struthus caniceps,* the "gray-headed snow finch." Five years later T. C. Henry (1858) described the southern subspecies also as a full species, *Junco dorsalis,* the "red-backed snowbird."

The two subspecies have since been considered together as: a single race of the Mexican junco, *J. cinereus* "variety" *caniceps;* two separate races of *J. cinereus* (later *J. phaeonotus*); and as races of the original *Junco* species, *hyemalis. Junco caniceps* has now for many years generally been considered a separate species, but one proposal made it a race of the Oregon junco, as *J. oreganus caniceps,* while *dorsalis* was left as *J. phaeonotus dorsalis.* Jonathan Dwight (1918) considered *dorsalis* a mere hybrid of two species, *J. caniceps* and *J. phaeonotus.* The fourth edition of the A.O.U. Check-List (1931) listed the two forms as *Junco caniceps* and *Junco phaeonotus dorsalis.* The present status, as two races of *J. caniceps,* was proposed by A. H. Miller (1932, 1934) and accepted by the fifth edition of the A.O.U. Check-List (1957), although even Miller (1941b) recognizes *dorsalis* as "a fully established form which gives evidence in its peculiar sublimation of characters of origin by the hybridization of *J. c. caniceps* and *J. p. palliatus,*" practically echoing Dwight's opinion. This turbulent history has resulted mostly from the fact that such field characteristics as eye color, voice, color of eggs, and manner of locomotion were lost in the skins upon which classification was based. Its taxonomic history emphasizes the position of *Junco caniceps* as the connecting link between the southern and the northern juncos, exhibiting the general plumage of the southern and the field characters, lost in study skins, of the northern groups.

The gray-headed junco is the only junco known to breed in its pure form in Colorado, Utah, and Nevada, with the minor exception of a race of the Oregon junco, *J. o. thurberi*, in extreme western Nevada. Pure, unmixed *Junco caniceps* in the northern and western parts of its range confines itself, even where junco habitat extends far beyond, within the limits of those three states. Practically all breeding records from near those state lines and adjoining parts of California, Idaho and Wyoming are of birds in populations mixed and interbreeding with *J. oreganus*, either *thurberi* west or *mearnsi* north. Junco habitat in southeastern Arizona and extreme southwestern New Mexico is occupied by the similarly plumaged, but yellow-eyed, northern subspecies of the Mexican junco (*J. phaeonotus palliatus*). Here there is no intermixing of the gray-headed and its neighbor, the breeding ranges of the two species being separated by hot desert, although one point of separation is no wider than 37 miles.

*Habitat.*—Miller (1941b) says of the habitat of *J. c. caniceps:*

The spotted distribution of this junco must be emphasized. It inhabits for the most part a series of mountaintop islands above 7000 feet in the arid Rocky Mountain and Great Basin ranges. Associations in which it breeds include coniferous forest types dominated either by spruce (*Picea*), *Pseudotsuga*, *Pinus contorta*, *Pinus ponderosa*, *Pinus flexilis*, or fir (*Abies*). It also breeds in pure stands of aspen (*Populus tremuloides*) and of mountain mahogany (*Cercocarpus ledifolius*). Compared with *Junco oreganus*, it shows high tolerance for arid forest and ground cover. It may occupy aspen groves where there is no surface water within two to five miles of the nest site. Unshaded forest floor with the ground poor in humus and nearly lacking in green plant cover is unsuitable for breeding.

While this subspecies has a high tolerance of arid conditions, its tolerance of moisture also is high, as is indicated by three nests R. B. Rockwell (1910) found June 16, 1910 at Columbine Lake, a 40-acre Canadian Life Zone lake in northern Colorado at 8,630 feet elevation surrounded by "a dense growth of pine and spruce extending in places to the water's edge." Of *J. c. caniceps* breeding in the Uinta Basin in northeastern Utah, A. C. Twomey (1942) reports: "The birds nested in all the mountains of the Basin from altitudes of 7,500 feet to timberline at 10,000 feet. Their range included the Douglas fir, yellow pine, blue spruce, aspen, lodgepole pine and Engelmann spruce-alpine fir forests."

In southwestern Utah, according to W. H. Behle (1943), the gray-headed junco occupies approximately the upper half of the Transition Zone ponderosa pine belt, which occurs between 6,200 and 7,600 feet, and the lower two-thirds of the Canadian Zone blue spruce, white fir, and aspen at 8,000 to 9,500 feet. Behle says:

PLATE 60

A. D. Cruickshank

GRAY-HEADED JUNCO AND YOUNG

Uinta Mountains, Utah

"The gray-headed junco is the summer resident of the juncos of the region. It occurs in the mountains from 7,000 to 9,000 feet. At lower elevations within the limits mentioned they are found most often in side draws arising from main canyons; at higher elevations they frequented the dense cover bordering meadows and occasionally ventured out along the edges of the meadows." Its failure to breed in southern Utah above 9,000 feet and into the spruce–fir of the Hudsonian Zone to timberline, as it does elsewhere, has not been explained. H. W. Henshaw (1886) found *caniceps* breeding somewhat lower in New Mexico "everywhere throughout the timber belt above an altitude of 6,000 feet."

Owen A. Knorr tells me of an exceptional nesting of *caniceps* on the University of Colorado campus at Boulder, Colo., in May and June 1955, at the relatively low elevation of 5,400 feet. The nest was on northward-sloping ground in low-growing myrtle (*Vinca*), near the shaded edge of a ½-acre pond. Tree cover was large American elm, western cottonwood, blue spruce, and a few small *Juniperus*. Here, on the plains a mile east of the Rocky Mountain foothills, several hundred feet lower than the usual Transition Zone habitat of the species, and only a few yards from a busy road, the birds found suitable conditions and fledged a brood.

Another low nesting, but in normal habitat, is reported by Louise Hering (1954) just within the lower limit of the ponderosa pine forest at approximately 5,900 feet ½ mile south of Boulder. Junius Henderson (1912) mentions a breeding, probably at the same place: "Bragg's summer record of the Gray-headed Junco at Boulder, altitude 5,700 feet, July 4, 1904, should be added to the list, as it indicates a probable breeding record much below the usual elevation."

For detailed breeding-bird population studies that show the habitat preferences of the gray-headed junco in the forest associations in the Colorado mountains see Hering (1948, 1954, 1956, 1958, 1961, 1962, 1963), Lawhead (1949), Snyder (1950), Cassel (1952), Thatcher (1954, 1955a, 1955b, 1956), and Beidleman (1960). These studies, covering all major forest types from 5,500 to 11,200 feet in altitude, show in essence that gray-headed junco populations may be found in varying numbers in forested areas of almost any tree species which are well but not densely stocked, have numerous openings to provide edges, and are not too arid.

Of the habitat of *J. c. dorsalis*, Miller (1941b) says:

There is a large area in the Mogollon Mountains of Arizona and New Mexico over which the distribution is nearly continuous. In addition to this, numerous isolated mountain ranges are occupied, much as in the breeding range of *J. c. caniceps*. Plant associations in which *dorsalis* breeds consist of coniferous forests wherein the following types predominate: *Pinus ponderosa*, *Abies*, and, less commonly, *Pseudotsuga*. Birds also breed in pure groves of aspens and in coniferous forests with some oaks intermixed. Compared with the habitats of *J. c. caniceps*, those in which I have found *dorsalis* are, if anything, less arid, more luxuriant forests, although occasionally birds will breed in the dry lower portions of the yellow pine belt. Ground cover is rarely as poor in grass, low bushes, and humus as in many parts of the range of *J. c. caniceps* in Utah and Nevada. However, the presence of good stands of yellow pine in the Transition zone provide [sic] junco habitat at lower zonal levels than in Utah and Colorado.

E. A. Mearns (1890a) found in east central Arizona that "Typical *dorsalis* breeds very plentifully through the northern Mogollon and San Francisco Mountains, but does not appear until one has ascended a considerable distance into the pine belt. It is the most characteristic bird of this higher region * * *."

The observations of these and several other writers indicate that the breeding range of *dorsalis* extends lower than that of *caniceps*. The ponderosa pine forest of the two more southern states, New Mexico and Arizona, is less arid and more luxuriant than most of that of Colorado, Utah, and Nevada, suggesting that the lower edges of the more northern pine forest may be too arid for suitable junco habitat. At the other altitudinal extreme, *dorsalis* seems generally not to breed as high as *caniceps*. W. W. Cooke (*in* Bailey, 1928) states its breeding range as "Transition and Canadian Zones of high mountains in Arizona and north central to southern New Mexico," but probably not "much if any above 9000 feet," while the breeding range of *caniceps* is given as "Hudsonian and Canadian Zones," up even to 12,400 feet at one locality.

*Spring.*—As spring approaches and the northern gray-headed junco (*caniceps*) starts northward and upward toward its summer home, the proportion of this species in the mixed flocks of juncos in their winter haunts thins noticeably. At Paonia, in central western Colorado, in the Upper Sonoran piñon-juniper and scrub oak country, Homer Griffin wrote me: "Gray-headed, pink-sided [*J. oreganus mearnsi*], and Oregon [*J. o. montanus*] juncos were present all winter; gray-headed juncos made up the majority of the population during March and pink-sided juncos during April." On the plains in the vicinity of Denver, Colo., the gray-headed has almost entirely left for the mountains by May 1, while the more northern Oregon and slate-colored (*J. hyemalis*) juncos are still present in numbers.

The gray-headed junco becomes plentiful in the vicinity of its breeding territories long before conditions are suitable for nesting. F. C. Lincoln (1920) took a specimen in Colorado at a garbage pit at 10,400 feet, Mar. 31, 1915, when "snow was from 3 to 15 feet deep and this bird's presence is more or less * * * a mystery to me." Up to timberline in the Colorado mountains the males sing freely in the tops of the tallest pines or spruces while the ground is still covered by two to three feet of snow. But during severe late snowstorms, which may occur as late as the last week in May, large numbers often reappear in the lower foothills or at the edge of the plains, wherever brush patches and bare ground offer food. At such times they seldom sing. The latest *caniceps* record on the Colorado plains is a female Niedrach and Rockwell (1939) report "taken in Denver, June 17, 1918." Joe T. Marshall (MS.) observed seven or eight *caniceps* in the Santa Catalina Mountains of southern Arizona Apr. 5, 1951, in a "very tame" flock with six or seven Mexican juncos, a *J. o. mearnsi*, and a *J. o. thurberi*. A month later, May 4, he saw a *caniceps* with Mexican juncos at a picnic table in the same locality. This is approximately 250 miles south of the breeding range of *caniceps*. In southeastern Arizona Seymour Levy (*in* Phillips, Marshall, and Monson, 1964) saw *caniceps* "to May 24 (1957 in Santa Rita Mountains * * *)" and there are exceptional dates of June 5 at Fort Huachuca and June 6 in Guadalupe Canyon, all some 250 to 300 miles south of the breeding range of *caniceps*.

The southern race, *dorsalis*, shows less seasonal movement than *caniceps*, and often winters with flocks of *caniceps* and Oregons in the pines and adjacent brushy places at or near its summer home. In March *dorsalis* individuals leave the mixed flocks and take up their summer territories while the higher country is still snow-covered. Edouard Jacot (MS.) writes that *caniceps* in the White Mountains of Arizona is "not as solitary as Red-backed [*dorsalis*], which is often seen alone in the timber." At Granville, Ariz., at the lower edge of the Transition Zone, he recorded the last *dorsalis* Apr. 19, 1935, in the "deciduous white oaks" (*Q. gambelli*), where wintering or migrating *caniceps* remained as late as May 7. On Feb. 13, 1937 Lyndon Hargrave (MS.) wrote of *dorsalis* at Flagstaff, Ariz., well within the pines of the Transition Zone: "Probably all my banded winter birds left last night. Abundant 12th." Allan R. Phillips recorded the "close of migration" there the previous year on April 23, after which date only one pair remained of the six or eight birds previously recorded daily in the vicinity.

*Territory.*—While the *caniceps* probably all leave their breeding territories for the winter, apparently many *dorsalis* that breed in the ponderosa pine forest remain throughout the year in the vicinity of the breeding grounds. Hargrave (1936) reported banding an adult male on its breeding territory in Flagstaff Jan. 30, 1935, which he retrapped several times from May 8 to September 3, and again November 8 and the following February 14 (MS.). Apparently it remained in the general vicinity the entire year. Its mate, however, was observed or trapped only from March 24 to September 3, and probably wintered elsewhere.

Some, probably most, *dorsalis* breed near the territory in which they were raised. Hargrave (MS.) reports, also at Flagstaff, a female he banded as a juvenile, Aug. 13, 1936, and which he believed nested the next year within 50 yards of the point of banding. The bird nested there 2, 3, and 4 years after banding, and was last seen there in May of the 5th year, 1941.

Recorded observations of territorial conflict between gray-headed juncos are few. During population studies by the writer (Thatcher 1955a, 1955b, 1956) and others in three areas in the eastern foothills of the Colorado Rockies, approximately 84 supposed territorial pairs were observed during 5 breeding seasons, in or immediately outside the study areas. Only one brief fight between two males of this species was recorded, June 18, 1953. On May 12, 1952, two gray-heads, apparently a pair in their nesting territory in open ponderosa pine, attacked and drove off a migrating slate-colored junco. In the same locality on Mar. 16, 1960 I attracted two gray-headed juncos and a single *J. o. mearnsi* with "tic" notes from a pewter-and-wood "bird call." The gray-heads ignored the migrant *mearnsi* but presumably regarded the bird call as a rival.

Louise Hering (1948) found five pairs of *caniceps* believed to be nesting on a 75-acre study plot in the Black Forest of Colorado. She reports: "Three pairs of juncos were far separated on the tract, while two breeding pairs remained near each other throughout the season. The males of the latter two pairs sang rather often but both families fed on the forest floor without any apparent territorial conflict." A. C. Twomey (1942) in Utah took a female hybrid *caniceps-mearnsi* "from a nest * * * within forty feet of a nesting pair of *caniceps.*"

*Courtship.*—The mating behavior of the gray-headed junco probably differs little, if at all, from that of the better known Oregon and slate-colored juncos. Twomey (1942) wrote of our species in Utah during the nesting season: "The birds at that time could be heard singing from all corners of the forest. The male always chose the top of a tall pine as a singing post. Considerable activity, consisting chiefly of pursuit and nest-building, was observed here."

Miller (1941b), in discussing hybridization between *J. c. caniceps* and *J. o. mearnsi* in northeastern Utah, describes interesting mating behavior of some of the hybrids:

A pair of birds about my camp west of Garden City was feeding young on July 22 [1931]. The male was collected at 5 a.m.; it was pure *mearnsi* on back and sides, but with head intermediate. The female, which could be seen to have normal *mearnsi* color on the sides and back, was left with the young. At 10 a.m. the small young were in the same group of bushes with the female, and a new male was on hand, singing, following her with tail fanned, and twittering with characteristic mating behavior; she did not drive him away. This bird was taken and found to have a mixed yellow back, *mearnsi* sides and intermediate head.   Female X, as she now became known, had another male attached to her party shortly after 11 a.m. This male was *mearnsi* in all characteristics except for intermediate tone of head. A fourth male came to female X at noon and proved to have pure *mearnsi* back, pure *caniceps* sides, and intermediate head.   I am doubtful that these males were all unattached previous to their interest in female X.   Males of various sparrows are known to be polygamous on occasion.   There was no doubt of the attraction of the female for all of them, however.   Not knowing the history of the case, an observer would have considered each to have been her normal mate.   No intolerance was evidenced by the female.   Some of the males gathered food for the young.   This indicates disregard on the part of the junco for differences in colors of sides and backs.

*Nesting.*—The gray-headed junco is with rare exceptions a ground nester and is ordinarily the only such passerine within its usual habitat, except the larger and much less plentiful Townsend's solitaire (*Myadestes townsendi*), whose nest is not likely to be confused with the junco's.   At timberline the junco's nest may be placed under a rock like that of the water pipit (*Anthus spinoletta*) and the two may be confused readily.   Ground nests of the Wilson's warbler (*Wilsonia pusilla*) and the Lincoln's sparrow (*Melospiza lincolnii*) in wet places, of the white-crowned sparrow (*Zonotrichia leucophrys*) at timberline and of the western flycatcher (*Empidonax difficilis*) in roadside or stream banks might be confused with the junco's.

Nesting activity commences as soon as most of the winter's snow disappears, and often before the last heavy spring snowfalls.   My earliest observation of *caniceps* nesting activity in north central Colorado was Apr. 28, 1954, when I (Thatcher 1954) saw one of a pair carrying nest material near the upper limit of the ponderosa pine, at 7,800 feet during a "warm, dry spring when breeding activity was two to three weeks earlier than usual."   The earliest nest in the same area had five eggs when I found it May 29, 1952, and young 3 days later.   Assuming 5 days for laying and 12 for incubation, the nest was probably completed by May 15.

The latest definite nesting activity date is contributed by Louise Hering (MS.) of two young that seemed "to be just out of nest" at Grand Lake, Colo., at approximately 8,500 feet, Sept. 4, 1949.   As parental feeding of the young probably continues 18 to 20 days more, the nesting period of *caniceps* in Colorado presumably extends through a period of at least 21 weeks: April 28 to September 22.

The May 29 *caniceps* nest mentioned above was at the edge of a large opening in the pines on a slight southwesterly slope, hidden in a shallow hollow beneath the downhill side of a clump of mountain muhley (*Muhlenbergia montana*), the major grass of the south-slope pine forest.   A heavy, 3-inch snowfall 6 days before the nest was discovered had no adverse effect on it.   Three other nests found nearby during 5 years of population studies were similarly located in smooth, rounded hollows under clumps of mountain muhley, with no other immediate protection.

The usual Colorado nest of the gray-headed junco is well described by Aiken and Warren (1914): "The nest is built on the ground, sometimes in a cavity in a roadside bank or a stream bank. One found by Rockwell and Warren in Jefferson County was sunken in the ground so that the rim was flush with the surface. The nest proper was made of grass, coarse outside, lined with finer, with a few horsehairs intermingled. This was under a Douglas's fir tree, and nearly covered by a spreading branch which grew out almost at the foot of the tree and actually rested on the ground over the nest. This nest contained four fresh eggs * * *. Taken May 30, 1912."

In northeastern Utah, Twomey (1942) found:

The first nests * * * at Green Lake, Uinta Mountains, on June 10 [1937]. * * * From June 17 to 20, at Indian Canyon, eighteen nests with fresh eggs were found in the mixed blue spruce, Douglas fir, yellow pine and aspen forest. The nests, averaging four or five eggs, were always on the ground, generally under a protecting shrub or a log. These were the most common nesting birds of this region.

At Paradise Park, between July 7 and 10, numerous nests were located, all containing eggs advanced in incubation. Birds in juvenal plumage were seen in large numbers at Bald Mountain in the Engelmann spruce-alpine fir forest from July 16 to 20. These juncos were nesting in larger numbers here than at any other place visited in the [Uinta] Basin.

Florence Merriam Bailey (1904) found several *caniceps* nests at 11,000 feet in north central New Mexico, near the headwaters of the Upper Pecos River, "nests being found everywhere in the open. * * * All of the nests were on the ground, completely hidden by tufts of grass or bunches of weeds, being discovered only by flushing the brooding bird."

Denis Gale (MS.) describes nests he found in the Gold Hill–Ward district of the Eastern Slope of the Colorado Rockies, at 8,000 to 10,000 feet: "Nests on the ground. Fond of selecting sheltered places, side of hill or bank, concealed with care and cunning, set well into the ground, with sometimes only the smallest aperture for the entrance and exit of the bird; seldom selecting a bare place, but preferring some shrub, plant, tree or stump or roots of such, under or close to which it excavates sufficiently for its purpose. Bird somewhat difficult to flush. Nest of coarse grasses outside, lined with fine grasses, hair and feathers sometimes. Eggs four and five * * *. One nest measured 4½ by 3½ inches outside—2½ by 1¾ inches inside." From Gale's data I estimate the earliest date of laying to be May 20, 1890 and the latest clutch was started July 8, 1886.

I found four nests of *caniceps* in 1958 on a north-facing slope in ponderosa pine at 7,800 feet 18 miles west of Denver, Colo. Nest 1, found May 25, contained four eggs and was in a slight hollow under a small, fallen, dead tree branch, overgrown with kinnikinnick (*Arctostaphylos uva-ursi*). When visited June 27, the nest had been torn apart and the young apparently taken by a predator; an adult was singing in a nearby tree.

The other three nests were in a somewhat more open area, 200 to 350 yards west from nest 1, and were in concurrent use in July, presumably for second, or possibly third, broods. Nest 2 had four eggs when found July 12, and three young July 19; one egg did not hatch. Built under a small common juniper (*Juniperus communis* var. *montana*) on level ground instead of in the more usual hollow, it was a large and bulky structure of grasses with a few pine needles and strips of inner bark. It measured: inside, 1½ inches deep by 2½ inches in diameter; outside, 3 inches deep by 4½ to 7 inches in diameter. Nest 3 was found July 19, hidden by grass and concealed beneath a Canada buffaloberry (*Shepherdia canadensis*), 50 yards down-slope from nest 2. It contained young both when found and 7 days later. This nest, too, was bulky, but had less than half the bulk of nest 2. Of the four, it was the only one containing hair, apparently of deer, and feathers, a few, gray and probably from the parent bird. This nest measured: inside, 1¼ inches deep by 2½ inches in diameter; outside, 2 inches deep by 4 to 5 inches in diameter. Nest 4 was 150 yards west of 2 and 3, surrounded by grasses, alongside a Douglas fir seedling 12 inches tall, and 8 feet from the nearest large tree, a 10-inch pine. As it was in a hollow, this nest consisted of no more than a lining, ½ to ¾ inches thick, of fine grasses and plant fibers and a few pine needles. It contained young 3 or 4 days old when found, July 27. The dissimilarity of nests 2, 3, and 4 can best be expressed by their dry weights, which were 33, 14 and 2 grams, respectively.

Nests 1 and 2 I found by searching when the parents scolded as I approached. The birds of nest 3 behaved much differently; the sitting bird flushed only when almost stepped upon, left without a sound, and never returned to scold on the three occasions I visited it. Nest 4 was found by watching one of the parents carrying food until it dropped from a pine overhead to the ground near the nest.

Neil Frederick Hadley recently spent two summers studying the species near Boulder, Colo. From about 7,000 feet altitude to timberline at 11,500 feet in the Colorado Front Range he found 34 gray-headed junco nests, most of them in the "upper montane" and "subalpine" zones between 9,300 and 11,000 feet. He has sent me the following notes from his unpublished study:

All the nests I found were on the ground and usually well concealed under some form of shelter. Favorite locations were beneath fallen logs, stumps, rocks, conifer seedlings, small shrubs, or tufts of grass, or in the banks of streams and gullies. Nests tend often to be somewhat "tunneled" into the ground, with only a very small aperture for the entrance and exit of the bird.

The outside of the nest is usually composed of coarse grasses and old decayed leaves; the inside is of finer grasses and always lined with some type of hair or feathers. Dr. Horace Quick helped me identify hairs from a number of different nests. We found not only the usually cited cattle and horse hairs, but also cervid hairs of either deer or elk, dog hairs, human hairs, hair from a snowshoe hare in winter pelage, and both fur and guard hairs of squirrels.

The nesting of *dorsalis* is similar to that of *caniceps*, but generally starts earlier in the spring, for this race winters either within or much nearer its summer range than does *caniceps*. Hargrave (1936) saw a *dorsalis* carrying nest material at Flagstaff in northern Arizona, Mar. 24, 1935. The first brood left a nest in a vine at the same place, according to Katherine Bartlett (MS.), on Apr. 28, 1940. E. C. Jacot (MS.) saw a *dorsalis* in the White Mountains of Arizona, at 8,000 feet elevation, Apr. 7, 1935 "carrying nesting material—a pine needle." Probably the latest recorded nesting date for *dorsalis* appears in F. M. Bailey (1928): "* * * On August 17, 1919, a nest with eggs was found 30 miles southwest of Chloride in southwestern New Mexico * * * at 7,200 feet (Ligon, 1916–1918)." Assuming a requirement of at least 30 days after hatching for completion of breeding activity, this would extend the nesting season for *dorsalis* over a period of 25½ weeks, March 24 to September 17, 4 or 5 weeks longer than that of *caniceps*.

Of *dorsalis* nesting in northern Arizona, Mearns (1890b) says:

> Sets of fresh eggs were found from May 22 to July 22, 1887, the nesting season varying considerably with the altitude, but the clutch seen on the last date probably belonged to a second brood. A typical nest was found on May 30, 1887, in pine woods near the bottom of a ravine on Mormon Mountain. At a short distance was a deep snow-bank. The male parent flew from the nest, beneath my horse's feet, where I found it concealed in a thick bunch of wire-grass. It was composed of fine roots, stems of plants, grasses, and an occasional feather, loosely put together in the manner of most ground nests. It contained four eggs * * *.

> I found its nest close to the upper edge of timber on San Francisco Mountain about the middle of June, and another nest on the very top of Baker's Butte [8077 feet], containing eggs, on the 22nd of July.

F. M. Bailey (1928) describes a *dorsalis* nest: "A typically well concealed nest of the Red-backed Junco found by Mr. Ligon in the Chloride region was hidden under a small pine that had spread over the ground and caught dead leaves, making a thick supporting mat as well as a dark base for the inconspicuous nest of bark and dead grass with its slight lining of hair. To further protect it from prowling enemies, a small bowlder [sic] stood beside it, blocking the entrance." Mrs. Bailey (1927) mentions that *dorsalis* also nests "in clumps of oaks on hillsides," as does W. I. Mitchell (1898):

"Abundant. Most common at 8,000 feet, breeding in clumps of scrub-oak on hillsides" in north central New Mexico. E. C. Jacot (MS.) describes an Arizona *dorsalis* nest found June 7, 1935, by Mrs. Jacot "in a thicket of 3- to 4-foot yellow pines; the nest was hidden near the foot of one of the small pines. It was composed almost entirely of very fine rootlets and some grass." One found in the same locality, Aug. 13, 1937 by Hustace H. Poor (MS.) near a stream was in a "dark, shady site under broad-leafed weeds."

Like the other juncos, the gray-headed sometimes nests off the ground. W. W. Cooke (1900) says of *caniceps*: "Breeds abundantly at Breckenridge [Colorado], and in 1898 one nested there under the eaves of Mr. [Edwin] Carter's house." One *caniceps* nest of 24 found by D. D. Stone (1884) in Colorado was "placed in a small pine, three feet from the ground, in a heavy bunch of timber." A note filed at the museum at Grand Canyon National Park, by K. Wing, June 5, 1950, mentions a nest "in the rafters of the cafeteria porch" at the North Rim of the Canyon. Lyndon L. Hargrave (1936) tells of a *dorsalis* "nest in vines under the eaves of the house" at the Museum of Northern Arizona at Flagstaff in 1934. Unpublished notes by Hargrave and others at the museum mention a later nest at the same location "in vine, northwest corner of patio," about 8 feet above the ground. Not only was this nest unusual in its location, but it was used several times: in 1937 (probably); in 1938, number of broods not known; in 1939, two broods; and in 1940, two broods. After the second brood left in 1940, a second nest, in which the third brood of that season was raised, was built on a roof plate "one foot over and two up" (note by Katherine Bartlett) from the first nest.

Although there seems to be no definite proof of *caniceps* raising more than one brood in a season, the many late nestings indicate that it probably raises at least two. As N. F. Hadley (MS.) comments: "The long period over which nests are found in Colorado suggests second broods are attempted whenever possible. The number of broods raised probably depends on how early the first nesting begins and the weather conditions when the second brood is to be started. If the first nesting is not successful, *caniceps* will attempt a second brood, as we observed several times. In each case the second nest was near the site of the first and built under a similar shelter, that is if the first nest was under a lodgepole seedling, so usually was the second."

Of *dorsalis*, however, we have Hargrave's (1936) detailed record, mentioned above, of the raising of three broods. Following is his summary, in part:

The summer's observations on breeding Red-backed Juncos at Coyote Range, Flagstaff, Arizona, have shown (1) that the male probably wintered within his prospective summer territory inasmuch as he returned to the locality on November 8, 1935, where he was banded on January 30 of the same year and where he was recaptured in early March; (2) that the female probably appeared on her breeding ground after the male had established himself; (3) that nesting activities were under way by March 24; (4) that one brood was hatched near the first of June, another in late July, and the last in late August; (5) that the male was father to three broods and the female was mother to the first and third and probably the second broods * * *.

*Eggs.*—The gray-headed junco lays from three to five slightly glossy eggs. They are usually ovate, although some may tend to short ovate. The ground is white, or very pale bluish-white, speckled, spotted, and occasionally blotched with "buffy brown," "sayal brown," "pecan brown," or "russet" with undermarkings of "pale mouse gray." These spottings may be scattered over the entire surface, but are usually concentrated toward the large end, frequently forming a wreath. The markings are often dull and somewhat clouded, and tend more toward yellow-browns whereas both *Junco hyemalis* and *Junco oreganus* have red-brown spottings. Sometimes a set or a single egg may be found that is plain bluish-white with only a few specks so small that they are hardly visible. The measurements of 47 eggs average 19.9 by 15.2 millimeters; the eggs showing the four extremes measure *22.0* by 15.8, 20.6 by *16.0*, *18.7* by 15.0, and 19.3 by *14.1* millimeters.

*Young.*—There appears to be no record of close observation of the complete nesting cycle of the gray-headed junco. Incubation time can be assumed to be 11 or 12 days, as given by Bergtold (1917b) for the slate-colored junco. Miller (1938) notes that two eggs laid in captivity by a "Point Pinos junco" (*J. o. pinosus*) mated with a male *dorsalis* hatched in 12 days. While determining the sex of an incubating bird is difficult, unless the bird is collected or the male is singing nearby, a bird flushed from the nest is generally assumed to be a female. Mearns (1890a), however, as noted above, says of *dorsalis*: "The male parent flew from the nest," while it contained eggs.

From his observations on *caniceps* near Boulder, Colo., N. F. Hadley (MS.) writes:

The female alone incubates the eggs. The male will occasionally fly down to the nest and feed her while she incubates and then fly away, or both may fly away together. The male sometimes remains at the nest edge while the female flies off, but I never saw one enter the nest and assume an incubating position. The female on the nest continually changes her position and turns the eggs, using both her bill and feet for the purpose, commonly once every five to ten minutes.

The male's arrival with food can often be foretold by the incubating female's actions. Alerted by some sort of signal from the male, not always heard, she perks up her head and turns it from side to side in anticipation. When ants or other insects pass by within reach, she will reach out to grab them. She also leaves the nest at intervals to feed herself. I observed one pair feeding together on the floor of a lodgepole stand over 200 yards from the nest. The frequency and duration of her absences from the nest and of her periods of attentiveness to incubation depend on time of day and weather conditions. During morning hours when the sun's illumination is at its peak due to slope and nest exposure, she tends to keep the eggs or young covered to prevent overheating. She tends to incubate longer and more continuously during raw, wet weather.

The eggs in a clutch seldom hatch simultaneously. Most hatch in the morning, but often one or two hatch in the morning and the remainder in the afternoon, or even the next day. After the first eggs hatch the female seems to move the others so that they receive optimal warmth. The actual emergence of the young from the egg is very rapid, often helped by the female pulling the shell with her beak. As soon as the fledgling is free, the female eats the egg shell.

Both male and female feed the hatchlings a diet that appears to be entirely of insects. When the female is brooding, the male sometimes deposits food at the edge of the nest where the female can take it for herself, or give it to the young. The female is very attentive to nest sanitation. At each feeding visit she scours the nest and removes the fecal sacs, usually depositing them on the limb of a nearby spruce or lodgepole. The young are apparently not fed in sequence; the same bird may be fed several times in succession if it proves the most aggressive. The nestlings' bright red mouth linings combined with their wide yellow bills give the feeding adult a large, easily visible target.

The young spend approximately 10 to 11 days in the nest after hatching, though one brood remained 13 days. The nestlings' eyes become slit-like on the fourth day, and open fully by the sixth day. As they become older (7 to 10 days) they venture out of the nest to receive food from their parents, sometimes as far as two feet, always returning immediately to the nest. They also leave the nest temporarily to try out their wings.

It was thought the nestlings would make their final move out of the nest in response to the parents' enticing them with food, but they sometimes desert it of their own accord when the parents are not present. Not all leave the nest at once; one or two may remain several hours after their more venturesome siblings have gone. Once out of the nest they become very difficult to follow. They spend at least three or four days hopping around on the ground before they can fly with any degree of coordination. During this time their parents watch them solicitously from nearby trees and bushes, flying down to feed them occasionally.

The following history of the young in a nest of *dorsalis* at Flagstaff, Ariz., is from unpublished notes by A. R. Phillips at the Museum of Northern Arizona. The nest containing four eggs was discovered May 25, 1936 under a tussock of grass, opening toward the west, which was shaded in the morning. The next day at 2 p.m. it contained four young "mostly naked with some gray down on head and rear end." May 29, at 3 days, the four young weighed 27.5 grams. May 30—"still nearly naked, eyes not open"; weight 35.5 grams. May 31—eyes still closed; weight 44.5 grams. June 1—eyes opening; weight 48 grams. June 2 (8:24 a.m.)—eyes open; feathers of belly tracts becoming prominent; weight 60.5 grams. June 3 (8:15 a.m.)— "One young squealed (first sign of fear instinct) and both parents came to the nest"; weight 62 grams. June 4 (11:40 a.m.)—weight 64 grams. June 5 (11:12 a.m.)—weight 70 grams; (1:25 p.m.)—only three young in nest, one probably having been "lured away by the parents"; at this time the young were 10 days old.

Hargrave (1936) found that the *dorsalis* male parent did most of the feeding of the first broods after they left the nest. The male in his report fathered three broods in one season (determined by trapping and banding with the young as decoys). After the third brood left the nest "both adults were observed" feeding them.

*Plumages.*—As previously mentioned, A. R. Phillips states that one-day-old young of *dorsalis* were naked with some gray down on head and rump. R. B. Rockwell (1910) described newly-hatched young he saw in Colorado as "pinkish little creatures irregularly covered with very fine grayish down." R. R. Graber (1955) says one of two Colorado *caniceps* nestlings had "smoky gray [natal] down on the rump," while the other had "down on the side of the crown." Graber describes the juvenal plumage: "Forehead and crown light gray, heavily streaked with black. Nape tinged with buff. Back mahogany red, streaked with black. Rump buffy, obscurely streaked with blackish. Upper tail coverts buffy gray, obscurely spotted with blackish. Rectrices blackish gray except outer two pairs white and third from outside about half white. Remiges black, narrowly white-edged (tertials edged with mouse gray). Coverts edged with gray. Secondary coverts tipped with whitish (two obscure wing bars). Lores dark gray. Auriculars gray, postauriculars like nape. Subauriculars streaked, blackish and white. Chin and throat white, obscurely spotted with gray. Underparts largely white, the sides and flanks light buffy. Chest and sides streaked with blackish (triangular marks with apex anterior). Belly and crissum white. Legs gray."

Two New Mexico *dorsalis* in juvenal plumage, apparently somewhat more advanced than the *caniceps* described above, were similar to the *caniceps* but in general lighter-colored. These Graber describes: "Forehead light gray. Crown and nape gray, streaked with black (nape more sparsely). Back light rusty (burnt sienna of Ridgway), sparsely streaked with black. Rump and upper tail coverts light, buffy-tinged gray, sparsely streaked with blackish. Rectrices largely dark gray, outer two pairs white (some white on third from outside). Remiges black, narrowly light edged (tertials broadly edged with gray). Coverts edged with gray and buff, secondary coverts tipped narrowly with white (narrow wing bars). Lores black. Auriculars and postauriculars gray, unmarked. Chin unmarked whitish. Other underparts white. Throat, chest, sides, and flanks finely spotted and streaked with blackish. Legs gray."

Miller (1941b) briefly describes the adult plumage for both races:

Iris dark brown; lower mandible flesh-colored, upper mandible black or flesh-colored. Back with sharply defined mahogany red area, confined normally to interscapular region; * * * tips of feathers grayish * * *. Lores and ocular region black, contrasting with neutral grays of head. Sides gray without line of demarcation separating them from upper breast. Tail always with two, and usually three, outer feathers partly or completely white. * * *

Sexual differentiation in plumage slight. Females average slightly lighter in colors of head and side in race *caniceps* only. Fourth rectrix more often pure black, fifth and sixth rectrices less often pure white in females than in males. Degree of sexual differentiation in rectrices variable, depending on population involved. * * * Females often have traces of buff on tips of feathers of sides, and reddish- or buff-tipped wing coverts. A distinctive immature or retarded plumage not recognizable; occasionally young males have buff-tipped sides, and this feature predominates in young females.

The red of the back alters with the season, becoming brighter and yellower to approach burnt sienna and Sanford's brown. The gray tips are worn off early, but this does not seem to affect the tone of color importantly. Brightening is not pronounced until late April, but in the succeeding six weeks the greatest alteration takes place. * * * The grays of the head pale slightly, so that the mass effect in worn plumage is that of lighter hood, except in the extreme state of wear of midsummer, when exposure of the basal downy barbules gives a sooty appearance.

For *J. c. caniceps*, Miller (1941b) continues: "Features present in all individuals that distinguish them from *J. c. dorsalis* are: (1) darker neutral gray (light neutral gray and neutral gray) of hood, especially that of throat, and (2) flesh-colored upper mandible." Miller also states that measurements of *caniceps* tail, bill, tarsus and middle toe average slightly less than those of *dorsalis*, and the "amount of white in the tail averages less." He says further, of *caniceps:* "Reddish color of variable extent is not uncommon on the pileum. It appears in all populations. In the total of 772 *J. c. caniceps* examined, 48, or 6.21 percent, have some feathers distinctly red, not merely buff tipped." Of *dorsalis*, he adds: "Red on the pileum occurs in 1.7 percent, compared with 6.2 percent in *caniceps* and 1.7 percent in *palliatus*.

I have seen in Colorado in early spring a *caniceps* with the entire pileum red, much like that of the chipping sparrow (*Spizella passerina*) in extent. Rockwell and Wetmore (1914) mention an "immature female [*caniceps*, taken in November, with] a rufous line on each side of the crown," and another female with "faint rusty tips to the feathers on the occipital and nuchal regions."

A regular but infrequent variation within *dorsalis* is the appearance of the mahogany red of the back "on the outer webs of the inner secondaries and greater secondary coverts," which appeared in 9, or 3.9 percent, of the 230 specimens Miller examined (1941b). This feature suggests affinity to *phaeonotus*, but places of its occurrence are not related to proximity to the range of that species. A. R. Phillips (MS.) at Flagstaff in March 1936, banded "a remarkably red bird [*dorsalis*], the color of the back invading much of the body—to be specific, the sides broadly tinged, the crown somewhat so, the secondaries edged and their greater coverts mostly the same color as the back!"

Another variation within *dorsalis* is the color of the lower mandible, which occasionally is dark, but probably never as dark as the black maxilla. Seven birds Phillips banded at Flagstaff, all but one in winter and hence not juveniles, had lower mandibles ranging from "pinkish lavender" through "bluish," "dark lavender" (a juvenile banded in June), "dark blue," "blue black," and "black."

F. M. Bailey's (1902) comment on the plumage of *dorsalis* applies equally well to *caniceps*: "The coloration of most of the juncos is not particularly protective except as the color pattern disguises the bird's form, but the red-backed on the pine plateau of San Francisco Mountain, Arizona, spends a large part of its time about the fallen pine-tops, where the red of its back and the red of the dead pine needles and old bark make a protective combination that, added to the gray of the body, which offsets the gray of the branches, results in a most effective disguise."

*Food.*—Juncos are mainly terrestrial and obtain practically all of their food on or very near the ground. Unless hard-pressed by hunger they seldom feed on a shelf or other raised feeding station, but prefer to pick up the seed spilled on the ground by other species. F. M. Bailey (1928) mentions *dorsalis* in July "feeding among the dead leaves, * * * scratching much like chickens" in the Capitan Mountains of New Mexico, and mentions Major Goldman's finding them in the Mogollon Mountains in late October, when "Small parties were everywhere hopping about, scratching among the leaves through the thin snow, and when startled rising and alighting in the lower branches of trees."

Unusual feeding behavior of a "red-backed" junco is reported by E. C. Jacot (MS.) in the White Mountains of Arizona on Mar. 13, 1935 "feeding from the bark of a pine tree 20 to 30 feet from the ground, as painted redstarts often do. Perched on a limb and flew to the trunk keeping tail somewhat fanned, then back to the limb."

No detailed study has been made of the food of the gray-headed junco, which probably differs little from that of the other, better-known northern junco species. Of *caniceps* in the Sangre de Cristo Mountains of New Mexico, F. M. Bailey (1928) says: "Among the insects fed to the young birds were a caddice [sic] fly and a green caterpillar." A. R. Phillips notes that the *dorsalis* young he studied at Flagstaff, Ariz., when 4 days old were fed green seeds and "apparently a green caterpillar." One of Miss Bartlett's Flagstaff notes says that at the "vine" nest previously mentioned Milton A. Wetherill observed that the female parent "fed young birds with soft parts of grasshoppers, carrying hard parts away." There, also, Hargrave

(1936) reports: "On one occasion both adults were observed carrying millet [from a trapping and feeding station] to young fifteen feet above the ground in a pine tree." William H. Behle (1943) says of *caniceps* in southwestern Utah: "Their diet seemed largely insectivorous while feeding young, for nearly every individual shot had the mouth and throat filled with bodies of moths, measuring worms, or larval insect forms." Louise Hering (1948) in her Black Forest, Colo., study noted young *caniceps* being fed "moths and worms" obtained from kinnikinnick. At a Colorado *caniceps* nest at timberline in July, I watched both parents bringing the young small grasshoppers.

In the White Mountains of Arizona, F. G. Watson (MS.) noted of *dorsalis* seen daily about a cabin at 9,400 feet elevation in July 1936, that "they feed on crumbs and grain * * *," and A. R. Phillips (MS.) on Oct. 20, 1936, mentions one (of two or three) eating dandelion (*Taraxacum*) seeds. F. M. Bailey (1928) says of flocks of *caniceps* driven to lower elevations in the Gallinas Mountains of central New Mexico by an early October snowstorm: "They were everywhere but especially abundant in the weed patches on the edge of the scrub oak thickets into which they flew when flushed, and the stomachs of two taken were full of seeds, including a large per cent of pigweed." Edward R. Warren (1910a) quotes John W. Frey, from central Colorado, regarding *caniceps:* "Thousands of these birds wintered here [1908–9] on the tumbleweed seed." I have observed wintering *caniceps* in Colorado eating the seed of an abundant species of cheat grass (*Bromus* sp.). According to D. I. Rasmussen (1941), who observed mixed winter flocks of Oregon and gray-headed juncos on the Kaibab Plateau, in northern Arizona: "They are active on the ground, and their food consists of all available plant seeds, grasses, herbs and shrubs."

E. D. McKee (1934) noted wintering juncos at Grand Canyon eating seeds of the piñons (*Pinus edulis* and *P. monophylla*): "When cracked nuts are put out it has been found, strangely enough, that natural seed-eaters such as juncos and chipping sparrows actually prefer them to various types of grain and that robins hold them in equal esteem with their much-loved raisins. Even bluebirds, Cedar Waxwings, and Cassin's Purple Finches will eat them with relish." At the South Rim of the Canyon, Oct. 20, 1948, L. Schellbach (MS.) "observed 2 [*dorsalis*] distinctly pecking open pinyon pine nuts and extracting the nut meat * * *." On a Colorado mountain top at 11,300 feet F. V. Hebard and A. W. Gardner (1954) observed a flock of *caniceps* in early April feeding with red and white-winged crossbills, pine siskins and pine grosbeaks, in Engelmann spruce and limber pine, where "spruce seeds were the main source of food."

*Behavior.*—Nesting gray-headed juncos, except when incubating closely, generally take alarm readily and scold an intruder vigorously with their characteristic, sharp, rapidly-repeated "tic" note, which E. C. Jacot (MS.) describes as sounding "like snapping two nickels together." A bird on the nest usually flushes only when nearly stepped upon, and in most cases remains nearby, scolding loudly. But an occasional one flushes silently and disappears until the intruder leaves. J. K. Jensen (1923) notes a New Mexico *caniceps* S. R. Hammitt found that "flew off the nest almost under his feet, and although he waited patiently for more than an hour, it never returned." Jensen adds, "I have several times seen the birds building, in which case the nests have always been abandoned." F. M. Bailey's account of H. W. Henshaw's flushing from her nest a female that "glided off through the grass, fluttering about and feigning lameness" is unusual.

In an account of pine grosbeak breeding behavior in northeastern Utah, Norman R. French (1954) writes: "A pair of Gray-headed Juncos nested near the base of the same tree in which the grosbeaks were nesting. The grosbeaks sometimes alighted low in the tree and worked up to their nest. The juncos invariably came into the tree and worked down to their nest. As a result the paths of the birds sometimes crossed. When a junco was on a perch and one of the grosbeaks came toward it the junco immediately flew, usually to a lower perch in the tree."

As mentioned previously, juncos will respond to "tic" notes made with a pewter-and-wood bird-call in their breeding territories. Once, in July, I used the call to attract mountain chickadees, unaware of two or three fledgling juncos near by. The parent juncos responded with vigorous scolding to the "tic" call. Wintering juncos generally ignore a call, but occasionally foraging mixed flocks, largely of Oregons, will respond to one as readily as do chickadees or nuthatches.

Although fairly tolerant of moderately arid conditions, the gray-headed junco makes frequent use of available water. L. Hering (1948) states that *caniceps* was one of six species of birds breeding in Colorado pine "seen bathing in the creek." C. W. Stillman (MS.) records "A group of at least six [*dorsalis*] close to a spring and small stream in bushes and grassland. Seen bathing in a stream" Aug. 5, 1937. A. R. Phillips "saw one or two bathing in Horse Creek," Nov. 22, 1936.

*Voice.*—The voice of the gray-headed junco is in most respects similar to that of the slate-colored junco as A. A. Saunders (1935) describes it:

The song of the junco is a very simple one. Normally it is a simple trill * * * or a series of rapid notes all on the same pitch * * *. The number of notes, when they can be counted, varies from eight to twenty or more. The quality is rather musical, decidedly more so than the quality of the Chipping Sparrow. There are occasional variations in time, with the notes at the beginning faster or slower, and pitch sometimes varies up or down a half-tone or a tone.

Occasional individuals have some peculiar abnormal form of the song, sometimes so different that one must see the bird to be sure of identification. Such individuals seem to sing in that way always, and may be known and followed from year to year by the peculiarity. An individual has little variation in its singing.

Early in the spring, when singing first begins, one may sometimes find a Junco singing a faint, varied song with mixed pitches. It is a highly attractive song when one is near enough to hear it clearly, but I am inclined to think it is primitive in character.

In winter, birds produce a note like *"tsehehehe"* which is rather musical and pleasing. Alarm notes are *"tsick"* and *"tŭtŭtŭtŭp"* the latter used commonly when the nest contains young, but rarely heard from winter birds.

In the Colorado foothill ponderosa pine forest where both *J. c. caniceps* and the chipping sparrow are numerous, I found that frequently the quality of a less musical song of the junco matches the chipping sparrow's song so well that distinguishing unseen birds is extremely difficult, even when the two are singing simultaneously. They can usually be told apart by the timing and duration of the songs. The junco's song generally consists of 1½- to 2-second trills, given eight to ten per minute, while the chipping sparrow's are of approximately three seconds duration given four to six times per minute. Later in July I found this relative timing not completely reliable when a supposed junco near a known junco's nest at timberline and singing at the rate of eight trills of 1½ to 2 seconds duration per minute turned out to be a chipping sparrow. It sang 191 times in 24 minutes, stopped for 1½ minutes, then resumed singing. Not only was this sparrow singing the junco's song, but it was 3,000 feet above its usual foothill habitat.

I consider the song of the gray-headed junco more varied than that of the slate-colored. A gray-head in early spring, Mar. 29, 1960, in its breeding habitat sang three different songs, all of the more musical, "junco" quality, averaging ten per minute. One variation, lasting approximately two seconds, consisted of a two-part trill, *swe-swe-swe-swe-swe-te-te-te-te-te;* the second, approximately one second long, was a simple trill of seven or eight notes, *te-te-te-te-te-te-te,* like the second part of the longer song; and the third, also of one second's duration, resembled the first part of the longer song, *swe-swe-swe-swe-swe-swe.* Another song, heard the next day at the same place, alternated two simple trills, one quite musical, typically "junco," and the other less musical, much like the chipping sparrow's. Four or five of these alternating trills comprised a series.

Joe T. Marshall, Jr. (pers. comm.) recorded an early July song of a *dorsalis* singing at noon and later in the day near the top of a dead aspen in the Canadian Life Zone of the Arizona White Mountains: "Steadiness, quality and variety suggest *phaeonotus: Tswee tswee tsee tswee chit chit chit chit.* There was another series of *tsuwee tsuwee tsuwee tsuwee chit chit chit chit* and one of just six *chits.*"

While the junco characteristically sings from tall trees in spring, it occasionally uses lower perches. One of a pair of *caniceps* I watched at timberline in Colorado June 24, 1958, sang on the ground as it foraged and occasionally from a twig a foot or two above the ground.

At Flagstaff, Ariz., in the Transition pine forest at 6,900 feet, L. L. Hargrave (MS.) in 1936 recorded the earliest territorial songs of two *dorsalis*, one February 14 and the other March 3. The next year he heard juncos (perhaps Oregons instead of "red-backs") singing a "soft twittering song, very faint—not heard far" on February 4; the first territorial song by a *dorsalis*, he heard the same date as the preceding year—February 14. E. C. Jacot (MS.) at Alpine, southeast of and 1,100 feet higher than Flagstaff, recorded the gray-headed junco, probably both subspecies, singing "since the 11th" of March 1935, when there were 10 to 15 inches of snow on the ground, with open patches at bases of trees and along streams and roads. On March 18, Mr. Jacot recorded of *caniceps:* "At Alpine as usual. Seem to be in full song," and of *dorsalis:* "red-backed in full song. They and gray-headed seem to sing almost as soon as they are perched in tree or bush after being flushed." The latest *dorsalis* singing dates also are from the White Mountains. F. G. Watson (MS.) at the Phelps Ranger Station at 9,400 feet heard them "singing about the cabin each day" July 9 to 28, and also on Baldy Peak at timberline, 11,200 feet, July 12. Thus the period of singing by *dorsalis* in 1936 included nearly twenty-three weeks—February 14 to July 28.

My earliest seasonal record for singing by *caniceps* in Colorado is Mar. 15, 1951, in its breeding habitat at 7,500 feet. On May 2, 1954, none of approximately 15 *caniceps* at the edge of the foothills at 6,000 feet, driven down from the mountains by a severe snowstorm, was heard to sing, although 7 weeks earlier on March 13 in 1955, at the same place several individuals of a mixed flock of approximately 35 *J. o. montanus, J. o. mearnsi,* and *J. hyemalis* (no *J. caniceps*) were in song. On May 21, in both 1955 and 1960, two of seven or eight birds seen each time in the Hudsonian Zone at 11,000 feet were. singing, although 2 to 3 feet of snow delayed nesting 4 or 5 weeks During a 5-year population study in ponderosa pine (Thatcher, 1956) the latest singing date was July 17, 1955, when the male of only one of six observed pairs sang. A few days earlier on July 12 in 1952, four of seven were in song. My extreme latest song dates are July 31, one in a cool aspen forest at 7,750 feet and one of eight adults at timberline, 11,700 feet. The song period of *caniceps* thus is approximately 20 weeks, March 15 to July 31, 3 weeks less than that of *dorsalis*.

While timing early morning singing in the ponderosa pine forest, June 6, 1954, I recorded the first song of *caniceps* at 4:23 a.m., 16 minutes after sunrise and 55 minutes after the first birds, western flycatcher and common nighthawk, were heard. I heard notes of 12 additional species before the junco's first song.

*Field marks.*—Juncos usually are readily distinguished from other small birds occurring in their range by the combination of white outer tail feathers and the characteristic *"tic"* notes they almost invariably give in flight. The combination of mahogany-red saddle, light gray head, and gray sides distinguishes the gray-headed from all other juncos except those that breed south of its breeding range. Some races of the Oregon junco have somewhat reddish backs, but their heads are black or nearly so. The "pink-sided" Oregon junco (*J. o. mearnsi*) has a light gray head, but its back is brownish with almost no hint of red, and its sides are distinctly reddish, more so than those of the black-headed Oregons. If the lighter gray head fails to distinguish the gray-headed from the slate-colored and the white-winged juncos when the red back is obscured, the lack of a sharp line between gray of breast and grayish-white of abdomen should do so.

The light, flesh-colored upper mandible of *caniceps* and its slightly darker head, "light neutral gray and neutral gray" of Miller (1941b), distinguish that race from the more southern *dorsalis* with its blackish upper mandible and "pale or pallid neutral gray" (Miller) head. The breeding gray-heads of the Kaibab Plateau in northern Arizona and of the Zuni Mountains in central western New Mexico are mostly intermediate. This condition is most obvious in the color of the upper mandible, which is flesh-colored or pinkish with tip and base black in highly variable proportions, as described by Miller (1941b), who later (1949) terms the Kaibab birds "a single hybrid swarm, not a geographic gradient either of blending or of alternating characters or both."

The pale upper mandible readily distinguishes those *J. c. caniceps* wintering in southern Arizona from the resident Mexican junco, but other characteristics must be observed for identification of the few *dorsalis* which winter there. These are, for the Mexican junco: yellow eye, yellowish feet and lower mandible, and considerable red on wings; and for the gray-headed junco: dark brown eye, flesh-colored feet, grayish lower mandible, and little or no red on wings. In addition the voices differ considerably. The song of the Mexican is more varied than that of the gray-headed, being described by R. T. Peterson (1948b), in comparison with those of the Oregon and slate-colored juncos, as "a more complicated finch-like song, which involves two and sometimes three pitches * * *," and the call resembles more the "*tsip*" of the chipping sparrow. The gaits of the two differ noticeably also, for, as Peterson (1948b) says: "Furthermore, the Arizona [Mexican] Junco *creeps* along in strange mouse-like fashion. * * * whereas other juncos habitually hop." According to L. N. Nichols (1936) the Mexican junco "is said to have less the manners of a Junco than of a Water Thrush," and Allan Brooks (1914) agrees that "it walks daintily and deliberately over the floor of the forest like a titlark or water-thrush, instead of the shuffling hop of the junco and sparrows."

Owing to the free interbreeding of the gray-headed and Oregon juncos where the breeding range of the former meets those of *J. o. thurberi* and *J. o. mearnsi*, birds of mixed plumage are numerous in the overlapping ranges and occur commonly throughout the winter range of *caniceps*. Many of these have the red back of *caniceps* with the pinkish sides of *mearnsi*. In some individuals the red back is diluted or mixed with yellowish, or the pink of the sides is spotty or on only a few feathers. A few may have the dark head of *thurberi* or the brown or yellowish back of the Oregons, with the gray sides of *caniceps*. Variations are almost unlimited and most confusing to the close observer. The mated female *J. o. thurberi* and male *J. c. caniceps* x *J. c. mearnsi* Miller (1935) collected at the meeting point of the ranges of the three forms could certainly have produced puzzling offspring!

*Enemies.*—The enemies of the gray-headed junco are presumably those common to most small ground birds, but we have little definite information on this subject. The eggs or young of only two of seven nests I have observed until completion were taken by what I have assumed were small mammals. Upon investigating an unusually vigorous scolding by a pair of gray-heads at 9,500 feet in Colorado, in mid-August, I found a fledgling junco a day or two out of the nest in the jaws of a large garter snake and released it, apparently unharmed.

One of the young of the campus nest, at Boulder, Colo., previously mentioned, was said by O. A. Knorr (pers. comm.) to have been taken by a screech owl nesting nearby. R. G. Beidleman (1957) mentions long-eared owls which "evidently preyed on the juncos" on a winter population study area in Colorado ponderosa pine, where four species of juncos, including *caniceps*, were present. Miss Oppie Reames (pers. comm.) reports a pygmy owl (*Glaucidium gnoma*) eating an Oregon junco in southern Colorado in late October, undoubtedly from a mixed flock with a high percentage of gray-heads. Denis Gale (MS.) presumed predation by the northern shrike in northern Colorado. His notes state for Oct. 17, 1889: "Saw a Northern Shrike * * *. Evidently has crossed the range in the wake of Juncoes [sic] and was making for the valley." Howard Rollin (pers. comm.) saw a northern shrike in January "chase and kill a pink-sided junco" at his ranch on the Colorado plains during severe weather when mice, the shrike's usual diet, remained in shelter. An occasional gray-head loses its life at a banding or feeding station; at the Grand Canyon a banded *dorsalis* was reported killed in November "by an Abert Squirrel in a trap" (unpublished banding notes), and at nearby Flagstaff, Hargrave (1936) reports an immature bird killed in a trap by a sharp-shinned hawk in February. Also at Flagstaff, Hargrave (MS.) says the first brood raised in 1940 in the "vine" nest previously mentioned was "killed by dogs the day after they left the nest."

Although H. F. Friedmann (1949) lists the white-winged and the Cassiar (*J. hyemalis cismontanus*) juncos as victims of cowbird parasitism, there seem to be no records of victimization of the gray-headed junco. The breeding habitats of this junco and the brown-headed cowbird (*Molothrus ater*) seldom, if ever, overlap.

*Fall.*—After completing their breeding activities the northern *caniceps* form small groups, presumably of adults and the young of the season, and start a southward movement. Such groups are frequently encountered weeks before late breeding is finished in the same area. Twomey (1942) observed small flocks as early as July 25 at 6,000 feet in northwestern Colorado. The late-summer migration appears to be southward and frequently upward as higher mountains are encountered. Occasionally small moving bands occur 2,000 feet or more above timberline, where I have seen them as late as August 29. The first birds usually reach the "lowlands" about October 1, but their advent may be hastened by an early mountain snowstorm. Gray-heads soon join the migrating flocks of other junco species from the north, which eastward are mostly *J. o. mearnsi*, and westward *J. o. montanus*. In Arizona and New Mexico, the *J. c. caniceps* and the Oregon juncos associate commonly with the local, less migratory *dorsalis*.

The latitudinal limits of the winter range of *caniceps* are well south of those of the breeding range—generally 100 to 150 miles in the north and 500 miles or more in the south. Thus presumably the birds migrate not only vertically but a considerable distance southward. In his study of the winter birds in Utah, Hayward (1935) concluded that heavy snowfall covering "a large part of the available ground food * * * for a considerable length of time" determines the northern limit of the winter range of the gray-headed and other juncos.

To learn whether the wintering or migrating gray-headed juncos at Boulder, Colo., breed, as is generally presumed, in the mountains immediately to the west or northwest, Dr. and Mrs. John N. Hough color-banded 234 birds from October through April of 1957–58 and

1958–59.   Not one of these birds was reported during the three summers, 1958–1960, though several observers watched for the colored bands west of Boulder and in Rocky Mountain National Park 20 to 40 miles northwest.   This suggests that the birds migrating through or wintering at Boulder breed some distance farther north in Wyoming or extreme northern Colorado.

*J. c. dorsalis* has more of a vertical than a horizontal migration, and few birds move any great distance outside the pine forest of the breeding range.   H. S. Swarth (1924b) writes from northern Arizona: "One specimen was collected in juniper woods September 28 * * *.   This was the only occasion on which *dorsalis* was seen below the yellow pine belt.   When the migrating northern juncos arrived, the mixed flocks of *caniceps, shufeldti* [probably *montanus* (Miller, 1941b)] and others were abundant at the lower edge of the pines and in the piñons and junipers, but no specimen of *dorsalis* was found in any of these aggregations.   I found *dorsalis* at a higher altitude, in small flocks, and never accompanied by any other species."   A. R. Phillips (Phillips, Marshall, and Monson, 1964) says *dorsalis* "* * * seems a fine example of an altitudinal migrant, at first glance.   During severe winters, at least, it occurs commonly in the Verde and upper Gila Valleys * * * just below the Mogollon and Natanes Plateaux. It is notable, however, that these valleys lie to the south of the breeding range. * * * the available evidence indicates that these birds move downward in a southerly direction only."

In summarizing his account of the raising of three broods of *dorsalis*, Hargrave (1936) comments on fall behavior: "* * * (6) that shortly after leaving the nest the young of all but the last brood moved out of the nesting territory; (7) that the third and last brood remained within the nesting territory until the postjuvenal molt was nearly completed; (8) that the parents apparently left the nesting territory together and ahead of their offspring of their third brood; (9) that, after the summer adults had left, the young of the third brood remained and mixed with others of their race; and (10) that the members of the third brood apparently left the nesting territory together after the fall migration was well under way."   The young of the second brood left the nesting territory August 3, 1935.   The first birds from outside were trapped September 10 and 11, "indicating that the fall movement was under way."   The next season, Hargrave and A. R. Phillips (MS.) noted that *dorsalis* juveniles became numerous at Flagstaff August 15, nearly 4 weeks earlier than the preceding year, but no adults were seen at that time.

*Winter.*—While in general the northern gray-headed juncos, *caniceps*, move downward and southward for the winter, a considerable number winter in the mountains, well into the Canadian Zone in suitable places such as near corrals and bird-feeding stations in towns. There the gray-heads are usually in company with smaller numbers of Oregon juncos and an occasional slate-colored or white-winged junco. Frequently one or two gray-heads and perhaps an Oregon or a slate-colored occur in company with the white-winged juncos that typically winter in flocks of 10 to 30 in the more open stands of ponderosa pine of the eastern Rocky Mountain foothills. In similar foothill situations I have seen small groups of gray-heads in mid-winter, usually unaccompanied by other juncos, in close company with mixed flocks of mountain chickadees and pygmy nuthatches, and perhaps one or two white-breasted or red-breasted nuthatches or brown creepers. Many gray-heads winter with the other juncos along the lower edges of the coniferous forest, chiefly in brushy ravines and patches of *Crataegus*, scrub oak, mountain mahogany (*Cercocarpus montanus*) and other "brush," which furnish both shelter and a plentiful food supply not covered by snow. Often what appear at first to be only three or four juncos will, upon taking flight two or three at a time to the next brush patch, turn out to be a mixed flock of fifty or more. Such flocks may also contain considerable numbers of tree sparrows.

Just as *dorsalis* migrates much less than the more northern *caniceps*, the latter is considerably less migratory than the more northern races of the Oregon junco, *shufeldti, montanus,* and *mearnsi*. Miller (1941b) says that "Compared with *J. c. caniceps, mearnsi* leaves the breeding range more completely in winter and spreads out on the plains in greater number. The extreme limits of record are similar in the two forms; they are commonly associated in flocks in winter in Colorado and in the oak belt of New Mexico and Arizona."

At Boulder, Colo., near the northeastern extreme of the winter range of *caniceps*, the John Houghs (pers. comm.) banded 4617 juncos from October through April, 1946 through 1959. Their relative frequencies were: gray-headed 24 percent, white-winged 6 percent, slate-colored 6 percent, Oregon 64 percent (approximately 8 percent *montanus* and 56 percent *mearnsi*). The average junco numbers for the 13 Christmas counts between 1945 and 1961 at and near Boulder as reported in Audubon Field Notes show the following frequencies: gray-headed 14 percent, white-winged 4 percent, slate-colored 4 percent, *J. o. montanus* 11 percent, and *J. o. mearnsi* 67 percent. Summaries of the Christmas counts of the past 30 years within the winter range of the gray-headed junco show its relative numbers increase southward to the region of greatest concentration, a small area in north central New Mexico around and including the Sangre de Cristo Mountains. There approximately 45 percent of the juncos east of the mountains and 75 percent of those west were gray-heads. Immediately to the south the northern Oregons outnumber the gray-heads, *mearnsi* east and *montanus* west of the mountains.

In the western part of the winter range of the species on the Kaibab Plateau in northwestern Arizona, D. I. Rasmussen (1941) found that "The most abundant birds found during the winter season in this [piñon-juniper-woodrat] association are the juncos. The red-backed junco [*dorsalis*], which breeds in the upper portions of the mountain, is present in winter along with Shufeldt's junco [actually *J. o. montanus* (Miller, 1941b)], with perhaps individuals of the pink-sided junco and the gray-headed junco [*J. c. caniceps*]. Flocks of juncos were observed in the snow-covered foothills in flocks of twenty-five to one hundred individuals in the winter of 1930–31. Both the 'black heads' and the 'gray heads' were present. The former exceeded the latter in numbers of three to one."

At Grand Canyon National Park 2,476 juncos were banded from October 1932 through February 1939. In round numbers 60 percent of these were *J. o. montanus* (recorded as "Shufeldt's") and 40 percent *J. caniceps*, plus four "pink-sided" and one slate-colored (totalling 0.2 percent). Observations made at the same place 20 years later in 1956 and 1957 by Louise Hinchliffe and W. E. Dilley (MS.) found *montanus* the most numerous junco, often 6 to 1 of the others, followed by *caniceps*, including *dorsalis* and intergrades, and *mearnsi* in varying numbers, with a few slate-colored and "Cassiar" juncos. Probably at least ½ of the gray-headed juncos banded at Grand Canyon were *caniceps-dorsalis* intergrades native to the vicinity. Records were kept of the color of the upper mandibles of 23 banded in November and December 1932. Miller (1941b) would probably have classified 10 of these as pure *dorsalis*, as the mandibles of six were entirely black and those of four "mostly black" or "nearly all black." Six presumably were Miller's pure *caniceps*, the upper mandible of one having been recorded as "pink" and those of five as "very little black," "practically no black," or "flesh-colored except black tip." The mandibles of the other seven were intermediate in color, the birds presumably being *caniceps–dorsalis* intergrades from the nearby Kaibab Plateau population.

In the San Francisco Mountains southeast of the Grand Canyon H. S. Swarth (1924b) found that "By the middle of October [1922] *caniceps* was present in fair abundance, in the piñon-juniper belt to some extent, but in greater numbers in the yellow pine belt. Flocks of juncos were frequently encountered composed of as many as fifty or sixty individuals. Nine-tenths of such a flock would consist of *caniceps* and *shufeldti* [*montanus*] in about equal numbers, with a few *mearnsi* and perhaps an occasional *hyemalis*". At Flagstaff a few miles south, in 1935, L. L. Hargrave (MS.) recorded that a flock of about 25 juncos, all *caniceps* and *dorsalis*, suddenly disappeared after a one-inch snowfall November 2, except two *caniceps* and one *dorsalis*, "even though the feeding station was well baited; very surprising," and that most did not return for nearly a month.

While gray-headed juncos accompany the other juncos in the winter, both races often are partly segregated within the flocks from the Oregon and slate-colored juncos. In early November in the Arizona White Mountains, A. R. Phillips (MS.) noted that a group "which detached itself from the main group and fed off to one side of the field among small yellow pines was composed of several *dorsalis* and a few *caniceps*." Phillips continues: "These two races often segregate within larger flocks, as do the *oreganus* group; thus a flock will contain several races, but often a part of the flock feeding in one spot will be entirely composed of northern or southern races." Later in November, he recorded that *dorsalis* outnumbered *caniceps* by two or three to one, and that the *dorsalis* "also seemed more active than any other race and were always chasing each other about." In February and March, on several occasions *dorsalis* was noted with other juncos, but almost always feeding aside from the main flock and staying closer to thick brush; on one occasion in late March they were, however, recorded as "not in brush this time, but feeding with others by the road." In the same area, E. C. Jacot (MS.) agrees that *caniceps* is "evidently rarer away from timber than *oreganus* group."

## DISTRIBUTION

### Northern Gray-headed Junco (*J. c. caniceps*)

*Range.*—Southern Idaho and southern Wyoming south to northern portions of Sonora, Sinaloa and Durango, and western Texas.

*Breeding range.*—The northern gray-headed junco breeds in mountains from southern Idaho, Nevada (Santa Rosa and Jarbidge mountains), Utah (Porcupine Ridge, Uinta Mountains), and southern Wyoming (Uinta Mountains, Medicine Bow Range) south through central and east central Nevada (Toiyabe Mountains, Wilson Peak), the White Mountains of California, Utah, and western and central Colorado to northern Arizona (intergrades with *J. c. dorsalis* on Kaibab Plateau) and northern New Mexico (Chuska Mountains; Pecos; intergrades with *J. c. dorsalis* in Zuni Mountains).

*Winter range.*—Winters in lower mountains and plains of breeding area, north to northern Utah (Utah Lake Valley), northern Colorado (Rocky Mountain National Park); and from western Nebraska (Scotts Bluff County) and eastern Colorado (Fort Morgan, Yuma) south to northern Sonora (Rancho Carrizal), northern Sinaloa (Babizos), northern Durango (Ciénaga de las Vacas), and western

Texas (Palo Duro Canyon, Chisos Mountains); rarely to southern California (San Diego, Los Angeles and San Bernardino counties).

*Casual records.*—Casual north to eastern Montana (Glendive) and east to south central Nebraska (Red Cloud), central Oklahoma (Norman), Arkansas (Little Rock), and Louisiana (Shreveport).

*Migration.*—The data deal with the species as a whole. Early dates of spring arrival are: Utah—Moab, April 2. Wyoming—Laramie, March 23 (average of 8 years, April 12).

Late dates of spring departure are: Nebraska—Red Cloud, April 18. Texas—El Paso, April 25. Oklahoma—Cimarron County, April 20. New Mexico—southern New Mexico, April 18.

Early dates of fall arrival are: California—Deep Springs, September 20. Arizona—Hualpai Mountains, September 27. New Mexico—Manzano Mountains, October 8. Oklahoma—Cimarron County, October 20. Texas—El Paso, September 13.

Late dates of fall departure are: Wyoming—Laramie, November 7 (average of 6 years, October 13). Utah—Roundy Reservoir, October 25.

*Egg dates.*—Colorado: 45 records, May 8 to July 18; 24 records, June 16 to July 4.

New Mexico: 3 records, July 15 to August 7.

Utah: 5 records, June 18 to July 19.

### Red-backed Gray-headed Junco (*J. c. dorsalis*)

*Range.*—Arizona, New Mexico, and western Texas.

*Breeding range.*—The red-backed gray-headed junco breeds from north central Arizona (south rim of the Grand Canyon) and central New Mexico (Magdalena Mountains) south to east central Arizona (Sierra Ancha, Hannagan Meadow), southern New Mexico (head of Mimbres River, Guadalupe Mountains), and extreme western Texas (Guadalupe Mountains).

*Winter range.*—Winters on or near the breeding grounds (north to the Grand Canyon), south in small numbers to southern Arizona (Pajaritos, Huachuca, and Chiricahua Mountains), extreme southwestern New Mexico (Big Hatchet Mountains), and southwestern Texas (Chisos Mountains).

*Egg dates.*—New Mexico: 3 records, July 15 to August 7.

JUNCO PHAEONOTUS PALLIATUS Ridgway

# Mexican (Yellow-eyed) Junco

PLATE 61

Contributed by OLIVER L. AUSTIN, JR.

## HABITS

This resident of the high montane conifer and pine-oak forests from southern Arizona and New Mexico southward through central Mexico to the Guatemalan border is one of the most distinctive and geographically isolated members of the puzzling junco complex. With its red-brown back and gray head and body, it most closely resembles the southern race of the gray-headed junco, *dorsalis*, from which it differs principally in its bright yellow eye. According to Miller (1941b):

It occurs in the pine association, Transition Zone, * * * usually above 7,000 feet, but occasionally as low as 6,000 feet. There is a winter record at 4,000 feet, below the pine belt, for the Santa Catalina Mountains of Arizona. The pine association may have a considerable mixture of deciduous oak. Prominent forest associates are *Pinus ponderosa* var., *Pinus chihuahuana, Pseudotsuga taxifolia,* and *Abies religiosa.* The forest floor which the junco occupies, though perhaps more arid on the average than that in the range of *dorsalis,* usually consists of pine needles and oak leaves, with some green bushes such as *Symphoricarpos, Garrya, Rhus, Ceanothus,* and brake ferns.

Though the species is mainly resident and nonmigratory, Phillips, Marshall, and Monson (1964) note: "Yellow-eyed Juncos descend below the forest at times, especially in severe weather, and have been noted there from *September 18* * * * to May 15 * * *."

*Courtship.*—The literature contains very little about courtship and territoriality in this species, other than H. S. Swarth's (1904) statement: "They begin to pair off about the first week of April * * *. In the spring the male bird frequently ascends high in the tree tops, and sits there motionless, uttering his short song at frequent intervals; and two or more may often be seen pursuing one another through the trees, seldom descending to the ground at such times." More details are available in the manuscript notes of James Veghte, who studied this junco in the Chiricahua region of Arizona under the guidance of Alfred O. Gross in 1948. Veghte writes:

"The courtship of the Arizona junco takes place in the middle or latter part of April. During this period the male abandons his terrestrial environment for the arboreal and sings his short song from the tree tops. I watched one male junco singing for 15 minutes in a large yellow pine at least 60 feet above the ground. These songs apparently play a prominent part in the courtship ritual.

"In a typical mating display, while a pair of juncos were feeding, the male flared out his tail and strutted around the female, alternately dragging his tail feathers on the ground and holding them upright from his body at a 45° angle. I watched one male strut with spread tail up and down the horizontal limb of a white pine, some 8 feet above the female who was feeding below. As he strutted he uttered a curious variation of the spring song.

"Fighting that appeared to be linked with courtship was observed rather frequently. Once when a pair of juncos was calmly feeding together, the male, on the ground, alternately feeding and singing to the female, another male lit near by for a moment and then dove at the male. The first male flew at the intruder, and both dropped to the ground fighting savagely with feet and bills. Breaking apart for a few seconds they faced each other defiantly with tails flared and mouths agape. Joining in combat again they rose above the ground in a miniature whirlwind of feathers while the female watched. Finally the two males flew wildly off through the trees with the female following. I saw this happen some five different times while we were in the Chiricahua region."

Herbert Brandt (1951) describes the same behavior thus:

In spite of its delicate dress and quiet manner, this junco is a tenacious fighter, settling its territorial disputes by locking bills with an opponent, rolling over and over on the pine needles, with short pauses between so that both birds may regain their breath. In one conflict behind our cabin, four juncos, probably two pairs, were seen on the ground; suddenly two birds flew at each other, and seizing hold, rolled about, with first one then the other on its back, the paler underpart being noticeably displayed. Finally a third bird, probably one of the females, flew in on them as though to separate the disputants; then shortly, as if nothing had happened, they all resumed walking about in their peculiar stride.

*Nesting.*—Almost all observers comment on the difficulty of finding this junco's nest, which is usually revealed only by flushing the sitting bird from it. As Brandt (1951) puts it, "to go into the field and deliberately try to find a junco's nest by systematic search is about as difficult a task as one would care to undertake, because the cradle is usually so well concealed that only by good fortune would the seeker be accidentally successful."

Swarth (1904) states: "The nest is usually built upon the ground, under a bunch of grass, a log, or as I have occasionally found it, under a flat stone; but this is not invariably the case, as I have known one or two instances of its being placed in some thick shrubbery, a drooping pine limb, or a young fir, a foot or two above the ground."

F. C. Willard (1923) comments:

Another bird which likes good solid ground under its nest is the Arizona Junco * * * , yet I once found a set of incubated eggs fifteen feet up in a hole in a dead pine branch * * * . A still more surprising find was a nest of one

PLATE 61

Arizona                                    F. E. Willard
NEST AND EGGS OF MEXICAN YELLOW-EYED JUNCO

Chiricahua Mountains, Ariz., May 1947              R. T. Peterson
MEXICAN YELLOW-EYED JUNCOS WITH YOUNG

PLATE 62

Bethel, Johnson River, Alaska, June 17, 1946                    L. H. Walkinshaw
WESTERN TREE SPARROW AT NEST

Churchill, Manitoba, July 8, 1933                    M. C. Baumgartner
JUVENILE TREE SPARROW LEAVING NEST

of these juncos nine feet up in a small oak tree alongside a well-used trail. The nest was placed on a small branch and against the trunk. The bird flushed as I passed. During the years from 1910 to 1916 a pair also built in a small Spanish bayonet which grew beside a trail at Berner's in Ramsay Canyon of the Huachuca Mountains. When cats were introduced at this place, they made short work of this pair.

Veghte (MS.) writes: "The four nests I located were all on the ground; one was cleverly hidden under a small log, another was partially concealed by a stone, a third was beneath a large piece of yellow pine bark, the fourth hidden under several grass clumps. The nest is built entirely by the female. I saw one male bird pick up a few pine needles and fly toward the nest, but he dropped them before reaching it.

"The first stage in nest building is hollowing and shaping the bowl. The female scratches the ground with her feet and bill and carries the undesired dirt away from the immediate nest site in the bill. She then shapes the hollow with her body to the proper size and shape before she starts to line it. These preliminary operations may extend over 2 or 3 days. Building the nest itself may take another 5 or 6 days. The outer cup is generally made of coarse grass stems intermixed with a few strands of moss. This, in turn, is covered with finer grasses. The final inner cup is a lining of soft deer hair. A few horse hairs and a bit of gray fur were in one nest. The average outside diameter of the bowl is 6⅛ inches, bowl depth averages 1 to 1⅜ inches, and the nest cup diameter is 4⅛ inches. After the nest is completed, 2 or 3 days usually elapse before the first egg is laid."

*Eggs.*—The Mexican junco lays three or four, and sometimes five eggs. They are ovate and slightly glossy. The ground is grayish-white, or very pale bluish-white with spots and specklings of yellow-browns such as "sayal brown," "pecan brown," and "buffy brown," with undermarkings of "pale mouse gray." The spottings may be scattered over the entire egg, but more frequently are concentrated toward the large end where they commonly form a wreath. The markings may be either dark and sharply defined or dull and somewhat blurred. The eggs of this species are indistinguishable from those of *Junco caniceps*. The measurements of 65 eggs average 19.9 by 15.1 millimeters; the eggs showing the four extremes measure *22.1* by 15.0, 19.5 by *15.3*, *18.3* by 14.6, and 20.5 by *14.2* millimeters.

*Young.*—Veghte (MS.) notes: "Incubation lasted 15 days at one nest I watched and was by the female alone. Although the male takes no part in incubating, he joins the female in the burden of feeding the young as soon as they hatch.

"At hatching the young have gray down on their capital tract and on part of the spinal tract on the lower part of the back, also smaller amounts of down on the lower portion of the ventral tract and on the humeral, alar, and crural tracts. The down disappears rapidly after the 2nd day, and on the 4th day the first feather sheaths of the juvenal plumage are visible on the dorsal region, with the primary sheaths showing the most growth.

"The eyes do not open until the 3rd day, and do not seem to be really functional until the 4th or 5th day. The irises of the juvenals remained a dark brown as long as I was able to observe them.

"By the 6th day the tips of the feather sheaths break and the feathers begin to appear. The nestlings feather out rapidly during the next 2 days. On the 10th day they begin to leave the nest. At this time they are unable to fly and barely able to flutter about. When I approached, the female gave an alarm call that attracted the male; then she hopped a few inches from the young with food in her bill and as the fledgling fluttered toward her, she hopped backward to lead it away from me."

*Plumages.*—R. R. Graber (1955) describes the juvenal plumage of *Junco phaeonotus phaeonotus*, which differs from that of *J. p. palliatus* only in being slightly darker throughout the upperparts, as follows:

"Forehead, crown, and nape gray, finely streaked with black. Back rusty red, streaked with black. Scapulars gray or buffy gray, streaked with black. Rump and upper tail coverts buffy gray, obscurely streaked with dark. Rectrices black, except outer two pairs largely white. Remiges black; primaries edged with white, tertials broadly edged with burnt sienna (rusty red). Lesser and median coverts gray, narrowly edged with buff. Greater coverts edged with chestnut, tipped with buff (narrowly). No wing bar pattern. Lores black. Black feathers nearly circumscribe eye (in a patch). Auriculars gray, obscurely streaked with dark. Chin and throat white flecked with black (especially on sides). Chest, sides, and flanks streaked with black (triangular marks pointing anteriorly). Underparts largely white, sides and flanks tinged with buffy. Belly and crissum largely unmarked. Leg feathers gray, edged white."

Graber comments that the tertial edgings are much more rusty red than in *J. caniceps dorsalis*, which has the tertials edged gray.

Swarth (1904) states:

About the middle of June the young birds in the spotted plumage begin to appear, and all through July they are quite numerous, often two or more broods running together, accompanied by the various parents. The young birds are at this time heavily streaked above and below, though less on the throat and adbomen than elsewhere * * * and, as the soft juvenile plumage wears away very rapidly, those birds which have nearly attained their full size have these markings much more faintly indicated than those which have just left the nest. * * * As the bird becomes older the iris gets paler, changing from brown to whitish, then to pale yellow, and finally, about the time the juvenile plumage is shed, to the bright yellow of the adult bird. * * * The juvenile plumage is shed in August, at the same time that the adults are undergoing their post-nuptial moult; specimens secured on September 2 being hardly distinguishable from adults, and with but a few faint spots remaining on the breast, sides of the head, and scapulars. The scapulars seem to retain the juvenile markings the longest * * *. An adult male taken September 2, has not quite completed the moult, some of the rectrices having not yet acquired their growth; and is practically indistinguishable from specimens taken in February, the principal difference being in the softer more blended appearance of the plumage.

*Food.*—According to J. T. Marshall (1957):

This junco feeds on the ground on seeds, other vegetable matter, and insects (seven stomachs, insects in summer-taken specimens only). Quantities of gravel also are ingested. A few instances were recorded of feeding above ground: in foliage of *Holodiscus* thickets; in foliage of Douglas firs; a family reaching from the ground to pluck flowers and pendant fruits from a small milkweed; one bird climbing into twigs of an oak and reaching up to pick something off the trunk bark; another bird climbing up a tall grass stem until the stem bent over. This last bird was later seen chewing a portion of the flower of this grass. On the ground these yellow-eyed juncos shuffle, the feet moving alternately, over the leaves, as they pick up food. They also run with long true hops after moving insects, which they catch, pound, and swallow,

Mexican Juncos can scratch their way down through thick leaf litter under bushes; they also scratch to find seeds in gravel and among pine needles. It looks as though each scratch is initiated by rocking forward to take the weight off the feet, with the head up while the feet are advanced. Then the feet are simultaneously scraped backward, kicking out gravel and catching the body again as the head end tilts down—a convenient position for picking up the seed. The feet are far apart and kept close to the surface of the ground.

The Mexican Junco is a resident of numerous Forest Service picnic grounds in pine-oak of the Arizona mountains, where it becomes very tame, taking crumbs from the table and feeding its young in camp. At one camp a junco repeatedly picked up and chewed the edge of a large piece of newspaper. Apparently food or salt was smeared on the paper.

*Voice.*—An early reference to this is W. E. D. Scott's (1885b) observation that "The male has an exceedingly pleasant song, not unlike that of *Pipilo maculatus megalonyx,* which bird he also emulates, perching on some prominent dead twig or limb, often at a very considerable height, whence his notes are heard perhaps most frequently just after sunrise." A recent summary is in Phillips et al. (1964): "Its varied song is usually in three parts of contrasting pitch and rhythm. Each male has several song patterns in his repertoire, but the observer soon learns to recognize them all as belonging to this species by their sweet, thin quality suggestive of a wood warbler." Miller (1955a) notes of this subspecies: "The birds were usually detected by their weak alarm note which is softer and less blunt than in northern species of the genus. Also the songs were typical of *phaeonotus,* never consisting of a simple trill but of a multiple trill usually of two or three segments of different pitch and rhythm." Brandt (1951) comments: "Generally the Arizona Junco is not in the least noisy, as its song is of such a high pitch that the faint trill can be detected only by a trained, keen ear.  In spite of the lack of volume, in April and May the bird pours forth its tiny heart many times during the day, with a vigor that belies its weak accomplishment." R. T. Peterson (1961) says the song is "musical, unjuncolike, more complicated; 3-parted, often thus: *chip chip chip, wheedle wheedle, che che che che che.*"

Veghte (MS.) writes: "When I first heard the song of this bird it instantly reminded me of the chipping sparrow's trill.  Shortly I had the good fortune to hear both these birds singing simultaneously, and the chipping sparrow's was sharper, clearer, more pronounced, while the junco's trill was lower pitched, not too loud, and had a rather ventriloquial quality. The song most frequently heard I transcribed in my notes as *kwill-ill-ill-ill-ill*, the notes blending together in a continuous trill.  A variation started with two lower, slower notes, *chwal-twill-ill-ill-ill*, with the accent on the *wal*.  Another, heard most often in the evening, was a soft, liquid *chwee-kee-kee-kee-kee-verit*, the notes going up and down the scale.  Three times during my stay I heard a curious finch-like song uttered by the male when he chased the female.  The alarm note was a sharp *chip* or a softer *tip* or *tsspt* either given singly or repeated."

*Behavior.*—Brandt (1951) characterizes the bird as one of "a quiet, unobtrusive demeanor * * * a bird of smooth, slow movement, little given to attracting attention * * * [which] differs from the more northern birds of its family also in that it usually walks with deliberation, rather than hops.  Its motion on the ground reminds one of the Ovenbird, for it moves about leisurely, never appearing to be in a hurry.  It is in the Arizona highlands the most confiding bird towards man, thus an enjoyable attraction at nearly every camp and cabin in its coniferous habitat."

Phillips et al. (1964) describe the gait as "a peculiar shuffle, between a hop and a walk," which Miller (1955a) also notes as distinctive and characteristic of the species.

Marshall (1957) states: "I was astonished to see three birds feeding in the water at Rucker Creek.  They picked up small light-colored objects (pollen or seeds) which were either floating in the slowly moving shallow water or were stuck against rocks at the waterline.  The birds jumped in and fed while standing in water covering the feet or which reached the belly; then they would hop or fly out again. Also they shuffled along the rocks that stuck out of the water, reached to the surface to pick up objects, and made prodigious leaps from one rock to another, sometimes aided by the wings."

*Winter.*—As noted above, the species is resident throughout its range, but occasionally moves vertically to below the forests during periods of severe weather. Phillip set al. (1964) note that when they do so "The birds do not join their dark-eyed cousins, but stay to themselves, in groups not exceeding family size."

## DISTRIBUTION

*Range.*—The Mexican junco is resident in the mountains from southeastern Arizona (Pinal Mountain, Santa Catalina and Graham mountains) and extreme southwestern New Mexico (Animas and Big Hatchet mountains) south through northeastern Sonora (San José Mountains), Chihuahua, and Coahuila (Sierra del Carmen, Sierra Encarnación) to southern Durango (El Salto).

*Egg dates.*—Arizona: 41 records, April 18 to August 1; 20 records, June 2 to June 14.

New Mexico: 3 records, May 3 to June 1.

## JUNCO BAIRDI Ridgway

# Baird's Junco
### Contributed by RICHARD C. BANKS

## HABITS

This species was described by Robert Ridgway (1883b; *see* Deignan, 1961) on the basis of two specimens taken in the Laguna Mountains of Baja California by Lyman Belding. A short while after the original description, two additional specimens were obtained and described by Belding (1883b). Further work showed that Baird's junco lives throughout the mountains of the Cape region of Baja California. It has never been found elsewhere.

This is one of the yellow-eyed group of juncos, most closely related to the juncos of Mexico and Central America (Miller, 1941b). In some of its characteristics it is similar to *J. alticola* of Chiapas and Guatemala, in some to *J. fulvescens* of Chiapas, and in some to *J. phaeonotus*, which ranges broadly through Mexico to the east of the range of *bairdi* (Miller, 1941b; Davis, 1959). A. H. Miller (1941b) notes that "It possesses several peculiarities of color and proportion that sharply set it off from all others, yet, speaking broadly, it is a pale, dwarfed representative of the Central American juncos."

Miller's (1914b) study of the genus *Junco* led him to conclude that the progenitors of *J. bairdi* had colonized the isolated mountains of the Cape region by direct flight from the east or south, in times earlier than Pleistocene. John Davis (1959) considered Baird's junco to be one of a number of species that originated in the Madro-Tertiary flora of Mexico and followed this flora into the Cape region, where later climatic changes left it isolated. In isolation it retained a number of features which characterized the original pioneering population.

Relatively few ornithologists have seen Baird's junco in its natural habitat, and even fewer have written about it. Much of the information in this report is taken from unpublished field notes of Chester C. Lamb, who collected in the mountains of the Cape region of Baja California in the winter of 1928 and the summer of 1929.

*Description.*—Back and scapulars cinnamon brown, becoming buffy brown on rump. Sides cinnamon, the color extending onto the breast and sometimes meeting in a band across the breast. The cinnamon fades with wear, becoming more yellowish. Lores blackish. Top and sides of head and hindneck uniform light gray, the nape often tinged with buff, at least in unworn plumage. Throat and upper breast pale mouse gray, lower breast, abdomen and under tail coverts white. Tail with outer two feathers partly, the outer often completely white, the third sometimes with a white spot. Iris yellow; lower mandible yellow, upper mandible brown. Wing and tail short, bill and feet moderately large, proportionately.

Sexual dimorphism is limited to size and tail pattern, the female being slightly smaller and averaging somewhat less white in the tail (Miller, 1941b; Ridgway, 1901.)

In juvenal plumage this is the least heavily streaked junco (R. R. Graber, 1955).

*Habitat.*—Nelson (1921) characterized this bird as an inhabitant of the Upper Sonoran Life Zone of the Cape region of Baja California. According to Miller (1941b), it is one of the few juncos that breed under zonal conditions lower than Transition. Frazer found it inhabiting the pine and oak woods (Brewster, 1902). Miller (1941b) amplified the description of the habitat: "The region inhabitated is forested predominantly with oak (*Quercus devia*), also with piñon (*Pinus cembroides*) and madroño (*Arbutus penninsularis*), and with cottonwoods (*Populus monticola*) in the canyons." He further states that "The nature of the region compares most closely * * * with the Upper Sonoran oak belt of Arizona * * *."

Belding (1883) found this species very common over 3,000 feet elevation, and Miller (1941b) reports that most specimens have been taken above 4,000 feet. Only a single bird has been taken as low as 1,800 feet, at El Triunfo (Brewster, 1902).

*Habits.*—Belding (1883), when reporting the capture of the third and fourth specimens of this bird, said that "Nothing worthy of note in connection with its habits was noticed." Brewster reported (1902) that like most juncos they were tame and familiar, and that "they often came into a shed where Mr. Frazer prepared his specimens, and hopped about his feet, under the table, or pecked at the dried venison suspended from the roof."

These juncos apparently stay close to the ground, often taking advantage of the lower, bare limbs of pines or oaks for perches. Chester Lamb's observations were consistently of birds "feeding on the ground," "perched on a low bare twig in an oak seedling," or "on an old stump among some brush." They readily responded to "squeaking." After a day of intermittent showers in early August, Lamb wrote: "During these rains all the birds but the Baird juncos and large-billed towhees [*Pipilo erythrophthalmus magnirostris*] disappear, but these birds can be seen at the edge of the meadows busily feeding during most of the storms." In mid-December, after noting observations of birds apparently singly rather than in flocks, he summarized that they were "common, but very shy and retiring at this time of year."

On May 22, 1965, seven juncos were foraging together in a space about 30 by 30 feet in the meadow, near a small group of pines. There was one encounter which seemed to enforce individual distance. When disturbed by my approach, they flew to a small pine where, after some initial squabbles in finding places, they remained quietly together. Despite the tendency for gregariousness, there were numerous chases during May that seemed to enforce territorial boundaries. One bird was involved in two such chases within a few minutes, about 40 yards apart.

On one occasion, a bird sitting in an oak flicked its wings rapidly when alarmed.

Baird's juncos remain in winter in the highest part of their breeding range. "Apparently there are no winter flocks of any proportion, the birds staying close to the nesting grounds * * *." (Miller, 1941b.) No seasonal movements are known.

*Nesting.*—Nesting apparently occurs in late spring and early summer. Brewster (1902) says that Frazer found no nests in the Sierra Laguna during his stay from late April to early June, but "late in May a bird was seen collecting building material." At Laguna Valley, at 6,000 feet elevation, Chester Lamb found nests in many stages during July, 1929, and was led to believe that the birds nest twice. On July 7, 12, and 15, he found nests with "heavily incubated" eggs, and on July 8 he "saw one carrying nesting material in its bill." Thayer (1909) mentions that W. W. Brown was too late for eggs of this species when he reached the mountains on August 2. Dependent young have been recorded from June 12 to July 17 (Miller et al., 1957), but the dependent period must extend into early August.

In contrast to this previously available information, which suggests a nesting season from late May through July, we found well-grown, but still dependent, young as early as May 20, which indicates that some birds, at least, start breeding early in May. Despite the fact that we saw young frequently, we were unable to find any nests.

Nests of Baird's juncos are either on the ground or in low trees. Of eight nests mentioned in Lamb's notes or collected by him, two he described as being "located in [the] leafy extremity of a branch 6 feet up in a small pine," and one was "6 feet up, against the trunk in a small pinyon pine." Two nests were hidden in depressions in the ground; one was "under a small stick" and the other "in a hole in the ground 3 inches back from [the] entrance." Another nest was "placed on the ground among some low flowering weeds." Two nests were "made of fine weeds and grasses, lined inside with horse hair."

*Eggs.*—Each of the nests Chester Lamb found in 1929 contained two eggs, and this apparently is the normal complete set. The eggs are whitish with small flecks of dark reddish-brown, most heavily spotted on the large end.

*Food.*—In May 1965, most foraging was observed on the ground, among dry leaves and weeds, but one bird was seen feeding on the terminal ends of oak limbs about 20 feet above the ground. One bird tried twice, unsuccessfully, to catch an insect (fly?) that was slowly flying about 4 inches above the ground.

*Voice.*—The song is described in my notes both as warbler-like and as reminiscent of that of the black-throated sparrow. It is a complex song, and is quite variable. It seemed that the song of every bird was different, and it is possible that individual birds sang more than one song, but that point was not determined.

*Weights.*—Weights of two adult males were 17.8 and 16.7 grams; an adult female weighed 16.7 grams.

*Enemies.*—Baird's juncos are undoubtedly exposed to all the hazards that beset other ground nesting birds. The only record of predation, however, is in Chester Lamb's notes for July 17, 1929: "Early this morning in the meadow [I] saw a large wild cat [*Lynx rufus peninsularis*]. It had just despoiled a ground nest of a Baird junco."

### DISTRIBUTION

*Range.*—Baird's junco is resident in the Victoria Mountains (La Laguna, Mount Miraflores) of the Cape district of Baja California; casual downslope to Triunfo.

SPIZELLA ARBOREA (Wilson)

# Tree Sparrow*

PLATE 62

## Contributed by A. MARGUERITE BAUMGARTNER

### HABITS

To anyone who has tramped our snowy fields and brushy hedgerows in winter, the little tree sparrow is a familiar and beloved bird. One of the most abundant winter residents over much of the northern and central United States, its gentle confiding ways and cheerful warblings have ever endeared it to those who go afield with binoculars or who feed the winter birds about their gardens. Easily identified by its pert chestnut cap, clear gray breast with a single black "brooch," white wingbars, and a bill dark above and yellow below, the tree sparrow is most frequently confused with its relatives, the somewhat similar but smaller chipping and field sparrows.

Two geographic races are now recognized, the nominate eastern *Spizella arborea arborea* and the western form, *S. a. ochracea*, with a wide belt of intergradation between them through the Prairie Provinces and the Plains States. With no perceptible differences in measurements or in the juvenal plumage, typical *ochracea* differs from the eastern race primarily in degree of color, having a slightly paler back, a richer wash of ochraceous buff on the sides, and a heavier veiling of buff on the crown. Although the line of demarcation between the two falls in mid-continent in winter, during the breeding season the eastern race sweeps far westward. It nests from the Atlantic coast to Anderson Valley, almost to the boundary of the Yukon Territory (Preble, 1908), while *ochracea* breeds across northern MacKenzie and the Yukon, throughout Alaska as far north as there is any scrubby growth, and down the mountain ranges of British Columbia in the sparse forests just below timberline.

The tree sparrow is another example of a misnomer by our pioneer forefathers, for few birds spend less time in trees, either in winter or summer. The early settlers saw in it a superficial resemblance to the chestnut-capped tree sparrow (*Passer montanus*) of Europe and, either in ignorance of specific differences or in nostalgic recollecton, called this little American sparrow by the same name. Actually our tree sparrow might more accurately be called brush sparrow, for its haunts include the scrubby edges of our fields and marshes, hedgerows, and fallow fields. In summer it travels far beyond the dense Canadian woodlands to the lake-dotted open forests of the

---

*The following subspecies are discussed in these sections: *Spizella arborea* arborea (Wilson) and *S. a. ochracea* Brewster.

upper Hudsonian Zone. Though it nests occasionally in the dense, stunted spruces characteristic of this region, it spends most of its time in the brushy willows and birches that fringe the pools and boggy meadows, and the overwhelming majority of nests on record have been on the ground.

An analysis of hundreds of faunal works, local lists, Christmas censuses, and field notes, shows the center of abundance of tree sparrows in a normal winter to be through central Nebraska, Kansas, Iowa, and Missouri, and across the corn belt to the middle Atlantic States (Baumgartner, 1939). An abnormally mild season finds a greater number wintering in the northern states and southern Canada, while early storms and excessive snows drive them farther south. In Oklahoma, near the southern border of their regular range, I have found their occurrence as variable as Oklahoma weather. In Tennessee, where they occur only rarely, they are generally associated with low temperatures and a blanket of snow (Laskey, 1934b).

*Winter distribution of sexes.*—In the course of two seasons of collecting at Ithaca, N.Y., it was discovered that the proportion of males ran considerably higher than females during the nonmigratory period, which I arbitrarily limited to the dates December 20 to March 1. In fall and spring the female population equaled or exceeded that of males. Postulating that this indicated segregation of the sexes during the winter, I wrote all the leading museums in the country for lists of their tree sparrow specimens, in the hope of plotting the respective ranges. While many did not have numbers adequate for any conclusions, the larger series corroborated the figures from my personal collecting and banding (indicated in the following list by *), showing that males tend to winter farther northward and females farther southward:

| Part of Range of Species | Locality | Number of Winter | |
|---|---|---|---|
| | | Males | Females |
| Northern | Ontario | 16 | 0 |
| | British Columbia | 11 | 2 |
| | Idaho | 16 | 9 |
| | Michigan | 28 | 5 |
| | *New York (1933–35) | 102 | 31 |
| | Connecticut | 21 | 1 |
| Central | *Indiana (1935) | 16 | 22 |
| | Pennsylvania | 26 | 27 |
| | District of Columbia | 17 | 17 |
| | Kansas | 185 | 158 |
| Southern | *Oklahoma (1940–41) | 31 | 78 |
| | *Oklahoma (1960) | 40 | 113 |

During late February and March of 1960 Oklahoma had a period of severe cold and heavy snows which brought in an unprecedented number of tree sparrows. During a single month I handled almost 200, most of which repeated several times a day. When my hands were not too numb nor my glasses fogged, I noted external sex characteristics (*see* Plumages), and recorded a tentative sex identification. While some were not differentiated sharply enough even to hazard a guess, I have 113 cards marked as unquestionably female with narrow crowns heavily streaked with dark shafts, and 40 possibly immature males or adult females, the group most difficult to sex by external criteria. Of the 168 tree sparrows I banded between 1948 and 1959, I designated 110 as females, the rest an indetermined proportion of adult females and males.

*Migration.*—Between the winter range and the breeding grounds of the tree sparrow stretch almost 1,000 miles of territory in which the species occurs only as a migrant. Alaskan birds must travel some 3,000 miles to reach their destination, but most of the birds that winter through central United States may be assumed to journey between 1,500 and 2,000 miles to nest.

In Oklahoma, in the southern part of their range, the first evidence of spring movement comes in late February, and the majority are normally gone by mid-March. Following the severe storms of March 1960, new birds continued to visit my banding station at Stillwater until March 26, and a dozen or more individuals remained until April 5.

In the Mississippi Valley, Cooke (1888) found the crest of the migration to pass between March 30 and April 8. Eaton (1910) lists migration in New York State chiefly through late March and the first three weeks of April; the latest is May 15 at Ithaca (Edminster, MS.). Traveling primarily by night, flocks of five or ten or hundreds arrive in waves, remain a few days or weeks, and drift away a few at a time.

The sequence of migrants and winter residents as presented by W. P. Smith (1926), Horsey (1926), and Austin (1932b), agrees substantially with the movements observed at Ithaca, N.Y. Five years of records from Dr. A. C. Frazer's station and a check group of 54 regular winter residents at my own traps showed parallel behavior: A sprinkling of the winter residents (birds banded between December 20 and March 1) disappeared during mid-February, which probably represents local wandering rather than true migration. During the third week of February a number of new birds were banded and a few more winter residents drifted away, consistently enough at both stations to suggest the vanguard of true migration. March saw a steady increase in migrants and departure dates of winter residents, with a pronounced crest the 4th week. Smaller crests occurred in mid-April for migrants, while the number of winter residents decreased steadily through the month. Interestingly, the last birds to leave on May 1 were on of my winter "standbys" and a winter resident from the Frazer station.

The proportion of the sexes during spring migration indicates that these birds do not travel as mated pairs. In late February at the end of the winter period, males constituted 90 percent of the birds collected from a flock near Ithaca. Thereafter the percentage of females increased steadily until it equaled the males in late March, the crest period for departing winter residents and incoming migrants. During the mid-April crest, proportions were nearly equal again with 45 percent male birds, many of which upon dissection showed evidence of immaturity. On April 26 the last collection netted 86 percent females and a sprinkling of small males, presumably first year birds (Heydweiller, 1936).

*Nesting.*—At the beginning of my graduate study on the life history of the tree sparrow, I wrote hopefully to Mr. Bent for any available information on the nesting habits of this species. He replied that there was little beyond locality records and descriptions of nests and eggs, adding tersely, "It is regrettable that you did not select a bird you could study in the field yourself." The following account is the outcome of that brief comment (Baumgartner, 1937b):

In the wet, brushy wastes of the Canadian Northland, beyond arable land or usable timber, from the northern third of the Hudsonian spruce timber as far north as there is any scrubby growth, the tree sparrows find optimum conditions for nesting and for rearing their young. Churchill, Manitoba, at latitude 58° N. halfway up the west coast of Hudson Bay and 5 miles beyond timberline, proved an ideal locality to study the nesting habits of this species. Connected by rail with the outside world in 1929, it was then the only spot that could be reached early enough in the season to trace the complete nesting cycle without spending a winter in the North. The embryo town was hospitable, and the nearby river flat, a bouldery, hummocky, pool-dotted stretch of tundra extending back to timberline, was interspersed with patches of scrub birch and willow, a maximum of 4 or 5 feet high, in which tree sparrows were one of the most abundant species.

During 5 months spent on the nesting grounds—throughout June and July in 1933 and from June 4 to August 21 in 1934—I found a total of 26 nests, 9 of which were kept under constant observation from the time of their discovery. While the birds were common, their nests, usually hidden in the densest tangles of the scrubby thickets, were difficult to find. The nests studied, however, showed such uniformity that I was satisfied they were both normal and typical for the species.

In 1946 Walkinshaw (1948) gathered nesting data on the western tree sparrow in western Alaska. His observations and data are remarkably consistent with my Churchill records and corroborate the close relationship of the two forms.

According to Taverner and Sutton (1934) the tree sparrow spends about four months at Churchill, arriving about May 25, and is seen last on September 29. The occasional few of the first two days (Sutton's field notes) were followed almost immediately by enormous numbers of both sexes, scattered (none in flocks) through the stunted willows of the river flats. In Alaska, Nelson (1887) likewise noted that flocks were broken up when they reached the breeding grounds and that the birds were mated soon after.

When I arrived at Churchill in early June, the tree sparrows were already established on their territories and had begun nest building. The successive stages of the reproductive cycle and their inclusive dates at three typical nests were:

*Dates of Period*

| Activity * | Nest I | Nest III | Nest IX | Average Length of Period |
|---|---|---|---|---|
| Nest building | Completed June 5 | Completed June 13 | | 7 days (at nest II) |
| Resting | 5 days | 2 days | | 2 to 3 days |
| Laying | June 11 to 16 (5 eggs) | June 16 to 21 (6 eggs) | June 25 to 28 (4 eggs) | 4 to 6 days, usually 1 egg each day |
| Incubating | June 16 to 28 | June 20 to July 3 | June 27 to July 10 | 12 to 13 days |
| Hatching | 1 at 4 p.m., June 28; 3 by 7 a.m. June 29 | 3 by 10 a.m., 2 by 2 p.m. July 3 | 1 at 9 a.m., 1 at 8 p.m. July 9, 1 by noon July 10 | all within 7 to 30 hours |
| Young leaving nest | last left at noon July 8 | 3 on July 11 (disturbed), 2 on July 13 | only 1 left, on July 18 | 9 to 9¾ days (8 days if disturbed) |
| Parents feeding fledglings | Until first week of August (a few to August 19) | | | 2 weeks |
| Molting | Throughout August by both adults and young | | | 3 weeks |
| Fall flocking | First seen August 17 and 19 | | | 1 month |

(*At Churchill, Manitoba; nest dates in 1933, August data in 1934.)

In the short northern summer it is highly unlikely that more than one brood is reared each year. As the earliest young at Churchill left the nest on July 8 and both parents continued to feed them for another two weeks or more, a second brood could not have been started before July 22. As it takes some 70 days after egg-laying to bring young through the postjuvenal molt, such a late brood could hardly be ready to migrate by September 29, the latest record for the species' occurrence there.

Song is the tree sparrow's chief asset in courtship display, for the species is plain colored and the sexes are alike. In courting either sex may be the aggressor, pursuing the other and flaunting its humble beauties. Of one pair observed for some time and finally collected, the pursued bird proved to be the male. One nest-building female approaching her nest with a ptarmigan feather was filled with a sudden excitement when her mate came to sing nearby. She dropped the feather, hopped to a twig about a foot from the ground, spread and fluttered her wings, and uttered an alluring "*wehy-wehy-wehy-wehy.*" The male sang on indifferently, and she picked up her feather and went onto the nest.

In another case the female fed quietly on the ground while her suitor, sitting on the bush above her, uttered a rapid series of stacatto chips, puffed his plumage, spread his wings, and then darted to the ground with much fluttering. In acknowledgment she preened daintily, fluttered her wings with neck much extended, and murmured the soft "wehy" notes which brought him to her. Fluttering over her for an instant, he copulated and darted back to his perch. He repeated the procedure several times in the next two minutes. There was no singing at this time. Sometimes copulation took place without display of any kind, the male simply flying to his mate while she was feeding or at the nest. The nest I pair were seen to copulate at the nest on three occasions, once during its building, twice within half an hour the day before the laying of the second egg.

The extent of the tree sparrow's summer territory proved to be considerably smaller than the winter feeding range, as anticipated. Two nesting areas were studied in detail: a stretch of open tundra bordered on one side by a small patch of brush, near which was a single nest (nest I): and a tangled thicket of low willows and birches, extending some 300 by 800 feet along the river flats, within whose confines dwelt four families in 1933 (nests III–VI) and three in 1934 (nests C, D, E).

Though I marked no adults the first season for fear of upsetting their natural behavior patterns, I could tell the males apart by their song patterns, and the females by watching them as they left the nest. In 1934 I decorated a few adults with gay chicken feathers to corroborate the first year's observations. Young birds were banded, but the tailless, soft juvenal plumage would not hold additional feathers (Heydweiller, 1935).

The size of individual territories was found to vary with the season and the location. During the first week in June, when birds were engaged chiefly in feeding together, courting, and preliminary building, territories were large and poorly defined. One male, feeding with his mate at a little pool, made vicious attacks upon a third bird and pursued it 400 to 500 feet before circling back. Then abruptly the pair flew ¼ mile downstream and disappeared in the brush.

With the onset of incubation, areas became more limited. Isolated nest I was surrounded by a territory some 600 by 700 feet in diameter, and both birds frequently fed and later obtained food for their young at a drainage ditch 450 feet from the nest. In the more congested thicket occupied by nests III–VI, the song perches of the various males encompassed territories only 200 to 300 feet in diameter. Occasional overlaps occurred without friction, provided the other male was singing at the opposite side of his territory; and in spite of close quarters very little fighting was observed.

While the young were in the nest, both parents foraged in the thick tangle of low leafy branches of the tiny birches and willows, frequently only 10 or 15 feet from their charges. Throughout the latter part of July 1934, the gay plumes with which the adults were marked waved from the same tiny territories while the fledglings scuttled among the underbrush.

During early August, when the young were fully fledged and able to feed themselves, the three 1934 broods in this area ranged freely throughout the 300- by 500-foot patch of thicket, though they still maintained family unity. Not until the 19th of August did they emerge from the thick cover and merge with the flocks that were gathering in the grasses and moss of the river flats.

The main defense of territory against invasion is song, strengthened by an occasional brisk assault upon an intruder. While this is usually by the male, his mate occasionally assumes the offensive. At nest I when the young were a day old, the brooding female suddenly darted from the nest and made a vicious attack upon another tree sparrow. At nest IV the incubating female flew at a yellow warbler that perched carelessly some 20 feet from her—her mate was singing only 150 feet from the nest, but she apparently considered the case too urgent to wait for him to expel the trespasser.

At my intrusion the parent birds chipped anxiously, but neither attacked, as will hawks, terns, owls, and jays, nor feigned injury as did their neighbors the shore birds, though if followed they would guilefully lead me farther and farther afield. The chief protection of the incubating female was her streaky coloration, which she relied on until almost stepped upon.

Specific sites for the 26 nests I studied at Churchill were of three types:

1. Dwarf willow–birch thickets—20 nests in tussocks of grass or depressions in the ground at the base of shaggy bushes, concealed by dry grasses and dead branches.

2. Open tundra, near patch of brush—four nests in depressions in mossy hummocks, concealed by grasses or semiprostrate shrubs.

3. Spruces at timberline—one nest at base of stunted spruce on open tundra; one nest 5 feet up in a small spruce under overhanging branches, built on the remains of an old redpoll nest.

All but the last of these were on or within a few inches of the ground. MacFarlane (1891) who examined more than 200 nests in the Anderson River valley, found most of them on the ground, but a few in dwarf willows 1 to 4 feet high.

The nest is usually built in three layers: an outer shell 20 to 40 millimeters thick, composed of heavy grass and weed stems, rootlets, bits of moss, lichens, shreds of bark, and an occasional leaf or twig; an inner coat of fine, dry grass stems, about 10 millimeters thick; and finally a soft lining of ptarmigan feathers. Generally the nests are compact, well-built, rather heavy, and open to the sky, though a few open at the side. One found in a deeper depression lacked the outer shell almost entirely and was lightly and loosely woven. The lining feathers, ranging from 29 to 152 in number, were frequently woven into the inner shell. Other materials than ptarmigan feathers may be used for linings—five nests had pintail feathers, one of them exclusively. Another had dog hairs interspersed among the feathers. One nest contained a soft mass of the thin, wiry mosses that carpet the ground. The presence of a small patch of lemming fur in the bottom of another suggests the birds sometimes raid this animal's old winter nests that are found everywhere above the ground. One enterprising bird that built near the railway station used shreds of waste cloth.

The average dimensions of tree sparrow nests at Churchill were as follows:

| | Exterior diameter (top, in millimeters) | Interior diameter (top, in millimeters) | Interior depth (in millimeters) | Depth overall (in millimeters) | Weight (in grams) |
|---|---|---|---|---|---|
| Average | 130 | 50 | 35 | 54 | 15. 6 |
| Maximum | 150 | 55 | 45 | 70 | 25. 9 |
| Minimum | 110 | 40 | 30 | 45 | 4. 9 |

Nest building is by the female alone, but her mate takes an active interest in her activities and is never far away. Singing a few feet above her while she works at the nest, he frisks dutifully after her when she goes for another feather or straw, then back to his perch when she returns, or sometimes down to the nest to mate with her. The source of the material is never far distant, for grasses and moss are the stuff of the tundra itself, and ptarmigan feathers are scattered everywhere as these birds shed their winter dress. Building is a leisurely process, and after three or four trips for material, the pair usually flits off to feed about the marshy edges of a pool, and the observer might sit and shiver for 2 hours or the rest of the day before they return.

The construction of a nest observed almost from its beginning was briefly as follows:

June 5 and 6—Pair seen feeding together; no indications of building though territory defined, as indicated by feeding range and attacks on others of this species.

June 11, 8:30 a.m.—Nest found, barely started, a small depression in the damp ground with moss padded partly across the back, bits of straw thinly woven across the front, and two or three soggy bits of dead grass on the floor. Female came to nest three times in 2 hours. 3:00 p.m.—Floor sparsely laid with soggy straws from the front to one-third of way back.

June 12, 7:30 a.m.—Nest much more rounded and built up in front. Yesterday's flooring covered with bits of moss and peaty sod. 7:30 p.m.—Rim built up an inch above yesterday's mark and broader, now ¼ inch thick in back as well as front of nest. Floor well padded with moss and sod. Length of time for building outer shell approximately 3 days.

June 13, 3:00 p.m.—Nest has a beautifully woven inner coat of fine dead grass, stems, and one ptarmigan feather. Inner coat practically completed in ½ day.

June 14, 6:15 p.m.—Three feathers in nest.

June 15, 7 p.m.—Ten more feathers and finer grasses added to inner shell, burying one feather.

June 16, 10:30 a.m.—One new feather.

June 17, 18, and 19—No change, nest looks complete. Lining completed in 3 days, followed by a rest of 5 days. When I examined this nest at the end of the season there were 43 feathers in it.

June 21, 12:30 p.m.—One egg.

*Eggs.*—The tree sparrow usually lays from three to five eggs, occasionally six. They are ovate with some tending toward short ovate, and they are slightly glossy. The ground is pale bluish or pale greenish-white, profusely spotted and speckled with "wood brown," "cinnamon brown," or "auburn." These markings are generously scattered over the entire surface, often entirely obscuring the greenish-white ground and giving it a light brown appearance. In addition to the heavy speckling there are frequently a few long thin black scrawls.

The measurements of 50 eggs of *S. a. arborea* average 19.5 by 14.3 millimeters; the eggs showing the four extremes measure *20.8* by *15.0*, *17.7* by 14.5, and 18.3 by *13.5* millimeters.  The measurements of 40 eggs of *S. a. ochracea* average 18.8 by 14.0 millimeters; the eggs showing the four extremes measure *21.3*, by *15.2*, *16.8* by 13.7, and 17.3 by *13.2* millimeters.

In color, size, and shape, the tree sparrow eggs at Churchill displayed a striking variation, not only in the different nests, but within a single set.  Ground color ranged from pale blue to greenish, and from a clear, almost bright hue to a dull, leaden appearance.  In some, the brown fleckings were so evenly washed over the whole surface that the ground color was almost obliterated, though generally they were more concentrated at the large end of the egg.  The shape has been described as oval, ovate, or ovoidal.  Frequently one egg in a nest was conspicuously more rounded than the others.

The following measurements were made during early incubation:

| | Length (in millimeters) | Width (in millimeters) | Circumference (in millimeters) | Weight (in grams) |
|---|---|---|---|---|
| Average | 19. 1 | 14. 2 | 44. 0 | 2. 12 |
| Maximum | 21. 0 | 15. 5 | 48. 0 | 2. 40 |
| Minimum | 17. 5 | 14. 0 | 41. 0 | 1. 82 |
| Variation in one set | 21. 0 | 14. 5 | long and oval | 2. 40 |
| (Nest VI) | 19. 5 | 14. 0 | normal shape | 2. 08 |

The average egg weight equals 11.37 percent of the yearly average weight of the female bird (18.62 grams).  At nest I weights were taken at intervals of 3 or 4 days to check the percentage of loss.  Total loss was 0.30 gram, or 14.63 percent.

A normal clutch of the tree sparrow at Churchill ranged from four to six eggs; the majority consisting of five.  MacFarlane's (1891) records for 216 nests were four to five, with occasional sets of six or seven.  Sets of two and three are apt to be incomplete.  In order to determine the capacity for laying of this species, the third egg at nest II was removed each morning.  Unlike the famous flicker that laid 71 eggs, the female settled down to incubate after her fifth egg and laid no more.  The experiment was not repeated, and may represent only an individual case.

Of 66 eggs in 14 nests that were watched through an undisturbed hatching, five eggs or 7 percent did not hatch and presumably were infertile.  Of these, three belonged to a 6-egg set, and one to a belated 4-egg set.

After the nest was completed, the birds usually rested for several days, during which they seldom visited the nest.  Thereafter an egg was laid daily.  At five nests observed, only one bird skipped a day (between the second and third eggs). The eggs were laid in the early morning, between 6:00 and 7:30 a.m. At nest I the second egg had not been deposited at 6:45, but was laid before I returned at 7:45. On the 4th day the new egg was in the nest when I arrived at 6:30.

During egg laying the birds show somewhat more interest in the nest. In 10 visits to nest I during this time, I found the female covering the eggs on two occasions, once from 5:30 to 6:00 a.m., returning at 6:25 to lay, and once in mid-afternoon. In addition the male visited her twice, and came once when she was absent. Other females were found on their nests at various hours of the day. When nest B contained one egg, the bird was flushed at noon, returning in about 15 minutes with a bill full of grasses. It is believed that the females roosted there at this time, as nest II with four eggs was occupied at 10:15 p.m., and another with one egg at 5:30 a.m.

Incubation is performed by the female only, and begins normally with the laying of the last egg. At nests III and IX another egg was laid after incubation had apparently commenced. It may be significant that at both nests one egg hatched much later than the others, and this last young died before its first day was over.

During the first days, the female at nest I was absent for long periods, and on the morning of June 18, 2 days after the set had been completed, the eggs felt ominously cold. Twenty minutes later I found her incubating persistently, and thereafter she was seldom long absent. About two-thirds of the working day she spent on duty, a ratio she maintained throughout the period. While the percentage of time did not vary appreciably, it was noted that during late incubation the periods on and off the nest were of much shorter duration. These facts are indicated by the following figures, compiled from 3- and 2-hour observations, respectively, at mid- and late incubation. Irrationally, the longest period away from the nest occurred during a brief cold shower.

| | 6 days of incubation | 11 days of incubation |
|---|---|---|
| Time on nest | 61.80 percent | 61.78 percent |
| Time off nest | 38.20 percent | 38.22 percent |
| Average length of period on nest | 21.6 minutes (max. 31) | 7.6 minutes (max. 34) |
| Average length of period off nest | 14.0 minutes (max. 33) | 5.2 minutes (max. 12) |

The incubating female crouches low in the nest with neck drawn in, wings laid compactly against the back, and tips of primaries crossed over the rump, only the bill and tail extending beyond the rim of the nest. This position is conspicuously different from the brooding posture, when she sits high over the nest, frequently panting from heat, neck outstretched, wings drooping over the rim of the nest.

At nest VII after one young had hatched, the parent alternated these positions at frequent intervals.

During incubation the male continues to show a direct interest in home and mate, visiting the nest frequently. At nest III he appeared three times during 2 hours, and the pair flitted away together to feed. During the gray dusk which is the northern night, males of four nests were flushed from 20 to 60 feet from their nests. From the ground or the base of the bushes, they scudded low a few feet ahead of me, silently or with a low tsip. One sang a few bars of song and trailed off to silence in the middle of a note.

*Young.*—Development of the young has been described in detail (Baumgartner, 1937). Summarizing the major points, hatching may occur at any time of the day, the sequence not dependent upon the order of laying, and the down dries in about 3 hours. The female subsequently swallows the egg shells.

Upon hatching the skin is yellowish with a pinkish undertone and is sparsely clad in tufts of fuscous down; bill and feet pinkish horn, lining of mouth orangish pink. The average length is 33.5 millimeters, weight 1.62 grams. Pin feathers begin to protrude at the age of 4 days on dorsal, ventral, and alar tracts, at 5 days on the caudal. At 6 days free feathers emerge beyond the sheaths of all tracts. At 8 days nestings are almost covered dorsally, the lower belly is bare, and the tail a stubby pincushion with feather tips barely showing.

At 9½ days, the age at which undisturbed young leave the nest, the back is fully covered, lower belly still slightly bare, wings two-thirds grown, and tail still a stub; weight is 16.70 grams, a 930 percent gain over the bird's weight on hatching, and equal to that of the average July adult.

Development of fledgling birds was traced in a brood confined to its nest area by a wire mesh cage, and through the recapture of banded young of known age. In both cases a loss of 1.5 grams was noted the first day out of the nest, then a gradual increase to 21 days with a total gain of 3 grams. Wings were then still slightly short and tails about two-thirds grown.

During August all birds were in heavy molt. In a series collected on August 19, measurements of the young were comparable to those of adults, and many were in almost complete adult plumage. Weights averaged slightly less than adults of the same sex.

| Number | Sex | Weight (in grams) | Number | Sex | Weight (in grams) |
|---|---|---|---|---|---|
| 6 | Male adult___ | 19.7 | 14 | Male immature | 18.1 |
| 4 | Female adult_ | 17.7 | 12 | Female immature | 16.8 |
| 10 | Average____ | 18.7 | 26 | Average_____ | 17.5 |

Both parents shared the task of feeding their young, at first equally, later with the heavier load falling on the male. During the first few days the nestlings were fed only three or four times an hour; thereafter, an average of 16 feedings per hour was maintained, at intervals ranging from 1 to 10 minutes between visits.

During the early days the female brooded the young 74 percent of the time. Periods averaged about 8 minutes, occasionally as long as ½ hour, with intervals of only 3 to 8 minutes away from the nest. After a few days, feeding occupied a greater proportion of her time, and brooding periods were short and infrequent, rarely exceeding 3 minutes. At 6½ days she was on 20 percent of the time during the very early morning, but not at all later in the day, though the female on nest IX was flushed from her nest on the 8th day. At night most of the birds remained with their young the full term of 9½ days.

At the age of 2 days the nestlings were sufficiently developed to stretch for food. From this time until fear was acquired, they responded with outstretched necks and gaping mouths to any motion. At 4 days the eyes were half open, and at the end of 5 were wide open, after which their responses were somewhat more discriminating.

They emitted no sound until the age of 5 days, and even at 8 days they usually simply raised their heads to accept what their parents brought.

Fear was acquired abruptly between 7½ and 8 days, correlating perfectly with the development of physical independence. In my daily rounds I had found them at first unalarmed by my presence and quiet during weighing. At nest III, where three banded young had hatched ½ day before the other two, weighings were made just before these birds were 8 and 7½ days old, respectively. By keeping them in a box they were retained long enough to weigh. As soon as they were returned to their nest, the three older birds scrambled off into the bushes, while the other two remained serenely their full term of 9½ days in the nest.

During the 9th day in the nest the young became quite active, shifting and stretching frequently, and greeting the parent bringing food by outstretched necks, fluttering wings, and noisy clamors. The undisturbed normal method of departure was observed at nest I. Arriving at the nest in the early afternoon of July 8, I found three of the brood already gone and the youngest, banded with a green thread at the time of hatching, sitting alone in the nest. The female bird came soon thereafter with food, which Green accepted quietly without moving to follow. His reaction was quite different when the male came. Immediately the young bird hopped past the proffered food and out onto the open tundra, peeping vigorously, sprawling and stumbling over the uneven ground 1 or 2 feet behind his father, who led him toward the nearby willow-birch thicket. About 20 feet from the nest he was fed, and thereafter he was given a morsel after every few feet, at intervals of 15 to 30 seconds. Occasionally Green wandered off the course and after considerable peeping by both parties, was finally found and fed. Thus it took them 20 minutes to traverse 100 feet of hummocky tundra. At the edge of the thicket the young bird was allowed to rest in the shelter of the hummock.

This performance was repeated almost identically when twice I brought him back to the nest. Green showed no desire to travel alone, nor to follow the female parent, whose instincts seemed to cling to the nest. Throughout my visit she chipped anxiously about it and fed her offspring several times while he was there. The third time that he was forcibly returned he concealed himself in the shrubbery directly behind the nest. The female came and did not see him, calmly swallowed the food herself and brooded for 2 minutes on the empty nest. Subsequently the male appeared and Green, now a true fledgling, hopped after him to the shelter of the thicket.

As has been indicated, young birds were quite unable to fly when they left the nest. The day following the departure from nest I described above, I found Green perched in a small tamarack about 15 inches from the ground in the same thicket to which I had followed him the previous afternoon. He was easily captured by hand, and upon his release he stumbled away over the uneven hummocks without trying to fly. Five days later a banded young from this same brood flushed 6 feet in front of me and flew laboriously some 30 to 40 feet. The development of caged young again corresponded with observations afield. Within the fenced corral droppings were first found on the branches a few inches above the ground level when the young were 15 days old, and they were thereafter conspicuously more active and quarrelsome. By the end of July young birds everywhere were flying about freely within the little thickets of their territory.

Fledglings over 2 weeks old, both at the cage and in the field, seemed to be fed as frequently as during their nest life. On July 26, when they were 22 days old, the male made three visits to the enclosure in ½ hour, although there was but one bird inside and three at large (the others had escaped). It was on this day that the young bird still in the corral gave the first indication of independent feeding. He was observed picking at the ground and was much attracted to a bread crust from my lunchbox.

Family groups farther afield were observed until August 15, but only occasionally was an adult seen gathering food for the young or feeding them.

On August 21, my last day in the field, the tundras were deluged with tree sparrows. Leaving the thickets where they had been reared, they were feeding now on the grass seeds of the open flats. The young were fully fledged, adults and immatures now indistinguishable, and the fall flocking had begun.

*Plumages.*—The natal down has been described above. The juvenal plumage, worn by the fledgling until about 4 weeks of age, is as follows (Baumgartner, 1938): Pileum dull cinnamon brown, streaked by the black shafts of individual feathers, and more or less edged with light buff; nape similar, the black shafts indistinct or lacking, becoming grayer or buffer on sides of neck; feathers of back and scapulars broadly centered with black, edged with light buff and occasional touches of chestnut, especially the latter; rump and upper tail-coverts light buff, indistinctly streaked or mottled with black; sides of head and whole underparts light buff (shading to light smoke gray on throat and becoming a rich buff on sides), heavily streaked with soft black, especially on the breast, but not on lower abdomen and under tail coverts.

Except for the heavy streaking on the breast, the color pattern is essentially like that of the adult plumage, with the distinct pileum color terminated by a grayer nape, the broadly streaked back and rich buff of the sides. The same facial expression is produced by a light superciliary stripe, an irregular dark line under the eye, and a definite postocular streak. The dark pectoral spot, contrary to Beebe's (1907) assertion, can be identified among the heavy streakings of the breast. A small patch of dull chestnut at the bend of the wing is streaked with black. The wings and tail are those of the first winter.

The first winter plumage is "acquired by a partial post-juvenal molt in August which involves body plumage but apparently not the wings or tail, young and old becoming indistinguishable" (Dwight, 1900). This molt begins on the back and sides before the young are fully grown, about the first of August, and does not reach its culmination until after the middle of the month. The last juvenal feathers to disappear are those of the nape, the dark postocular stripe, and scattered streaky feathers of the throat and breast. None of the Churchill birds collected up to August 19 were in complete winter dress, and feet and bills were still pale.

When the species arrived in Ithaca in October, traces of the molt could still be discerned in 10 percent of those collected, of which 3 were young birds.

The nuptial plumage, for old and first year birds alike, is "acquired by wear, the buffy edging of the back becoming grayish and the chestnut everywhere slightly paler" (Dwight, 1900). A certain amount of this is due to fading, as Dwight intimates, but the chief change is by actual wearing away of the feather edges.

During the spring there is in addition a restricted molt of which Dwight (1900) says: "New feathers regularly grow on the chin in March, but apparently not in the other tracts and their appearance indicates, as in some other species, renewal rather than molt, for they are very few in number." It was found, however, to be more extensive, for of 130 specimens examined, fresh sheaths were evident regularly on cheeks and chin, later on the throat, and other tracts were affected in the following proportions (in this count scattered feathers were not considered, but only definite areas of new quills):

| Tract | Number of Specimens Showing Molt |
|---|---|
| Crown (sides and back only) | 5 |
| Superciliary stripe | 6 |
| Lores | 3 |
| Nape | 10 |
| Dorsal tract | 19 |
| Scapulars | 4 |
| Rump | 2 |
| Sides | 5 |
| Belly | 6 |

Adult winter plumage is "acquired by a complete postnuptial molt, undistinguishable from first winter dress" (Dwight, 1900). At Churchill the first evidences of this plumage were detected on July 31, 1933, and on Aug. 3, 1934. Sequence was irregular, but in general contour feathers preceded the flight feathers, and the molt progressed from the anal region toward the head.

Although tree sparrows are described as "sexes identical," a determined effort disclosed minor differences in plumage and measurements, a combination of which may distinguish up to 90 percent of birds at banding stations (Heydweiller, 1936). Using specimens which were later dissected to determine sex (by gonads) and age (by skull), a practical test with 129 birds gave the following score:

Male adult _____ 36 birds, all judged correctly
Male immature _____ 43 birds, 5 incorrect
Female adult _____ 19 birds, 7 incorrect
Female immature _____ 31 birds, all judged correctly
Percentage of error _____ 9.3 (due to overlap of characteristics
                               of young males and adult females)

Criteria used in distinguishing sex and age are primarily lengths of wing and tail, width of crown, and amount of veiling of the crown. In general the largest birds are adult males, the smallest ones with distinct dark shafts on the crown feathers are first-year females. A wider crown usually indicates a male, a narrow crown a female. Male birds frequently show a loose flecking of buff over the whole crown, which in the female tends to be more heavily concentrated toward the center. The distinct dark shafts in the center crown feathers, though not invariable, are characteristic of first-year females. Operators of banding stations interested in sexing their tree sparrows should refer to the original article (Heydweiller, 1936) which gives measurements, a sketch of four typical crown patterns, and further details.

The western form, *Spizella arborea ochracea*, was recognized as a distinct subspecies by William Brewster in 1881. In describing it, he (Brewster 1882) remarks:

"The ground color of the back is decidedly paler than the eastern examples, bringing out the dark streaks in sharper contrast, which is heightened by the absence of their usual chestnut edging; ash of throat and sides of head is much fainter, in many places replaced by brownish fulvous; the underparts, especially the sides and abdomen, are more strongly ochraceous; and the broad ashy crown patch gives the head a very different appearance."

The types of *ochracea* are now in the Harvard College Museum of Comparative Zoology: co-types from Fort Walla Walla, Washington, collected by Captain C. E. Bendire, male—Nov. 8, 1881; female—Dec. 13, 1881.

*Food.*—Beal (1897) found that a single tree sparrow eats about one-fourth ounce of seeds per day. Estimating conservatively that ten birds per square mile spend an average of 200 days in Iowa, then this species alone destroys 875 tons of weed seed annually. This figure, he thought, could without exaggeration be multiplied by four. In the stomach of an individual bird he recorded 700 seeds of pigeon grass. A specimen I collected at Ithaca, N.Y., contained 982 seeds in the crop alone, with another 200 in a crushed mass in the stomach.

During its stay in the United States, the tree sparrow subsists almost entirely on weed and grass seed (Judd, 1901), with 98 percent seed food, about 2 percent animal matter, and an insignificant quantity of fruit. This species differs from associated fringillids in the large proportion of grass seed it eats, which makes up fully 50 percent of its vegetable diet. Panicums, pigeon grass, and allied grasses seem to be preferred, after which ragweed, lamb's quarters, and the polygonums comprise another 40 percent, with the remaining 10 percent a variety of seeds, berries, buds, catkins, flowers, and waste grain.

Animal food found by Judd consisted chiefly of weevils and other beetles, ground beetles, rose beetles, wasp-like insects, ants, caterpillars, bugs, grasshoppers, and spiders. Knight (1908) adds flies, grubs and larvae. Hamilton (1933) found small stoneflies in the stomachs of four out of five tree sparrows collected in midwinter near a small stream near Ithaca, N.Y. He suggests that any warm day throughout the winter will bring thousands of transformed imagos to the vegetation surrounding such streams, and may account for the little flocks of birds that haunt such situations.

Knappen (1934), in summarizing the material in the Biological Survey files, states that in the 14 midwinter stomachs containing animal food, proportions varied from 1 to 90 percent of the total stomach content. Insects and spiders were found in adult form, as eggs, larvae, and pupae. Of a total of 550 stomachs on file, 38 contained animal food. During October animal matter comprised a third of the total. From November through March it ranged well below 10 percent. By April it had increased to almost a third again, and a single May specimen from North Dakota contained 100 percent animal food.

When they arrive on their northern breeding grounds, however, tree sparrows find conditions nearer winter than summer. Seeds continue to form the greater part of their diet until past the middle of June, when insects first become active (Baumgartner, 1937c). By mid-August the brief nesting season is over, and the proportion of seeds consumed again approaches the 98 percent maintained during the winter.

Young birds up to 3 or 4 weeks old are fed almost 100 percent animal matter, with a trace of Rosaceae leaves for their greens. When they begin to forage for themselves about the first of August, seeds and fruit are taken to a limited extent, their proportions gradually increasing. The last stomachs examined, on August 19, still showed a considerably larger proportion of animal food than did those of the adults of the same date.

A trace of gravel is first found in young birds of 3 days. At 5 days and thereafter gravel may compose from 10 to 15 percent of the stomach content. In August when they are feeding independently the gravel content increases to adult proportions, ranging from 15 to 70 percent, the majority about 35 percent.

In summarizing the summer food, it was noted that the outstanding vegetable item was the seeds of the genus *Carex*. These were found throughout the summer in all adults and juvenals that contained any vegetable matter, though they were not found in the nestlings. At least six species of *Carex* were distinguished in a single bird. In late July and August seeds of the crowberry (*Empetrum nigrum*), cranberry (*Vaccinium vitus-idaea*), and bulblets of the alpine knotweed (*Polygonum viviparum*), became an important part of the menu. Grass seeds, which form such a large proportion of the winter food, were strikingly scant in the summer diet, being found in only one individual in late August. Besides seeds, plant matter was found in the form of soft bits of wood or chips, fibers, leaf fragments, galls, and unidentified debris.

The insects represent a large number of families and genera, among which the following groups are most conspicuous: Arachnida, Coleoptera (especially Donacia), Ichneumonidae, Lepidoptera, Nematinae, and Trichoptera. The adult stage predominated, but eggs, larvae, and pupae were also taken. A complete list of food species of the tree sparrow is included in Baumgartner (1937c).

In observations at the nest, the adult birds came repeatedly with bill overflowing with small green and brown caterpillars, as well as flies, mosquitoes, and other adult insects. At first the material is partially masticated, and the pulpy mass is jammed far down the young bird's throat. Several birds may be fed at a single visit. Later great billfulls of more or less entire insects are brought to the nest. But however great the quantity, it seems scarcely enough to satisfy one or two gaping mouths. The immensity of the old birds' task was shown by a male collected in the field holding in its bill 41 adult insects, 4 larvae, and fragments of others, all captured presumably within 3 or 4 minutes.

Although during June and July in the North almost full daylight extends from 2:00 a.m. until 10:00 p.m., tree sparrows do not begin feeding until 3:15, and cease shortly before 9:00, a "working day" of 17.75 hours. From this it may be computed that, at an average of 16 feedings per hour, some 275 feedings are made daily, divided among the four or five young. It is interesting to compare with this the parental care given by that closely related species of more temperate latitudes, the chipping sparrow (Weed, 1898). Averaging 12 visits per hour, divided among only 3 nestlings, each individual young of this species seems to be fed as many times per hour as do individual young of the tree sparrow. But here the working day begins at 5:00 a.m. and closes at 7:30 p.m. with only 14.5 hours in which to work. It is strongly suggested that these 3 extra hours a day make it possible for young tree sparrows to leave the nest at 9½ days, two days earlier than chipping sparrows at 11½ days. Thus the longer hours of daylight compensate in a measure for the briefness of the nesting season.

*Economic importance.*—Because of the vast quantities of obnoxious weed seeds the tree sparrows consume during their winter sojourn in the States, much has been made of the economic value of this species. The Department of Agriculture estimates that the sparrow tribe—of which the tree sparrow is one of the most abundant species—saves the farmer $90 million a year. Judd (1901) describes the thoroughness with which they clean up a patch before moving on. On an area 18 inches square in a weedy ditch where they had been feeding, he found 1,130 half seeds, only 2 whole ones, and only 6 seeds left in the whole field, which, he says, was devoid of weeds the next year.

Since Judd's time some doubt has been expressed of the value of the sparrow tribe. Certainly Judd overestimated the thoroughness of their gleanings, else they could not return year after year to the same areas, nor would they wander so freely over their little territories, only to cover the same ground another day. And certainly there is no scarcity of weeds in the country regardless of the great hordes of these birds. The reproductive capacities of the plants easily outdo the eating capacities of the sparrows, and there will probably always be enough weeds left to bother the farmer and propagate the species. Indeed, if there were no sparrows, the overcrowding of the plants themselves would soon establish a balance.

But if not actually beneficial, these birds are certainly harmless. They occasionally sample grain, but to no appreciable extent. The charge has been made that they distribute rather than destroy the seeds, but this accusation was refuted by Judd's study. He found that in the thousands of stomachs containing ragweed, there was never an unbroken seed. The thoroughness of avian digestion prevents the evacuation of anything but a most insignificant portion of the food ingested.

In the summer the tree sparrow is of no economic significance, as it nests beyond the reaches of civilization. But whether or not we can evaluate the species in cold dollars and cents, it will always be welcome as a gentle, cheerful little creature in our winter fields and gardens.

*Behavior.*—Since the earliest days of nature lore in America, writers of the winter fields have thrilled to the cheerful warble of these hardy little visitors from the North. I shall never forget my first flock of tree sparrows, feeding companionably at the weedy border of the marsh, hanging on the weed tops like animated Christmas tree ornaments, dropping lightly to the ground and etching their delicate tracery of claw prints in the snow. The air was mellow with their soft warbles, and to me they have always said "Marguerite, Marguerite." Erect, dignified, they are at some times more vivacious than others. On stormy days in midwinter they may huddle quietly in the lee of a wall, while in the springtime, or indeed any sunny day, we may find them playing a gay game of tag through the shrubbery.

Keynotes of the tree sparrow's character are gentleness and unsuspiciousness. Easily baited in large numbers, quiet in the hand,

and a frequent repeater, this species has long been a favorite at banding stations. Both at feeding stations and on the nesting territory they are amiable and unaggressive, going their quiet way without the nervousness and fussiness of so many species.

When flushed, tree sparrows swoop up into the nearest bush or tree and perch quietly from 3 to 10 or 12 feet from the ground. If the intruder stands quietly, they will soon forget him and return to their endless banquet. During the migration they tend to be more shy and secretive, flushing sooner and flying greater distances. In summer the incubating female flushes usually at 4 to 6 feet, and reappears a moment later, chipping with gentle anxiety from the top of a scrub birch a few feet away. The male, less nervous, less vociferous in his protests at an intruder, is more direct and presumptive about the nest. Even in feeding the young, when duties of the sexes are identical, he can easily be distinguished by his perkier air, erect crown, and more direct manner of approaching the nest, while the female fusses and chips and finally creeps through the grasses to her young.

The tree sparrow's flight is unhurried, graceful, and slightly undulating. In a normal day's foraging, the birds fly no great distances, drifting through hedgerows or marshes, passing and repassing one another in their irregular advances. When traversing pronounced distances across bare areas, the flock rises with a circling, swirling movement to about 100 feet and sails off in irregular formation to points unknown.

When food is abundant or winds are biting, they may perch quietly for 20 to 30 minutes at a time with neck drawn in, tips of the primaries slightly crossed over the rump, and contour feathers fluffed to twice their normal size, almost covering wings and legs. For such extended rests a small limb in denser shrubbery is usually chosen, from three to ten feet from the ground. For short stops any twig will do, usually near the ground, but not infrequently in the higher tree tops.

As their winter diet consists principally of weed seeds, tree sparrows feed largely on the ground, scratching among the dry grasses or hopping up at bent-over weed-heads. They are less inclined to dig than song sparrows, and when food is plentiful will pass lightly over the more obvious patches. Often one balances on a weed top, swaying in the wind and scattering the seeds on the snow below, where they are promptly appropriated by his companions. That one bird deliberately performs this function for the others, as has been sentimentally inferred, is unlikely. On the contrary, it has been observed that the foraging birds rarely encroach within six inches of one another, and maintain small and definite feeding territories for themselves.

In the early summer at Churchill they were seen, usually in pairs, feeding about the grassy edges of little pools and, not infrequently, picking the fresh buds and catkins off the stunted willows and birches. These they obtained either by perching on the branch or by hopping up from the ground, sometimes to a height of several inches. Later, when the young had hatched and the diet had changed to chiefly animal food, the parents were seen gleaning caterpillars and small insects among the leaves and branches of the nearby thickets. Occasionally one darted into the air for a mosquito or moth, but these forays were short, and if the prey escaped it was not ardently pursued.

Water is as essential as food, and in winter when there are no open pools, I have frequently watched tree sparrows about my station swallowing snow, either from the ground or from the crotches of trees. They enjoy bathing even in the coldest weather, nor are they content merely to wade, but hop to their middles and splash and duck and flutter like diminutive ducklings.

While tree sparrows are gregarious at night as well as by day, they seem to prefer a solitary roost, for tramping through their haunts frequently after dark I flushed only scattered individuals. I believe they prefer cattail marshes when these are available. Here they creep into little cavities on or near the ground, protected from storms, wind, and enemies. Weedy fields, corn shocks, and haystacks are also popular. Dense growths of young white pine offer shelter not unlike their northern home. A flock of a hundred or more I watched near Ithaca, N.Y. usually assembled in the late afternoon in a weedy corn patch, and at dusk drifted up the valley to a stand of young pines over a half mile away. Straggling in loose formation, yet with some definiteness of purpose, they spread out over the whole area so that only single individuals could subsequently be flushed.

*Voice.*—Across the barrens of the North, the little song of the tree sparrow rings as clear and sweet and simple as one who loves its gentle ways could desire. Though quite different in pattern, its song resembles that of the field sparrow in pitch and intensity, and it has that silver, bell-like quality that is at the same time both plaintive and serene. There is also a decided resemblance in accent and rhythm to the final notes of the chestnut-sided warbler. In length its song ranges from 3½ to 4 seconds, with an occasional rollicking variation of only 1½ seconds.

Some of the variations in my field note book are: *tsee tsee-ah, tsi tsit su; tsee tsee-ah, tsit sut sut; tsee tsee-ah, tsi tseedle-eedle-ah; tsee tsweee tsi, tsi tswit su trtrtrtrtr* (end a clicking trill) (these are variations at a single nest); *tsi tsi tsweeeee, tswee tswee tswee tswit tswit-sut,* and a brief warble-like *tse-weet, tse-weet, tse-wi-tse-tse-tsweet.*

During June the males sing continuously, one song following another in rapid succession. On one occasion I counted four in a minute, followed by a brief interval while the bird flew to another perch. There is no siesta period in this cool climate. Night singing, in spite of the half dark twilight of the midnight sun, is infrequent. On several occasions when I watched nests all night, singing decreased conspicuously after 9:15 and the last song was heard at 10:15 p.m., although other species were still active. Although there was full daylight at 2:15 a.m. the first tree sparrow song was not recorded until 2:45.

In mid-July singing becomes less frequent as males take over their share of feeding the young. During August the song can be heard occasionally on warm still days.

During fall migration the song is heard not infrequently during November, a thin, wiry note that rarely reaches the fullness of the true breeding song. February is the beginning of the spring tune-up, and by mid-March the hedgerows ring with the true summer song. With the passing of most of the males, singing becomes less frequent after the middle of April.

That melodious, warbling twitter of a winter flock which Thoreau (1910) so aptly describes as the "tinkle of icicles" cannot, according to Saunders (1929b) be considered true song, as it is not a courtship performance but merely the contented utterance of a well-fed flock. It can be heard at any time and in any weather throughout the winter a cheerful, tri-syllabic warble, *teedle eet, teedle eet.*

Call notes include the soft *tsip* on winter feeding grounds, a somewhat sharper alarm note heard both winter and summer, an imperious little breeding call of the male *chek-chek-chek, chek, chek,* the female's response, a soft *whey-whey-whey-whey-whey,* and whispered *ts-ts-ts-ts-ts.* Sometimes when the male came to feed the young, the brooding female uttered rapidly and with rising inflection, a series of consonants which I recorded in by field notebook as *"pppppppt,"* or a low ticking note. Sometimes both parents came to the nest simultaneously and stood fondly over their family, uttering low cooing notes and touching bills tenderly.

Development of voice in the young was traced from the first soft *tseeeeeeee* at 5 days (Baumgartner, 1938a) to the noisy food call at 9½ days as the young left the nest, when both adult and nestling uttered a raucous *aah aah aah aah.*

*Enemies.*—Man, the archenemy of many birds, affects the tree sparrows very little. Too small for game, beneficial in habits, inconspicuous in manner, they are seldom noticed in winter, and in summer retreat mainly beyond the reaches of civilization. Predatory animals, such as the bird hawks, owls, shrikes, weasels, and the domestic cat account for a few in winter. In summer they are beyond the domain of snakes, cats, most crows, jays, and squirrels, and such competitors as English sparrows, starlings, and cowbirds. I found nest mortality and infertile eggs to be 21.3 percent.

Parasites, both external and internal, were found to be relatively few (Baumgartner, 1937a). Of some 600 specimens carefully inspected, many were entirely free and none harbored more than a scattering. Of 26 nests observed at Churchill, none showed evidence of infestation.

The most serious enemies of this species are the elements—snows that cover the food supply, and storms and sudden cold spells, particularly during the long migration. While the birds can withstand temperatures to −28° C. (West, 1960), they cannot survive without food. A late traveler in the fall, an early one in spring, they run the gantlet of the equinoctial storms at both seasons. W. E. Saunders (1907) counted 358 dead tree sparrows in 3 hours after an October storm on Lake Huron.

Of the thousands upon thousands of this species that have been handled at banding stations, only a small porportion survive to their 4th year. A handful have returned a 5th and 6th year, and the oldest birds on record are a return-8 taken by B. S. Bowdish of Demarest, N.J. (in litt.) and another by Paul Nighswonger (1959) at Alva, Okla. Assuming that these birds were banded in their first winter, they would have been between 8½ and 9 years old on last appearance.

Survival ratio of tree sparrows has been computed by Baumgartner (1937a) based on nest mortality, proportion of first year and adult specimens collected through the season, and banding returns, both personal and those recorded in the literature.

Calculating the fate of a potential 750 eggs from 150 nests:

| | |
|---|---|
| 78.7 percent survive the nestling period | =590 birds |
| 50 percent of these 590 survive the first migration and winter | =295 birds |
| 40 percent of these 295 make winter R1 | =119 birds |
| 43 percent of these 119 survive to R2 | =  51 birds |
| 34 percent of these 51 survive to R3 | =  18 birds |
| 28 percent of these 18 survive to R4 | =   5 birds |
| 16 percent of these 5 survive to R5 | =   1 or 2 birds |

By the sixth summer only one old veteran remains, who may live one or two more years.

*Fall and winter.*—Beginning the southward trek in September, the hordes of tree sparrows reach southern Ontario about the first of October (Taverner and Sutton 1934) and by the end of the month are flooding the States. They normally reach Oklahoma, near the southern part of their range, by early November and remain until March.

Traveling, apparently, in family and neighborhood groups, the flocks upon arrival at Ithaca, N.Y., were composed of almost equal proportions of males and females, with a 16 percent dominance of males (Baumgartner 1937a). First-year birds (with skulls incompletely ossified) exceeded old birds 3 to 2 between mid-October and mid-December. During the non-migratory period between January and March, the proportion dropped to almost equal numbers of young and old birds, indicating a higher mortality of first-year birds. Females, traveling farther south, dropped to a 3 to 1 proportion until near the end of March.

The extent of winter territory and flocking habits has been the subject of several intensive studies, following different techniques and with a variety of conclusions. At Ithaca, N.Y., in 1933, 1934, and 1935, I marked individuals at four stations by gluing different colored feathers to their tails (Baumgartner, 1938b). By following these marked individuals and by retrapping at other stations, I found that the normal feeding range in winter was 500 to 1,700 feet in diameter, average 1,000 feet. Extensions from 3,000 to 6,800 feet, recorded for 40 percent of the birds, were associated with fall settling, spring excitement, or heavy snowfalls. A few individuals appeared to be regular wanderers.

Winter flocks appeared to be loosely defined units of varying numbers and individuals, with a fairly definite flock territory, from which, however, individuals strayed at will. Flocks inhabiting open country ranged more widely than those in denser cover such as marshes. In severe weather, flocks split into smaller groups and wandered more widely.

The histories of individually marked birds suggest several explanations for low return ratios at banding stations. Besides migrants, which are unlikely to make the same stop-overs a 2nd year, this study recorded several of each of the following types:

(1) Trap-shy individuals that were caught only once or twice a season, though observed regularly in the vicinity.

(2) Wanderers that covered so large an area they missed their original station another season.

(3) Regular residents of another area that meandered only once into the trap where banded.

(4) Emigrants that shifted from year to year.

A project at Amherst, Mass., during the winter 1957–58 (Sargent, 1959) used colored bands at five stations. Sargent likewise considered flock structure unstable, with no fixed associations within a flock, or regular times of day for visitations to the traps. He also attributed wandering to winter storms, with consequent influxes of new birds to a station. Fifteen of his birds wandered over ½ mile, seven wandered over 2 miles and one to a point 7½ miles away. He suggests that the social organization, described as a straight-line pecking order modified by reverse pecks (Sabine, 1949), may be partially responsible for wandering, as over-crowding at a feeding station might induce social intolerance and force away individuals near the bottom of the social hierarchy.

Helms and Drury (1960), working at South Lincoln, Mass., color-banded 477 tree sparrows, with almost 2,000 handlings to gather data on measurements, weights, and fat deposition. Field observations were made on a fairly stable winter population of about 50 birds to determine size, behavior, composition, and changes of winter flocks. They describe foraging groups as loosely integrated groups, usually four to eight birds, traveling and feeding together for most of the winter. The reason these birds do not coincide regularly in the traps, they believe, is because the foraging group remains only 10 to 20 minutes in a feeding area, and thus the likelihood of recapture together is slight. During a normal winter day, foraging individuals spend a maximum of 6 to 10 minutes in feeding activities, followed by a 12- to 20-minute period of either perching, preening, bathing or social activity that may carry the group to another foraging area.

Tree sparrows appear to have a strong homing instinct. Not only do they return year after year to banding stations; experiments in transporting birds varying distances indicate that they return with astonishing rapidity (Heydweiller, 1935). A bird transported 5 miles was back the following morning. An individual taken 10 miles covered the intervening fields in 16 days. Of 14 birds carried from 17 to 100 miles, 3 returned the following winter. A fourth was collected the following year from a flock 3 miles from the station.

Sargent (1959) transferred six color-banded regular winter residents of one of his stations 7½ miles to another. Three were retrapped at the original station from 2 to 18 days later. Another traveled an additional 3½ miles in the opposite direction from its original area, and was observed twice at this point. On February 9, he similarly transferred 20 birds new to the station following a snowfall. Some remained at the new station for about a month. None returned to the original station, for which, presumably, they had no home attachment.

### DISTRIBUTION

Eastern Tree Sparrow (*S. a. arborea*)

*Range.*—Mackenzie, Keewatin, northern Ontario and Labrador south to Oklahoma, Tennessee, and Virginia.

*Breeding range.*—The eastern tree sparrow breeds in central and eastern Mackenzie (mouth of Coppermine River, Fort Rae, Hanbury River), northern Saskatchewan (Fort Fond du Lac, Reindeer Lake), central western Keewatin (Hoare Lake), northeastern Manitoba (Churchill, Cape Tatnam), northern Ontario (Fort Severn, Little Cape), northern and central eastern Quebec (Lake Minto, Fort Chimo, Paint Hills, Old Romaine, Bradore), and Labrador (Okak, Battle Harbor).

*Winter range.*—Winters from central Minnesota (Sherburne and Isanti counties), Wisconsin, northern Michigan (Schoolcraft and Luce counties), central Ontario (North Bay), southwestern Quebec (Montreal), Maine, New Brunswick, Prince Edward Island, and Nova Scotia south to Oklahoma, Arkansas (Winslow), Tennessee (Memphis, Nashville), western North Carolina (Asheville, Winston-Salem), and Virginia (Blacksburg, Quantico); casually south to southern Nevada (Lake Mead), southeastern Texas (Hardin), north-western Mississippi (Rosedale), central South Carolina (Summerton), and Bermuda.

*Migration.*—The data deal with the species as a whole. Early dates of spring arrival are: Maine—Bangor, March 20. Quebec—Montreal area, March 17 (median of 8 years, March 22). Illinois—Chicago, February 26 (average of 16 years, March 15). Ontario—Ottawa, average of 18 years, April 12. North Dakota—Cass County, February 23 (average, March 10).

Late dates of spring departure are: Alabama—Gadsden, March 16. North Carolina—Cherokee County, March 9. Virginia—Lexington, April 9. District of Columbia—April 24 (average of 29 years, March 27). Maryland—Prince Georges County, April 14 (median of 6 years, March 28); Allegany County, April 12. Pennsylvania—State College, May 22. New Jersey—Troy Meadows, May 12 and May 5. New York—Ontario County, May 11; Westchester County, May 8. Connecticut—South Windsor, May 3; New Haven, April 28. Massachusetts—Nantucket, May 29; Martha's Vineyard, May 3 (median of 6 years, April 10). New Hampshire—New Hampton, May 12 (median of 21 years, April 25); Concord, April 30. Maine—Bangor, May 16. Quebec—Montreal area, May 9 (median of 14 years, April 30). New Brunswick—May 28. Nova Scotia—Wolfville, April 30. Arkansas—Fayetteville, April 3. Tennessee—Athens, April 22 (average of 5 years, April 8); Nashville, March 27. Kentucky—Lexington, March 30. Missouri—St. Louis, April 28 (median of 15 years, April 20). Illinois—Chicago, May 10 (average of 16 years, April 26); Urbana, April 25 (median of 19 years, April 8). Indiana—Wayne County, April 14 (median of 11 years, April 6). Ohio—Buckeye Lake, May 7 (median of 40 years for central Ohio,

April 20). Michigan—Detroit area, May 13 (mean of 10 years, May 7); Battle Creek, May 2 (average of 30 years, April 17). Iowa—Sioux City, April 21 (average of 32 years, April 1). Minnesota—Minneapolis-St. Paul, April 25 (mean of 6 years, April 8). Kansas—northeastern Kansas, April 14 (median of 14 years, April 4). Nebraska—Red Cloud, April 20. South Dakota—Sioux Falls, May 7 (average of 8 years, April 23). North Dakota—Cass County, May 5 (average, April 29). Wyoming—Laramie, April 14 (average of 9 years, April 6). Idaho—Lewiston, April 10 (median of 11 years, April 1).

Early dates of fall arrival are: Idaho—Lewiston, October 16 (median of 11 years, November 1). Wyoming—Cheyenne, September 28 (average of 11 years, October 17). New Mexico—Rio Grande Valley, November 6. Manitoba—Treesbank, September 9 (average of 21 years, September 26). North Dakota—Jamestown, October 1; Cass County, October 1 (average, October 6). South Dakota—Sioux Falls, October 4 (average of 7 years, October 19). Nebraska—Red Cloud, October 11. Kansas—northeastern Kansas, October 7 (median of 16 years, October 21). Texas—Fort Worth, November 14. Minnesota—Minneapolis-St. Paul, October 5 (mean of 12 years, October 17). Iowa—Sioux City, October 8 (average of 32 years, October 15). Michigan—Detroit area, September 25 (mean of 10 years, October 7); Battle Creek, October 15 (average of 29 years, October 27). Ohio—central Ohio, September 27 (median of 40 years, October 20). Indiana—Wayne County, October 8 (median of 10 years, November 19). Illinois—Chicago, October 1 (average of 16 years, October 10). Missouri—St. Louis, October 10 (median of 15 years, October 25). Kentucky—Bowling Green, November 7. Tennessee—Clarksville, November 21. Arkansas—Fayetteville, October 18. Nova Scotia—Margaretsville, October 23 (average of 11 years, October 27). New Brunswick—St. Andrews, September 16; Scotch Lake, September 23. Quebec—Montreal area, September 27 (median of 14 years, October 13). Maine—Lake Umbagog, October 9. New Hampshire—New Hampton, October 15 (median of 21 years, October 21); Concord, October 21. Massachusetts—Martha's Vineyard, October 5 (median of 5 years, October 19). Connecticut—East Windsor Hill, September 30; Farmington, October 1. New York—New York City, September 16; Ontario County, September 17. New Jersey—Island Beach, October 4. Pennsylvania—State College, October 1; Renovo, October 16. Maryland—Allegany County, October 18; Laurel, November 6 (median of 5 years, November 7). District of Columbia—October 3 (average of 16 years, November 10). Virginia—Shenandoah National Park, October 31. North Carolina—Arden, November 25.

Late dates of fall departure are: Manitoba—Treesbank, November 15 (average of 20 years, November 6). North Dakota—Cass County, November 24 (average, November 12). Illinois—Chicago, December 7 (average of 16 years, November 17). Newfoundland—St. Anthony, October 9. Prince Edward Island—Murray Harbour October 26. Quebec—Montreal area, November 19. Maine—Lake Umbagog, November 9.

*Egg dates.*—Alaska: 128 records, May 27 to June 29; 68 records, June 4 to June 16.

Labrador: 16 records, June 10 to July 11; 11 records, June 20 to June 29.

Manitoba: 14 records, June 12 to June 26.

Ontario: 1 record, July 1.

### Western Tree Sparrow (*S. a. ochracea*)

*Range.*—Northern Alaska, Yukon, and northwestern Mackenzie south to northeastern California, Arizona, New Mexico, and central Texas.

*Breeding range.*—The western tree sparrow breeds from northern Alaska (Kobuk and Colville deltas), northern Yukon (Firth River), and northwestern Mackenzie (Mackenzie Delta, lower Anderson River) south to southwestern and central Alaska (Naknek, Wrangell Mountains), northwestern British Columbia (Atlin), southeastern Yukon (Sheldon Lake), and central western Mackenzie (Fort Franklin).

*Winter range.*—Winters from southern British Columbia (Vancouver, Okanagan Landing), southwestern Saskatchewan (Cypress Hills), South Dakota (Harding and Hutchinson counties), and north-central Iowa (Sioux City) south to northeastern California (Fort Creek, Wendell), central western Nevada (Carson City), northern and central eastern Arizona (San Francisco Mountains, San Carlos), central New Mexico (San Antonio), and central Texas (San Angelo, Giddings); casually north to Alaska (Fairbanks, Wrangell) and south to southern California (Riverside, Death Valley).

*Casual record.*—Casual north to Banks Island.

*Egg dates.*—Mackenzie: 29 records, June 6 to July 4; 14 records, June 14 to June 21.

SPIZELLA PASSERINA (Bechstein)

# Eastern and Canadian Chipping Sparrows*

PLATE 63

Contributed by WILLIAM DeMOTT STULL

## HABITS

The specific name Alexander Wilson gave this little sparrow, *socialis*, aptly describes the close relationship many later authors have noted between its habitations and those of man.   None has expressed it better than Forbush (1929), who wrote "The Chipping Sparrow is the little brown-capped pensioner of the dooryard and lawn, that comes about farmhouse doors to glean crumbs shaken from the table-cloth by thrifty housewives.   It is the most domestic of all the sparrows.   It approaches the dwellings of man with quiet confidence and frequently builds its nest and rears its young in the clustering vines of porch or veranda under the noses of the human tenants."

The early writers spoke of it as the most common bird in their areas. Audubon (1841) wrote "Few birds are more common throughout the United States than this gentle and harmless little bunting."   But soon after the turn of the century a sharp decline in numbers was noted in formerly populous areas (R. F. Miller, 1933; H. F. Price, 1935; L. Griscom, 1949).   The explanations given usually include cowbird predation or competition from English sparrows.   Yet in 1954–58 the chipping sparrow was the most abundant nesting bird on the campus of the Lake Itasca Forestry and Biological Station in Hubbard County, Minn., in an area where there were many cowbirds and no English sparrows.

While we continue to think of this bird as preferring man's door-yards, lawns, and orchards, we wonder where it existed under primeval conditions.   In Itasca State Park, Minn., it occurs in small numbers in stands of jack pine, in virgin black spruce bogs, and in stands of virgin red pine.   In the more favored developed areas it lives in abundance.   Forbush (1929) says that, "Here and there in the wilder parts of New England Chipping Sparrows may be found in forest openings or along the shores of lakes and streams."   On Lake Mistassini, Quebec, Godfrey (1949a) found it confined to a narrow clearing which was "densely populated in summer by noisy Indians and their dogs and enclosing the trading posts of the Hudson's Bay Company and the free trader."   The same writer (Godfrey, 1950) found it a "common summer resident in aspen and coniferous forest edges and tall shubbery on the margins of roads, streams and lakes"

---

*The following subspecies are discussed in this section: *Spizella passerina passerina* (Bechstein) and *S. p. boreophila* Oberholser.

throughout the Flotten Lake Region of Saskatchewan, and Rand (1946) found it fairly common along Canol Road in the dwarf-birch and spurce flats bordering a river as well as in muskeg type forest and in open mixed forest.   In western Montana Saunders (1914a) records it as a common summer resident in the cottonwood groves in the prairies.

Burleigh (1958) suggests that in Georgia the open pine woods were probably its original habitat, for it is still plentiful in this type of woodland that once covered much of the state and is somewhat similar to the aforementioned stands of jack pine and mature red pine in Itasca Park, Minn.

The evidence indicates that, from one end of its range to the other, the chipping sparrow probably originally inhabited open woodlands or the borders of forest openings produced by rivers and lakes.   When man appeared on the scene and began to make clearings for his villages, he created additional open areas which the birds quickly occupied. The axes of the European settlers made a hundred clearings where the aborigines had one, and undoubtedly the chipping sparrow population of today is many times that in pre-Columbian North America.

The chipping sparrow population of west-central Canada was distinguished by H. C. Oberholser (1955) as *Spizella passerina boreophila* with the following diagnosis: "Similar to *Spizella passerina passerina*, but larger, and ground color of upper surface, except pileum, paler, more grayish, near drab.   Like *Spizella passerina arizonae*, but darker above, particularly the pileum; sides of head and the hind neck more clearly gray (less brownish) and somewhat darker; postocular streak wider."   The race is at best a very fine split; it cannot be identified except in the hand, and wide areas of intergradation exist between it and the other two North American forms.   In habits and behavior the Canadian birds do not differ materially, if at all, from the eastern and western chipping sparrows.

*Spring.*—The wintering population begins to migrate from the southern coastal plain in late winter, and the last stragglers have usually left the coastal regions of Georgia by the middle of April. Farther inland in the uplands of the middle coastal plain, they are usually gone by May 1.   In the south the males are singing on their territories by late March.   Trautman (1940) has the following to say of their arrival in central Ohio:

It was sometime between March 17 and April 2, usually the last week of March, that the first Eastern Chipping Sparrows arrived.   A few days after April 1 a small wave appeared, and by April 10 the species had become numerous.   The peak of migration began about April 12 and continued until April 30.   Usually, all transients had disappeared by May 5.   During the largest flights 5 to 35 could be daily encountered.   The earlier arrivals were in groups of 3 to 6 individuals of their own kind, or in flocks of Eastern Field and Allegheny Song sparrows. They could be found about weed patches, weedy and vine-entangled fence rows, and brushy thickets near woodlands. After mid-April individuals and pairs were most frequently observed on lawns, in trees, in shrubbery, and in fields, and about farmhouses, cottages, and villages. In the spring the species preferred uplands and well-drained situations.

The average date Walkinshaw (1944b) reports for first arrivals in southern Michigan is April 13. Roberts (1936) gives April 5 as an average arrival date in southern Minnesota. In central Saskatchewan, over a 4-year period, the average for first arrivals fell in the 2nd week in May (Houston 1953, 1954, 1955, 1956). Usually within 2 weeks after the first arrivals the males are on their territories.

*Territory.*—The following description of territory is quoted from Walkinshaw (1944b):

> When first observed each spring male Chipping Sparrows have been already attached to certain territories, which they proclaim by singing from some perch during most of the daylight hours. In Battle Creek they were not always completely surrounded by other Chipping Sparrows, so that their territories, although limited on one or more sides, were quite flexible on the others. Territorial defense consisted chiefly in chasing intruders, which then usually left at once. I have often observed a trespasser depart on the mere approach of the resident male with wings slightly lowered and feathers slightly raised * * * . On one occasion a resident male drove away a trespassing female.

Louise de Kiriline Lawrence has submitted the following notes on an encounter she observed between an invading male and a pair that had just fledged its first nestlings: "A chase, then halt on twigs with the strange male singing loudly and vigorously several songs. Chase again, then halt on twigs followed by impudent singing by the strange male and the home male silent. This has gone on for several hours (it went on from 1 p.m. until night-fall) with only short intervals for feedings. Both birds were panting from the heat and exertion * * *. Sometimes the female takes part in the chasing." Mrs. Lawrence adds that the next day the strange male had retired from the scene and the pair was busy building the second nest.

My own observations made in Itasca State Park, Minn., indicate that the female defends at least the area of the nest tree. Two instances occurred while I was trying to trap the parent birds for banding, using the nestlings to lure the parents into the trap. In the first instance I had placed the male in a cage to keep him out of the trap and thrown a jacket over the cage. A neighboring unmated male soon entered the territory and sang. As it approached the nest tree, it stopped and sang at intervals. The female was at the nest and paid no attention until he entered the tree adjacent to the nest tree. She then attacked and he retreated to his own territory. On the second occasion, with a different pair, I released the male from the

PLATE 63

Butler County, Pa., June 8, 1945                 H. H. Harrison
EASTERN CHIPPING SPARROW AT NEST (NOTE COWBIRD EGG)

Pike County, Pa., July 1957                 D. S. Heintzelman
CHIPPING SPARROW WITH FLEDGLINGS

PLATE 64

Crawford County, Mich., July 1937          L. H. Walkinshaw

### NEST AND EGGS OF CLAY-COLORED SPARROW

Crawford County, Mich., June 23, 1944          L. H. Walkinshaw

### CLAY-COLORED SPARROW FEEDING YOUNG

trap. He flew directly to the nest where again the female was at the empty nest. She immediately drove him out. He soon returned, giving the twitter the male usually uses when approaching the incubating female, and she showed no aggressiveness toward him.

Territories are about an acre in extent. Walkinshaw found them to be between 1 and 1½ acres at Battle Creek, Mich. In 1953 at the Lake Itasca Forestry and Biological Station, 21 pairs nested on 52 acres, but much of this area was unoccupied and some territories were about one-half acre. At the Edwin S. George Reserve in southeastern Michigan, Sutton (1960) concluded that one territory was 70 yards by 45 yards, or approximately two-thirds acre.

*Courtship and mating.*—Bradley (1940) reports that in the pair she observed at Douglas Lake, Mich., courtship took place while the female was nest building. "It consisted of outbursts of song by the male from the top of a cabin, interspersed with quick flights to the ground where the female was pulling up weed stalks for the nest. Copulation took place on the ground soon after this display." Walkinshaw (1944b) observes that copulation "which usually took place on the ground, but sometimes on a horizontal branch, wire, or roof, is frequent during the days preceding egg laying and often occurs several times in succession. The female assumes a crouching posture with head and tail slightly raised and wings rapidly vibrating; the male approaches and hovers over her for a few seconds. During copulation the female (and perhaps the male) utters a rapid call, *see-see-see-see-see.*"

*Nesting.*—The female does all the gathering of nesting material. All observers agree that the female does all the nest building and while the male often accompanies her on her trips to gather nesting material, he usually does not return to the nest tree with her. Nest building goes on throughout the day with greatest activity before noon. Walkinshaw (1944b) states that "most of the nest building was done in the early morning hours." In the single case I observed, nest building was greater during mid-morning than during the first ½ hour of the day. The greatest frequency of trips was 11 in 30 minutes. Walkinshaw (1944b) found that nests in May were completed in 3 to 4 days, while the one July nest observed was completed in 2 days. A single observation of what was probably a second nesting in Minnesota in the 2nd week of June indicated that the nest was built in 2 days.

The nest is almost invariably constructed of dead grass, weed stalks, and rootlets and lined with fine grasses and hair. Horsehair seems by all odds the favorite nest lining material and when available is always the principle component of the lining. When horsehair is not available, the birds will use human hair or that of cattle, deer, raccoon, or other animals. In one case, a nest adjacent to a pen of bison was lined with bison hair. Itasca State Park, Minn., is so remote from horses that no nests found in 1954 contained horsehair. In the summer of 1955 a friend generously gave me some black hair from the mane of his horse to take to Minnesota to use as a lure to trap the females for banding. It worked very well. At nest lining time the females readily entered traps containing a few strands of horsehair. Even after I stopped trapping most newly built nests continued to contain the horsehair, for these sparrows commonly remove the lining from old nests when rebuilding.

The size of eight nests Walkinshaw (1952) studied varied between 80 and 150 millimeters (average 112 millimeters) in outside diameter at the top, between 40 and 60 millimeters (average 48.3 millimeters) interior diameter at the top, between 45 and 75 millimeters (average 56.8 millimeters) exterior depth, between 30 and 50 millimeters (average 37.3 millimeters) interior depth, and between 3 and 5.8 grams (average 4.7 grams) weight.

Chipping sparrows nest in a variety of situations and of trees and shrubs. The favored nesting site seems to be in conifers—pines in the Southeast, junipers where they are common, and spruces in the North. Orchard trees and vines are also high on the list of preferences. Of 115 active and inactive nests located in 1954 and 1955 in and around Itasca State Park, 85 were in spruce, 11 in jack pine, 6 in fir, 6 in juniper, 4 in white pine, 1 in red pine, 1 in low willow, and 1 in an Ampelopsis vine. Walkinshaw (1944b) lists 51 nests found near dwellings at Battle Creek, Mich.; of these 14 were in spruce, 8 in arborvitae, 5 in juniper, 8 in grape vines, 7 in the horizontal branches of horse chestnut, pear, or apple trees, 5 in rose or spirea bushes, 2 in the side of old straw stacks, 1 on a mowing machine in a semi-open tool shed, and 1 on the ground in dead grass. Burleigh (1958) states that "Pairs frequenting the open pine woods almost invariably build their nests at the outer end of a limb of one of the larger pines, the height varying from ten, to not infrequently, thirty or forty feet from the ground."

A number of observers in addition to Walkinshaw have reported nests built on the ground. Other unusual nesting sites reported were at the bottom of a hairy woodpecker's winter roost hole 6 inches deep (R. F. Miller, 1923), in a hanging basket filled with moss on a stoop within a foot of the door (F.O.H., 1884) and for 3 years in a row a chipping sparrow nested in pepper plants hung to dry in later summer not far inside a shed on a Philadelphia County, Pa., farm (R. F. Miller, 1911).

Most nests are built at low to moderate heights. At Lake Itasca, of 83 nests measured from May 17 to July 23, 1955, 51 (61.5 percent) were lower than 6 feet and 11 (13.3 percent) were higher than 11 feet. Eighteen of these nests were found between May 17 and June 8 by following individual birds until they flew to their nests instead of searching in what might be considered the most likely places. Of the 18, eight were higher than 10 feet, three were between 19¾ feet and 25½ feet and five were between 30 and 36 feet. Of these last five, three were within 8 feet of the top of 35' and 40-foot spruces and firs. In the summer of 1956 Robert Galati found two chipping sparrow nests near the tops of black spruce trees in a mature black spruce bog in Itasca State Park—one was 56.5 feet from the ground in a 58.5-foot tree, the other at 54.5 feet in a 56-foot spruce. They were 70 feet apart and were both being built on July 2 when Galati first observed them. He later witnessed a territorial dispute that began 30 feet up in a dead black spruce and ended with the combatants rolling on the ground. Maurice Broun reports two high nests at Hawk Mountain Sanctuary, Pa., one 30 feet up in the top of a maple overgrown with grape vines, and a second 50 feet from the ground in the top of an oak.

Walkinshaw (1944b) found that the average nesting height became progressively higher during the summer; 15 May nests averaged 3.6 feet from the ground, five June nests averaged 5.0 feet, and seven July nests averaged 7.5 feet.

*Eggs.*—The chipping sparrow usually lays four eggs, but sometimes only three or as many as five. They are slightly glossy, and ovate with some tending to short ovate. The ground is "bluish glaucous" or "Etain blue," with speckles, spots, blotches, and a few scrawls of dark browns such as "auburn," "Brussels brown", "Argus brown", "mummy brown", or "snuff brown", and black, with undermarkings of "pale neutral gray." They are rather sparingly marked, and most of the spots are confined to the large end where they frequently form a loose wreath. This wreath may be of very small spots or quite long interlacing scrawls. In most instances the spots are rather sharply defined and in many cases the undermarkings are absent. Occasionally an egg will be unmarked. A set of three eggs in the American Museum of Natural History is pure white and unspotted. The measurements of 90 eggs average 17.6 by 12.9 millimeters; the eggs showing the four extremes measure *20.3* by 12.7, 16.8 by *15.2*, *15.2* by 12.5, and 16.8 by *11.2* millimeters.

The first egg is laid on the morning following completion of the nest. One egg is laid each morning usually before 7:00 a.m., though sometimes later (Walkinshaw, 1952) until the clutch is complete. In most cases four eggs complete the set; three-egg sets are common, and clutches of two and five are rare.

Street (1954) reports on 63 clutches in the vicinity of La Anna in the Pocono Mountains of northeastern Pennsylvania and Walkinshaw (1944b) reports on 45 complete clutches in southern Michigan as:

|  | Clutch Size | | | | |
|---|---|---|---|---|---|
|  | 2 | 3 | 4 | 5 | Average |
| No. of sets (Street) | | 17 | 42 | 4 | 3.79 |
| No. of sets (Walkinshaw) | 1 | 15 | 29 | --- | 3.63 |

Walkinshaw found that the average clutch size decreased from 3.81 in May to 3.00 in July.

Sets containing five eggs have been reported from Newton, Mass. (G. M. Allen, 1892), Buckeye Lake, Ohio (Trautman, 1940), St. Louis County, Minn. (Roberts, 1936), and Flotten Lake, Saskatchewan (Robert P. Allen, *fide* Godfrey, 1950).

Some variation in egg color and marking has been found. Over a 5-year period Walkinshaw (1952) examined 35 eggs from the same female and found them all darker blue than the usual chipping sparrow eggs, and the markings, usually sparse scrawls, were heavy black. A clutch of unspotted eggs has been reported (Oologist, 1884:70).

*Incubation.*—Incubation begins on the day before the last egg is laid. Usually the female does all the incubating, but Walkinshaw (1944b) reports one instance of the male incubating.

Walkinshaw (1952) determined the incubation period for nine nests and found a relationship between the air temperature and the length of the incubation period. The four nests that were incubated during the period of highest average mean temperature (66.2° to 76.0° F.) had 11-day incubation periods, while when the average mean temperature was lowest (48.7°) the incubation period was 14 days.

As with many song birds, the male feeds the female while she incubates. As he approaches the nest tree he utters a series of low chips, sometimes rapidly. At the sound the female becomes alert and restless, and sometimes leaves the nest to feed near by. At other times she remains on the nest. In one case the male came to the nest and fed the female only 3 minutes after she returned to the nest from being with him. She often chips rapidly, flutters her wings, and begs as he arrives.

The incubating female often can be approached quite closely, which I found most convenient. I marked a number of females on the nest for identification by applying model airplane dope to them with the tip of a stalk of timothy grass.

*Young.*—When the eggs hatch the female eats the shell (Walkinshaw, 1944b). The young, which are capable of only one activity, feeble gaping, are fed almost immediately. Walkinshaw (1944b) watched a female feed one young 20 minutes and another 28 minutes after hatching. I have observed two first feedings. In one case the male brought food to the nest, the female flew off, and he fed the hatchlings. In the second instance the male brought food and gave it to the female on the nest; she then hopped up on the rim and, while the male stood by, fed the newly hatched young.    In nests that I have observed the male did most of the feeding for the first few days, and the female brooded the young.    Toward the end of the 3rd day she brooded less and fed the young more often, until, by the last days before the young fledged she brought food as often as the male.    The rate of feeding ranged from 2 trips per hour the first day to 17 per hour toward the end of the nesting period.    Some individual differences occur in the roles of male and female in the early feeding.    In a nest observed by Bradley (1940) the pattern was the same as in those I watched, but Walkinshaw (1944b) reports a nest where the female did nearly all the early feeding.    This was an August nest when the pattern may be somewhat different, especially when the male is still tending young from a previous nesting.

The female does most of the brooding.    Walkinshaw (1944b) found that "on a cool morning the male occasionally brooded for a very few minutes."    On the first day the young are brooded about 90 percent of the time.    This declines until after the 4th day there is little brooding, except when the sun is directly on the nest, at which time the female often stands over the young.

Weed (1898) recorded the activity at a nest containing three young that fledged 2 days later.    The observations were made on June 22 and extended from 4:06 a.m., when the brooding parent first left the nest, until 7:50 p.m., when a parent settled down for the next night of brooding.    During this period of nearly 15¾ hours the parents fed the young 189 times.    During the first hour they were fed 13 times. The lowest number of feedings was between 6:00 and 7:00 a.m. when there were 7 trips; the highest was 21 trips between 1:00 and 2:00 p.m.    During the last hour of the day the rate was the same as for the first, 13 times.

William R. Dawson and Francis C. Evans (1957) conducted a study on the growth and development of nestling field and chipping sparrows. At hatching the muscular system is poorly developed and the nestlings remain inactive except for gaping for food.    The muscular system develops rapidly and by the 4th day they can hold up their heads and are attempting to stand.    The capacity for temperature regulation begins to appear on the 5th day and it is quite effective by the 6th. On the 7th the birds are "essentially homeothermic."    Dawson and Evans report that on the 6th day they were so active they had to be confined to boxes to prevent escape.    I found that in northern Minnesota the 6th day is the best time to band nestlings, for at that age they are large enough to band and may still be easily returned to the nest; 7-day-old nestlings often abandoned the nest after being handled.    Dawson and Evans (1957) report that "touching or jarring the nest generally produced a gaping response in 5-day-old or younger individuals whereas such a stimulus caused older birds to crouch low and huddle in the nest."    In the nests they studied 2 individual nestlings fledged at 8 days, 18 at 9 days, 20 at 10 days, 10 at 11 days, and 2 at 12 days for an average age at fledging of 9.85 days.    The nestlings increased from a mean weight of 1.7 grams at hatching to about 10 grams at fledging.    Walkinshaw (1944b) found several nestlings still wet from hatching to weight 1.1 grams.

Walkinshaw (1944b) reports that "When only two or three days old, the young uttered a low *zeee-zee-zee-zee* call when they were fed.    On leaving the nest they immediately began to use a *zip-ip-zip-ip-zip-ip* or *chip-chip-chip* call."

He describes the nest-leaving as follows: "They hopped to the edge of the nest and remained there for some time.    Then they moved gradually out into the branches of the nest tree.    Sometimes one fell to the ground, and it was then led by one of the adults, usually the male, into a brushy area.    By 10 days of age they could hop into the lower branches of bushes, where they sometimes remained for long periods on one perch.    By 12 days of age they could fly a few feet, and at 14 days of age they were capable of sustained flight."

*Plumage.*—Dwight (1900) describes the juvenal plumage, which is acquired by a complete juvenal molt, as follows: "Above, wood-brown, grayish on nape and rump, heavily streaked with dull black, faintly tinged on scapularies and crown with chestnut.    Wings and tail dull black, rectrices and primaries ashy edged, the secondaries and tertiaries chestnut edged, wing coverts and tertiaries terminally edged with buff.    Ill-defined superciliary stripe, dull grayish white spotted with black.    Auriculars wood-brown.    Dusky loral and postocular streak.    Below, white, streaked except on abdomen and crissum, with dull black.    Bill and feet pinkish buff, the former growing dusky and the latter wood-brown with age."

In juvenal plumage the chipping sparrow is most like the field sparrow, but can be distinguished by the fact that it is "much more heavily streaked, both above and below, than in the young field sparrow, the dark markings being much sharper and more distinctily blackish."    (Sutton, 1935.)

Sutton (1937) observed the plumage development and molts of a young chipping sparrow, of precisely known age, from the time it left the nest at 8 days of age until it was 8 weeks old.    He summarizes the changes as follows:

The postjuvenal molt begins when the bird is about thirty days old. The post-juvenal molt thus must begin in late June and early July in young of normal first broods * * *.

The plumage worn by the eight-day-old Chipping Sparrow is not, strictly speaking, a complete plumage of any sort. Not until the bird is about three weeks old does it don its first set of lesser wing coverts. As the total skin area of the growing bird increases new rows or sets of feathers appear, particularly in the region of the lower breast and belly.

The juvenal middle and greater coverts drop out almost simultaneously when the bird is about six weeks old. Molting of the body plumage takes place much more gradually, but the streaked feathers of the under parts are all gone by the time the bird is forty-five days old.

The postjuvenal molt does not involve the remiges and rectrices, but it does involve the tertials, the dropping out of which is subsequent to that of the middle and greater coverts.

The plumage acquired by this partial molt is the first winter plumage which Dwight (1900) describes as similar to the juvenal plumage "but with the chestnut crown veiled with buff edgings and narrowly streaked with black. Below, uniform grayish white, unstreaked, washed with buff on throat and sides. Superciliary line dull white buff tinged. Loral, postocular and indistinct submalar streaks black."

The first nuptial plumage is acquired by a molt in March and April confined largely to the head, chin, and throat. This results in the chestnut crown, the white superciliary lines and the white chin with the adjacent cinereous gray characteristic of the adults (Dwight, 1900). Other changes involve increased streaking of the back brought about by abrasion and a general paling of the buff and chestnut caused by gradual fading.

Adult winter plumage is acquired by a complete postnuptial molt, and the adult nuptial plumage by a partial prenuptial molt (Dwight, 1900).

*Food.*—Judd (1900) examined the contents of 250 stomachs taken from March through November from New England to California. He found that for the whole sample the food was 62 percent vegetable and 38 percent animal. The vegetable component was made up largely of grass seed (48 percent of total food) which included 26 percent (of total) crab and pigeon grass seed; the rest was grain (4 percent) and a miscellany (10 percent of total) of the seeds of clover, ragweed, amaranth, wood sorrel, lambsquarters, purslane, chickweed, knotweed, and black bindweed. The animal component contained weevils (6 percent), leaf beetles (2 percent), other Coleoptera (3 percent), caterpillars (9 percent), grasshoppers (10 percent), and 8 percent made up of such organisms as leafhoppers, true bugs, ants, spiders, and parasitic wasps. He found that in June the food was 93 percent insects—63 percent grasshoppers, 25 percent caterpillars, and 6 percent leaf beetles.

At Lake Itasca in summer the chipping sparrows often fed by the doorsteps where the table cloths had been shaken, and it was supposed that it would be simple to trap them with bread crumbs or oatmeal as bait. When neither of these proved effective, we tried fine chick feed with equal lack of success. These chipping sparrows were apparently nearly exclusively insectivorous in the breeding season, for they readily enter grain-baited traps at other times. Burleigh (1958) writes, "Stoddard, in his manuscript on the bird life of Grady County, tells us that, during the late winter and early spring months from 1924 to 1930, many Chipping Sparrows were caught and banded that had entered the quail traps operated by the Co-operative Quail Investigation." Stoddard (1931) baited the traps "with a half-and-half mixture of 'baby chick' feed and 'hen chow,' or in wet weather with a combination of wheat, sorghum, millet, popcorn, and similar whole small grains that do not sour so badly."

Mrs. Louis de Kiriline Lawrence writes that she watched a pair, feeding young 9 or 10 days old, pecking at a salt block. Notes submitted by A. D. Du Bois record "The chipping sparrows are frequent and welcome visitors in the vegetable garden. In the nesting season, when they have nestlings to be fed, they patrol the row or two of cabbage plants looking for and picking off the cabbage worms, the troublesome green larvae of the cabbage butterfly. A chipping sparrow that I saw eating dandelion seeds seemed to swallow the downy tufts and all."

*Behavior.*—On two occasions I have seen an incubating bird tumble from the nest and flutter along the ground. One nest was in the lowest limb of a white spruce at Itasca Park, 6 feet from the ground and 10 feet from the trunk. Each time I approached this nest the occupant dropped out and fluttered hesitatingly along the ground in a direction away from my approach. The second nest was about 6 feet from the ground near the top of an ornamental juniper along the west wall of a building in Delaware, Ohio. This individual behaved in the same manner as the Minnesota bird.

Cases of "flycatching" have been reported from at least two widely separated points. Laurence B. Potter writes from Eastend, Saskatchewan, "This spring I remarked for the first time chipping and clay-colored sparrows springing out from a fence in approved flycatcher style." F. H. Allen (*in* litt.) reports from Massachusetts: 'Like so many passerine birds the chipping sparrow occassionally catches insects on the wing. On a September day I saw one associated with cedar waxwings and a phoebe that was flycatching from some telegraph wires.  The chippy followed suit but always landed on the ground instead of returning to the wires."

The chipping sparrow is numbered among those birds that have been observed sparring with their reflection in a pane of glass (Forbush, 1929).

Robert A. Norris submits the following interesting note on their behavior in the winter flocks:

"One characteristic that I have noticed repeatedly among winter flocks of chipping sparrows is the proneness of individuals—usually but two at a time—to engage in brief, almost momentary, aerial disputes or 'clashes' involving excited call notes and agile maneuvers— sometimes upward, sometimes in other directions.  While still in the air the birds separate so that their dogfight, if it may be so called, seems to end as suddenly as it begins.  The reasons for flight combats in chippies are not at all clear; they do not seem to be directly associated either with food supply or with temporary territorial holdings.  I have not observed field sparrows giving these aerial performances at any time.  Indeed, these actions, if seen among members of a distant flock of small sparrows, enable one to predict with confidence that the sparrows will turn out to be chippies."

*Voice.*—Donald J. Borror analyzed 461 chipping sparrow songs by means of an audiospectrograph from recordings of individuals in Maine, Pennsylvania, West Virginia, Ohio, and Michigan.  The following account is taken from his work (Borror, 1959):

Songs of the Chipping Sparrow * * * have been described * * * as a simple trill or rapid series of notes, all on one pitch, and of a dull and unmusical quality. The only variations mentioned are in speed ("fast" or "slow") and in the number of notes in the song. * * * Chipping Sparrow songs are generally simple trills * * *.

The individual phrases of the song contain from one to three slurred notes. The slurring is usually quite rapid, in some cases over an octave or more in 0.01 second; it is this rapid slurring of the notes that gives the song its dull and unmusical quality. The notes are usually clear, but in a few songs each phrase contains a buzzy note. The notes may be up-slurred or down-slurred (or both); the phrases in most songs contain both up-slurred and down-slurred elements.

* * * Very little variation, never more than a few thousandths of a second, was found in the length of different phrases in the same song.

* * * The number of phrases in the songs studied varied from 9 to 72, and averaged 33.31. A few songs whose phrases were two- or three-noted had the last phrase incomplete.

* * * The phrase length, measured from the beginning of one phrase to the beginning of the next, varied from 0.044 to 0.145 (average, 0.087) second; this corresponds to a variation in rate of from 22.5 to 6.9 (average, 11.5) phrases per second. * * * In general, the shorter the phrases the more phrases there were in the song. * * * The songs varied in length from 0.94 to 6.86 (average, 2.61) seconds. * * * There was no evidence in the recordings studied of any significant geographic variation in song pattern in this species.

It is interesting to note that the songs of eight individuals recorded in Mexico and analyzed by Marler and Isaac (1960) fall within the range of variation Borror found in his recordings from the northeastern United States.

Borror describes the songs of one individual which began with a short series of long phrases and then abruptly went into a series of short, more rapid phrases. For two seasons I observed a male at Lake Itasca that had the opposite pattern. He began with a series of rapid short phrases and abruptly changed to a series of longer slow phrases. The change was so marked that one observer concluded that two individuals were singing in the same tree. Forbush (1929) remarks that "rarely a bird will interpolate or add some unusual improvised musical notes."

Beginning with Audubon (1841) observers have noted that the chipping sparrow occasionally sings at night. Mr. Bent recorded the following in his notes: "May 13, Dudley St., 10 p.m. Pitchy dark— heard a chipping sparrow sing one strain." At Itasca State Park a bird not infrequently sang a single song from the ridge of our cabin roof at night.

In a letter, A. A. Saunders writes, "On a number of occasions, in the very early morning, I have heard birds singing a series of short songs, each one of eight notes, and each one beginning with a strongly accented note. This may be a sort of twilight song, but if so it is not common." This may be the same song that F. H. Allen describes when he writes, "The early morning singing of the chipping sparrow consists of a rapid repetition of much shorter songs than the songs we hear at other times. I have on at least one occasion heard this manner of singing late in the afternoon."

*Field marks.*—The two sexes are marked and colored alike. The species may be readily distinguished from other *Spizellas* by the reddish brown cap, the darker lower edge of which sharply delimits it from the whitish superciliary line, which is bordered below by the black eye line. The plain underparts are gray to grayish white. The bill is black.

The song is most apt to be confused with that of the pine warbler. Competent ornithologists have been misled by a chipping sparrow singing in a pine warbler habitat.

*Enemies.*—Statements on the importance of the cowbird as a factor in limiting chipping sparrow population seem to vary considerably. Friedmann (1929) lists it as one of the five species most commonly parasitized in New York State. He reports "It is an extremely common sight to see one of these familiar little birds feeding a big, clumsy Cowbird." In a study of nests in southeastern Michigan, Berger (1951a), in a small sample of eight nests, had five parasitized, while of 66 Walkinshaw (1944b) found in southwestern Michigan only three were parasitized. Sutton (1960) reports that on the George Reserve in southern Michigan he found only 1 of 38 nests with a cowbird egg in it, and although he saw one young cowbird out of the nest being fed by a chipping sparrow, he did not find a nest containing a young cowbird. He attributes the low parasitism to the fact that in the red cedars of the George Reserve the nests are very well concealed. The success of the cowbirds in chipping sparrow nests seems to be low.

About 60 percent of chipping sparrow nests are successful (Walkinshaw, 1944b, 1952) and the failures may be attributed to many different factors of which predation is only one. Snakes (Sutton, 1960), birds (Dixon, 1930), and cats (Walkinshaw, 1944b) have been observed preying on eggs or young. Maurice Broun writes me from Hawk Mountain, Pa., that "Our chipping sparrows are often victims of predation by the black and milk snakes. We have noted that when first nestings fail, the birds usually build their second nest at higher elevations."

Chipping sparrows are subject to a number of external parasites. H. S. Peters (1933) lists the following parasites collected from birds during banding: two species of lice (*Philopterus subflavescues* (Geof.), *Ricinus* sp.); two species of flies (*Ornithoics couftueus* Say, *Ornithomyia avicularia* Linn); one species of tick (*Ixodes brunneus* Koch); and two species of mites (*Analgopsis* sp., *Liponipsus sylviarum*).

A foot disease, often called "foot-pox," is common in chipping sparrows in the southeast in late winter and early spring. At Summerville, S.C., 13.6 percent of the 323 William P. Warton banded in 1929 (Warton, 1931) were afflicted, while another 9.3 percent showed evidence that they had recovered from the disease. In 1930 the disease was less prevalent, active in only 5.09 percent of the 255 birds Warton banded that year. Robert A. Norris, while banding a smaller sample, found a much higher incidence in 34 adults and first-winter birds trapped near Tifton, Ga., from Feb. 29 through Mar. 24, 1952. He reports (Norris, 1952) "Twenty seven birds or about 82%, including both age groups, were afflicted with foot-pox (*epithelioma contagiosum*), having discolored tumors on one or more toes and occasionally at the end of the tarsus. Some had lost a claw or two, and some parts of toes * * *. 1952 appears to be a peak year for this disease * * *. The overall average weight of 12.5 grams is very close to that of April trapped, non-diseased birds from Cleveland, Ohio (Baldwin and Kendeigh, *Auk*, 55:436, 1938). Both this fact and the data from Tifton suggest that, in general, diseased Chipping Sparrows weigh about the same as non-diseased ones."

*Fall.*—After nesting the family groups wander about feeding, usually in weedy fields, along fence rows and forest edges where they often join company with other family groups of their own species and also song sparrows and field sparrows until they form flocks of considerable size.  They wander about until they are ready to migrate in late September or early October.  In the North, migration usually begins in early October and the last individuals are seen in late October or the first weeks of November.

Audubon (1841) was of the opinion that this species migrated by day and he wrote: "These gentle birds migrate by day; and no sooner has October returned and mellowed the tints of the sylvan foliage, than flitting before you on the road, you see family after family moving southward, chasing each other as if in play, sweeping across the path, or flocking suddenly to a tree if surprised, but almost instantly returning to the ground and resuming their line of march.  At the approach of night they throw themselves into thickets of brambles, where, in company with several other species, they keep up a murmuring conversation until long after dark."

While the feeding flocks may work their way south in the manner Audubon described, Clarence Cottam (1953) describes large flocks of night migrants at the Capitol in Washington, D.C.  He says: "windy night of October 23d * * * fully a thousand Chipping Sparrows were swarming in the lighted areas from the statue of Freedom on the apex of the dome, outward over the Senate and House wings and on to the lighted terrace and walks surrounding the building.  * * * the floodlights * * * were turned off shortly after midnight * * *.  By 1:00 A.M. there was very little activity and the birds seemed to be settled for the night.  Consequently the observer left, but when he returned about sunrise not a Chipping Sparrow could be found. * * * on the night of October 29th * * * another huge flock was reported at the Capitol."

A. A. Saunders writes that "birds rarely sing in the fall, in late September or early October."  Forbush (1929) says that the young males begin to sing in August.

*Winter.*—Most chipping sparrows winter in the southern states. A few stragglers often linger along the coast as far north as New Hampshire and inland as far north as southern Ohio, Indiana, and Oklahoma.  They do not remain as far north as the field sparrow, and they do not ordinarily winter in large numbers north of the North Carolina coast.  From this point on south, along the east coast, they outnumber the field sparrow on the coastal plain, but are not so common on the piedmont and are generally absent from the western North Carolina and South Carolina highlands.  They become less common down the Florida peninsula.  They seem to avoid the southern tip of Florida and the coast line of the gulf states, although they winter in some numbers on the coastal plain just inland from the coast and as far north as northern Alabama and southern Arkansas.

The first winter visitors arrive on the coastal plain of Georgia in late October or the first days of November or at about the time that the last ones are leaving the North (Burleigh, 1958).

## DISTRIBUTION

### Eastern Chipping Sparrow (*S. p. passerina*)

*Range.*—Minnesota, Ontario, southern Quebec and Newfoundland south to Nuevo León, the Gulf coast, and southern Florida.

*Breeding range.*—The eastern chipping sparrow breeds from northeastern Minnesota, northern Michigan (Isle Royale), central and northeastern Ontario (Big Wood, Kirkland Lake), southern Quebec (Lake Mistassini), and southwestern Newfoundland (Tompkins, Codroy Valley) south to eastern Kansas, central southern Oklahoma (Lawton), southeastern Texas (Huntsville), central Louisiana (Florien, Baton Rouge), southern Mississippi (Gulfport), northwestern Florida (Pensacola), central Georgia (Columbus, Camp Stewart), and southeastern South Carolina (Mount Pleasant).

*Winter range.*—Winters from central Oklahoma (Oklahoma City), southern Arkansas (Delight), southwestern Tennessee (Memphis), central Alabama (Birmingham), central western Georgia (Columbus), Virginia, and southeastern Maryland (Berlin), rarely farther north from Michigan (Locke), southern Ontario (Toronto), Connecticut (New Haven), Massachusetts (Boston), and Nova Scotia (Wolfville), south to Nuevo León (Linares), the Gulf coast, and southern Florida (Fort Myers, Jupiter).

*Casual records.*—Casual in Arizona (four localities), Utah (Navajo Mountain), northern Newfoundland (St. Anthony), Cuba, and Bermuda.

*Migration.*—The data deal with the species as a whole. Early dates of spring arrival are: North Carolina—Raleigh, February 23 (average of 16 years, March 8). Virginia—Cape Henry, March 6. District of Columbia—average of 39 years, March 22. Maryland—Charles County, March 2; Baltimore County, March 7; Laurel, March 17 (median of 8 years, March 25). Pennsylvania—Beaver and Sewickly, March 19. New Jersey—Cape May, March 22. New York—Tompkins County, March 29; Essex, March 30. Connecticut—Glastonbury, March 12; New Haven, March 28. Rhode Island—Pawtucket, March 1. Massachusetts—Belmont and Concord, March 26; Martha's Vineyard, April 1 (median of 7 years, April 6). Vermont—St. Johnsbury, March 31. New Hampshire—New Hampton, April 2 (median of 21 years, April 21). Maine—Bangor, April 10.

Quebec—Montreal area, April 15. New Brunswick—St. Andrews, March 23; Summerville, March 28. Newfoundland—Tompkins, May 15. Arkansas—Little Rock, February 23; Fayetteville, March 12. Tennessee—Athens, March 2 (average of 6 years, March 12); Nashville, March 3 (median of 11 years, March 9). Missouri—St. Louis, March 25 (median of 15 years, April 13). Illinois—Urbana, March 8 (median of 20 years, March 23); Chicago, April 5 (average of 16 years, April 20). Indiana—Wayne County, March 16 (median of 18 years, April 6). Ohio—central Ohio, March 11 (median of 40 years, March 31). Michigan—Detroit area, March 6 (median of 10 years, March 28); Battle Creek, March 25 (median of 59 years, April 12). Ontario—Ottawa, April 12 (average of 21 years, April 20). Iowa—Sioux City, April 3 (average of 32 years, April 18). Minnesota—Minneapolis-St. Paul, April 6 (mean of 15 years, April 21). Kansas—northeastern Kansas, March 6 (median of 20 years, April 23). South Dakota—Sioux Falls, May 7 (average of 3 years, May 12). North Dakota—Jamestown, April 25; Cass County, April 28 (average, April 30). Manitoba—Treesbank, May 2 (average of 15 years, May 7). New Mexico—Los Alamos, April 4 (median of 8 years, April 19). Wyoming—Torrington, April 19 (average of 9 years, April 28). Idaho—Moscow, April 11 (median of 11 years, April 25). Montana—Columbia Falls, April 26; Libby, April 28 (median of 10 years, May 3). Washington—Everson, April 1 (median of 9 years, April 19).

Late dates of spring departure are: Florida—Daytona Beach, May 13. Alabama—Baldwin County, May 1. Georgia—Grady County, May 4. Maryland—Laurel, May 4. Illinois—Chicago, June 1 (average of 16 years, May 21). Ohio—Buckeye Lake, median, May 8.

Early dates of fall arrival are: Ohio—Buckeye Lake, median, September 10. Illinois—Chicago, average of 16 years, September 20. New York—Tiana, September 5. Maryland—Laurel, September 14. Georgia—Grady County, October 20. Alabama—Dauphin Island, October 11. Florida—Tallahassee, October 6; Orlando, October 15.

Late dates of fall departure are: Washington—Pullman, October 2. Montana—Columbia Falls, October 7. Idaho—Lewiston, October 16 (median of 11 years, October 9). Wyoming—Laramie, October 18 (average of 6 years, October 10). Utah—Salt Lake City, November 20. New Mexico—Los Alamos, October 26 (median of 8 years, October 10). Manitoba—Treesbank, October 4 (average of 14 years, September 22). North Dakota—Cass County, October 1 (average, September 20). Kansas—northeastern Kansas, November 15 (median of 11 years, October 20). Minnesota—Minneapolis-St. Paul, October 8 (mean of 7 years, October 1). Iowa—Sioux City,

October 24 (average of 32 years, October 10). Ontario—Ottawa, October 17 (average of 6 years, October 2). Michigan—Detroit area, November 11 (mean of 10 years, October 25); Battle Creek, November 1 (median of 31 years, October 14). Ohio—Buckeye Lake, November 2 (median, October 25). Indiana—Wayne County, November 2 (median of 8 years, October 10). Illinois—Chicago, November 6 (average of 16 years, October 22). Missouri—St. Louis, November 1 (median of 15 years, October 10). Tennessee—Nashville, November 21 (median of 27 years, November 2); Knox County, November 13. New Brunswick—Fredericton, November 11. Quebec—Ulverton, November 3. Maine—Isle au Haut, November 21; Westbrook and Brunswick, November 16. New Hampshire—New Hampton, November 26 (median of 21 years, October 31); Dublin, November 20. Vermont—Putney, October 26. Massachusetts—Martha's Vineyard, November 30 (median of 5 years, September 18). Rhode Island—Providence, October 28. Connecticut—East Hartford, November 19. New York—Westchester, November 9; Ontario, November 1. New Jersey—Cape May, November 9. Pennsylvania—State College, November 4; Beaver, November 3. Maryland—Baltimore County, December 4; Anne Arundel County, December 3; Laurel, November 29 (median of 6 years, November 9). District of Columbia—December 17 (average of 18 years, November 10). Virginia—Richmond, November 21. North Carolina—Raleigh, November 25.

*Egg dates.*—Illinois: 17 records, May 8 to July 11.

Maryland: 240 records, April 14 to August 28; 120 records, May to June 2.

Massachusetts: 76 records, May 12 to June 21; 50 records May 27 to June 6.

Michigan: 166 records, May 1 to August 20; about 85 records, May 21 to June 22.

New Brunswick: 25 records, May 21 to July 15.

New York: 38 records, May 15 to July 11; 19 records, May 30 to June 16.

Ontario: 72 records, May 16 to July 10; 36 records, May 29 to June 14.

West Virginia: 22 records, April 16 to June 7; 12 records, May 6 to May 20.

## Canadian Chipping Sparrow (*S. p. boreophila*)

*Range.*—Alaska, Yukon, Mackenzie and Manitoba south to southern Baja California, Michoacán, Puebla, and central Texas.

*Breeding range.*—The Canadian chipping sparrow breeds from east-central Alaska (Tanana Valley), central Yukon (Dawson), central Mackenzie (Fort Reliance, Fort Good Hope, Dickson Canyon), northeastern Alberta, northern Saskatchewan (Sandy Lake, Reindeer Lake), and northeastern Manitoba south through British Columbia and Idaho to northern Utah, northern Colorado, and central Nebraska, ranging east to west central Ontario, central North Dakota, and central South Dakota.

*Winter range.*—Winters from southern California, northern Sonora, and north central Texas to Michoacán, State of México, and Puebla.

*Casual records.*—Casual in Mississippi (Deer Island). Accidental at Point Barrow, Alaska.

*Egg dates.*—Alberta: 30 records, May 30 to June 17; 20 records, June 6 to June 13.

Mackenzie: 8 records, June 9 to June 24.

## SPIZELLA PASSERINA ARIZONAE Coues

# Western Chipping Sparrow

### Contributed by R. Roy Johnson

#### Habits

The western race of the chipping sparrow differs from the nominate eastern subspecies chiefly in being slightly larger in size and paler in color, differences that are seldom discernible in the field. It resembles its eastern relative very closely in practically all aspects of habits and behavior. A bird of wide range and great adaptability, it is essentially an inhabitant of woodland clearings.

In Washington state, Jewett, Taylor, Shaw, and Aldrich (1953) consider it a "common migrant and summer resident from April to September in open timber and brushy situations from Upper Sonoran to Hudsonian Zones." In Oregon, Gabrielson and Jewett (1940) state that it "is one of our most abundant summer resident birds and is one of the familiar lawn birds of the valley towns throughout the State, where it may be found hopping about in the grass, collecting insects and seeds to feed the youngsters in the hairlined nest built in some low-hanging bough. It is equally abundant and unsuspicious about the mountain meadows of the Cascades and in the parklike vistas of the yellow-pine forests of the Blue Mountains, where it is present at all but the highest elevations."

Of its status in California, Grinnell and Miller (1944) say: "Summer resident, migrant, and winter visitant; in some lowland localities in southwestern section present throughout year. Appears in areas of summer residence in April, or at higher elevations in May; leaves in September and early October. Usually common on nesting grounds, sometimes abundant; in winter sparse to fairly common; numbers vary greatly according to area within the extensive and diversified range." Of its habitat they add:

Of great variety, but in summer seemingly always includes the following elements: trees, scattered or in open stands through which much light penetrates to the ground; ground forage area essentially bare or covered with sparse or dense grass, but usually not with continuous, tall grass; the ground usually is not heavily shaded or extensively bush covered. Preference for the more exposed sunny parts of forest and woodland is shown in the high mountains and near the coast. Habitat requirements are met by orchards and oak woodland at lower elevations and in coniferous forests of all zones up to the timber line. The trees seem to be essential as retreats, for song posts and for nest sites, although bushes may also be used for nesting. Foraging is carried on principally on the ground, but also in spring in the foliage of the trees when insect food and buds are there readily available.

In Idaho, M. D. Arvey (1947) calls it a "very common resident in the Transition Life-zone." In Montana according to A. A. Saunders (1921) it is "A common summer resident throughout the state. Breeds commonly in mountains, in mountain valleys, and in the prairie region, in pine hills and cottonwood groves of the Transition zone, and in Douglas fir or lodgepole pine forests of the Canadian. * * * Less common in cottonwood groves of the prairie region than elsewhere, but still very numerous; often abundant in the mountains." He adds that "migrations take place mainly in May and September" and that "nesting takes place mainly in June and July, and there are usually two broods."

J. M. Linsdale (1936a) writes that in Nevada it is a "Summer resident; common on middle slopes of most of the mountains ranges in the state. Present in winter in the Colorado Valley. * * * The species is especially numerous on timbered portions of the mountains in July and August when the young are concentrated in flocks. The mountain mahogany makes up the main portion of the vegetation where chipping sparrows live on the Nevada mountains. However, the birds are often found also in yellow pines, limber pines, aspens and even in sagebrush."

A. C. Twomey (1942) remarks that in the Uinta Basin in Utah the birds follow the water courses into the mountains in spring and nest from the belt of yellow pines to timberline. A. M. Woodbury and H. N. Russell, Jr., (1945) state this race is a common breeder in the Navajo country of Utah, principally between 5,000 and 9,000 feet and especially in the pine and pygmy forests and sagebrush, but it also extends sparingly into the spruce-fir forests above and into the streamside trees below.

In Arizona it "is one of the tamest, most familiar, and also one of the commonest sparrows" according to Phillips, Marshall, and Monson (1964), who specify: "Abundant summer resident in open parts of the Transition and boreal zones, and rather common in open wooded parts of Upper Sonoran Zone, of northern Arizona * * *. Migrates throughout the state. Winters abundantly * * * throughout southern Arizona * * *." F. M. Bailey (1928) says it is also "one of the commonest breeding birds" in New Mexico, where it "breeds as low as 4,700 feet near Montoya * * * up to 11,000 feet near Pecos Baldy, on Jack Creek."

## DISTRIBUTION

*Range.*—Washington and Oregon south to southern Mexico and central Texas.

*Breeding range.*—The western chipping sparrow breeds from Washington, Oregon, northern Utah, southwestern Colorado and western Kansas south to southern California (San Clemente Island, Escondido, San Bernardino Mountains), northern Baja California (probably Sierra San Pedro Mártir), central western and southeastern Arizona (Hualpai and Huachuca mountains), northeastern Sonora (south to latitude 30° N.), northwestern Chihuahua (Pacheco), and western and central Texas (Chisos Mountains, Kerrville, San Antonio).

*Winter range.*—Winters from central California (Snelling), southern Nevada (lower Colorado River Valley), central Arizona (Camp Verde), central New Mexico (San Antonio), and western and central Texas (El Paso, Ingram) south to southern Baja California (Cape San Lucas), Veracruz (Las Vigas), Guerrero (Chilpancingo), and Oaxaca (Tamazulapam).

*Egg dates.*—California: 102 records, March 24 to July 8; 35 records, May 10 to May 30; 40 records, June 10 to June 28.

Oregon: 24 records, May 6 to July 16.

Washington: 12 records, May 15 to June 12.

## SPIZELLA PALLIDA (Swainson)

## Clay-colored Sparrow

### PLATE 64

### Contributed by OSCAR M. ROOT

## HABITS

I have found the quest of clay-colored sparrows on the Canadian prairies a delightful experience. On all sides and overhead the prairie birds join in a joyous symphony—the tumbling liquid chant of the western meadowlark and the fairy piping of the prairie horned lark, the mellow "sliding down the scale of his own notes" of the chestnut-collared longspur, the mournful "wolf" whistle of the upland plover, the earnest minor key of the Savannah sparrow, the exquisite lays of the vesper sparrow, the distant tinkling of the Baird's sparrow, above the Sprague's pipit's wild trillings cascading earthward in a silvery torrent—these are the sweet melodies that Ernest Thompson Seton called the "prairie bells."

As one nears a snowberry patch, he hears yet another song, a persistently repeated, high-pitched "*zee, zee, zee*" with a dreamy, almost soporific timbre, the territorial song of the clay-colored sparrow. The sound is pleasing, but scarcely comparable in musical quality to the rhapsodies that accompany it, just as he who sings it is pleasant without being spectacular. The clay-color is a trim little fellow, neat of form, clothed mostly in shades of brown and gray, with clay-colored trimmings and a three-cornered ear patch of darker brown. A gray and buffy streaked crown helps to distinguish him from his city cousin, the chipping sparrow.

The clay-colored sparrow is one of the common field sparrows in our midwestern plains. It also occurs in the mountain valleys of Alberta and British Columbia. Widmann (1911) reported it breeding at Estes Park, Colo., at an altitude of 7,500 feet in 1910. *S. pallida* is not generally as companionable or familiar with humans as its congener, the chipping sparrow. It seeks the wild prairies rather than the protective warmth of human habitation. By no means a solitary, timid, or unfriendly bird by nature, it tends to avoid humans during nesting season because it requires a brushy type of habitat not ordinarily found in centers of population. Rarely the clay-color nests in public parks, vacant lots, and yards, and catches insects in neighboring gardens. During fall migration it sometimes comes to lawns, bird baths, and sprinklers.

On migration *S. pallida* travels in flocks with its congeneric relatives, the chipping and Brewer's sparrows, and associates freely with a wide variety of other birds. On its breeding territory it lives in close harmony and friendly association with a large number of avian species. Observers have seen clay-colored sparrows pay little attention to indigo buntings, redwinged blackbirds, and eastern kingbirds that shared their perches.

The first specimen of the clay-colored sparrow (sex undetermined) was collected by one of the two daring English explorers, Dr. John Richardson and Thomas Drummond, at Carlton House (burned in 1885) on the North Saskatchewan River, in what is now the province of Saskatchewan, on May 14, 1827 (Houston and Street, 1959). Dr. Richardson was a surgeon and naturalist, and the second-in-command; and Thomas Drummond was assistant naturalist and botanist on the second of Sir John Franklin's three hazardous and tragic Arctic Land Exploring Expeditions. The clay-colored sparrow specimen and hundreds of other plant and animal specimens were carried thousands of miles by canoe and portage, and eventually to England. Here William Swainson, the eminent English zoologist, described the species and named it *Emberiza pallida*, the Clay-coloured Buntling (Swainson and Richardson, 1831). The type was deposited in the University Museum, Cambridge, England.

John J. Audubon (1844), thinking he had discovered a new species, named the bird *Emberiza Shattuckii*, Shattuck's bunting, after his young friend, George C. Shattuck, M.D., of Boston, who accompanied Audubon on his voyage to Labrador in the summer of 1833.

Sir John Richardson (Swainson and Richardson, 1831) writes: "It frequents the farm-yard at Carlton-house, and it is as familiar and confident as the common House Sparrow of England." J. J. Audubon (1844) states: "Abundant throughout the country bordering the Upper Missouri." Apparently this sparrow has held its own against the pressure of civilization, for the species appears to be almost as abundant as when first discovered. Loss of breeding sites was inevitable as brushy land was converted to crop land; *S. pallida* no longer breeds in Iowa and Illinois. Compensation for the loss of breeding territory is the extension of breeding range eastward and northward during the present century. J. Van Tyne (1941) cites as evidence records in Michigan in 1901, 1904, 1914, and 1925, and suggests, as a cause of the spread, lumbering that was followed in ecological succession by a habitat in which the clay-color is usually found. Similarly, L. L. Snyder (1957b) details its range extension into the lower Great Lakes region of southern Ontario in recent years.

*Spring.*—Leaving their main winter home in Mexico, migrants regularly cross our southern border from Texas to Arizona during late March and April. For more than 2 months the birds move northward in successive waves across the Great Plains and prairies. William Youngworth writes me that at Sioux City, Iowa, he observed two to three mass flights of 25 to 100 birds each spring from 1929 to 1957. Arrival dates there ranged between May 8 and 20, with scattered arrivals building up to a mass movement, then diminishing. Mrs. I. D. Acord reported peak numbers still at Amarillo, Texas, on May 10–11, 1958, although a mass first arrival of *S. pallida* and *S. passerina* had occurred at Regina, Saskatchewan, on May 9, 1958, as reported by Robert W. Nero (Aaron M. Bagg, 1958). W. Ray Salt (1966) states that *pallida* arrived in the Edmonton, Alberta, district during the first week of May in 1964, but that the males did not firmly establish their territories until about the middle of the month.

In migration the species occurs commonly in mesquite and other desert shrubs, in thickets, copses, weed patches, and grass, and shows a preference for borders of fields, woods, roads, and streams. The bird is one of the many passerine species that migrate by night in spring and fall. Evidence of diurnal migration in the spring comes from Frances Clopton (Mrs. H. L.) Williams of Midland, Texas, who writes me that late on the morning of Apr. 23, 1959, she watched 52 birds flying from bush to bush up a draw toward the northwest.

In 1952 Lester L. Snyder wrote me: "Records from Point Pelee suggest that the species now migrates into and out of southern Ontario via this 'port.' There are two other obvious 'ports of entry' into Ontario, however, namely in (1) the Sault Ste. Marie and Manitoulin region, and (2) the Minnesota and Manitoba areas." Frank A. Pitelka (1947) suggests that these sparrows reach the interior of British Columbia via the northern end of the Rocky Mountain mass and the Peace River district.

George F. Simmons (1925) describes the unusual occurrence of a huge flock of 3,000 birds that stayed for 2 weeks at Austin, Texas, in the spring of 1907. George M. Sutton (MS.) saw about 400 near Arnett, Ellis County, Okla., on May 11, 1936. Professor Orin A. Stevens (1950) shows that at Fargo, N.D., arrival dates for 26 years average May 5 with the earliest April 30, 1934, and the latest May 12, 1919. He informs me that the average variation for 2.7 days is the third smallest he has recorded for 49 species.

*Territory.*—The clay-colored sparrow, unlike the field and Baird's sparrows, has a rather small territory. The size varies from about ¼ acre to 1 acre. Near Brandon, Manitoba, in 1962 I found the distances between the singing perches of five males to be 40, 60, 65, 70, and 120 yards respectively. John Lane found three nests forming a triangle with sides of 30, 40, and 50 yards, in 1960. Nine miles west of Brandon on June 5, 1960, 11 searchers found nine nests in 1½ hours in a remote 9-acre patch of snowberry and wolf willow, a first class type of cover. In the same patch, on June 28, 1962, I counted 15 singing males.

Throughout the nesting period the male defends his territory vigorously against his own species. He has also been observed chasing chipping sparrows (Terrill, 1952) and song sparrows (Fox, 1961) from his territory. Lawrence H. Walkinshaw (1944a) states that territorial behavior is much like that of the field sparrow. His notes taken May 29, 1944, follow:

An empty nest was found. The male and female were near. The male trying to attract me from the nest, flew around and around his territory calling the attraction call "zip-zip-zip-zip-zip", much like the song of the Black-poll Warbler. Occasionally both birds called to each other a low "zeep" "zeep". When the male neared a neighboring territory, male two settled quickly on a nearby limb, head stretched forward, very alert. On closer approach, male one was attacked by male two. They flew around and around in a group of six-foot trees, the attacker dashing at him in a more aggressive manner than he returned.   Finally, male one returned to his own boundary, male two leaving him.

Gary C. Kuyava writes me from Duluth, Minn., that on May 25, 1959, birds had begun to stake out territories.   He says: "One bird flew continually between two bushes about 100 feet apart."   He also describes defense of territory: "Saw a pair of males fly along and suddenly dart at each other in a struggle.   When they hit the ground, they were still pecking at each other.   The struggle lasted about 2 minutes, after which both birds flew off in opposite directions."

*Courtship.*—Elliott Coues (1874) states that in South Dakota the pairing season is in the latter part of May, and throughout its short duration males continually chase the females about in bushes.   John Lane, of Brandon, Manitoba, at my request studied clay-colored sparrows in 1960.   On May 8 he saw a male interrupt his singing to make a short flight over an adjacent field.   Returning, he made a swooping dive at his mate, who sat quietly on a low perch all the while; then he resumed singing on his perch.   On May 25, 1960, Lane watched a mated pair as they silently flitted from bush to bush and frequently to the ground, apparently seeking a suitable nesting site. On two occasions the pair alighted on the same branch and lightly touched bills.   On May 24, 1962, Lane watched courtship activities involving three birds.   A female sat motionless in a low red willow. Two other birds, apparently males, sat and eyed each other; then one dived at the other, which shifted to another branch.   The first male repeated the dive and made contact with the second bird, which again moved a short distance.   Finally the first male and the female flew to the ground.   The second male made no move to follow, and in a few minutes flew away.

L. H. Walkinshaw (1944a) comments on a male observed by Mr. and Mrs. N. T. Peterson in Calhoun County, Mich., in 1943.   The bird, lacking a mate, was apparently trying to court female field sparrows. The clay-colored sparrow was on a shrub-covered field and continually tried to drive nearby male field sparrows from his vicinity, but the latter paid him little attention.

*Nesting.*—For nesting, the clay-colored sparrow generally seeks dry uncultivated shrubby land such as pasturelands, parklands, hillsides, edges of fields, roads, swamps, woodlands, and poplar-willow bluffs, burned over areas, forest openings, and plots overgrown with weeds. In the Canadian prairie provinces, both on dry ground and in buffalo wallows, the bird favors areas of low western snowberry and wolf willow (silver berry), in North Dakota "areas covered with sumac" (Lincoln, 1925), and near Edmonton, Alberta, land supporting rosebush, snowberry, and willow-aspen bush (Salt, 1966).

The nest is cup-shaped and generally supported and hidden well.

It resembles closely that of the chipping sparrow but is not so compact. The nest site is often a tuft of dead grass swathing the base of a shrub such as wild rose, snowberry, willow, or gooseberry; or the base of a grass tuft, thistle, sweet fern, goldenrod, or other herbaceous plant; also a low branch of shrubs or small trees including hawthorn, serviceberry, and conifers. Height from the ground varies from a fraction of an inch to 4½ feet. When near the ground the nest may be entirely covered with dead grass. When built elsewhere it is usually well concealed by leaves. E. T. Seton (1891) writes: "When first the discoverer draws aside the brush and exposes the nest with its complement his feelings are as of finding an exquisite casket of jewels." During incubation and early brooding a searcher can find the nest easily because the female generally flushes when the intruder is close to the nest. On a calm day one may see the matted leaves of a bush quiver a few feet ahead as the female prepares to flush.

L. H. Walkinshaw (1939d) summarizes a study of 10 nests in a dry brushy prairie area 5 miles long and 2 or more miles wide (swept by fire during early 1930s) immediately west of Lovells, Crawford County, Mich. He says that each structure is usually raised from a base. One nest was very conspicuous because of many long grass stems in the base, 10 or 12 measuring 35 to 58.2 centimeters. Above were shorter grasses in a circular formation lined with finer tops of the same type of grass, from 3 and 4 up to 15 centimeters in length. The nest contained 384 pieces of grass.

Observers have found grass, fine twigs, weed stalks, and rootlets in the main structure; and fine grasses, fine rootlets, horsehair, deer hair, and cattle hair in the lining. John Lane found horsehair in 19 of 31 nests in southern Manitoba in 1960. He writes me that earlier in this century, before the use of motorized farm equipment, clay-colored nests in Manitoba contained much more horsehair than today. He says that then most nests were well lined with shiny black hair, a few with gray or white hair or a combination of gray and black. Salt (1966) found no hair or other animal matter in any linings in 24 nests near Edmonton, Alberta, in 1964.

L. H. Walkinshaw (1944a), after a study of 40 nests near Lovells, Mich., says that the female builds the nest but is often accompanied by the male on her short trips for material. Usually first nests are much closer to the ground than later ones. The average heights in centimeters from the ground to nest rim were: May, 3 nests, 15.6; June, 15 nests, 49.6; July, 22 nests, 45.4; 40 nests, 44.75 (10–105). Average dimensions in millimeters of 34 nests were: interior diameter at top, 45.9 (40–54); interior depth, 37.6 (25–48); exterior diameter at top, 105.5 (80–140); depth overall, 65.6 (55–90). The average weight of six nests was 3.95 grams (2.1–7.3).

W. R. Salt (1966) at Edmonton, Alberta, noticed a similar increase in height of nesting site with the advancing season. He states that during the last week of May, when foliage is sparse, nest shelter is provided chiefly by dead grass, matted by winter snows and winds into clumps in stems of rosebush or snowberry. Here some nests rested practically on the ground, while others were 10 inches above ground. The average height was 5 inches. No nest rested in a scrape. As growth became more luxuriant with the advancing season, the nesting site became rosebush or snowberry, and the average height was 13 inches. Salt suggests that the clay-colored sparrow is more responsive to distance from the surface of the vegetation than from the ground. The majority of the clay-colors in his area nested within 9 inches of the surface of the vegetation. Salt, Walkinshaw (1944a), and Fox (1961) all record the tendency within a local population to select one type of nesting site above all others.

Angus H. Shortt observed 50 nests during 1932 and 1933 at Deer Lodge, Manitoba, a suburb 1 mile west of Winnipeg, in an area now residential. He reports (MS.) the heights of nests above ground as follows: up to 5 inches, 9; 6–10 inches, 34; 18 inches–4 feet, 7.

Nest building requires 2 to 4 days and usually is done during the morning (G. A. Fox, 1961). Pershing B. Hofslund at Duluth, Minn., observed a female still building a nest that contained one egg.

Nest failure, followed by renesting, is common. Pairs generally renest promptly, within a day or so, and usually close to the original nest site. G. C. Kuyava writes me describing three nesting attempts near Duluth in 1958. After a storm destroyed the first nest containing four eggs on June 30, the birds built another nest about 10 feet away. Two of three eggs hatched, but 2 days after hatching, a predator rifled this nest. After about a week the birds built another nest almost equidistant between the first two sites. Two eggs hatched 12 days after laying. Both adults had been banded and were caught several times in nets around each of the three nests. A. H. Shortt informs me that he watched one pair make four attempts at nesting. The adults deserted the first two nests because of cowbirds, but succeeded with the third and fourth nests.

W. R. Salt (1966) found seven clutches, known to be first ones, completed in the period May 27 to June 11, and felt that the remaining 11 clutches completed between June 11 and July 2 were second or third layings. He cites an instance in which a new nest was built and four eggs laid in only 7 days after destruction of the first brood. The greatest distance between sites of the original nest and of the second nest was 110 feet.

Recorded evidence that clay-colored sparrows attempt second broods after successful nestings is scarce. John Lane tells me that repeated visits to nesting areas near Brandon, Manitoba, during July of 1960 and 1961 did not yield even one nest.  In some localities, on the other hand, *pallida* appears to attempt two broods.  L. H. Walkinshaw (1944a) gives proof, based on observation of a color-banded pair, of a second brood in Michigan.  He writes: "One pair of birds definitely feeding young, had eggs in a second nest during July 1944."  He adds: "Nests have been found as late as August 1, during 1937 with young."  Clara Hussong (1946) provides evidence of second broods in Wisconsin.  On June 13, 1945, in Green Bay she tried to band two full grown juveniles leaving a nest in an unkempt vacant lot 150 by 250 feet.  On July 7, in a nest 50 feet from the first nest, in the same back yard, she found four eggs in the process of hatching. In both cases the male used the same elm tree as a singing post. From St. Paul, Minn., Hubert Lewis (1943) reports five nests in which eggs hatched on or about August 14, 24, and 28.  These late dates suggest second broods.

*Eggs*.—The clay-colored sparrow usually lays three or four and occasionally five slightly glossy eggs.  They are ovate with some tendency toward short ovate.  The ground color is "bluish glaucous" or "Etain blue" with spots, speckles and blotches of dark brown such as "mummy brown," "auburn," "Dresden brown," "snuff brown" or "Brussels brown" and with a few scrawls of black.  The undermarkings, which are not always present, are "pale neutral gray."  The eggs are rather sparingly marked, rarely unmarked, and the majority of spots are confined to the large end where they often form a loose wreath.  The markings are usually sharply defined and may be in the form of a few quite large blotches mixed with small spots and an occasional scrawl.  These eggs are indistinguishable from those of *Spizella passerina* except that series average slightly smaller.  The measurements of 50 eggs average 17.1 by 12.7 millimeters; the eggs showing the four extremes measure *18.5* by 13.0, 17.6 by *15.0*, and *14.5* by *11.5* millimeters.

L. H. Walkinshaw (1944a) says that the female lays one egg daily during the earlier morning hours.  His average weights of eggs in grams were: eggs quite fresh, 1.534; 19 at laying, 1.594; 6 at hatching, 1.26.  In tabular form he shows that egg sets decrease in size with the advance of the summer.  The average number of eggs per set, per month in 25 sets were: May 4, June 3.87, July 3.21.  G. A. Fox (1961) reports that in three nests in Saskatchewan, June 6–11, 1959, the females began to lay eggs 1 and 2 days after completion of the nests.  W. R. Salt (1966) reports an instance in which the fourth egg of a clutch was laid at least 3 days after the third one.

*Incubation*.—L. H. Walkinshaw (1939d) writes that on two occasions at Lovells, Mich., incubation started the night previous to laying of the last egg. Incubation periods were 11 and 11½ days in 1937 (Walkinshaw, 1944a). In a letter Walkinshaw defines the incubation period as "that period between the laying and hatching of the last egg laid in a set." On the other hand, G. C. Kuyava, using a similar definition, writes me that near Duluth the period was 14 days in each of 11 nests he observed in 1959. G. A. Fox (1961) gives an incubation period of 11 days in Saskatchewan, and W. R. Salt (1966) cites approximately 10 days near Edmonton, Alberta.

Frederick E. Warburton (1952) states that both parents incubate, but one much more often and for longer periods than the other. The birds change place silently, the incubating bird leaving the nest as soon as the newcomer approaches. At one nest each bird had its own approach route, about 18 inches in length, consisting of perches used in an almost invariable sequence. By the last day the birds often skipped half the usual stops. When young could receive food, the parents used a new approach, less well defined. G. A. Fox (1961) found that on the first day of incubation at one nest in Saskatchewan between 2:00 and 5:00 p.m. incubation time was divided as follows: female 81 percent; male 13 percent; nest uncovered 6 percent.

During both incubation and brooding the female sits close, and, if one is cautious, he may part the branches and photograph her before she flies. After an incubating bird flushes, both parents flit from bush to bush, silent but watchful. Birds may return and resume incubating 45 seconds after being flushed. The male frequently carries food to an incubating female, who often leaves the nest to meet him.

G. C. Kuyava writes me that the three eggs in one clutch all hatched between 9:10 and 9:40 a.m. on the same day; the time from the first pipping to complete emergence of the three was respectively 11, 11½, and 10 minutes. Clara Hussong (1946) describes a different hatching pattern; she writes that of a four-egg clutch in Green Bay, Wis., two hatched on July 7, one on July 9, and the fourth on July 10. W. R. Salt (1966) points out the unevenness of the hatch, stating that hatching of each of four clutches was completed in 2 successive days.

A. H. Shortt writes me that in 1932–1933 at Deer Lodge, Manitoba, where cowbirds were active, of 50 nests found, 22 (44.0 percent) produced fledglings. Of 27 first nests only 8 (29.6 percent) were successful. Of 21 renesting attempts 12 (57.1 percent) succeeded. Two nests could not be classified as either first or second nests. Of 158 eggs found in 50 nests, 80 (50.6 percent) hatched; 73 young fledged, a reproductive efficiency of 46.2 percent. The reproductive efficiency of renestings (62.3 percent) was greater than that for first nestings (34.9 percent). Shortt gives the causes of 52 eggs lost as follows: removed by cowbirds, 25; lost in deserted nests, 12; lost in destroyed nests, 10; infertile, 5.

John Lane reports that of 34 nests (firsts and renests) found near Brandon, Manitoba, in 1960, 14 (41.2 percent) were successful. Two of the nests produced no eggs, 2 nests were destroyed, 8 abandoned, and 10 rifled. Of 90 eggs found in 31 nests, 59 (65.6 percent) hatched; 34 young fledged, giving a reproductive efficiency of only 37.7 percent. The hatching and efficiency percentages are probably inflated because in nine successful nests 12 cowbird eggs or young (to some extent probably replacements of clay-colored eggs) were already in the nests when found. In 11 nests not parasitized by cowbirds success was greater; 6 (54.5 percent) were successful. Of 40 eggs, 28 (70.0 percent) hatched, and 19 fledglings were produced, a reproductive efficiency of 47.5 percent. Neither human interference, storms, floods, nor droughts was a factor affecting nesting success near Brandon. L. H. Walkinshaw (1944a) writes that young left from only 10 of 19 nests, or 52.5 percent, near Lovells, Mich., where none of the nests suffered from cowbirds. Of 56 eggs found in 19 nests, 41 (73.2 percent) hatched; 30 young fledged, for a reproductive efficiency of 53.6 percent.

Near Edmonton, Alberta (Salt, 1966), nestling losses were considerably lower than egg losses. Of 11 nests in which 38 young hatched, only two nests suffered losses. A loggerhead shrike took five nestlings, and one died from parental desertion.

*Young.*—At hatching, the body and legs are flesh colored, and the skin covering the eye appears bluish-black (Walkinshaw, 1939). Weight for 11 individuals at hatching varied between 1.1 and 1.4 grams, averaging 1.2 grams; at 8 days around 10 grams (L. H. Walkinshaw, 1944a).

G. A. Fox (1961) describes the rictal area as white, and the mouth lining a bright orange-red with black and yellow palate. On the 3rd and 4th days the mouth lining darkens, and the rictal area turns yellow. The tarsus averages 6 millimeters at hatching and 16 millimeters on the 5th day. At one day the alar, humeral, caudal, spinal, and ventral tracts show as dark dots beneath the skin. G. C. Kuyava describes the bill of a newly hatched bird as cream-colored; a day later the bill turns light brown in the central region, remaining cream-colored around the edge.

Both adults brood the young. G. A. Fox (1961) gives the distribution of brooding time during the 2nd day at a nest in Saskatchewan between 1:45 and 3:45 p.m. on June 22 as: female 71 percent, male 9 percent, young uncovered 20 percent.

L. H. Walkinshaw (1944a) shows in tabular form the results of four periods of observation at two nests. Direct feedings of eight nestlings, ranging in age from 1 to 6 days, averaged 16 per hour by both parents from 4:45 to 6:50 a.m., and 6.85 to 9 feedings per hour by both parents from 8:00 to 10 a.m. On one occasion the male came in to feed the young, which were cold and did not eat. So he brooded them from 8:55 until 9:10 a.m., holding the food in his bill all the time, and then left without feeding them. The number of feedings per hour increased as the nestlings became older. The earliest feeding, on July 23, 1944, was at 4:50 a.m. (sunrise was at 5:25 a.m.). The young remained in the nest 7 to 9 days. A. H. Shortt (MS.) says that the males first came to the nest on the 4th day, and began to share in feeding activities on the 5th day.

Nestlings first receive food about ½ hour after the last egg hatches. The male sometimes brings food to the female, who may meet him as far as 30 feet from the nest and either swallow the food or carry it to the young in the nest.

W. R. Salt (1966) writes: "The young grow rapidly. A newly-hatched Clay-colored Sparrow weighed 1.13 g. Eight days later three young Clay-colored Sparrows had an average weight of 10.3 g, just 0.3 g less than the average weight of two adult males taken about the same time."

Both parents continue to feed the young for at least 8 days after they have left the nest. Sometimes the male gives food to the female, who carries it to the young. Adults are very solicitous for their young, and show great anxiety and reluctance to feed them while being watched. Fledglings are very active in snowberry, which affords good hiding cover. Even during feeding activities the male pauses long enough to give territory and warning calls.

Two incidents give evidence of parental concern. F. E. Warburton (1952) writes: "A Marsh Hawk, *Circus cyaneus*, flew over the nest that evening as one of the sparrows was about to feed the nestlings. Immediately the sparrow crouched and froze, uttering three thin calls resembling the syllable *'eek'*. When the hawk had passed, feeding was resumed." L. H. Walkinshaw (1939d) describes injury-feigning behavior: "When I captured a young bird yet unable to fly one of the parents, presumably the female, flew down to the ground, dragging her wings and advancing slowly, chipping constantly. She continued this as long as the young bird uttered a distress note * * * which lasted several minutes."

Concerning nest sanitation, L. H. Walkinshaw (1944a) says that parents carried away the excreta, flying about 3 to 5 feet above the ground. As a rule, parents swallowed the smaller fecal sacs, but always carried away the larger ones, usually about 150 feet, although a male dropped one only 69 feet from the nest. F. E. Warburton (1952) limits eating of excreta to 3 days after hatching. One adult, probably the male, picked a piece of eggshell from the nest, "chewing" the shell for a few seconds. "He then flew six feet with it, apparently ate it, wiped his beak, and disappeared."

*Plumage.*—At hatching, according to Walkinshaw (1939d, 1944a), the young are adorned only with a few dark gray neossoptiles about 10 millimeters long on the frontal, occipital, scapular, and sacral regions. Newly hatched clay-colored sparrows resemble hatchling field sparrows; their down is neither as dark nor as dense as that of new-hatched chipping sparrows. David K. Wetherbee (1957) states that the clay-colored is more similar to field sparrows in the small amount of down than either of these species is to the Brewer's or chipping sparrows. When leaving the nest, Walkinshaw (1944a) notes, the young show characteristic face markings and a buffy central crown stripe; one had the primaries unsheathed about 10 millimeters and the tail 4 millimeters. W. R. Salt (1966) says that at the time of leaving the nest: "the contour feathers are well developed but the bases of many of them are still ensheathed. The wing and tail feathers, however, are still largely ensheathed except for about one-half inch of vane exposed at their tips."

Richard R. Graber (1955) describes the juvenal plumage, based in part on a direct-from-life painting of a Michigan juvenile by G. M. Sutton, as follows:

"As in adult, crown three-parted with pale buffy or whitish median streak, and lateral darker brown or gray brown parts, all uniformly streaked with blackish. Nape silvery gray with little or no streaking. Back streaked buffy brown and black. Rump and upper tail coverts buffy, obscurely streaked with blackish. Rectrices blackish edged with buffy (median), or buffy white (lateral). Remiges blackish, light edged. Uppermost tertial edged with light buff, others with light rusty. Coverts edged with light rust, secondary coverts tipped with buff (two wing bars). Lores buffy or whitish, eye ring buff. Superciliary buff or whitish. Auriculars buffy, or light brown, irregularly marked with darker brown. Postauriculars like nape, subauriculars similar, or whitish. Hint of dark mustache on chin. Chin and throat white, obscurely marked with pinpoint gray flecks. Chest, sides, and flanks markedly tinged with buffy, suggesting pattern of *Melospiza lincolni*, and streaked with dark brown or blackish. Belly and crissum white. Legs white, marked with brownish. Tail (ventrally) light gray."

Robert Ridgway (1901) gives the following description of the plumages:

*Adults in summer (sexes alike).*—Pileum light brown (pale umber, wood brown or isabella), more or less heavily streaked with black (black sometimes prevailing), with a more or less distinct medium stripe of pale gray or buffy grayish; a broad and very distinct superciliary stripe of pale buffy gray, grayish buffy, or dull buffy whitish; hindneck and sides of neck grayish, the former more or less streaked (narrowly) with dusky; back and scapulars pale buffy broccoli brown, broadly streaked with black; rump pale broccoli or hair brown, the upper tail-coverts similar but with darker mesial streaks; tail dark hair brown, the rectrices edged with pale grayish; lesser wing-coverts brownish gray or hair brown with darker centers; middle coverts dusky, tipped with pale buffy; greater coverts dusky centrally, broadly edged with pale buffy brown, becoming still paler (pale dull buffy or buffy whitish) on terminal margins; tertials dusky, broadly edged on outer web with brownish buffy or light isabella color, paler on innermost feathers; primaries grayish dusky, narrowly edged with very pale buffy grayish; auricular region light buffy brown or pale wood brown, margined above by a distinct postocular streak of dusky brown and below by a supramalar streak of the same; malar region dull white or buffy whitish, margined below by a more or less distinct dusky or brownish streak along each side of throat; under parts dull whitish, tinged pale grayish buffy on chest, sides, and flanks; maxilla brown with dusky tip; mandible paler brown; legs and feet very pale brownish.

*Adults in winter.*—Similar to the summer plumage, but black streaks on crown narrower, never (?) exceeding the brown ones in width, and plumage more tinged with buffy.

*Immature (young in first winter?).*—Decidedly more buffy than adults, the back and scapulars with the ground color nearly the same light wood brown or isabella color as the pileum, the latter with the paler median stripe indistinct and buffy instead of grayish, and the black streaks narrower; chest decidedly buffy.

Plumage variations, I find, are rather usual. Of 70 adult fall plumage skins in the Museum of Comparative Zoology 11 lack one or more of the five head characters described under *Field marks*. One January skin has a small amount of rufous in the crown. J. Van Tyne and G. M. Sutton (1937) write: "The female taken April 17, 1935, varies from the normal plumage of the Clay-colored Sparrow in the character of the crown which is narrowly streaked with black and almost lacks the median stripe of gray, precisely as in many specimens of *Spizella breweri*. In fact, on the basis of the color and pattern of the upper parts one would unhesitatingly place it in a series of *Spizella breweri* rather than among the other specimens of *Spizella pallida*."

Laurence C. Binford examined for molt the 23 specimens of *S. pallida* in the Louisiana State University Museum of Zoology. He writes me that four specimens, September 10 to October 15, show varying degrees of retention of immature ventral streaking. One is molting heavily on back and ear coverts, another has only two new feathers growing in, both on the crown. No molt appears on the other two. Binford says that three early October specimens, probably adults, have apparently just finished a complete molt. All are in fresh plumage, including wings and tail. R. R. Graber (1955) states that stub-tailed *pallida* and *breweri* have shown a precocious development of winter back plumage. Harrison B. Tordoff and Robert M. Mengel (1956) state that two feathers were being replaced in the tail of an immature October 6 bird, which was also in body molt and had some juvenal feathers on the body and flanks.

Binford states that some birds have a nearly complete spring molt, involving all portions of the plumage except the primaries. Five birds undergoing such a molt showed wear in the unmolted wing and tail feathers.

Binford adds: "A second and larger group of birds (11 specimens), taken at approximately the same time of year (spring) as the five molting birds discussed previously, shows no apparent molt. An apparent tendency in some individuals to retain some juvenile feathers into the spring is shown by one male, which has a few dark immature streaks on the flanks. All 11 specimens have moderately worn body plumage and tail feathers. A comparison of the three spring series (nonmolting males, nonmolting females, and molting birds) shows that those molting tend to have a greater amount of rufous edging on wing, back, and crown feathers, and ear coverts; also whiter supercilliaries. This greater degree of rufous gives the sides of the crown a darker color and sets off the light median crown stripe."

Allan R. Phillips writes me that two birds from South Dakota, May 16, 1933, show fresh body plumage and tertials, and the tail varies; the female has replaced only one central rectrix, the male all the tail except the outer two pairs of rectrices. "To what extent, if any, accidents affected these replacements," he says, "I do not know, but the asymmetry of the female is suspicious."

T. S. Roberts (1932) states that a partial spring molt and wear produce the first nuptial plumage, which is like the adult except for the rufous wings. These are retained until the first postnuptial molt.

The following records shed some light on spring molt dates. G. M. Sutton (MS.) reports a female molting heavily about the head shot near Arnett, Okla., May 15, 1936. The late George O. Hendrickson wrote me of an adult male in full breeding plumage on May 14, 1931, and a young male not yet in full nuptial plumage on May 11, 1931.

G. C. Kuyava has sent me the following average weights in grams of birds at Duluth, Minn., the adults sexed by examination of the cloacal protuberance: seven males, May 10–June 17, 1959, 11.55 (9.80–12.50); four females, May 13–June 6, 1959, 12.83 (10.80–14.50); six juveniles, July 26–August 16, 1958, 11.16 (9.51–12.76). L. H. Walkinshaw (1944a) gives the weights in grams of six adult nesting females at Lovells, Mich., as 11.8 (10.7–12.7). A male at Fawcett, Alberta, weighed 12.8 grams on May 20, 1942.

*Food.*—Most of the food of the clay-colored sparrow is vegetable matter, including a wide variety of seeds. Mrs. H. L. Williams writes from Midland, Texas, and lists the following: seeds of sweet alyssum, *Alyssum sp.*, and cockscomb, *Celosia sp.*; tumbleweed, *Salsola kali*; Bermuda grass, *Cynodon dactylon*; gamagrass, *Boutelous sp.*; fingergrass, *Chloris sp.*; bladder-pod, *Lesquerella gracilis*; pepper grass, *Lepidium alyssoides*; mustard, *Sophia sp.*; leaf buds of soapberry, *Sapindus saponaria*; and mesquite, *Prosopis juliflora*. Stuart

Criddle, of Manitoba, provides the following list: lambs quarters, *Chenopodium album*; Russian pigweed, *Axyris amaranthoides*; redroot pigweed, *Amaranthus retroflexus*; false flax, *Camelina microcarpa*; tumbling mustard, *Sisymbrium altissimum*; green foxtail, *Seraris viridis*. Gary C. Kuyava writes me that in his banding traps clay-colored sparrows eat finely cracked corn, millet, sunflower seeds, bread crumbs, and occasional berries. In early spring they eat willow catkins and buds of elms and other trees. In the fall they particularly relish seeds of crabgrass (Youngworth, 1959).

William Youngworth informs me that this sparrow feeds freely on canker worms in Iowa in the spring. George F. Knowlton (1937b) states that one specimen from Dolomite, Utah, Sept. 21, 1934, contained two beet leafhoppers and six false chinch bugs, besides numerous insect fragments. Various observers have reported both adults and young eating large and small insects, including grasshoppers, ants and other Hymenoptera, both adults and larvae of Lepidoptera, also spiders. A. H. Shortt (MS.) states that grasshoppers, abundant in Manitoba during the summers of his study in 1932–1933, were the chief item of food. During the last 4 days of nest life the young received grasshoppers exclusively.

*Behavior.*—Dr. Nathaniel R. Whitney writes me that in May in South Dakota the feeding birds remained on the ground with white-crowned sparrows, but when alarmed, or apparently to rest or sing, they flew up into the lower trees, where their most conspicuous associates were the yellow warblers.

Two instances of hybridization are on record. E. L. Cockrum (1952) lists a hybrid clay-colored and Brewer's sparrow. Robert W. Storer (1954) identified a hybrid clay-colored and chipping sparrow that Almerin D. Tinker collected in Lovells, Mich., where the chipping, field, and clay-colored sparrows all occur as breeding birds.

Mrs. Malcolm (Dorothy Wellington) McIlroy (1961) describes the association of a singing clay-colored and a chipping sparrow. The nest was in a red cedar tree about 12 feet from the ground in a weed-grown field in a settled residential area in Ithaca, N.Y., in June 1960. The clay-colored visited the nest regularly during 3 days while the chipping sparrow was incubating. Arthur A. and David Allen photographed both sparrows feeding three young in the nest on June 23. The fledglings were put in a cage where both adults fed them, but the young soon disappeared for reasons unknown. Mating of the two adult birds was not witnessed.

That clay-colored sparrows reach the age of five years was proved by Mrs. Hannah R. Gray, who banded one on July 30, 1946 at Wilton, N. D. The bird returned to her traps on June 30, 1947, and again on July 20, 1951.

*Voice.*—The territorial song, given by the male only, is unique in quality. The notes are simple, hard, fairly loud, leisurely, high-pitched buzzes, which may be translated as "zee-zee-zee" or "bzzz-bzzz-bzzz." A territorial song generally consists of one to six notes. The commonest are the two- and three-note songs. Songs vary more than is generally realized. Those given in close succession may vary in the number of notes per song. Single notes may vary in length and volume. Buzzes are longer when they are fewer in number per song. Songs, regardless of the number of notes per song, average 7 to 9 per minute. L. M. Terrill (1952) heard a male sing 71 times successively, 8 to 9 songs per minute, in early July, 1951, in Lanark County, Ontario; four evenly-spaced buzzes, less commonly three, composed the usual song.

Aretas A. Saunders (MS.) states that pitch varies rather slightly from G''' to C'''', a range of only four tones or ½ an octave in the 3rd and 4th octaves above middle C on the piano. Single songs range from 1½ to 2 tones, but change of pitch during a song is uncommon. Songs vary in length from 1⅛ to 3⅜ seconds, with the average about 2 seconds.

D. J. Borror (1961a) analyzed, with a Vibralyzer sound spectrograph, seven recordings of clay-colors from Michigan and Ontario. He gives the pitch range (in cycles/second) as 2,500–8,500 and states that buzzes vary in length up to about one second. Most songs are 1.5 to 2 seconds in length. The buzzes consist of a series of similar phrases uttered 42 to 146 per second; each phrase is of two to three very abruptly slurred notes.

Saunders (MS.) cites two variations: a single rather long buzz that swells and then dies away, and a single-note song that fades abruptly in the middle, sounding from a distance like two notes. G. C. Kuyava, in a letter, describes two variations in Minnesota: (1) one bird, songs of five to seven notes, last notes extremely thin, almost inaudible; (2) one bird sang one note in low tone and one note in high tone alternately for seven notes and then a thin, intermediate tone with each note about twice as long as either high- or low-tone notes.

At Neudorf, Saskatchewan, in 1959, John Lane heard a song that seemed to have a noticeable, distinct *ting* effect at the end of each *zee*. At Wapello, Saskatchewan, on May 13, 1960, he heard two males in adjoining fields answer each other song for song, the south bird with a two-buzz song, the north bird's song varying from two to four buzzes. The latter dropped to the ground and began scratching in the grass, still answering the south bird, and shortened his reply to a single buzz as he ate a black beetle.

During nesting season males greet an invader of the habitat with loud, warning notes that well up on all sides as other males take up the cry.  The warning song varies from a hard-sounding, low-pitched "bzztt-bzztt-bzztt" to a less common, thinner, higher-pitched "beez-beez-beez"; either may be repeated rapidly without pause up to 13 times at a rate greater than one note per second.  The warning call fades out behind the intruder as he advances.  Warning notes differ between individuals in inflection, intensity, and duration.

Recordings in *Sounds of Nature*, volume 6, by Donald J. Borror and William W. H. Gunn, and *A Field Guide to Bird Songs* by Peter P. Kellogg and Arthur A. Allen present both the territorial song and the warning notes of the clay-colored sparrow.  The narrators, however, do not point out the difference in the nature of the two sounds.

Males generally sing intermittently throughout the day.  Songs have been heard from 1:45 a.m. to midnight.  A male may use several perches and generally remains in one place until disturbed.  The perch may be a low tree or shrub, or a weed, fence, or occasionally a telephone pole or wire.  Perches average 1 to 7 feet in height, though they may range to 20 feet.  The male stands erect and tilts his head at an angle of 30° to almost 90° above the horizontal.  Between songs he often spreads his tail and both wings, and preens and shakes himself.  Mr. and Mrs. John Lane report that on a quiet evening in Manitoba the song is clearly audible 150 yards away, above the songs of western meadowlarks, redwinged blackbirds, and vesper, Savannah, and song sparrows.

In May, before establishing territory, males sing sporadically.  Singing reaches its height during the first half of June.  On hot afternoons in June and July the clay-color is one of the few birds that sings on the Canadian prairies.  After mid-June singing is less persistent until sexual activity wanes at the end of the breeding season, when both territorial songs and warning calls cease for the most part.  A late song date on the breeding grounds at Brandon, Manitoba, is August 6.  Singing is irregular at other times, as early as March 31 or as late as October 15 in the fall, when juveniles may be making their first attempts at song.  G. M. Sutton (1951b) heard birds in song near Monterrey, Mexico, on a warm, sunny January day.

Both parents and young utter low *tsip-tsip* calls.  Parents give them at mating time and after the eggs hatch, even while carrying food.  A slight change in the *tsip* of a parent will cause sudden abandonment of the nest by all the young.  The fledglings first utter the *tsip* call while leaving the nest.  When hidden among vegetation the young continually sound the note, which appears to be a hunger call, an alarm call, and a "keep in touch" call.  Both adults occasionally reply with a *tsip*, and will call rapidly and loudly when alarmed, changing their note to a sharp *chip*.  Later, in the fall, the *tsip* becomes a flocking call.

*Field marks.*—Breeding plumage: The clay-colored sparrow is slightly smaller and paler than the chipping sparrow. Five head characters are important in field identification: (1) a median crown stripe of pale gray or buffy; (2) brown ear patches outlined with black lines; (3) a prominent white malar stripe on each side of the throat; (4) a light superciliary stripe; (5) a gray nuchal collar extending to the sides of the neck.

Fall and winter plumage: Adults may lack one or more of the head characters, especially the crown stripe. Field identification in first winter plumage with absolute certainty is sometimes impossible, because of the general similarity to the first winter plumages of chipping and Brewer's sparrows.

*Enemies.*—During the nesting stage clay-colored sparrows are most vulnerable when nests are close to the ground or in areas of high nest concentration. Stuart Criddle, veteran Manitoban field naturalist, has provided the following list of mammals that may be considered predators of the eggs and young of *S. pallida*: Drummond's vole, *Microtus pennsylvanicus drummondii*; Baird's white-footed mouse, *Peromyscus maniculatus bairdii*; short-tailed ermine, *Mustela erminea bangsi*; prairie long-tailed weasel, *Mustela frenata longicauda*; least weasel, *Mustela r. rixosa*; northern plains skunk, *Mephitis m. hudsonica*. Other sources of destruction are garter snakes, loggerhead shrikes, black-billed magpies, fire, and trampling by cattle and horses.

Severe weather is a serious menace to eggs and young. G. C. Kuyava informs me from Duluth that three storms totaling over 7 inches of rainfall in 2 weeks commencing June 30, 1958, destroyed 14 of the 17 nests under observation.

The clay-colored sparrow is a common victim of the cowbird. I have records of imposition in British Columbia, Alberta, Saskatchewan, Manitoba, Ontario, Montana, North Dakota, Minnesota, Michigan, and Wisconsin. According to Herbert Friedmann (1963) *S. pallida* is frequently victimized in Alberta. In Saskatchewan, Fox (1961) in one season found eight of nine nests parasitized. None of the 10 cowbird eggs hatched. In 6 nests the cowbird's eggs were laid when the sparrow eggs were fresh, but no sparrows hatched from any of these six nests. In the seventh nest a cowbird egg was laid after four young sparrows had hatched. In the eighth, a replacement nest, three cowbird eggs were laid before completion of the nest.

The cowbird frequently parasitizes the clay-colored sparrow in Manitoba. Mr. and Mrs. John Lane sent the following report on 31 nests near Brandon in 1960:

"Twenty, all near heavy tree cover, contained eggs of *Molothrus ater*, while 11, all well away from heavy cover, were unparasitized; 14 held one egg, 4 held two eggs, and 2 held three cowbird eggs. Of these, two nests held one and two cowbird eggs respectively but no clay-colored eggs.  Both nests were abandoned.  Three nests containing both clay-colored and cowbird eggs were abandoned; 5 nests successfully fledged one cowbird each, both alone and in company with fledging clay-colors; one nest vacated three cowbirds.  From 28 eggs, eight cowbirds were fledged, or a reproductive efficiency of 28.5 percent.  One nest had a cowbird egg imbedded in the lining; in another, two of the four *pallida* nestlings were removed simultaneously, presumably by a cowbird, and one cowbird egg was substituted.  Only 6 of the 20 parasitized nests contained the full complement of four clay-colored eggs, suggesting the removal of one or more *pallida* eggs by the cowbird.  The latest egg-laying date for the cowbird was July 4."

W. R. Salt (1966) states: "in two cases after a cowbird's visit, eggs of the Clay-colored Sparrow were found just outside the lip of the nest but held by the surrounding grasses."

A. H. Shortt (MS.) states that the cowbird was the most persistent enemy of clay-colored sparrows at Deer Lodge, Manitoba, in 1932–1933.  Of 50 nests he studied 26 were parasitized; 13 were deserted after being parasitized.  From 31 cowbird eggs, eight young were reared (none in the same nest with young clay-colors), or a reproductive efficiency of only 25.8 percent.  The sparrows seemed more tolerant of parasitism toward the close of the nesting season, for reproductive efficiencies of cowbirds were 10.5 percent during the first nesting of the clay-color; 50.0 percent during the second nesting.  Young cowbirds left the nest on the 10th day.

L. H. Walkinshaw (1944a) found no cowbird eggs in 40 nests near Lovells, Mich.

Six recently fledged juveniles that G. C. Kuyava banded at Duluth in July and August 1958, were each host to from one to three small green adult hippoboscid flies, *Ornithomyia fringillina*.  Kuyava also noted many unidentified parasite eggs on the underside of one bird's wing.  Near Duluth in June 1950, P. B. Hofslund found several insect larvae in the nostrils of a solitary but very active nestling.  G. Robert Coatney and Evaline West (1938) report that the only clay-colored sparrow examined in the Lincoln, Nebr., region was negative for blood-inhabiting organisms.  While migrating, adults may suffer casualties from TV towers (H. B. Tordoff and R. M. Mengel, 1956).

*Fall.*—After nesting is finished, clay-colored sparrows move about in small, loose flocks in shrubbery, fields, gardens, and among trees, uttering a constant *tsip* much like that of the field sparrow.  When flushed they tend to fly low instead of high.  Southbound migrants arrive in Texas between August 3 (El Paso) and November 18 (Tarrant County), while other adults are still attending young in Minnesota as late as August 28 (Lewis, 1943). Florence M. Bailey (1928) states that *pallida* ranges in fall migration to at least 8,000 feet at Black Lake, N.M. L. Irby Davis writes me that in Texas flocks up to 100 birds sometimes remain in a rather definite territory for some weeks, and sometimes seem to move on almost at once. He thinks the seed crop may be a causal factor.

Adolf J. Krehbiel, of Clayton, N.M., has witnessed large-scale diurnal migrations. On the afternoon of Aug. 22, 1954, about 4 miles west of Clayton, he and Dr. Neland Gray saw thousands of clay-colored and chipping sparrows continually bounding and tumbling in low wavelets across the open prairie, moving almost straight south. Low flights of 50 to several hundred feet by individual birds constantly overlapped each other. The observers estimated the rate of mass movement at about 5 miles per hour. On Sept. 14, 1958, 20 miles northwest of Clayton, the same observers estimated more than 2,000 clay-colored sparrows in a general drift southward as they fed upon sunflowers.

F. C. Lincoln (1939) reports that a clay-colored sparrow banded at Northville, S.D., on May 2, 1934, was found dead at Cuautla, Jalisco, in southern Mexico on Dec. 23, 1934.

Evidence suggests that in the Great Plains region the main mass of birds may shift westward in fall migration. A. J. Krehbiel writes me that relatively few clay-colored sparrows visit the Clayton area in the spring. The fall migration there is much longer and noticeably heavier. William Youngworth writes me that at Sioux City, Iowa, the bird is primarily a spring migrant. He has 105 spring records (not individuals) to 13 fall records from 1928 to 1958. John M. Bates (1901) states that *S. pallida* was the commonest bird of the brush on Aug. 25, 1901, at Long Pine, in western Nebraska.

The clay-colored sparrow is a regular though rare fall migrant along our eastern coast from Massachusetts southward. The first Massachusetts specimen record comes from North Eastham, on Sept. 20, 1930 (O. L. Austin, Jr., 1931; O. M. Root, 1952). Paul A. Buckley (1959) writes that "during the past ten years" the clay-colored sparrow has become a regular occurrence in small numbers in autumn on the south shore of Long Island and on the coast of New Jersey. He cites specimen records to support his statement. Richard W. Castenholz (1954) describes an exhausted bird on board the University of Miami Marine Laboratory's research vessel T–19 in the latitude of Ft. Lauderdale, Fla., on Oct. 17, 1952. Recent specimen records from Nantucket, Mass., 1957; Bermuda, 1958; Florida, 1958, 1960, and 1963; Rhode Island, 1960; Virginia, 1961; and Maryland, 1961, give further evidence of this sparrow's regular fall occurrence along the

Atlantic coast. Whether the bird is a newcomer to the East, or has always filtered eastward in small numbers in autumn but just has never previously been reported, we shall probably never know.

*Winter.*—Early arrivals reach Sonora by September 15 and remain as late as April 30, the latest reported date of spring departure for the North. A. R. Phillips writes me: "Like all *Spizellas* they go in flocks during the winter. The habitat in Mexico is open weedy country or the main highlands, not the wooded coast lowlands. The species occurs west almost to the coast, as far as there are open valleys. I find it in weedy fields, stands of sunflower, and in just plain, weedy, brushy hillsides." In the neighborhood of El Paso, Texas, according to a letter from Mrs. Lena McBee in 1959, clay-colored sparrows consort through the winter with Gambel's and Brewer's sparrows in stands of mesquite and tornillo on the desert, or feed in clumps of tumbleweed and wild grasses along the levees of the Rio Grande or along the numerous irrigation ditches that thread the area.

### DISTRIBUTION

*Range.*—Northeastern British Columbia, southern Mackenzie, central Manitoba, and northern Michigan south, mainly east of the Rockies, to southern Mexico and Guatemala, and in small numbers to the Gulf and Atlantic coasts.

*Breeding range.*—The clay-colored sparrow breeds from northeastern British Columbia (Minaker River, Charlie Lake), central southern Mackenzie (Hay River, Fort Resolution), central Saskatchewan (Flotten and Emma lakes), central Manitoba (The Pas, Hillside Beach), western Ontario (Kenora, Port Arthur), and northern Michigan (L'Anse, McMillan) south to southwestern Alberta (Waterton Parks), south central Montana (Huntley), southeastern Wyoming (Laramie), southeastern Colorado (Pueblo), southern Nebraska (Red Cloud, Belvidere), northern Iowa (Sioux City; Jackson County), southern Wisconsin (Baraboo, Madison, Racine), central Michigan (Roscommon, Ogemaw, Iosco and St. Clair counties), and southern Ontario (Grey County, Trafalgar); sparsely west to central British Columbia (Bulkley Lake, Okanagan Landing); taken in the breeding season in Illinois (Urbana) and Indiana (Dune Park).

*Winter range.*—Winters from southern Baja California (La Paz), northern Sonora (Bacoachi), northern Durango (Rosario), southern Coahuila (Saltillo), central Nuevo León (Monterrey), and southern Texas (Laredo, Falfurrias) south to Guerrero (Chilpancingo) and Oaxaca (Mitla), casually north to Massachusetts (Amherst) and south to southwestern Guatemala; in migration recorded east to Quebec (Metis), Maine, New Hampshire, Massachusetts, New York, New Jersey, Maryland, Virginia, North Carolina, South Carolina,

Florida, Georgia, Bahamas (New Providence), Bermuda, Cuba, Alabama, Mississippi, and Louisiana.

*Casual records.*—Casual west to Washington (Spokane), southwestern California (Imperial Beach; Berkeley County) and northwestern Utah (Dolomite), and north to northern Ontario (Fort Albany).

*Migration.*—Early dates of spring arrival are: New York—South Ozone Park, April 16. Missouri—St. Louis, April 20. Illinois—Urbana, April 5; Chicago, April 29 (average of 14 years, May 6). Ohio—Ottawa County, May 12. Michigan—Battle Creek, May 16. Iowa—Sioux City, April 24 (median of 38 years, April 27). Minnesota—Minneapolis-St. Paul, April 24 (mean of 14 years, May 6). Kansas—northeastern Kansas, April 3 (median of 15 years, April 29). Nebraska—Red Cloud, April 13 (average of 15 years, April 25). South Dakota—Sioux Falls, average April 30. North Dakota—Cass County, April 28 (average, May 2). Manitoba—Pilot Mound, April 8; Treesbank April 24 (average of 24 years, May 4). Saskatchewan—McLean, May 1. New Mexico—Los Alamos, April 9. Colorado—Beulah, April 14. Utah—Pinto, April 23. Wyoming—Laramie, April 29 (average of 6 years, May 3). Montana—Albion, April 30.

Late dates of spring departure are: Florida—Melbourne Beach, April 23; Sarasota, April 18; Gainesville, April 14. New Jersey—Beach Haven, May 8. New York—Far Rockaway, May 14. Louisiana—Cameron, April 16. Mississippi—Benton County, April 29. Missouri—St. Louis, May 12. Illinois—Chicago, June 1 (average of 14 years, May 21). Iowa—Sioux City, May 30. Texas—Sinton, May 9 (median of 5 years, April 25). Kansas—northeastern Kansas, May 19 (median of 15 years, May 10). Arizona—southeastern Arizona, March 29.

Early dates of fall arrival are: California—Point Loma, San Diego County, September 19. Montana—Missoula, August 18. Utah—Dolomite, September 21. Arizona—Tucson, September 10. New Mexico—Los Alamos, September 5. Nebraska—Holstein, August 27. Kansas—northeastern Kansas, August 4 (median of 7 years, September 23). Texas—Sinton, October 22 (median of 6 years, November 8). Iowa—Sioux City, September 16. Illinois—Chicago, September 6 (average of 6 years, September 18). Missouri—St. Louis, September 9. Massachusetts—Nauset, September 9; Martha's Vineyard, September 11. New York—Riis Park, September 7; Tiana, September 10. New Jersey—Island Beach, September 13. Maryland—Ocean City, September 11. Alabama—Dauphin Island, September 16. Florida—Leon County and Rockledge, September 25.

Late dates of fall departure are: Montana—Bozeman, October 13.

Wyoming—Laramie, October 20 (average of 4 years, September 24). Colorado—Denver, October 25.  Saskatchewan—Eastend, September 26.  Manitoba—Treesbank, October 4 (average of 23 years, September 22).  North Dakota—Cass County, October 6 (average, September 26).  South Dakota—Sioux Falls, September 24.  Nebraska —Holstein, October 19.  Kansas—northeastern Kansas, October 19. Minnesota—Minneapolis-St. Paul, October 5 (mean of 5 years, September 15).  Iowa—Sioux City, November 13 (median of 38 years, October 17).  Illinois—Chicago, October 6 (average of 6 years, October 4).  Missouri—St. Louis, October 28.  Mississippi—Saucier, October 26.  Massachusetts—Martha's Vineyard, November 10. Maine—Castine, October 18.  New York—Short Beach, November 19.  Maryland—Libertytown, November 11.  Alabama—Dauphin Island, November 8.  Florida—Lower Florida Keys, November 9; Leon County, November 5.

*Egg dates.*—Alberta: 12 records, June 5 to July 7.

Mackenzie: 3 records, June 9 to June 15.

Manitoba: 37 records, May 23 to July 13; 22 records, June 2 to June 15.

Michigan: 40 records, May 29 to July 24.

Minnesota: 21 records, May 22 to June 13; 12 records, May 31 to June 6.

North Dakota: 21 records, June 1 to July 15; 10 records, June 7 to June 14.

Ontario: 1 record, June 3.

## SPIZELLA BREWERI Cassin

# Brewer's Sparrow*

### PLATES 65 AND 66

### Contributed by ROBERT T. PAINE

### HABITS

John Cassin discovered this drabbest of North American sparrows in 1850 and named it in honor of the Boston physician and naturalist Thomas Mayo Brewer.  His recognition of the range as essentially western North America remains unchanged, especially with the discovery in 1925 in the Canadian Rocky Mountains of a montane race. No other bird is more characteristic of the arid sage country of the Great Basin and Pacific slopes, where Brewer's sparrow is often abundant both as a migrant and resident.

*The following subspecies are discussed in this section: *Spizella breweri breweri* Cassin and *S. b. taverneri* Swarth and Brooks.

I am considering the two named races, *breweri* and *taverneri*, together here because the paucity of life history data warrants no separation and, in fact suggests an essential uniformity in the habits and behavior of the two forms. *S. b. taverneri* differs from nominate *breweri* in having broader black streaks on the back, a darker gray breast, a slightly longer tail, and a shorter, stubbier bill.

The race *breweri* breeds within the continental United States, excluding Alaska, and the more southern portions of western Canada. It is often the most common summer resident in open, brushy habitats of the Sonoran and Transition zones in these regions, where many authors have noted its close association with sagebrush (*Artemesia tridentata*). J. Grinnell and A. H. Miller (1944) write that in California, where the species breeds within an altitudinal range of 350 to 10,400 feet, it may even follow the *Artemesia* association into the Boreal zone. Although the relationship between bird and plant is close, the presence of the latter does not imply the former, nor are there any indications of an obligative relationship. For instance, R. E. Snodgrass (1940) records that in Yakima and Franklin counties, Wash., Brewer's sparrow is replaced by the chipping sparrow in sagebrush desert habitats; L. Wing (1949) found them in considerable abundance in bunch grass prairie; and Wauer (1964) records them breeding in piñon pine-juniper woodlands. *S. b. breweri* breeds south throughout the central plateau of Mexico to Jalisco and Guanaguato, where it goes under the name of "chimbito de Brewer" (A. H. Miller, 1957).

Just as *breweri* is characteristic of the arid sagebrush, the slightly larger, more northern race, *Spizella breweri taverneri*, formerly known as the timberline sparrow, is typically associated with the balsam-willow habitat of southwestern Yukon, northwestern and central British Columbia, and the Canadian National Park regions of Banff and Jasper. H. S. Swarth and A. Brooks (1925), who described the race, call it "an inhabitant of the Alpine-Arctic zone on mountain tops," and they and subsequent observers have found it breeding above timberline. Although these races are not known to overlap during the breeding period (I. M. Cowan, 1946), a population of *breweri* living at 6,000 feet in the Lassen Peak region of California was found by Grinnell, Dixon, and Linsdale (1930) to approximate or even duplicate most of the peculiarities of *taverneri*'s coloration. This fact suggested to the above authors "a 'tendency' in birds from the extreme northwestern outposts in the general range of *breweri* toward *taverneri*."

*Nesting.*—In its typical haunts of exposed scrub vegetation, whether on the desert to the south or above the timberline in Canada, Brewer's sparrow acts in a shy, retiring manner, and if its nest is approached it disappears readily into the brush.  J. S. Appleton (1911), finding *breweri* to be a rather common resident of the Simi Valley, Ventura County, Calif., writes: "The birds are very shy, sneaking from the nest and running through the grass instead of flying; consequently the nests are rather difficult to locate.  All the nests that I have found have been on a south slope, sparsely covered with sagebrush and cactus, with a thicker growth of smaller plants and shrubs between. The nests were in these smaller shrubs, generally not over a foot above the ground."  The nesting site is usually within the favored sagebrush habitat and almost always within four feet of the ground.  I have found only one report of a nest actually on the ground, that by F. Kenagy (1914) for a normally constructed nest in a slight depression in an alfalfa field.

John G. Tyler (1910) records it breeding in vineyards near Clovis, Fresno County, Calif.  All the nests there were much alike in place-ment and construction, being typically composed on the outside of dry grass stems and a few grass blades and roots, and lined with very small, dry brown rootlets and a few long horsehairs.  The neat, compact structures impressed Tyler as being almost exact miniatures of nests of the California jay.

The nesting of *taverneri* has been described in some detail by H. S. Swarth (1930) in the Atlin region of northern British Columbia where, except for habitat, the details could apply to *breweri* as well.  There, above timberline at 4,500 feet altitude, and in a dwarf fir-birch-willow habitat, Swarth was forced to work patiently to discover the nest. He writes:

A cautious return later resulted in flushing my bird at close range from a nest with four eggs.  Even then, the bird arising not more than three feet away and directly in front, I had to make a careful search on hands and knees.  The birch was only partly leaved out, but the closely interlaced branches made a perfect cover from above.  The nest, its bottom a scant six inches from the ground, was loosely placed among the supporting vegetation, not fastened to the twigs.  When the surrounding branches were cut away the nest was removed separately; it could not be kept associated with the shrubbery in which it had been placed.

The nest is constructed almost entirely of rather stiff dried grass stalks and gray shreds, apparently from the fire-weed.  The lining is of fine dried grass and a few moose hairs.  Average external diameter (excluding long, protruding stalks) 130 millimeters; inside diameter, about 50 mm.; inside depth, about 30 mm.

*Eggs.*—Brewer's sparrow lays from three to five eggs, with three or four being the usual number.  They are ovate and slightly glossy. The ground of "bluish glaucous" or "Etain blue" is speckled, spotted, and blotched with such dark browns as "Brussels brown," "mummy brown," "snuff brown," or "cinnamon brown" with occasional under-markings of "pale neutral gray."  They may be either very finely speckled, or marked with a few blotches and scrawls.  In most cases

PLATE 65

A. D. Cruickshank

Lake Bowdoin National Wildlife Refuge, Malta, Mont.
BREWER'S SPARROW FEEDING NESTLING COWBIRDS

PLATE 66

Mono County, Calif., June 24, 1940                    J. S. Rowley
NEST AND EGGS OF SOUTHERN BREWER'S SPARROW

Calhoun County, Mich., July 25, 1935              L. H. Walkinshaw
NEST AND EGGS OF FIELD SPARROW

these are sharp, well defined and concentrated toward the larger end. The eggs of the two subspecies, *breweri* and *taverneri*, are identical to one another and indistinguishable from those of *Spizella pallida*. The measurements of 59 eggs average 17.0 by 12.6 millimeters; the eggs showing the four extremes measure *18.8* by 13.2, 17.8 by *14.7*, and *15.2* by *11.4* millimeters.

*Plumage.*—D. K. Wetherbee (1957) described the downy tufts of natal plumage as "light drab to drab gray" in coloration. Jean Linsdale (1936b) in a study of heat exchange and color of nestlings recorded the color of the downy young as "dark, slate gray." The juvenal plumages of both *breweri* and *taverneri* are described in detail by R. R. Graber (1955). According to him *taverneri* can be distinguished easily by the very heavy black streakings of the chest, upper belly, sides and flanks. In *breweri* these areas are only lightly streaked.

Brewer's sparrow starts losing the streaked juvenal plumage in a postjuvenal molt soon after leaving the nest. H. S. Swarth (1930) notes in *taverneri* that "Young in streaked juvenal plumage were out of the nest by the middle of July, the postjuvenal molt was in progress the later part of July and early in August, and birds in first winter plumage, completely acquired, were collected by the middle of August. An adult in the midst of the annual molt was shot August 6, and others in fresh winter plumage throughout, on September 1 and 5." There also is a partial prenuptial molt which, according to F. M. Chapman (1910), "appears to be confined to the head, where there is a slight feather-growth, and one April specimen has been examined which is acquiring new tertials, but the change to summer plumage is affected chiefly by wear and fading."

Ridgway (1901) states that the sexes are similar in coloration. He gives the color of the bill in life as pale lilaceous brown, darker at the tip and along the culmen. Sometimes the maxilla is blackish with a pale commissure, and the mandible lilac grayish. The legs appear to vary from pale brownish flesh to grayish horn color. Fuller and Bole (1930) describe the iris as hazel in both sexes, and the female as having a flesh-colored mandible and legs either "pale pinkish dusky flesh or pale horn color."

*Food.*—Stomach analyses, supported by a minimum of field observations, indicate that Brewer's sparrow is a "beneficial" species subsisting on a varied diet of plant and animal foods. The most thorough study was conducted by E. R. Kalmbach (1914) in an effort to discover the agents of natural control of the alfalfa weevil *Phytonomus poticus*, in which Brewer's sparrow may be important. He examined the stomach contents of 46 Brewer's sparrows during the summer months. In May weevils comprised 43.4 percent of the food and occurred in all but one of the 14 stomachs, averaging 2.2 adult and 6.9 larval weevils per bird. One bird which had not fed on the weevil was nine-tenths full of plant lice, a food item which occurred in 7 of the 14 stomachs and amounted to over 38 percent of the average diet. "Caterpillars were present in five stomachs, forming 7.7 percent. Spiders and miscellaneous beetles were estimated at about 3 percent each, and the remaining animal food was of small quantities under several heads. The vegetable portion (1.1 percent) was entirely weed seeds." In June the sparrows' diet was 64.6 percent weevils and 14.5 percent caterpillars, with again only a trace of plant material. In July weevils composed 44.8 percent of the birds' diet, one individual having consumed 45 weevils' larvae, but in this month plant material, mainly weed seeds, amounted to about 20 percent of the diet. These indications of a seasonal shift in dietary composition are borne out in a further analysis by Martin, Zim, and Nelson (1951): in the fall months 53 percent of the food was plant material, and in winter, 90 percent.

Kalmbach also examined the stomach content of three nestlings during June and found that their diet differed little from that of the adults. Other observers have seen only insects being fed to young birds at or near the nest. For instance, Grinnell, Dixon, and Linsdale (1930) noted an adult at Lassen Peak, Calif., carrying large insects to a recently fledged young bird. Isolated observations do not alter the pattern. A single specimen collected among Russian thistles at Flux, Utah, in September 1934, by G. F. Knowlton (1937b) contained 5 adult and 21 nymphal beet leafhoppers, 13 seeds, and numerous plant and insect fragments. Stomach analyses of three specimens obtained in summer in northern California (H. C. Bryant, 1911) disclosed that, despite insect abundance, these individuals had fed primarily on weed seeds augmented by a few small beetles.

J. Grinnell (1914b) notes that birds wintering in the Colorado Valley preferred to feed among the bushes on the desert and only visited the river for water.

*Behavior.*—Although Brewer's sparrow is the characteristic bird of sagebrush country, its drab coloration and generally shy manner do not attract much attention. Most observations, which all speak well of the sociability of this small sparrow, have been made on migratory flocks, to which attention is drawn by group size and vocalization. Brewer's sparrows have been observed wintering in Texas in the company of white-crowned, black-throated, vesper, and Savannah sparrows (Van Tyne, 1936). A. C. Twomey (1942) records migrating flocks regularly of from 50 to 100 individuals in the Uinta Basin, Utah.

J. Grinnell (1923b), who considered *breweri* to be the most abundant sparrow in Death Valley, Calif., records his observations on a transient flock as follows: "These sparrows showed a great weakness for bathing.

They seemed to be spending most of the forenoon hours every day in the mesquites along the overflow ditches, thoroughly wetting the plumage in the shallow streamlets and then perching in the green canopied branch-work above to preen at great length. Sometimes such bathing parties would be perfectly quiet save for the sound of fluttering wings. Then again some certain individual would break into prolonged singing * * *. Occasionally many, occupying adjacent mesquite thickets, would sing ecstatically in chorus, giving an effect of the bedlam of canary songs one hears in a bird store."

Once on the breeding grounds, however, these sparrows become quite inconspicuous, ducking into bushes at the least provocation and keeping warily close to shelter when feeding on the ground. Flock activities cease, except for communal singing, and loosely defined territories are set up, with singing males occupying some regular vantage point, usually on the end of a branch in the vicinity of the nest. Few data are available on territory size or the extent to which these may be defended. L. Wing (1949) indicates that there may be as many as 47 breeding pairs per 100 acres in eastern Washington.

The timberline sparrow behaves similarly. H. S. Swarth (1930) writes: "It was evident that singing males were occupiyng perches in fairly close proximity, a bird, perhaps, to every five or six acres, where conditions were favorable. They were wary, and generally flew before they could be closely approached, but always moved about within a rather short radius, unwilling to be driven far afield. For each singing male it seemed likely that there was a mate upon a nest near by * * *."

It does not seem to be known whether natal care is by the female alone or by both parents, and I find nothing in the literature on the behavior of a parent towards its offspring.

W. P. Taylor (1912) describes the flight pattern of *breweri* on its northern Nevada breeding grounds: "The birds made rather nervous movements, often flying irregularly into the air to a height of fifteen feet or more and then shooting straight down and coming to rest in a sagebrush. Certain variations in flight were observed. For instance, at times a manner of movement resembling that of a vesper sparrow was noted, the Brewer flying in a zigzag manner towards a bush at some distance and sinking to the ground behind it, repeating the operation on being flushed again." The timberline sparrow acts in the same manner when flushed from the top of one of the balsam thickets on which it perches when suspicious of danger. H. S. Swarth (1926), impressed by the wariness of these sparrows, writes that when flushed they fly long distances and then dive into birch thickets. He found it difficult to dislodge and follow a bird from such a refuge, as they tended to run beneath the shrubbery and take flight from some distant point.

Both races of Brewer's sparrow apparently behave similarly when an intruder approaches the nest. Many authors, among them J. G. Tyler (1910) and Grinnell, Dixon, and Linsdale (1930), have commented on the apparent reluctance of an incubating *breweri* to leave its nest. Thus, approaches of less than 2 feet are sometimes possible if no rapid movements are made. These latter authors note that brooding birds driven from the nests fly off silently and sometimes return to a nearby bush "protesting weakly at the intrusion." One bird returned quickly, and, hopping on the ground within 2 meters of the intruder, chirped excitedly. When disturbed, *taverneri* will occasionally remain near the intruder. H. S. Swarth and A. Brooks (1925) observed pairs of excited birds "perched on the tallest bushes, jerking their tails in a manner seen in no other *Spizella* save *monticola*."

*Voice.*—Brewer's sparrow is said to be vociferous, especially on the breeding grounds, where it often engages in flock trilling. The greatest volume of song is attained in the twilight and dawn chorus, which on dark days will extend almost to noon, although individuals can be heard from time to time even during the night. W. P. Taylor (1912) writes that in Nevada during the latter part of May and the first of June *breweri* is a most vocal species, and can be heard earlier than 3:00 a.m. and later than 8 p.m. At this locality some singing continued until at least August 10, though it was certainly not so prominent at that date as earlier in the season.

The complicated phraseology of the song has made schematic representation difficult, and many authors have resorted to a verbal interpretation. F. A. Pitelka (1951) describes the song as weak, monotonous and not very noticeable, while Hartshorne (1956) states it "implies marked continuity and variety." W. L. Dawson (1923) interprets the song as "weeeezzz, tubitubitubitubitub," which indicates its repetitive nature but not the variations in pitch that may usually be heard.

To H. S. Swarth (1930) the song of *taverneri* suggests a cicada-like trill, with many interpolations suggestive of a canary's song and, as with the canary, it was long-sustained. There seemed to be a fairly regular sequence of trills and stops, but it was not a short, definite and unvaried song, as with the golden-crowned and white-crowned sparrows. I. M. Cowan (1946), although not stating whether *taverneri's* song is continuous or broken into phrases, gives its duration as 10 seconds.

At the close of the breeding season the song chorus stops, and the most common notes are an abbreviated song or twittering and slight note given as "tsip" (Rockwell and Wetmore, 1914). L. Griscom (1928b) notes that "the call note was a weak one for a sparrow," and he describes it as about halfway between those of the Savannah and field sparrows.

*Field marks.*—This species is a small, pale, grayish-brown sparrow of a very nondescript nature. The upper parts are brownish, streaked evenly with black on the back, hind neck, and scapulars. The top of the head is finely streaked, the side of the head unstreaked. The greater wing coverts are tipped with buffy white, which forms an indistinct wing bar. The tail is long and notched. The underparts of adults are unstreaked. The sexes are similar. The crown shows no hint of the rufous found in chipping sparrows. The adult clay-colored sparrow is similar except for a light stripe through the center of its crown and a well-marked cheek pattern, both of which Brewer's sparrow lacks. The juvenal plumage is similar to the adult but is less sharply streaked above, and the chest may be streaked with a dusky color.

R. T. Peterson (1961) points out it "resembles Chipping Sparrow but sandier, *crown finely streaked*, no hint of rufous or median line. Young Chipping and Clay-colored Sparrows in fall or winter might be confused with it, but their crowns are usually browner with a pale median line."

*Enemies.*—Little is known about this aspect of Brewer's sparrow's biology, although undoubtedly individuals are exposed to about the same attacks by predatory animals as other small sparrows. Allan R. Phillips tells me that he collected a "red racer" with a still undigested Brewer's sparrow in its stomach at Cofer Hot Springs, Mohave County, Ariz., about Sept. 23, 1948. Phillips had noticed two or three *breweri* in the top of a sparsely leaved, half dead bush, and then turned away for a few minutes. On his return he saw the snake stretched out among the upper branches about 1 or 1½ meters from the ground. Because he did not witness the capture, he was unable to state where the snake actually caught the bird.

H. Friedmann (1963) writes: "Brewer's sparrow is a poorly known victim of the brown-headed cowbird. It has been recorded in this capacity only in Wyoming and New Mexico."

## DISTRIBUTION

### Timberline Brewer's Sparrow (*S. b. taverneri*)

*Range.*—Southwestern Yukon and western Alberta to Arizona, New Mexico, and western Texas.

*Breeding range.*—The timberline Brewer's sparrow breeds in mountains of western Canada from southwestern Yukon (Kluane), northwestern and central British Columbia (Atlin region, Hazelton), and central western Alberta (Jasper region) south to mountains of southeastern British Columbia (19 miles west of Invermere) and southwestern Alberta (Banff region).

*Winter range.*—The winter range is not known in detail; migrants have been taken south to Arizona (near Morenci), New Mexico (Escondido), and western Texas (Van Horn, Alpine).

*Migration.*—The data deal with the species as a whole. Early dates of spring arrival are: Oklahoma—Kenton, March 20. Nebraska—Hastings, May 10. Saskatchewan—Eastend, May 3. New Mexico—Los Alamos, April 27. Arizona—Wupatki National Monument, March 20; Fort Apache, March 27. Colorado—Fort Morgan, April 16. Utah—Washington County, April 21. Wyoming—Albany County, April 22; Laramie, April 28 (average of 6 years, May 3). Idaho—Moscow, April 23. Montana—Missoula, May 7. California—San Diego, March 7. Nevada—Carson City, April 10. Oregon—Lava Beds National Monument, March 23; Klamath Basin, April 9. Washington—North Yakima, March 30. British Columbia—Kittitas County, April 10.

Late dates of spring departure are: Texas—El Paso, May 14. Arizona—Fort Mohave, May 28.

Early dates of fall arrival are: Arizona—Douglas and Sonoita, July 31. Oklahoma—Kenton, August 25. Texas—El Paso, September 11.

Late dates of fall departure are: Oregon—Harney County, September 26. Nevada—Carson City, October 15. California—Hollywood, September 28. Montana—Fallon, September 12. Idaho—Lewiston, September 24 (median of 11 years, September 5). Wyoming—Laramie, October 21 (average of 5 years, September 25). Utah—Salina, September 5. Colorado—Weldona, September 30. New Mexico—Los Alamos, October 11.

## Southern Brewer's Sparrow (*S. b. breweri*)

*Range.*—Southern British Columbia, southern Alberta, and southwestern Saskatchewan south to central Mexico and southern Texas.

*Breeding range.*—The southern Brewer's sparrow breeds from central southern British Columbia (White Lake, Midway), northern Idaho (Moscow), southern Alberta (Deer Creek, Sweetgrass Hills), southwestern Saskatchewan (Eastend), central eastern Montana (Fort Keogh), southwestern North Dakota (Marmarth), western South Dakota (Belle Fourche, Black Hills area) and northwestern Nebraska south, east of the Cascades, through Washington and Oregon, to eastern California (south to San Jacinto Mountains), central Arizona (Fort Whipple, Camp Verde), northwestern New Mexico (Fort Wingate, Santa Fe), and central southern Colorado (Fort Garland).

*Winter range.*—Winters from southern California (San Fernando Valley, Providence Mountains), southern Nevada (Nelson), western and central Arizona (Hualpai Mountains, Safford), southern New Mexico, and western and central Texas (El Paso, Guadalupe Mountains, Boerne) south to southern Baja California (San José del Cabo), Jalisco (Juanacatlán), Guanajuato (Irapuato), and southern Texas (Brownsville); casually north to northern California (Glenn County). In migration through western Kansas and western Oklahoma.

*Casual records.*—Casual (this race?) in Louisiana (Cameron). Accidental in Massachusetts (Watertown).

*Egg dates.*—California: 84 records, April 19 to July 16; 9 records, May 13 to June 3; 34 records, June 7 to June 17. Colorado: 5 records, May 24 to July 21. Montana: 3 records, May 29 to June 16. Nevada: 6 records, May 28 to June 22. New Mexico: May 20 to July 10 (number of records not stated). Oregon: 36 records, May 18 to July 22; 19 records, May 24 to June 16. Texas: 6 records, May 21 to June 12. Utah: 20 records, May 6 to July 18; 10 records, May 29 to June 7. Wyoming: 13 records, June 1 to June 25.

## SPIZELLA PUSILLA PUSILLA (Wilson)

## Eastern Field Sparrow

PLATE 66

Contributed by LAWRENCE H. WALKINSHAW

### HABITS

Though it is a fairly common bird in old fields and brushy fence-rows in much of temperate North America, the field sparrow is not so well known as some of its relatives. It rarely nests near houses as do the chipping and song sparrows, it is not brightly colored, and its voice is neither loud nor striking. Yet its plaintive spring song does attract some attention, and interested persons eventually become aware of the singer. Many people know it as a likeable, friendly little bird living in and along the edges of their open, unplowed fields, and its gentleness is often commented on.

T. D. Burleigh (1958) writes of the species in Georgia: "As its name implies, it is a bird of fields and pastures overgrown with briar thickets and deciduous underbrush. Open pine woods are avoided unless changed into open slashings by logging operations, but when this happens, the Field Sparrow soon takes advantage of the new, favorable environment. It is noticeably more retiring than the Chipping Sparrow, and rarely if ever will be seen far from the brushy fields that it prefers. Here it can be found in small flocks during the winter, and here it nests during the summer."

I had the pleasure of studying this bird for 11 years on an old uncultivated farm near our home in Battle Creek, Mich. Much of the following account is drawn from my published reports (1939b, c, 1945) of those studies. I have also drawn extensively from the unpublished master's thesis of Malcolm P. Crooks, who studied the species on its breeding grounds near Ames, Iowa.

Lumbering in northern Michigan in the nineteenth century, followed by fires, produced thousands of favorable acres for this species which, together with the towhee, clay-colored sparrow, and indigo bunting, followed the lumbering operations north to the Straits of Mackinac. Much of this land has now grown back to forest, but many brushy spots still remain where field sparrows summer. When the young planted pines were small, the field sparrows nested in them; as they became taller the chipping sparrows replaced the field sparrows in them.

My study area, near the northern edge of the species' range in Michigan, consisted of about 100 acres of which (1939b) "about sixteen were woodland and marsh and thirty acres covered merely with grass, so that fifty-four acres, uncultivated and grown up to shrubs proved the most suitable to the species. * * * Through the tall grasses of these regions were to be found patches of blackberry (*Rubus*), staghorn sumac (*Rhus typhina*), dwarf sumac (*Rhus copallina*), New Jersey tea (*Ceanothus*) and bush clover (*Lespedeza*). Small trees, oak (*Quercus*), hickory (*Carya*) and hawthorn (*Crataegus*) were scattered along the side hills and valleys. On this favorable 69 acres, 23 pairs of birds were known to nest [in 1938], a ratio of one pair to each three acres."

Crooks (MS.) writes that his "principal area studied is 31 acres of abandoned pasture land at Ames, Iowa. It is virgin prairie soil and has been used as pasture for many years, including the summer previous to the study. The terrain is very rolling and includes three separate hills. An oak woods borders half of the southern part of the area with a heavily grazed pasture on the remaining part. * * *

The grassy cover of the area itself is mainly Kentucky bluegrass, *Poa pratensis*, in the valleys and on the hillsides, and needlegrass, *Stipa spartea*, on the hilltops. Some wild barley, *Hordeum jubatum*, was found ln the valleys while the following plants grew mainly on the hillsides: prairie larkspur, *Delphinium carolinianum*, daisy fleabane, *Erigeron ramosus*, many-flowered aster, *Aster multiflora*, honey vervain, *Verbena striata*, harsh-leaved goldenrod, *Solidago patula*, wild indigo, *Baptisia leucantha*, evening primrose, *Onagra biennis*, bindweed, *Polygonum convolvulus*, and bull thistle, *Cirsium lanceolatum*.

The south central to southeastern part of the area is level and is thickly grown with crabapple, *Pyrus ioensis*, and wild hawthorn, *Crataegus mollis*. Most of the trees in this area are from 2 to 20 feet tall, much larger than the same species of trees in other sections of the area. Each of the eight small valleys has numerous hawthorns with a few crabapples interspersed. Often these trees grow in clumps, giving very thick cover, but they are also scattered over the hillsides so there are no large areas of open land. The trees generally grow taller in the valleys than on the hillsides.

Another area is a pasture of about 25 acres used by 14 cows. The lower part is in woodland, and only the upper 15 acres were used by field sparrows. The type of cover these birds used was sparse with only occasionally hawthorn shrubs that survived the grazing and trampling of the cows. * * * The predominant cover is Kentucky bluegrass. Hawthorn shrubs are scattered thinly over the area, while the overstory is mainly English walnut, *Juglans repustris,* cottonwood, *Populus deltoides,* and green ash, *Fraxinus lanceolata.*

*Spring.*—From their wintering grounds in the southern United States the field sparrows closely follow the warming spring northward.

They migrate mostly at night, traveling in small flocks, often with other sparrows. They do not first appear on their northern breeding grounds in flocks, however, but arrive a few individuals at a time. Suddenly one nice warm morning, an area where hitherto no birds were in evidence is found to have three or four singing males scattered widely over several hundred acres of brush-grown fields. If the weather turns cold, no new birds appear until the next warm spell brings additional males. They continue to trickle in until soon territories are established in most of the available habitat. When in a few weeks the females begin to arrive, they come in more rapidly, but still individually and not in flocks.

The average date of arrival of the first males at Battle Creek was March 31 over a 43-year period; the earliest date was Mar. 14, 1957, and the latest was Apr. 15, 1924. The females generally arrive 3 weeks later, in late April.

*Territory.*—Though not so belligerent about it as many other species, the field sparrow is strongly territorial. Immediately on arrival each male selects a territory which he proclaims and defends against encroachment by other males. He flies from one tree or bush to another on the area he wishes to claim and sings from four or five favored spots, usually the tops of prominent shrubs or saplings. From each of these he pours forth his plaintive little song, most actively during the early morning hours.

If a new male arrives and tries to settle adjacent to his territory, the two birds begin to establish a definite boundary between their domains. This may take several days of intermittent conflict. The established male chases the new bird back and forth along the boundary whenever he encroaches on it until one or the other tires and both stop to rest. The new male sings a low song again and again; the established male sings less frequently. The chase renews, and sometimes the new male chases the established one. Seldom do the two come into bodily contact, the pursued bird managing to keep just out of reach, 2 to 5 feet ahead of the other. Occasionally, however, they do clash in mid-air, and fall to the ground in a flurry of beating wings and scratching feet. For several days they chase each other for hours along the boundary until it is apparently established. Then both stop chasing and fighting and return to singing, unless one wanders over the line.

Should another male move in on another side, the established bird has the same procedure to go through again. Sometimes when several new males try to establish themselves in the vicinity the chasing conflicts are almost continuous and revolve from one bird to another. It may take the first bird many mornings to maintain his territory, which may also have become much smaller than the many acres he claimed on his first arrival, though still adequate for the needs of a family.

The sizes of the individual territories I found varied somewhat during the 11-year study. Which they seemed to average about 3 acres, some years most were less than 2 acres in extent, and in other years, after a severe fire had swept the area, territories were of 5 or 6 acres.

Stewart and Robbins (1958) report breeding population densities in Maryland varying from a low of 7 territorial males per 100 acres of "damp deciduous scrub with standing dead trees" to highs of 79 males per 100 acres of "abandoned field with open growth of young scrub pine" and 80 per 100 acres of "unsprayed apple orchard with unmowed ground cover."

Observations on color-banded birds showed that usually the older males were the first to return in spring, and each invariably came back to the identical spots he had defended the previous year. Younger males coming to breed for the first time had to find leftover spots or try to squeeze into suitable places between already established territories. Banded birds that did not return I felt certain had perished, and the varying percentages of birds returning each year suggested the death toll was higher some winters than others. Of 50 banded birds that returned in subsequent years, all but one of which was banded as an adult, 27 returned the 2nd year, 12 the 3rd, 5 the 4th, 4 the 5th, and 2 the 6th year.

One of these 6-year birds, as I have detailed elsewhere (1945), reared two broods successfully with his mate that year. The other 6th-year male tried repeatedly to maintain his territory, but was unable to do so against the much stronger new unbanded males. He tried to chase them, but soon they were chasing him the most. After the encounters he flew to the ground and rested, panting as though he was very tired. He remained only a few days, then disappeared, and I never saw him again.

Often between territories were stretches of ground that neither male defended and on which both fed, sometimes only a few feet apart.

Later these feeding grounds were sometimes used by three or four pairs, none of which acted aggressively toward the others on it. Each pair worked along the ground only a few inches apart while another pair fed similarly a foot away.

*Courtship.*—After the male has sung steadily each morning for about 3 weeks during which he has established and defended his domain in innumerable territorial squabbles, one morning a new bird appears on it, the female for whom he has been waiting and singing. At first he flies at her as if trying to drive her away, but she merely dives into a bush and hides near the ground. When she reappears he may pounce at here again, but still she does not leave, and his attitude quickly changes to one of tolerance and then of acceptance. In a few hours the two become inseparable, and as a rule they remain so for the entire summer.

The return percentage for females is much smaller than for males. This is perhaps to be expected, for the male usually accepts the first female that arrives on his territory. If his previous year's mate does not arrive in time to mate with him a second year, she often settles on a nearby territory with a new male, who may or may not have been there the previous year.

As soon as pairing is accomplished, the male sings much less often and less vociferously. The change is so marked that I have usually been able to tell which males are and which are not mated by their singing behavior. For the next several days the two birds stay close together. They fly around the territory only a few feet apart, spend much daylight time feeding together, and they roost very close to one another, usually in the same bush. The male continues to maintain his territorial integrity closely, and chases every other field sparrow that ventures over his boundaries. Sometimes he is extremely busy indeed, tending his mate and fighting territorial battles with one or possibly two neighboring males simultaneously.

Pairs start copulating usually during the nest-building period, from 2 to 5 days prior to egg laying. The act is generally performed early in the morning. Typical were the actions of a female I watched working on her nest at 7:00 one early May morning. Sitting on a low branch, she crouched into the receptive stance, body held rather low across the branch and head extended. The male trilled, fluttered carefully down, mounted her for a few seconds, then flew away with rapid wingbeats and trilling softly. She sat still a moment, then also flew away chipping softly.

Early one morning I watched another male copulate with his mate on the ground and then fly to a far corner of his territory. After he left his mate continued chipping softly and maintained her receptive pose. A neighboring male flew across, copulated with her, and immediately returned to his own territory. She still maintained her position, and a second neighboring male came and copulated with her. Her rightful mate then came flying swiftly back, and drove the second intruder away. He then returned to his mate, and both fed together as usual on the ground, softly chipping to each other.

M. P. Crooks (MS.) states: "Copulation usually occurred while the female was perched on a low limb or a small shrub, though occasionally on the ground. All but three of the many copulations witnessed took place during the nest-building period and between 6:45 and 9:30 a.m. I saw one pair copulate April 27, 11 days before the female began nest building and 15 days before she laid her first egg. Two other acts took place July 31, after the females had completed laying all the eggs for the season.

"One pair was seen copulating at 7:15 a.m. on the 3rd and last day of nest building. They had been feeding together for the previous 10 minutes. After the act the female sat quitely for about a minute, then resumed feeding. The male flew a short distance away and preened, chipping very softly meanwhile. At 7:47 they copulated again, and once more at 8:03 a.m. After this both continued to feed and preen, and the female did not go back to nest building the rest of the morning."

*Nesting.*—During normal seasons the field sparrows start nesting in northern United States and Ontario before the trees and shrubs start to leaf out. Consequently the first nest is almost invariably built in a thick clump of weeds or under a grass tuft on or very near the ground. On my Michigan study areas most of the first nests were built beneath the drooping leaves of fall witch-grass, *Leptoloma cognata* that grew on the sides and tops of the hills. As the season advanced later nests were built off the ground in small thick shrubs.

From 1938 through 1948 I measured and recorded the heights of 661 nests. Of 173 May nests, 135 were on the ground, the highest was 31 centimeters above it, the average height was 7.46 centimeters. Of 239 June nests, 36 were on the ground, the highest was 84 centimeters, the average was 21.35 centimeters. None of the 240 July nests was on the ground; they ranged from 8 to 97 centimeters high and averaged 30.64 centmeters. The nine nests built in August ranged from 15 to 58 centimeters high and average 30.8 centimeters.

The nests were built in the following vegetation: 124 in New Jersey tea bushes, 122 in or under fall witch grass, 80 in blackberry bushes, 61 in small hawthorns, 45 in cinquefoil, 42 in small oaks, 30 in goldenrod clumps, 19 in small hickories, 13 in hazelnut bushes, 11 in sweet clover clumps, 10 in black raspberries, 10 in grape vines, 10 in grass clumps other than *Leptoloma*, 9 in dwarf sumac, and less than 4 each in Canada thistle, elderberry, catnip, wild rose, wild lettuce, wild spirea, box elder, lespedeza, lilac, and dewberry.

The early nests were made largely of coarse dead grass stems and leaves interwoven with finer grasses and lined with rootlets and hair. Some were lined entirely with black horsehair, some with very fine grass, others with rootlets or a combination of these materials. Later nests usually contained some live grasses. Measurements of 90 nests were: outside diameter 85 to 210 millimeters, average 124.3 millimeters; outside depth 47 to 110 millimeters, average 63.8 millimeters; inside diameter 43 to 55 millimeters, average 50.2 millimeters; and inside depth 25 to 62 millimeters, average 39.3 millimeters.

After examining a number of locations, the female chooses a site and starts building the nest. She does all the work on it, but the male is almost always close by, especially at first nests. Before she starts building, I have seen the male occasionally pick up bits of nesting material and offer them to her, but he always dropped them in a few seconds. He usually flies back and forth with her on her trips for material. At later nests he is often busy tending the young of a prior brood, and the female builds anew without his company. He stays in the vicinity, however, and warns her of approaching danger— mammals, hawks, cowbirds—by chipping in alarm. Both birds seem acutely aware of cowbirds, and when one appears nest building ceases and the birds start innocently feeding.

Most of the work is done between 6:00 and 11:00 a.m., and periods of construction are interrupted by periods of rest. The female will suddenly start working, build for several minutes, then stop just as suddenly and begin feeding. She may gather some material within a few feet of the nest, but usually gets it from 20 to 65 yards away. She may spend considerable time selecting and gathering it, but then flies directly to the nest, often landing momentarily a few meters away before flying into it. The coarser material for the exterior she usually brings a piece or two at a time, drops it at the site, and goes back for more. As the nest takes shape she brings finer and finer materials, until by the time she is working on the lining, she often brings it in large beakfuls. When interrupted by a cowbird or other intruder, she drops the entire mass, and begins anew later on.

First nests may take 3 to 7 days, usually 4 or 5 days to build. Later nests are generally built in 2 or 3 days, with some lining material occasionally added the 4th morning. Almost invariably after a nest loss, the female lays the first egg in the new nest on the 5th morning.

*Eggs.*—The field sparrow usually lays from three to five and rarely six eggs. They are ovate and slightly glossy. The ground is creamy, very pale greenish or bluish white, and speckled, spotted, or occasionally blotched with "army brown," "Verona brown," "sayal brown," "russet," or "hazel." Undermarkings are "light mouse gray," but these are often absent. The eggs are somewhat delicately marked, and the spots may be either sharply defined or clouded. The markings tend to be concentrated toward the large end, where they may form a loose wreath, but they are often scattered over the entire surface. The measurements of 58 eggs average 17.6 by 13.1 millimeters; the eggs showing the four extremes measure *19.8* by 14.0, 17.8 by *14.8*, *15.8* by 12.5, and 17.3 by *11.9* millimeters.

A total of 446 clutches in my Michigan study area varied from two to five eggs with an average of 3.37 eggs per set; early nests contained more eggs, later ones fewer, as the following table shows:

| Month | Two-egg sets | Three-egg sets | Four-egg sets | Five-egg sets | Total sets | Average per set |
|---|---|---|---|---|---|---|
| May | 0 | 23 | 78 | 7 | 108 | 3. 85 |
| June | 6 | 55 | 79 | 2 | 142 | 3. 54 |
| July | 19 | 148 | 17 | 0 | 184 | 2. 99 |
| August | 3 | 9 | 0 | 0 | 12 | 2. 75 |

The measurements of 1,308 eggs averaged 17.9 (16.1–21.0) by 13.5 (12.3–14.7) millimeters. Their average weight was 1.73 (1.35–2.1) grams. As described above, the eggs vary considerably in color, and those laid by each female were often so distinctive I was confident which female laid them in many nests I found, even before I had positively identified her. Eggs in the same set were often similar in size, and I found no discernible trend in measurements and weights of eggs as laid in the set; some first eggs were smaller, some larger than those laid later.

Almost invariably one egg is laid per day until the set is completed. Eggs were laid early in the morning, some before 5:00 a.m., but the majority between 5:00 and 6:30 a.m. Occasionally the last egg of a clutch was laid slightly later, even after 8:00 a.m.

Incubation is entirely by the female, but on rare occasions a male may be found on the nest. One male I watched spent the entire night over young that had just hatched when the female was afraid of the trap I had placed over the nest. But if a female was killed, rarely did the male continue the nesting activities until he acquired a new mate. One male fed the small young but did not brood them, and they soon died.

Though the female may be found on the nest almost any time after the first egg is laid, she usually does not start incubating steadily until the night before she lays the last egg. Crooks (MS.) found that females incubated 70 percent of the daylight hours and were off the nest only 30 percent. While the female incubates the male sings near by, stopping occasionally to feed. At times he brings food to the female on the nest, usually large larvae. When the female leaves the nest to feed, the male joins her and they go to the feeding grounds together. While she feeds he remains very alert, and gives a low warning "Zeee-zeee-zeee" if an enemy appears, especially a hawk.

In 74 sets of marked eggs I found the incubation period ranged from 10.5 to 17 days and averaged 11.6 days. In 44 of the 74 clutches the last egg hatched 11 days after it was laid.

*Young.*—On Aug. 7, 1938 an egg hatched while I held it in my hand. Pushing with its head, neck, feet, and wings, the young bird finally split the egg near the larger end where the shell had been incised by the egg tooth. It took several minutes to emerge because it rested for a few moments between each attempt. The empty shell weighed 0.3 gram. I placed the fledgling in the nest with a sibling that had hatched an hour earlier, and it curled up in the bottom. When I touched the nest it responded immediately by raising its head and opening its mouth. From my notes I (1939c) described it as follows:

The color of the skin and legs is pinkish, the bill pinkish, grayed near the tomia. The lining of the mouth is yellowish, pinker near the side. The small egg tooth, near the tip of the maxilla, is white and soon disappears. The eyes show in large gray areas beneath the skin and are closed. No suggestions of feather tracts are visible.

The weight of the young bird which hatched in my hand was 1.5 grams. His wing measured from the bend to the tip, 6 mm. The tarsus measured 5 mm. and the culmen 3 mm. * * *

By the second day the primaries showed in dark lines through the skin. The dorsal feather tracts were discernible. The ventral regions showed merely as lines but were easily seen on the third day. The occipital regions were dotted black at two and one-half days.

Newborn nestlings varied in weight from 0.9 to 1.5 grams and averaged 1.62 grams on the day of hatching. On the 2nd day they weighed 3.67 grams, on the 3d day 5.43 grams, on the 4th 5.43, on the 5th 7.31, 6th 8.61, 7th 9.64, 8th 10.2, and 9th 10.1 grams. They attained the full adult weight of 13 grams on the 13th day.

The female stays on the nest and broods the young at night until they are 6 days old; females were found on the nest over 6-day young at night only about 50 percent of the time, and over 7-day young only 25 percent. She also broods the young a great deal during the daytime during early nestling life, and especially during periods of inclement weather. This decreases steadily as the young feather out, and ceases entirely by the 6th day.

Both parents feed the young and tend to nest sanitation. As the fledglings mature they are fed more and more frequently. At a nest with three young under 3 days old, the parents brought food 23 times (the female 18 times, the male 5) and removed excreta 3 times during 312 minutes of observation. When the young were 5 and 6 days old they were fed 11 times in 100 minutes, an average of once every 9.1 minutes. At 7 and 8 days of age they were fed 25 times in 253 minutes; the shortest interval between feedings was 1 minute, the longest 23 minutes, and the average 10.1 minutes. Young were also fed more often late in the day than at mid-day. Three young about 6 days old in a nest I watched in early August between 7:50 and 8:20 p.m. were fed 7 times or once every 4.2 minutes.

Lynds Jones (1913) watched a pair of field sparrows feeding four 6- to 8-day-old nestlings for 19 hours and 12 minutes. "During that time 237 pieces of food were delivered and 31 excreta removed. The shortest time between feedings was one minute and the longest 21 minutes, the average being 10 minutes between feedings. If each of the four young were [sic] fed in regular rotation each received food once in 40 minutes. There were 154 Geometrid larvae (104 green, 37 brown, 13 white), 45 grasshoppers, 24 moths, 3 scattering, and 11 unknown."

Undisturbed young usually left the nest when between 7 and 8 days of age, and when disturbed, often at 6 days. The departing fledglings hopped first to the nest rim, then to the ground. When disturbed they often erupted from the nest in a group, tumbling out awkwardly, each heading in a different direction. They usually hopped unsteadily on the ground a short distance and then stopped. Sometimes the female would lead them farther away from the nest and then leave them. They kept within their own territories as a rule, and seldom wandered into neighboring ones.

After leaving the nest the young remain near it on the ground or in a low bush, where the parents feed them about once every 5 to 10 minutes. If they are not fed often enough they begin to "chip," which they never do in the nest, and the parents seem to try to keep them quiet by continuous feeding. When they have been out of the nest 5 days they can fly short distances, but the parents still keep them together in their territory. The male now assumes more and more of the care of the nestlings, and all of it when the female starts to renest.

By the time the young are 25 days old, their tails have reached approximately adult length, and shortly thereafter they are on their own. Malcolm Crooks (MS.) gives the age of independence in Iowa as attained between 26 and 34 days. I have watched adults feeding young from 25 to 30 days of age at different nests gradually acquiring their independence. At this point in my study area the young gathered in small flocks of 10 to 12 individuals in the dense thickets of hawthornes in the general nesting area. The male field sparrows to whom the territories belonged did not bother them, and the young birds, now fully grown, fed and played together, often flying up and down at each other, and then returning to perch in the hawthornes.

Late in the summer some of the young males occasionally sang brief snatches of sweet song, much shorter than the adult version.

If undisturbed by predators and other mishaps, field sparrows in Michigan probably raise three broods of young each summer. I have known two pairs to accomplish this during my 11-year study. I found the nest of one banded pair May 28, 1939 with four young that left the nest June 4. Their second nest I found June 28, and its four young left July 2 and 3. On July 21 I found their third nest, whose three eggs hatched July 28, and all three young left the nest successfully August 4th.

The usual field sparrow pair is seldom this fortunate. Too many enemies are searching for food, too many cowbirds are looking for foster parents for their eggs. Consequently the female field sparrow often builds many extra nests during the summer. The most I recorded for one female was seven in one season. I found her first nest May 24, 1945; its three eggs hatched May 28, and the nestlings were gone May 30. On June 1 she was building a new nest, in which she laid two eggs June 4 and 5; these were gone on June 6. I found her third nest newly completed on June 11; she laid one egg in it June 13 which was gone June 14, and she deserted. Her next nest I found June 26 with one egg; the next morning, though she had laid her second egg, a cowbird had also laid one and her first egg was gone, and again she deserted. She finished her next nest July 1 and laid three eggs in it July 2, 3, and 4; when two of these disappeared July 5 she left it and started the next day on a new nest, which she finished July 8. In this she laid three eggs July 9, 10, and 11, but the morning of July 18 it had been destroyed. She built her seventh nest July 20–21 and laid three more eggs in it July 22, 23, and 24, which hatched August 3 and 4. On August 9 the nest was torn to pieces and the young gone. Thus from May 14, when I estimate she laid her first egg, through August 9 when her last nest was destroyed, a period of 87 days, she laid a total of 17 eggs in her seven nests; 6 of her eggs hatched, but she fledged no young. I have records of females laying 18 eggs in a single summer.

My (1945) published totals on 462 nests observed showed 159 or 34.41 percent of them successful, and from 1,235 eggs laid, 447 young fledged, or 36.19 percent. In Malcolm P. Crooks' (MS.) Iowa study six nests of 17 fledged young, yielded an almost identical 35 percent nest success. Of the 45 eggs laid in these 17 nests, 27 or 60 percent hatched, but only 12 young, or 26.66 percent survived to migration time.

*Plumages.*—Dwight (1900) gives the color of the natal down as "mouse gray." D. K. and N. S. Wetherbee (1961) describe the hatchling as "light orange with down that varied from light to dark gray.

The upper mandible was gray on the anterior half; the mouth was bright red and the rictal flanges yellow." The natal down is replaced by the heavily streaked juvenal plumage, which G. M. Sutton (1935) describes as follows:

* * * In general appearance the eight to ten day old birds are more streaked than are older birds, especially on the crown and chest. By the time the juvenal plumage is fully unsheathed there is practically no streaking on the crown and hind neck, and the streaks of the underparts have much the appearance of *spots* or *flecks*. The postjuvenal molt begins when the individual is about sixteen days old, toward the end of June or early in July in young of the first brood. This molt involves only the body plumage (including the wing coverts) as a rule, though Dwight tells us that "the middle pair of rectrices is occasionally renewed."

* * * Four specimens at hand, all with fully developed juvenal flight feathers (July 14 to 30), are in various stages of the postjuvenal molt, the back in every case having two distinct types of feathers: the comparatively dull, buffy-edged, loose, plumulaceous type characteristic of the juvenal plumage in all Fringillidae; and the sleek, firm, red-brown type that is characteristic either of this species' first winter plumage or of some intermediate, *postjuvenal* plumage. The specimen taken July 30 (U.M.M.Z. No. 75012), is naturally the brightest of these, about a dozen new red-brown feathers showing plainly in the back.

In a series of 15 juvenal field sparrows Sutton found a considerable variation in the amount of streaking below. Not one of his Michigan specimens showed any streaking on the throat as Dwight (1900) mentions.

Of the first fall and winter plumage T. S. Roberts (1932) notes. "The stripes on underparts are lost at the postjuvenal molt and the young closely resembles the adult, which, in the fall and winter dress, are more rusty and buffy than in the spring and summer plumage." The breeding adult plumage which, as Dwight noted, is acquired largely by wear, Roberts goes on to describe thusly:

Crown and nape rusty-brown with a more or less evident median gray stripe; sides of head gray with a rusty-brown stripe back of eye and a small spot in front of eye; an indistinct buffy eye-ring; back and scapulars rusty-brown, streaked with black, rufous, and buff; rump and upper tail-coverts light grayish-brown, lightly if at all streaked; below grayish-buff on breast and sides, paler on throat, and shading behind into white or grayish-white on abdomen, belly, and under tail-coverts; wings dusky, primaries narrowly edged with light, secondaries and tertiaries more broadly with rufous; coverts dark centrally, edged with rufous, and the middle and greater tipped with white or buffy-white, forming two more or less conspicuous wing-bars; tail grayish-brown, outer feathers narrowly edged with white. Bill pinkish; legs and feet pale flesh color, darker on feet; iris brown.

*Food.*—In his classic work, Judd (1901) notes that the field sparrow eats about 41 percent animal and 59 percent vegetable matter. The animal food consists of weevils, beetles (May, click, leaf, ground, and tiger), grasshoppers, caterpillars, leafhoppers, ants, flies, wasps, and spiders. The vegetable matter is made up of grass seeds (crab, pigeon, broomsedge), chickweed, purslane, lamb's quarters, gromwell, knot-weed, wood-sorrel, with some oats after harvesting time.

Martin, Zim, and Nelson (1951) state of the field sparrow's animal food: "Insects eaten consist chiefly of beetles, grasshoppers, and caterpillars. Various other invertebrates, including ants and other *Hymenoptera*, leafhoppers, true bugs, and spiders are also consumed." Plant food from 137 specimens from the northeast consisted mainly of bristlegrass, crabgrass, broomsedge, panicgrass, some oats, and lesser amounts of dropseed grass, sheep sorrel, pigweed, ragweed, wood sorrel, timothy, and goosefoot. From 38 stomachs from the prairie states, the main plants eaten were bristlegrass, panicgrass, dropseedgrass, and crabgrass, with lesser amounts of vervain, goosefoot, wheat, redtop, and gromwell.

Crooks (MS.) noted that the field sparrows began feeding before it was completely light in the morning; they fed a great deal up to about 9 a.m., intermittently for brief periods during the day, and then heavily again from 6 to 6:30 in the evening. He also noted that the female fed for longer periods, up to 14 minutes at a time, while the male's feeding periods averaged around 4 minutes.

My observations confirm those of Malcolm Crooks. Pairs often fed for many hours during the early morning before they nested, and seemed to be picking up grass and other seeds. During nesting they continued to feed on seeds, but began eating many more insects, including grasshoppers and large larvae, and the incubating female devoured any ants that ventured into the nest. The nestlings, as stated above, are fed entirely on insect food. Later in the summer as the flocks began to form they again fed largely on grass seeds.

*Voice.*—Much has been written of the song of the field sparrow, which Cornelius Weygandt (1930) epitomized most aptly as "a little song, a trembling and lonely melody, minor, but never uncheerful." To me the song sounds like "seeea-seeea-seeea-seeea-wee-wee-wee-wee." The male usually begins to sing just as day begins to break, usually from a prominent perch on his territory, and, if he is not mated, he continues on and off during the entire day, though noteably less in the afternoon. After he is paired he sings little after daybreak until nestings starts, when he sings more often, and always most during the early morning, usually at the rate of about three or four times per minute.

F. H. Allen, in notes to Mr. Bent, describes the commonest song of the field sparrow as "several long, slow notes with falling inflection followed by a rapid trill on a higher pitch." A bird he heard at West Roxbury, Mass., July 17, 1916 "held himself erect, threw back his head, and kept his bill open while singing, the mandibles moving only slightly at the beginning, and gradually closing with the final trill."

Aretas A. Saunders (1922b) writes: "The Field Sparrow song is of short duration. The average length of the song, based on the one hundred and forty-nine records I now have, is 2.7 seconds. The longest song of all is 4.6 seconds, and the shortest 1.6 seconds. * * * One specific time character, that holds in practically all songs, is acceleration. The introductory notes are the longest and the terminal notes the shortest of the song, the latter often so rapidly repeated that they cannot be counted and must be recorded as a trill." He notes that the pitch of a single song never varies greatly. The range is exactly one octave, from $D''''$ to $D'''$; most songs range between $C''''$ and $F'''$. The song varies little in intensity, and its quality of a clear, sweet whistle makes it very attractive.

A. R. Brand (1938) reports the approximate mean vibration of a field sparrow song at 4,100 per second, with the highest note 5,100 and the lowest 3,650.

In addition to the song, the field sparrows have a number of other notes. When they are 4 or 5 days old, nestlings utter a low "Zweep" or "Zeeep" when the parent approaches with food. As the female feeds the young she gives a low "Zeee, Zeee." While searching for food for the young the male and female call to each other with a low "zee-zee-zee-zee" or a "chup-zup-zup-zup-zup." After the young leave the nest they give a sharp "chip" when they are hungry. The adults use a similar sharp "chip" for an alarm note, often repeated in a rapid chipping. When a hawk appears over the breeding area, all the field sparrows give a penetrating "zeeeeeeee" and disappear into the cover. A male trying to entice a neighboring female was heard to give two calls, a "chip-chip-zip-zip-zip-zip," or just a plain "zip-zip-zip-zip-zip."

*Behavior.*—J. S. Y. Hoyt (1948) reports a pair of field sparrows nesting within 18 inches of the nest of a pair of red-eyed towhees in a small white pine. Both species fed the young in both nests at time; if the young in one nest did not offer to take food from the parent, the old bird went over and fed the young in the other nest.

An outstanding characteristic of the field sparrow is its gentleness. It is seldom aggressive toward other species or its own kind. It feeds amicably through the fall and winter in mixed flocks of its own and other species. Its cheerful yet plaintive song, usually given 5 to 25 feet up in a tree on its territory, adds much to its personality.

*Field marks.*—The field sparrow is most apt to be confused with its congeners, the chipping and clay-colored sparrows, with which it is often found in fall and winter. Its most striking field mark is its pink bill. Its chestnut cap is not so bright as that of the chipping sparrow, and lacks the center stripe of the clay-color's cap. Peterson (1947) also stresses: "Except for the pink bill, it resembles the Tree Sparrow and the Chippy. It has less noticeable facial striping; this and the *eye-ring* gives the bird a blank expression,

Young birds in summer are finely streaked below like young Chippies, but lack the well-marked head-stripings."

*Enemies.*—Field sparrows are subject to predation by the usual animals capable of catching small birds. Cats, dogs, foxes, raccoons, skunks, and weasels must all take the contents of ground nests occasionally. Evidence points to cats killing a number of females on their nests at night in my study area. Dogs destroyed at least one nest, and probably more. Once a weasel working through the neighborhood of several nests came to my squeaking. Smaller mammals such as spermophiles, chipmunks, and field mice were also present, and I was sure some of them took eggs or young at times, usually when the nest contents disappeared one at a time.

Among bird predators, Cooper's and sharp-shinned hawks were present during most of the nesting season, and whenever they appeared the field sparrows took to cover. They also showed alarm when blue jays came near. Jays foraged commonly in family groups over the sparrow territories from mid-summer on, and definitely destroyed at least one nest. Crows also appeared now and then, but seldom fed in the sparrow nesting area. M. P. Crooks (MS.) watched a house wren destroy a set of field sparrow eggs in Iowa. E. A. Mason (1938a) reports a loggerhead shrike capturing a field sparrow he had just banded and released in Summerville, S.C.

Snakes also take a considerable toll of birds nesting on or near the ground. I (1943) reported incidents of nests of the chipping sparrow, prothonotary warbler, and goldfinch despoiled, respectively, by a garter snake, a pilot snake, and a blue racer in Michigan. On July 11, 1943, I found a milk snake swallowing the eggs from a field sparrow nest in my study area; I killed the snake, extricated the eggs, and put them back in the nest. E. D. Nauman (1929) reports a rattlesnake eating an adult and a nestful of nearly grown young field sparrows in Iowa.

Unquestionably the chief enemy of the field sparrow in northern United States is the brown-headed cowbird. Cowbirds are almost always present in or near the fields where the sparrows, whose nests are not too hard to find, are among the commonest breeding small birds. Though I have seen them outwit the cowbirds many times, nevertheless 182, or 27.4 percent of 664 nests in my study area were parasitized. G. O. Hendrickson (1953) reports 80 percent of 16 nests parasitized at Ames, Iowa, and R. T. Norris (1947) only 15.8 percent of 57 nests at Butler, Pa. In my 182 nests the cowbirds laid 234 eggs—135 had one, 42 had two, and 5 had three eggs. The field sparrows immediately deserted 100 of the 182 nests (with 134 cowbird eggs) and from the 234 eggs fledged only 27 cowbirds, a nesting success of 11.6 percent. While the average production of only

2.45 young cowbirds per year for the 100-acre tract over the 11-year period does not seem overly serious, nevertheless cowbird interference retarded the field sparrow nesting cycle and production of young considerably. As the cowbirds usually laid no eggs after mid-July, the sparrows did not have this trouble to contend with during their last nesting.

H. S. Peters (1936) lists 13 different ectoparasites found on the field sparrow, including four species of biting lice (Mallophaga), two of flies, four of mites, and three of ticks. R. O. Malcomson (1960) adds another Mallophaga to this list, and C. Herman (1944) reports finding the blood protozoan, *Plasmodium* in the species twice.

Unseasonable spells of inclement weather such as extreme cold with snow or sleet, extreme heat, and heavy wind and rain all take their toll of this species. M. P. Crooks (MS.) reports all the eggs and young he was studying were lost during a late spring snowstorm. In early nests before the vegetation has leafed out enough to provide shade, the hot sun may cause the young to leave the nest prematurely. I have found a number of such young dead within a short distance of the nest, killed either by the heat or by small red ants which had already partly devoured them. These ants were found to kill healthy small young, left unprotected in the nest by adults, in an hour. Heavy downpours with high winds often wrecked nests in bushes or dumped eggs or young out onto the ground.

I have found many field sparrows killed by cars on the roads. The most recent modern perils for these and other night migrants are the ceilometer beams at airports and tall television towers. A. R. Laskey (1957, 1960) reports at least 23 field sparrows killed by flying into the tower at Nashville, Tenn. H. L. Stoddard (1962) reports 24 field sparrows among the some 15,200 individual birds of 150 species killed at a television tower 20 miles north of Tallahassee, Fla., between 1955 and 1961.

*Fall and winter.*—After nesting activities in Michigan cease in late summer adults and young start forming flocks that remain on their favorite brushy fields throughout most of September. Hundreds may be found together in especially good feeding areas. They roost at night in small trees or bushes still heavily covered with leaves. Banding operations show the birds start moving southward in mid-September, and the population changes continually as the migrants keep coming through until the 2nd week of October. Though individuals occasionally linger into November, most have left by mid-October.

In Nashville, Tenn., where the species both breeds and winters, Mrs. Laskey (1934b) found, through banding, that the population changed regularly. Though she captured immature birds she considered to be migrants as early as July 19, most of the migrants came through in October and returned again in March.

In Alabama Imhof (1962) says: "In winter it is abundant and widespread throughout the state. Usually it occurs in brushy fields, old overgrown pastures, wood borders, and the like, and it is the most common sparrow of broomsedge fields." Burleigh (1958) says about the same of it for Georgia: "During the winter, the Field Sparrow is an abundant bird over the entire state, its numbers being increased by numerous flocks of transients from farther north." In Florida Howell (1932) says "The birds are rather shy and retiring, and are found usually at some distance from farm buildings. * * * In winter they often associate with Chipping Sparrows and other ground-feeding species."

## DISTRIBUTION

*Range.*—Minnesota, Michigan, southern Quebec and southern Maine south to southern Texas, the Gulf Coast, and southern Florida.

*Breeding range.*—The eastern field sparrow breeds from central Minnesota (Nisswa), north central Wisconsin (Holcombe; Oconto County), north central Michigan (Crawford County), southern Ontario (Wasaga Beach, Arnprior), southwestern Quebec (Montreal), and southern Maine (Bangor) south to eastern Texas, northwestern and southeastern Louisiana (De Soto Parish, Hohen Solms), southern Mississippi (casually at Biloxi), central and southeastern Alabama (Greensboro, Abbeville), and Southern Georgia (Savannah); casually in northern Florida (Waukeenah).

*Winter range.*—Winters from eastern Kansas, central eastern Iowa (Davenport), southern Wisconsin (Beloit, Lake Geneva, Racine, Milwaukee), central Michigan (Traverse City, Midland), southern Ontario (London, Hamilton, Richmond Hill, Toronto, Pickering), central New York (Rochester, Syracuse, Dutchess County), Massachusetts (Belmont, Newburyport), and coastal New Hampshire south to southern Texas (Brownsville), the Gulf coast, and central Florida (Tarpon Springs, Winter Park); casually south to Nuevo León (Linares) and southern Florida (Cape Sable).

*Migration.*—The data deal with the species as a whole. Early dates of spring arrival are: District of Columbia—March 5. Maryland—Laurel, March 8. Pennsylvania—Somerset County, March 6; Beaver, March 12; State College, March 15. New Jersey—Cape May, March 22. New York—Tioga County, March 4; Westchester County, March 7. Connecticut—New Haven, March 14. Massachusetts—Concord, March 26; Martha's Vineyard, March 28 (median of 7 years, April 5). New Hampshire—New Hampton, March 27 (median of 21 years, April 14). Maine—Lewiston, April 14. Quebec—Montreal area, April 20 (median of 7 years, May 2). Illinois—

Urbana, February 20 (median of 20 years, March 22); Chicago, March 10 (average of 16 years, March 27). Indiana—Wayne County, March 16 (median of 8 years, March 26). Ohio—central Ohio, March 9 (median of 40 years, March 12). Michigan—Detroit-Windsor area, March 3; Battle Creek, March 14 (average of 43 years, March 31). Iowa—Sioux City, March 27 (median of 38 years, April 10). Minnesota—Minneapolis-St. Paul, March 23 (median of 15 years, April 19). Kansas—northeastern Kansas, March 4 (median of 13 years, April 10). Nebraska—Douglas, March 26. South Dakota—Sioux Falls, April 14 (average of 7 years, April 28).

Late dates of spring departure are: Florida—northern peninsula, April 21; Gainesville, April 17. Alabama—Gulf Shores, May 1. Georgia—Fitzgerald, April 30. Maryland—Laurel, April 29. Illinois—Chicago, May 31 (average of 16 years, May 23). Ohio—central Ohio, median of 40 years, May 3. Texas—Sinton, April 12 (median of 5 years, April 9). Nebraska—Webster, May 2.

Early dates of fall arrival are: Nebraska—Logan, September 15. Ohio—central Ohio, median of 40 years, September 15. Illinois—Chicago, average of 16 years, September 22. Mississippi—Gulfport, October 28. New York—Tiana Beach, September 27. Maryland—Baltimore County, September 13; Laurel, October 2. Georgia—Fitzgerald, October 6. Alabama—Foley, August 28. Florida—Tallahassee, September 22; Pensacola, November 2.

Late dates of fall departure are: South Dakota—Millette, October 7. Nebraska—Red Cloud, November 22; Lincoln, November 9. Kansas—northeastern Kansas, November 12 (median of 11 years, October 26). Minnesota—Minneapolis-St. Paul, October 17 (median of 6 years, September 17). Wisconsin—Milton, December 1, Waukesha County, November 11. Iowa—Sioux City, October 29 (median of 38 years, October 17). Michigan—Battle Creek, November 7 (average of 36 years, October 18). Ohio—Buckeye Lake, November 12 (median, October 30). Indiana—Wayne County, November 15 (median of 5 years, November 11). Illinois—Chicago, December 9 (average of 16 years, October 28). Tennessee—Nashville, November 16. New Brunswick—Kent Island, October 14. Quebec—Montreal area, October 23 (median of 7 years, October 8). New Hampshire—New Hampton, November 6 (median of 21 years, October 17). Massachusetts—Concord, November 25; Martha's Vineyard, November 12. Connecticut—New Haven, November 30. New York—Rockland County, November 19; New York City, November 13. New Jersey—Cape May, November 21. Pennsylvania—McConnellsburg, November 29.

*Egg dates.*—Connecticut: 20 records, May 18 to June 13.

Georgia: 35 records, April 7 to August 12.

Illinois: 79 records, April 20 to August 11; 40 records, May 17 to June 10.

Iowa: 17 records, May 12 to July 30.

Kentucky: 10 records, May 7 to June 5.

Manitoba: 1 record, June 30.

Maryland: 265 records, April 21 to August 25; 105 records, May 10 to June 8.

Massachusetts: 35 records, May 15 to July 25; 18 records, May 21 to June 10.

Michigan: 708 records, April 28 to September 18; 55 records, May 15 to June 30.

Missouri: 7 records, May 4 to May 17.

New Jersey: 35 records, May 5 to July 13; 19 records, May 15 to May 31.

New York: 23 records, May 3 to August 10; 11 records, June 10 to July 22.

Ontario: 21 records, May 9 to July 19; 11 records, June 10 to July 22.

Texas: 3 records, April 22 to May 4.

West Virginia: 65 records, April 30 to July 16; 36 records, May 15 to May 31.

## SPIZELLA PUSILLA ARENACEA Chadbourne
### Western Field Sparrow
#### Contributed by LAWRENCE H. WALKINSHAW

### HABITS

Arthur P. Chadbourne described this western race of the field sparrow in 1886 from wintering specimens taken in Laredo, Texas. He diagnosed the subspecies as "Similar to *S. pusilla* but with the rufous replaced by brownish-ash, and of slightly larger size, with decidedly longer tail and somewhat heavier bill." The following year C. Hart Merriam gave specific rank to breeding specimens from South Dakota and Nebraska. Later evidence showed the form to be only subspecifically distinct, and it has been so recognized by the A.O.U. Check-List ever since.

Little has been published about the ecology or the breeding habits of this form, which presumably do not differ materially from those of the eastern race.

### DISTRIBUTION

*Range.*—Montana and North Dakota to Coahuila, Nuevo León, Tamaulipas, and Louisiana.

*Breeding range.*—The western field sparrow breeds from north-western (rarely) and southeastern Montana (Billings, Paris) and northern North Dakota (Charlson, Minnewauken) south to north-eastern Colorado (Boulder, Fort Morgan), western and central south-ern Oklahoma (Arnett, Arbuckle Mountains, Lake Texoma), and Kansas (intergrades in east with *S. p. pusilla*).

*Winter range.*—Winters from Kansas, central Oklahoma (Oklahoma City; Creek County), northern Arkansas (Winslow), and north-western Mississippi (Rosedale) south to northern Coahuila (Sabinas), central Nuevo León (Monterrey), northeastern Tamaulipas (Mata-moros), and southeastern Louisiana (Mandeville).

*Casual records.*—Casual in migration west to New Mexico (Lea County, Los Alamos) and east to eastern Iowa (Giard) and western Tennessee (Tiptonville, Hickory Withe).

## SPIZELLA WORTHENI WORTHENI Ridgway

### Worthen's Sparrow

#### Contributed by J. DAN WEBSTER

#### HABITS

It sounded like a chipping sparrow; however, there was a peculiar initial phrase—a slur that was most unchippy-like—and so I investi-gated. The sparrow sang from a waist-high thorny bush, and scrutiny with binoculars convinced me that the bird was one I had been anxious to meet—the little known Worthen's sparrow. This spot where I first encountered the species is still the only one where I have ever seen it, and other recorded localities are few. The only record from the area of the A.O.U. Check-List is the type specimen, which was collected by C. W. Worthen at Silver City, N. Mex., June 16, 1882; otherwise the species has been found only in Mexico.

There is some doubt as to whether the Worthen's sparrow is distinct from the field sparrow. Burleigh and Lowery (1942) hold that the two are conspecific; whereas Webster and Orr (1954a) argue that they are not. Present information is inadequate for any real conclu-sion. However, the present investigation turned up one more argu-ment in favor of specific status for *wortheni*, viz.: there is definite sexual dimorphism in plumage coloration in *wortheni*—more, in fact, than in any other species of the genus *Spizella* excepting, possibly, *atrogularis*. Ridgway's (1901) statement, "Sexes alike," is erroneous.

*Ecology.*—Brown (*in* Thayer, 1925) found the species near Miqui-huana, Tamaulipas, breeding in weedy, overgrown cornfields and in prickly shrubs in uncultivated foothills. Ray (*in* Burleigh and Lowery, 1942) collected a specimen in shrubby desert near Saltillo,

Coahuila, in April, which was probably a migrant. My own observations (Webster and Orr, 1954a; Webster, 1954, 1958, and MS.) concern a colony, estimated at eight breeding pairs in 1954, 9 miles northwest of Sombrerete, Zacatecas, at 7,800 feet elevation on the northeast shoulder of Cerro Gordo. Here the birds occupied a tract of heavily grazed open rangeland or grassland which was dotted with small trees and bushes. Shrubby junipers (*Juniperus deppeana*) were the chief woody plants, averaging from 15 to 35 yards apart; most of them were 6 to 8 feet tall, the highest 12 feet. Other shrubs, sparsely distributed, were *Cowania mexicana, Acacia* sp., *Opuntia* sp., and *Pinus edulis.* Ground cover consisted of numerous tufts of the shrub *Brickellia spinulosa* 6 to 12 inches high, and a sparse sod of grama grass (*Bouteloua* sp.) and herbaceous weeds. The commonest associated birds in June and July were the brown towhee, bush-tit, lark sparrow, eastern meadowlark, house finch, and chipping sparrow.

*Habits.*—On sunny mornings in June and early July the male Worthen's sparrows sang almost continually from daylight until 10:00 or 11:00 a.m. One territory was 100 by 25 yards, and others seemed about the same size; several shrubs or trees served as song perches. Feeding was ordinarily on the ground, but once a bird jumped into the air to capture two flying insects and once one was seen foraging in a low bush. Singing was invariably from a perch, and danger always caused the birds to take refuge in a bush. Feeding was on the territory, except that once a rival male was tolerated for a few minutes while both fed on the one's territory. There was usually no water on the nesting area in June and July, and occasionally one or another bird flew off toward the creek ½ to 1½ miles away, presumably for a drink. Usually rival males were driven off vigorously with an aerial chase and fight, followed by strong singing by the victorious defender.

Brown (*in* Thayer, 1925) writes, "I found the Worthen Sparrow breeding in overgrown cornfields where it nested—invariably in low weeds of the mint family.* * *

"In habits the Worthen Sparrow is almost exclusively terrestrial, though during the nesting season it sings from the tops of high weeds. Its song is a faint trill. In one instance I saw a Worthen Sparrow, perched on a high weed, dart into the air several times after insects, like a flycatcher.

"Outside of the cornfields, in the foothills, where the land is uncultivated and conditions are natural, this bird nests in prickly shrubs, the highest being about four feet from the ground."

*Voice.*—The song of the male Worthen's sparrow is sometimes a trill indistinguishable to my ear from that of the chipping sparrow. More often, however, there is an initial slurred-down note followed by the trill— ⟨ ‗‗‗‗ or *pee chrrrrrr*.  The entire *peee* is usually pitched lower than the trill, but one bird sang the initial phrase several tones higher than the trill which followed.  Most birds sang the initial phrase softer, with less carrying power than the trill.  As compared with the field sparrow, the middle notes are lacking and there is no gradual *accelerando*.

*Nest.*—The nest of the species is unknown save for the several Brown collected at Miquihuana, Tamaulipas, in 1924.  Brown (*in* Thayer, 1925) describes the nest as "well made, compact, and well concealed.  It is constructed of rootlets and grasses and lined with fine fibers and sometimes with horsehair and is placed without exception within six inches of the ground.  Sometimes it even rests upon the ground like a Song Sparrow's nest, but supported by the weed in which it is built."

Charles H. Blake, who kindly examined for me the 27 nests complete with eggs in the Thayer Collection at Harvard writes: "In dimensions and wall construction I doubt that the nests could be told from those of field sparrows.  The lining is a little more like that used by the chipping sparrow, mostly composed of very fine rootlets.  Some nests include a few long, black hairs.  The external diameter runs from 75 to 95, mostly about 80 to 85 millimeters.  The internal diameter is 45 to 50, and the depth 25 to 35, mostly 30 to 35 millimeters.  The smallest nests are about 65 millimeters in external diameter, but without reduction of the internal diameter."

*Eggs.*—Worthen's sparrow usually lays three or four eggs.  They are ovate with some tending toward elongate ovate, and are slightly glossy.  The "bluish glaucous" or "Etain blue" ground is speckled, spotted, and occasionally blotched with "natal brown," "snuff brown," "Mars' brown," or "Brussels brown."  The majority of eggs do not seem to have undermarkings, but when present these are "light neutral gray."  The spottings, either sharply defined or somewhat cloudy, are generally concentrated toward the large end.  The measurements of 50 eggs average 18.1 by 13.4 millimeters; the eggs showing the four extremes measure *19.7* by 13.9, 17.9 by *14.5*, *16.2* by 13.1, and 18.3 by *12.1* millimeters.

*Field marks.*—A slender, clear-breasted sparrow with a pink bill and a white eye ring.  Persons from the eastern United States will note the resemblance to the field sparrow; the differences are the grayer, more ashy shade of the back, the lack of the brown postocular stripe, and the presence of the eye ring in the Worthen's sparrow.  Adult males are marked, in addition, by a prominent gray nape, or collar, and a gray forehead, rather sharply setting off the chestnut pileum.

*Plumages.*—The immature plumages have never been described. A female taken July 5, 1924, at Miquihuana and now in the Museum of Comparative Zoology, is similar to a juvenal-plumaged field sparrow, but differs in possessing a prominent, pale buffy eye ring and a more prominent and more buffy postocular stripe. The flight feathers are full length, but only a few postjuvenal feathers can be distinguished— on the crown, amongst the scapulars, and possibly the tertials. The general effect of the dorsum is nearest buffy brown. The ground color of the crown, back, and wings is close to buffy brown, streaked prominently on the back and moderately on the crown and nape with a blackish brownish olive. The nape and forehead are not very distinctly set off; they are between dark gray and brownish olive in color. The underparts are generally a pale smoke gray, darker anteriorly and tinged slightly with buffy and streaked prominently on breast and flanks with blackish olive.*

An adult female in rather fresh plumage (December 10) is nearest buffy brown on the back, with the ground color a little more cinnamoneous and blacker than that shade and streaked prominently with blackish olive. The scapular, secondaries, and coverts are edged with buffy brown, which forms very indistinct wing bars. The crown is buffy brown, obscurely streaked with a blackish shade of the same. The nape is a little grayer than the crown and back, but is not well differentiated. The forehead is dark gray with a buffy brown tinge. The side of the head is medium gray, except for a narrow white eye ring; the auriculars are tinged with buffy brown. The underparts are clear, pale gray on the belly and under tail coverts darkening to smoke gray on the breast and throat and between smoke gray and buffy brown on the flanks. The flight feathers are dark blackish olive, the rectrices and primaries narrowly edged laterally with smoke gray.

No male specimen in completely fresh plumage has been seen. Specimens taken from March to July differ from females in the coloration of the head; the pileum in males is more chestnut, less streaked, and more distinctly demarcated from the more purely gray nape (collar) and forehead. Specifically, the pileum of adult males in nuptial plumage is between chestnut and tawny or blackish between chestnut and tawny, more or less obscurely streaked with a darker shade of the same tint. The nape is medium gray or dark gray, sometimes obscurely streaked with blackish. The side of the head, save for the white eye ring, is pure gray, from dark gray to medium gray. However, one specimen (Louisiana State University Museum)

---

*All colors in this section were compared directly with the Palmer and Reilly (1956) color standards.

taken in April, has the auriculars, especially dorsally, tinged with buffy brown.

Examination of most of the extant specimens (42) of Worthen's sparrows provides the following information on molts: as in the field sparrow (Sutton, 1935) the juvenal body plumage is at least partially lost and replaced from July to September by an adult-looking first winter plumage. I took two females in postjuvenal molt in Zacatecas, Aug. 16, 1961. A scanty prenuptial molt in May, sometimes extending into June and even July, includes primary 1 and secondaries 1–3 and sometimes also primary 2 and secondaries 4–7 and 1 or 2 or all 12 rectrices. The postnuptial molt begins on the head in June or July and extends posteriorly, probably not being completed until November. Two specimens (June 7 and July 12) showed what was apparently an overlap of the prenuptial molt (1 rectrix and 1 tertial, 1 rectrix and 2 tertials) with the beginning of the postnuptial molt (forehead).

## DISTRIBUTION

Apparently Worthen's sparrow is endemic on the high, temperate grasslands of northern and central Mexico, and formerly, the United States border. The only definite breeding localities are Miquihuana, Tamaulipas, and near Sombrerete, Zacatecas. However, the June specimen from Silver City, N. Mex., probably represents an extirpated breeding population in the United States, and the August specimens from Salinas, San Luis Potosí, probably indicate a breeding colony there. March specimens from Chalchicomula, Puebla, and Ojuelos, Jalisco, and a December skin from Tepetate, San Luis Potosí, represent our only knowledge of the winter range.

A specimen taken Apr. 16, 1941, on the desert near Saltillo, Coahuila, was either a migrant or a wintering bird. Dates on Brown's, and Nelson's and Goldman's specimens from Miquihuana range from May 27, 1924 to July 12, 1924. Near Sombrerete, my records range from June 19, 1952 and 1954 to Sept. 6, 1955.

Two subspecies of the Worthen's sparrow are recognized: the paler-colored nominate *S. w. wortheni* in New Mexico, Tamaulipas and (in winter) Puebla; and a darker race (*S. w. browni*) in Zacatecas. Specimens from San Luis Potosí are apparently intermediate and one from Coahuila is unassignable to race.

*Range.*—The species breeds in southwestern Tamaulipas (Miquihuana); possibly formerly to New Mexico (one record, the type specimen taken at Silver City, June 16, 1884); Zacatecas (Cerro Gordo).

Recorded in Coahuila (Saltillo), San Luis Potosí (Tepetate, Salinas), Puebla (Chalchicomula), Jalisco (Ojuelos), and Veracruz (Limón).

*Egg dates.*—Miquihuana, Tamaulipas, Mexico: 27 records, June 4 to July 15; 15 records, June 15 to June 30.

## SPIZELLA ATROGULARIS EVURA Coues

## Arizona Black-chinned Sparrow

### Contributed by JOHN D. NEWMAN

#### HABITS

In 1851, while on an expedition in Mexico, J. Cabanis discovered this species and named it *Spinites atrogularis*. Although the type locality is not precisely known, van Rossem (1935b), who examined the type specimen at the University Museum in Berlin, believes it is likely that this specimen was collected near Mexico City. Baird (1860) mentions a specimen taken in Coahuila, Mexico in 1853 by D. N. Couch. The first specimens for the United States appear to be those taken by Coues (1866b) at Fort Whipple, Ariz., which he designated as *Spizella evura*. By 1898, the species was known to be common along the southern border of the United States from the Lower Rio Grande Valley to southern California, and its nest and eggs were described in the literature (Davie, 1898). In 1913, Grinnell and Swarth published the first detailed information on its habits and song. Further work has been very scarce, however, and today the black-chinned is probably one of the most poorly known sparrows north of Mexico.

The common name of this bird tells us its most characteristic feature, which sets it apart from the other members of its genus. Sexual differences in the size and intensity of the chin patch make this the only sexually dimorphic *Spizella*. In nearly all other aspects of its appearance, however, it is a typical *Spizella*.

Perhaps one reason why the black-chinned sparrow is so little known is its choice of habitat, the tablelands and rugged mountain slopes of southwestern United States and Mexico. Grinnell and Miller (1944) describe its habitat in California as "Tall fairly dense sagebrush (*Artemisia tridentata*), or other brushland types of similar physical aspect. Usually the cover contains a variety of plant species, such as purshia, ephedra and coffee berry in addition to the prevailing artemisia. Sloping ground and rocky outcrops or scattered piñons and junipers interrupting the brush cover are characteristic." Johnson, Bryant, and Miller (1948) describe their encounter with this species in the Providence Mountains of California: "Black-chinned sparrows were summer residents throughout the Upper Sonoran Zone, at elevations between 5,000 and 7,500 feet. They stayed in brush-covered areas for the most part, nesting in sagebrush * * *. A few were seen in brush patches in the bottoms of rocky canyons and on ridges, but the greatest numbers were in situations * * * where stands of tall and fairly dense sagebrush grew in isolated shallow basins among rocky, piñon-covered hills."

F. Stephens writes in a letter to D. A. Cohen (1899): "In a general way this species is more or less distributed over the brush-covered hillsides (chemisal) of Southern California, between 1,000 and 3,000 feet altitude. * * * I have seen small companies of fewer than a dozen birds in the migration, but usually not more than one or two pairs inhabit any one hillside."

Phillips, Marshall, and Monson (1964) call it a "fairly common summer resident in Upper Sonoran chaparral across Arizona," while in New Mexico according to Ligon (1961) it is found up to 6,000 or 7,000 feet and "seems to prefer the brushy, rugged mountains and ridges, shunning forested areas."

The species appears to be relatively uncommon wherever it is found, but this may be a result of its scattered distribution. As Dawson (1923) writes: "Like so many of the chaparral- and sage-haunting species, the Black-chinned Sparrow colonizes loosely. Here on a hillside may be found half a dozen pairs, and upon the heels of this good fortune, a silence of a dozen miles, or forty, may ensue."

*Nesting.*—Although little is known of the nesting activities of the black-chinned sparrow, all writers agree that the nest is of typical *Spizella* character. Dawson (1923) describes it as "a compact cup of dried grasses, lined—or not—with horsehair; placed in sage or other shrub of the dwarf chaparral, often well concealed."

In a letter to Mr. Bent, Wilson C. Hanna writes that the nests are sometimes fairly compact but usually of rather loose construction, and long grass stems may extend 4 inches from the rim. A "typical" nest is "made of long grass stems in loose construction with lining of similar material and shredded fiber; outside diameter 4 inches, inside diameter 1.75 inches, outside depth 2.75 inches, inside depth 1.3 inches. In one case the outside diameter is recorded as 8 inches by 12 inches over all. The inside diameter may be up to 1.75 inches. The lining often has long strands of hair."

James B. Dixon of Escondido, Calif., in a letter to Wendell Taber, says that in 50 years of field work he has found only three nests. One of these, found on June 6, 1937 near Hesperia, San Bernardino County, Calif., was 3 feet up in a sage brush. The nest was composed of dry, hard weed stems on the outside, and lined with soft vegetable fiber and a few feathers. The site, on the edge of the Mohave Desert, was at an altitude of about 4,000 feet. Dixon also mentions a nest C. S. Sharp found in 1907 in Escondido at the remarkably low altitude of 800 feet above sea level.

Johnson, Bryant, and Miller (1948) found, in the Providence Mountains of California, "a nest with three eggs * * * on May 28 [1938] at 5,500 feet. It was wholly concealed from view in the center of one of many dense clumps of sagebrush that grew near the bed of a small wash. The nest was 26 inches from the ground in a bush 40 inches high. The outside diameter and depth were each 4 inches, the inside diameter and depth each 1⅝ inches. The framework consisted chiefly of closely woven dry fibers from leaves of *Yucca baccata;* the lining was of brown and white cow hairs."

Laurence M. Huey (1915) describes what appears to be an atypical nest, found by a friend inside the city limits of San Diego on May 9, 1912: "The nest was in an extremely open spot, it being easily seen for fifty yards in any direction, and was entirely built of grasses and placed about 18 inches above the ground in an upright fork of a slender chaparral."

*Eggs.*—The black-chinned sparrow lays from two to four, and occasionally five ovate eggs. They are very pale blue and slightly glossy. The majority are unmarked, while others have a few small scattered spots of brown such as "mummy brown" which are often so dark that they appear to be black. Wilson C. Hanna, who has had considerable experience with this species writes that of the sets he has examined "38 percent contained eggs without any markings; 32 percent had both marked and unmarked eggs, and in 30 percent all eggs were spotted." The measurements of 74 eggs average 17.6 by 13.3 millimeters; the eggs showing the four extremes measure *19.3* by 12.6, 18.5 by *15.1, 15.5* by 13.0, and 16.1 by *12.3* millimeters.

*Young.*—No information seems to be available on length of incubation, hatching, or care of young in the nest. It seems fairly well established, however, that fledglings are cared for by both parents. Miller (1929) reports both a male and a female feeding young just out of the nest. Bailey (1928) observed young being fed out of the nest in the Big Hatchet Mountains, N. Mex. And Frank Stephens (1903) writes: "Saw a female carrying a larva of some kind in her bill, on Providence Mountains [California], about June first. She came quite close to me and acted as if her family were near. A month later I saw several at about the same altitude (6,000 feet) on the Hualapai Mountains [Arizona]. These appeared to be parents and young of the year."

*Plumages.*—Ridgway (1901) says that the young in juvenal plumage are "Very similar to adult females without black on chin, etc., but streaks on back narrower and less sharply defined, edges of wing-coverts and tertials more rusty, and gray of underparts paler, the chest nearly white, very indistinctly streaked with light gray."

Ridgway describes the adult male as follows:

Lores, anterior portion of malar region, chin, and more or less of the throat, black; rest of head and neck gray, darker (slate-gray or slate-color) on pileum, where sometimes narrowly and indistinctly streaked with dusky, fading into lighter gray (no. 7) or olive-gray on chest and other under parts, the abdomen white; back light rusty brown or cinnamon (sometimes mixed with broccoli brown) streaked with black; scapulars similar but with outer webs more decidedly rusty or cinnamomeous; rump and upper tail-coverts plain gray or olive-gray, the latter sometimes with darker mesial streaks; tail dusky, the rectrices edged with light gray; lesser wing-coverts gray; middle coverts dusky centrally, broadly margined, and tipped with pale cinnamon-buffy; greater coverts dusky centrally broadly edged with pale buffy brown or wood brown; tertials dusky, edged with pale wood brown; primaries dusky edged with pale grayish; bill vinaceous-cinnamon, more or less darker at tip; tarsi deep brown or dusky, the toes usually darker * * *.

He describes the adult female as "Similar to the adult male and not always distinguishable, but usually with the black of chin, etc., duller and much less extended (hardly extending to upper throat), often entirely wanting, the entire head being gray (usually the black is indicated by a darker shade of the gray), and the gray of pileum and hindneck rather browner * * *."

Dawson (1923), in describing the adults of this species, says that "the black [on the face] of the adult female * * * is probably not attained before the second season."

*Food.*—Nothing seems to have been published on the food of this species. We can only assume that it feeds on items similar to those consumed by other chaparral-inhabiting finches.

In the summer, black-chinned sparrows are known to forage through piñons, junipers, coffee berry, sagebrush, and ephedra. Johnson, Bryant, and Miller (1948) saw a few birds in brush patches in the bottoms of rocky canyons, and these birds may also have been foraging. They report shooting a female on June 9, 1938 whose beak was full of insects, "evidently for nestling birds."

*Behavior.*—The few available reports allow only a brief glimpse of this species' behavior.

Of its manner of moving about, Grinnell and Miller (1944) write: "In moving through the brush cover, chiefly on forage missions, the flight may be near the ground, through alleyways, or in the open over the bush-tops. Individuals are wide-ranging for a brushland species."

Of behavior during the nesting season, Dawson (1923) says: "Not from him [the singing male] shall we receive any information as to the dainty nest * * *. And if we flush the female, sitting tight till close approach, she will disappear upon the instant, and as like as not for good." Huey (1915) adds of an incubating female: "The bird was rather tame, allowing me to get within a few feet of her. But when she left the nest, it was a rapid downward flight into the nearest brush, and she would then return like a Bell Sparrow, hopping on the ground most of the way."

The black-chinned sparrow apparently does not isolate itself from other bird species during the summer, for Hardy (1949) observed one drinking in the company of house finches in southern Nevada during July and August.

*Voice.*—Joseph Ewan (1928), in relating his experiences in the southern California mountains, says: "Few bird songs can compare with that of the Black-chinned Sparrow. His trill is noticeably canary-like, crystal-clear, and its melody often carries far down the mountain glades. Beginning with emphasis, descending gradually, and ending with low full tones; resembling sweet-sweet-te-te-te-tt-tt-t-t-t. The length of the trill, and the richness of each note are remarkable."

Dawson (1923) notes that there are actually two songs. The major one is usually given in the morning: "Shrill, vibrant, penetrating, with the incisiveness of a whip-crack, but infinitely sweeter, comes each note, *accelerando*, until the trill is reached. Here the singer becomes disheartened, and lets his melody peter out to an inglorious finish." The second song alternates irregularly with the first, and is "little more than a simple (and altogether different) trill. This phrase begins with a single inspirated note, those which follow are just distinct enough to be separated by the ear, while the terminal portion becomes rapid and *diminuendo*, as before. This echo song, moreover, is oftenest terminated, after the tiniest interval, by a single *cheep* or *tsweet* of characteristic quality. It is as though the singer had signed his name with a flourish to a performance which we should not otherwise have recognized." Dawson heard this "echo song" in the evening from chaparral high on a hillside and transcribed it *"TSEET chweet chweet chweet trrrrr."*

Dawson also describes the manner in which the male delivers the song: "As a singer he performs conscientiously, and with an eye single to duty. He chooses elevated stations, a yucca stalk, the tip of the tallest chamisal, or, rarely, a tree. He is quite demure in manner, sitting pensive or turning calmly in the intervals which succeed his song. But every five or ten minutes, prudence enjoins that he shift his station, even though it be to another of equal prominence."

*Field marks.*—The gray head and breast and pink bill give both sexes a superficially junco-like appearance. The brown, streaked back, white wing bars on brown wings, and habitat identify them. Adult males, with their black chin patches except in winter, are distinctive.

*Enemies.*—Of its enemies, only the cowbird is known. Friedmann (1963) writes: "This little known bird has been recorded only twice as far as I know as a victim of the dwarf race of the brown-headed

cowbird [Molothrus ater obscurus].   In the files of the U.S. Fish and
Wildlife Service there is a record by Stokeley Ligon reporting a
parasitized nest which was found 18 miles above Santa Rosa, New
Mexico, on July 6, 1913." The other record is of two parasitized
nests collected by Hanna in San Bernardino County, Calif.

### DISTRIBUTION

*Range.*—Eastern California and southwestern Utah south to
southeastern Sonora and western Texas.

*Breeding range.*—The Arizona black-chinned sparrow breeds east
of the Sierra Nevada in central eastern California (east slope of
southern Sierra Nevada; White Mountains south to Providence
Mountains), southern Nevada (Grapevine, Charleston and Sheep
mountains), southwestern Utah (Beaverdam Mountains, Leeds),
northwestern, central and southeastern Arizona (Hualpai Mountains,
Prescott, Chiricahua and Mule mountains), southern New Mexico
(Cuchillo, Sierra Capitan), and western Texas (Chisos and Guadalupe
mountains).

*Winter range.*—Winter range poorly known, but includes southern
Arizona (Ajo and Santa Catalina mountains, Natanes Plateau),
northern Sonora (Sierra Carrizal, Sierra de San Antonio) and western
Texas.

*Migration.*—The data deal with the species as a whole.   Early dates
of spring arrival are: Arizona—Baboquivari, March 24; Huachuca
Mountains, April 4.   Utah—Washington County, April 8.   California—Monrovia, March 31; Pasadena, April 6; Mt. Diablo, April 16.

Late date of spring departure is: Arizona—Sahuaro Lake on Salt
River, April 28.

*Egg dates.*—California: 91 records, April 23 to July 7; 46 records,
May 11 to June 6.

### SPIZELLA ATROGULARIS CANA Coues
## California Black-chinned Sparrow
#### PLATE 67
#### Contributed by JOHN D. NEWMAN

### HABITS

Miller, Friedmann, Griscom, and Moore (1957) give the range of
this subspecies: "Breeds in inner coastal mountains (Monterey
County southward) and on west slopes of southern Sierra Nevada of
central and southern California, extending south to northern Baja
California.   Winters from coastal southern California (rarely) south
through Baja California to Cape San Lucas."

Van Rossem (1935b) describes this race thusly: "Briefly, it is a small race with a slightly darker and less purely gray coloration as compared with *evura*. The characteristics are most pronounced southerly. From Ventura County northward there are slight but definite tendencies toward *caurina* of the San Francisco Bay region."

Measurement by van Rossem of 18 males from different localities yielded an average wing length of 61.7 millimeters and an average tail length of 63.3 millimeters.

This race is found in habitat typical of the species elsewhere. Grinnell and Miller (1944) describe it as "Arid, fairly tall and at least moderately dense chaparral, usually situated on sloping ground. Frequently the chaparral is of distinctly mixed composition and old burned-over tracts, well along in recovery of vegetation * * *. Most prevalent plant associates are *Adenostoma, Artemisia, tridentata,* species of *Ceanothus* and scrub oak." They note that this race ranges during the nesting season from within a few hundred feet at sea level (San Diego) up to at least 6,800 feet (San Bernardino Mountains); individuals occasionally wander to 8,000 feet in late summer.

Very little is known of the seasonal movements of this race. Jack von Bloeker obtained a male *cana* at Priest Valley, Monterey County, on Oct. 9, 1937. This region is only a few miles to the south of the mountains of San Benito County where the race *caurina* breeds. There appear to be only two winter records: one, from the San Fernando Valley, Los Angeles County, Feb. 18, 1922, and a second from San Clemente Island, Dec. 5, 1908.

### DISTRIBUTION

*Range.*—Southern California and Baja California.

*Breeding range.*—The California black-chinned sparrow breeds in the mountains of south central and southwestern California (Big Sur River and Coulterville south to San Diego County) and south to northern Baja California (Sierra San Pedro Mártir).

*Winter range.*—Winters from southwestern California (San Fernando Valley, San Clemente Island) south to southern Baja California (Cabo San Lucas).

### SPIZELLA ATROGULARIS CAURINA Miller

## San Francisco Black-chinned Sparrow

### Contributed by JOHN D. NEWMAN

### HABITS

This, the most recently discovered race of the black-chinned sparrow, was described by Alden H. Miller in 1929.

First found on Las Trampas Peak, Contra Costa County, Calif., this subspecies is now known from Alameda and Contra Cosa counties south to southern San Benito County.

Its choice of habitat parallels that of other black-chinned sparrows, being, according to Grinnell and Miller (1944) "Arid chaparral, in which adenostoma, ceanothus and scrub oak predominate. In one instance has nested in a tract of *Baccharis pilularis*. Bushes are fairly dense and 3 to 6 feet high, and occasional trees may be intermixed."

A. H. Miller (1929) in his original diagnosis describes this race as follows:

A subspecies of *Spizella atrogularis* characterized in comparison with the other races by dark and less brown coloration. Neck, lower throat, and breast between no. 6 gray and a light neutral gray * * *; whitish area of belly narrowly restricted, and tinged with gray; flanks and under tail coverts pale neutral gray. Pileum and hind neck near deep neutral gray, usually lacking shades of brown; black, cinnamon, and cinnamon brown tones of back deep; rump and upper tail coverts neutral gray. Wing and tail long as in *S. a. atrogularis* [the Mexican race]. Breast and flanks of juvenile with pronounced streaks of dark neutral gray.

Miller, in the same paper, compares *caurina* with the race *cana*:

*Caurina* differs from *cana* * * * in a decided general lack of brown and buff colors on the body plumage and in the smaller area of white on the belly; the gray of the head is distinctly darker. The cinnamon of the back of *cana* usually becomes more nearly cinnamon-rufous in *caurina*.

* * * The immature plumage of *caurina* stands in sharp contrast with the same plumage of *cana* in that the underparts are neutral gray with almost a total lack of the buff tippings so extensively seen in the fresh fall plumage of the southern California birds. The pileum is decidedly darker in the new race, the new feathers being only slightly tipped with brown.

The few available dates suggest that *caurina* departs early from its breeding grounds. In Alameda County, the latest date is August 13, and in Los Angeles County, September 10 (Grinnell and Miller, 1944).

### DISTRIBUTION

*Range.*—The San Francisco black-chinned sparrow breeds in coast ranges of central western California (Oakland south to San Benito Mountain); the only winter record is from Santa Cruz Island, California.

PLATE 67

Claremont, Calif.                                    W. M. Pierce
NEST AND EGGS OF CALIFORNIA BLACK-CHINNED SPARROW

D. Bleitz

JUVENILE AND ADULT BLACK-CHINNED SPARROWS